ACLS History E-Book Project
Reprint Series

The ACLS History E-Book Project (www.historyebook.org) collaborates with constituent societies of the American Council of Learned Societies, publishers, librarians and historians to create an electronic collection of works of high quality in the field of history. This volume is produced from digital images created for the Project by the Scholarly Publishing Office and the Digital Library Production Service at the University of Michigan, Ann Arbor. The digital reformatting process results in an electronic version of the text that can be both accessed online and used to create new print copies. This book and hundreds of others are available online in the History E-Book Project through subscription.

Many of the works in the History E-Book Project are available in print and can be ordered either directly from their publishers or as part of this series. For information refer to the online Title Record page for each book. Inquiries regarding this series can be directed to info@hebook.org.

ACLS
HISTORY E-BOOK

http://www.historyebook.org

SOUTHERN HONOR

SOUTHERN HONOR

Ethics and Behavior in the Old South

BERTRAM WYATT-BROWN

OXFORD UNIVERSITY PRESS

Oxford   New York   Toronto   Melbourne

Oxford University Press

Oxford   London   Glasgow
New York   Toronto   Melbourne   Auckland
Delhi   Bombay   Calcutta   Madras   Karachi
Kuala Lumpur   Singapore   Hong Kong   Tokyo
Nairobi   Dar es Salaam   Cape Town

and associate companies in

Beirut   Berlin   Ibadan   Mexico City   Nicosia

Library of Congress Cataloging in Publication Data

Wyatt-Brown, Bertram, 1932–
Southern honor.

Bibliography: p.
Includes index.
1. Southern States—Civilization.   2. Southern
States—Moral conditions.   3. Honor.   I. Title.
F209.W9   975   81-22448
ISBN 0-19-503119-9   AACR2
ISBN 0-19-503310-8 (pbk.)

Printing (last digit): 9 8 7 6 5 4 3 2 1

Printed in the United States of America

Dedicated to

Natalie Wyatt-Brown

and

in Memory of Laura Wyatt-Brown

white Southerners were not harboring a convenient myth. To us, though, inequality of condition, early and late, is a palpable affront. Only a fool would defend any scheme of tyranny. But to label slavery a crime is to insist that its white beneficiaries should have known what we know, should have done as we do (or at least pretend to do). The philosopher of history could explain the fallacy involved. Recapturing the mood of the past is hard enough without indulging in the should-have-beens.

In light of these opening remarks, it is only fair that the reader be apprised of my own perspective, since it may be significant in the appraisal of the work itself. I was not born in the South, but in Harrisburg, Pennsylvania. My parents were from southern Alabama and, though somewhat "Yankee-fied" themselves by long Northern residence—at least so my uncles maintained—they were intensely loyal to the South and the Democratic party. Surrounded by Pennsylvania-Dutch Hoover Republicans, my father was a truculent progressive who regarded Woodrow Wilson and Franklin Delano Roosevelt and his wife Eleanor as deities of political humanitarianism. Yet there was always some guilt about the migration from Southern penury and limited opportunity. My father's brothers certainly took a dim view of his departure. Uncle Hoyt, by all accounts a soldier of fortune who had something obscure to do with stringing telegraph wires through the Philippines, used to tease his brother about the move. On a rare visit, Uncle Hoyt could not subdue the spirits of the children running in and out of his room. Finally, he exclaimed, "Shut de do', boys, shut de do'." "Oh mother-r-r, come hear how Uncle Hoyt says shut the door-r-r." Over and over they begged him to say the magic phrase, and brought playmates in to hear it repeated. Later Uncle Hoyt regaled the members of the Southern branch of the family with retellings of the incident, one that suggested how the Northern members of the clan were losing their heritage along with their Southern accent.

To compensate, perhaps, for the alleged betrayal, my father tried to instill Southern ways in our household routines and attitudes, with biscuits and hominy (*never* called grits) at most suppers (*never*

Preface

For some thirty or more years, historians of the South, with few exceptions, have relegated the most important aspect of antebellum ethics to the trashbin of history. Honor, keystone of the slaveholding South's morality, has been called a chimera, one that was imposed to hide the region's guilt over race domination. The ethic was so clearly incompatible with the moral thrust of civil rights and democratic hopes that Southern-born scholars joined with Northern students of the region's past to eliminate the ethic from serious consideration. As its power diminished and even seemed to slip out of sight, those academicians who were not proud of the Southern record sought to exorcise its ghostly shape. It would not do to recognize its former existence as a determinant of behavior for fear it might obtain renewed legitimacy. Since World War Two, the reluctant entry of the South into the moral assumptions of the nation as a whole required, it seemed, a drastic rewriting of the past. Better to call the manifestations of honor the "cavalier legend," the "plantation myth," the "patriarchal dream" than to see how and why an American people once fought to the death for principles no longer deemed valid.

From the founding of Jamestown to the mid-twentieth century, called dinner). Nor were we to call him Daddy, only Father, at risk of almost painful ticklings. But among the vestiges of the old life, there was certainly no redneck racism. Cole Blease, Theodore Bilbo, and Gene Talmadge were anathema to him, as they were to most gentle Southern souls of the 1930s. It scarcely occurred to my parents that there was any incongruity in venerating the memory of the "glorious cause," chastely damning the "infamous" misdeeds of Generals Sherman, Sheridan, and Wilson, and yet deploring the horrors of lynch law. My parents accepted Jim Crowism. Yet they applauded the tentative first steps to breach racism during the first New Deal, then during Harry Truman's Fair Deal. Had he lived, my father would have approved the course of Rosa Parks and Martin Luther King, albeit gingerly. Such attitudes were neither prescient nor timid, neither egalitarian nor altogether patrician.

Yet aside from an almost irrational devotion to English culture, my parents never swerved from admiration for their ancestors who had left farms in South Carolina for frontier Alabama in the 1810s and who had made a contribution, however undistinguished, to the Confederate war effort. Throughout the 1930s a steel engraving of Robert E. Lee hung in the vestibule of the house in Harrisburg, staring bleakly out the front door toward the Susquehanna riverbank just beyond. A small Confederate flag was draped, slightly askew, across a corner of the picture. The first poem that I ever tried to memorize was Father Ryan's "The Conquered Banner." My father and another uncle, an Episcopal missionary in Tarboro, North Carolina, used to recall in my hearing the family story about Jefferson Davis's visit to their hometown, Eufaula, Alabama, on his trip in 1881 to a celebration in Macon, Georgia. He had tea in the house of their father, my grandfather, the town's assistant postmaster. (During Grover Cleveland's terms in office grandfather took the top spot, and the community's sole—and half-literate—Republican became his assistant.) The local Episcopal minister, a Yankee, fulminated about the county's reception and parade for the "traitor," my uncle recollected. Politeness—what would you expect of Yankees anyhow?—had demanded that the children be silent throughout the clergyman's tirade, but nevertheless my uncle Bertram had spoken up in a passionate defense of Jeff Davis. He was almost sure that his father secretly approved the outburst.

In the early 1940s my family moved to Sewanee, Tennessee. We lived under the shadow of Breslin Tower, landmark of the University of the South, mountain refuge for post–Civil War Carolinians who had seen better days and whose descendants lived there still. Summers, as before, were spent at Blue Ridge Summit, on the Maryland-Pennsylvania border, within walking distance of the Mason-Dixon line. My parents ensured that I had a Southern education, sending me to the Sewanee Military Academy (recently disbanded), then to St. James in western Maryland, near Antietam, then back to Sewanee for college. The choice of attending Johns Hopkins University in Baltimore for graduate study under C. Vann Woodward was my own. These experiences in the North, in a border state, and in the lower South no doubt shaped my thinking as much as the unforgettable inspiration that Professor Woodward imparted to all his students in the late 1950s and early 1960s. If such a background may seem inappropriate, the circumstances cannot be rectified at this late hour.

Thus I cannot claim ideal credentials for the task ahead. Perhaps no one can. No historian can attain pure impartiality, not in the face of the cruelty, violence, distortion, and venality to be found among any people alive or dead. But about the Old South a new objectivity which is not to be confused with indifference or insensitivity may now be possible. Even former segregationists recognize that American racial customs must continue to change. The battles for equality have been and still are being fought, and there are great imperfections yet to be conquered. But for all the temporary setbacks that may ensue in the present and future, there is a national confidence about democratic values, a certainty that did not exist ten or fifteen years ago. Under these circumstances, we can more clearly perceive how far we have traveled and look backward without feeling dismay at the deeds of ancestors, good and bad.

The present volume is divided into three major parts. The first four chapters comprise a section called "Origins and Definitions."

They deal with the common moral thrust of the country, from the plantings of the seventeenth century to the establishment of the early Republic. The ethic described is a harsh code, traceable to the Indo-European tribes that created Homeric Greece and destroyed the power of Rome. Chronology, the reader will find, is subordinated to comparisons of past times and societies and demonstrations of similarities. The purpose is to stress the continuity of human ethical principles. These orderings of conduct, thought, and ritual make possible, for instance, our enduring appreciation of great literature from one age or another. What Homer, Tacitus, Polybius, Montaigne, Shakespeare, Molière, and others had to say spoke directly to cultivated white Southerners as clearly as they do to us, though economic, social, and political conditions varied one from another and from ours. We have not left the old ethic entirely behind even today. For better or worse, we are its heirs.

Literary sources in the first section and also thereafter are treated almost as if the fictional characters were once alive. Through metaphor and felicity of language, the novelist's imagination can recreate the way people once thought and acted, so ordering matters toward an ethical veracity that the historian could never achieve. The scholar is dependent upon written records, whereas feelings and even the dramas of daily routine often were conveyed by gesture, look, or silence, or words that no one saw fit to write down. We do, however, have an underutilized body of materials—courtroom testimony hidden away in county seats and state repositories. These often verbatim samples of ordinary speech, particularly valuable for reaching those who were not much given to using the pen, have been an indispensable aid, most especially in the second and third sections.

The second division of the book, "Family and Gender Behavior," explains the pervasiveness of the ancient code and its nineteenth-century accretions of humanitarian and Christian gentility. At once it will be observed that I have broken with two traditions. I have not tried to trace out the role of politics in the culture of honor as it affected home and community life. Political expressions and causes arose from these sources—defense of family and community. If honor had meant nothing to men and women, if they had been able to separate it from slavery, there would have been no Civil War. Proof of that point, however, I do not attempt here.

The second noticeable deviation from current historical practice is that I have not placed slavery at the center of Southern concern. White Southerners seldom forgot the presence of blacks; nevertheless, what mattered most to them was the interchanges of whites among themselves. This is what dominated whites' everyday life, no matter how dependent so many were upon the unceasing toil of the unfree. Had it been otherwise, slavery would have been even more oppressive than it was. Whites' jockeying for position in their own world gave the underclass some room for fashioning lives apart. Intrusiveness and overconcern, sometimes well intentioned, must have been a serious vexation for those in the slave quarters. They preferred to be let alone.

The last section, "Structures of Rivalry and Social Control," treats a vital aspect of the Southern ethic: the relation of the community to the individual, free and slave, and the family to which he or she belonged. All traditional societies, the slaveholding South among them, provided little space for the individual, at least by present-day standards of privacy. Tradition has it that no man or woman ever was—or should be—an island. Instead, one's existence and even one's capacity or right to survive are determined in the public forum—the *deme* or larger "family" of peers and superiors called community. Deviance from accepted norms can only be tolerated if the offender somehow conveys a sense of powerlessness. Otherwise the nonconformist, whose misdeeds may be real or socially conjured up, faces ostracism or worse.

A third point of departure, especially noticeable in the final part of the book, involves the use of some interpretations provided by behavioral scientists. I share some of the skepticism that has greeted productions in "psychohistory"; whether as practitioners or theorists, psychoanalysts are seldom sensitive to historical change or to cultural differences among people. By contrast, in these pages such matters as oedipal conflict are not treated as purely Freudian manifestations. Rather, they are perceived as social, even economic issues separating the generations. There can be no doubt whatsoever, though, that white Southerners, highly conscious of even the subtlest distinctions in rank among themselves, exhibited evidence of father-son ambivalence along with other kinds of rivalry at home or in the world. An understanding of such patterns is best achieved through anthropology and sociology, insofar as these fields may be applied to historical circumstances with common sense. In this regard, I have been influenced most especially by Julian Pitt-Rivers and other anthropologists specializing in the study of Mediterranean cultures. To be sure, the Old South was neither so rigid in hierarchy nor so intensely concerned with honor as those currently living on the Mediterranean littoral. Yet similarities are evident, not because of any direct linkage between two regions so alien in history and religion, but because primitive conditions of life often produce elemental social values sometimes roughly parallel from one society to another. We have tended to interpret many Southern and American traits as consequences of our frontier heritage—including a tendency toward violence. However, American continuities of conditions, forms of violence, and social patterns from the prehistoric Indo-European culture, and more directly from the British Isles, also played a crucial role. The connections have yet to be thoroughly explored in scholarly depth, but an attempt has been made here to point the direction to others.

In addition, a debt to the modern followers of Emile Durkheim should be acknowledged. Kai T. Erikson, whose *Wayward Puritans* (1966) was among the first books to combine history with analyses of "boundary maintenance," helped to illuminate the patterns of Southern punishments for deviants, white and black. In applying ideas from other disciplines, the historian is tempted to adopt language and, alas, selection of facts to suit the exigencies of the alien field. I trust that these dangers have been avoided, so much so that experts in the other social sciences will have more reason to find fault than the traditional historian or general reader will.

Finally, a particular use of narrative should be mentioned. Although much of this book is unexceptional in the application of short examples to illustrate a general point, extended treatment of events sometimes appears as well. The purpose is not so much to entertain as to explicate major themes. Storytelling is the oldest form of history, and a genre that has long associations with honor itself. Heroes and villains, statesmen and turncoats, heroines and harlots—these figures around whom stories were built have served as personifications of honor and shame throughout Western civilization. Their deeds or misdeeds celebrated the triumph of revered values, the defeat of wrong. Needless to say, the use of stories here does not carry that traditional moral purpose. Adoption of the narrative form, even partially, does not involve an uncritical endorsement of values and individuals as they were judged in prior times. Instead, honor and its opposite can be observed with detachment and yet with a sympathy that implies no approval. The context, or plot line as it were, often determined how people in the past interpreted events and judged actors. Thus, we must tell stories—some long, some short—to understand how honor and shame were once experienced. I shall expend precious space, for instance, on a story by Hawthorne in the first chapter, on Bacon's Rebellion in early Virginia in the second, and on an obscure nineteenth-century planter family's tragedy in the last.

Storytelling, fictional or historical, satisfies a basic human curiosity to learn how it all came out. Modern historians and readers seek something more significant: an understanding of social structure and the changes and tensions that constantly undermine the walls until they crumble and new ones take their place. Lucidity and coherence may suffer if, within the narrative mode, facts and artistic touches are added to enliven the recounting. "Plot" and analysis are at cross-purposes. Nonetheless, extended examples with intertwined argument—what David Hackett Fischer calls "braided narrative"—are offered in place of hard statistical data, the evidence that modern social historians prefer over literary impression.* Ethics are grounded in situations, as Joseph Fletcher, the American theologian, has explained, and situations do not lend themselves to

* David Hackett Fischer, "The Braided Narrative: Substance and Form in Social History," in Angus Fletcher, ed., *The Literature of Fact* (New York: Columbia University Press, 1976), pp. 109–33.

quantification. Even so, probably more in that line of verification could have been introduced into the text than what the reader will actually find there. Worth noting, though, is the fact that on many matters—first-cousin marriages or bride-groom age discrepancies in the Old South, to name only two—scholars have just begun the necessary work. It is hoped that when we have more such information, the results will bear out the findings here.

An explanation of the various terms in the title should be offered at the outset to prevent early misunderstanding. Although more elaborate explorations of honor will be forthcoming, the word must be defined here. As used in the text, honor is essentially the cluster of ethical rules, most readily found in societies of small communities, by which judgments of behavior are ratified by community consensus. Family integrity, clearly understood hierarchies of leaders and subordinates, and ascriptive features of individuals and groups are guides for those evaluations. By "ascription" is meant such biological determinants as race and color, gender, bloodlines, physique and physical skill, age, and inherited position. It cannot be too strongly emphasized that honor is not confined to any rank of society; it is the moral property of all who belong within the community, one that determines the community's own membership. Even those who rebel against the society and its conventions or who stand outside or below the circle of honor must acknowledge its power. Southern yeomen, no less than rich planters, found meaning in honor's demands. Thus, honor served all members of society in a world of chronic mistrust, particularly so at times of crises, great or small.

The ancient ethic was the cement that held regional culture together. At one time other Americans, not Southerners alone, expressed concern for honor. Despite allegiance to Christian conscience and to increasingly secular ways of perceiving social values, even colonial New Englanders adhered to the traditional ethic of honor. Many continued to do so well into the nineteenth century.

Yet the traditional credo lasted longer and in more pristine form in the slaveholding section than it did elsewhere in America. We cannot understand the role assigned women in America, for instance, without reference to honor. Nor can we grasp the persistence of racism in American life generally without recognizing its intimate relation to the code.

The subtitle "Ethics and Behavior" will alert the reader to the fact that this study is not exclusively devoted to one class or another, not to one part of the South or another. But my focus is entirely upon white people's notions of right action; no attempt has been made to include free blacks or slaves. In regard to the white race, the South was no more uniform on moral than on economic issues. Some communities were more simply organized than others. Poverty-stricken hillfolk and wealthy Charlestonians lived substantially different lives and entertained quite distinctive opinions about one thing or another. This study scarcely refutes so obvious a point. But our attention must be directed toward those ethical patterns that gave coherence to the region's culture. In doing so, greater attention has been paid to the Southern interior and Southwestern slave states than to the more sophisticated plantation homes of Tidewater Virginia and Maryland. The reason is that the great majority of white Southerners did not enjoy the wealth, comforts, and educational advantages of that tiny, overstudied group of gentlefolk. Moreover, according to recent investigations those Tidewater squires and their ladies were a good deal less refined than prior generations of scholars were accustomed to think. In adopting a nonaristocratic and "hinterland" bias, if that is a fitting description, I have been guided by W. J. Cash's example in *The Mind of the South,* which greatly influenced the writing of this work.

I have chosen the term "Old South," one identified with the years 1800 to 1860. The designation is more broadly interpreted in this work because persistence of custom is a central theme. Limiting a topic to exclusive periods is a convenient but sometimes doubtful usage. Certainly it makes little sense in regard to matters of ethics. As a rule writers of history overplay abrupt change, symbolized by neatly bracketed "eras" or dates. Often scholars ascribe responses to conditions which they believe peculiar to the short span of years under scrutiny or to particular circumstances that do not include such factors as folk memory and habits passed down through the generations. This work does not employ that approach. Therefore, "Old South" refers to traits and styles of actions with distant origins and with manifestations still observable in Southern life today. As a result, I have sometimes made use of investigations undertaken by twentieth-century rural sociologists. The remarks of farming folk whom they have interviewed often reflect attitudes of a "pre-modern" character. In fact, "pre-modern" might have been used instead of "Old South," but that neologism is very infelicitous and probably confusing.

As a result of decisions reflected in the title, certain issues have been omitted. I leave to another volume, in preparation, the discussion of honor, race, and slavery, although some aspects of the subject are explored in this book. In addition, a third monograph is planned to deal with honor in decline. The process of decay began in the Jeffersonian era, if not sooner, as more and more whites were evangelized by the revival movements and secularized by the forces of democracy and economic development. The pace quickened in the 1850s, causing so much consternation among advocates of traditionalism that it helped to precipitate secession. Although the turmoil of Reconstruction led to temporary regression, the ethic of honor continued to weaken ever more speedily as class consciousness, secularism, and other forces hastened its departure, especially after World War I. The volume will carry the topic into the 1950s. It will emphasize the influence of religion, urban life, and economics in a way not found herein. In contrast, the task of the moment is to show how honor functioned in the first place.

Another departure, which social and intellectual historians will be the first to notice, is the emphasis placed upon law, particularly family and criminal law. It is impossible to study husband-wife relations, for instance, without taking account of the persistence of common-law practice. Likewise, criminal codes and practices were fundamental in the determination of acceptable and unacceptable forms of personal violence. By and large, social and intellectual history has usually been presented without sufficient regard for the legal system and its demands. Instead, scholars have counterposed popular behavior to the strictures of the church, whose task it was to set standards almost beyond human capacity. Thus Protestant thought, particularly Calvinism, has served as the baseline; if practice scarcely ever matched ideal, surely it was no wonder. First, only a fifth to a third of all Southern whites before the Civil War were churchgoers. Second, even the faithful did not always do even the least that was expected of them. But all, whether faithful disciples of God or not, were subjected both to formal law and to community rule. One should not ignore the steadily growing power of the various denominations in the First and Second religious Awakenings. Nonetheless, the legal and community sanctions against deviancy were the chief regulators of conduct, not the church. The courthouse, not the clapboard church, the gossipers at the tavern or in the parlor, not the frowning deacons, exercised primary influence. When matters seemed to get out of hand, Southern whites resorted to trials at law or, more grimly, to communal forms of justice—the charivari (tar and feathers), public whipping, or lynch law. Churchmen either were themselves involved or stood quietly aside, recognizing the superior moral force of the circle of honor itself.

Finally, this study, moving as it does backwards and forwards in time and place, does not directly chronicle the coming of the Civil War in its ethical, economic, or political phases. But it should be evident that I believe that a major and unstudied aspect of that struggle was the region's abiding faith in honor. The inhabitant of the Old South was not inspired to shed his own or another's blood for the right to own slaves. Ever since man first picked up a stone to fling at an enemy, he has justified his thirst for revenge and for popular approval on the grounds of honor. A close reading of Southern rhetoric on the eve of war should make clear the fact that white Southerners were certain their cause was justified by that prehistoric code. My intention, however, is not to explain the course of a conflict that only Cassandras and hotheads thought irreversible. Rather it is to illuminate the continuity and social utility (as South-

ern whites thought) of moral rules often at war with the secular and
evangelical ethics of the dynamic North.

The sole advantage in undertaking a project requiring much research, writing, rewriting, and, agonizingly, additional rewriting is
that one gains more friends than a speedier productivity would permit. Though engaged in her own professional pursuits in literature,
my wife Anne has endured the ordeal with aplomb and patience.
Part Southern, part Northern herself, she brought many rich insights, especially about Southern womanhood and childrearing, to
the materials, as well as her own literary skill. Equally useful as
editor and critic was her father, William L. Marbury, an accomplished lawyer who insisted (alas, sometimes vainly) upon clarity of
thought and expression. His legal expertise saved me many times
from embarrassing error. Also I acknowledge with much gratitude
the information that Professor Terry Alford so kindly and gen-
erously provided for the final chapter.

Three colleagues read all the chapters as they were produced,
and sometimes the extensive revisions as well: Lawrence J. Friedman, David Hackett Fischer, and Stanley L. Engerman. Busy with
his own *Gregarious Saints,* an antislavery study soon to appear,
Larry Friedman found time to make extensive, always helpful criticisms. Stan Engerman did likewise, with remarkable speed and
precision. Dave Fischer was instrumental in a restructuring of the
book that entailed an additional six months of labor on the first
section. The experience was worthwhile if only because I learned
more about honor's evolution. Finally, I must mention the distinguished professors and promising graduate students at these
institutions where parts of the book were given in seminar or lecture: Princeton, Case Western Reserve, Johns Hopkins (especially
Ron Walters), Bowling Green State, Brandeis, North Carolina at
Chapel Hill, Akron, Pennsylvania (especially Drew Faust), and the
Newberry Library.

Foundations and grants supplied assistance without which the book might never have been completed. A John Simon Guggenheim Foundation Fellowship made possible the initial research. The National Endowment for the Humanities and the Woodrow Wilson International Center for Scholars both provided a crucial summer stay in Washington. The Shelby Cullom Davis Center, under the masterful direction of Lawrence Stone, not only offered a second year away from teaching but also the critical appraisal of the Princeton history faculty, graduate students, and fellow visitors at the center, both in seminar and in useful private exchanges. But perhaps most significant of all was the Charles Rieley Armington Program on Values in Children, with Professors Morrell Heald and Barry Levy of Case Western Reserve University in charge. Financial assistance and a forum for the work in progress, presented in cross-discipline seminar, were important as the work neared completion. I note, too, the help of Professors Van Tassel, Ubbelohde, Zain-aldin, and Grossberg of the Case Western Reserve history department. Finally, Dean Dixon Long of Western Reserve College and Eldon Epp, dean of faculty, provided timely grants for typing and administrative help.

Librarians and archivists must receive notice, too. Carolyn Wallace and her staff at the Southern Historical Collection, Chapel Hill, were, as always, gracious and helpful. The same can be said of E. L. Inabinett and Allen H. Stokes at the South Caroliniana Library, University of South Carolina, Columbia; Michelle Hudson and Clinton Bagley at Mississippi's state archives, Jackson; Larry E. Tise and staff at North Carolina's, Raleigh; and Virginia Jones, archivist, and Milo Howard, director, at Alabama's, Montgomery. Other institutions' reference staffs and archivists are also gratefully mentioned: those at the Library of Congress; the Maryland State Archives, Annapolis; the Supreme Court of Baltimore Law Library; the Swemm Library, William and Mary College; the Virginia State Library and the Virginia Historical Society, Richmond; the University of Kentucky Library, Lexington; the Kentucky Historical Society, Frankfort; the Tennessee State Archives and Tennessee Historical Society, Nashville; the South Carolina State Archives, Columbia; the Louisiana State University Library, Baton Rouge;

the Petrie Room of Auburn State University; the archives of the Baker Library, Harvard University School of Business; the Western Reserve Historical Society, Cleveland; and the Law School Library, Case Western Reserve University, Cleveland. Last but by no means least in this category, at Freiberger Library of Case Western Reserve, Ann Drain and her efficient staff of reference and interlibrary loan librarians have been most generous in offering office space and prompt, cheerful service. County officials are always preoccupied with more contemporary pressing issues than rummaging rat-infested basements for an old docket book and suchlike. Yet, with the help of Campbell Miles, I learned how to navigate through the Adams County, Mississippi, deed books and other documents in the Natchez courthouse. Also, special praise is registered here for the history-conscious county clerks in these Louisiana parishes—St. Mary, at Franklin; St. Landry, at Opelousas; and St. Martinsville and Lafayette—where the extant records are well preserved. I thank Doris Tomburello and Maureen Weigand of the History Department, Case Western Reserve for able typing and good-natured response to crises of various kinds, and Sarah Poole for her careful reading of proof. Tessa DeCarlo has rendered highly professional service as copy editor for Oxford University Press. It was a pleasure to work with her. Without Sheldon Meyer's semiannual inquiries over the years about my progress on this study, this book might have been even longer in the making than it was. An author who has so helpful and solicitous an editor as Sheldon Meyer is indeed a lucky one.

Cleveland, Ohio   B.W.-B.
March 1982

Contents

Part One

•

Origins and Definitions

1

Honor in Literary Perspective

Paradox, irony, and guilt have been three current words used by historians to describe white Southern life before the Civil War. They are popular terms because it is hard for us to believe that Southerners ever meant what they said of themselves. How could they so glibly reconcile slaveholding with pretensions to virtue? We prefer to assume that their defenses were either lies or self-delusions. If neither of these alternatives meets the complexities of the circumstances, then their mental gymnastics and their habits may be characterized as unintended paradox—a discrepancy between boasted ideals of freedom and a contrary assumption that those values could forever rest upon the enslavement of blacks.[1] Apart from a few lonely dissenters, Southern whites believed (as most people do) that they conducted their lives by the highest ethical standards. They thought that they had made peace with God's natural order. Above all else, white Southerners adhered to a moral code that may be summarized as the rule of honor. Today we would not define as an ethical scheme a code of morality that could legitimate injustice—racial or class. Yet so it was defined in the Old South. The sources of that ethic lay deep in mythology, literature, history, and civilization. It long preceded the slave system in America. Since the

earliest times, honor was inseparable from hierarchy and entitlement, defense of family blood and community needs. All these exigencies required the rejection of the lowly, the alien, and the
shamed. Such unhappy creatures belonged outside the circle of
honor. Fate had so decreed.

For all the many meanings that the word "honor" has been
given, the ethic for centuries was fairly stable. Ages differed on
which aspect should have priority: inner feelings of self-worth, gentility, and high-mindedness, or public repute, valor for family and
country, and conformity to community wishes. Each of these aspects of the ethic might conflict with others, and much of Western
literature is concerned with how and why such antinomies have
both helped and hindered men's choices of action. Nevertheless,
honor has retained over centuries a character that most could comprehend. That is no longer true. Our view of honor is so rarefied
that we do not see how it could really coexist with violence and the
complacent subjugation of so-called inferiors. Since paradox, irony,
and guilt tell us more about our modern ethics than about the antebellum Southerners', we need a better strategy to reach the heart of
the past. The most efficacious means is through literature, at least
at first. For introductory purposes, I will not begin by defining
honor, or even by offering specifically Southern examples of it. To
do so might at once resurrect long-standing moral preconceptions,
before we are ready to rediscover the South that once existed. It is
best to look elsewhere.

We will start by observing honor at a moment of crisis. It is one
in which a ritual, tragically common in the American South but at
one time more widespread in the Western world, helped a community to overcome its fears and reassert its primal values.

In 1832 Nathaniel Hawthorne, explorer of the New England soul,
published a short story that well illuminates the role of traditional
honor and shame in human affairs. The setting for "My Kinsman,
Major Molineux" is a colonial New England port (Boston, though
unnamed.) True, the site of the tale bears no physical resemblance
to the agrarian South about which this study is concerned. None-

theless, the principles of conduct that guide Hawthorne's characters were ones quite familiar to white citizens of the slave states.
They too knew the exigencies of honor, the horrors of shame. In
fact, Southerners saw them as means of holding fast to the social order that they so deeply cherished. It was threat of honor lost, no
less than slavery, that led them to secession and war.

At the beginning of the story, Hawthorne assures the reader that
the incidents to be described are not conscious foretellings of the
coming American Revolution. The message, he implies, lies elsewhere. He is concerned with the relations of individuals to their
community, one that had not yet broken the cake of custom. He
places the sketch at 1732 or thereabouts. Throughout the early history of the colonies, Hawthorne says, officials of the provincial government displeased both their English masters in London by failing
to carry out orders and their American subjects by attempting to do
so. The result, Hawthorne concludes by way of dismissing politics
from center stage, was "much temporary inflammation of the popular mind."[2]

The narrator then introduces Robin, an eighteen-year-old youth
who has walked from his distant forest home to the somnolent port
with its wooden buildings, narrow streets, and odors of pitch and
the sea beyond. Night has just descended. His mission is to locate a
respected first-cousin-once-removed—Major Molineux. "The Major,"
Robin later tells a kindly gentleman, "having inherited riches, and
acquired civil and military rank, had visited his cousin, in great
pomp, a year or two before; had manifested much interest in Robin
and an elder brother, and, being childless himself, had thrown out
hints respecting the future establishment of one of them in life."

According to old and early New England customs, Robin's elder
brother was to inherit the family farm. In those days, many American young men would receive less of the patriarchal bounty than
the firstborn. Though neither in the North nor South was primogeniture ever popular, inheritances were not always evenly distributed, especially when a father's resources were severely limited. The
second son had to settle for unimproved acres or a chance for apprenticeship at a trade. Some, like Robin, relied upon a patron. The

prominence and wealth of an uncle or another relation could assist the advance of a kinsman on the threshold of career and adulthood. Reliance upon family connections was not a sign of weakness, but a necessity. Such was the pattern in the South long after these common practices had begun to erode in the antebellum North.[3]

First, Robin encounters a dignified gentleman, jealous of his rank and rude to inferiors, an attitude symbolized by his manner of walking with a long, polished cane and a pompous "hem, hem" punctuating his stately tread. When Robin boldly asks directions to the major's dwelling, the periwigged old man turns in outrage. "I know not the man you speak of! What! I have authority. I have—hem, hem—authority," he shouts. Robin hastens away as two barbers standing nearby roar with laughter at his predicament. Throughout his ill-directed wanderings in the town, those overhearing the exchanges, like a Greek chorus, echo the derision of the barbers. Robin encounters a pretty prostitute, whose blandishments he virtuously rejects, a tavern-keeper and his rowdy guests, a watchman, and a representative of the law, who all refuse to answer his simple question. Other townsmen, one and all, eye him with unfeigned suspicion. In exasperation, Robin belligerently halts a stranger who, he perceives, had been among the scornful revelers at the inn. Now, however, the stranger's countenance has been made grotesque, with some black substance smeared down one side of his face and red dye down the other. A violently misshapen nose separates the two colors. The cloaked masquerader gruffly tells him to wait an hour and the major will pass by. The figure vanishes.

While waiting, Robin sees a church standing desolate, faint moonbeams playing over the pulpit and open Bible within. The cold solitude of the church and nearby cemetery remind him of the contrasting warmth of religion at home. He half-dreams that his family is gathering under an ancient oak where his father, a penurious clergyman, customarily holds summer prayer. In the pastoral tableau, his father strains against his emotions for the missing son and the others indicate their grief in stolid but poignantly revealing ways. Then the family enters the house, but in his mind's eye Robin is "excluded from his home."[4] The adventurer knows that he cannot, or at least should not, return in defeat. He must be on his own, however much he misses the innocence and domestic joys of the simple country life that he has left behind.

Another gentleman passes. This time when the request is made, however, the newcomer is cordial, though he urges Robin to wait for the Major just as the previous stranger had commanded. The brief, cheerful interlude ends as a trumpet bleats oddly. Then distant shouts are heard. The people in the imposing houses in front of which Robin and the genial companion linger step out to join the approaching procession with its discordant music. Robin sees "a dense multitude of torches." At the head is a single horseman, the grim figure with the particolored visage. He is "clad in a military dress" and carries a drawn sword, "and, by his fierce and variegated countenance, appeared like war personified; the red of one cheek was an emblem of fire and sword; the blackness of the other betokened the mourning that attends them." Others are dressed as Indians. Some have costumes and faces made up in totally meaningless perversity, as incomprehensible as the passwords that groups of rowdies had earlier whispered to Robin as they passed. Then the leader steps directly in front of Robin, as if the whole pageant were for his edification. The noise diminishes to a low hum deadlier than silence. The torches flicker on the sole occupant of a wooden cart in the midst of the crowd. There sat Major Molineux "in tar-and-feathery dignity."[5]

> He was an elderly man, of large and majestic person, and strong, square features, betokening a steady soul; but steady as it was, his enemies had found means to shake it. His face was pale as death, and far more ghastly; the broad forehead was contracted in his agony, so that his eyebrows formed one grizzled line; his eyes were red and wild, and the foam hung white upon his quivering lip. His whole frame was agitated by a quick and continual tremor, which his pride strove to quell, even in those circumstances of overwhelming humiliation.[6]

A poignant, climactic moment follows: the major's recognition of his kinsman. "The foul disgrace of a head grown gray in honor" was now compounded; the cousins "stared at each other in silence, and Robin's knees shook, and his hair bristled, with a mixture of pity and terror." Robin realizes that all those who had tormented him earlier are nudging each other and leering at him from various points in the immense throng: the watchman, the strumpet in the scarlet dress, the innkeeper, the tavern guests, and the barbers. From underneath the balcony of a mansion that Robin had earlier imagined belonged to the major, there rings out a laugh—"Haw, haw, haw,—hem, hem,—haw, haw, haw." The peal of raucous mockery comes from the first ancient Robin had met. A nightcap has taken the place of the periwig, and his silk hose hang loosely about his legs. But the old man is leaning on his polished cane, scepter of power. Against his will, against all rationality, Robin bursts into uncontrollable laughter, as if in answering bray. All join in, most especially those whom Robin had previously encountered. But Robin's shouts are the loudest of all. The rite ends. The crowd disperses. The cart bears the major away. Drained of all feeling, Robin turns to his companion and says with finality, "Thanks to you, and to my other friends, I have at last met my kinsman, and he will scarce desire to see my face again. . . ." He asks for directions home, but the kind gentleman demurs. Instead he suggests that Robin stay longer; "as you are a shrewd youth, you may rise in the world without the help of your kinsman, Major Molineux."[7]

The story is a fantasy. The masquerading, deceptions, shadowy confusions might be appropriate to a mystery story such as Edgar Allan Poe's "Gold Bug." Colors, and their absence, also suggest the Gothic mode. The writer calls attention to the primary reds of the whore's dress, the crowd's torches, the horseman's half-face, the thrusts of light from the barbers' windows, the harsh glare of lamps and fires at the tavern. These contrast with the blackness of unlighted passageways, the other side of the horseman's visage, the gloom of the mansion opposite the church. The narrator's description of fitful moonbeams upon church and cemetery are also dramatic devices. But myth and reality are curiously conjoined. When people knew only of wooden carts, rude houses, filth-runneled al-

leys, and meager sources of illumination, the flash of color and the
pomp of ceremony were greatly prized. Romance was intended, but
it was the romance enlivening a medieval life of grayness, rotting
wood, deadly odors, and drab existence. It was a world with little
safety or light, one where honors were few but so preciously regarded that cruelty was born of fear for their loss.

The focus of the story is upon Robin's coming of age. The pastoral reverie reveals the disorientation that naturally would arise
when a boy far from home meets unexplained rebuff. He is home-
sick, but also feels somewhat abandoned, even by those who love
him. Yet he takes strength from their memory. Loyalty to family, to
the father who had sacrificed part of his meager salary to send him
thither, was a virtue highly respected, and infidelity was to be
greatly condemned. By the time the kind gentleman arrives, Robin
is already subdued. He supplicates rather than demands help. Robin
is a child still: he even jumps up to show the stranger that he is
full grown. The response of Robin's new friend is genial, but the
initiation into corporate life is just begun. When the noise of the
paraders grows louder, Robin disputes his companion's observation
that it is only a handful of ruffians making fun. No, he says, the tumult must come from a "thousand voices." The kind gentleman
asks, "May not a man have several voices, Robin, as well as two
complexions?" One must learn to accept men as they are, even
though their actions belie their outward claims. Just as some men
are religious and God-fearing, others pay only lip service. It is only
the foolish and the misguided who dare challenge all the ways of
the world. Robin is forced to agree. Then the youth replies with
spirit, "But Heaven forbid that a woman" should be so deceptive as
well. He has in mind the pretty prostitute's "seductive tones" when
she pretended to be the major's housekeeper. A woman's honor, he
means, is much more circumscribed than a man's. She cannot act
shamelessly and yet retain respect. The gentleman does not dispute
his observation. It was a universal judgment.

Although the perspective is that of a very young man meeting a
cruel world, in a few pages Hawthorne has also described the basic
moral theme of early Anglo-American popular culture: the sover-

eignty of a primeval community in the distribution of honor—and dishonor—and the effects of that coercive spirit upon the subjects of the community's rulings. The author makes it abundantly clear that the ritual saturnalia—the mock crowning of the Scapegoat King—has the acquiescence, if not the connivance, of the local establishment. The constabulary was present, not to repress the cruel merriment but to join the proceedings. The single horseman at the head of the crowd represents the fraternity of the colonial militia, the citizen army by which a semblance of order was maintained. The figure with the cough and cane testifies to the complicity of the highest local authority. For the sake of preserving ordinary governance, he permits, and probably had even instigated, the sacrifice of Major Molineux, one of his own councillors. The townspeople who join the procession just as it reaches Robin and his companion live in fine houses near the church and presumably worship there. They would not have initiated so crude a rite, which had its beginning in the meaner districts. Nonetheless, the upper-class folk were scarcely averse to applauding the show.

The tale has been seen almost exclusively as a classically Freudian rendition of the oedipal myth[8]—Robin laughs because the "son" is celebrating the defeat of the surrogate father, Major Molineux. But it must be remembered that while we see events through Robin's eyes (with occasional authorial departures) there is a veiled drama contained in the action, too. It is the struggle, offstage, between the major and Authority, personified by the old gentleman with the cane. Old age has triumphed over Molineux the councillor, himself a man of graying hair but at the height of his powers, until enemies found his vulnerability. Jealous of rivals, determined to retain the preferments of office, the old man under the balcony has found the means to fend off a challenge, perhaps for the last time before death. At the very least, he has preserved his rapport with the vulgar elements of the town under the strange horseman's control. It is this victory, the success of near dotage, that Authority finds so delicious. Fortuitous circumstances—Providence—had placed a young kinsman of the enemy on the scene to witness the ruin of Authority's victim. Since both the cane-carrying official and Major

Molineux were long in years, we cannot assert unequivocally an oedipal relation between them. But still, there is a hint that whatever the situation was prior to the scapegoating ritual, established authority in the town has won a struggle. Robin, still the innocent, sees the pageant as a child would, with himself the center of adult concern, but clearly the old man under the balcony and the demonic militiaman had more serious business to perform. The oedipal factors, if present, must be considered, at least in part, as the reverse of a son's triumph over a patriarch. The "father" of the community is the victor; he makes Robin the child laugh. We shall discover in the Old South that the refusal of the old to surrender power sometimes led to the frustration and degradation of the young. As the figure of Authority exemplified, men deny death's inevitability even when the effects of age confront them. As it has ever been, the relation of father and son could be corrupting, not solely because the young wished the death of the old but also because the old could not always recognize the ravages of age and relinquish power to the young. Triumphs such as that of Authority in "Major Molineux" were hollow. The son, when his turn finally came, either learned to exercise power with similar ruthlessness or, because of a dependency lasting too long, felt unable to replicate the father's success. Hawthorne's story masterfully gives rise to such thoughts, while permitting other possibilities to seem equally valid.

In any case, the climax of the story demonstrates a social fact of traditional life. When crises arose, Hawthorne implies, rich and poor, high and low, join together in the selection of a person to blame. Someone, anyone, should pay for the collective sense of apprehension and outrage. Through the victim, their anxieties are personified and exorcised for the sake of all. At earlier times in New England, wretched old women and zealous Quakers had served similar purposes. Why Molineux should have been chosen is not important. Hawthorne disdains even to offer a clue. The politics of the moment do not concern him, or us, but rather the inexorable will of the populace, whatever the reason, however guilty or innocent the party selected might be.

It is a literal world that Hawthorne describes, but one not seeking justice so much as the facsimile of it. It is all one could expect in a world of risk and vulnerability to misfortune, human and natural. Justice was only public retribution, not abstract principle. If these inclinations were peculiar to New England in its pre-Revolutionary years, the story would be a curious comment on antique ways and little more. But the ethic that produced Molineux's distress lived on in the slave South. It endured, in fact, long afterwards too. The active participation of one part of a white community and the silence or even hidden manipulations of the rest in such affairs were a means of preserving communal solidarity. The invocation of the Lord of Misrule for the maintenance of order was usually directed toward the underclass of blacks. But whites too, on occasion, were its victims. Without such demonstrations the social and racial order itself, it was thought, would founder or drift toward chaos. Everyone had to subordinate personal autonomy to the collective will. It was the task of leaders to carry out the community's desires, to uphold its sacredness; otherwise they would find that they themselves were the sacrifices offered up to the sanctified ideals.

The weight of the community upon the individual is most dramatically demonstrated in Robin's reaction to the sight of the mob and its prize. Not once does the youth question the social order, only his personal disillusionment, which Hawthorne hints will not last long. Nor, in Christian fashion, does he bind his cousin's wounds or follow the cart to offer the kind of aid that he himself, ironically, had journeyed to obtain. Instead Robin joins the laughter of the ruler, who stands in symbolic disarray. Robin's shout is the catharsis attending any tragedy. First there is the pity and terror of watching someone die, either physically or spiritually, an emotion that Southerners sometimes experienced in much the same way. A boisterous release of tension follows. Someone else has been chosen by Providence, and the creature's misfortune somehow enhances one's own sense of safety. That security, which a system of honor and shame provides, is evinced in Robin's successful initiation into the community. By laughing, Robin acknowledges his oneness with the rest. Hysterical though it is, his response was what the crowd anticipated. In bowing to the onlookers, Robin is morally compromised: he is tainted with their complicity in his own kinsman's downfall. Robin is placed in a double bind. The only way provided for his entry into the community is to join in humiliating his cousin. In a society in which family ties are so intense, family betrayal, even under pressure of community opinion, becomes corrupting. Robin's tormentors appreciate the irony. They enjoy his embarrassment and his submission to their will. He only gains the status of bare toleration, but it is a step up from his earlier isolation.

Even as his kinsman is ushered out of decent society—and out of Robin's family—the youth is welcomed, though scarcely warmly, into the new surroundings. In Robin's reaction there is indeed a hint of oedipal triumph over the major, his sought-for guardian. Robin's shout celebrates the transfer of power from the major to the community. In societies of few opportunities, minimal institutions, and low productivity, the death or removal of any office-holder opens a position that advances by one rung those further down the ladder. That exigency, as much as a son's unconscious resentment of a father's power over him, is a factor in Robin's compulsive laughter.

In a sense, Robin is Everyman on a pilgrimage not toward God but toward place in society, passing youthfully through vales of disorder, vice, and unpredictable evils—the common lot of mankind. One message of the tale is the same as that of *The Scarlet Letter:* "Be true! Be true! Be true! Show freely to the world, if not your worst, yet some trait by which the worst may be inferred."[9] That is a universal maxim, applying not to eighteenth-century New England alone. The closing lines about Robin's prospects in the town may suggest that a new, less vicious approach to life lies in the town's future, one in which some of the virtues of the forest order are brought to the city. But Hawthorne forgoes didacticism. Instead, he deals with human isolation—the great dread of being alone in the midst of many, a theme that runs through much of American literature and life. Robin and his kinsman, the major, are both severed from family ties and from community fellowship. But Robin's future, unlike the major's, is hopeful. The stranger offers him the chance to remain. In effect he says, "If you do as we do, you may be one of us." Also, he implies, "Your success will depend upon your own efforts and rectitude, and not upon the favors of a patron."

Nevertheless Robin, though a good lad, belongs to the world of honor, not of conscience. By no means is he to be seen as a figure transcending the multitude. By similar pressures upon the individual, Southern whites held a race in bondage. To make one's way in Robin's setting or in the antebellum South, one had to adopt the principles held sacred by the community.

At the heart of honor, then, lies the evaluation of the public. It may seem paradoxical but it is not so, as Hawthorne's story reveals. Honor has three basic components, none of which may exist wholly independent of the other. Honor is first the inner conviction of self-worth. Seemingly, that sense of personal completeness would comply with modern notions of individuality: all men are created equal. Robin entered the town certain of himself and of his place in society. But he is not yet modern man, who is fully equipped with independent judgment, ready to experiment, reform, innovate. (So at least we like to imagine modern attributes.) The second aspect of honor is the claim of that self-assessment before the public. Robin calls on others to recognize who he is by announcing his kinship with a powerful local figure. The third element is the assessment of the claim by the public, a judgment based upon the behavior of the claimant. In other words, honor is reputation. Honor resides in the individual as his understanding of who he is and where he belongs in the ordered ranks of society. (When society has pretensions that there are no ranks, honor must necessarily be set aside or drastically redefined to mean something else.) It is, at least in traditional terms, both internal to the claimant, so that it motivates him toward behavior socially approved, and external to him, because only by the response of observers can he ordinarily understand himself. The internal and external aspects of honor are inalienably connected because honor serves as ethical mediator between the individual and the community by which he is assessed and in which he also must locate himself in relation to others.[10]

Honor is therefore self-regarding in character. One's neighbors serve as mirrors that return the image of oneself. This submission to public evaluation prevented outrageous haughtiness and encouraged affability, for if one used the self as mirror as Narcissus did, then self-love would become destructive. It is, for instance, the theme that Jane Austen often explored in her novels: the incompleteness of character divorced from social convention. A point that Hawthorne makes, therefore, is the accepted congruence between personal values and the conventions imposed upon the individual by society. The internal man and the external realities of his existence are united in such a way that he knows no other good or evil except that which the collective group designates. He reflects society as society reflects him. To a large degree, that same morality and psychology applied to the Old South as it once did to the New England that gave Hawthorne his historical and literary inspiration.

The decision to begin with a story by Nathaniel Hawthorne was based upon several considerations. First, the tale seems timeless because the author has universalized its meaning by blurring the specifics of location and time. The action of the story is mythic, partially independent of changes in the social order and disconnected from geographical, religious, political, and economic factors. In truth, the ritual of scapegoating was more typical of the South than the North, at least as we recollect such ceremonies from the past, even the recent past. It is hard to imagine the pagan rite's survival in so sternly Calvinistic a setting as the Boston of 1730, where the vision of a New Jerusalem still lingered from the more idealistic days of the colony's first fathers. In other words, Hawthorne's story reminds the reader, therefore, that the morality of a people—at any time, at any place—may have historic roots and elemental features that civilization and religious doctrine can never wholly efface.

In that light it is possible to say that honor complemented, superseded, and challenged the contemporaneous institutions that men and women carefully nurtured and passed on to descendants over the centuries. Just as ancient social customs persisted despite the hegemony of New England church and state in the story—as it did, on occasion, in history—honor existed before, during, and after slavery in the Southern region. Bondage was an answer to an economic need. The South was not founded to create slavery; slavery was recruited to perpetuate the South. Honor came first. The determination of men to have power, prestige, and self-esteem and to immortalize these acquisitions through their progeny was the key to the South's development. Of course, slavery was wholly compatible with honor in ways that were not so apparent in the godly and commercial settlements of New England and Pennsylvania. In fact, over the course of a parallel and mutually sustaining existence, white man's honor and black man's slavery became in the public mind of the South practically indistinguishable.[11]

Yet the South was not always a biracial or slave society. From the founding at Jamestown to the reign of Charles II it had been as homogeneous as the New England communities continued to be until the Irish invasion of the nineteenth century. With a valuable commodity to sell—tobacco—Virginians first employed apprentices and indentured servants. By such means masters could maintain the honor of unsoiled hands exclusively for themselves. But labor shortages developed in the latter half of the seventeenth century. The supply of poor immigrants declined. There was no choice but to buy Africans in the marketplace. Thereafter whites who did migrate southward, particularly the Scots-Irish in the eighteenth century, settled less often as bonded servants than as free peasants. They either subsisted in the uplands as squatters or smallholders or else ambitiously sought to become slaveowners themselves. They too, no less than Tidewater planters, were imbued with the principles of honor.

At first the legal status of the imported Africans was rather uncertain. In a sense, such confusions did not matter greatly. What was important was that servants—regardless of their standing in law—did the indispensable labor. Probably the introduction of Africans was a reluctant step because of the long-standing distaste of English people for the culture, color, and language of a folk so different from themselves. But what mattered to the whites, as to Hawthorne's Authority, was power, honor, and respect, for which riches and a body of menials were essential no less than in New or Old England of the same era.

Even in the Boston that Hawthorne described, slavery existed without much comment one way or the other. In 1701 Judge Samuel Sewall of Boston offered some pious criticism, but he was at once challenged by an advocate of the acceptability of bondage in the eyes of God.[12] In other communities, even among the Quakers above and below the Potomac, the holding of Africans in perpetual chains aroused little if any initial complaint. But in the eastern provinces, climate, economic tendencies, and, to some degree, a moderate rather than intense commitment to honor hobbled large-scale use of Africans. For the most part, the healthier air of New England and the Middle Colonies drew sufficient numbers of laborers from familiar Old World sources.

These thoughts, induced by a close reading of Hawthorne's text, outline a basic premise of this study: the distinct existence of honor apart from a particular system of labor, a special region of the country, and a specific time in history. Just as Hawthorne universalized the point of his narrative, so we too must see honor as greater, longer, and more tenacious than it has been viewed before, at least in relation to the slaveholding South. It was not merely a Southern phenomenon, though in that part of the continent its tenets were more sacrosanct, more integral to the whole culture than they were elsewhere. After all, in the South today devotion to family and country, restrictive views of women's place and role, attitudes about racial hierarchy, and the subordination of all to community values still remain in the popular mind to an extent not altogether duplicated in the rest of the land. Hawthorne, were he alive to observe this set of Southern patterns, would not be at all surprised. His mythic vision points to the endurance of popular morality against the forces of change.

A second reason for beginning in this fashion is that the present study of Southern honor ends with an incident similar to the one in Hawthorne's story. The pair of stories frames the study and its themes. The latter narrative, a real, not fictional event, concerns a Mississippian who in 1834 killed his wife near Natchez; he paid the same price as that which was inflicted upon Major Molineux in Hawthorne's imagination. The first account leads us into matters of definition and origin. The second brings together the various threads of personal, family, and group life in the Old South, threads that made up the texture by which the Southern ethic was sustained. In history, as in fiction, there is a mythic element, one which the charivari of Natchez exemplified as truly as that presented by Hawthorne.

A third advantage of using Hawthorne's tale grows out of the second. Historians are once again debating the long-disputed question: were the North and South different or the same in most essential features? Was slavery alone the cultural and political dividing line, or was it one major point of departure among others? Like Hawthorne's masterpiece, the topic embraces more than a single, plausible interpretation. From one perspective the answer would have to be a resounding No, they were not at all alike. In regard to the colonial centuries, how could New England, for instance, steeped in religious concerns, organized around tightly knit, orderly villages and well-tended farms, have much resemblance to Southern society? There the church played little role in men's calculations. (Piety and churchgoing were for women and dependents.) Towns were almost nonexistent. The population was scattered thinly throughout the countryside. Rather than raise cereals for local consumption, as was done in New England, planters sought quick profits from cash-cropping. When differing racial mixes in populations and the values emerging from contrary labor systems are added to the equation, one would have to conclude that the issue bears little argument. Besides, as historians are now at last beginning to understand, not only were the initial reasons for the early migrations diverse, according to colonial region, but so too were the populations attracted to these shores. Southern colonists were much more likely to come from the more conservative, rustic, and wilder areas and households of the British Isles. By contrast, the settlers of Massachusetts largely emigrated from the more domesticated areas surrounding London and other relatively sophisticated districts. Likewise it may be said without unnecessary exposition that in antebellum times the quickly industrializing North, with its urban, polyglot populace, had increasingly little in common with the still agrarian, underpopulated, and deeply parochial South.[13]

However, if one were to restate the question of sectional characteristics, adding the dimension of time, the answer might well be quite different. Though the peculiarities that had separated the slaveholding and the free parts of the country from their earliest settlement cannot be forgotten, there once had been a moral perspective that embraced both North and South. That ethical unity, a mixture of traditional Protestantism and folk tradition, made possible a united front against the crown in the American Revolution. A common heritage from Great Britain—devotion to common law and the rights of free men, commitment to familial styles of patriarchy, common language and literary culture—assured a harmony of political interests. Had there been no such ethical consensus, the two sections would have parted company long before they did. Hawthorne's story and its companion at the close of this book illustrate the point. Boston in 1732 and Natchez in 1834, to allude to the pair of ceremonies, resembled one another in terms of popular morality much more than the old colonial Boston resembled its transformed self a hundred years later.[14] Like the latter-day Natchez, the Boston that Hawthorne used as his setting was not the thriving town it was later to become. Young men like Benjamin Franklin found greater opportunities in Philadelphia, New York, or the march westward. Early Boston's institutions were not much stronger than those in the somnolent town of Natchez in 1834. To put the matter as simply as possible: Southern mores did not change, at least not very fast; Northern conventions did.

By the time Hawthorne published his story, his Yankee readers had already begun to repudiate the ethical code that the tale so economically describes. The old means of publicly shaming the deviant had disappeared and been replaced by the relative privacy of the penitentiary system, and an almost exclusive reliance upon the legal apparatus rather than community justice. A "cult of humane sensibility" was so firmly entrenched in the free states by 1832 that Southern habits seemed to many as alien, in some respects, as the

customs of Hindus. As one historian has put it, Anglo-American reactions to slaveholding cruelties—for instance, the buying and selling of human beings as chattel—had "the reflexive force of the taboo
against incest."[15] Northern ideals of equality of all men before the
law, though imperfect in practice as always, undermined the privileges of the wealthy and wellborn. To get ahead required skill at intellectual tasks, not just expertise at manipulating others—or at
least so the ideal became. Honor in the antebellum North became
akin to respectability, a word that included freedom from licit vices
that once were signals of masculinity. The process was not toward
human perfection, as some of Hawthorne's intellectual contempo-
raries dreamed, but at least there was an erosion of earlier forms.
True, as late as the 1790s a sea captain of Marblehead was tarred
and feathered for failing in his duty to rescue victims of a ship-
wreck. The local minister was gratified to report in his diary that
the captain had "experienced . . . just deserts."[16] Nevertheless, mob
actions and this form of lynch law were increasingly condemned, especially by the church. The Rev. Lyman Beecher's assault on dueling after Alexander Hamilton's fatal encounter with Aaron Burr
met a widespread popular response. The custom, which was based
on the ethic of honor, became exceedingly rare thereafter in the
free states. These and other signs of social change in the relatively
short span of one hundred years indicated that honor in Yankee-
dom had become another word for domestic and civic virtue. No
longer did it mediate between a rude, sometimes passionate public
and a belligerent, self-regarding manhood.

The older concepts continued, however, to thrive in the Old
South (albeit with some lessening of their strength by the same humanitarian and rationalizing tendencies that the free states experienced). It was this discrepancy between one section devoted to conscience and to secular economic concerns and the other to honor
and to persistent community sanctions that eventually compelled the
slaveholding states to withdraw. Though they were gradually emerging from the archaisms that Hawthorne describes, pre–Civil War
Southerners had to calculate the value of union when their claims

to respect were met in the North with skepticism, condescension, and finally, contempt.

Another noteworthy aspect of the Yankee author's romance is its demonstration of how a writer can make use of the tension between dying social conventions and those that take their place. Only when traditional honor had expired as a dominant force was Hawthorne able to make such impressive use of it, casting his story back in the time when the ethic was much alive. The New England Renaissance, of which Hawthorne was a leading figure, was an outgrowth of that tension between old and new, a transition largely for the better but with costs that sensitive minds like his understood. Southern writers of the same period were denied that interpenetration of changing social and moral systems, and mourned the departure from old ways without having much vision of what was the matter with the slaveholding status quo. The Southern literary renaissance came much later. William Faulkner wrote of honor with a hard-won, anguished detachment not unlike that of the reclusive New England writer: honor in both its heroic and inglorious aspects was the central theme of so much of his work. There was also the same underlying regret for what had disappeared, the same discontent with a new order that was crass, impersonal, with money, not honor, its chief god. Honor had always required wealth but only as a means to an end. It was not the end itself. In fact, there was even a place for honor apart from wealth—when wealth had been lost or not yet fully reached. Moreover, wealth was always relative, so that in a society of poor folk, the most effective wielder of power laid claims to honor even if his property was not great. But possessions for the mere sake of having and enjoying them was secular accumulation, amoral and self-indulgent, as churchmen as well as men of honor never tired of stressing.

What the North experienced in the 1830s and 1840s of Hawthorne's prime, the South would not reach until one hundred years later—the same span as that which separated Hawthorne from the setting of his story. That persistence of honor as the keystone in the arch of social order prevented Southern writers from achieving much authentic voice in the antebellum days, and even long after. The patterns were too much a part of one's being. They could not be touched dispassionately. To do so would have thrown unwelcome, critical light on the concept itself.

To be sure, exaggerations of honor—excessive touchiness, uncontrolled ambition, shameless servility to a fickle public, self-destructive hospitality, and other manifestations of honor distorted—had always been a major theme of human discourse and representation from classical times to the South of the nineteenth century. These evils were always set in opposition to what was thought to be true honor: the unity of inner virtue with the natural order of reason, the innate desire of man for the good, and the happy congruence of inner virtue with outward, public action.

But as Hawthorne's story subtly explains, honor itself was defective. Its reliance on shame distorted human personality and individualism, forcing even the good man, like Robin, to lose himself in the cacophony of the crowd. The interior contradictions of honor held men in shackles of prejudice, pride, and superficiality. It often existed not in authenticity of the self but in symbols, expletives, ritual speeches, gestures, half-understood impulses, externalities, titles, and physical appearances. All these might conform with rational, innovative thought and action, but often enough they were diametrically opposed. Thus holding men in bondage could not have worried too many Southerners so long as they were committed to the age-old morality. Honor, not conscience, shame, not guilt, were the psychological and social underpinnings of Southern culture.

Finally, Hawthorne's story casts light upon the concept of honor, one too long misunderstood. On a popular level, honor conjures up familiar quotations: Falstaff, "a word . . . a mere scutcheon"; Norfolk in *Richard II*, "Mine honour is my life . . . Take honour from me, and my life is done"; Lovelace, "I could not love thee (Dear) so much, lov'd I not honour more"; Antony, "If I lose mine honour, I lose myself."[17] We think of it more or less as our nineteenth-century ancestors did: knights on prancing steeds, battling futilely as Don Quixote did or nobly in the manner of Walter

Scott's Ivanhoe. Reading Chaucer's prologue to the *Canterbury Tales,* we assume that the knight on pilgrimage rather resembled a stained-glass Victorian representation of a handsome crusader serving God. Chaucer's figure "loved chivalrie, Trouthe and honour, fredom and curteisie." But actually those words have a meaning quite a bit harsher than the attributes of Christian gentility that a modern reader might imagine. Chivalry meant mounted warfare and tourneys, truth was fidelity to a lord, honor and freedom meant reputation and self-sufficiency, and courtesy was deferential manners at court.[18] Clearly honor was not always simply a resistance to cheating on exams, the holding of doors for ladies, or even a quaint prickliness about insults. It was much more complex and also much more pervasive than these images indicate.

This is not to say that Southerners lacked any conception of Christian usages. "Respectability" was as popular a term in the South as anywhere else in America. Influenced by religious advances, transatlantic commercialism, and a secular gospel of humanitarianism, Southerners found themselves—like it or not—being homogenized in the modes of Victorian thought and values. At the same time, the resistance to changes that would otherwise have eroded slaveholding remained a powerful force. The result was admiration for two types of honorable conduct, not just gentlemanliness alone. William J. Grayson, an antebellum South Carolinian thinker, was among the few to put succinctly the two concepts before the public. "What is this quality so Protean in its nature as to be prominent and essential in the christian and the man of the world?" he asked in 1853. "In what does this Janus-faced honour consist? It is not honesty; for nothing is more common, both here and in Europe, than for men of honour to contract debts without intending to pay them. Nor can it be veracity, for the falsehoods of gallantry . . . or diplomacy, are sometimes matters of triumph with honourable men." Swearing, gambling, drinking, wenching, and rejection of the Sabbath custom, Grayson observed, "are not incompatible with the character of a man of honour." Before he closed his essay, however, Grayson meekly accepted the new version of virtuous manhood in which Christian qualities outweighed the older, lustier kind.[19] Southern intellectuals were not much given to challenging customs and forms.

Even in the fast-changing North there continued to be a mingling of older and newer versions of honor. Not all Northerners were pious Victorian gentlemen. Not all were outraged by Southern slavery. Some Yankees even joined the ceaseless flux of plantation expansions west, and most of them were quite at home with Southern popular values. Yet despite the diversity that existed in both sections, the crucial difference between them remained a matter of ethical more than economic priority. As much as the regions shared a common legacy, they yet parted to some degree on perceptions of right and wrong. Differing economic systems may coexist peaceably in the same country. But when moral assumptions diverge, the chances for disunion are much greater. Without grasping the ancient, even pagan origins and continuities of honor, we cannot comprehend the endurance of racism as a sacred, intractable conviction, or the approach of civil war, or the desperate commitment of Southern whites to hold black Americans forever in their power.

2

Primal Honor:
Valor, Blood, and Bonding

Like Major Molineux's ordeal, popular concepts of honor grew out of traditions stretching back to far-distant times, to early modern England and even earlier. Southerners were children of the Reformation and humanistic learning no less than other Americans. Like Northerners, they perceived themselves as Protestant in thought, custom, and faith. No other God but the true God ruled their forests and lives. They had a sense of oneness with ancient values—both Old Testament and classical—concepts that still had pertinence in lives of hardship and inequity. "Honor thy Father and Mother," an eye for an eye, the subordination of Eve's daughters to Adam's sons, the shamelessness of Jezebel, the hard vengeance of Jael, the Abrahamic sacrifice of Isaac, the expulsion of Ham, the anointing of David—these and countless other stories, maxims, and rites had a depth of meaning they no longer sustain. Just as some Southerners were religious and others indifferent, so too some whites believed in honor and shame as the biblical stories presented them, whereas others took the ethic lightly. Yet, as evinced in biblical, classical, and popular lore, honor was for all hard law, but inescapable. As the ancient Romans put it, *dura lex, sed lex.* Like the air one breathed, the demands of honor were no more to be doubted than the pursuit of justice, virtue, and godliness, aims with which it was supposed to be compatible.

Two ethical strands that coexisted in Western culture had relevance to the South. The first may be called pagan or Indo-European ethics; the second, a departure from the first, was Stoic-Christian. The latter, more familiar strand was not always distinguishable from the first. The two were thought to be reconcilable, at least to a degree. Like other aspects of human endeavor, honor was subject to evolutionary changes, most especially in the epoch just before American settlement began. In sixteenth-century English court circles, learned men following the humanistic trends of the Continent began to refine the concept of honor from its primitive, familial origins. As the church had long sought to adapt the warrior motifs of chivalry into the Christian credo, so the intellectuals of the Renaissance hoped to broaden the definition of honorable behavior. Such thinkers as Sir Thomas Elyot, in *The Boke named The Governour* (1531), advocated loyalty to church and crown as nobler manifestations than fidelity to clan, lord, and personal family. The traditions of a provincial patriarchy, based on blood lineage, slowly declined as the autonomy of lords diminished. The English crown, uniting state and church, grew in power under Henry VIII and Elizabeth and inspired the work of such men as Elyot and Sir Philip Sydney. To military valor, prime requisite of ancient honor or "glory got by courage of manhood," the humanists added the prestige and virtue of learning, especially legal expertise and service to civil government. "Nor place I the honour of Nobilytie in hawkynge, huntynge, pastimes . . . traynes of horses and servauntes . . . or grate lyne," declared Laurence Humphrey, an early Puritan, in 1563. Yet the transition was hardly radical. Even Humphrey, like many scholastics before him, claimed that "renown and fame of auncestry" was a valid motive, but he added that it was especially so when combined with "Chrystian and farre spred vertue." Out of this matrix emerged the concept of gentility, an ideal that eventually evolved into that of the Christian gentleman of Victorian England and America. The application of "right reason" and acquisition of scientific knowledge amplified the character of honor to in-

clude the scholar in the cloister as well as the royal servant on the
bench or battlefield.[1]

Parallel with the increasing reliance upon formal learnedness
was the continuation of oral tradition, versification, and romance
as moral instructors in early modern England. A classic example
was Thomas Malory's *Le Morte D'Arthur*, which explored through
legend the conflict between old lineage culture and the rising demands of central kingship. As a rule, the upper classes of Great
Britain, particularly those far from the universities and the court at
London, were scarcely sophisticated intellectuals. Although historians have concentrated upon the philosophies of Richard Hooker,
Puritan divines, and of course John Locke, it is well to remember
that the English rural squirearchy, from which many Southern
families sprang, more frequently made use of tales, literary and
folk ballads, and, later, eighteenth-century novels as sources of
entertainment and social instruction. John Adams, Thomas Jefferson and the other founding fathers belonged to the humanistic tradition, but many if not most of their neighbors sought less demanding repositories of wisdom. For instance, the famous diarist Mary
Boykin Chesnut recalled how her grandmother in up-country South
Carolina had set her (age eight or so) to singing of "cruel Barbera
[*sic*] Allen—& Lord Lovel" or to reading favorite romances aloud
while the company of black "semptresses" and their mistresses cut
out and sewed clothes for the slaves to wear. To be sure, there was
also the Bible, and in very pious quarters some volumes of sermons.
Taking the genres of social and ethical inspiration together, one
can readily see that they covered a wide range of literary and aural
experience. Some, like the ballads and stories, spoke to the rightfulness of revenge, others to the glory of martyrdom for God's sake.
Some were weighty explications of moral law; others addressed the
need for rebellion against tyranny. Yet all were incorporated as
truths to be revered in a quite unselfconscious but functional way.[2]

So much has already been written about the high cultural forms
for inculcating right conduct that the persistence of the popular
version of honor will require some examination in the next chapter
as well as this one. A central feature of that ethic was its pessimism.

Despite the transformation of pagan notions of Fate into that of Divine Providence, the ancient concept still had its adherents in the colonial and antebellum American South. Like the early modern gentry and commoners of Great Britain, white Southerners (as well as other rural Americans) were aware of the whims of fortune, quite beyond human understanding and control. Forces of a mysterious character predetermined events. All could agree that the villain got his due reward because Providence or God had condemned him for his sins. But what could explain why good men fell despite rectitude and valor? How, for instance, was one to account for the unrelenting series of wartime disasters that befell the Confederacy? God, reasoned the disbelieving Rebels, surely could not think so ill of those who had shown such valiant steadfastness. Faced with what she regarded as the oppressions of Union occupation forces in 1862, a Tennessee Presbyterian minister's wife complained, "I can't think God in his 'tender mercy' will allow such a state of things to last much longer . . . 'The prayers of the righteous availeth much.' " Christian though her petition was, she, like most Confederates, did not acknowledge that the South had sinned in the holding of slaves and therefore deserved the trials of bloody war and Yankee vengeance. Almost every culture in which honor has held sway reveals the same repudiation of penitence as it is demanded of the conquered by the victors. Contradictory though it might seem, success was always attributed to nobleheartedness duly rewarded by divinity. On the other hand, defeat meant no disgrace, no godly judgment, for instance, upon Southern devotion to the slave institution. Fortuna—arbitrary forces of some supernatural kind—had so decreed, but Fate was arbitrary, morally blind, and indifferent. Yankees, most especially the antislavery reformers, expected Southern contrition for wrongs of the slaveholding past, but that would have violated Southern honor and collective self-esteem. Reflecting both religious and pre-Christian feelings, Cornelia Spencer, a Civil War matron of North Carolina, conceded that the South had indeed sinned, but not in the ownership and treatment of slaves, not in the vices that Northerners had so long identified with Southern barbarity, violence, and ungodliness. "I believe," she wrote at the close

of the war, "that the South sinned. Sinned in her pride, her prosperity, her confidence. Sinned in the way she allowed a few fanatical demagogues to precipitate her into the war. God has humbled
her. But strongly as I feel all this, so strongly do I feel that, though
we have fallen we shall rise again. God chastens whom He loves . . .
I would rather be the South in her humiliation than the North in
her triumph. . . ."[3]

Behind this selective, honor-bound fatalism lay centuries of experience with disasters. Recurrent scourges of war, disease, flood,
drought, and other natural calamities made impossible a firm sense
that progress, whether secular or divine in origin, was a reasonable
conjecture. A sense of resignation pervaded Southern colonial and
antebellum popular thought. As historians now understand, for instance, the Chesapeake settlers of the seventeenth century died faster
than natural increase could replace them. A vulnerability to local
diseases only abated toward the close of the first century of white
habitation. Smallpox, dysentery, typhoid, malaria, childbirth complications, and a low ratio of women to men were all inhibiting
factors. Colonial historians Darrett and Anita Rutman have shown
that in a sample of marriages in one eastern Virginia county in the
seventeenth century, 91 percent of the white families had only one
surviving natural parent to care for minor children. "Before I was
ten years old . . . I look'd upon this life here as but going to an
Inn, no permanent being," confessed William Fitzhugh, a wealthy
Chesapeake planter, in 1698. In one household, the Rutmans write,
"the progeny of six marriages among seven people amounted to
twenty-five known children," none of whom reached adulthood
without mourning at least one parent. In the course of the following centuries, conditions improved: men and women lived longer
and parentlessness declined. Yet Southerners' life expectancies con-
sistently trailed those of Northern whites. Southern crops and cattle,
too, were subject to predators and blights that proved less virulent in the temperate zone northward. There frosts, careful hus-
bandry, and shorter growing seasons checked the advance of para-
sites, viruses, and other lethal organisms.[4] Desperation more than
boundless hope inspired Southern whites at work, an approach that

engendered heavy exertions for the short term, perhaps, but apathy and even a sense of helplessness over the long stretch.

At least among the ambitious, the vagaries of world markets for cash crops contributed to life's uncertainties. Bad luck and accidents also played havoc with the future. As a result of these factors, it was not hard for Southerners to remember how fragile human affairs could be, how fleeting joy, how ephemeral popularity, how mortal any system of government, how transient wealth. To be sure, white attitudes were anything but peculiar in this respect. The New England Calvinist tradition provided a similarly medieval view of human hardship and moral inability. But especially after the American Revolution, Northerners, particularly prosperous ones, adopted more sanguine views than those entertained by their early Puritan forbears. Even in the slave states, evangelical impulses and secular trends brightened the prospects for a more predictable, orderly world, but resignation to fate and mortality was deeply ingrained.

Apart from the unpredictability of nature, there was also the unreliability of man. Cynicism was not much in fashion anywhere in the upper classes of Anglo-American society. Nonetheless, the untrustworthiness of others was very much on the minds of Southern planters. As late as 1860 one Texan wrote a friend, "The chief end of [men's] existence is to get money, honestly if they can, dishonestly if they must; and the latter seems the most popular." In advice to his daughter, J. W. Womack wrote, "You must remember as we pass along in the world that people we see are not in earnest—not playing their real parts like the actors on a stage in a theatre. When Mrs. B. meets you," he continued, "and rushes up to you with an air of great affection . . . you may feel certain that she has some plan on foot to deceive you. You must not believe a word she says."[5]

Finally, the mutability of family fortunes—despoiled by the caprice of nature or by some personal degeneracy—was a circumstance well known to the white ruling class. For Landon Carter in the mid-eighteenth century, for John Randolph in 1831, for other Virginia squires from the founding of Virginia to the close of the Civil

War, there was a sense of marked contrast between current deterio-
rations and prior happiness and prosperity, the inevitable falls
from grace that lessons from pagan history and from Scripture so
remorselessly predicted. Thus at a political rally at Prince Edward
County in November 1831, John Randolph "passed in review all
the old families of Virginia, alluded to the fathers and grandfathers of many then standing around him; spoke of their energy, sa-
gacity, and efficient usefulness of character." However, the present
generation, Randolph said, fell far below "their forefathers' standards."[6] Such expressions were meant to invigorate the spiritless by
lashing them verbally with claims of former splendor. Virginia's
economic and political decline from the mid-eighteenth century to
the third decade of the following one was especially demoralizing
for the "old elite," that is, the distinguished families of whom Randolph spoke. But that prospect of declension—the fall of empires,
peoples, and clans—had been the destiny of mankind for ages past,
as Randolph and his kind constantly reminded themselves. Typically, the moral lesson cast the Southern mind backward, not forward to better times ahead.[7]

   If we bear in mind the Southern conviction of life's transiency,
the persistence of archaic values should not seem surprising. Like
conditions produced like moral perceptions, but rather than follow
the ethical transmissions from prehistory to the Civil War, the earliest forms of honor will be seen largely as bench marks for antebellum attitudes. They are reference points against which to set
white behavior before the defeat at Appomatox. The purpose is to
show the lack of uniqueness in Southern custom, its compatibility
with long-held popular perspectives from the Old World. Nineteenth-century New England and much of the rest of America were
the aberrations, not the South. C. Vann Woodward perceptively
noted that Southern distinctiveness in the American setting rested
upon its commonality with world history, a record of class upheavals and betrayals, political dislocations, poverty, and oppres-
sion. But in addition to these woes, which Yankees were generally
spared, the South also shared with other lands an unbroken train
of ethical patterns. These traditions of social instruction and judg-

ment gave Southerners reassurance. Security resided in knowing that insecurity was the lot of mankind; holding fast to the familiar was the best means of salvation.[8]

Constancy of this kind involves no mystery. At one time, however, ancient origins for modern developments were viewed almost as some form of race determinism. In the 1880s Herbert Baxter Adams of Johns Hopkins University urged his graduate students to locate the seeds of American institutions in the heroic, racially superior Germanic past—the New England town meeting's embryonic form in the Anglo-Saxon folkmoot, for instance, as harbinger of American liberty.[9] That exercise quickly proved ephemeral. In reaction, Frederick Jackson Turner, one of Adams's ablest students, turned his attention to indigenous American traits. His celebration of the frontier and the democratic spirit that it supposedly created became a dominant theme for at least a quarter-century after his famous essay on the frontier's closing was published in 1893.

In subsequent years, though, Turner's influence waned, and a different explanation for American national characteristics became popular: the Protestant Ethic of work, entrepeneurship, and consequent town and industrial growth. Even the slaveholding South was partially included in the synthesis. Yet the elemental factors that checked the advance of what was called "bourgeois" ideals have received too little attention. Both Turner and those who took his place rejected Adams's position on the grounds that it rested on insecure social-Darwinist foundations and fantasies of "Aryan" roots. Rather than compare common folk beliefs in the Old World and New, they contrasted the high culture of Boston, Philadelphia, and Monticello with the rough ways of the pioneer trapper, miner, and farmer. Yet American backwoodsmen (ofttimes new arrivals from the Old World themselves) did resemble the peasants and lower order of city dwellers of Great Britain and eastern America, in customs, routines, and beliefs. If scholars have been able to trace American black folkways to African traditions, it stands to reason that similarly oral-based transmissions had an impact upon white Americans, especially in the deeply conservative ranks of poor and middling folk. Ethical risk-taking was never confined to the prosperous classes, but wealth does tend to stimulate innovation and experiment. Thus "habits and customs of older civilizations were" by no means "momentarily forgotten" in the succession of American frontiers in the way Ray Billington, last of the Turnerians, recently claimed. Instead the frontier, especially in the South, was the locale for recapitulating the social customs that settlers brought with them to the wilderness.[10]

Among the attitudes brought from the Old World was the ancient system for determining who belonged among the worthy and who did not. The first signs of an archaic honor appeared in the forests—not where Hawthorne's story opens, but in regions beyond the Alps, before Christ, before Rome. The ethic of honor had Indo-European origins. From the wilderness of central Europe and Asia a succession of conquering tribes had come into prehistoric Greece, then, millennia later, into Roman Gaul, Spain, Italy, and Great Britain, and finally, in the last upheaval, by sea from Scandinavia into parts of the once Roman world. These peoples shared a number of ideas about how men and women should behave. They had thoughts in common about the nature of the human body, the mind, the soul, the meaning of life, time, natural order, and death. The linguist Richard Broxton Onians has described these primitive concepts, finding a unity among the Greeks, Romans, "Celtic, Slavonic, Germanic and other 'Indo-European' peoples" and even those dwelling in "early Egypt and Babylonia and among the Jews." Myths, rituals, oaths, grave sites, artifacts, and most especially word roots all indicate a common fund of human perceptions that lasted in popular thought from antique to recent ages.[11]

The overriding principle for these generations of human beings was an ethic almost entirely external in nature. It was easily comprehended and was considered physically demonstrable without resort to abstraction, without ambivalence or ambiguity. Differentiations between what belonged in the public or the private realm were very imprecise. Evaluations depended upon appearances, not upon cold logic. Southern whites retained something of that emphasis. As Walker Percy, the contemporary novelist, once remarked about the South of not long ago, there was an "absence of a truly public zone" completely separate from the interior life of the family, so that the latter "came to coincide with the actual public space which it inhabited." Family values differed not at all from public ones. The attitude helps to explain folk intransigency about race-mixing, for instance: threat to community was danger to home and vice versa. The absence of a public sector, Percy observed, made possible the coexistence of Southern hospitality and "unspeakable violence" in the same cultural matrix, without paradox, without any sense of contradiction.[12]

With these thoughts in mind, the honor derived from the Indo-European system of ethics will be called "primal honor." From the Stoic-Christian system that the English humanists began to cultivate there arose the concept that hereafter will be spoken of as "gentility." The latter notion of honor became the more familiar one, associated with the upper ranks of Southern society from the eighteenth century through the Civil War. The darker, more unpleasant aspects of Southern life betokened the continuation of the archaic forms, kept alive by the exigencies of an inhospitable, dangerous world where masters had to rule in fear. The following elements were crucial in the formulation of Southern evaluations of conduct: (1) honor as immortalizing valor, particularly in the character of revenge against familial and community enemies; (2) opinion of others as an indispensable part of personal identity and gauge of self-worth; (3) physical appearance and ferocity of will as signs of inner merit; (4) defense of male integrity and mingled fear and love of woman; and finally, (5) reliance upon oath-taking as a bond in lieu of family obligations and allegiances.

In regard to primal honor as personal bravery, Southerners of the nineteenth century boasted that they stood next to no other people. Examples could be cited from almost any public address or ceremony. For instance, J. J. McKilla, at an Independence Day militia banquet in Sumterville, South Carolina, in 1854, offered a typical toast: "*The Palmetto State:* Her sons bold and chivalrous in war, mild and persuasive in peace, their spirits flush with resentment for wrong." Heaping scorn on the "athlete Sumner," the Massachusetts abolitionist, Lucius Quintus Cincinnatus Lamar told Mary Chesnut in 1861 that if the Yankee senator "had stood on his manhood . . . and struck back when Preston Brooks assailed him" on the floor of Congress in 1856, the "blow need not have been the opening skirmish of the war. . . . We are men, not women. . . . Even Homer's heroes after they had stormed and scolded, fought like brave men, long and well." So too would Southern heroes, but if Charles Sumner had only defended his virility, his state would not have had to take up the quarrel, Lamar theorized. For him, as for many, the Civil War was reduced to a simple test of manhood. As Kenneth Lynn ably argues in a study of regional humor, Southerners' touchiness over virility, stemmed from deep anxieties about how others, particularly Northerners and Englishmen, saw them. Yet the braggadocio, the role-playing, the self-deception should not be seen as "gentlemanly masquerade," as Lynn asserts. They meant every word. Look, for example, at Edmund Ruffin, the fiery nationalist who blew out his brains in rage against Confederate surrender. "With what will be my last breath, I here repeat and would willingly proclaim my unmitigated hatred to Yankee rule—to all political, social and business connections with Yankees, and the perfidious, malignant and vile Yankee race": these were the words of his epitaph.[13] Ruffin was no masquerader.

Intimately related to brave conduct and a capacity for hatred was family protectiveness. The impulse was not only a means to assure survival but also a way to avoid criticisms, especially those voiced by one's own family. Thus when the Civil War began, Samuel David Sanders of Georgia mused about Confederate enlistment, "I would be disgraced if I staid at home, and unworthy of my revolutionary ancestors." Moreover, these strictures kept armies in the field. Said a kinswoman of Mary Chesnut in 1865: " 'Are you like Aunt Mary? Would you be happier if all the men in the family were killed?' To our amazement, quiet Miss C took up the cudgels—nobly. 'Yes, if their life disgraced them. There are worse things than death.' " These thoughts differed little from the forms of pagan honor whose descriptions can be found in almost any relevant source. Just as Sanders identified his fortunes with those of his kinfolk, so too did ancient Greeks, for example. "Family attachment," says Moses I. Finley in reference to the Odyssean world, was based upon the conviction that "one's kin were indistinguishable from oneself." As Xenophon phrased the glory of warriors, "And when their fated end comes, they do not lie forgotten and without honor, but they are remembered and flourish eternally in men's praises." The personal and familial were wholly united with the fate of the *deme* or kin-related community, whose defense was brave men's obligation.[14]

Southern demands of courage had ethnic sources. Many of the settlers, especially those in the interior, had roots in the unsophisticated parts of the British Isles, coming particularly from Scottish, Scots-Irish, and Welsh stock. Following the migration patterns down the spine of the Appalachians in the eighteenth century, two investigators, Grady McWhiney and Forrest McDonald, have recently claimed that settlers from the old "Celtic Fringe" of Great Britain comprised a substantial proportion of the whites in most Southern states. Using the 1790 census, Forrest and Ellen McDonald estimate that over half of Southern Carolina's freeholders, and over a third of Maryland's, consisted of individuals of Celtic extraction. The term "Celtic," though, should not be taken too literally. The peoples on both sides of the Atlantic were too mixed to make such a genealogy very clear. Moreover, those of purely English stock, whatever their origins, also found the demands of rural isolation very exacting in terms of bravery and physical stamina.[15]

Nonetheless, illiterate and semiliterate folk tend to hold fast to those values that are functional and practical. Not surprisingly, then, Celtic herdsmen who migrated to the American South carried on those simple, manly skills for which they were noted in the hills of Scotland, Wales, and Ireland. Cattle-raising and, by adaptation, hog-raising were the frontiersman's chief business, forming a pastoral economy parallel to the tobacco and cotton cropping undertaken by venturesome agrarian settlers both Celtic and English by extraction. For instance William F. Claiborne, an early settler and historian of Mississippi, recalled that "Long Johnny McLeod," a state legislator, owned 2,000 head of cattle in the Piney Woods district of the state during the early part of the nineteenth century. Sheep also were plentiful; said Claiborne, "one may graze 5000 sheep without owning a rood of land; from the eastern bank of the Pearl your flock may roam from county to county, till it reaches the margin of the Mobile River, and never be put off the public domain. . . ."[16]

A people devoted to pastoral life may live in abundance, yet they have little need for schools, regularity of work habits, and other marks of economic sophistication and personal comfort. Hillfolk "laziness" owed much to the undemanding character of the up-country economy. The values of honor, the temptations of whiskey, and an abundance of time to enjoy the controversies arising from both assured a continuity with ancient habits wherever Southern herdsmen, half-nomads, gathered for their rowdy amusements.

These Celtic folk had come from a people long inured to hardship and rough ways. Their social attitudes, according to some recent scholars, very closely resembled those of the kinsmen they had left behind the borderlands of the British Isles. (It should be quickly added, however, that from these same areas—Yorkshire, Cornwall, lower Scotland, Ulster, and the lowlands of Wales, most especially—English influence and native enterprise combined to produce others who were not wedded to a primitive pastoralism and were able to adapt to city life, commerce, and steady farming. Their descendants could be found in the Southern ports and on cotton, sugar, and hemp plantations, easily mingling with those of English descent.) Whether these upcountry settlers in the Southern region were Celtic or otherwise, they all shared conservative ideals. For instance, what bound the Scots, whether Highland or Lowland, was the tie of "a widely extended" kinship, "associations common to inhabitants of a rude and wild" land, declared Sir Walter Scott, a novelist whom Southerners greatly admired. The same was true of the Louisiana Creoles, since the French peasants from which so many of them had sprung were also bound by a devout loyalty to immediate kinfolk.[17]

Thus diverse as the Southern people were, at least by European standards, they had a common fund of values that overcame differences in economy and style of living. But certainly the Celtic influence was a most salient feature of antebellum Southern life. Andrew Jackson, Jefferson Davis, John C. Calhoun, James K. Polk, and Sam Houston, to name only a few, were reared on Old World stories of warrior heroism, notions of the correct role for women as mothers, wives, and daughters, and the duties attending manhood. Davis's grandmother, for instance, was Scottish. His father was Welsh. Davis's mother told him legends from the land of her birth, and even taught him a few words of Gaelic that Davis later took pleasure in teaching his own children.[18]

In the case of the Scots-Irish pattern, a direct linkage can be confidently asserted between traditional habits and the Southern style of the mid-nineteenth century. Historians have been slow, however, to recognize the Old World influences upon white Southern culture, largely because such groups as the Scots-Irish melted so readily into the American populace. The Virginia novelist George Tucker, in his 1824 *Valley of the Shenandoah,* noted the tendency and claimed that it arose from feelings of inferiority to the metropolitan culture of the conquering English. Hence, he said, the Scots-Irishman "readily identifies himself with the country he adopts." Nevertheless, the same violent spirit, inattentiveness to regularity of farming, and clannishness persisted.[19]

Insistence upon valor was especially evident in moments of crisis when outside forces threatened Southern integrity. In 1811, as the nation struggled with an ineffective policy toward England's war with Napoleonic France, young John C. Calhoun replied to the Anglophile John Randolph's caution against fighting the British by exclaiming, "Sir, I here enter my solemn protest against this low and 'calculating avarice' entering this hall of legislation." Peace with submission was "only fit for shops and countinghouses. . . . [The nation] is never safe but under the shield of honor." Many years later, William L. Yancey echoed opinions similar to Calhoun's and to those that have inspired loyalists to the ethic of honor ever since Polydamus lost the debate with Hector and the Trojans imprudently followed Hector's impassioned cry for action and left their walls to contest Achilles on the battlefield. The Alabama senator warned the 1860 Democratic convention in Charleston:

> Ours is the property invaded; ours are the institutions which are at stake; ours is the peace that is to be destroyed; ours is the honor at stake—the honor of children, the honor of families, the lives, perhaps, of all—all of which rests upon what your course may ultimately make a great heaving volcano of passion and crime. . . .[20]

These were not romantic sentiments. They were not merely frightened words at the prospect of slavery's economic and political demise. Rather they were the quite unextraordinary notions that always appeared when a people, ancient or more recent, felt the necessity to defend familial and *deme* integrity.

Such heedless bellicosity had its positive side. The virtues of the battlefield ensured that men could rely on each other in time of need. Although perpetual rivalry for position among men of honor resulted in intracommunity violence, a cultivation of ferocity meant that when attacked from without, men could trust each other, almost as brothers. The Mediterranean aphorism was "My brother is my enemy, but the enemy of my brother is my enemy." This style, though not so intensely followed in the Old South as in present-day North African and Middle Eastern countries, might seem repugnant to modern sensibilities. Yet it was essential to a martial people that men be warlike, for the sake of the *deme*'s security. Through warfare, just as through personal tests of strength in peace, white Southerners constantly found reasons to trust one another and to punish the untrustworthy. The overcoming of hardships enhanced personal and group fellowship. War was ennobling, and the necessity for discipline strengthened character. If men believed these notions to be true, in some measure they were self-fulfilling.

Yet community pressures, not personal preferences, were often the basis for military valor. So it had been in ancient times, when the women and children at the battle site denounced the cowardice of their Germanic male protectors when the fight was going poorly.

Likewise in 1709, returning militia troops who had failed to dis-
lodge the hated French from Nova Scotia received an unexpected
welcome from Boston housewives. From second-floor windows the
women emptied chamber pots upon the veterans on parade, crying,
"Is your piss-pot charged, neighbour? So-ho, souse the cowards."
Fear of reproach for failing to fulfill one's duty to serve family and
community at war was so great that antebellum Southern whites,
like these earlier peoples, questioned the value of peace in submission. War was a way to put aside luxuries and idleness, vices that
weakened resolve.[21]

The truculence of the Nullifiers had much to do with this concept of morally purifying violence. In 1827, for instance, when
South Carolina debated whether or not to challenge federal authority to impose the hated tariff, Robert B. Rhett urged constituents, "If you love life better than honor,—prefer ease to perilous
glory, awake not! stir not! . . . Live in smiling peace with your insatiable oppressors, and die with the noble consolation that your
submissive patience will survive triumphant your beggary and despair." Whether Nullification or, later, secession was wise or fraught
with risks mattered little to those zealots determined to retrieve
honor, with which slavery was inextricably tied. What concerned
them was the necessity for valiant action. Without it, the rest of the
world (they asserted) would deem the white populace cowardly and
their leaders recreant to duty. The "Submissionists," the opponents
of secession, Albert Gallatin Brown of Mississippi claimed in 1860,
were the worst enemies the South could have. "If it should cost us
the Union, our fortunes, our lives, let them go," he fumed; better
that than meekly to "submit to a disgrace so deep and damning."[22]

Southerners were not peculiarly romantic in voicing these sentiments. Equally hyperbolic language came from the lips of Northerners during the American Revolution. Just as impetuous and
honor-conscious as a South Carolinian, the Boston leader Josiah
Quincy spoke out in tones that a planter would have applauded.
"Go, thou dastard! Get thee home!" Quincy exclaimed during the
anti-British crisis of 1767. "A rank adulterer [the Tory neighbor]
riots in thy incestuous bed, a brutal ravisher deflowers thy only

daughter, a barbarous villain now lifts his murtherous hand and stabs thy tender infant to the heart—see the sapphire current trickling from the wound, & the dear Boy, now as he gasps his last, cries out the Ruffian's mercy." Quincy was a Puritan at heart, but he saw no dichotomy between the rhetoric of honor and his religious convictions. For those who urged a more prudent, calculated course, Quincy had a ready retort: "If this, thou blasphemer! is enthusiasm, then will we live and die enthusiasts." It was on such popular notions of valor and bloody conviction that American Revolutionaries relied to unite the colonies to overthrow tyranny. That shared fund of experience and language would eventually be dissipated in recriminations over slavery.[23]

These warrior convictions were ancient. For instance, the morally purifying nature of military action was the theme that Geoffrey of Monmouth placed in the mouth of the legendary Cador, Arthur's Duke of Cornwall: "I have been afraid that the life of ease which the Britons have been leading might make cowards of them. . . . Indeed, when it is obvious that men are no longer using their weapons, but are instead playing at dice, burning up their strength with women . . . then without any doubt their bravery, honour, courage and good name all become tainted with cowardice." Similarly, during peace drinking and gambling had long served as moral equivalents of war. The purpose of excessive bouts was to steel the nerves of heroes and also to express the relative worthiness of those who took the punishment and gained the winnings over their rivals. Alcohol was supposed to provide the courage to meet upcoming challenges. To Tacitus, German tribesmen of his time carried matters beyond all reason. Frequently they drank themselves into insensibility and then boasted of stamina. Some even gambled their lives into slavery, accepting the outcome with remarkable aplomb. The debt of honor, the gambling debt, was a figurative death; it had to be paid, just as one sacrificed life in battle, heedless of result. Such distractions, Tacitus admitted, were thought immoral if they became a permanent preoccupation. But, he said, ancient Germans loved games and wild banqueting better than domestic routine; only war was a greater pleasure. By "dawdling away their time they show a strange inconsistency—at one and the same time loving indolence and hating peace." Descriptions of Southern inclinations along these lines were often quite exaggerated. Such habits, however, were too often observed and even complained about by Southern whites themselves to be wholly mythical.[24]

Honorable revenge, regardless of consequences, had not only political implications but social results as well. It justified many kinds of cruelty toward native Americans. Spoiling the slain was a common custom that enhanced the esteem of those who were victorious by demeaning the fallen. When Patroclus was killed, Hector stripped the corpse, cut off the head, and left the body for the dogs of Troy. Americans treated Indians to similar ignominies. In response to the Creeks' murder of a white family in 1812, Andrew Jackson, for instance, wrote, "When we figure to ourselves our beloved wives and little prattling infants, butchered, mangled, murdered, and torn to pieces, by savage bloodhounds, and wallowing in their gore, you can judge our feelings. . . . we are ready and pant for vengeance," for "the brave sons of Tennessee" were compelled "by their prowess and heroism" to "wipe from the national cherector, this blushing shame." In Jackson's eyes, no less than in those of ancient peoples, man was born to die. But to die in defense of kinsmen or to humiliate in vengeance an enemy was to win eternal glory. Beowulf, the Norse hero, told King Hrothgar, "Better is it for each one of us that he should avenge his friend, than greatly mourn. Each of us must expect an end of living in this world; let him who may win glory before death, for that is best at last for the departed warrior."[25]

It was that spirit which inspired the famous "Rebel yell" on the battlefield. Warlike screams to unnerve the enemy and arouse the fighters had also been part of the ancient German repertoire, as Tacitus marveled. They helped to make possible the atrocities committed upon the battlefield dead. In one's own eyes, defeat did not destroy honor, but when visited upon the enemy defeat was without redeeming feature, and corporal humiliations were justified. The violence of the German epics, the Book of Kings, and the *Iliad* and *Odyssey* all bear witness to the delicious rejoicing in physical revenge. "Hippolochus," celebrated Homer, "darted away," and Agamemnon "smote to the ground; slicing off his hands with the sword and cutting off his neck, he sent him rolling like a round log through the battle-throng."[26]

Southern whites were just as ready to take matters into their own hands when revenge for familial loss was required in their relations with each other. A crime of passion in response to a family wrong was often greeted with acquittal. If the law intervened at all, the penalty was often slight. At the close of the seventeenth century, for instance, a wealthy North Carolinian planter, Jacob Blount, was indicted for " 'an Assault & Grievous Battery' on one Robert Campain, whom he 'did beat Batter bruise and Sorely wound with Sticks, Clubbs and fist insomuch that his life was despaired of.' But no disgrace followed," remarked the family's historian.[27]

Violence of this kind often arose from verbal insult. Any word of calumny required immediate response among white Southerners, just as among pagan German tribesmen centuries before. Tacitus observed that Germanic warriors were "not cunning or sophisticated enough to refrain from blurting out their inmost thoughts in the freedom of festive surroundings, so that every man's soul was laid bare." The result was often bloodshed in the course of drunken feasts. The style became known as the "point of honor" in Germanic medieval culture, in contrast to ancient Rome, where words did not have so powerful a force that redress was at once required. There the proper response was sheer disdain, a refusal to recognize the legitimacy of the challenge. It was quite otherwise in seventeenth-century England and eventually in the American South as well. Yeomen, no less than rich folk, reacted to defamation harshly and immediately.[28]

Courage in the Old South, as in ancient times, was a personal attribute, but it could not be wholly separated from the familial context. Therefore it was important to have kinsfolk who needed valorous protection and who could undertake justifiable revenge when the hero was himself slain. Without relatives one was helpless, and shorn of a major reason to exist. Illegitimacy of birth had the same effect. An appropriate example was the situation of Alexander Hamilton. Although not a Southerner, he had come from the rather similar slaveholding society of the British West Indies. His putative father was the fourth son in a lesser branch of a powerful Scottish clan. Incompetent and idle, James Hamilton had not made a success of his exile to the Leeward Islands. He lived with one Rachel Lavien, who had deserted her legitimate husband. Her morals were not irreproachable, and Alexander may have been fathered by another man. In any event, the son grew to maturity burdened with the stigma of being an "obscene child." Through fortuitous circumstances and his own brilliance, he overcame the uncertainty of his origins. Such miracles occurred, everyone recognized, but being kinless or ill-born was a heavy reproach in traditional Western societies. "There is more pity shown to a clod than to an orphan" was a French peasant saying.[29]

No doubt, as recent biographers have observed, the compulsion behind the touchiness of men like Alexander Hamilton, Louis T. Wigfall, William L. Yancey, and Andrew Jackson, to name only a handful, was because of an acute awareness of their vulnerability and solitariness. These men, noted for their high-strung sensibilities, hot tempers, and depressed spirits, had forebears little respected in the community, or else had lost parents early in their lives. Though each posed different psychological complexities, kinlessness and the stigma attached to it affected the attitudes of all of them toward the world. Truculence became something of a compensation. The defect was seen in this light because, according to ancient tradition, environment, blood, and moral bearing were inseparable. In ancient German, a *wrekka* or "wretch" was defined as a kinless figure. Later, under Christian influence, the term implied pity as well as contempt. Nevertheless, "wretch" was the epithet for one who was powerless and untrustworthy, having no relative to stand guardian, no dependent to be defended, a task that was a duty conferring honor.[30]

In contrast, those with numerous kinspeople were assumed to have moral stalwartness unless they proved false in some way. Living up to the familial ideals was therefore a common requirement. Veneration of dead ancestors had practical uses. In ancient Rome, for instance, at the funerals of distinguished figures, relatives marched carrying death masks that were arrayed in wooden shrines. The mourners also wore masks and togas to represent the deceased luminary's forebears, rode in chariots preceded by the dead hero's insignia of office, and seated themselves on ivory chairs at the site chosen for the oration. Young men, said Polybius, could see nothing so edifying as these solemn rites. Although, like the ancient Germans, white Southerners did not use so rich a display of pomp, they too revered the dead for the sake of instruction. The living were the dead, the dead the living when old Southerners recalled the adventures and deceased heroes of their youth and the boys played games of war as brave centurions from the *Gallic Wars* or generals of the American Revolution. As an adolescent in backwoods Tennessee, Sam Houston, later the founder of the Texas Republic, used to escape the torments of his elder brothers by living and hunting with neighboring Indians for weeks at a time. He often carried a copy of Alexander Pope's translation of the *Iliad,* "a pretty strange business," he later said. The choice fed his fantasies of action, fame, and antique heroism. William Faulkner's the Rev. Gail Hightower, though mad in his confusion of past and present, served to represent that desire for retrieving the élan of the dead, mythic and ancestral. From the pulpit he relived, over and over, the dramatic entry of his grandfather's Confederate cavalry unit into the county seat of Jefferson so many years before.[31]

Primal honor also made the opinion of others inseparable from inner worth. For instance, whereas a modern speaker would refer to conscience and guilt, the ancients, to avoid shame, used such expressions as "I wish to be regarded as honest," not "I am honest." It was not that inward virtues were wholly absent. Rather, virtue and valor, apart from social utility, simply were unimportant. Antebellum Southern whites were not, of course, so unsophisticated as the ordinary post-Homeric Greek citizen. Nevertheless, the public character of inner virtue was evident, for example, in a valedictory speech that John Randolph of Roanoke gave in 1828: "I shall retire upon my resources: I will go back to the bosom of my constituents as man never had before . . . and I shall receive from them the only reward I ever looked for, but the highest that man can receive,—the universal expression of their approbation, of their thanks." A man of piety would not have placed human praise so high; God's alone would be sufficient. Likewise, Mississippi politician Albert Gallatin Brown pointed out in the closing days before the Civil War that the "one standard of social merit" in his region was "integrity," by which he meant "unsullied reputation." On that basis, any white man of reasonable status stood "on a social level with all his fellows." Similarly, Charles Casey, an English traveler, noted that Southerners judged one another by outward criteria: "Your temperament, speech, look and act, are all taken by him; and if you can get at the tablet of his mind, you will find . . ., your exact worth written there upon."[32]

It followed that those who lacked honor also lacked reputation. Slaves, in both the ancient world and later centuries, were deemed incapable of reliability and therefore impervious to the dictates of community judgment. Similarly, poor whites in the Old South were subjected to the ancient prejudice against menials, swineherds, peddlers, and beggars, who, said William Perkins, an English divine, in 1632, were "as rotten legs and arms that drop from the body." Daniel R. Hundley applied these strictures to the South's hog-driving hill folk in 1860: "Who ever yet knew a Godolphin that was sired by a miserable scrub: or who ever yet saw an athletic, healthy human being, standing six feet in his stockings, who was the offspring of runtish forefathers, or wheezy, asthmatic, and consumptive parents?" As Hundley pointed out, to his own consternation, democratic ideals had modified the older notions of blood purity and asserted the equality of every idler with every hero. By no means was the South, conservative as it was, given to the strict aristocratic principles that had separated peasant from lord since time immemorial. Yet vigorous traces of the archaic stigma against the honorless could be found, particularly in the animadversions against slaves and white "tackeys" or "crackers."[33]

The opinion of others not only determined rank in society but also affected the way men and women thought. The stress upon external, public factors in establishing personal worth conferred particular prominence on the spoken word and physical gesture as opposed to interior thinking or words and ideas conveyed through the medium of the page. At the heart of the matter was the archaic concept that thought itself was a form of speaking. Deep reflection was imagined in very ancient times as a conversation with oneself, rather than a process of ratiocination. After all, this is the very way that children understand the thought process. A psychiatrist once illustrated the notion in the form of a father-daughter exchange:

Father. *What is thinking really?*
Hilda (aged four years, nine months). *Don't know.*
Father. *Well, what do we think with?*
Hilda. *Animals think with their mouths.*
Father. *And people?*
Hilda. *With their tongues.*
Father. *What does a man do then when he thinks?*
Hilda. *He speaks.*[34]

Of course, Southerners were not as unsophisticated as this example suggests. But thought and speech had an intimate relationship that literate cultures no longer sustain. Acquired virtues were therefore most especially recognizable if a man was an eloquent orator, enchanting storyteller, or witty raconteur. These attributes aroused deep admiration. As a writer in *DeBow's Review* pointed out in 1849, like other Southern states "Virginia has a system of oral instruction which compensates for the want of schools, and that is her social intercourse." Family and neighborly visits were not just social events, but training grounds where young and old alike "are taught," the *DeBow's* writer said, "to think and converse," a pairing that demonstrated the assumed congruity between the life of the mind and the life of the community. The writer boasted that this happy sociability gave "intellectual tone" to Virginia society. The oral expressiveness of "an agricultural people" intrigued the writer, though visitors to the South would hardly have characterized the trait as "intellectual." To some degree, then, thought *was* speech; reputation arose in large part from skill in its exercise at gatherings large or small. For the politician in the antebellum South, declared the historian William Garrott Brown in 1902, "There could be no hiding of the personality, no burying of the man in his art or his mission. The powerful man was above all a person; his power was himself." What he was was intimately related to how he used his tongue.[35]

The third organic part of honor requires elaboration: bodily appearance as outward sign of inner merit. Northerners like Hundley were impressed with Southern stature and strength. Perhaps the sedentary styles of Northern living made them feel physically at a disadvantage in relation to the allegedly healthy specimens from the slave states. Hundley stressed the hardihood of Southern sport as the reason for the white male's prowess, but superior breeding was cited, too. The stereotype was much exaggerated, especially in light of the semitropical diseases and enervating summer climate that afflicted the South's inhabitants. Nevertheless, physical presence was no less a sign of worthiness in the Old South than it had been in ancient times. Tacitus, for instance, found German tribal commanders peculiarly tall and well built—revoltingly so, he reassured himself. When Arthur's grave was opened at Glastonbury in 1278, the bones were said to be "of great size." Charlemagne stood over six feet, towering over his courtiers. Whether legend or reality, impressive stature was clearly thought a signal of divine favor. Those less well endowed had to withstand ridicule. Hunchbacks, for instance, were disbarred from inheriting property in ancient Germany. Entry into Valhalla depended upon being fair-skinned and red-haired or blond. Penetrating eyes, emblematic of inner strength, would betray a disguised hero, according to legend.[36]

Poor health, small stature, or any other physical defect carried special opprobrium in the Old South, just as kinlessness did. Yet it could be a spur for achievement. Such was the case with Alexander Stephens, Henry S. Foote, and Robert J. Walker, all of whom suffered unusually from having slight frames and physical disabilities from an early age. Stephens, for instance, always regarded the puniness of his body as a sore trial. A reporter once observed him, late in life, swathed in flannels and an "immense cloak," but his eyes,

peering beneath a tall hat, he said, "seemed to burn and blaze," be-
tokening the "invincible soul that dwells in this shrunken and
aching frame."[37]

In its most fundamental form, honor was a state of grace linking
mind, body, blood, hand, voice, head, eyes, and even genitalia. The
blood of a self-regarding nobility transmitted the appropriate qualities. The heart held the intentions that had to be open and honest
toward friends and superiors and closed and implacable toward the
honorless. The right hand gave the signal of respect in friendship,
revenge in enmity. The eyes witnessed honor and looked down in
deference or shame. Thus a steady gaze from a slave signaled
impudence.

Most important was the head, seat of the social self. Not only
was its covering a sign of status—tricorn, periwig, or whatever—but
also of sacredness or profanation, by which another's guilt or innocence might be ascertained.[38] In the Waxhaw backwoods of South
Carolina, where Scots-Irish Presbyterians had settled, the widow of
a clergyman was forced to touch the decayed skull of her murdered
husband in 1767; the woman had married a wealthy planter suspi-
ciously soon after her first husband's death. Among the Celts in the
community where Andrew Jackson grew up, it was believed that if
the woman were guilty her right hand, when placed on the skull,
would bleed, identifying her as a violator of nature's law, a murderous woman. For American Indians the scalp lock served as a
trophy for the same reason: the magical properties of the head.
Whites also used heads as trophies. For instance, the body of an alleged insurrectionary leader of 1835, John A. Murrell, a Tennessee
ne'er-do-well and penitentiary inmate, was dug up in 1845. The
graverobbers severed the head from the corpse, which had been half-
eaten by hogs, pickled it in some way, and displayed their prize at
Southern county fairs for ten cents a look.[39]

The genitalia were at once the most sacred and the most vulnerable aspect of the body. Ham had ridiculed his father Noah's naked-
ness and was banished; he had desecrated the patriarch's most sacred loins, from which descendants sprang. The seventeenth-century
French essayist Montaigne described how a young man who had

successfully convinced a girl to bed with him was so mortified when
he was unable to complete the seduction that he went home, cut off
the offending part, and sent it to her out of shame. Quoting from
the poet Tibullus, Montaigne concluded, "Not in manly style / Had
his limp penis raised its senile head." The French thinker thought
the gesture un-Christian but admirable.[40]

There was a most immodest interest in the private parts of the
deceased John Randolph, owing to the Virginia senator's bachelor
status, odd personality, scanty beard, and high tenor voice. According to William C. Bruce, an authoritative Virginia historian, a
physician's autopsy in 1832 revealed that Randolph's "testicles at
the time of his death were mere rudiments. These facts simply confirm a popular impression which was universal during the latter
part of Randolph's life." The point is not to prove Randolph's defect, but to note the premium placed upon the congruity of outward manliness and its hidden source. It goes almost without saying
that the penalty for a slave who dared lust after white women's flesh
was castration, first by the law of the slave code, later by community
justice alone. The grisliest example of this barbarity occurred as
late in Southern history as 1934. A black farmer named Claude
Neal, suspected of raping and murdering a white child near Greenwood, Florida, fell into the hands of lynchers. They cut off his penis
and testicles, forced them into his mouth, and made him eat and
say that he enjoyed it. The next day Neal's body was strung up,
nude, in the Jackson County courthouse square.[41]

Not surprisingly, sexual honor was the most curiously ambiguous
aspect of the whole concept in the American South, as it had been
in prior centuries. The Southern adulation of women needs little
elaboration here. But it should be stressed that there was a dual vision of the ideal, one always present in Western popular thought.
The Southern woman was supposed to be not only ethereal but also
hardworking, politically aware (though never "to mingle in discussion"), and prudent in household management. These were virtues
of subservience. "The husband of her bosom," rhapsodized a Southern writer in 1850, "is a man of strength. He has been the partiarch

in her abodes. . . . He has kept foes and poverty alike from the door." Her task was to raise sons who would be brave protectors able to meet the intruding world. Thus, he concluded, "day by day, will she train her young spartans to the trial—to the endurance of privation—cold, hunger, toil—no less than the danger and the brunt of the battle." These remarks from a reviewer of a book on women of the American Revolution were not just suited to the subject at hand. They reflected a common, venerable perception: the mother as the moral arbiter of bravery. For instance, during the War of 1812 Sam Houston joined the army. His mother, who had urged him to do so, handed him a musket. Houston recalled her saying, "Never disgrace it; for remember, I had rather all my sons should fill one honorable grave, than that one of them should turn his back to save his life." Then she presented him with a plain gold ring, "with the word 'Honor,' engraved inside it."[42]

Unequal though male and female were supposed to be by the laws of nature, man and woman were expected to make single unions. The heritage of the ages, as Southerners believed, had or-dained the rule of monogamy. During the mid-century before the Civil War, pious sentiment softened some aspects of women's traits, stressing their moral purity rather than their weak resistance to temptations. But too much can be made of the Southern notions of woman's irrelevance to the main concerns of life. They were not ex-pected to be mere ornaments, but were to fulfill duties commensu-rate with male prestige. In noting the German tribesmen's fidelity to a single mate, Tacitus marveled that praises from the wife, mother, and sister were the ones that the warrior most greatly cherished. Women were present at battles, wailing to remind the fighters that slavery or death awaited them if the men proved to be cowards. The German tribesmen believed, Tacitus said, "that there resides in women an element of holiness and gift of prophecy; and so they do not scorn to ask their advice, or lightly disregard their replies," holding them in some awe though not as "goddesses." One may question Tacitus's accuracy (he may have had polemical mo-tives), but when necessity required, Germanic women were known to join the battles as warriors.[43] Likewise, Southern women were expected to show courage and to remind men of their martial, protective duties.

Owing to this dual character of woman—both her power and her powerlessness—there was bound to be considerable misogyny. The origin of male anxiety along these lines resided in two elemental and complementary sources: male physical dread of what seemed alien in a woman's biological functions, and male fear of woman's ability to shame him before other men—both attitudes much older than the settlement of the Southern frontier. The fates of Siegfried, Launcelot, Ulysses, the Trojans, and, of course, the biblical Adam all testified, through myth, to male vulnerability and fear of exposure to humiliation. Southern feelings about the adulterous wife, the cuckolded husband, the successful gallant or base seducer (depending on viewpoint) varied not at all from what had always been Western popular basic reaction to sexual rule-breaking. The attitude was not so much indignation as it was a fear that the community might find a head of household who was traduced by a bold lover to be a poor disciplinarian and an even poorer defender of his family's honor. It was scarcely a wonder then that men, both in ancient and more recent times, were often hostile to women, even as they could also be loving parents, husbands, and brothers.

Women's sexual powers were formidable. They could damage or destroy male reputation, that of their own men or of others. They could make complaints publicly about men's failings as providers, lovers, and family leaders. Under ancient Anglo-Saxon law such defamers, as these women were viewed, were subject to fierce penalties, and in colonial Virginia and Massachusetts women accused of being common scolds and slanderers suffered duckings. The Virginia legislature in 1662, for instance, pointed out that "many brabling women often slander their neighbours for which their poore husbands are often brought into chargeable and vexatious suites. . . ." Men who were indicted for gossiping also risked punishment, but not of the same severity. For example, in 1642 Robert Wyard of Accomac, Virginia, was required to wear a white garment and hold a "white wann [wand] in his hand" for impugning the character of another's wife. He was given the option of apologizing.[44]

At the same time it was true, without paradox, that nothing could arouse such fury in traditional societies as an insult hurled against a woman of a man's household, most especially his mother. In the Old South, as in the ancient world, "son of a bitch" or any similar epithet was a most damaging blow to male pride. The intensity of feeling arose from the social fact that a male's moral bearing resided not in him alone, but also in his women's standing. To attack his wife, mother, or sister was to assault the man himself. Outsider violence against family dependents, particularly females, was a breach not to be ignored without risk of ignominy. An impotence to deal with such wrongs carried all the weight of shame that archaic society could muster. The symbols of failure were the phallic horns of the cuckold, the jeers of children, the ringing of cowbells and banging of pots, and sometimes ostracism or retribution at the hands of other family heads. At the same time, seduction was the aim of the young man seeking to prove his manhood and challenge the authority of the older generation, a tension that provoked ribald humor, for laughter then, as in Hawthorne's story, was mockery.

Fierce retaliation was therefore mandatory when a daughter, wife, or mother had been dishonored. So it had been in ancient German and Celtic tribes, and so it continued to be in antebellum society. Shakespeare's Leonato mourned his daughter's sexual degradation in a way that many Southern fathers would have recognized:

> Why had I not with charitable hand
> Took up a beggar's issue at my gates
> Who smirched thus and mired infamy,
> I might have said "No part of it is mine;
> This shame derives itself from unknown loins"?[45]

What was at stake in the promiscuity of a dependent woman was her protector's status, without which he could not remain an effective member of society. The unchaste wife or daughter did not betray herself alone. She exposed her male family members to public censure. The inner life of the family was inseparable from its public appearance. Since there was little recognition of a morality apart from community custom, the erring woman had to be condemned along with the husband, father, or brother who was unable or unwilling to control her or to avenge the seducer or rapist. Suits for sexual slandering were epidemic in seventeenth- and eighteenth-century England, particularly Yorkshire, a borderland whence many settlers in the colonial South had come.

The fear of woman entertained by archaic man—and the antebellum Southerner—stemmed from this very real situation. Women *were* dangerous. They could present a husband, father, or brother with an illegitimate child and thereby cast doubt on the legitimacy of the line and desecrate the inmost temple of male self-regard. Male Germans, Tacitus reported, took a woman's adultery as a profanation of themselves. He noted that "punishment is prompt and is the husband's prerogative: her hair close-cropped, stripped of her clothes, her husband drives her from his house *in the presence of his relatives* and pursues her through . . . the village." The need for public exposure of his indignation was evident.[46] Under such circumstances, which, though to less dramatic degree, also applied in the American South, it was no wonder that men feared women.

It might seem paradoxical that men should make demands for sexual restraint on their female relatives, when giving themselves a right to license. But to the traditional mind there was no "double standard" of morality. The sexes differed. They lived separate lives—one in the world, the other in the home, one in exterior circumstances, the other in the inner sanctuary that required vigilant safeguarding. As John C. Calhoun once said, "The moral is like the physical world. Nature has incrusted the exterior of all organic life, for its safety. Let that be broken through, and it is all weakness within."[47]

The male identified that inner part of himself with his women. The woman's responsibility was solely to make sacred that internal space. They should have little cause to defend themselves, a male imperative.[48] This differentiation in moral duty elicited both pride and worry from their sometimes not so self-confident menfolk. In a world without safety, fidelity, privacy, or permanent plenty, the moral order could not be imagined in more benevolent, sexually egalitarian terms.

The last feature of primal honor to be treated here is the role of oath-taking. In most societies the rite of swearing on sacred honor is highly ceremonial, with a rich display of vestments, signifying rank, and of liturgy and ritual, signifying high erudition. Such was not the case in America, however, partly because of the rawness of life there and partly because of the Protestant mistrust of symbol and panoply. At the opening of quarter-sessions in colonial Virginia's county seats, for instance, says a recent investigator, "there was no preliminary sermon, no formal procession from parish church to shire hall, no parade of judicial gowns or gold-laced coats, no tipstaffs leading the way." Nevertheless, the high point of pretrial drama was the official oath-taking, when "each justice by order of seniority" swore to uphold the majesty of the law.[49] The sacerdotal nature of the oath, supported by a ritual no matter how depleted, was something impressive, particularly to Southern whites, and especially to the less well-to-do, who prized oral, personal ways over rationalistic, formalistic ones.

Most important in the life of the ordinary British or American subject was the oath taken in marriage. But the duties pledged in the civil and military sphere, rather than in domestic transaction, will be the focus of attention here. To be sure, fealty to family was the first law of honor. Close kin needed no oath-takings to seal mutual loyalties. The oath given to outsiders, even on such minor issues as petty indebtedness, was a replacement for the primary bonding. The oath was meant to surmount the dangers of nonfamilial relationships. It was, said an English writer in 1614, "the safest knot of civil society, and the firmest bond to tie all men to the performance of their several duties."[50]

The oath could not, however, meet such expectations, because fealties to family, to community, to a local figure of power, or to personal advantage so easily superseded the pledge. Moreover, particularly in the seventeenth century, the rite became so often repeated that its character was compromised. Strict policing, standing armies, and other expensive, institutional means of social control were beyond the resources of Tudor-Stuart Society, but the oath was a poor substitute. Even men of impeccable credentials took the obligation lightly if a test-oath law rankled. For instance, at the close of the Civil War former Rebels were obliged to swear loyalty to the Union. The penalty for defiance was the punishing disgrace of disfranchisement and the loss of other civil rights. The honor-bound Southerner ofttimes went through the motions that President Andrew Johnson had ordered, and did so with little qualm of conscience. Catherine Edmondston, a North Carolina plantation mistress, explained the perjury in these graphic terms:

> We feel a deep & abiding resentment towards a nation who thus debases our sense of personal honour & weakens the heretofore sacred obligation of an oath taken in the name of Almighty God. Who considers it binding: No one. . . . [I]s it not a fact made to a nation of thieves who say to us, 'Your property, your existence, nay protection to your person, to your honour, to that of your wives & children or this hated oath . . . this oath—or a life of exile & dependence.' Rather than this, welcome the oath. . . . You have sullied the purity of our integrity. You have us promise what we will not pay, & for all this we hate you![51]

The imputation of shame was to be rejected instantly as unworthy of a proud people.

It would be hard to prove that Southern whites, both colonial and antebellum, were more addicted to the rites of affirmation than other Americans. But there can be little doubt that the matter was taken extremely seriously in many aspects of daily Southern life. An oral pledge from a gentleman was thought to be the equivalent of a signed oath, particularly in regard to gaming debts. Southern college students, perhaps more than any other single group, were obsessed with the formulary. Thomas Cooper, president of South Carolina College, once remarked to Thomas Jefferson, "Every student in College holds himself bound to conceal any offence against the Laws of the Land as well as the Laws of the College." This clubbiness excused a good many pranks, even assaults upon professors who allegedly doubted the offender's honor. The rise of Greek-letter fraternities and men's clubs in the mid-nineteenth century carried on the supposedly sacred obligations to one's peers, against the world if need be.[52]

In political life, too, the oath often had a crucial role to play. An important aspect of the Nullification controversy in South Carolina was the battle over the state's test-oath, one that raged even after the famous ordinance was repealed and a congressional compromise worked out. On a more personal level, oaths among gentlemen also figured in political activities. In 1823, for example, Willie P. Mangum, a North Carolina planter and politician, came to an agreement with Daniel L. Barringer, a militia general and rival for a local office. The pair swore before Sheriff H. B. Adams not to campaign for votes—canvassing being considered beneath dignity in low-country North Carolina. But later, before the election, each accused the other of violations. Adams certified that, though both had "pledged their honours . . . in a most sacred manner," Barringer had violated his oath. Furious and embarrassed, Barringer challenged Mangum to a duel, but friends intervened successfully to prevent it.[53]

As this story illustrates, only those within the circle of honor were entitled to participate in the oath-swearing rite, an exclusionary rule that had applied since the earliest of times. Those outside the community ranks, most especially blacks in the American South, were ineligible for oath-taking. For that reason, among others, slaves and free blacks could not serve as witnesses in trials of whites. Nor could one expect, so it was thought, that sworn marital obligations had any meaning among bondspeople—a convenient surmise, since a recognition of fidelity might jeopardize masters' rights to dispose of human property at will. Fear of punishment had always been regarded as the sole means to assure loyalty and truthfulness among the honorless.

The most serious breach of submission in America, of course, was slave insurrection. Incendiarism, real or imagined, for instance, excited wild anxieties, to such a degree that in 1740 a slave who had burned a white's dwelling was ordered by a South Carolina court to be burned alive. The penalty was not part of the slave code. Nonetheless, declared Edward McCrady, a late-nineteenth-century historian, that form of execution was excusable as authorized "under the ancient law of England . . . as a kind of *lex talionis* under the statute of Edward I." Like arson, forgery, and counterfeiting, poisoning was categorized as petty treason: a black woman under that indictment went to the stake alive in Wayne County, North Carolina, in 1831. The severities of punishment were the response to the shameless villainy of those who could not be relied upon to fulfill duty except under threat of brutal retribution.[54]

Horrible as they were, these penalties were derived from ancient usages, as the South Carolinian McCrady pointed out. In the Germanic forests, noted Tacitus, deserters and other oath violators were hanged on trees or drowned under wattled hurdles in bogs. The English also used hurdles, to draw the guilty to the site of execution. By judicial discretion, the traitor could be partially hanged, then have his bowels cut out and burned before his eyes. After the subsequently completed hanging, the authorities removed the head and divided the body, for distribution to the city gibbets. To preserve the traitor's head for public shaming, reported the Quaker Thomas Ellwood in 1662, one hangman boiled it in "Bay-Salt and Cummin-Seed." These depredations proclaimed the sacredness of sworn obedience that could only be rescued by the polluting of the violator's body.

Needless to say, these emblematic, painful ceremonies reflected the uncertainties of social order and the inadequacy of oath-swearing as a bond of peace and fellowship. The system that created honor as a virtue of submissiveness to higher powers also equipped the recreant with justification for his crimes. "Damn your eyes" was the murderer's curse upon those witnessing his hanging, according to a popular Anglo-American ballad. Their eyes beheld his shame, but he defied them by condemning sight itself. Reliance upon shaming led at times to bold determination to deny guilt, even to a reveling in rebelliousness. Though some abjectly participated in their own public degradation, others found honor in rejecting conventional obligation. Pirates' honor took that form. Upon that premise, too, it might be said that Mrs. Edmondston and other stalwarts of the dead Confederacy felt free to swear to anything. It retrieved honor in defeat.[55]

This presentation has offered some unappealing aspects of honor, at least to modern tastes. It has not tried to show the evolution of honor over time, in order to give precedence to the fundamenals. It must be understood, however, that such transformations did modify the starkest elements. Loyalty to family was transformed into duty to country. Ancient largess became, under Stoic influence, Aristotelian magnanimity, which in turn grew into Christian charity. Virtuous revenge gave way to more abstract concepts of justice. Primitive boasting and haughtiness evolved into condescension toward inferiors, affability toward peers into egalitarianism, courtesy toward superiors into general graciousness. Nevertheless, traces of the old ethic continued, especially in times of crisis such as war or when whites' mastery over blacks was threatened. These trends, admittedly rendered in the sketchiest way here, separated the customs of the South from their most primitive origins, but not by so great a degree that the resemblance between the old and more recent ethical patterns was entirely lost from view. The textures of honor were many, and some of the threads were more colorful and pleasing than others. But the vitality of the whole cannot be questioned for a moment.

In summary, the consequence of primal honor was the ordering of life into alternations of attitude. Looking from a modern perspective, a historian might readily suspect Southern whites of gross irrationality, erratic conduct, and hypocrisy. That interpretation imposes alien moral values upon the past. Like the Germanic tribesmen whom Tacitus described, Southerners loved both idle peace and soul-stirring action. They genuinely trusted their own slaves and loved those they knew best, yet were convinced that the race was vile, bestial, and fit for nothing but bondage. They dared not challenge the family rule of fathers; instead they sought out rivalries as a way to give vent to repressed passion. They cherished, even revered their women, yet dreaded the power that women could exercise over them. These were not opinions held at one and the same time, but evoked as occasion seemed to dictate.[56]

As a way to gather these values in a familiar framework, one could propose a second Sermon on the Mount. Jesus had meant to repudiate the ethical standards of the traditional world, but if a man of primal honor had written the homily, it would have taken a form similar to literary historian George Fenwick Jones's rephrasing of Matthew 5 : 2–11:

Blessed are the rich, for they possess the earth and its glory.

Blessed are the strong, for they can conquer kingdoms.

Blessed are they with strong kinsmen, for they shall find help.

Blessed are the warlike, for they shall win wealth and renown.

Blessed are they who keep their faith, for they shall be honored.

Blessed are the open-handed, for they shall have friends and fame.

Blessed are they who wreak vengeance, for they shall be offended no more, and they shall have honor and glory all the days of their life and eternal fame in ages to come.[57]

The primeval code not only affected the way Southern whites thought of themselves and others, but also influenced how they viewed hierarchy, government, and rebelliousness. The concept of honor was designed to give structure to life and meaning to valor, hierarchy, and family protection. But its almost childlike clarity, its seeming innocence, contained inner contradictions. Within the ethic, there was a conflict never wholly mastered, a point at which the resolutions and the alternations of the system broke down. The contradictions became too overwhelming for easy solution. The chief problem was the discrepancy between honor as obedience to superior rank and the contrary duty to achieve place for oneself and family. In the American South before the Civil War, those belonging to the circle of honor were much greater in number than in any other traditional society. Democracy, that is white democracy, made that possible. But even in colonial times, claimants to prestige extended beyond the rigid hierarchy of the gentry class. The result could sometimes be highly violent. The ethic of honor was designed to prevent unjustified violence, unpredictability, and anarchy. Occasionally it led to that very nightmare.

3

Primal Honor:
The Tensions of Patriarchy

In *Absalom, Absalom!* William Faulkner describes the curious relationship between leader and follower in the rural South just after the Civil War. In his remorseless determination to found a dynasty, Colonel Thomas Sutpen, a nouveau riche member of the Mississippi planter class, seduces Milly, granddaughter of Wash Jones, the caretaker of Sutpen's Hundred. Milly gives birth to a daughter in the stable straw. Sutpen had sought a son and heir, to give his name perpetuity, and in disappointment he callously tells her, "Well Milly; too bad you're not a mare too. Then I could give you a decent stall in the stable." By community standards, Wash Jones is poor white trash, friendless and kinless, only marginally independent. He had not served with his employer in the war; his only contribution had been an occasional request for Sutpen to kill a Yankee or two for him. Inwardly he knows his position, too. But the colonel had never forced him to confront his worthlessness, had never driven him to self-despisement before. The brutish remark that Jones overhears shows how matters really stand. In mad reprisal, Jones seizes a scythe and slays his chief. Then, once again as passive as he had been throughout his years of mean subservience, he sits on his haunches awaiting the inevitable arrest.[1]

Sutpen's murder reminds us that Sutpen himself had come from exactly the same class that Wash Jones represented. As the young son of a shiftless, poverty-stricken hog-tender and small farmer from the Virginia hills, Sutpen had been rebuffed at the entrance to a big planter's mansion in the Tidewater, when the slave door-keeper had haughtily ordered him to knock at the back. Numb, unaware of his inner fury, Sutpen had translated outrage into cold ambition, and had become determined to achieve that mastership to which the likes of Wash Jones and the Virginia houseservant would have to bow. Yet as Faulkner makes clear, Sutpen—not being raised to *noblesse* and the art of leadership—cannot acquire the necessary bearing as he strives to move ahead. It is a deep repression of self-knowledge, not his class origin, that prevents him. Faulkner calls this insensibility Sutpen's "innocence." General Compson, one of Sutpen's neighbors, remarks that Sutpen "believed that all that was necessary was courage and shrewdness and the one he knew he had and the other he believed he could learn if it were to be taught." Morality, gentility, and compassion were irrelevant. When all his attempts to make good his pledge from his youth fall apart, he does not understand, and asks, "What did I do or misdo? . . . I had a design. To accomplish it I should require money, a house, a plantation, slaves, a family—incidentally of course, a wife. I set out to acquire these, asking no favor of any man."[2] Thomas Sutpen is a fictional character, but his traits, even his "innocence," a simplicity in the quest for power, can be found in the lives of some nineteenth-century Southern whites.

Faulkner's story illustrates a significant pattern of Southern relationships that was not confined to the planter-yeoman connection. Deference—and sometimes resentment about having to offer it—permeated the exchange of all men of differing ranks along the social spectrum. The requirement was greatest in the seventeenth-century American colonies, but it continued to be important in the Old South even beyond the Civil War. The greater the space along the moral and social continuum, the more the respect due the higher, the less the regard owed the lower. Being affable and condescending was required of the man with rank, but clearly the lower the subject of such attention was, the less solicitous one had to be. Being personal in nature, such a system was bound to be uneasy and, at times, unpredictably violent. As Johann Huizinga, the Dutch historian, observed, American individualism "reveals itself as much more of a primitive, limiting, and negative force" than that of the European Renaissance; it was "medieval individualism," a "spirit of strict, intolerant enforcement of religious authority and public morals within their own circle and resistance to any authority from outside." Huizinga suggested that the "tar-and-feathering of Loyalists" during the Revolution was indicative of this temperament. Certainly, deference was not always a guarantee of American social order.[3]

The social structure of the Southern states appeared to be so simple as to call for little scrutiny. Actually, however, the simplicity hid deep complexities that generated infinite questions about who stood where in the antebellum pecking order. When did a friend become a rival, a rival a trusted ally? When did a leader confound followers and turn tyrant? When should subordinates break allegiance and risk disorder in the search for justice?[4] There were no easy answers to these questions. Honor, however, provided a framework for handling social problems. A discussion of the relation of honor to social order can best be arranged with regard to these three factors: first, the nature of rankings in the patriarchal household, and, by analogy, in the community; second, the connection of wealth with community power; and third, the dilemmas implicit in protest and rebellion against the rule of family and government, the two agencies of patriarchy that on a popular level were considered complementary.

In regard to the first issue of discrete rankings, the customs that linked planter and yeoman in the antebellum South were based upon ancient traditions, ones requiring common and mutual respect for manliness within the circle of associated followers and leaders. W. J. Cash called this set of rubrics the Savage Ideal. Like Faulkner in *Absalom, Absalom!*, Cash argued that the Southern environment, untamed and forested, preserved but did not create *sui generis* the ordering of agrarian society. "The way of life was his," Cash said of the Man at the Center, or typical Southern white, "not because he himself or his ancestors or his class had deliberately chosen it as against something else, not even because it had been tested through the centuries and found to be good, but because, given his origins, it was the most natural outcome of the conditions in which he found himself."[5]

Just as German tribesmen expected their leaders to be men of wealth, large kinship networks, and charismatic appeal, so too did Southern whites. Wealth had always conferred high status, especially if the properties were inherited. Even so, in the Old World and even more in the New, possessors of present power could not invariably trace their lineage much further back than could the fictional Sutpen. True, one suspects that younger sons of the English gentry helped to populate the early leadership ranks of Virginia, Barbados, and the Carolinas, although at an earlier point in Southern historiography such New South liberal scholars as Thomas Wertenbaker suggested that the seventeenth-century planter class arose from English "middle-class" families rather than from "cavalier" sources, as nineteenth-century romanticists claimed. In a sense the issue, though intriguing, is not significant from the ethical perspective concerning us here. After all, even those like William Byrd I, whose sire was a London goldsmith, accepted the rural ethic. The line between it and the customs of the city was much less distinct than were differentiations between town and country of a later epoch. English burghers, if wealthy enough, became aristocratic or "gentrified," exchanging their natal culture for the one into which they were entering. They moved from the calculations of the marketplace to the privileges of the landholder class. As the English historian Lawrence Stone has noted, the College of Heralds and the process of entitlement during the late Tudor and Stuart eras had as their purpose to maintain "a precarious social balance between a rigidly unalterable hierarchy, and a situation of absolute mobility." Gentry folk sent their younger, dispossessed sons into trade, by which they either rose to retrieve the life they had once known as children or fell to lower depths. Some of their descendants, in turn, found it practical to leave the country altogether and try to make their fortunes abroad, as Alexander Hamilton's father had. If one could master the techniques for advancement in ways Sutpen could not, the standing of parents mattered chiefly as inspiration—in the absence of large material legacies.[6]

In early colonial America, few could boast of exalted station. Even thereafter, by European standards, the great Southern families could not claim to belong to the nobility, as distinct from the gentry class. Nevertheless, honor by lesser means than the peerage flourished throughout the period, though with ever-decreasing social esteem for family lineage. From first to last, there was the honor of having a white skin—what one historian has called "*herrenvolk* democracy," the fraternity of all whites against all blacks.[7] Its importance never ceased, and even grew in strength as other forms of privilege fell away.

The married state and fatherhood, regardless of one's social place, offered further prestige. According to George Mason, a Virginia delegate to the Constitutional Convention of 1787, simply being head of a household was sufficient for responsible exercise of the suffrage. Arguing against the view expressed by the English suffrage requirement of a forty-shilling freehold, Mason pointed out that such people as "the married man, the parent of a number of children whose fortunes are to be pursued in their own [country]," should scarcely be seen as "suspicious characters," since the duties involved made any man a governor in his own small province.[8] These were essentials to community repute.

Southern historians have long pondered the means by which slaveholding planters held other men in their sway. Were they patriarchs to the vast numbers of yeomen and poor whites, or was there a more democratic style by which they retained control? In *The Mind of the South*, Cash rejected the "paternal" analogy, one that has enjoyed some popularity in recent years. Although the rich have claimed to stand guardian over the poor ever since the beginning of recorded history, the democratic impulse in America was strong enough—and land was available enough—to prohibit European and feudal modes of hegemony. Cash wisely recognized the difference, and maintained that inroads on aristocratic *noblesse* had firmly diminished the separate roles of deference and condescension. Referring to the post-Jeffersonian South, Cash remarked, "I call the term ["paternalism"] inaccurate because its almost inevitable connotation is the relationship of the Roman *patron* and *client*," that is, the imperial model that Tacitus had long before contrasted with the reciprocal exchanges among German tribal ranks. Paternalism, Cash continued, "suggests with a force that has led to much confusion, that there existed on the one hand an essential dependence, and on the other a prescriptive right—that it operated through command . . . and rested . . . on compulsion."[9]

As Cash so perceptively explained, every man, according to his station, expected and ordinarily received respect for individuality. The arrangement, though more self-conscious in the antebellum period, was scarcely new. Throughout the eighteenth century, both in the New World and the Old, former notions of the implacable rule of blood had gradually given way to the rule of environment. The poor remained a subject of contempt, but mingled with the old despisement was a growing appreciation of environmental factors. Harry C. Payne, a literary historian, argues persuasively that during the eighteenth century the leaders of Western society—such men as the French *philosophes*, Richard Steele, and Henry Fielding—reflected a new ambiguity about the lower classes. On the one hand there was a growing awareness of the differences in culture between themselves and those far below; on the other there was a greater desire for involvement with the uplift of the poor. In the late colonial South, as elsewhere, reforms in education, strictures against supernaturalism, and denunciations of blood sports became more vigorous than ever before. At the same time, on a daily level one simply had to deal with the masses of poor folk, and take account of their needs. Even in the South, where educational resources for the poor were limited, literacy, at least by Continental and perhaps British standards, was sufficient by the time of the Revolution to modify old assumptions about the moral backwardness of ordinary farming people. The rise of the Baptist faith, the somewhat more modest advance of Presbyterianism in the backwoods, and the late upsurge of Methodism during and just after the Revolution assisted the transformation of upper-class attitudes. At first the result was surprise and deep worry. The wellborn Anglican gentry of mid-eighteenth-century Virginia, for instance, found it disconcerting when pious poor farmers adopted forms of self-discipline and began abjuring the blood sports, heavy drinking, and gambling that gentlemen were as yet unprepared to relinquish. One may overestimate the impact the Great Awakening had in reordering the priorities of Southern middling ranks and poor. Nevertheless, the struggle between men of new-found faith and the traditional Anglicans gradually earned for the lower ranks of Southern society a respect formerly denied them.[10]

These changes in social perception, some of them self-induced by the rich and some imposed from below by demands for recognition, vitiated the concept of patriarchy as the principle for governing the lower orders of whites. (Patriarchy remained the guide for slave control, however.) It was replaced by a more democratic outlook, one that still stressed hierarchy, but the old, rigid styles of an earlier day were generally blurred, almost beyond easy recognition. Antebellum Southern gentlefolk, like their Northern counterparts, no longer enjoyed the respect once accorded their forefathers. But among gentlemen themselves the old habits of deference persisted, as if to distinguish them from the vulgar. For instance, Maunsel White, New Orleans factor for Andrew Jackson's estates, received in 1845 a very complimentary letter from the aged general on his valor at the Battle of Chalmette years before. Jackson's unexpected words of praise were prompted by a sense of gratitude for White's generous assistance to Jackson in overcoming a particularly embarrassing disarray in his finances. Those words meant much more to the recipient than any payment in money ever could have. White, in return, promised his former commander that he would ever cherish the commendation and would bequeath the document to his descendants "to inculcate sentiments of Integrity, Honor and Patriotism." Beneath the formalities of the exchange between the two gentlemen, one can detect the genuine love and respect that could exist within the hierarchy of superior and subordinate. That ranking—along with those manners—was still functioning in the antebellum South and North, but more egalitarian notions were quickly eroding it, most especially in the free states.

Although broad generalizations are dangerous, the best term for the antebellum Southern style of leadership was not "patriarchal," except at the farthest extremes of the social spectrum, and then only with such men of prominence as George Washington and Andrew Jackson, or, on a more regional level, figures such as John C. Calhoun, John Randolph, and the heads of the great Virginia and Carolina families. On a more modest scale, at the county and district level, where duties were less august, the squire and his lesser neighbors were fraternally rather than patriarchally bound. By familial analogy, all white freemen, particularly after the American Revolution, were brothers. While they shared common cultural assumptions, some had the advantage of education, greater wealth, and a sense of command, with preferments ordinarily given the eldest. When a man had power but no office, his neighbors saw to it that he deviated very little from community custom. Though self-sufficient, he was not to put on airs. He was dependent upon their esteem and acted accordingly. "The populace" of frontier Mississippi in the 1820s and 1830s, declared Reuben Davis, "might be ignorant of many things, careless and indifferent about many more, but where honor and honesty were concerned, the great heart of the masses beat true and fearless. Any man who aspired to lead them must be above reproach, according to their standards," by which he meant, "outward conformity with the popular ideal. . . ."[11] In effect, such a leader served as head of a "moral team," a position less commanding than that of someone acting in an official capacity. Those with a title or an office—magistrates, judges, militia officers—obviously enjoyed greater authority than did the neighbors' head man. But whether one held rank by appointment or election or enjoyed less formal prestige, the loyalty of the subordinate was based upon the assumption that the leader could never, as Cash observed, "run counter to his aims or desires." Democratic changes throughout the colonial and early national periods only reinforced that expectation.[12]

The second element of honor in the Southern scheme of social and political hierarchy was the relationship of wealth to claims on governmental power. The same reciprocations that marked the connection between planter and yeoman also applied to those with possessions and to their connections with the state. The exchange of duties was supposed to be at least partially volitional, even after oaths, written laws, and other ways of regularizing matters had been established over the centuries. Tribal chieftains in Germany, as Tacitus observed, could require and receive complete devotion, but only so long as they met their obligations in turn by offering gifts to their superiors. The practice extended into the feudal era as well. Otherwise the neglectful ruler was likely to be removed, deserted, or killed. At the same time, free warriors of rank made gifts to their lord, supposedly voluntarily and in proof of gratitude and fealty.[13] But if the "gifts" were treated too readily as a right of the ruler, the Germanic vassal felt degraded. Taxes and tribute were signs of slavery; "gifts" were honorable. Although the topic is highly complex and involves much more than can be dealt with here, it is worth noting that taxation and honor were fundamentally incompatible throughout the long history of Western Europe, a tradition that colonial Americans, and white Southerners in particular, inherited.

In 1728 William Byrd II, to offer an early and typical example, discovered on his famous tour of North Carolina that the residents, both great and small property holders, were "rarely guilty of Flattering or making any Court to their governors, but treat them with all the Excesses of Freedom and Familiarity. They are of Opinion their rulers wou'd be apt to grow insolent, if they grew Rich and for that reason take care to keep them . . . dependent. . . ." There was no direct link between ancient Germans and North Carolinian settlers, but the ethic to which both people adhered facilitated the construction of arguments against the power to tax.[14]

It is far beyond the purpose of these extended definitions to trace the history of the "rights of Englishmen," that is, the honors due every freeman, against arbitrary rule and resented taxation. Yet there was certainly irony in the fact that late-eighteenth-century notions of liberty for all whites (particularly those with property) should arise from the hierarchical values of honor, not only in this country but in England as well. That same attitude—the duty of rulers to have their own resources for running the government and enjoying the preferments arising therefrom—prevailed throughout the Southern states during the post-Revolutionary years. Frugality at the centers of authority was a virtue that Southern citizens believed essential to the preservation of their own integrity. Those who raised military units in time of need should bear at least some of the expense, it was thought, in exchange for the entitlement and dignities enjoyed. Governors and judges should have their own means of carrying out many of the duties of their respective offices. Self-assessments on a local level were accepted as important if everyone saw the benefit, but otherwise severe qustions were asked. As a brilliant young historian of frontier Alabama (1820–60) has noted, the rich had to tax themselves in order to avoid imposing any demands upon lesser folk, who were equipped with the means to defend themselves through the franchise. Government activities were therefore minimal, since a consensus about such issues as taxation for public education or other common goods could not be permanently or readily secured.[15]

One basis for these suspicions of government and the privileged few who ran it was the ethic of honor. As a result, deference to law was not always a matter of habit and routine. As Julian Pitt-Rivers, an English scholar, has observed, "the constancy required by honor prefigures the law's demand for regularity." The man of honor is inclined to give deference to individuals above him, whereas the law-abiding citizen pays due to abstract principle. In circumstances that set honor against law, Pitt-Rivers says, the code "re-emerged to allocate the right of precedence and dictate the principles of conduct: among aristocracies and criminal underworlds, schoolboy and street-corner societies, open frontiers and those closed communities where reigns the 'Honorable Society,' as the Mafia calls itself."[16]

Mistrust of governments, of administrators, and of commercial and financial interests that required special protection and help from legislators was a natural consequence of the ethic. Even Yankees, at least those in the Democratic party, subscribed to these convictions, ones that assisted in holding the federated states together for over half a century. This interpretation helps to reinforce Eugene D. Genovese's argument concerning the "precapitalistic" and "prebourgeois" or "seigneurial" character of the planter class. However, it must be stressed that diversifying planters, who were usually closely tied to centers of authority, found themselves of two minds, particularly in the rapidly developing economy of the late antebellum period. The ethic to which all subscribed could not be squared with modern trends that some, especially in the port towns, were themselves hastening along. Planters whose interests did not include banks, mills, railroads, or canals discovered that yeomen shared their discomfiture; they too opposed modernity if it meant loss of autonomy and higher taxes. Periodically, the forces aggrieved with such changes enjoyed election victories that symbolized the allegiance to tradition. The opposition to internal improvements, bank charters, tariffs, and other measures, both state and national, thus reflected a moral as well as an economic concern: opposition to what was thought inimical to the primeval heritage handed down by the fathers.[17]

Despite these later trends in Southern antebellum history, Southern whites, whether rich or poor, believed that the chief duty of government was the protection of men's property, by which honor was sustainable. Possessions were an essential component of personality, family identity, and moral position. In the uncomplicated world of the eighteenth-century South, Landon Carter expressed the matter as well as any. *"Independency"* was his, he said in 1759, so long as he held his "excellent little Fortress," his plantation holdings, which were "built on a Rock." Self-sufficiency, he reiterated a decade later, was "the base or footstool on which Liberty can alone be protected." The thought was a common one; it conformed with the political and social theory of an emergent republicanism during subsequent years.[18] A quarter-century later President John Augustine Smith of William and Mary College, for instance, maintained that since most legislation was concerned with property, laws should be written by those who held it. The Jeffersonian enthusiasm for agrarian pursuit was based upon property holding. To the modern mind, the moral element in widespread land ownership is not totally clear unless the feature of personal honor is understood as an essential ingredient. Although Southerners of the Revolutionary and post-Revolutionary years conferred upon landholding a prestige that Northerners were already beginning to withhold, both sections were united in viewing republicanism, property, and personal honor as mutually supportive.

In time, of course, as Alexis de Tocqueville noted in 1835, the natural association of honor with possessions (especially if inherited) gave way to a different concept of personal identification. American individualism, the French thinker explained, stressed new uses of wealth. A "boldness of enterprise," commerce, and manufacturing separated moral worth from specific forms of property. Riches could be transferred from one enterprise to another as shrewd management dictated. Special prestige no longer inhered in land, which simply became another commodity to be traded. Tocqueville failed to see that Southerners in some respects moved less quickly to the new ground than other Americans. Ownership of slaves and land continued to offer a distinction and moral imprimatur beyond their monetary value. But on the major issue, he correctly saw that economic misfortune—filing for insolvency, for example—was no longer a personal mortification. But in the South, the old ways predominated: Southern legislatures did not enact bankruptcy laws, preferring instead debtor-relief devices. Meantime, in the North a dynamic economy encouraged the necessary changes in contract law to enable the bankrupt to get a second start. Until the advent of the early nineteenth century, however, both sections had agreed that defense of one's "little Fortress," whatever its size or character, was a virtuous undertaking.[19]

Ambition to achieve self-sufficiency posed some dangers even as it was indispensable for social prestige. Sutpen, in a sense, may serve to symbolize that antisocial factor. Virgil A. Stewart, a West Tennessee counterfeiter, was one of many real-life illustrations of how the ethic could provide justification for getting ahead without regard for others. On an expedition through the "Morass" district of Arkansas in 1834, Stewart turned to his traveling companion and said, "What is it that constitutes character, popularity, and power, in the United States? Sir, it is property; strip a man of his property in this country, and he is a ruined man indeed—you see his friends forsake him; and he may have been raised in the highest circles of society, yet he is neglected and treated with contempt. Sir, my doctrine is, let the hardest fend off." These were not just the sentiments of a self-important scoundrel. One finds greater men—Alexander Hamilton or James Henry Hammond—voicing similar notions of the perfidy, venality, and malice of others and using those vices to excuse their own behavior. Property was the key to esteem, and deplore it though one might, there was no gainsaying the matter. As Landon Carter complained in the mid-eighteenth century, the desire for advantage animated most men regardless of status. "Men of low and selfish Notions," the Virginia planter often insisted, were "well vined in the sinister modes of gain," and impelled "by an uncommon Kind of Partiality." Like most others, he denounced jealous rivals for the fault, seldom himself. Fear that others would gain ascendancy at personal expense could become obsessive.[20]

It might be thought that this desperate concern for personal acquisitiveness among Southern whites, most especially the planters, was "modern individualism." Indeed, some scholars have so argued. But the term cannot be so glibly applied. Large families, limited opportunities, constricted options, and early death all created a context of severe limits that lent a particular intensity to the pursuit of gain. How one fared, as Stewart observed, depended less upon one's own exertions than on how those endeavors were perceived in an ever-watchful community of men ready to find weakness. Neighbors, not the individual himself, decided when he was a fool, a hero, a useful ornament, or a creature unworthy of comment.

In regard to the third point, how honor affected the relation of men to government and authority, to clarify matters it will help to look in some detail at the forms of protest that occurred in seventeenth-century England and America. During that period the fundamental principles of honor were laid down in plantation Virginia and the basic moral antithesis to the primal code appeared in the Puritan colonies of the Northeast and the Quaker province of Pennsylvania. The first example of crises in honor to be discussed here was passive, domestic, and purely English. The second was aggressive, public, and Anglo-American. Both, however, were the same in this regard: they reflected the fundamental struggle of old against young, father against son, authority against ambition for either heavenly or worldly glory. Moreover, the form the disputes took, the "script" for the protagonists, was shaped by the language of honor and shame, prestige and ignominy.

The first illustration is related to the requirement of obedience to household patriarchy, the analogical microcosm of the larger state.[21] The background to this conflict, between a magisterial father and a Quaker son in England, was no less important than the incident itself. The orthodox Englishman's reaction to his son's radical faith sheds light on the assumptions that governed traditional life.

In almost every feature, the Quaker credo directly challenged the tenets of honor. Though condemned as subversive for shattering custom, the Friends made themselves walking testaments of pious shamelessness. They adopted the Beatitudes and tried to live by them. In fact, the most zealous among them elevated shame, translated into humility, to the penultimate in virtue, second only to godliness. In public, plain clothes, plain speech, and the use of the intimate form of address and greeting were all designed to set Friends apart, but also to serve as implicit criticism of a world of ranks, brute strength, and self-aggrandizement. Like the early Christians, Quakers appealed largely to the honorless—the servant and tenant classes, the cottagers of Wales, the small artisans of England. (There were also, however, a few notables in their midst.) All things have their price, even in moral affairs, and not even the most earnest Quakers were able to sustain a complete refutation of the world's ways. William Penn, for instance, in his design for a government for Pennsylvania, proposed an upper house constituted of the "most eminent for vertue Wisdom and Substance." There was no sense, even among Quakers, that poverty was a sign of purity, particularly as Pennsylvania Quakers prospered in the eighteenth century. But another failing grew out of the repudiations themselves. Inner repression of violence and of hopes for status resulted in a certain sanctimoniousness and satisfaction in misery. Group solidarity led to group conformity. Moreover, passive styles of aggression often accompanied sainthood in the Quaker mode.

Yet whatever its faults, Quakerism was initially an effective and thoroughgoing challenge to primal honor. First and foremost, the Friends repudiated the intimate connection between community approval or rejection and the individual. Worldly reputation imputed no glory or ranking (at least in theory). Instead, one's duty was the solitary business of seeking God, for all men were equipped with a divinity permitting the search for the Light Within. Although rejecting the usages of "the Honourable of the Earth," as the English Friend John Crook put it, the radical sectarians steadfastly believed in deference, when it was shorn of display. Sons, for instance, were to obey fathers, out of respect arising from acknowledged early dependency and from the wisdom, born of experience, attending seniority. Also, respect was to be given to those who deserved it on grounds of inner worth, not simply by reason of birth or dignity of office. Though this was not always observed in practice, as Penn's remark revealed, entitlement was perceived as distinct from personal character. Hospitality or honorable largess was to be offered only to those in need, without tacit expectation of return. Charity was to be dispensed out of scarcity, not out of plenty, as in circles of honor. In sexuality, continence before marriage was to be observed regardless of one's gender. Women were accorded the right to speak in meetings. In dealings with outsiders and menials, one was to recognize that all human beings, were children of God. In short, there was scarcely any aspect of primal honor, including military virtue (though not at first), that the Quakers did not drastically transform, modify, or reject outright. Opposition to slavery, a much later development, eventually became part of the Friends' challenge to worldliness.[22]

The contrast between the man of honor and the Quaker was most vividly illustrated in the confrontations between Thomas Ellwood

(1639–1714) and Walter Ellwood, his father, a Cromwellian magistrate. Son Thomas converted to Quakerism in 1659. He soon realized that "the honour due to parents did not consist in uncovering the head and bowing the body to them, but in ready obedience to their lawful commands, and in performing all needful services unto them," out of love of God and parent. "Hat honour" and "Knee honour," as Friends called them, were profane, not sacred rituals; God alone should receive such courtesies, but in inward obedience, not outward sign. Still wearing his hat, Thomas stood before his father. Outraged, the old man fell upon his son with both fists, "plucked off" the headgear, "and threw it away."

Over the next several days the curious struggle continued: Ellwood lost two more hats and finally was reduced to wearing a "montero-cap," or riding hat with ear flaps. Choleric once again, his father hurled the cap to the ground as well. Young Ellwood remarked, "I was forced to go bareheaded when ever I had occasion to go within doors and without." He caught a severe cold and was confined to his room for several weeks. On one occasion, the elder Ellwood nearly killed his son with a heavy cudgel; his sister and the servants had to pull him away. Yet the old man, obsessed though he was, was not insane. Instead, he was frightened: if his son's behavior became known, other men would ridicule him, the father, for impotence in his household management.[23]

As one might expect from this brief exposition, Southern antipathy to Quakerism long preceded the sect's sympathy for slaves, having its roots in the Friends' repudiation of the ancient ethic of honor. As the social historian Philip A. Bruce pointed out, mistrust of Quakerism began with first acquaintance in seventeenth-century Virginia. Under Governor William Berkeley and other conscientious authorities the Friends were punished, although none were hanged as a means of instruction, a policy sometimes adopted in Puritan Massachusetts. When the antislavery reform arose in the Revolutionary and post-Revolutionary era, however, southern Quakers were subject to more searching inquiry. Until then, though, their numbers were too small, their settlements too scattered for them to represent a major risk. For the most part, Southern planters both in and out of colonial government had more serious problems to face in regard to social order.[24]

As Hawthorne's story suggested, early America—and contemporary England—suffered acutely from unruly populations as well as self-protective, frightened, and arrogant rulers. Neither the exercise of authority nor public peace was predictable. Low expectations and high mortality rates made men, whether rich or poor, desperate, fearful, and violent. In England, disgruntled sailors were inclined to mutiny, slum-dwellers to bread riots, tenants to quitrent protests, foresters to poaching and warfare against gamekeepers, and the dispossessed to highway robbery, smuggling, and piracy. To deal with these outbreaks the English authorities were given not to charity but to the use of whip, gallows, and gibbet. Even gentlemen, as Lawrence Stone observes, were sometimes barbaric. He offers the example of one Sir Germaine Poole, who "bit off a good part" of Thomas Hutchinson's "nose and carried it off in his pocket."[25] Such behavior was later confined to the lower classes in both England and America, about which more will be said later.

In America, whites both high and low marauded against Indians, contrary to government importunings. Like Englishmen, they protested tithes, taxes, rents, and low prices for crops, often resorting to mob violence. Government rested even more lightly on American than on English shoulders, and there was fierce opposition to allegedly tyrannical standing armies, which were a constant source of Anglo-American resentment against central government. There was little in the way of preventive surveillance. Instead, order in both countries was after the fact: helter-skelter mustering of forces to quell riot, raid, rebellion, or disorder. Ofttimes a few leaders, sometimes men of high rank, would be punished from amongst "soe many Seduced Anxious Subjects," as Lord Culpeper of Virginia explained to London authorities in 1683. But the prevalence of policies of mercy, once order was restored, indicated that central authorities had neither the strength nor will to take draconian steps against popular upheavals.[26]

Bacon's Rebellion, the second example of crises of honor in relation to authority, was more serious than most other such outbreaks, but it was by no means unprecedented.

Some of the trouble that Virginia governor Sir William Berkeley faced was of his own making. An astute politician, he had once maintained a delicate balance among local factions and interests in the New World and in London. But beset by the dwindling faculties and stubbornness of old age, he grew increasingly self-inflated. For instance, he raised planters' taxes to make Jamestown handsome with new buildings. The planter taxpayers, seeing no advantage in town life or central administration, were angrily uncomprehending. Berkeley had his polished cane of office, but he had lost touch with popular opinion. A younger man would shortly build his career upon the crumbling foundations of Berkeley's prestige.[27]

Like Hawthorne's protagonist Robin Molineux, Nathaniel Bacon had come to his new residence in 1674, as the kinsman of a wealthy patron, another Nathaniel Bacon, who sat on Berkeley's council. The newcomer was also related to the governor himself. True to family ties, the two elder officials did well by their young protégé. Though less than thirty, Bacon was placed on the council and given a choice of fertile lands on the upper James River. But young Bacon, who had come from England, had not done so on his own volition. His father, a substantial gentleman, was highly displeased with his son's prodigality and inattention to his studies at Cambridge University. Moreover, Bacon's bad reputation had induced Sir Edward Duke to refuse consent for his daughter Elizabeth's marriage to Bacon. When she defied him and married Bacon anyway, her father disowned her, a further blow to the young man's self-esteem. As punishment, the elder Bacon had dispatched his son to the western wilderness, a circumstance that the son greatly resented, despite the paternal gift of money that accompanied his banishment.

A grim, sulking, obdurate individual, Nathaniel Bacon "could not contain himself within bounds," said one chronicler. He was ambitious for glory and vindication. Unlike Robin Molineux, this stranger brought no country naiveté to the town. Instead, he carried the impulses of court honor—the search for place and power— to the forest. At first the welcome he received was gratifying. As one observer remarked, the "honor" of being named a councillor "made him the more considerable in the eye of the Vulgar, and gave some advantage to his pernicious designes." Moody, he was sometimes of "an ominous, pensive, melancholly Aspect"—godless, impatient with unsophisticated planters, and generally "arrogant." But when drinking or if pleased with turns of events, he was extravagantly merry. Unlike the pious Thomas Ellwood, Bacon had more than one complexion, more than one face to show the world.[28]

The immediate cause of what became known as Bacon's Rebellion was, as often it was in "public inflammations," a petty business. A planter on the upper James had failed to pay the Doeg Indians for some hogs. Though ordinarily peaceful, the Doegs slew the planter's herdsman. "Honour and intress," declared the squires, required blood vengeance for this and other alleged atrocities. Soon the Susquehannocks, a more formidable tribe, were drawn into the conflict. The conflagration spread throughout the Chesapeake, and the authorities were unable to suppress or control it.[29]

Having barely repressed a planter uprising over similar Indian and fiscal difficulties the year before, Governor Berkeley proposed lavish fort constructions, a defensive and not altogether efficient policy. But once the plan was underway, Berkeley could not easily change course, despite popular disapproval. As one chronicler put it, "How should [the governor] satisfie his honour with the undertakers of the worke" if he acceded to public wishes and abandoned the experiment? On the other hand, to persist was to lose his "Repute" which "he all ways held, in the [popular] judgment for a Wise Man. . . ." Honor determined policy; retreat meant shame. In March 1676 a call for troops was much more gratifying to public opinion. It offered the chance for white retribution, and for the heaping of blame upon the Indians for all the colony's perplexities. Moreover, the yeomanry would have an opportunity to earn militia pay—and gain from plunder—just when low tobacco prices were driving common folk to despair. If Berkeley had used the Indians as scapegoats sooner, he might have avoided what developed into a challenge to his rule.[30]

There were always grievances that could be exploited at any time in so risky and hierarchical a world. But the emergence of head-strong leadership for rebellion was often largely fortuitous. The personal element counted much more in human affairs then than it did in later, more complex circumstances. At any rate, young Nathaniel Bacon quickly took command of a "giddy and unthinking multitude." He demanded a commission to head the fight against the Indians. When it was not at once forthcoming, Bacon acted as if the power were already his. Affronted, Berkeley denounced him as a traitor, removed him from the council, and resolved that there could be no peace until either the rebel submitted or one of the two of them was dead.

Like Hawthorne's character representing Authority, Berkeley had to face the unpleasant fact that the mystique of royalty, the weight of law, and churchly strictures about honoring fathers on earth as in heaven were inadequate defenses against dissidence and rebellion. They alone could not bring Bacon to the gallows or to his knees. In fact, the initial confrontations between the two placed Berkeley at the mercy of the mob. At Jamestown, in June, surrounded by Bacon's military forces, Berkeley apparently conceded. He did so with characteristic seventeenth-century pomp, declaring, " 'God forgive you, I forgive you,' thrice repeating the same Words," as the assembly watched. Like an obedient son, Bacon knelt before the governor, swearing fealty. Berkeley had no choice; the rebel and his followers were restored to favor. A realist, Bacon left town before Berkeley mustered the power to retaliate.[31]

As each prepared for the next encounter, Bacon increasingly found himself caught between the demands of his troops for action, plunder, and glory and the risks of being arrested for treason against the crown and local authority. In late June he returned to Jamestown determined to gain legitimacy by means of the necessary commissions. The scene was worthy of a Renaissance drama. Six hundred men accompanied their hero to the ramshackle capital on the lower James. This time Berkeley, still poorly supported, greeted the demands by "uncovering his naked Bosome," daring Bacon's men to "shoot him, before ever he would" sign the commissions. Patricide, as it might be called, would bring ruin on them all, as the cagey old politician knew. Bacon understood. He pledged not to "hurt a haire of your honor's head," but like a petulant schoolboy he finally shouted in exasperation, "God damne my Blood, I came for a commission, and a commission I will have before I goe."[32]

Negotiations over the commissions ensued, but finally Berkeley, with stiff hauteur, strutted away, followed by his councillors and some burgesses. Seeking to regain the initiative, Bacon pursued him "with outragious Postures of his Head, Arms, Body, and Leggs, often tossing his hand from his Sword to his Hat" in exasperation—men of Bacon's nature did not hide their emotions. His men-at-arms followed closely behind, exclaiming menacingly, " 'We will have itt. We will have itt,' " and pointing their guns at the faces of the burgesses peering through an assembly chamber window. The show ended with Berkeley's surrender. Yet although "Ignorant People" thought Bacon's triumph was permanent, the leader himself knew better. His legitimacy remained in doubt: Berkeley had only to repudiate the commissions. After all, they had been signed under unlawful duress. As a result, Bacon had to rely upon sheer personal magnetism. He rallied his men by invoking the ancient spirit of valor. At Green Spring he told them, "Come on, my hearts of gold; he that dies in the field lies in the bed of honor."[33]

The events of the rebellion included looting and atrocities against indwelling, friendly Indian tribes and even against Berkeley's planter allies; the razing of part of Jamestown to vandalize Berkeley's urban dream; and several attempts to arouse white and black servants against their masters. Once they were organized, the government's forces were soon likewise engaged in riotousness. Resort to lawlessness showed the weakness of both factions. The allegiances of common folk and even of some planters shifted as quickly as summer breezes, and men took the line of least resistance to save themselves. To secure loyalty, Bacon and Berkeley both had to placate their backers with prizes, liquor, and a sense of immediate triumph. The crowd that Hawthorne was to imagine in his story as followers of the devilish militia officer represented the same psychology. Such was the nature of the "Giddy headed Multitude" in traditional society, one that "unless restrayned" might "prove ye

Ruin of a Country," as two friends of Governor Berkeley had warned him as early as January 1673. Though grievances were many and plausible, leaders were not always in firm command. It was only natural to search out some scapegoat, even the governor himself, to name as the great devil. The struggle of youth against age, poor against rich, settler against officialdom was both mythic and real in character. The strictures of patriarchy seemed to invite that interpretation of this kind of crisis.

In this case, as in Hawthorne's story, it was reigning, aged Authority that triumphed. On October 26, 1676, Bacon died, the sudden victim, Berkeley gloated, of the "bloody Flux" and "lousey Disease; so that the swarmes of Vermyn that bred in his Body he could not destroy but by throwing his shirts in the Fire as often as he shifted himself." The black-haired, scowling "demon," as Berkeley's faction called Bacon, had tried to stigmatize the governor as foolish, senile, incompetent, corrupt. But for the moment, at least, it was the aged governor's turn to rejoice, as Authority had in Hawthorne's tale. He crowed in doggerel, "Bacon is Dead I am sorry at my hart/ That Lice and flux should take the hangmans part." Clearly Berkeley's mockery expressed both fury and delight—he hid neither emotion. A party searched for Bacon's remains, planning to expose them, a chronicler said, "to public infamy," but the corpse could not be found.[34]

The attitudes about authority, the rituals of allegiance, their quick repudiation, and the curiously inchoate dispersals and realignments of factions all indicated an English (as opposed to purely American) style of uprising. It was one in which commoners and some gentlemen expressed in violence their dissatisfactions with crown policy, without serious intent of overthrowing monarchy itself. Such rebellions had occurred many times before and after, both in England and America. For instance, Cade's Rebellion, the Pilgrimage of Grace in 1536, and the Northern Rising of 1569 displayed patterns remarkably similar to the Bacon affair in Virginia, not only in the almost ritualistic forms of violence by both rebels and government supporters and the personal nature of leadership but also in the ambivalence that all these things reflected about central authority. Throughout the Tudor and Stuart eras, obedience to established authority was the uppermost civic virtue. The schoolmen never wearied of reiterating that point. Shakespeare's historical dramas presented the issue in popular form. At the same time, it was recognized that outbreaks and commotions were reminders to the crown and its officers to correct the faults of misrule and not rely upon draconian measures alone. Of course, the containment of dissent within ritual bounds did not always succeed. The English Civil War, which occurred before Bacon's Rebellion, and the American Revolution, which happened many years afterward, were both situations where the acting out of protest got out of hand. On both occasions the central power failed to heed the signs of virulent, popular outrage. Forgetting the institutional weakness of their police power, the royal authorities reduced the problem to that of the villainy of demagogues, vicious and ignorant peasants, and corrupted local magistrates. Certainly Berkeley saw matters in this light. So had Charles I at the start of the English Civil War. A rigid, even fatuous sense of royal honor led him to discount the economic burdens of the London lower classes in 1642. His blunders cost him the loyalty of the city, and eventually his throne and his life as well.

But if the signs of disquiet were ofttimes misread by those in power, dissenting members of the local elite also had much to worry about. Propertied rebels had to confront the fact that the crowd, once roused, might turn against themselves. The possibility was real. As Peter Shaw has so ably shown in his study of American Revolutionary crowds, the annual festival to celebrate the repression of revolt—Guy Fawkes Day—also paid homage to the act of rebellion itself. The Boston mob of the 1760s, whether engaged in a Pope's Day bacchanalia or a Stamp Act riot, followed the traditional practice of reenacting disorder with effigy burnings, a not very subtle reminder to the elite that power of the lower orders resided in numerical strength. Because of that power and because of the general ambivalence about authority itself, one can clearly see why there was such side-switching and uncertainty of relations between the

Virginia gentry and the yeomanry throughout the Bacon episode. Ritual actions such as the forced oath-takings were supposed to give guidelines and coherence to the protests. They were, however, insufficient; class ambiguities and resentments remained. But once the eruption was contained, the wise ruler and his faction threw all blame upon a few leaders and on the "brutish" and misled commoners. A handful of dissident gentlemen would be rounded up and hanged. Meantime, and more significantly, the ruler—Henry VIII, for instance, in the Lincolnshire Rebellion—would correct the most easily remedied abuses.

Thus the successfully repressed uprising did not result in the rooting out of every rebel, and most especially not of the most powerful ones in the local elite. It would have been foolhardy to try. Good leaders were never in great supply in a society with so many at the bottom of the social pile, so few at the top. The damage had to be held to the minimum. Mercy was shrewd policy, and moral lessons of governance had to be contemplated. "Yet this I note concernynge rebelles and rebellyouns, although the deuyll raise them," declared a sixteenth-century humanist, "yet God always useth them to his glory, as a parte of his Justice. For whan Kyngs . . . suffer theyr under officers to mysuse theyr subiectes, and will not heare nor remedy theyr peoples wrongs whan they complayne, than suffereth God the Rebell to rage, and to execute that part of his Iustice that the parcyall prince would not."[35]

Berkeley, though, proved heedlessly vindictive. There were too many hangings, even for the taste of Charles II. A royal commission, the customary means for mending the damaged fabric of social order, investigated Berkeley's rule and found it severely wanting. Berkeley returned to England very much in disgrace. He spent his final years vainly wheedling the crown for vindication. There was as much rude justice in his fall from royal favor and command as there was in Wash Jones's wielding the scythe. The governor's hauteur proved his undoing no less than Sutpen's had.

Nevertheless, as policy and English custom seemed to dictate, the great landholders who had been involved in Bacon's rebel camp (at one point or another) did not suffer severe consequences, despite Berkeley's vindictiveness. Some of them even received royal pardons; among the lucky were William Byrd I and Colonel Giles Brent.

This style of rebellion, with its imperfect use of ritual, demonstrated the instability of order, the fear of unpredictability in human affairs. In order to provide themselves with an explanation for what seemed to be demonic, observers turned to supernaturalism, as if men such as Bacon were manifestations of some terrible, uncontrollable force in nature as much as in man. Thomas Mathew, one of Bacon's neighbors, began his recollection of the troubles by listing the "Three Prodigies" which the public claimed were "Ominous Presages." The first was the appearance of a comet in 1675. Then a large flight of pigeons, similar to the one preceding the Indian massacre of 1640, stirred anxiety among "the old Planters," he said. Finally, the colony was attacked by swarms of flies that emerged mysteriously from the ground. During the harvest of 1676 it was evident that the dry summer had severely damaged the crops of Indian corn and tobacco. The people, observed Mathew, were certain that the *"Pawawings,* i.e. the Sorceries of the Indians," were responsible. In reaction to events that could not be controlled by the institutions available, the Virginia colonists thought spirits of another world had added to their woes, no less than the people of Salem believed in the Satanism of the women there accused of witchcraft.[36]

No doubt the rebellion represented a major shift in the direction of Virginia history, which was never so anarchistic or so unsophisticated again.[37] Nonetheless, the rebellion passed on the legacy of stylized rituals from the past. The ethic of honor and shame was displayed not just in the language used but also in the actions of both authority and rebellion. Some have stressed that Bacon and his friends were Western pioneers—rough examples of the new America. That would miss the rebellion's Old World derivations and their mythic character.[38] These rebel Virginians were no less English than Berkeley and his allies. Rebels and Robin Hoods, pirates and heroes then belonged to the transatlantic world, not to one country or another. It was no easy matter to tell villains from worthies; all made claim to honor.

At the same time, Bacon should be seen not only as a reflection of the past but also as a herald of the future in the South. Just as their yeoman ancestors had followed Bacon, nineteenth- and twentieth-century small farmers and laborers were to be galvanized by other demagogues. Gene Talmadge, Cole Blease, and Theodore Bilbo, like Nathaniel Bacon, knew how to make commoners proud of their color and their social values. Bacon offered no real reforms. Nor did the latter-day political leaders. Their "program" was chiefly inspirational—the sense that one could partake in the magic of brave fellowship for redress of grievances. The aim left much to be desired. Yet the men who could evoke the age-old principles of honor became legends.

If Southern history were merely the record of conflict that the primal ethic engendered, it would have been a bloodier, more repressive society than ever it was. Instead, the elements of the archaic code were mingled with those of a higher moral system, of a style of life and a way of thinking about law, religion, and society that were of a richer cast. Although "gentility," a version of honor more refined than the archaic code, is a more familiar word in the Southern historian's lexicon, it must be posed as a complement, and sometimes a challenge, to the code described here so far.

4

Gentility

Honor in the Old South applied to all white classes, though with manifestations appropriate to each ranking. Few could escape it altogether. Gentility, on the other hand, was a more specialized, refined form of honor, in which moral uprightness was coupled with high social position. Such a joining of rank with acquired virtue was vulnerable to all sorts of confusions and self-doubts. As Kenneth S. Lynn has observed, the seventeenth-century Virginia planter was never wholly sure that he was truly a gentleman, at least by the standards of London, the society to which he looked for approval. Often enough the American colonial visiting England met open contempt, and the ridicule rankled. Gentility, most especially its English form, involved mastery of quite subtle marks of status—the proper accent, the right choice of words and conversational topics, the appropriate attire, an acquaintance with various kinds of social proprieties and other rules not easy to follow with aplomb. The mimicking of English customs, styles of architecture, furnishings, and portrait hangings was, for wealthy men like William Byrd II, a way to demonstrate to themselves and others that gentility had been achieved. Byrd was particularly determined. "I rose at 4 o'clock this morning and read a chapter in Hebrew and 400 verses in Homer's

Odyssey," he noted in his diary in a quite typical entry. Such activity had social more than intellectual meaning for him. Nevertheless, the stigma of being a colonial remained. Likewise, in the nineteenth century the Southern gentleman, unless very cosmopolitan, was not always comfortable about his place in the larger context of Anglo-American respectability, however secure he felt at home.[1]

Even as a simple mark of status within the various and distinct parts of the South itself, gentility was sometimes problematical. On the one hand, eighteenth-century Virginia and South Carolina planters established close-knit marital alliances that restricted the circle of gentility to the very wealthiest and wellborn families. There was little difficulty in ascertaining who belonged and who did not in long-settled communities or even districts. But with the territorial expansions of the nineteenth century, the perceptions of gentility underwent corresponding changes. In the newer states of the early nineteenth century, sang their chroniclers, "men of talent and enterprise and women of beauty, intelligence, and virtue" from worthy eastern lineages brought civilization and refinement to the backlands. But it was quickly apparent that the sobriquet "Virginia gentleman," for instance, had become so commonplace as early as the second war with Britain in 1812 that it had lost much of its exclusivity. When the Virginia writer Anne Royall traveled through frontier Alabama in 1818, she identified nearly every fellow countryman as "gentleman," even if he was a tavern-keeper or boatman. Northern visitors were less chauvinistic and more skeptical. In 1858 Corydon Fuller, a book salesman from Ohio, managed to find an occasional "specimen of the best class of Southerners," like Judge Norman of Union County, Arkansas, who was "a Georgian," but "intelligent" nonetheless.[2]

Difficult though it was to tell the genuine article from the fake, three components appeared to be necessary for public recognition of gentility in the Old South: sociability, learning, and piety. Northern gentlemen also assumed these graces, but the order of their priority was quite different, and therefore to them Southern gentility appeared in a curious refraction. Moreover, Southerners themselves did not give the virtues equal weight. Piety was a late addition, a result of the Second Great Awakening early in the nineteenth century. Learning, an expensive commodity throughout the plantation South's history, did not command as much prestige as it did in the New England states. But sociability was the *sine qua non,* from the seventeenth to the late nineteenth centuries, from Charleston to New Orleans, from Richmond to the Ozarks. Despite the different priorities assigned each of the qualities, a favored few seemed to embody them all, thus giving the Old South a reason for pride far beyond what the actual number of such people would have warranted. The culmination of the three graces of gentility was best exemplified in the figure of Robert E. Lee, the man as well as the legend.

The antebellum frame of reference in regard to sociability needs little amplification here. We all know about Southern hospitality—pulling out the wine bottle, opening wide the larder, and plumping up the pillows for any and all strangers. The custom had a darker side that will be treated later. But sociability—"affability," the eighteenth-century gentleman called it—involved more than that. It was a way of identifying the Southerner and distinguishing him from the Yankee. To the Northern observer, the ideal of gregariousness seemed as much a defect of character as a reason for admiration. As early as 1773, for instance, Josiah Quincy, Jr., who was visiting South Carolina to ascertain patriotic sentiments, was appalled—as were many later Yankees—by the prevalence of "men of the turf and gamesters." It worried him that matters of political philosophy and religion were so frivolously set aside for lighter subjects of conversation. At the same time, the New England revolutionary found himself strangely drawn to a Colonel Howe, "a very extraordinary character." Howe was at ease both "in the company of the philosopher and the libertine—a favorite of the man of sense and the female world." If he had faults, who, after all, was spared them? "In short his character seemed an assemblage of a Grandison and Lovelace." Many years later his son, Josiah Quincy, had similar feelings toward the Southern style of gentility. President Andrew Jackson was nothing more than a western savage to Quincy and his conserva-

tive Whig friends. Upon meeting the general on his New England
tour in 1833, however, Quincy observed that he "was, in essence, a
knightly personage—prejudiced, narrow, mistaken on many points,
it might be, but vigorously a gentleman in his high sense of honor
and in the natural, straight-forward courtesies which are easily to
be distinguished from the veneer of policy." The old criticism of
Southern graciousness, with its hint of impetuosity, was still there.
Yet a strong attraction was felt, too. "Cotton Whigs" like Quincy
were not so pious that slaveholding disturbed their equipoise. They
comfortably retained some of that worldliness that had always posed
a counterpoint to the Puritan and later evangelical style in New
England. Aware of these complex reactions in the Yankee soul,
Henry James drew a curious portrait of the Southern gentleman in
the figure of Basil Ransom, hero of *The Bostonians*. Ransom's touch
of violence, like Jackson's, made "courtesy in the hall," as Emerson
put it, seem an artifice. So at least it appeared in the eyes of Olive
Chancellor, Ransom's obsessively feminist rival for Verena Tarrant's
heart. Just as Olive Chancellor rejected her femininity in favor of
the suffrage cause, so Ransom needed to proclaim his masculinity in
refutation of any and all abstractions. These sectional compulsions
were ones that James found fascinating.[3]

By far the most celebrated example of the ambivalence registered between the Northern and the Southern gentleman was Henry
Adams's recollections of his Virginia friends at Harvard College in
the mid-1850s. A "trio of Virginians as little fitted" for the rigors of
intellectuality "as Sioux Indians to a treadmill" enlivened campus
life. Especially impressive was "Roony" Lee (William Henry Fitzhugh Lee), "tall, largely built, handsome, genial, with liberal Virginian openness towards all he liked," a figure, in short, who in-
stinctively took command. The youth, said Adams, "had no mind;
he had temperament." The Southerners drank, wenched, and got
into scrapes over some "imaginary grief," but Roony customarily
managed to head off serious confrontations when his cronies stepped
out of line. Yet Adams admitted that he found something in common with these unpredictable young men. They were eighteenth-
century characters like himself, figures ill-equipped by temperament

and class to meet the challenge of the modern world. "No doubt the self-esteem of the Yankee, which tended naturally to self-distrust, was flattered by gaining the slow conviction that the Southerner, with his slave-owning limitations, was as little fit to succeed in the struggle of modern life as though he were still a maker of stone axes, living in caves, and hunting the *bos primigenius,* and that every quality in which he was strong, made him weaker." But Adams had begun to fear that even in this respect one eighteenth-century type might not differ deeply from another. Yankees, he lamented, already preferred "economists over diplomats or soldiers," a shift that left the old gentility irrelevant. Whether or not Adams was wholly accurate either in his assessment of himself or of these specific Southerners, he was keenly aware "how thin an edge of friendship separated them in 1856 from mortal enmity." If matters had been left to the Northern and Southern elite alone, such mixed feelings would scarcely have led to hostilities in 1861. The differences would have simply remained a source of amusement. There was nothing at all fallacious about Adams' stereotype: some Southerners were exactly like Roony Lee—wild but polished, "childlike" but commanding. Yet their ranks were thin, much thinner than legend would have it.[4]

As Adams suggested, the Cavalier was more than a little discomfited when it came to learning. To be sure, Southern ideals of education differed not at all from what early Republican Yankees believed was necessary to equip young men for the world. Study of the classics had always constituted most of what a gentleman, British or American, was supposed to know from books. As President William Brattle of Harvard remarked in 1689, *"Liberali liberaliter instituendi—*Gentlemen must be educated like gentlemen." Over a hundred and fifty years later, William J. Grayson echoed the same sentiment with a South Carolinian accent. "The end of education," he declared, "is to improve the manners, morals, and mind of the Student."[5] Yankee professors would have rearranged the sequence, but it was an acceptable trinity.

Although classical literature endured as the foundation of the

Southern college curriculum much longer than it did in the technically oriented free states, learning itself was not greeted with uniform enthusiasm. Easy reference to Homer, Plato, Horace, and Livy
assured Southern gentlemen of one another's trustworthiness, but
only so long as the quotations and allusions were familiar. What
would the Southern funeral orator have done without a reference
to Nestor as a last wreath to fling upon the bier of a "polished
statesman"? No encomium to Southern womankind was complete
without a reminder of Sparta's brave mothers. To justify nearly any
act of self-defense or vengeance, Hannibal's dying words to son
Hamilcar or some choice thoughts about Thermopylae always
seemed appropriate. It did not take a scholar to report what Cicero
had to say about a policy of honor and immortal fame in immediate
war as opposed to strategies of peace, wise expediency, and careful
military preparation. Far from it. These and other catchwords and
maxims from the ancient past were simply part of everyday par-
lance, along with familiar lines from Shakespeare and Scott's *Lay of
the Last Minstrel*. Even gamblers named their horses Bucephelas
and hunters called their dogs Scipio.

It was all very well for Southern whites to boast of the high-
toned character of their "civilization," but such references signified
very little. Nevertheless, year in and year out the *Southern Literary
Messenger* and other publications fiercely defended the old curriculum, even if their handfuls of subscribers were already convinced.
Willoughby Newton, at the Virginia Military Institute's 1858 com-
mencement exercises, was still extolling the primacy of the classics.
Such studies, he told the cadets, prepared them for a military career
at least as well as courses in modern mathematics and engineering.
Just three years before the war broke out he was urging that what
the South needed was a thirst for brave achievement as intense as
that which provided "the highest incentives to public virtue" among
the ancients.[6]

The purpose of these ritual words was not to sentimentalize the
past but to reassure listeners that nothing much need change; the
past was yet alive. If it all seemed boring, that too had its uses. New
moral thoughts, like new religious inspirations, could be dangerous,

but heavy blankets of ancient moral orthodoxies, largely from the Stoic tradition, could stifle uncommon opinion.

Learning, especially of the venerable kind, marked the possessor as a gentleman. Yet in the South at least, too much of it allegedly spoiled the result. There was a strongly anti-intellectual streak in Southern society, one that generations of college students perpetuated so that sociability—and reputation for manliness—would have no rival. Deploring the consequences, Grayson, one of South Carolina's few intellectual squires, blamed the old-fashioned methods of instruction for the problem. Recalling his own days at South Carolina College in the 1820s, Grayson thought an hour or two of recitation with a half-bored professor much too brief and unproductive. Thereafter the student, barely adolescent, was left to his own and others' "boyish devices." Free of adult checks on his behavior, the young man "makes rapid advances in smoking, chewing, playing billiards; concocting sherry cobblers, gin slings and mint juleps; . . . to say nothing of more questionable matters and takes degrees in arts and sciences about which his diploma is altogether silent." Within a year or two, he forgets most' everything. At age thirty, nineteen of twenty graduates can no longer "construe an ode in Horace," Grayson lamented in 1862.[7]

To claim that literary pursuits had no effect at all would seem entirely unfair. At the very least, setting the standard of some degree of learning was bound to exhilarate a few and lead others to grudging admiration for those who did come close to the ideal. Certainly, Thomas Jefferson was totally unselfconscious in advising his nephew Peter Carr (no towering intellect) to study the classics well. His list of authors to be tackled at once was very formidable: Goldsmith's *History of Greece,* Herodotus, Thucydides, "Xenophontis hellenica. Xenophontis Anabasis. Quintus Curtis. Justin." Then on to the Greek and Latin poets, and thence to the moderns—Milton in particular. "In morality read Epectetus Xenophontis memorabilia, Plato's Socratic dialogues, Cicero's philosophies."[8] For a young man of Virginia, the advice was probably more depressing than inspirational.

It is never possible to determine how much literature affects behavior. Yet if the choice of subjects to study ever has a close relationship to felt needs and experiences, it could be argued that the South's concern with classical sources reflected the continued relevance of Stoic traditions of honor and virtue. Thinkers of the ancient world had come to realize that primal honor was an insufficient guide: pursuit of the just, the beautiful, and the true took precedence over popular acclaim for valor. The broader vision was expressed in the Aristotelian ideal of *megalopsychia*. It signified high-mindedness, pride in one's self-worth and achievements, greatness and openness of heart. In the Renaissance, the Stoic concept represented a rejection of self-depising Christian asceticism, the *contemptuus mundi* of the monastery. At the same time, it was a repudiation of ancient Teutonic and Celtic boasting; instead, one's self-assessment should correspond with one's actual, inner worthiness, not with public reputation, as in primal honor. An ability to suffer misfortunes graciously and rejoice in good times moderately was based upon appropriate, modest self-appraisal and becoming restraint. As Montaigne, the French Stoic, put it, "Aristotle thinkes it an office of magnanimitie to hate and love openly, to judge and speak with all libertie."[9]

Southerners often wrote each other as if they were applying copybook lessons from these expositors of humanistic behavior. While the descriptions may have been quite accurate, often enough the language was stilted and unconvincing. For instance, in 1854 Charles C. Jones, a young Georgian of very high breeding, happened to meet Colonel Charles Suttle, whose fugitive slave, Anthony Burns, was the subject of considerable agitation at the time. Outraged that Yankees could dare think ill of so representative a Southern planter as Suttle, Jones, in a letter home, heaped praises upon him. Suttle, he said, "is a perfect Virginia gentleman, of high standing, well educated, fine commanding, prepossessing appearance," who had to be regarded as "high-minded" as anyone could be. In a word, he was "a gentleman of the *first class*. Perhaps he was. But the description better fit the Aristotelian ideal than any unpretentious Virginia squire. Hyperbole, though, should not be thought simply a sign of Southern romanticism; rather it was a part of the ritual speech that invoked ancient humanism for current application. Lord Bolingbroke, Edmund Burke, and other advocates of gentility who preceded the romantic era would have understood and approved Jones's choice of compliments. At the same time, such uses of language and models no longer held their appeal in the North. By confusing humbler aspects of honor with lofty gentility, Jones seemed morally insensitive. Even sympathetic Yankee conservatives were beginning to weary of such stalwart defenses of slaveholders on the grounds of a spurious "high-mindedness."[10]

In reviewing the more admirable characters of the American past, however, Southern and Northern gentlemen could come to quick agreement about the appropriateness of the Stoic model. George Washington, John Marshall, and other exemplars of the role aroused orators to flights of erudition, regardless of their sectional origins. For instance Edward Everett, the New England attorney, dwelt upon George Washington's Ciceronian qualities. "The ancient philosophers," he said, "placed the true conception of perfect manhood in the possession of those powers and qualities which are required for the honorable and successful discharge of the duties of life, each in the golden mean, equally removed from excess in either direction, and all in due proportion." Washington, he continued, fulfilled these traits better than "any other chieftain or ruler of ancient or modern times." Such inner strength did not, Everett said, find popular support. "Thoughtful valor" in a chieftain gains only modest approval; whereas "gallant rashness" takes the laurels. In magistracy, "discreet" measures for the public good win meager assent, but "selfish management" is easily condoned. In council, the "well-urged" argument for reasonableness obtains faint applause, while the emotional appeal "delights the ear, and sometimes maddens while it charms." The gentleman, he summarized, was one who "disarms Fortune" with the power of prudence, regardless of its unpopularity. The Northern version of gentility stressed dignity, reason, sobriety, and caution; the Southern ideal made more concession to warm-heartedness, generosity, and expressiveness. But in either case high-mindedness, a summation of all these traits, was the social ideal, one that combined grace with honor as the Stoic tradition had fashioned it.[11]

The difficulty was, however, that in the antebellum South gentility and learning became increasingly incompatible as white democracy eroded the old deferences to hierarchy. Even after new schools and colleges were established, the leaders were defensive. When the University of the South was founded, for example, the early recruiters catered to the raw planter mentality. They arranged the school year so that in the winter months the student could "engage in the sports which make him a true Southern man, hunting, shooting, riding; when he can mingle freely with the slaves who are in the future to be placed under his management." School studies would occupy the summer and fall, when the young man was of little use to anyone on the plantation.[12]

If many planters were skeptical of learning, so too was the yeomanry. The University of the South's founders could not repel an intruding world. Hundreds of Episcopalians gathered on the Sewanee mountaintop in 1860 to lay the first cornerstone for the "heavenly city." But mountain folk trooped to the windy site as well, attracted by the chance to gape at militia uniforms, well-dressed matrons, and processions of bishops in billowing vestments. They soon wearied of prayers and long speeches. "I saw fighting, horse-trading, gambling, all conducted openly and vociferously and without the least regard for the ceremonies that were being conducted around the cornerstone," one participant later recalled. No one dared silence the "country-people" or tried to stop the drinking and gaming. The juxtaposition of the fancy and plain, the decorous and the vulgar accentuated the code of gentility—setting its adherents apart from lesser folk—but also served to remind them of the social fragility that so limited Southern genteel learning.[13]

The chief problem facing the gentleman who wished to be known for his learnedness and erudition was not solely the presence of slavery in the society. Matters scarcely improved when that institution was gone. Rather it was the stress upon sociability and manliness as the highest significations of honor that obstructed a free pursuit of the life of the mind.

As a result, even the defense of the South's most cherished institution—slavery—earned the intellectual few tangible rewards. As Professor Drew G. Faust has observed, those who undertook the task of demonstrating the legitimacy of slaveholding did so in order to prove their loyalty to the South, a fidelity rendered suspect by their concerns for high culture. Surrounded by a "brainless" squirearchy and mired in the routines of country living, such thinkers as William Gilmore Simms, William J. Grayson, and Beverley Tucker commiserated endlessly with each other in long, self-pitying letters. They disliked the vulgarity and ignorance that they discerned in the Southern masses, even in the planter class itself. The Southern thinker was always a man apart, covering his vulnerability as an intellectual by glorifying the "home institution." Aloof by necessity, he could not share the boisterous pleasures of the neighboring squires and yeomen. "Shy when they are frank; sad and thoughtful when they are uproarious; solitary when they crowd together," a Southern intellectual like Simms, even as a boy among playmates, recognized his differentness. As a youth, Simms recalled, it had made him feel resentful and morbidly despondent, attitudes of mind lasting a lifetime. Still more provoking to Simms and his friends was the intellectual's impotence in politics and even in regional letters. Quarterlies drew few subscribers. "There is something wanting among us," lamented Simms's fellow sufferer William J. Grayson. The "quarterly review," said Grayson, "is a head without a body, a portico without a temple. It is not Hamlet without the ghost; but the ghost without Hamlet. We have little to review."[14]

Westerners dwelling in plantation societies in the West Indies, Ceylon, and other far-off places have generally lacked the self-confidence, sophistication, and intellectual stimulation necessary to match the creativity of metropolitan centers. The South was no exception, though the Revolutionary Fathers briefly provided a remarkable deviation. But in the more democratic milieu of the antebellum South, when Southern life was under fierce criticism abroad,

that Revolutionary heritage died out. Paralyzed by recognition of
his own irrelevance to planter society, the gentleman-intellectual
claimed to have no ambition for "the admiration and subserviency
which great wealth secures its professor," as William J. Grayson
loftily declared.[15] But another device for reconciling oneself to ineffectuality was to mask learning in personal eccentricity, an approach that John Randolph, Edmund Ruffin, and Beverley Tucker
adopted. Such methods ensured that planting neighbors, easily
affronted by erudition that they could not understand, would not
be resentful.[16]

By the late antebellum period evangelical Christianity had severely
altered the characteristics that defined the ideal Southern gentleman. "High-mindedness," magnanimity, and a sense of self-worth
continued to be adjuncts of manly gentility, however imperfect
their realization in practice. But much more easily discernible and
therefore more readily acquired was piety. That virtue, however,
was also the subject of some ambivalence in the public forum. A
long anticlerical tradition among the upper classes of Virginia and
the Carolinas was bound to affect the way men perceived religious
attributes.

During the eighteenth century, under the influence of the ratio-
nalism of the Enlightenment, the Southern model of honorable conscience conformed with the classical heritage. For instance, Jefferson
advised his nephew Peter Carr in these secular terms: "Give up
money, give up fame, give up science, give up earth itself and all it
contains, rather than do an immoral act. And never suppose that in
any possible situation or under any circumstances that is best for you
to do a thing tho' it can never be known but to yourself, ask yourself
how you would act were all the world looking at you, and act accordingly." The inner motivation rested upon Stoic, not Christian precept. One was to imagine public scrutiny, not expect alienation
from God or even one's own sensibilities. While Yankee schoolmasters, fathers, and clergymen would not have any objection to
such propositions for right living, they were much more likely to
include Scripture and works of the church fathers in their lists of

suggested reading, particularly Richard Baxter, Philip Dodderidge, and other Protestant advisers to the soul. The supremacy of honor as the criterion for excellence of character was much more intense in the Southern gentry code than in the puritan moral scheme. "Health, learning and virtue will ensure your happiness," Jefferson later urged his nephew; "they will give you a quiet conscience, private esteem and public honour."[17] Not surprisingly, the skeptical squire of Monticello said nothing about either divine blessing or the curse of alienation from God in the event of failure.

The difference between conscience as part of honorable bearing and conscience as an inner voice of God might seem slight as far as the actual way gentlemen behaved. One could forgo the committing of wrong as easily by one injunction as the other. Nevertheless, the Christian approach quite clearly had a more telling effect in encouraging moderation, sexual continence, repression of anger, and postponement of desires, because guilt is a more internal and self-dependent mechanism than shame.

In contrast to the eighteenth-century deistical notion of conscience, the diary of Michael Wigglesworth, written in mid-seventeenth-century Massachusetts, exemplified what Henry Adams, two centuries later, called the cultivation of "self-mistrust," an essential ingredient in Christian guilt. *The last night a filthy dream and so pollution escaped me in my sleep for which I desire to hang down my head with shame and beseech the Lord not to make me possess the sin of my youth and give me into the hands of my abomination,"* wrote the Boston merchant. "I despair of ever pleasing God by my endeavours in the world. . . ."[18]

Whether Wigglesworth's remarks were heartfelt, or merely ritualistic, one seldom found similar expressions among churchgoing aristocrats of Virginia in the seventeenth or the eighteenth centuries. Though devout in his own way, Landon Carter took a much more sanguine view of his relations to God. "Dispair," he said, almost in conscious reaction to the New England mode, "is the worst disorder that a human Creature can fall into; but in a planter it is a disease unto death; therefore God keep me clear of that." The difference was not just a matter of personality. Carter was concerned with thanking God for blessings received and pondering the meaning of human mortality. His soul took care of itself, in a way Wigglesworth would have found most capricious and self-centered.[19]

These distinctions in the sources of inner motivation were evident in the way the upper classes of North and South viewed institutional religious life, particularly in the colonial and Revolutionary era before the Second Great Awakening. In both parts of the country gentlemen were convinced that good order required regularity of Christian doctrine and stable hierarchy. " 'Take ye wise men . . . known among your tribes' for their great abilities and good deeds, 'and I will make them rule over you,' " intoned Elizur Goodrich in 1787 in an election-day ceremony at Hartford, Connecticut. "Such an aristocracy is founded in merit and designed by the God of government and order . . . Riches are so far necessary as to raise the judge and counsellor above the temptation of transgressing for the peace [*sic*] of bread." Society had need of the "title of eminence," Goodrich insisted, for rulers deserved "honour and respect," in a republic no less than in a monarchy.[20]

Certainly no Southern planter of ample means would quarrel with such sentiments. Nevertheless, hostility toward the clerical office was more deep-seated in the Southern colonial squirearchy than among the "river gods" or aristocracy of the New England valleys. For much of the colonial epoch the Anglican church was scarcely an agency of social and moral uplift. As in England, its leaders labored under the domination of the rural gentry, with Sir Roger de Coverley a pious stereotype whose real-life counterparts were seldom in evidence. The few Anglican ministers who served the needs of the settlers were often as likely to engage in blood sports, drinking, and similar recreations as to attend to more lofty affairs.

In the eighteenth century the most gratifying sermon, by gentry lights, was one that little disturbed the listeners' equanimity. In 1766, for instance, George Washington, scarcely noted for the depth of his religious feeling, remarked that two sermons which he had heard "were good and sensible Discourses but a little Metaphysical." Neither profundity nor enthusiasm was much in demand. When earnest Virginia divines urged a reformation of manners, they could expect indifference or outrage. A most notable case was one that set Colonel Landon Carter against his minister, William Kay, in 1747. Kay had inadvertently provoked the wealthy squire because, said Kay, "I had preached against pride." Carter retaliated by mustering "his kindred relations, or such as were subject to him" and had them nail Kay's churches shut. The incident highlighted the strong current of anticlericalism in Virginian Anglican life. The ministers could scarcely command respect unless they had independent means to be treated as "Gentlemen, Christians and Clergymen," yet squires gave them little chance to play the role.[21]

Gentry suspicion of the ministers was not simply a manifestation of Enlightenment rationality and deistical thought. Rather, it stemmed from the same discomfiture that had always set aristocrats in opposition to established clergy, whether Papist or Anglican: the struggle over power, church taxation, and patronage. As late as 1829, for instance, John Randolph at the Virginia Constitutional Convention opposed a measure to enable clergymen to hold elective office. They belonged, he insisted, in the "domestic circle" with the womenfolk. "If ladies will plunge into the affairs of men, they will lose all deference they now enjoy; they will be treated roughly like men. Just so it is with priests." Though couched in terms of solicitude for the sacred office, the argument betrayed a fear of unsettling fanaticism and a worry that clerical influence in the pulpit could mislead a gullible public through the mysteries of "priest-craft."[22]

By the 1830s, however, religious precept, somewhat democratic in character, transformed the ideal of gentility. As Professor T. R. Dew of William and Mary College put it in 1836, "He who obtrudes upon the social circle his infidel notions, manifests the arrogance of a literary coxcomb, or that want of refinement which distinguishes the polished gentleman."[23] Aside from a few genuine intellectuals like Jefferson, most eighteenth-century gentlemen were deistical only out of convenience. With revival enthusiasms at work among Baptists, Methodists, and Presbyterians, the ranks of the gentry gradually came to accept Dew's position, which was only slightly premature.

Southern colleges, seminaries, and academies all sought to inculcate the new evangelical prescriptions. For instance, in 1839 Francis Lieber, a German refugee and professor of philosophy at South Carolina College, tried to combine the Stoic and Christian traditions for the edification of young college men. His advice was a prediction of the cosmopolitan style that clergy and laity alike would admire in the coming Victorian age. The gentleman, he said, was self-disciplined, uncomplaining, modest, but firm in rectitude. He was dedicated to progress, and he rejected the "splendors of plume, lace and cut" of his forbears in favor of democratically "plain attire." Influenced by another professor of moral philosophy, Robert Henry, a young student at South Carolina College named James Henry Hammond, reflected the new democratic and Christian orientation. In his class notes from 1828 he wrote, "Honor is that principle of nature which teaches us to respect ourselves, in order that we may gain the respect of others. No man desires the respect of one class of Society exclusively and therefore the law of honor will influence our conduct towards persons of every quality." Lieber would have agreed. Even a slave, Lieber said, could manifest the nobility of gentle conduct despite his lowliness, gaining esteem from those below and above himself no less than a master could. As William J. Grayson later observed, the Southern gentry would appreciate Lieber's effort because "a religious spirit has interfered" with the old understanding of gentility and "modified the temper of society."[24]

Bookstores in the South found a ready market for sermons suited to pious tastes, at least in the well-settled Eastern communities. Men who would spurn the emotion of camp meetings would place a devotional book by their bedsides. In 1830 Hugh Grigsby of Norfolk, for instance, confided in his diary his intention to find more of "Allison's sermons. They suit my taste wonderfully. They breathe a spirit of moral excellence and manly piety," being the work of "an elegant scholar and accomplished gentleman." Grigsby was one of many who combined gentility with evangelicalism in the South. Such men as he and General John H. Cocke of Fluvanna County, Virginia, had their counterparts in other Southern states. They gave to benevolent societies, subscribed to religious journals, and welcomed missionaries to their parlors.[25]

Looking backward, Southerners of refinement marveled at the change that had come over their region during the prior fifty years. In 1862 William J. Grayson recalled the evils that once had detracted from the cultivation and Christian aspirations of Carolina gentlefolk. As a young man, he remembered, he had stayed at the house of a Major Hazzard, an elderly veteran of the Revolutionary War, and Grayson's first cousin once removed. One night the major had secretly left the house to join other irate planters in pursuit of supposed black insurrectionists. Seized, tortured, and condemned in a perfunctory freeholders' trial, the slaves were hanged. Then "their heads were cut off, stuck on poles and set up along the highway." To their credit, Grayson boasted, the young gentlemen there were so disgusted by the sight that they took down "the hideous butcher's work" and buried the remains.[26]

In addition, the "churches were filled. Sunday was kept sacred," Grayson noted; also the Yankee invention of the Temperance Society had become a fixture in some quarters of the gentility. Whereas in Revolutionary times men were "more jovial and talked louder as they drank deeper," one seldom heard any more a "smutty allusion" in decent company. These remarkable changes, attributable to growing associational life, he thought, made mockery of the laments sometimes heard about the loss of old-fashioned virtue in the Carolina low country. Grayson's pontifications, however, were considerably overdrawn. Even he was not altogether convinced that progress and Christian evangelism were unmitigated blessings. Like others of intellectual bent, he mourned the fact that lesser men adopted these imports from the Northern cities to gain the social power to replace older families like his own. Nevertheless, he welcomed the changes and pronounced them advantageous for the genuine attainment of "a noble purity, strength, and elevation of character."[27]

Nearly every Southern community could boast a representative of Christian gentility. Such individuals went far beyond the usual customs of a grudging charity. Instead, they were kindly toward lesser folk, strangers, and even neighbors whom others despised. Their self-regard was very much involved in the doing of good works, in both formal and informal ways. They gave substance to the meaning of gentility. Such figures as John Belton O'Neall, General John Hartwell Cocke, Chief Justice John Marshall, and Charles Cotesworth Pinckney exemplified the role with the naturalness of manner that only a few gentlemen genuinely possessed. Moreover, they supported noble, often national causes—for black colonization, Bible societies, temperance organizations, and the other paraphernalia that the rich in both sections thought necessary for God's glory and patriotic advance. Their efforts were not always appreciated, but they had the social rank and necessary self-possession to stare down complaints. Likewise, clergymen like Charles Colcock Jones of Georgia and Bishops Barnwell, Otey, Elliott, Pettigrew, and Wilmer—all well placed and well intentioned—provided a satisfying retort to those who perceived the South as godless, licentious, and indifferent to nineteenth-century progress. The presence of such men must be noted, but it would be travesty to claim them as the sole representatives of Southern honor. There were other kinds considerably less pious, benevolent, and self-sacrificing.

As a means of contrasting the ideal model of gentility with the ordinary styles to which most Southerners were loyal, the familiar example of Robert E. Lee seems the most efficient. We shall not meet in these pages many others of his stature or moral bearing. Yet it is important to remember that such figures, as even the Ohio book agent in Arkansas recognized, set a standard that affected Southern life far out of proportion to their number. Though Lee assumed legendary proportions in the hands of Southern—especially Virginian—historians after the Civil War, the myth was based upon genuine attributes. Jefferson Davis summed them up in 1880 when he called Lee "a gentleman, scholar, gallant soldier, great general, and true Christian." Lee's scholarship left much to be desired, but on the other points he was a figure of considerable interest, however hackneyed the portrait has become in the redrawing.[28]

Lee's father, "Light Horse Harry" Lee, might be said to have typified the eighteenth-century squire as accurately as his son set a model for the next generation. Born of distinguished Virginia lineage, Richard Henry Lee had left his Princeton studies to serve in

Washington's army at the outbreak of the Revolution. With customary bravado, he refused Washington's offer to make him his aide-de-camp, declaring, "I am wedded to my sword and my secondary object . . . is military reputation" with hope of deserving "your Excellency's patronage" as "a stimulus to glory, second to none in power of the many that operate upon my soul."[29] His fulfillment of that pledge need not concern us here. Hero and three times governor of Virginia in the 1790s though he was, Light Horse Harry had no gift for business. Ann Carter, his second wife and the mother of Robert E. Lee, watched helplessly as he despoiled his own and her ample estate in unrealistic speculations. Still worse than the constant, humiliating dunning by irate creditors was the serious maiming suffered in a Baltimore anti-Federalist riot over entry into the war with England. Unwisely he had taken the unpopular side in the dispute; one man stabbed him twice in the face and another tried to remove his nose with a knife. The humiliation broke Lee's spirit. He went into self-imposed exile to the West Indies and died in 1818 in Georgia not having rejoined his Virginia family.

Perhaps the fact that he was little acquainted with his own father was one reason for Robert E. Lee's devotion to children, something he had not experienced firsthand. Once early in the Civil War, when he was stationed in western Virginia, Lee came upon two dozen little girls in "white frocks and pantlets," running and giggling about the yard at a large party. "It was the prettiest sight I have seen in the West, and perhaps in my life," he remarked.[30] Such a sensibility was rare among Army men. In any event, Lee was endowed with an unusually affectionate nature. Reared as much as a member of the Carter family as of the Lees, young Robert showed early all those graces that a proper Christian gentleman should manifest—with children, slaves, women, and fellow men.

In contrast to the diffidence of his father, Robert E. Lee was particularly attentive toward his progeny. Military duties, however, kept him away from the home he loved. When his son and namesake was three years old, Lee returned to the Arlington plantation from the Mexican War. The boy, dressed in the customary frock and with hair "freshly curled in long golden ringlets," waited impatiently for the father whom he had not seen for two years and did not remember. Amidst the greetings, Lee exclaimed, "Where is my little boy?" He then seized the child of a visiting relative and kissed him. "I was shocked and humiliated," Lee's son recalled, but quickly added, "I have no doubt that he was at once informed of his mistake and made ample amends to me." Judging from his further recollections and the affectionate letters that the younger Lee received, his surmise was certainly accurate. In the accepted style of the day the father showered advice upon his children. "Honor and fame are all that men should aspire to," Lee asserted. With steady application and valor, "they will at last be won. . . . Hold yourself above every mean action. Be strictly honorable in every act, and be not ashamed to *do right*," he wrote his son Custis in 1851. Absence from home made such suggestions poignant reminders of an involuntarily neglected role. But even at a distance, Lee was determined that his youngsters should grow in grace. When present to supervise them, he did not, as his own father had done, act indifferently. He was especially keen that the boys should learn sports. Robert, Jr., for instance, reminisced that his father "gave me my first sled, and sometimes used to come out where we boys were coasting to look on." Moreover, he allowed them an intimacy not altogether common in that day of austere patriarchy. He even let the little ones "climb into bed in the morning and lie close to him, listening while he talked to us in his bright, entertaining way."[31]

Though not the scholar that Davis claimed, Lee was indeed the Christian. He read devotional volumes, from the Bible to the Book of Common Prayer, from Thomas a Kempis to pamphlet sermons. His faith was largely emotional, not cerebral or rationalistic. As pious as any Northern evangelical, Lee constantly resorted to prayer, for friends and kinfolk, for his state and country, for the men he led and those he fought. There was a "primitive" quality to Lee's piety, according to one scholar, but resignation to God's will, faith in the literal word of scripture, and a sense that the "fratricidal" war was a divine visitation upon the land for the sins of all Americans were common opinions among the religious folk of the time. One could not really be a Southern gentleman without such views, according to many in the upper ranks of late antebellum Southern society.

Lee's attitude toward slavery and its relation to Divine Providence was typically Anglican, a mixture of condescension and twinges of guilt of an indefinite sort. "In this enlightened age, there are few I believe, but what will acknowledge, that slavery as an institution, is a moral & political evil in any Country." But his sympathies, he admitted, lay chiefly with the owners, for, after all, the slaves were better off in America than in Africa. He relied, he said in 1856, upon "the mild & melting influence of Christianity" to effect any progress toward emancipation. Christians, he wrote his wife, should press for "the final abolition of human Slavery" but look always to the God "who Chooses to work by slow influences; & with whom two thousand years are but as a Single day."[32] Lee was unexceptional in maintaining such views: they were the standard opinions of a class that exploited black laborers, but wished them well, that bowed to fast-gathering metropolitan opinion but did nothing to hasten the hour.

Lee was not one to allow personal feelings to interfere with his high sense of duty. For him as for many of his kind, honor was not "my family, right or wrong." The Stoic and Christian traditions would not permit that ancient rubric to prevail if honor itself was jeopardized by a selfish aim. During his tenure as superintendent of the United States Military Academy, Lee faced such a dilemma. His nephew, Fitz Lee, son of his favorite brother Smith Lee, and a group of fellow cadets left the barracks on December 16, 1853, without permission, returning with liquor in the early morning hours. They were all caught, and Lee had to recommend their dismissal or trial before a court-martial. Fitz Lee, like his cousin Roony, of whom Henry Adams had written, gained friends easily. The entire third-year class pledged its honor not to commit such offenses for the remainder of the school year if young Lee and his companions were excused. The superintendent made no effort to lighten his nephew's difficulties. But being a firm believer in the sworn word of a gentleman, Lee recommended to his superior, Jefferson Davis, the secretary of war, an acceptance of the pledge. Davis, who had the final authority, refused because the fourth-year class had not done the same for its offenders who had been caught at the same time. The court-martial imposed a stiff penalty on Fitz Lee, but since he had had no liquor on him when caught, allowed him to remain, whereas the seniors were forced to resign. While serving out his demerits the following summer, Fitz Lee once again went off one night without leave; once more his uncle had to forward a request for court-martial. Again the superintendent did not for a moment consider asking for special treatment for his kinsman. Fitz Lee's friends rallied again, however, and upon reconvening in the fall, the full senior class renewed the offer of obedience to regulations. This time Davis agreed to accept the pledge, and young Lee was allowed to graduate; he later served in his uncle's army with distinction.

When his own son, Robert E. Lee, Jr., enlisted in the Confederate Army as a private, Lee made no effort to secure him an easy billet. A young man had to make his own mark, according to lights of the refined code of honor. "I do not suppose," the son recalled, "it ever occurred to my father to think of giving me an office, which he could easily have done." Nor did any of Lee's kinspeople or friends suggest that he should have done better by the young man.[33]

We need not dwell on Lee's other much-praised attributes. Douglas S. Freeman explained them well. "If blood means anything," wrote the great Virginia historian, "he was entitled to be what he fundamentally was, a gentleman." Nevertheless, his connection with the ancient ethic deserves comment. Without that tie, his decision to join the Confederacy would be inexplicable. Lee's partial doubts about slavery scarcely relieved him from the weighty obligation that the tradition of honor imposed. "I wish to live under no other government," he wrote in the last days before secession, "& there is no sacrifice I am not ready to make for the preservation of the Union save that of honor." The stipulation was irremovable. He was no Southern nationalist. Few Southerners were. Lee always viewed the struggle as a "civil war," not a "war between the states," or for "Southern rights."

Though a much more complicated figure than his image as the "marble man" suggests, Lee was utterly simple in choosing his destiny. He had no faith in the cause he served. None was needed. Two interconnected factors, and those two factors alone, explained his decision to resign his commission, return to Virginia, and accept appointment under the new government. He wrote Anne Marshall, his sister, about one of them: "I have not been able to make up my mind to raise my hand against my relatives, my children, my home."[34] From the days when Tacitus wrote *Germania,* the cardinal principle of honor was family defense. To war against one's own family was a violation of law—a law that, unwritten and often unspoken, superseded all other claims. To Lee, as to nearly all Confederates, that commandment, whatever its source of inspiration, pagan or Old Testament, could not be violated. It helped to drive the upper South out of the Union. Who did not have kinsmen further South? In time a sense of abstract nationality, transcending family and *deme,* might have been constructed upon the secession effort, but certainly not in 1861, when archaic honor and a sense of insult superseded notions of a truly separate nation.

The second reason was equally a matter of conscience—one arising from the primal code as much as from Christian heritage. As Mrs. Lee wrote a friend, "My husband has wept tears of blood over this terrible war, but as a man of honor and a Virginian, he must follow the destiny of his State." The Old Dominion was not an abstraction in Lee's mind. Inextricably it was bound up with the life and heritage of the Lees, Carters, and other clans with which he was associated, the living and the dead. Lee had no choice in the matter. Culturally, morally, spiritually, he was compelled to forsake the Union. On this count he is sometimes accused of a narrowness of vision, but the complaint itself is parochial. Lee could not escape either fighting for or against his kin. The option simply to exile himself would not have occurred to him. By any standard that was the coward's way out, a rejection of what Lee's God had set before him as moral choice.[35]

This brief description of General Lee has not been included in order to throw a sentimental light upon the Southern code or to prove that such old Southern apologists as Freeman, Ulrich B. Phillips, and Philip A. Bruce were wholly justified in highlighting

the magnanimity, kindliness, and childlike innocence of the plantation order as a whole. Rather it is designed to show the range of the
Southern system. Honor was always more than the sum of its parts,
and it could bring out the best in men as well as the worst. Many
Southern gentlemen would have agreed with Lee, however, when
he said in a wartime reflection, "A true man of honor feels humbled
himself when he cannot help humbling others." For him "the forbearing use of power does not only form a touchstone, but the
manner in which an individual enjoys certain advantages over
others is a test of a true gentleman."[36] Such men resided throughout
the South, even in its roughest, most unformed regions, a point that
the modern cynic might deny. But unhappily the number of such
men was small, their influence sometimes circumscribed more than
legend would concede.

Nevertheless, for all their imperfections, gentility and honor together were not only functional aspects of Southern life but, at
times, creative ones as well. Without the conflicts arising from the
two intertwined ethical patterns, without the intimate context they
provided for natural reactions and passions, without the sense of
family and communal continuity they afforded, a major source of
American nationalism would be missing. One of the most serious
problems that faced the ancient Greeks was the difficulty ordinary
citizens had in recognizing duties and fidelities higher than those to
immediate kin and locale. To some degree the same kind of virulent
particularism that had made union of city-states against common
enemies so hard to achieve also afflicted the Confederacy. Dissidence
and even rebelliousness behind Rebel lines were not invariably
signs of an emergent, modern style of individualism and diversity,
but rather of an ancient localism, one that had plagued all sections
of the country during the American Revolution. But the Southern
states that experienced war and then Reconstruction, as W. J. Cash
had observed, developed in the Redeemer period and after a greater
sense of regional identity than that which had led to secession.
However fractious Southern whites had been during the fighting,
the war experience provided memories and myths upon which a
sense of sacred collectivity was based. As initial bitterness faded

and celebrations of old glories became ever more stylized, that impulse for valor and immortal honor—what the Greeks had called *arete*—was transformed into a sense of national loyalty, without loss of its regional origins. The Southern concept of patriotism was constructed upon faithfulness to a particular place and people and their past, not upon some abstract idea such as "democracy" or "freedom," principles generating few sparks in ordinary men's minds unless they were conceived as synonyms for personal and familial security and self-regard. It is no accident or irony that the region most renowned for its particularity, its separateness, its experience with both glory and defeat should also be the most nationalistic, not only in the last century but in the present one as well. It was never the abstraction of "liberty" that animated Southern patriotism, but rather the concrete determination to uphold personal and community independence from overt or insidious attempts to destroy it.

William Faulkner, in *Intruder in the Dust,* recognized this circumstance when, drawing upon his memories of boyhood, he wrote these words about the impact of that old, primal sense of honor on young Charles Mallison, one who was raised to make no distinctions between his forefathers' past and his own life:

> It's all *now* you see. Yesterday wont be over until tomorrow and tomorrow began ten thousand years ago. For every Southern boy fourteen years old, not once but whenever he wants it, there is the instant when it's still not yet two oclock on that July afternoon in 1863, the brigades are in position behind the rail fence, the guns are laid and ready in the woods and the furled flags are already loosened to break out and Pickett himself with his long oiled ringlets and his hat in one hand probably and his sword in the other looking up the hill waiting for Longstreet to give the word and it's all in the balance. . . . *Maybe this time* with all this much to lose and all this much to gain: Pennsylvania, Maryland, the world, the golden dome of Washington itself to crown with desperate and unbelievable victory the desperate gamble, the cast made

two years ago. . . . A small voice, a sound sensitive lady poet
of the time of my youth said *the scattered tea goes with the
leaves and every day a sunset dies:* a poet's extravagance which
as quite often mirrors truth but upside down and backward
since the mirror's unwitting manipulator busy in his preoccupation has forgotten that the back of it is glass too: because if
they only did, instead of which yesterday's sunset and yesterday's tea both are inextricable from the scattered indestructi-
ble uninfusable grounds blown through the endless corridors
of tomorrow. . . .[37]

History shorn of all myths and emblems is, happily, impossible.
New ones replace the old. But beneath the "scattered leaves" of
dead events and their legends lie genuinely noble aspirations, such
as those that Charles Mallison envisioned in Faulkner's story. One
may seriously question if, going farther back in time from Gettys-
burg and Lee's great throw of the dice, there ever would have been
a notion of liberty for Americans had not Thomas Jefferson and
others, both Northern and Southern, been spurred to statecraft on
the basis of that high-mindedness and honor that humanists of
Renaissance England had fashioned from sources "ten thousand
years" old. Yet there was irony, in C. Vann Woodward's sense, in the
results. The same impulses toward honor and gentlemanly rule that
established the new government and prompted the Declaration of
Independence also inspired the Southern course toward secession.
As Southern historian William Garrott Brown declared in 1903,
"To the Southerner, liberty meant nothing less than the right of
himself and his community to be free from all interference by the
peculiar outside world," a determination that nearly wrecked the
greater cause of honor in which all Americans, regardless of color
or condition, could share.[38]

Before we proceed to the familial and community aspects of Southern ethics, one final observation is mandatory. The ancient philosophers and their humanistic interpreters, in early modern England
and in the South as well, often spoke of the "laws of honor" as if

they were as readily apparent as the Ten Commandments. They were not. Honor was accorded on the basis of community decision. The method of reaching that conclusion involved many contingencies. Any action, *ex post facto,* then seemed logical if it was regarded as conforming to those "laws." In like manner, writers of history, like those in other social sciences, must impose a coherence, regularity, and rationality upon the subject at hand. In both cases, however, the process of necessary ordering distorts, because, as Faulkner intimates, much of human existence is really inchoate even if it lives on in memory. We speak of rules of behavior in the past. They were not rules, not immutable or even logical. At best they were acceptable options. The strategies and the priorities were more like trails across a field. In the South the "rule" was, in fact, simply the unplanned, customary path that in most instances enabled the antebellum sojourner to avoid rough terrain and dangerous cliffs in the course of moving over the social landscape. If for some reason the road was blocked, less desirable detours could be taken. To stray too far from the familiar way, however, was to confuse the order of nature. These paths were not always well marked. Misjudgments were frequent, and community evaluations were sometimes ambiguous, perhaps wrongheaded. One had to improvise. Yet the main objective of fidelity to custom could not be cavalierly repudiated.[39] In any event, why people behaved as they did cannot be entirely encompassed in so broad a category as "strategies." One must allow for irrationality—including collective irrationality, as in Hawthorne's story.

Yet honor, for all its variations—from primal valor to Christian graciousness, from bloody deed to "right reason"—provided a means to restrict human choices, to point a way out of chaos. Thus it helped Southern whites to make life somewhat more predictable than it would have been otherwise. It established signposts of appropriate conduct. It staved off the danger of self-love and vainglory and in the circles of the genteel, it elevated moderation and learnedness to virtues of self-disciplined community service. Since honor gave meaning to lives, it existed not as a myth but as a vital code.

Part Two

·

Family and Gender Behavior

BLANK PAGE

5

Fathers, Mothers, and Progeny

In his apologia for the Southern Way, Daniel R. Hundley declared in 1860 that "in the South the family is a much more powerful institution than in other portions of the Republic" and "the parental discipline more rigid." Amidst the decay of old values in the Northern states, where boys were rude to elders and women were "inclined to enter the lists" in competition with men, these old-fashioned virtues appealed to Southern enthusiasts like Hundley. He believed stern childbearing practices ensured social stability and respect for order. Yet as Clifford Geertz has declared, "No social arrangement is or can be completely successful in coping with the insoluble antinomies" it inevitably faces. The Southern dilemma on this score may have been no worse than any other society's difficulties. Yet the concentration of wide power in the hands of a single head of household entailed strains, particularly when the individual was ill equipped to handle the duties involved. Even if a wife or helpful relative were able to compensate for some of the Southern patriarch's frailties, their roles had to be played out within the context of the legitimacy of his rule. Quite naturally, the plantation sovereign tended to heap blame on anyone but himself in an effort to transfer responsibilities that might be overwhelming. "Did you ever see a really respectable, responsible, revered and beloved head of a family, who ever opened his mouth at home except to find fault," asked an acquaintance of Mrs. Chesnut.[1]

At the heart of the Southern family lay a problem not always satisfactorily resolved. At what points and to what degree should a father exercise his authority? When should he transfer his property and his power to the upcoming generation so that the sons, most especially, could learn how to command with dispatch and confidence? The problems inherent in the cycle of growth—the transition of child to man, and thence to father—were not peculiar to the South. As Ruth Benedict points out, the natural process is handled in different ways according to the cultural and economic determinants of every society. As a patriarchal order, the Southern scheme added to the ordinary oedipal resentments of fathers and sons the persistence of fatherly claims to power that sons found difficult to surmount even as their time of maturity arrived. As a result, some households were thrown into near chaos by generational disputes. William L. Barney, the historian of secession, has noted the prevalence of younger sons in the ranks of the Deep South fire-eaters, suggesting that their animus was at least partly derived from their enforced idleness and their frustration with fathers who refused to relinquish their control of property and their monopoly of power.[2]

The origins of these familial tensions lay in two aspects of social life. First, there was the veneration of forefathers and their traditions, a genetic foundation that provided sons with inspiration but also the formidable challenge of living up to almost mythological heroes from the family past. Second, and more importantly, child-rearing practices in the antebellum South subjected the young to flawed prescriptions of shame and humiliation and the ideals of hierarchy and honor, a mode in sharp contrast to the conscience-building techniques of pious Yankees. Even Southerners realized that the manner of inculcating youth to conform with familial and public customs and values was not always efficacious, but though they recognized deficiencies they resigned themselves to the evils, regarding them as being as incurable as human nature itself.

The weight of tradition within a family was the first yoke upon the rising generation. "Blood" was not an abstract concept but a determination that could so type a child that a sense of unworthiness could well develop. Like horses, human beings were supposed to exhibit traits of lineage. "I know him very well," wrote James Simmons to Governor John Manning in reference to a young aspirant for political appointment. "He comes of first rate Carolina stock and his breed is good. You can rely on him." On the other hand, "bad blood" was also supposedly a fair predictor of future prospects. Typical were the derogatory comments of Samuel A. Townes of Alabama to his brother George in regard to their sister's children. She had married a General John Blassingame, whom both brothers despised. Unfortunately, gossiped the rising young planter, "Blassingame blood circulates" in the youngsters' veins, and two of "Elizas children have already developed some of the villanous [*sic*] blood. Maria & John take after our family in our warm, open & honest intercourse with the world, but Elizabeth in some degrees & Aurelia *particularly* has all of the low cunning slandering & mean propensities of her detestible [*sic*] father and poor Eliza does not attempt to eradicate them."[3]

The parades of patriarchs stretching back sometimes to ancestors in Scotland, Ireland, Ulster, Wales, or England provided standards of accomplishment, status, and character to be matched—or, as in Samuel Townes's estimation, to be overcome as best one could. Family declensions, attributable to some deficiency of genetic inheritance or personal waywardness, could be located on every hand. They provided signposts of danger to be avoided. Meanwhile, newcomers to higher rank seemed to arrive from nowhere and assume vacated positions, defying the supposed laws of inherited characteristics. As James H. Hammond wrote his son Harry, "Genius and imbecility, Chivalry and poltroonery and meanness were always strangely mixed up among the Salt water people. . . . There were old families undecayed—decaying and decayed and new families founded by successful overseers and factors, and then an unusual amount of loafing fishermen, hunters etc." The historian Chalmers Davidson has observed that of the four hundred large slaveholding families in South Carolina in 1860, only fifty had roots traceable to great wealth in colonial days. Their gains, however, were someone else's losses, and the danger of slippage was never far from the thoughts of wary elders in the upper classes. Like Hammond, who had warned that idleness slackened "every nerve moral and physical," John Randolph of Virginia urged a young nephew to beware those who idled their lives away in expensive habits. They would "become in form, as well as in fact, poor folks." Anxiety to preserve and ambition to recover family fortunes were constant refrains in advice to the young. Somehow the "good blood" had to predominate over the bad.[4]

A most telling sign of the special intensity of family lineage was the pattern of naming newborns. Ofttimes distinguished surnames replaced the ordinary Christian name—Peyton Randolph, Langdon Cheves, Preston Brooks, Whitemarsh Seabrook, Otway Byrd, Beverley Tucker, Landon Carter—a custom not so readily found in polite Northern circles. By these talismans, perhaps, the threat of family dissolution could be prevented, as if there were some special magic in the christening itself. The surname taken from the maternal side and used as first name did not necessarily represent veneration of the mother, but rather honored her father. Women contributed to the honor of the family name chiefly through these means, since their own accomplishments were so strictly confined to the traditional duties.

More than in the free states, the mystique of names carried considerable meaning in the family and the community. If the bearer of the name came a cropper, the original figure so honored felt sorely abused. For instance, a distinguished judge in a western North Carolina county, where Scots-Irish family loyalties were especially strong, had been pleased to let his name be used by common folk as a hopeful prediction of a newborn's character and future renown. But one day Judge Saunders addressed the courtroom before passing sentence on a man convicted of larceny: "Hear all you people present; when you go home, tell your wives and neighbors to name no more children after me. Consider the situation in which I am placed; compelled in discharge of my duty, to pass sentence on this poor wretch to receive thirty-nine lashes on his bare back, and he is a man bearing my full name, Romulus Mitchell Saunders."[5]

More commonly, sons received family names, not those of prominent individuals, local or national, and upon them the fathers' immortality rested. In a letter to Theodore Dudley, John Randolph, for instance, advised the young man to make a name for himself not solely for the good of mankind but for the glory of his family, too. Randolph presented a list of all their important relatives, as inspiration and also as practical notification about whom to reach for cousinly assistance as occasion might arise. First, Randolph called attention to their mutual connection with Dr. Bolling Hall, "a valuable counsellor." Bolling's "great grandfather, on the mother's side" was one Robert Bolling, Randolph continued, "brother to Drury Bolling, my maternal great grandfather . . . which Drury and Robert were sons of Robert B[olling] . . . by his second wife, Miss Slith [*sic*, Stith?]; (his first being the grand-daughter of Pocahontas, by whom he had one son, John, from whom, by his first wife Mary Kennon, my paternal grandmother sprang.)" The ritual incantation of "begots" might appear to be a casual recital, yet whether it came from a querulous maiden aunt or from a wealthy bachelor uncle, the implications could not be lost on the dullest lad. Randolph then pointed to the various branches stemming from that impressive trunk: "Bollings of Chesterfield and Buckingham, in the male line" and "Curles Randolphs, Flemings, Gays, Eldridges, and Murrays in the female." Throughout the stress was upon the males of the tribe, whether on the maternal or paternal side.[6]

This tendency was still observable as late as the 1930s. In a letter to "Cousin Eloise" a North Carolina clergyman recalled how, a few years before, a Mrs. Jacobs of Wilmington had written to say that "she was a grand-daughter of Col. Axalla Hoole who was killed at Chickamauga. I never had heard of her before," the minister said, but she declared that "I was her only relative in North Carolina" and should baptize her little daughter. Thus, last Sunday "I Baptized the great-grand-daughter of Col. Axalla Hoole who died at

Chickamauga. Mrs. Jacobs is the daughter of Cousin Ada Lawrence, who is the daughter of Col. Hoole. Col. Axalla Hoole was my grandfather's half-brother, and also your grandmother's brother, wasn't he?" The repetition of Hoole's name, rank, and manner of death revealed the talismanic nature of family pride. Such incidents were fondly recalled because the rituals of family remembrance assured continuity and the preeminence of fathers past in the lives of their progeny. Scarcely a Southerner today could not repeat some similar anecdote.[7]

By emphasizing male ancestors on both sides of the family tree, several aims were accomplished. First, it helped to cement solidarity between grandchildren and grandparents, whose attitudes toward their offspring's mates were often crucial to family harmony. Second, it gave mothers and wives reason for pride as bearers of their fathers' names. And finally, it served as guide for the sons. Abiel Abbott, a Yankee clergyman in Charleston, remarked how the children of David Ramsay, historian and planter, conducted themselves in the knowledge that they were "the offspring of illustrious ancestors & parents whose names are embalmed in the national history. . . ."[8] The relation of the dutiful child to ancestors and to community was thus made clear; one could not easily escape to pursue one's own hopes under such circumstances. Duty to fathers came first. The future, even the present, rested on the past.

In contrast, Northern naming practices were swiftly changing during the early years of the nineteenth century, part of an evolution that had begun much earlier. According to historian Daniel Scott Smith, the shift demonstrated the waning power of the father and the growing sense of freedom from the past. Each individual looked toward a future in the pursuit of personal, not strictly familial interests. In Hingham, Massachusetts, a fairly representative New England community, the increase in nonfamily Christian names was dramatic, particularly after the American Revolution. The ratio changed from 10 percent for males and 30 percent for females at the turn of the century to 30 percent and 40 percent respectively in the Civil War era.[9] The transformation suggested a desire to promote an instrumental kind of individuality.

Identification of moral worth by blood and name was by no means a peculiarity of the slaveholding elite. Although historians have often narrowed the compass of patriarchy and family commitments to the Southern upper ranks, poor whites displayed similar concerns. Quite early in childhood, family members of the yeomanry also learned respect for the patriarchal name and the values that it embodied. No one, for instance, was quite so paternalistic as one George Reynolds of Pickens County, Alabama. Father of seventeen children, the illiterate farmer held sway over 234 descendants, all living in Bostic Beat and obedient to his wishes in family matters. A long-standing Unionist during the prewar and wartime struggles, he went unmolested by fire-eaters and Confederate officials, out of deference to his local power. Even the Ku Kluxers of Reconstruction left this Republican stalwart alone. Perhaps more than in the higher reaches of society, the stress upon family ties in the yeoman class confined one's specialness to a kin-group context. Noting that his child had died from a refusal to take a prescribed medicine, a backwoods father at Bullskin Creek, Kentucky, observed proudly, "No one couldn't make her take no medicine; she . . . was a Baker through and through, and you never could make a Baker do nothin' he didn't want to!"[10]

Just as rich folk enjoined their children to match the high achievements of the family ancestors, so too did the poor refer to some kinsman as representing the best ideals of their clan. The ownership of slaves, it is often asserted, was the aspiration of such people, a factor helping to mitigate envy and resentment of the planter ranks. But actually the prospect of respectability identified with a particular ancestor or kinsman, who may or may not have owned slaves, urged the poor boy to match that record. The example might not be very grand: a summer service in the Revolutionary War as private, or superior hunting skill. Sometimes a reputation for leadership in an obscure backwater or even a claim to have been reared in a prestigious part of Virginia before a westward relocation stirred pride. Glorious or objectively petty, the claims were revered all the same. "My mother was a Gholson," boasted Riley Wyatt, a Mississippi doctor of humble Alabama stock. A maternal first cousin, Samuel J. Gholson, who had served Mississippi in Congress, provided him with a sense of family prominence that could yet be retrieved, despite his father's obscurity and widowed mother's abject poverty. Likewise John Hewitt of Tennessee recalled a kinsman named Reaves who was two generations away from "ancestors of high birth and education." Both Reaves and his wife, "three generations" from literacy, subsisted in the hills on a "hog and hominy diet" until Reaves defied his less ambitious mate and set off alone to become a typesetter in an obscure village scores of miles away. Later he called for her and the children to join him, after he had mastered the craft. His inspiration came from a crankish great-grandfather, a recluse who had had considerable education.[11] Thus the aspiration to change and get ahead was not necessarily a purely bourgeois objective, as a modern perspective might lead one to assume. It could be an outgrowth of family pride—simply the ancient desire to be *somebody,* to create a lineage.

Just as some rich families sought merely to retain status that was inherited, so too did poorer folk find well-being in just holding on. Family honor of this kind did not require soaring objectives. Belonging to an old and large clan was sufficient. Such was certainly the case in the Scots-Irish settlements that dotted the Southern hinterlands. In Mecklenburg County, North Carolina, for instance, John McKnitt Alexander and William Baine Alexander populated the region so thoroughly that they and their neighbors no longer even used the surname, so common had it become. Legal documents sometimes identified Alexanders by their middle, not their last names. Likewise, in Cumberland County, a recent study points out, a Scottish name was almost an assurance of election to local office during the early nineteenth century. After all, who could vote against a fellow clansman?[12]

As late as 1940 this kind of adherence to family names and their evocations still endured. In Kentucky, a rural sociologist discovered that only 5 percent of all males had names not affiliated with traditional family first and middle names. Over 70 percent of the men were named for their fathers. Like their ancestors before them, Kentucky hill people used the word "generation" to mean common lineage from a single patriarch, not a certain age group (for example, the "older" or "younger" generation). A great-grandfather and great-grandson belonged to the same "generation," with "sets" grouped by different family heads distinguishing one line from another: the "Old Dick set" of Browns, for instance, "Old Dick" being the common progenitor. The same pattern had existed in Mecklenburg, with the "Clerk Isaac" set and "Long Creek Isaac" set of Alexanders. These customs suggest the persistence of very elemental means of preserving patriarchy. They helped to make everyone feel loyal not to an immediate father alone, but to a whole weighty series of fathers.[13]

For the most part naming patterns reflected the strength of the patriarchal order across the gradings of wealth and rank. No doubt when elaborate studies are conducted—none currently exist for the antebellum era—class and geographical variations will be found. But the key pattern, naming sons for paternal forebears, will no doubt show little change over time, except in districts where unusual urban growth and a new order of things was underway. Moreover, the naming patterns will probably be found to have little relationship to the ownership of slaves or the lack of that form of property. For the poor, the weighty responsibility to live up to ancestral standards of performance did not impinge upon the upcoming generation as much as it did in old families of power. Nevertheless, in the South the compulsion to advance was particularly tied to familial considerations. This attitude spanned the social classes and helped to give the South its sense of regional wholeness. At the same time, it encompassed a basic social ambiguity: one could only be truly individualistic by conforming to ancestral prescriptions.

If there were some ambiguities in the emphasis on ancestral success and personal autonomy, there were even more contradictions in the manner of childrearing. Contrary to what Hundley declared, the style was not "rigid," at least not in the way he meant it. The patterns were very similar to the habits of western Europeans and British folk stretching back to the precolonial era. In essence the approach, like the society itself, relied chiefly upon principles of shame rather than conscience, with three clearly identifiable components: (1) the early and continuing ambivalence of mothers toward their offspring, leading to a combination of near-smothering love and emotional withdrawal; (2) the abrupt assertion of fatherly authority at the "clothing" stage, approximately four years of age; and (3) socialization into a community in which sexual differentiations were demanded, with honor and shame the chief principles upon which social and moral hierarchies, including those of race, were insistently enforced.

Southern white mothers, rich or poor, had reason for dissatisfaction with their fate. Although some writers have maintained otherwise, these matrons had little conscious awareness of what should take the place of their rounds of drudgery and their subservience first to father, then to husband.[14] Their little stage for life's dramas was confined to the family circle. There was no escape. Yet it would hardly be fair to claim that Southern mothers were incapable of unqualified love for their children. On the contrary, mothers lavished caresses upon their little "Cherry Cheeks," as one plantation matron called her youngest. Whether rich or poor, there was no lack of fussing over small ones, especially when they were peevish. In fact, babies were almost public property, so fondled were they by neighbors, kin, slaves, and visiting strangers. White plantation children were even more indulged than yeomen's infants. After all, there were the ubiquitous mammies to give succor and nourishment. For instance, William Faulkner, like generations of Southern men before him, declared his loyalty to the memory of his "Mammie," Callie Barr, who "gave to my family a fidelity without stint or calculation or recompense and to my childhood an immeasurable devotion and love." In his opinion, Callie Barr was "brave, courageous, generous, gentle, and honest . . . much more brave and honest and generous than me." The sentiment was heartfelt but not unusual.[15]

On the male side, too, there were also "significant others," as if fathers alone could not fill the role assigned them. The attention given to infants and toddlers by "uncles," both kin and black, as well as grandfathers, cousins, and tutors to the older children, had a more reserved character than that offered by the women, but there was nothing at all lacking in the way of genuine attachment. J. G. Clinkscales, for instance, attributed his own understanding of manhood less to his neurasthenic father than to "Unc' Essick," whom he called "one of the best and truest and noblest men I ever knew— white or black."[16] As the child grew older, these male figures became increasingly important in the formation of the child's character and social demeanor. By such means the child learned early his role as a member of a community of men, not just of a parental and sibling group. He also learned that houseservants were considered members of the household; they were the master's "black family," just as the master's offspring belonged to the "white family."

In order to understand the Southern mode, it is necessary to explain its Northern antebellum counterpart. Roughly speaking, in the Jacksonian era a pious, mother-centered form of childrearing was gradually replacing the older traditions of coercive, father-centered practice. To be sure, there was no categorical uniformity in the homes of Yankees any more than in the South. Some Northern families were as conscious of lineage, honor, and patriarchal authority as Southern families were. Nevertheless, one may safely refer to the Northern evangelical scheme, with its origins in Quaker, Congregational, and Presbyterian theology and ethics. Whereas the Southern child was to learn the rubrics of honor and shame, the religious mode set the criterion of conscience and the imposition of guilt. Devout parents did not rely so much upon whippings, slaps, and furious verbal abuse, but upon internal, self-regulative prescriptions. Sermons, tracts, and exchanges of advice among pious mothers in a community all stressed the centrality of conscience-building, based upon the individual's relationship to God rather than an identification with community values of honor and reputation. The inculcation of conscience was a time-consuming, onerous task. It required patience and skill, whereas the Southern style was much less calculating and reflected more concern for the convenience of the adult than for the instruction of the child. Only mothers had the time, or, frequently, the interest to perform the duties demanded of the pious approach. In the South, fathers still held the reins of power, even over child discipline, but their concern was all too often intermittent. As a result, there was some uncertainty in Southern mothers' minds about how strict or lenient they should be in the absence of paternal advice or direction.

To raise up God-fearing, hard-working, and well-motivated children, the evangelical Yankee mother sought to channel the young person toward wholly effective self-mastery. Mrs. Taylor, a Boston adviser, for instance, recommended in the fashion typical of her times that early schooling could do much to restrain "the violent and obvious acting of *self-will*," but the process had to begin much sooner—as soon as the baby left the crib and began to move about. "A mild system," in which fathers were prepared to "strew a few flowers" and not always play the part of "master," was "always to be preferred, if possible: yet . . . [discipline] must be firm," she argued. "System," not inconsistent reaction to childish behavior, was all-important, with each child treated with impartiality, regardless of sex or age. Mrs. Taylor warned that parents who had come into new wealth were likely to be uncertain about how to raise their children to the standards appropriate to their new station. Yet religion, rational planning, and acceptance of good advice on parental practices could overcome the deficiency, she said in her 1825 book.[17]

A major means of achieving these lofty ends was to withhold affection from the wayward child, rather than to react with a boxing of the ears in the heat of the moment. In 1832, by which time the style was thoroughly developed, the parents of a deceased four-year-old New England boy published a memoir of his upbringing. The regimen for John Mooney Mead included "withholding from him whatever he cried for, and when he was fretful, they did not pacify him by caresses, or by bestowing what he desired, but by directing his attention to something else." Only once in his brief life did the child feel the sting of the switch, at fourteen months of age. The punishment, however, was accompanied by appropriate words of admonition, not just a grumpy "don't do that." His father, a Congregational minister, and his mother constantly assured him that he had erred but could be restored to favor by making amends to his loving parents, who were ready to embrace him at the first sign of contrition.[18]

As the child of evangelical parents grew more independent, the imperative to reflect upon consequences became more insistent. Gradually the young person discovered that the checks on conduct grew from within and were no longer related to fear of provoking adult anger. Theodore Parker, the abolitionist and fiery preacher of Boston, remembered how at age five he had nearly killed a turtle. But he had surprised himself when he had refrained. Racing home, he breathlessly asked his mother Hannah why he had not struck the turtle that had frightened him. She exclaimed, "Some men call it conscience, but I prefer to call it the voice of God in the soul of man. If you listen and obey it, then it will speak clearer and clearer . . . but if you turn a deaf ear or disobey, then it will fade out . . . and leave you all in the dark without a guide." In many respects the story could have been told by a planter's son, for in the antebellum years more and more plantation families fell under the evangelical sway, with conscience the objective sought. Yet not many Southerners would have considered the incident a turning point in their moral and religious development, as Parker did. Although there were anxieties aplenty in such inculcations, Parker and many like him felt their wills reinforced by encounters with temptations overcome. From such experiences they learned that parents cared very much about them and their future prospects, even if there was little outward show of affection in the form of kisses and hugs.[19]

In contrast, white Southerners reared children to value honor as much as, if not more than, godly conscience. Like the Puritan conscience, honor could be internalized, and when it was violated, guilt was likewise the response. It did require self-restraint, but based upon pride, not divine commandment. Honor reconciled both habits—to make all due allowances for another's provocations with self-denial and restraint and, when required, to react impulsively for the sake of self-esteem and public reputation. Although there might seem to be a dichotomy between adult violence—the Southern record of personal altercations and duels—and the parental demands for

children to forswear aggression, there was none. The North Carolinian William Pettigrew advised his younger brother that "as far
as it can be done, we should live peaceably with our associates; but,
as we cannot always do so, it is necessary occasionally to resist. And
when our honor demands resistance, it should be done with courage."[20] Nor was it impossible to promote both Christian conscience
and the conscience of honor in nearly indistinguishable ways, as
Lee's advice to his sons evinced.

In regard to deference for the older generation, conscience and
honor arrived at the same point from somewhat different perspectives. Conscience-building evoked respect for old age as a general
abstraction. One should be kind to the poor elderly, not just to
the wealthy aged. Honor, however, was much more discriminatory.
"Honor thy father and mother," but it was considerably less important that one be deferential to the "uncle" in the cabin, the stranger
at the gate. Nevertheless, among gentlefolk of the South, whether
the source was Christian or simply traditional, the well-bred child
was expected to manifest courtesy. Familial pride demanded it. But
it was also simply the right thing to do, and by all and sundry it
was thought to be both Christian and honorable, as if the two ethical patterns were always one and the same. The strategies for judging and exemplifying personality in relation to status were part of
a young Southerner's training from the earliest age, but it was also
a matter of plain moral duty.

The raising of children to a code of this variety by no means implied that parents rejoiced when youngsters were brutal toward the
helpless and alien. Nor should it be inferred that the Southern gentility lacked conscience, as some critics of slaveholding, then and
more recently, have maintained. Yet the early introduction of the
modes of honor did serve to blunt sentimentality about the unfair-
ness of hierarchy. Thus honor was more than a manifestion of
Southern high-spiritedness and community prejudices about race,
sex, and family pride. It entered the very texture of upbringing.

Insofar as honor was woven into the lives of very small children,
it was a source of familial and personal strengthening. Among the
natural benefits—and they were substantial—was the full expression

of love between parents and children. There was a natural outpouring of spontaneous feelings, for, as was mentioned earlier, to speak was to think, to feel was to express emotions openly. Whereas fathers in Northern and evangelical households tended toward distance and reserve, and mothers worried lest they allow maternal indulgence to jeopardize God's favor upon the small one, Southern parents were almost too devoted to their children. In particular, the eldest child, as one would expect in a patriarchy, enjoyed special interest. As Freud once said, "A man who has been the indisputable favorite of his mother keeps for life the feeling of a conqueror." That was indeed the hope of the Southern parent. But one could be equally favored by an adoring father, too. "If only I could get a squeeze at that little fellow, turning up his sweet mouth to 'keese baba!' " wrote Robert E. Lee to his wife when far from the home that he loved. At its best, a lofty appreciation of personal worth and status could grow out of that sense of familial belonging. "A certain high-mindedness"—Stoic and humanistic *megalopsychia*—one Southern writer has said, "went with Corinthian columns and self-immolating black mammies."[21]

In terms of social ideals, one could do much worse than to set before the child those principles of gentility already described. In homes where piety as well as patriarchy reigned, the Christian ethos and the concept of genteel honor could seem almost perfectly in harmony. Such a style contrasted with the stiff demeanor and sometimes destructive inhibitions that a rigorous and overly introspective "self-mistrust," as Henry Adams said, engendered in Yankee souls. For the children of the Rev. Charles Colcock Jones, Presbyterian and slaveholder of Georgia, or of the North Carolina Pettigrew family, or of many other planter families, conscience and honor could be and were wisely combined. Patriarchy did not necessarily involve a complete submission to parental will. Southern fathers expected a degree of liveliness, even independence from the young. But among those who belonged to the high gentility especially, the child was to honor the father's position as much as the father himself. Much was often said in correspondence and diaries about letting the children find their own way in the world—on the plantation and at school as youngsters, in the larger sphere when young adults. Indeed, fathers were even willing to gamble on their sons' success by presenting them with patrimonies to manage at a surprisingly early age. Nevertheless, an egalitarian or even brotherly relation between father and child was not the aim (even were it possible in any society). No less than in Northern, evangelical households, the Southern parent of high gentility perceived the child as a moral figure to be molded as if made of clay, not as an independent personality with talents, interests, and temperaments to be developed for individualistic rather than family needs.

Some fathers assured themselves of filial respect by withholding intimacy. This was also meant to be instructive, insofar as it encouraged the child to seek self-protective reserve in relations with others. Advice reinforced this parental example. In 1850 a planter wrote to his son, "Be kind and civil to every one but intimate with none." A Mississippi plantation mother in 1864 told her daughter, "It is best not to be Intimate with any body nor confide to[o] much in anyone" because "our best friends are our greatest enemies."[22]

Other parents took a less formidable line. But in either case, there was always much intrusiveness and constantly repeated advice about conduct. Many if not most parents presumed that whatever the manner of their own behavior, it was worth emulation. Cultural relativism had not yet arisen: there was, most believed, only one way, one road to achieve success. The consequence was, on the whole, fairly salutary. Children are amazingly adaptable, Southern whites no less than any others. But for some, the burdens that moral parents laid upon the child were too absolute. They could be torn between love and shame, respect and rebellion, especially when parents discovered that ideals had not been met and personal whims and desires had been allowed to run free. At such times, in families where honor was the chief goal, the admonitions took this form: "Avoid as much as possible low company," advised a Natchez plantation mistress in 1859; "[A]ssociate with the refined for your manners soon tell what company you keep—Recollect dear Son you have a name to preserve." Characteristically, there was no mention of a jealous God to serve, an immortal soul to save.[23]

The reins of guilt and shame, internalized from an early age, could be extremely dangerous, especially if the "significant other"—fathers, mothers, widows, guardians—placed severe moral demands upon themselves and expected offspring to do likewise. "Overindulgence" was often thought to be the reason for so many sons having become prodigal in the upper social ranks. But they also appeared in highly upstanding families, to the grief of distinguished fathers and grandfathers. Thomas Jefferson, for instance, was often didactic in his solicitude for his daughters and their children as well as for the offspring of his sisters and brother. Yet he was generous-hearted and informal in personal relations with the young. How it grieved him, though, when, as so often happened in planter families, the young did not grow in maturity and self-discipline. Charles Lewis Bankhead, his grandson-in-law, Lilburne and Isham Lewis, his nephews, and other relatives were involved in spectacular scrapes, usually a consequence of alcoholism. Such ne'er-do-wells were a special curse in the rural South, though Northern families of similar repute had their share as well.[24]

In households where fathers were not so distinguished, not so committed to public service, high aims were perhaps less determinedly set before the growing youngster. Some fathers offered examples of manliness so physical and primal that the young son had little difficulty duplicating in his small world what he observed in his father's behavior. "Minister as he was," recollected Reuben Davis, a Mississippi lawyer from middling stock, "my father never doubted that it was part of his Christian duty to knock down any rascal who happened to deserve such discipline." His code did not resemble that of Thomas Jefferson, nor that of a Boston Brahmin. For the former, a Roman disdain for insult and a certainty of inner integrity forbade such unseemliness. For the latter, time itself was too valuable to be wasted in minor disputes. Sense of self was such that the slights of others were not to be taken seriously, in the fashion of a gamecock. But for the late-eighteenth- and early-nineteenth-century Southern planter class on the frontier, the rules to impart to the young were simple, clear, and, in context, healthy. Andrew Jackson recalled the advice of his widowed mother before her death, when he was still very young: "If ever you have to vindicate your feelings or your honor, do it calmly," she had warned. "Avoid quarrels as long as you can, but sustain your manhood always." Equally uncomplicated was Reuben Davis's credo: "A man ought to fear God and mind his business. He should be respectful and courteous to all women; he should love his friends and hate his enemies . . . eat when . . . hungry, drink when . . . thirsty, dance when . . . merry . . . and knock down any man who questioned his right to these privileges."[25] For an oral, rather fluid slave society, these were all virtues that made good sense, unrefined though they were. Perhaps there was the danger of a childish naiveté implicit in so transparent a scheme. Still, it had a vitality, and as long as men and women so raised were in touch with their feelings, it could produce admirable results.

As in the North, Southern mothers played the dominant role in the care of infants. But in the South, among both rich and poor, fathers were not invariably diffident about their offspring. Demonstrative themselves, they expected to see early signs of manliness in sons and vivacity in girls. "Give little Molly a thousand kisses for me," wrote George Braxton, a Virginia planter, to his wife in 1755. "Remember me to the children and tell em I will be mad if they are naughty," declared Levin Joynes affectionately in 1788. The pattern rather resembled modern-day rural father-child relations. According to a recent anthropological study, black fathers in northern Florida treat their progeny similarly. The father "holds the baby, kisses him and talks to him," but when the baby becomes "hungry, tired, or needs to be changed he is returned to the mother." Nevertheless, the father "demonstrates pride in him, relates to him in an affectionate way, and provides emotional . . . support for him."[26]

Although proud of their youngsters as extensions of themselves, Southern antebellum fathers devoted little routine time to them. The same was equally true of upper-class Northern fathers during the period. Busy with financial and commercial enterprise, the Amorys, Appletons, and Lawrences and similarly well-placed fathers had no time for superintendence of their young. Besides, it would have been indecorous to show too much affection, which was best left to nurses and mothers to provide. In the South, fathers were busy with less profitable but equally gratifying and socially functional duties—muster rolls, courthouse visits, hunting parties, and other activities that conferred status but not always reward in coin. Whatever the utility of their excursions abroad might be, Southern fathers were not as tied to plantation and hearth as modern historians have pictured them by way of contrast to the work-home dichotomy of the antebellum Northern and modern style. By whim more than by design, fathers lavished affection on their young one moment and were utterly preoccupied with other matters the next. The haphazardness in Southern father-child relations was in stark contrast to the Northeastern upper- and middle-class, evangelical norms of behavior. Travelers frequently remarked upon the irregularity that characterized so much of white Southern life, including childrearing. For instance, children of merchant bankers in Boston were very early introduced to the notion of keeping strict accounts, accepting the parental idea that they should note *"every cent* you receive, and *every cent you expend."* Rare was the Southern planter who required such monetary exactness. An early introduction to the stables was more appropriate.[27]

In times of crisis fathers often demonstrated the utmost concern, as if, perhaps, to make up for prior inattention. When William Beverley of Virginia buried an infant boy in the mid-eighteenth century, he wrote a close friend, "I vainly thought he would be an exceeding great comfort to me in my old age . . . but now he is gone the way of all flesh, I shall endeavour not to be fond of any thing in this world." Two months later he still was inconsolable and mourned that he had not himself "died in his room," instead of the boy. Antebellum fathers, no less than their colonial forebears, were distraught in crises of illness and death.[28] Yet fathers spent little time hovering over the cradle; it was not quite respectable or manly to be too domestic. At the same time, the child was frequently seen as an extension of themselves.

Family historians have lately insisted that in traditional societies such as seventeenth-century England and eighteenth-century Vir-

ginia parents showered little love or attention upon their young because high mortality rates allegedly precluded intense emotional investment in the young. Whatever the situation might have been in
England, Virginia parents, colonial and antebellum, were highly
concerned about the survival of their progeny *at the time of crisis.*
In the early eighteenth century, William Byrd II and his wife went
to considerable lengths to save their child Parke, who died at eighteen months. When in 1815 John C. Calhoun's little girl expired
suddenly of fever, he wrote his mother-in-law, "She is gone alas!
. . . So fixed in sorrow is her distressed mother that every topick
of consolation, which I attemp[t] to offer but seems to grieve her
the more. It is in vain I tell her it is the lot of humanity; that almost all parents have suffered equal calamity; that Providence may
have intended it in kindness to her and ourselves. . . ." Calhoun's
sorrow was real. Nor could it be said that parents looked only upon
the dynastic aspect of child survival. Instead, early and late, the
dead youngster's attainments toward individuality were fondly recalled. In the same letter Calhoun observed that before the final
seizure, "she had just begun to talk and walk; and progressed so fast
in both as to surprise every one."[29]

Mothers were prostrated with grief; fathers were not abashed to
shed tears. Moreau de St. Mery, a visitor to America in the 1790s,
noted what he thought was a salutary venting of feeling when a
planter wept in his presence for the loss of a child—a contrast with
the taciturnity of French aristocrats. When in 1772 a kinswoman of
Landon Carter seemed to take the loss of her baby too much in
stride, Carter was mortified for the sake of his family as well as the
child, needlessly lost, he thought, because the mother had failed to
call an experienced physician in time. We do not know, however, if
she had been negligent out of sheer selfishness or because of a complex state of mental depression to which women, given the seemingly endless cycle of birth and pregnancy, were sometimes subject.
In any event, Carter's reaction was certainly the ordinary response
of shock toward the neglectful mother, whether or not his complaints were just.[30]

No doubt some poor whites were subjected to impoverishments

of spirit and body when insurmountable burdens deadened feelings. An example from the 1850s comes from a poor illiterate white woman in East Texas who was hosting Frederick L. Olmsted and a physician in her tiny flea-infested cabin. They inquired about her feverish child, and her response was distressingly monosyllabic and casual. "Well," she drawled with glazed eyes, "it's been going on some days now and keeps getting worse . . . I reckoned I should lose it one spell." She had lost two children earlier from the same cause. When the physician asked her if she had medicines, she opened a drawer full of powders and potions. It turned out, however, that she could not read the labels. But once the doctor told her what to do, she went about it with a will. Obviously her indifference was merely a natural response to the feeling of helplessness, to which fatalism was a logical reaction.[31]

In the nineteenth-century South fathers continued to be no less solicitous about sick children than William Beverley had been eighty years before. Governor Israel Pickens of Alabama had not only lost his wife but was about to lose his youngest son William, ill with "bilious fever." Rather than entrusting the infant to "the carelessness of a nurse," for several days he stayed up all night with him. "These dear little ones are now my only objects of affectionate concern," he wrote a close friend, General Walter Lenoir, "and the very trouble they afford me is perhaps at this moment a blessing, as they furnish subjects of attention both to my body and mind" in time of grief. Although neighbors urged him to disperse the children among them, he refused: "I would prefer giving them my own personal care."[32] Pickens, a man of sensibility and intellect, had not learned such lessons in domesticity from New England advisers. He was simply reacting in a very natural, humane way to circumstances.

Men and women did not fear to invest their emotions in such transitory beings as children. A willingness to gamble with Providence—taking risks with one's emotional equanimity—was not confined to the racecourse and gaming table. It was part of living and dying. The losses of loved ones mattered. Yet death had to be borne bravely, with resignation. Nothing could possibly be so arrogant as the claim that only modern man knows how to grieve.

Beyond the efforts to keep a child alive, a chief objective in child-rearing was to encourage the very young to be aggressive, even ferocious. Otherwise, reasoned the traditionally minded parent, the male child would be so severely checked and overprotected that effeminacy might ensue. Thomas Jones, a Chesapeake planter, rejoiced in the eighteenth century that his two-year-old "runs about the house, hollows and makes a noise all day long, and as often as he can, gets out of Doors." Very young children learned that they were supposed to grab for things, fight on the carpet to entertain parents, clatter their toys about, defy parental commands, and even set upon likely visitors in friendly roughhouse. Girls acted with the same freedom from restraint as boys. Their introduction to the proprieties of ladyhood came much later.[33]

According to Landon Carter of Sabine Hall, Virginia, in 1774, children were so much incited to impudence that ones "just cloathing are instructing their Parents" in his part of the world; "and what is worse these Parents who practiced this when Children themselves, know not how to curb their Children now they attempt it." (The observation was sound and its applicability extended well into the next century. By then, however, evangelical principles were gradually replacing the traditional style in many Southern homes.) Carter also understood the reason for the indulgence. A change in management would by implication be a severe criticism of the eighteenth-century parents' own upbringing and its outcome. "Nothing is so common," he explained, "as to hear Parents say, to curb their children is to spoil their genius and tapapers [?]. But is not this, because these Parents have not yet forgot their own childish dispositions?"[34]

Unconscious imitation of the parents' own experiences as children was one factor, but it was also true that allowing youngsters to have their own way was a form of denying responsibility and rejecting unacceptable feelings of exasperation. Children were then, as always, demanding creatures. How easy it was to leave the answering of needs to slaves, or simply let the child have its way. Even so, upper-class Southern mothers were often ambivalent about their youngsters, especially the boys, whose uninhibited play was both a trial to bear and a sign of future manly virtue.

In the lower classes, however, repressed discontent with the parental role found voice in a way that refined folk spurned: a belief in witches. As anthropologists have long known, a function of what was called "the evil eye," usually attributed to women, was the splitting of the mother image into the good, solicitous mother and the bad, subversive witch. Zillah Brandon of Alabama provided an example. Parentless, she and her younger brother had been raised by very poor foster parents on the early nineteenth-century Southern frontier. She disliked them, especially in later life, for not being religious enough to give her proper instruction or to understand the torments to which their supernatural notions subjected the pair of orphans. "The daughter of the gentleman by whom we were raised," she declared, "made my life miserable by telling me about ghosts and witches, she made me believe they thronged the earth and ruled it." Leaving the child in the charge of this elder daughter in the family, the foster parents exposed Zillah to the inconsistency of one who was supposed to be loving but could not be. The phenomenon of transference to some outside evil was hardly unusual in agrarian societies. Two purposes were served: the fantasies of hexes and devouring demons were used to frighten the child into temporary obedience and at the same time provided an outlet for unmanageable adult emotions. One need not wholly adopt Melanie Klein's theory of the role of infant aggression in biting during the nursing period to accept the idea that the strategy of projection upon an outside force was at work when mothers or surrogate mothers conjured up witches to explain their own hostilities. Such anger was not unnatural; it stemmed from the responsibility of childcare itself, a tedious, sometimes unfulfilling experience. Mothers had good reason to rage against their circumscribed fate and their dependence upon often untrustworthy men whom they could hardly help but envy for their freedom of movement and power.[35]

At the same time mothers, both rich and poor, tried with varying success to compensate for such attitudes in positive ways, especially self-sacrifice, giving their all in physical and outwardly affectionate demonstrations. So overeager were mothers toward their sick children that in 1844 the Raleigh *Star* complained that the results were counterproductive. Maternal fussiness was a reason why, the editor asserted, one-fifth of the North Carolina infants died before reaching a year of age. They are "over-fed, over-clothed, take too little exercise in the air." Swaddling was not common, so far as we know, but obviously the mothers of whom the writer spoke were killing their young with kindness and restricting their movements in some way. It would have been the height of disgrace for a responsible mother to confess anger about helpless little ones, fretful from illness, but sometimes negative feelings took a disguised form. Sensing this, a Scottish divine visiting in Alabama urged a mother to ignore a child screaming itself into a fit. She insisted that the girl had scarlet fever and required her pampering. The next morning the clergyman felt vindicated: the three-year-old seemed to him just as perky—and obnoxious—as ever. The mother's concerns may have been exaggerated but her twittering solicitude and impulsive caresses were intended less for the nurturing of the child than for the easing of her own ambivalent feelings. The effect on this particular child might not have been damaging, but, if the observer was accurate, the potential for trouble was certainly there.[36]

Heaping great affection and interest upon the child, however, had another effect. Parents worried that the male child's sexual identity might be seriously compromised if he was so indulged: it might lead to dependency in later life, even effeminacy. Therefore, along with the tendency toward binding the child to the parents, there was the contrary drive to insist that masculinity appear early and unmistakably. For instance, on a plantation near Savannah in 1863 Josephine Clay's "Mr. One Year Old" received from a fond grandmother "a pretty whip, which he uses very fiercely in his carriage." Quite clearly, though, the identification of manliness with guns, whips, bowie knives, and other weapons was impressed upon toddlers who saw fathers, uncles, and elder brothers carry and use them as part of their regular equipage. "A most martiall Genious" was the characterization given a toddler in the Byrd family in eighteenth-century Virginia. Later in the same century a three- or four-year-old girl named Eliza Custis had to act in ways unbecoming a girl, so disappointed was her father not to have a son to rear in the arts of war and manly self-expression. He had her entertain his hunting guests by singing ribald and military verses.[37]

In order to encourage their babies' drives, mothers tried not to bruise their egos too soon. This, coupled with their own ambivalences about the raucousness and the fragility of children, led mothers to let small ones have their own way. "I snatch a moment," wrote one colonial matron, "from a crying infant, and the noise of two or three ungoverned children, which is so distracting to the brain as a confused din of arms to a timid soldier." Her analogy was appropriate. Ofttimes mothers did feel intimidated even by their smallest boys. Ineffectuality of discipline was a Southern hallmark, observed Sir Charles Lyell. On a steamboat in the 1840s, the English visitor had passed a stateroom packed with squalling children, still in their sexless frocks, and their much distracted mothers. On every side he heard "the threat of 'I'll switch you,' " announced in peremptory Southern tones. But "never" was the warning "carried into execution." Examples could be multiplied, from eighteenth-century through Civil War sources.[38]

The haphazard character of motherly correction of the very young had its inner rationale, though along with it went long conversations in women's circles about the absolute need for stern obedience from children if ever they were to amount to much. Mary Austin Holley, a Yankee in the deep South, was disgusted with the talk she heard about "whipping them, & breaking their spirits as you do horses & dogs." All that resulted from such imbecility, she huffed, was to teach the child to "hate *you*, not the doing wrong, & lose all the nice feelings which make excellence of character. Who does not spurn a blow if there is true pride?" Once she heard a friend's child exclaim after being forbidden some activity, "After she is gone, *I will do it*." Thus the objective of indulgence was to ensure aggressiveness.[39]

Mrs. Holley mistook mothers' exchanges with the realities at home. Everyone seemed to wish a public repute for being a sturdy disciplinarian. Whether they were or not was quite another matter. When overwhelmed with other duties, mothers could be very abusive. At times, they were prone to sudden anger, and slapped their children harshly. But so long as the child's aggression was directed toward another child or perhaps a stranger, the parent was pleased with these clear signs of sturdy willfulness. In this respect they met the criteria of Stephen Penton, a late-seventeenth-century spokesman for traditional childrearing. He urged parents to let boys run free, at least with peers and pets. Even street urchins, he argued, could be trained to command thousands and tens of thousands, simply by letting natural male impulses for power find suitable outlets.[40]

Even as late as the 1830s the Presbyterian leader John Holt Rice of Virginia worried lest Southerners become too bookish and regimented so that they saw the world in a "metaphysical," schematic, inhibited, and Yankee way. A reflective approach to childrearing, he thought, would "simplify too much" and *"explain* too much." It was far better that parents should allow their children wide latitude for self-expression and learn through the give and take of social relations. Even Southern evangelical parents could be somewhat indulgent about the way small children acted toward each other, though insistent upon respect for elders and authority above.[41]

Looking backward with both regret and, probably, secret pride, Southern evangelical clergymen, the group most conscious of changes in the moral climate, recalled barbaric times as a way of encouraging parents to inculcate conscience and control. The Rev. Sidney E. Bumpas, for instance, declared, "My parents were very indulgent. . . . I was never compelled to read my book or go to church; and Sunday with me was usually a day of visiting, fishing & hunting. . . ." The "godless" community of the 1790s, he said, was more to blame than his own parents. The neighbors held "the mistaken notion that we could not be strict with our children." At a higher end of the social scale, the Rev. William Porcher DuBose, from one of Carolina's oldest families, remarked of his upbringing in the 1840s that neither of his parents had ever done "a Severe thing to me." At the very bottom of the social ladder, Peter Cartwright, a low-born revivalist of Kentucky and Indiana, reminisced about his frontier upbringing in the early 1800s. Said he, "My father restrained me but little," although his mother piously sought to counteract the influence of his gambling, drinking father. William Winans, later a Methodist missionary in Mississippi, was raised in the same period, without benefit of religion or such discipline that stimulated self-restraint, he recalled. He attributed his adolescent years of heavy drinking, gambling, and struggles under "the magic influence of Female solicitation" to his poor training as a small boy. These were common recollections of a later generation of Southerners, particularly of those from backlands. Yet such was the imperative of being manly, even belligerent when occasion demanded, that these clergymen were boasting of their prowess even as they presented themselves as overindulged, nearly lost young souls whom God had finally rescued.[42]

Though they sometimes worried that their children might slip too far into an abyss of savagery, parents—especially those in the wilder sections of the lower South—raised their young in a manner paralleled by the methods of aboriginal people. "Grandparents might complain that small children got into everything but the small child was free to romp, pry into things, to demand what it wanted, and to assault its parents." So writes Anthony F. C. Wallace of the Iroquois. Erik Erikson gives similar evidence from his studies of the Sioux. The pattern may also be found elsewhere.[43]

The result of this attitude of bemused indulgence, pride in aggressiveness, and distracted childcare was sometimes close to tragic. It led children to frequent accidents—falling from great heights, getting lost in the woods, being thrown from ponies, hurting themselves with firearms left casually about. Fire was the greatest risk of all. With apparent impunity children played with firebrands as recklessly as later Southern youngsters set off fireworks, without adult supervision. It did not occur to some parents that children might lack the necessary maturity to understand the dangers involved. One eighteenth-century Virginia parent, for instance, delightedly told her husband that the children were "imployed all day making bonfires." Another example was the sister of John J. Pettus, a governor of Mississippi just before the Civil War and son of a small farmer; she lost an eye by fire when just a toddler. Yet it would not do to curb spunkiness. After all, life was a gamble. The greatest sign of providential favor was survival under duress. A signal of special curse was a hapless accident. The rationale was at least partly self-serving; it allowed parents to do as they pleased, on the assumption that children should learn early to care for themselves or pay the consequences. The policy was applicable to little girls as well as little boys.[44]

When a boy developed speech and was presented with his first pair of breeches, an early sign of manhood for four-year-olds, his parents' impatience to see him a self-reliant, competent, and virile soul grew apace. Moreover, it seemed only proper to entrust young children to the care of older siblings and young slaves. Busy with household and farm duties, mothers thrust children into sometimes irresponsible hands. Serious confusion of roles, one suspects, arose from the practice of burdening older children with the supervision of the younger ones, who were their rivals for familial and adult favor. In William Faulkner's *The Sound and the Fury*, the problem was vividly portrayed. Young Caddy had to serve as surrogate mother for the mentally retarded Maury (Benjy) and little Quentin in the stead of the neurotic Compson mother, while Jason, the eldest brother, was forced to be a replacement for the alcoholic father. Both children—in fact all four—were severely scarred by the distracted, self-regarding habits of the parents. It forced upon them unnatural feelings of dependency upon each other, resentments and defenses mingling anger, revenge, and perplexity against the outside world as well as confusions within. One may conjecture that early close ties arising from the isolation of plantation life and the insensitivity of parents to childhood needs sometimes did bring brothers and sisters into emotionally confusing situations, as Faulkner discerned.[45]

At the same time, it must be quickly asserted that affections between brother and sister were not always perverse, not by any means. Brantley York of early nineteenth-century North Carolina, for instance, had a healthy and straightforward love for his older sister.

He remembered how at age four he had to accompany her to the Old Field School in frontier Randolph County; she was "minding" him for mother. He did not object to the tedium of school, an activity in which he could not then share. He noted that she had always been "my nurse." There was a "rough sympathy and helpfulness," a Yankee visitor thought, in the way poor white children acted toward their younger siblings. The same was true for the vast majority of gentry families in the nineteenth-century South, the themes of incest which Edgar Allan Poe and William Faulkner explored notwithstanding.[46]

It is always risky to generalize about such matters as childrearing. Every family, ancient or modern, has its own peculiarities. Moreover, different styles were coming into fashion in the mid-nineteenth-century South, ones largely connected with the advance of evangelical religion. It would be an error to insist that honor alone was the principle guiding Southern white childcare. Particularly in the upper South, but elsewhere too, Southern matrons and fathers sometimes recognized the failings of the traditional approach. "How bad it is," said one Virginia mother in 1804, "for children to be so giddy & extravagant." But for an extended example, we return to the case of Robert E. Lee, because he so well epitomized the way Southern gentlemen were becoming accustomed to react toward the young. Lee's solicitude about how problems of discipline ought to be handled in a very young child's life was evident in a letter of 1837, posted to "Dear Markie," his aristocratic wife Mary Custis. "Our dear little boy," wrote the pious young father, "seems to have among his friends [i.e., his elders] the reputation of being hard to manage,— a distinction not at all desirable, as it indicates self-will and obstinacy." Lee readily admitted that the world saw in such behavior of a three- or four-year-old healthy signs of aggression. Nevertheless, the army regular continued, "it is our duty, if possible, to counteract" such feelings and impulses so that they could be quickly brought "under his control." Lee explained that he tried to reason with the youngster and to warn him against letting "his little faculties" become "warped by passion."[47]

Most Northern as well as Southern evangelical parents thought early checking of that vice was an absolute necessity. Parents with more traditional views also agreed, but they often lacked the psychological strategies to instill it. Also, the parents' daily example was likely to undercut their words. Turning his attention to the topic on a much later occasion, Lee wrote "Markie," "You must not let" the youngest boy "run wild in my absence, and will have to exercise firm authority over all of them. This will not require severity or even strictness, but constant attention and an unwavering course. Mildness and forbearance will strengthen their affection for you, while it will maintain your control over them." These sentiments indicated that in the South, among the small number of evangelicals in the upper class, inner integrity, self-discipline, and personal achievement were all goals to which parents and children were to aspire.[48] In this they differed not at all from the Northern evangelical pattern. Similar regularity could be found, too, among some of the families in the Southern yeomanry.

One should not assume, though, that Lee's style of fatherhood was the rule to which all other forms of childcare were exceptions. In making that assumption, as we in this age may be inclined to do, we should recognize two factors. First, Southern scholars today are likely to have been raised in rather similar ways, ones that encourage educational, possibly high religious objectives. To universalize those attitudes and to transpose them back in time would be all too natural. Second, Southern archives are full of family papers in which these same principles are set forth in letter after letter. After all, the kind of people who would leave voluminous testimony to their achievements and thoughts, for later family—and eventually public—edification, were already predisposed to strive for great, often godly ideals. But what of the thousands who did not squirrel away family treasures in ribboned bundles? There is no way of knowing how representative the paper-keeping evangelical whites were in the Old South. One must suspect, however, that there were more traditional parents—ones who were not careful about keeping home records—than there were those who did so.

Typical of the better sort of old-fashioned father (one who did write down his thoughts for posterity) was John Horry Dent. An

Alabama slaveholder originally from low-country South Carolina, Dent established an uncommonly efficient plantation in Barbour County, near Eufaula. Sober, industrious, civic-minded, and well read, he was probably more typical a Southern parent than Robert E. Lee.

In childrearing, as in life, the rugged aristocrat from South Carolina believed that neither church nor womankind should interfere too much in checking manhood in the very young. For him, worship services were accommodations to the needs of matrons, old people, and other dependents. Personal uprightness, he maintained, had almost no connection with Sabbath observances. Unless one had to be present for a marriage, christening, or funeral—all of them family more than spiritual events—he believed the wise planter should stay clear of church, where hypocrisy and sanctimoniousness flourished. In that respect he carried on the traditional anticlericalism of the eighteenth-century squires of the Carolinas and Virginia. Dent would have been horrified, however, had anyone suggested that he was repudiating conscience or denying its importance in the moral development of the young. Nonetheless, he rhymed his deepest convictions in 1858:

> Honor and shame from all conditions rise;
> Act well your part and their [sic] the honor lies.[49]

In keeping with these views, Dent's affection for his young was ordinarily casual. He made an exception, however, of his eldest son Horry. Upon him he lavished his hopes, until Horry died in Confederate service. According to Dent's recent biographer, his papers made few references to the others. The unhappy results of parental insensitivity were evident as the other two boys grew up. The youngest son showed no promise at all; he clerked in a small store. The second eldest, Herbert, was a constant trial, misbehaving from an early age. When a teenager, he killed a horse, lost another, and shot a slave in the leg—all accidents, perhaps. No doubt such scrapes were intended to catch the father's attention, by these if no other means, but Dent scarcely blinked an eye. After the Civil War Herbert, unable to hold a steady job, was still dependent upon the old man. In 1880 Dent lamented that he had "spoiled" Herbert. He consoled himself that most other planters of his generation had also overindulged their sons. Like other former slaveholders, he mused that slavery had been a curse after all: it had sapped the will of the young to learn self-reliance.[50] Actually, the fault lay elsewhere.

6

Male Youth and Honor

One of the key objectives in the raising of Southern white children was the early enforcement of sexual ascriptions, a prerequisite for the maintenance of the traditional ethic. The process began in earnest when a little boy "dropped the slips," that is, received his first pair of pants and no longer wore a small shift. The change usually occurred about age four. Alexander Stephens recalled the event, which had an almost ritual significance for him: "This was a momentous event with me, changing my ideas, giving me entirely new notions of myself, hitherto undreamed of."[1]

With the change in status and dress came also a sterner attitude on the father's part. Obedience was more regularly demanded. The switch appeared with greater frequency. Nevertheless, corporal punishment was not much more than a reactive device, in contrast to the pattern of the Northern evangelical household. There the usual practice in the decades of the early nineteenth century was to resort to the birch rod when all else failed and to accompany the beatings with lectures on the meaning of vice and the rightfulness of adult displeasure.[2] By such means the justice of the adult choice was supposed to be internalized. The child knew what to expect but also how to exercise self-control and forswear immediate gratification.

In the South, as in many other, chiefly nonevangelical households elsewhere, corporal punishment conformed with the primacy of shame. After "clothing," the child learned not to confess and be forgiven but to avoid detection and humiliation. Alexander Stephens, later vice-president of the Confederacy, offered an example that contrasted with the approach that Northern (and some Southern) evangelicals adopted. Stephens's father was a stern Scots-Irish farmer and schoolmaster in north Georgia. Charged with evening chores, as poor boys usually were, the young Stephens once neglected to search for a ewe missing from the herd. When his father discovered the unconfessed loss the next day, he turned brutally on the lad. The "anger of my father," Stephens remarked many years afterwards, "caused me much severer pain than did the stripes he inflicted." Together they located the dead ewe, lying in a ditch "with a lamb she had borne lying dead beside her." He revered his father, but the experience humiliated him. "I thought then, and still think, that if he had not whipped me, but had explained the reason of his injunction to me to report any missing sheep," and then had accompanied me "as he did and we had found the sheep dead from my negligence this would have had all the effect upon me that the punishment was intended to produce." Only in the more morally self-conscious Southern households—the homes of the Pettigrews, Lees, and Joneses of Liberty County, Georgia, and similarly rare and cultivated families—were more benign views entertained.[3] Alexander Stephens's tribulation was representative of how conventional parents raised their young.

By contrast, the Quaker style, mentioned earlier, offered a different way. "When children misbehaved," advised William Penn, "show them the folly, shame and undutifulness of their faults rather with a grieved than an angry countenance." "Personal honor," as historian Barry Levy phrases it, "was less emphasized" in Quaker homes "than the 'honor of truth.'" That approach had its disadvantages, too: it seemed to deny the child the legitimacy of his or her feelings. Fear of genuine self-knowledge could be the unfortunate consequence. The dangers of the traditional approach were uncontrollability and denials of fear; the risks of evangelical and

Quaker modes were denials of evil and violent thoughts, leading to a possibly self-destructive turning inward. Although Stephens thought that the overuse of corporal punishments had an unhealthy effect, many other Southerners believed that "order is Heaven's first law," that "there can be no order without law . . . no law without punishment, and no punishment without pain." Besides, declared a traditionalist in the columns of the *Southern Literary Messenger* in 1841, the ordeal "is soon over" and the "culprit is now conscious that it was deserved." The ancients had done it—" 'fortes, fuere ante Agamemnona,' " the writer intoned, "—there is nothing new under the sun. And others will be whipped hereafter." As former recipients themselves, the parents will do the same to their children, "so it is all fair and equal in the long run."[4]

Perhaps so, but the advantage of the shaming method was its satisfaction for the wielder of power, not the moral training it supposedly gave the young. In a fury typical of ill-controlled adults, William Byrd of Westover in the early eighteenth century sought to cure an apprentice boy of bedwetting by twice forcing him to drink "a pint of piss." In the 1780s the widowed mother of Robert Bailey, a professional gambler in later life, lashed out at the boy, not for fighting his sister, as she might have, but for refusing the mother's command to fetch water for the tavern she ran. Having just lost his alcoholic father, the seven-year-old cried all the way to the spring. Suddenly the heavens seemed to open. "I saw that good man," he recalled, in reference, one surmises, to his dead father. Then he heard "a loud voice saying 'I will catch you . . . You must go to hell!' " He screamed and ran back to his mother without the water. She punished him again. Rather grandiosely, Bailey mourned that he owed his life of sin to the injustice of his childrearing—an abusive mother and a still more abusive stepfather whom she married shortly after the incident. Indeed, his understanding of the difference between honor and shame, gaming and cheating was highly confused, an example of the ill effects of the shaming approach.[5]

Even in less chaotic households, corporal punishment reflected the anger and shame of parents more than a calculated determinant of child training. In the 1820s the mother of J. G. Clinkscales was so humiliated and vexed with her son's fear of the weekly public speech he had to make before the school authorities that she beat him soundly every Friday afternoon. It was not the best mode for helping him to overcome the phobia, as he later recognized himself. In the 1850s Mrs. Craft of Memphis, wife of a young and unusually domesticated husband, quarreled endlessly with him about her whimsical habits of disciplining their young son. At times over-indulgent and at others singularly brutal, she claimed to judge matters on the basis of Christian duty. However, her husband, Henry Craft, complained that "our earthly parents do not always chastise judiciously or solely for the good of their children," letting "caprice" guide them instead. Likewise, in the 1840s, Thomas Chaplin, a near-alcoholic of St. Helena's Island, South Carolina, fought his wife over how best to treat their son Ernest. Once he explained in his diary that he had beaten the boy so that he should not "escape always through the interference of his mother & by that means form an idea that I would not be allowed to whip him. . . ." No wonder both little Douglass Craft and Ernest Chaplin suffered from tantrums: they had not learned the means to control their own feelings, so disordered were their parents' signals to them. The lack of self-restraint in Southern adults' behavior owed much to the ambivalences and inconsistencies of parental discipline.[6] Conflicts of the heart were deeply embedded in the way children were raised.

During the preschool years (before age eight or ten in the antebellum South), white children discovered that they could exercise the same power over those beneath them that elders employed to rule their own tumultuous world. Southerners themselves often lamented that the presence of slaves gave a child a convenient scapegoat, a means to vent frustrations and test boundaries of acceptable conduct toward inferiors. Those habits of physical violence and overlordship continued into adult life. As psychologists well know today, the more violence seen, the more arbitrary the pain experienced, the more rooted the pattern of belligerence that may be instilled in the young. Seeing parents chastise slaves was sure to have an effect upon young imitators. Even Southerners thought so. John

Dickinson, a Revolutionary Whig and Philadelphia lawyer, had been raised on the eastern shore of Maryland in the mid-eighteenth century. He argued that early experience with slavery accounted for Southern "pride, selfishness, peevishness, violence" and other wrongs. Thomas Jefferson echoed the lament in *Notes on Virginia,* and Josiah Quincy reached similar conclusions on a visit to the Carolinas in 1773.[7] Actually, it was less slavery itself than the permissiveness about childish aggression against peers and underlings, white or black, that encouraged egocentrism and violent self-expression. Children want to know the limits of conduct; when none are set they frighten even themselves when they lose control. Nevertheless, the availability of slaves and the "duty" of whites to command them —some thought it could not be learned too soon—put a premium on chastisement by the young of those beneath them. Sometimes parents let slaves act in ways that whites could not. In 1839, Mrs. Holley noted that youngsters "commit a fault," and outraged elders "knock them down" for it, but ignore the slave child's misbehavior because it conformed with the supposed barbarism of the underclass. Such signals were no doubt confusing to the white child, but they learned by such means that vices were supposed to suit particular hierarchies on the plantation.[8]

As Southerners liked to boast even as they complained, young slave boys and girls often played happily with white companions from the Big House. Antebellum counselors like Mrs. Virginia Cary objected that the contacts would undermine the spiritual health of the planters' children. In the same period, Frederick Law Olmsted and others also heard planters lament the dire moral effects of undiscriminating racial ties.[9] Yet, contradictorily, one of the alleged advantages of slavery was thought to be childhood bonds, ones that adult white Southerners cherished in recollection. After the Civil War James Battle Avirett of North Carolina recalled benignly, "In this portion of the South there was an unwritten law by which the boy child born on the plantation nearest the birthday of the young master was his, and as the two came along together through childhood, boyhood, and all along through manhood, they were closely associated, having taken their first lessons together in riding, swim-

ming, fishing, boat sailing, and in the various employments of outdoor life." To him and to many others it was a glory of the old
regime. He insisted that the white naturally assumed command in
play and sport owing to superior genetic endowment, and the black
naturally learned the proper role of subordinate.[10]

In *The Unvanquished,* however, William Faulkner gave a much
richer portrait of such intimacy. Bayard Sartoris and his slave friend
Ringo collaborated in wartime adventures until an eventual parting of ways. Educational and social discrepancies gradually drew
them apart, until the association was broken in early manhood. Perhaps the most poignant and revealing description of these common
childhood ties appeared in the autobiography of Fields Cook, a
slave who wrote his memoirs while still in bonds. Recently discovered by the historian Robert Calhoon, this rare document revealed
the authenticity of white boastings about the fraternal ties across
racial lines: "I never knew," wrote Cook, "what the yoke of oppres-
sion was in the early part of my life for the white and black children all faired alike and grew on together highfellows." But, he
went on, those happy times did not last. Gradually the white friend
came "to feel . . . like the peafowl in the midst of a brude of
checkens" and he "raise his feathers and boast of his superiority
. . . over me." In justice to himself, he felt obliged to add "that if
there be anything in the world that is hertful to one . . . it is . . .
that after one has formed a real attachment to an individual that
they should after wards appear to have forgotten all friendship and
kindness and treat you with contempt."[11] The slave society required
the eventual sundering of those young affiliations.

No less intense than the influence of slavery was the parental insistence upon early signs of aggressiveness, demanded by notions of
white masterhood, before the child met the outside world at school.
The male child was under special obligation to prove early virility,
an obligation in which shame and honor played a crucial, if not
exclusive role. It should be added that in the antebellum North,
such demands upon the child were also made, with shame and honor
the means and ends. But the tendency, at least in middling and
upper-class Northern household, was to seek ways whereby children

would internalize virtues and fears of wrongdoing, chiefly through conscience and guilt.

Shame and guilt are not exactly the same, as psychologists today well know. Conscience commands recognition of doing wrong, in which there can be a demarcation between what the world condemns and what the individual feels is correct and right. Guilt entails a sense of discrete violation, even if society at large might not judge the misdeed so severely. Shame, on the other hand, involves a congruence of social and personal perceptions. As Helen B. Lewis notes, "The self does not feel autonomous or independent, but dependent and vulnerable to rejection." One feels recreant not for a particular misdeed but for one's complete existence, a totality of unworthiness because the fault or misconduct fully defines the individual in others' eyes and therefore in one's own. Because a person is most vulnerable when his or her back is turned or when he or she is unclothed, physically or in the mind's eye, these states of being are those most associated with shame. The turned back, the exposed rear is the position of disgrace, for child or adult. Honor is forward, open-faced, and outwardly trustful, even if only a mask, but the honor-conscious individual must show surprise at betrayal and express horror at the thought of vulnerability. If an honor-centered person is guilty of some wrong, his or her primary desire is to escape the implications of weakness and inferiority, the lash of contempt. The threat of shame, under such circumstances, would encourage resort to any means of deceiving the all-prying, ever-judging public or, in the case of children, the parents and elders.[12]

Aware of the role expected of him, the Southern boy could not easily confess a failure to his father, particularly in regard to some manly test such as horsemanship. A fear of horses would suggest cowardice, an affront to family and forebears; a boy had a duty to ride with expertise, a military virtue. In wilderness Virginia in the mid-eighteenth century, Peter Jefferson taught Thomas "to sit his horse, fire his gun, boldly stem the Rivanna when the swollen river was 'Rolling red from brae to brae,' " as one biographer rhapsodized. Fearing exposure of his unmanliness, Thomas, age ten, dared not return to his father without the expected game in his bag. Luckily, he later reminisced, he found a caged wild turkey, tied it to a tree with his garter and killed it, then "carried it home in triumph." The deception was fondly recalled. Jefferson's grandson Thomas Jefferson Randolph remembered that his grandfather "advised that boys but ten years old should be given a gun and sent into the forest alone to make them self reliant," a recapitulation of Jefferson's own upbringing.[13]

Though most boys found the task an easy one, not all could live up to the ideal. Some, of course, chose not even to try, having the confidence to be somewhat deviant in this respect. John Sharp Williams, a later Mississippi senator, hated to hunt both as youngster and adult. Fishing bored him to distraction. (But he proudly recalled his wrestling and butting matches with black companions.) Others simply could not cope, often because of persistent childhood illnesses and disquieting circumstances at home. For instance Edmund Ruffin, the Virginia fire-eater, had been a very sickly child and could not live up to the rough and tumble of plantation living. In addition, he had lost his mother at age four and his stepmother, harried with a brood of her own, gave him little emotional support. Rather than admit his waywardness, as Williams did, he repressed it with determination. Ruffin's permanent sense of inferiority also arose from early loss of his father, but in addition his poor health found compensation in a touchiness about his and the South's honor. Often enough those who, like Ruffin, insisted upon general admiration for their forthrightness and manliness were individuals with an early and damaging inability at athletics. Sometimes they overcame inner distress by engaging in duels, fights, and fractious disputes that seemed to arise from depressions and anger partly traceable to childhood unhappiness and illness.[14]

For more typical boys, informal training for valor began early and the conquest of fear and shame were appropriately met. An illustration contrasts with the parallel imperative for conscience-building in Theodore Parker's forbearance over the turtle cited earlier. On Millwood plantation in antebellum South Carolina there lived a squawking drake, which frightened the heir to the Hampton holdings, age five. Intimidated but determined to over-

come his fear, Wade Hampton, later a hunter of international renown, selected a toy sword, sheath, and belt during a shopping expedition with his parents. Upon his return home he attacked the
drake with "a terrific downward sweep" of his "young arm." Soon
the "web-footed bully" lay dead at his feet. "His elders had the good
taste," records his admiring biographer, "to congratulate him, and
to say things about a chip off the old block." The incident and the
subsequent praise were not significant in themselves, any more than
was Parker's refraining from killing the snapping turtle. Yet they
indicated a social and ethical tendency.[15]

A military submissiveness to those in higher authority was part
of the training in honor and the avoidance of shame, based as much
on fear as on love of the father. "When Pa raised his voice and
called me I answered respectfully, 'Sir?' " recalled a son of a backwoods Primitive Baptist preacher in Alabama. "Had my answer
been 'what?' a reprimand would have promptly followed." "I always knew that it was impossible to disobey my father," declared the
son of Robert E. Lee. To do otherwise was to be thought a family
disgrace. Reverence for parents was a classless ideal. Few questioned
the right of fathers to demand instant, outward deference. Under
the rubric of honor, parents could insist upon the honesty of children as much as of slaves, but the code did not require parental
reciprocation by any means.[16]

Children also learned the significance of entitlements by which
honor was translated into forms of address. One had to greet " 'Miz
Campbell'; 'Uncle Jim'; 'Aunt Mary'; or 'Cousin John!' " recalled
an Alabamian of Hatchet Creek. "A child of ten who addressed a
man or woman of fifty by his or her first name without attaching
thereto some title of respect would have been regarded as an ill-
mannered brat." These signs of deference, first required at home,
prepared the child for later pledges of submission to community
authorities, with their honorific titles of colonel, judge, and other
manifestations of power.[17] Again, demands to honor elders were not
solely upper-class duties.

In like manner, the child absorbed the proper relation to those
beneath, for the man of honor *assumed* a posture that encouraged

inferiors to defer. Once while on horseback Thomas Jefferson and his preadolescent grandchild passed an old slave who greeted them with a smile, doffed his cap, and give them a hearty greeting. Jefferson acknowledged the pleasantry; the boy, hiding shyness in hauteur, did not. Afterwards Jefferson quietly asked, "Do you permit a negro to be more of a gentleman than yourself?" As an eighteenth-century English adviser suggested, children had to learn to "make their Honours gracefully." Knowing when to be courteous, when to show *"spirit* and *firmness,"* as John Randolph urged, took as long to develop as conscience and guilt did in an evangelical household—and with the same degree of success and failure.[18] Planter gentility emphasized this rubric; the yeomanry did not.

In well-ordered antebellum Presbyterian and Episcopalian homes the stress was upon careful self-control, in the evangelical circles of both the South and North. Recalling his young years during the late antebellum period, Woodrow Wilson valued the restraint his father, a prominent Presbyterian minister, had insisted on. It was not only a character-building necessity but also a means of communicating ideas and experiences to others.

> When I was a boy, my father would not permit me to blurt things out, or stammer a half-way job of telling what I had to tell. If I became excited in explaining some boyish activity he always said, "Steady, now, Thomas: wait a minute. Think! Think what it is you wish to say and then choose your words and say it!" As a young boy, therefore, even at the age of four or five, I was taught to think about what I was going to say. . . . Before I was grown it became a habit.

Such transactions were encouraged by both parents in the Wilson household, but it was the stern, commanding father who seemed to exercise the greater influence on disciplinary matters, the mother who helped the youngster acquire his sense of selfhood. The orthodox divine was a firm believer in corporal punishment. A daughter reminisced, "His idea was that if a lad was of fine tempered steel, the more he was beaten the better he was." The result was that ofttimes boys so raised felt awe, repressed anger, love, dependence, and yearning for paternal notice. These were not necessarily emotionally damaging reactions by any means, but the potential for difficulties was certainly there. Wilson later called himself a "mamma's boy," suggesting both gratitude for and resentment about his mother Janet's frequent, possessive interventions on his behalf against his stern father. In light of Wilson's remarkable career, these tensions should not be seen as necessarily debilitating, but perhaps as stimulating.[19]

In the lower classes the rearing of children did not involve such punctilious lessons as that which Jefferson gave his grandson and the Rev. Joseph Wilson offered his son. Yet honor was by no means absent. Instead it took what may be called "ungrammatical" form. Thus in rearing their children poor whites and small farmers roughly paralleled the habits of their richer neighbors. In her 1959 study, for instance, Marion Pearsall observed that babyhood in mountain communities of North Carolina was a time of "great attention and indulgence" for both sexes. But once boys of three were taken out of their little frocks and given breeches (the old custom still persists in the hills), they followed their mothers about the farm. Gradually they learned to perform small chores. At six or perhaps a little later they occasionally went to the fields, disdained female ways, and stopped playing with sisters. Just like the upper-class women whom Sir Charles Lyell observed making idle threats, yeomen's wives carried on the "same popular game" of "I'll whup you, if you don't mind" without invariably doing so. An observer of poor whites in the 1930s reported that mothers usually chastised their young because fathers had license to escape the unpleasant duty. The mothers only intervened, however, when the children's squabbles made their busy mothers cross. " 'You know how a big family is—always fussing,' " declared one farm woman. But when a boy was about eight or ten—when he had grown accustomed to male associations on hunts, fishing trips, and in farm chores—the mother's authority diminished. A boy of that age would no longer submit to female authority, in imitation of the family males with whom he identified. To permit a woman to hurt him physically would be a dire humiliation.[20]

However, poorer folk did differ from richer ones in the manner of discipline. Believing in supernatural beings themselves, they invoked witches, the "Big Nig" (ofttimes portrayed as a runaway), "Guinea" blacks, headless horsemen, and Indian warriors as threats to discipline an erring child. Local conjure-doctors, sometimes reared in Africa, also were supposed to have a great supernatural power that children were to beware. Needless to say, the upper-class members of the community, as well as the God-fearing church-goers among the yeomanry, disparaged such parental threats and denied the validity of supernatural folk belief, not only because it was thought irrational but also because it was "vulgar." To the degree that fear of the supernatural encouraged timidity about being abroad at night and a feeling of vulnerability to nature's whims, a yeoman's lad raised on such antique notions of the world beyond was not well equipped to meet the criteria of gentlemanly self-possession. Brantley York, later a Methodist circuit rider, recalled, for instance, that "when the neighbors came together, the most prominent topic of conversation was relating some remarkable witch tale, ghost stories and conjurations of various kinds. . . . Often have I sat and listened to these stories till it seemed to me that each hair upon my head resembled the quill of a porcupine. I was afraid to go out of doors, afraid to go to bed alone, and almost afraid of my own shadow." Children of well-educated parents were taught to disregard what slaves and poor whites said of such things; lesser folk, however, perpetuated supernatural custom in the raising of their young.[21]

Self-possession was also somewhat undermined in the close bond that many poor yeomen boys had to form with their mothers and sisters out of fear of a father's tirades. Whiskey drinking and the demoralizations of poverty in general stimulated a good deal of wife and child abuse in the lower ranks of society. (It certainly happened enough in disordered households in the upper ranks as well.) In the first decade of the nineteenth century, for instance, William Brown of rural Kentucky, son of a drunken iron-worker of uncertain rank in the community, had to hide when the old man got into a rage. Mrs. Brown used to conspire with her boy to water the father's brandy, to little observable effect. "Mamma brought Morgan to [my] bed about 3 o'clock. Morgan [age three] said pappa kicked him," the ten-year-old wrote in his diary. The power of the father often engendered an intimacy between son and mother, as in this case. The father, says Marion Pearsall, was "genuinely feared," in yeoman households. In other families, she reported, however, fatherly strictness was more verbal than real.[22] Though poor whites were rather fearful of outside authority, they also harbored mistrusts closer to home. Fathers used their power, at times, to keep sons strictly in place beneath them. Family honor and pride were inculcated into the young, but its character was elemental.

The advent of school age (about eight or ten) marked the next major stage of socialization after "clothing." Lessons of deference and self-assertion learned at home had to be applied in a new, less predictable setting. "Starting to school," remembered Alexander Stephens about his early nineteenth-century upbringing, "was a great epoch with me. New fields of perception and reflection were opened before me." If, as sometimes happened, boys were still sleeping in the same bedchamber with their mother, they gained their privacy at this juncture. James Claiborne, a late-nineteenth-century physician of Virginia, recalled how fifty years before his father had abruptly removed him from his mother's room. Providing him with his first mount, the father escorted him to a boarding school in western North Carolina. It was time, thought the formidable patriarch, to wrench him from his slave playmates. Also, he sought to cut the boy, as Claiborne said, "from 'my mother's apron strings' . . . and to wean me from my dependence on, and my adoration of her."[23] At eight years of age he was to begin his manhood in earnest.

Children without much earlier experience with whippings were especially vulnerable to the school regimen that one adult bitterly called "reading, writing, ciphering, and flogging." Testing wills by defying all four subjects, but especially the last, became itself a lesson in honor. In 1831 Ashley Curtis had to beat a small boy unmercifully at his school in Wilmington, North Carolina. Curtis was delighted when the other boys stopped cheering the yowling victim on and instead applauded Curtis himself. The boy's parents had urged their son to stand up to the teacher as a point of family pride. Their perversity, Curtis gloated, made his victory over the son's challenge all the sweeter.[24] Schoolmasters elsewhere in the South faced the same issue: parental and child defense of honor against outside authority.

For boys, defiance of adult school authority had wide implications. Disobedience to the teacher helped to distinguish rich from poor and prepared the young planter's son to assume command over lesser folk in the social hierarchy, white and black. The instructor abetted the ritual, not necessarily because he or she accepted the justice of social discriminations, but because livelihood depended upon the favor of the powerful. Teachers, as well as their subjects of instruction, were not held in much esteem: pay was low and performance often incompetent. But even in well-ordered academies it was not always easy to assert the claim *in loco parentis*. For instance, before the Civil War nine-year-old James Claiborne of Virginia led a cavalry charge of youngsters at his North Carolina boarding school. They quickly dispersed the parading plebes, injuring several. The school authorities did not expel him; his father was on the board of trustees. In one case a Kentucky planter's adolescent son shot and killed a teacher for having dared to whip his younger brother. The jury acquitted him, accepting the defense counsel's plea that he had acted to avenge family honor.[25]

Such demonstrations of planter power in behalf of juvenile assertions of honor left no doubts about who had the right to defy nonfamilial authority. Inability to match that level of social self-confidence was one reason small farmers were so reluctant to send their boys to school. Those who did brave the obstacles discovered exactly what planters hoped they would—and should—discover, "that the privileged few must govern," as a Carolinian educator proclaimed in 1852. In Pickens County, Alabama, during the Civil War, Riley Wyatt and his brothers attended a school under the unlikely-named Miss Betty Turnipseed. On one occasion, Wyatt recalled, she had a showdown with Jim Robertson, son of the only wealthy member of that barren community and the leader of class-mates engaged in some prank. "My mother and father never whipped me on bare legs and I am not going to let anybody else do it," Wyatt recorded that Robertson announced. Miss Turnipseed sent him home unpunished. But, along with Riley Wyatt, the other mis-creants, a shoemaker's son and Wyatt's brother Jim, had to undergo the humiliation. Riley and Jim reached their mother's earth-floor cabin with backsides and "undernourished legs" covered with blood. "We were the ultra poor of the school, and had to pay the penalty," Wyatt reminisced. To the classmates, Jim Robertson was no less heroic than Mark Twain's Tom Sawyer. "It was a manly act in so small a boy," Wyatt remarked. Defiance lent stature to the planter's son and gave confidence in his leadership, leaving the poorer ones feeling appropriately inferior. "Poverty made us all timid as it does grown-ups to this good day," Wyatt concluded. Upon such incidents rested many a career in local politics—stories retold thereafter and used to justify support for a former school-mate.[26] Those who had been degraded into obedience looked up to those who repudiated humiliation.

Of course, not all masters and students were locked in perpetual antagonism. The ferrule often met the needs of the moment, re-storing order and ensuring respect for physical force, even when wielded outside the family. Julien Cumming, a little boy of Mt. Zion, Georgia, wrote his mother in 1842, "Mr. Johnston has whipped me once about knocking my old enemy Tom Wade in school. . . . I was very mad at first but after I had thought a little I saw that he was perfectly right in whipping us both." J. G. Clinkscales's South Carolina teacher had a novel way to stop schoolyard disorders: he beat the spectators, not the fighters, in the accurate belief that the group promoted these affairs. Training in the uses of honor was as much a part of the Southern school curriculum as the lessons.[27]

As one would expect, the coming of adolescence opened new de-mands upon and opportunities for male self-expression. In the North, at least among pious families, the entry into puberty was marked by the first religious conversion. It was an occasion to be treasured for a lifetime. Some went through the ordeal of anxious soul-searching in a conventional manner, much as if it were a ceremonial rite of passage. Others took the matter more seriously and suffered acutely. At thirteen, for instance, Henry Lyman, an early-nineteenth-century Connecticut boy, happened to swear aloud in front of friends. According to Lyman's biographer, they teased him with such remarks as, " 'Oh! Henry Lyman, what will your father say if he heard that?' 'My moral nature' quivered and trembled 'under the shock like an aspen,' he recalled. 'I hear even now that oath ringing in my ears . . . that *horrible heavy* mountain that rolled back upon my soul—that withdrawal of the restraints of divine grace.' " Such was the mental state of one bright New England teenager. Lyman later became a foreign missionary.[28]

In Northern mercantile households the rite of passage was often an apprentice clerkship. In Boston of 1827, James Amory, for instance, described the experience in advising a younger brother. It was an early introduction to a lifetime of regularity, punctuality, and close attention to detail. "When 'you go into a store you are [the] youngest apprentice for 2 years. [D]uring that time in summer the store must be opened by 6 o'clock[;] in winter swept & fire made by 7. [Y]ou are then allowed one hour for breakfast[. Y]ou return to the store [,] remain on duty until 2, obliged to run of errands (& unless your writing improves very much not allowed to even copy letters.) [,] return to the store at 3 [,] stay till dark & sometimes till 9 or 10 o'clock." If the apprentice was a success, the merchant might give some instruction in "book-keeping," Amory said.[29]

Neither the religious nor the commercial experience was a common one in the Old South. Instead, boys' entry into young manhood took more social forms, ones that had also marked the youngster of the prior century. Fighting, horse racing, gambling, swearing, drinking, and wenching were all activities that tested the schoolboy's honor among his peers. Philip Fithian, tutor to the Carter boys in the 1770s, described the kinds of "manly" deeds that Virginia teenagers of the gentry class relished so much. Ben Carter, his eldest charge, Fithian said, "has an unconquerable love for Horses," as much an obsession with him as arithmetic and Latin were anathema. "Bobs passion for the same Animal is no less strong, but it is furious & cruel," whereas "Harry's Genius seems toward Cocks, & low Betts, much in company with Waiting Boys, &, against my strongest remonstrances, & frequent severe corrections, he will curse, at times, horribly & swear fearfully!"[30] No waves of remorse rolled over these boys such as did over Henry Lyman.

As for fighting, Ben Carter took the same expressive attitude as he did toward the world of horses and good company. He thought it "best," Fithian reported, "for two persons who have any dispute to go out in good humour & fight manfully, & says they will be sooner and longer friends than to brood and harbour malice." Indeed, that was often the result. Boyish battles were the effective Southern substitute for the religious revival experience. The fights led to long-standing male friendships of an intense, fraternal kind.[31] They prompted ambitions for leadership and provided experience in physical defense, something that even the adult Southern white needed. These were all ways of gaining security in a harsh world, just as the religious conversion was functional in a commercial world in which personal reliability determined one's place in creditors' eyes and in society.

Thus when Northerners were preparing themselves for a career, Southern boys were furthering their experiments in adulthood of another kind. By age fourteen or so many of them had learned to drink, swear, gamble at cards, fight and wrestle, and imitate the mannerisms of older brothers and fathers. In poorer families a dram of whiskey was the early antebellum schoolboy's fare for breakfast. Brantley York, a North Carolinian yeoman's son, seldom left for school, he recalled, without first having a stiff glass. In addition, sexual experiments began. In 1774 Ben Carter, Philip Fithian's charge, took after a slave named Sukey in typical fashion, first pulling her hair and teasing the black girl, then invading the girl's room, where others also were sleeping. Wrapped in a sheet, a *"Thing"* clumped up the back stairs and lay beside her, then escaped when the alarm went up that "a Man was among them. . . ." Not long after Fithian came to suspect that the mysterious intruder was Ben Carter, who by then was slipping out for secret rendezvous with the vivacious Sukey. Indeed, one suspects that planter's sons were more likely to be involved in such affairs than older men. But the nature of miscegenation and its relation to honor must await later discussion.[32]

In regard to most of these activities—drinking, visiting brothels, placing bets at cockfights—parents, especially mothers, carefully shielded themselves from any knowledge. Carter's father, for instance, warned that if the "Ghost" appeared again in Sukey's room when the doors were barred, he would see to it that the culprit was "hanged!"[33] The object was to scare the son into more discretion, for that too was part of growing up a gentleman. The mother's honor was to be protected from the grossness of manhood, the lustiness that was both deplored and celebrated by the men themselves.

As the young male reached the threshold of adulthood, two interrelated problems faced him: how to cope with his feelings of admiration and resentment toward his father, and how to relinquish his dependence upon the family in order to affirm his own right to reputation and deference among peers. "We are thrown upon the performance of the solemn duties of *thinking* and *acting* for ourselves," declared Thomas Jefferson Withers, later a distinguished Carolinian judge. "Boyish trifles are to yield to substantive materials which are to determine the character of our histories. . . ."[34]

In the thrusts toward manhood, particularly in the late teens, the schoolyard handfight of a year or two before became the punctilious duel—at least for those boys raised in homes where church disapproval carried little weight. The purpose of these engagements was no different from that of the earlier fights—the sorting out of who ought to be made leader, who did not qualify. Fathers and concerned kin condoned, even encouraged such behavior, for it connoted a coming of age. For instance John Cantry, a Camden planter, approved his son's upcoming challenge of another teenager, though he begged, through Governor John Manning as intermediary, that the duel be postponed long enough for son James to visit his mother at the family plantation. While there the boy caught a cold. His father claimed disappointment that the illness

had prevented him from drilling his son "in the use of the pistol."
The delay led to a settlement agreeable to all concerned.[35]

Teenage duels were not uncommon, at least in South Carolina
and New Orleans. In 1855 Alfred Huger of Charleston, for instance,
rejoiced in the news that the son of a friend had killed his rival in
a contest. The boy had showed commendable willingness to be "cut
to pieces rather than give an inch or abate a tittle" of his honor,
Huger declared. When James Legaré's son was killed in a similar affair, Huger commiserated with the father, but pointed out,
"Would you call him back today, with his noble spirit tamed or
with his brave & manly bearing humbled! to see him 'live' without
the sensibility to perceive what was due his Honour?" Years of duels
under paternal surveillance produced adventures that excited the
pride of the gentility. Huger rhapsodized, "Give me such a One as
your Brave Boy, aye, in his winding sheet and Napkin, sooner than
another who prefers Existence to *that*, which confers upon Existence its only value."[36] It could be claimed that these sentiments, as
well as the duels themselves, were merely fancies peculiar to romantic personalities. Such was not the case. From sons' early childhood, fathers prepared their boys to observe the rules by which
honor was upheld, as a mark of status and a claim to leadership.

For the small but influential number who attended college,
honor was an unannounced part of the curriculum, both in the
classroom, as a subject revealed in the classics mentioned earlier,
and in the doings of the boys themselves. College students in those
days were much younger than they would be in the twentieth century, and therefore the pranks and scrapes had an adolescent, even
childish character. William J. Grayson recalled how at South Carolina College, President Thomas Cooper, in heavy irony, used to address the students at postchapel assemblies. He called them *"young
gentlemen,"* knowing full well how inapplicable the term was in
light of the previous night's off-campus frolic. At such times, Grayson fondly remembered, "the heart of the boy glows with generous
pride at being treated as a gentleman," especially since the good
feelings were accompanied by a delicious "misgiving, that, at the
moment, the honour bestowed was not altogether merited."[37]

Some antebellum Southern observers recognized that Southern child-rearing methods were inefficacious. Although worries about the young have afflicted aging males of every civilization, there was something rather immediate in the gloomy forecasts of the antebellum years. "More than half the young men raised in the Southern States," declared Elisha Hammond, a schoolteacher, "are sooner or later ruined by dissapation [sic]," and the problem was "too much *dependence* on others." William S. Pettigrew of North Carolina found that too many wealthy fathers had reared not genuine men, but "drones" who were merely "nuisances in the community in which they lived." John Randolph cursed the parasitic *"clodpoles"* who moved from one plantation house party to the next, haunted taverns, and otherwise made mockery of good sense and honest ambition.[38]

Some rightly traced the causes back to early childrearing practices. The Rev. Moses Curtis of Wilmington suggested that active incitement to violent behavior in the first years of life played a major part in Southern aggressiveness. In 1831 he had witnessed a nearly fatal struggle between two young brothers. Though the wife of one of them tried to stop the fracas, their sister urged the younger to kill the older before the reverse occurred. "Their violent tempers have been encouraged by lack of discipline at home," Curtis declared. The problem was not so much a matter of parental laxness, he thought, but a toleration of boyish aggression by everybody—including doting mothers, elder sisters, and grandmothers. Fathers too readily welcomed signs of virility, even before they were appropriate to the child's age. John Randolph noted that too many planters' sons "early assumed airs of manhood; and these premature men remain children the rest of their lives."[39] The reliance upon honor as a social-control mechanism almost assured that young male inclinations for violence, excess, and impulsiveness would arouse mingled admiration and worry in the community. All societies require order, but such affronts to order were themselves the means for preserving it. Self-possession was a Southern virtue, yet it easily became self-aggrandizement. Defense against wrongs was a manly prerogative, though it might quickly degenerate into mean bullying. These were the risks of the Southern style of childrearing, and of the culture as a whole. Few, however, sought to change the priorities; to do so would jeopardize familiar expectations and weaken the resolve to uphold racial and class hierarchy.

In pondering the dilemmas posed by individual assertiveness and group needs, men found a ready scapegoat for the excesses of the young. Conventional opinion blamed the women for feminizing the young men and giving them wrongheaded notions of reality. If only fathers would assert their rightful authority, proclaimed antebellum judges, planters, and editors, Southern manhood would yet revive to meet the challenges of a world gone mad for innovation and venality. The complaints were old ones. Landon Carter in the 1770s had said much the same about motherly indulgences. He was particularly acerbic about the way his son's wife raised his grandchildren. He fumed that "from the knowledge I have of some Ladies' tempers, I don't think there could be a more treacherous, interprising, Perverse and hellish Genius than is to be met with in A Woman," an insidiousness traceable to "Madam Eve" herself. From mothers such as she, he argued, what good could possibly come? On another occasion of rancorous dispute two years earlier, Carter had sarcastically called attention to the way his granddaughter imitated her mother's poor manners at table in the "smearing" of butter "over the plates." The old man's criticisms were greeted with tears and recriminations; to this affront to his dignity he replied by intoning that women "cheat the world by their tears" and "then Pass off their crying [as] a tenderness of their disposition."[40]

Years later, in 1842, in a child adoption case in Mississippi, Chief Justice William L. Sharkey voiced the same long-standing criticism: "A system of training must be adopted which is often repugnant to the wishes of the child. Which is best calculated to do these things, the doting, partial mother with whom every fault is a virtue, every wish a command, or the less partial father who looks to future welfare rather than the gratification of childish folly?"[41] There was already a large degree of antifeminism built into the code of honor that the growing power of women did little to alleviate.

Although there was some truth in the notion of feminine protectiveness toward sons, that too was a part of the very order that men had fashioned. They had made it necessary by their own formidability and also by their fear of curbing their sons' manliness. Beyond that, however, lay the possibility for a woman to express hidden aggressiveness against her husband by uniting with her child in assailing the authority of the father. The patriarchal scheme demanded such manipulations of feeling, similar to those that twisted and discolored the relations of masters and slaves.

The boy and young man had to beware the arbitrary hand of the father, but also the seduction of becoming just like him. "When a father turns a gamester," mused Landon Carter in the mid-eighteenth century, "if he has any children, he must ruin them either by his losses or his example. . . ." Thomas Dew agreed with the sentiment fifty years later. In his view, "lazy, idle fathers" set the example for their sons. But he went beyond the conventional criticism to denounce what he called "the hotbed system." The "plants" within it grew fast under the artificial stimulation of parental license that permitted boys to enjoy men's pleasures while still equipped with only children's emotions. Once in the world, the cold blasts of reality destroyed them. Parents, Dew advised, should not listen to neighbor's foolish advice that " 'it is a shame to keep their boys so long in leading-strings—they should be doing something for themselves.' " Dew charged that the fear of incipient effeminacy "settles every doubt, and the unfortunate youths, in all the perilous immaturity of boyhood, are forthwith converted into men, left to think and act for themselves."[42] They were not always up to the task. In fact, one suspects that in many cases they were not supposed to be. The inherent ambivalence in the father-son relationship was bound to create special difficulties in a slaveholding, patriarchal society.

On the other hand, there were also dangers in the acceptance of a mother's protection. Perhaps because of some keen observations of his son Woodrow's dependence upon his highly protective mother, the Rev. Joseph Wilson of Wilmington, North Carolina, addressed a sermon to the topic in October 1881. He described the ambivalences that existed between mother and boy. Trust, he maintained, was the first requirement for personal growth from infancy. Yet how rare it was, he told his congregation. Mothers withheld ultimate trust, he said, so that even their "most soothing touch" could not allay the child's sense of apartness and nameless dread. He attributed this inner unease to an instinctive search for a "presence whose love is beyond a mother's." But perhaps Wilson's father understood on some level that the ambiguity lay with the mother: a feeling of incompleteness arising from the role assigned her. An unacknowledged resentment of men, even of babies, had to be repressed and hidden in outward shows of affection, a denial to oneself as well as to the object of the manipulative love. The boy sensed it, as did the Rev. Joseph Wilson. "Is there not (always) a draw back sometimes nameless yet real and felt? Is there not, often, an ache like that of the child which no quantity or quality of human love even the most assiduous and most self-sacrificing can soothe— an ache which belongs to the souls own personality independent and unapproachable *individuality* and which accordingly it must just learn to *endure* . . . ?" Wilson had not anticipated Freud, nor did he fully explore his insight into the early signs of sexual conflict and parent-child mistrust. But he did speak of individuals having "a number of selves," not just a sinful one and another capable of reformation, the familiar Christian dichotomy. He had in mind those separate "selves" or drives that arose from the fancies, yearnings, and dreads that modified and sometimes even mocked the outward shows of "feminine" and "masculine" traits. Wilson dared not say that there was much of the "feminine" in men— a curious passivity, a paralyzing lethargy even as a danger approached—or that in women there could be a hardness of soul, an ability to cripple the most masculine of men using only words, looks, and demeanor. These "selves" could hardly have appeared in a Presbyterian clergyman's lecture to a Southern audience in 1881. But Joseph Wilson's habit of introspection, a rare characteristic in Southern life, had brought him close to the essence of the matter. He at least saw dilemma and tragedy where others recognized only overindulgence, dissipation, villainy—terms stark and one-dimensional.[43] But even this Old School Presbyterian divine, whose son would one day rule the nation, did not wholly grasp the emotional brittleness of Southern men, fathers and sons. Their fragility in relation to each other, their common ambivalence about mothers and wives who might unman them, exposed their vulnerability and led to fierce defensiveness.

Mothers had to cheer their sons' little victories of pride or stand apart in mortification and silence. They too admired the male honor that deprived them of all but vicarious pleasure in the achievements of their men. Yet beneath it all there was the same kind of ambivalence that the Italian novelist Leonardo Sciascia has portrayed in regard to Sicilian mothers. For him "many wrongs, many tragedies of the South, have come to us from the women, above all when they become mothers. . . . How many crimes of honor has she provoked, instigated or encouraged! . . . They are capable of the worst kinds of wickedness just in order to make up for the vexations they themselves were subjected to when they were young, as part of a terrifying social conformism. 'Ah, yes,' they seem to be saying, 'you are my son's wife? Well, he's worth his weight in gold!' " Living up to that demand was not easy for the son in the antebellum South. Once John Sharp Williams asked an old veteran of the Civil War why he and his fellow troopers had fought so desperately, so bravely, when they knew all along the cause had already been hopelessly crushed. " 'We were afraid to stop.' Afraid of what?" asked the Mississippi senator. " 'Afraid of the women at home, John. They would have been ashamed of us.' "[44] For this same reason the Germanic tribes of long ago had fought so fiercely, as Tacitus reported.

Although it was true that the patriarchal scheme in which children were nurtured chiefly benefited the men, women had their largely unconscious revenge. They compelled the men to live up to virtues that often enough could kill as well as sanctify. The historian William L. Barney describes a flag presentation on Independence Day, 1856, in Cahaba, Alabama, a ceremony in which the women took the chief parts. As she gave the battle flag to the commanding officer, Mrs. Lizzie English enjoined those present to "remember that we placed it in your hands, and bade you never yield it but with your lives; and if it must fall, let it only be to cover the lifeless form of him in whose charge we gave it." Captain Dawson made the appropriate reply to "the fair donors" and promised that "the agonies of death will be softened in the reflection that our pledge is redeemed; that we have obeyed your injunction to preserve it pure and stainless, at the price of our lives."[45]

Beneath such feminine advocacy of male valor there lay, perhaps, a hidden bitterness. Daughters, sisters, and wives were held in high esteem, but it was the men who counted in life within as well as outside the family. From childhood to young maturity girls were constantly reminded not to compete for male honors but to show love and submission to fathers, brothers, and husbands. A ladylike humility about mental agility, creative talent, and other marks of distinction beyond domestic skills earned the girl and woman praise, particularly if it enhanced the contrasting accomplishments of their men. Mary Chesnut, the South Carolinian diarist, sometimes grew impatient with such talk, being herself quite proud of her wit and social acumen. In wartime Richmond she and her friends spoke of these circumstances. "But you know, our women all speak in that low, plaintive way because they are always excusing themselves for something they never did." Another in the sewing group said, "Knit your stocking. We have had enough for today." A third added, "And the Yankee women are loud and shrill because they fight it out—fair field and no favor—and when incompatibility comes in, they go out for divorce." The Southern feminine recourse was, rather, limited to silent anger. One suspects that Southern women's vicarious bloodthirstiness had its origins in these demeaning conditions. On one occasion, Mrs. Chesnut reported, a Confederate officer grew a little alarmed at the constant female boasting about male prowess at war. "Those women who are so frantic for their husbands to join the army would like them killed, no doubt," he said. Certainly they had no such conscious thoughts, but there was an ambiguity about the business all the same.[46]

Conformity to community expectations required that the women be ever watchful of their own actions, suppressing in themselves any wayward signs and cajoling the men they loved to pay strict attention to the social ideals. Though on some level they may have had doubts about the duplicities and vainglory that male honor so often embraced, Southern matrons spun webs of illusions of their own. They sheltered from themselves the truth of their menfolk's inner misgivings and weaknesses, bravely smiling away disappointments and chagrin for appearances' sake. They were no more in touch with their feelings than were the boys they raised. Instead, both genders relied upon conventional community wisdom about death, honor, and battle glory to let them know how they were supposed to feel. The scheme of honor, the fear of shame gave too much play to jealousy, malice, and physical and social competitiveness by endowing these basic human sins with the rationale of sensitivity to self-esteem. The ambivalences of mothers toward their young sons, their dependents and their future masters; the latent hostilities of boys toward their fathers, their models and their rivals; and the mixed emotions of fathers toward their sons, their replications and their future replacements—all these familial strains had few direct outlets. They had to be hidden from society and from inner consciousness. Families were supposed to be refuges of love and protection, but did not always meet this lofty standard. The early pressures on a child to conform to gender role were almost bound to find expression in the family that he or she created in adulthood. Young men carried into their marriages the same compulsions that parents had borne in themselves and expressed in their childrearing practices. The lineage of fathers and forefathers, whose accomplishments weighed so heavily, continued to be a source of pride, but also of persistent compulsiveness and sometimes tragic disorder.

7

A Young Man's Career:
Cultural and Familial Limits

In all the strategies for individual male advance in the South, from the choosing of a career to marriage to a wealthy first cousin, as the case might be, the party ordinarily to be reckoned with was the young man's father. He ensured the stability of the family system, even when he was sometimes a cause of frustration. The situation very much resembled the English gentry world, with its desperate and hard-headed young people and mistrusting elders. One can find them well described in such novels as Jane Austen's *Sense and Sensibility* and Anthony Trollope's Palliser series and *Castle Richmond*. So slow was the young man's professional advance, blocked by older occupiers of positions standing in the way, that enforced idleness and the need for security and wealth often prompted even respectable men to bend principle to whatever opportunities arose, however slim they were. The pressures at home and in the world at large were such that the system generated quantities of that familiar Southern figure, the "black sheep." There seemed to be at least one in every generation of established families: men who repudiated religious precept and conventional morality and gave authenticity to the common sobriquets of the day: scoundrel, rogue, ne'er-do-well.

Not everyone was equipped to be a successful planter. Speaking of two of his sons, James H. Hammond complained that they were mismanaging the estates he had provided for their experiments in adulthood. The pair was "all sham, fudge gammon & every *negro* knows it to be so," he fumed. "They don't pull off their coats or go at it. They shoot birds, buy fish & gerrymander the County," and the neighbors, overseers, and slaves were fast becoming aware that they were destined to be "dilletanti—theatrical planters." It did not occur to Hammond, or to many fathers similarly vexed, that their own attitudes toward their sons might have stimulated the inappropriate responses.[1]

The first obstacle a young man faced was the narrowness of opportunity that both fathers and society provided him. The slave economy, traditional values, and the intrusions of family all conspired to leave the ordinary youth with a single alternative: farm, as Hammond's sons pretended to do, or starve. Raised to live an outdoor life and exercise power over slaves, most young planters' sons were not much concerned to try other possibilities. With wealth so concentrated in the form of slaves, there was an insufficient incentive to embark on unfamiliar commercial ventures. The actual number of plantation households was surprisingly small and restrictive. Seventy-five percent of the male population owned no slaves at all. Seventy-three percent of those who did held fewer than ten. Yet those fortunate enough to be raised in large-scale planter families were in a most enviable position. Even in frontier Texas, 2 percent of the heads of households held one-third of the state's wealth. According to Gavin Wright, the economic historian, 90 to 95 percent of all agricultural wealth was in the hands of slaveholders by 1860. Most of the rest of Southern whites simply farmed or raised cattle and hogs.[2]

Hindered by educational disadvantages, the consequent psychic obstacles, and maldistribution of wealth, not many whites below the high gentility were in a position to gain status or livelihood by entering some occupation outside agricultural or pastoral enterprise. Thus by the 1850 census, for example, Alabama had only fifteen college professors, Mississippi sixteen. In journalism matters were no better. Georgia had only 190 newsmen, whereas Maine, a comparably rural, underpopulated state, boasted 258. In the southwest printers were exceedingly few: thirty in Alabama, thirty-four in Mississippi.[3] Fairly representative of the problem, these figures signified the structure of power as well as the essential priorities of the society. The uniformity of objectives, with career options narrowed toward planting, was a commentary on the kind of individuality the South produced. For all the pride in self-reliance and liberty, few Americans were as devoted as Southerners were to the economic shackles of tradition. That sort of restrictiveness about livelihood was also bound to affect the general willingness of individuals to strike out on different moral, cultural, and social paths.

In contrast to the developments of a diverse Northern economy, planting was a specialty without professional spirit. Whereas Yankees were learning how to separate family from work, professional criteria from parochial values, individual preferences from community sanctions, Southern planters rejoiced in the persistence of old habits. "They all like to follow the same beaten track," remarked a Southern girl, just married.[4] Custom played so marked a role in most men's careers that it was hard to inject the most rudimentary notions of a professional nature. Few low-country communities lacked an agricultural society. These organizations might have developed into more than gatherings where squires congratulated each other in good years, commiserated in bad, yet by and large the agrarian chapter languished. As one scholar has observed, they survived, in South Carolina at least, chiefly to hold annual banquets to praise the glories of rustic stability in a fast-changing world. Those who bothered to attend were often told of the sins of the absentees, mired down in lethargy and backwardness. Stephen Elliott, planter-bishop of Georgia, for instance, noted how difficult it was for the sovereign "Lord of all he surveys" to break out of "the routine of old practices and traditional modes of action, especially as he had a profound contempt for . . . book farming of any kind. His father grew rich upon such an experience and it would be filial irreverence for him to engage in any new fangled schemes for the improvement of his homestead and grounds."[5]

In the Southwest, Charles C. Langdon, agrarian reformer, re-marked that it took "no mental effort, no study, no observation, hardly the labor to think" to raise cotton. Southern historical re-positories are laden with the meticulous records of a tiny number of professionally minded planters who seem to have given the lie to Elliott's and Langdon's words. Yet raping the land made profits for anyone with capital and spirit. Southern wealth was as great as modern economic historians claim, but not because of scientific planning. Most cash-cropping slaveholders owed their good fortune to insatiable European and New England demand for cotton tex-tiles, to protective tariffs on imported sugar and hemp, or to grow-ing urban centers in need of truck produce and grains. For every experimentalist like Edmund Ruffin of Virginia, William S. Petti-grew of North Carolina, or John H. Cocke with his estates in Vir-ginia and Alabama, there were three-score planters who never kept more records than a crude account book and a list of slaves and im-plements. Often they left it to the courts to document more exactly their credits, debits, and total holdings in wills, deeds, and in-dentures.[6]

Decisions against systematizing were not just based on ignorance or laziness. Some, at least, were deliberately, even truculently op-posed to the ways of the "manufacturing and large commercial centers" and their allegedly stultifying and impersonal values. Farm-ers, even large planters, refused to subscribe to agricultural jour-nals "on principle," as one historian recently concluded. "Now let me tell you," declared the old state's rights Jeffersonian Nathaniel Macon at the close of the War of 1812, "that on one plantation, the war system has been continued, that is, not raise much for sale, & buy less; it is true the land is poor & stoney, but it is honestly made, enough to have full bellies and warm clothes for any time of the year."[7] Most planters willingly tied themselves to the market econ-omy, but preferred defensive over innovative tactics.

Farming was a constant drama of death and birth—the violence of hog-killing, the tasks of calving, even the "correction" of unruly slaves—all part of the same comforting routines and duties. They were life itself. In a breezy conversation, Louis T. Wigfall made fun of "Farmer" George Washington who, with his "beautiful English hunting watch," used to time "Cuffy" to increase the labor of his hands—a practice out of line with the Carolinian Way, Wigfall claimed. Besides, overwork by either master or slave was thought "impractical." "Dr. William Porcher used to plant only three acres of cotton to the hand, against the advice his brother, Mr. T. Porcher," wrote T. W. Peyre of Statesboro, South Carolina. Since then, the plantation, called Sarrazins, had come under T. Porcher's management. He "planted a great deal more & does not make as much." Moreover, Peyre argued, a leisurely pace had its consolation—"that your negroes are not hard worked. And if your overseer is wanting in experience, it is particularly desirable to plant little to the hand" because "none but an experienced man can manage a large crop. We have commenced hunting fox. . . ." Pleasure, prestige and profit were all supposed to be happily combined in the farming enterprise. Edmund Ruffin, the Virginia agrarian reformer, also included "the cultivation of mental and social qualities," a way of living he regarded as far superior to the Yankee compulsion to organize and make the silver clink. He even brought a son back to Virginia from studies in Connecticut when the youth showed too much admiration for Yankee habits. In the opinion of Ruffin's planting colleague and fellow polemicist George Fitzhugh, farming "is the recreation of great men, the proper pursuit of dull men."[8]

High calling though planting was, old, distinguished Virginia families had to face severe declensions in the post-Revolutionary era. Population increases, narrowed economic opportunities, and worn-out lands were among the factors that reduced wealth. In a very persuasive study of Tidewater Virginia, Lorraine Eva Holland has recently shown that members of the "Old Elite" of whom John Randolph had spoken in 1831 had found themselves in increasingly straitened circumstances as the years passed. Fortunes like those of the Byrds, Nelsons, and Pages had been built upon diversified investments in land, slaves, merchandising, and cash-cropping. But economic and agricultural conditions had not kept pace with family needs. Some sons went west to new lands. The solution for those remaining, especially sons low in the birth order, was often professional training and migration to county seats and to such towns as Norfolk, Richmond, Petersburg, and Baltimore. But the fields of law and medicine were so crowded as a result that the move did not bring riches equal to those of the prior generation. Even for someone as gifted as Beverley Tucker, son of the famed Judge St. George Tucker, country practice at law proved no remedy, providing him with neither "honor nor profit," as he said. Whether in country or town, physicians fared little better.[9]

By contrast, firstborns were more fortunate because, unless the estate had been thoroughly dissipated, the eldest in the family line ordinarily received the prime holdings. Family strategy, not some rigid veneration for primogeniture, required that old wealth be vouchsafed to a single heir if family honor were to be preserved. The last in the birth order, Holland observes, was most likely of all sons never to have the means to attract a suitably prominent bride; the ratio of bachelors among younger sons was greater than among firstborns. If the noninheriting sons did marry, they did so much later than their elder brothers. As a result their families were usually smaller than the ones into which they were born. In fact family size declined among the Old Elite over the generations, indicating the declension of profitable planting. Holland's statistics show the figures gleaned from forty-nine Virginia blueblood households: first generation (when the estate was first created), 2.3 children; second generation (one that enjoyed the fruits thereof), 4.1; third generation (in which wealth was diminishing or static), 3.4; fourth generation (in decline), 2.9. Despite the gloomy circumstances, descendants of the once powerful clans did not readily move into trade, unless lucky marriages provided fresh capital on a large scale. In Charleston, for instance, James Johnston Pettigrew complained in 1849 that a male cousin had married into a common trading family. "The fact of [her father] having exercised a menial occupation is enough for me; for although some of the Pettigrews have been starvingly poor, and great drunkards, yet none ever condescended to buy and sell or engage in any business of life, which was not compatible with thorough and perfect independence. Though poor, they have always farmed their own soil and stepped [into?] . . . their own inheritance as Cincinatus [*sic*] or our own Teutonic ancestor."[10]

By the 1840s and 1850s, however, there was considerable loosening of such antique prejudices, much to the distress of the older planter circle. Some gentry folk were indeed bitter, most notably that crotchety bachelor David Gavin of South Carolina. In 1856 he lamented, "Times are sadly different now from what they were when I was a boy." At that time, "you had the oldest grant then," and "the younger would give up, but now you must prove possession. . . . [N]ow many live on credit, or by some swindling process. . . ."[11] In the Southwest such sentiments were rare, and scions of old families as well as upcoming small farmers trafficked in any enterprise that could make a profit without any stigma being attached. Nevertheless, the primary vocation remained planting.

In light of the transciency of agrarian wealth, historians have lately discerned deep-seated anxieties in the constant boasting about the superiority of the country life. Indeed, in the older states of the South worry was masked by references to Jeffersonian virtue. But in the Southwest, where fortunes could still be made in relatively short order, the rhetoric struck chords of self-confidence, even complacency. Colonel John L. Hunter of Eufala, Alabama, a Carolinian planter who had helped to drive out the Creeks from the vicinity, exemplified in 1840 the positive attitude about plantation living. Wholly unconscious of any contradictions or misgivings, he rhapsodized about its many blessings. "The Management and labors of the field expand the mind—elevate the thoughts—inspire the energy and promote the health of the scientific cultivator," he declaimed.[12]

Though careful management might make even the long-cultivated plantation thrive, not everyone was very skilled at the business. Thomas Jefferson, for instance, loved the life but not its financial side. Similarly, James L. Petigru of South Carolina, had talents only for the law, not for plantation responsibilities. Yet he could not relinquish the latter obligation without seeming to betray Carolinian sanctities. Whether one was a skillful lawyer, doctor, or clergyman, such an occupation was often a means to gain planter status, rather than to desert it. "As soon as the young lawyer acquires sufficient to purchase a few hundred acres of rich alluvial lands, and a few slaves," wrote a Yankee observer living in Adams County, Mississippi, "he quits his profession at once, though perhaps just rising into eminence, and turns cotton planter."[13]

By the 1850s, however, some rarer spirits were beginning to adopt a more programmatic view of their calling. Mrs. Mary Jones, wife of the Rev. Charles C. Jones, astutely perceived the conflict between slaveholding and professional life. "As your brother and yourself are professional men [physician and lawyer]," she wrote her son Charles C. Jones, Jr., "we have desired that you should never be involved in planting or the management of Negroes. Properly attended, it brings great care, great anxiety, expenses that must be met. . . . All these you will realize more and more . . . especially if you are an enlightened, conscientious master. . . ." Charles, however, felt the pressure to do as others did. He planned on a venture in Bryan County, Georgia, but finally did abandon it because, as a well-educated and devout young man, he felt out of place amidst the crudities of a typical planter neighborhood.[14] Although personal specializations were no doubt increasing just before the war, only the most self-possessed young man, like Jones, could defy sacred custom to pursue his own course without fearing neighborhood criticism.

The same conservatism that limited men to planting also found expression in other professions. Armand de Rosset, a planter and physician of Wilmington, North Carolina, boasted in 1847, "My grandfather, my father and myself and both my sons have been practitioners of medicine in this place." All of them had been and were plantation owners as well. In the Marbury clan of Prince Georges County on the western shore of Maryland, there was at least one planter-lawyer in four successive generations. Even after some members had moved to Baltimore at mid-century the ties to the land remained. The pattern was anything but exceptional. The reason was not just a romantic attachment to land, however much that sentiment was proclaimed in the South, but also economic. Part-time plantation management provided income and security in a very uncertain world, especially in the declining years of life. A father could look forward to retirement on the plantation while the son took up the duties of his law or medical practice. Traditionalism and practicality were mutually reenforcing.[15]

Such traditions no doubt encouraged some sons to strive for excellence—a desire to be worthy of so strong a family heritage. But inherited occupations could also lead to nepotism and tolerated incompetence. In the tight little world of Southern gentlefolk, the very weakness of nonfamilial institutions made them very vulnerable to family manipulations. Well-placed young men benefited from the easy opportunities that kinship offered them, but nonfamily institutions were bound to be vulnerable to powerful family pressures. George F. Holmes, for instance, owed his professorship at the University of Virginia not to his talents (although he had some), but to his wife's belonging to the influential Floyd clan.[16] Such things were also possible in Northern circles, but the North's more diverse vocations, insensitivity (at times) to the claims of family bonds, and more ingrained notion of work meant that the young man there more often had to rely upon other means to make his own way.

The Southern bank was peculiarly subject to family exploitation, being a relatively untried and usually undercapitalized institution. "Strictly speaking," boasted Governor Whitemarsh Seabrook of South Carolina, "there are no capitalists among us. Men whose profession is to deal in monied securities are rarely found in an agricultural community." He was right. A reason for it, though, was that family patronage interfered with the growth of professional methods and standards. The problem was not just a matter of class and planter interest in restricting financing to the agricultural community, as historian Eugene Genovese has explained, but also a lack of knowledge about other possibilities and a commitment to helping "friends," that is, relatives who belonged to the same social and political circle as the banks' managers. So at least complained former Governor Hammond of South Carolina. The founders of the state bank, he fumed in his diary, had sought chiefly to preserve their familial wealth (jeopardized "by the repeal of primogeniture of 1790"), provide jobs for young relatives, and maintain political power by these means. Only a few able spirits had prevented it from "exploding as would have happened before now." Likewise the Bank of North Carolina offered convenient patronage posts for the powerful Erwin clan from its founding in 1810 to 1859. In 1829 the mismanaged branch in Burke County nearly closed; nonetheless a son-in-law of the disgraced bank president was chosen his successor.[17]

In Alabama, Andrew Pickens, the brother of Governor Israel Pickens, was first president of the state bank. Based upon the South Carolina model, the bank followed the same exclusive style, though directorships and staff posts were allocated according to networks of neighbors as well as kin. No wonder banks were not popular. They serviced the needs of some clans and their intimate friends, but those who were left out had reason to complain. Though the whole society suffered from the deficiencies of the system, it was the unconnected young man trying to make his way in life who found his chance for employment or for financing most painfully restricted by monopolies of this kind.[18]

The occupation of politics had a familial, closed character no less than banking. A young aspirant for office almost had to have a large and strategically placed set of kinfolks. Young candidates without them had a much harder time breaking into the fairly small circle of local officeholders. Entry into such a clique was necessary before the officeseeker could even think of moving up into the larger spheres of public service. Freshmen candidates were expected to have the active support of a whole clan; they in turn were supposed to be as faithful to local traditions as the neighbors were to their candidacy. The effect was to narrow the purposes of officeholding. In a sense, elections were not just opportunities for civic improvement in a locale, but ratifications of a family's claim to honor. They also provided some visibility for its young representative in his struggle for place and position.

In working out family relations for political advantage, a novice officeseeker had to be assiduous in extending claims for kin support. Older politicians, with alliances of more complexity, could take such loyalties for granted, but not younger ones. For instance, the youthful Mrs. Benjamin Perry had to carry matters rather far in drumming up support for her husband in his first try for state office from Greenville, South Carolina. George Whilleman, a mattress maker of their acquaintance, mentioned a connection to one of Mrs. Perry's kin. She reported the conversation to Perry: "*Mrs. Peters!* Why she married mamma's cousin so only think I found out that George Whilleman is related to the Whilleman's in Charleston, who are a very respectable family now," though of "low origin." She urged her husband to cultivate the illiterate craftsman.[19]

Under these circumstances, family connections counted as much as or more than platforms, professional qualifications, and character, especially in those state positions that young men sought to fill. As often as not the incumbent had family ties that shut out the untried and ill-connected young careerist. When Alabama was first settled, the entire state, according to a recent study, was dominated "politically, economically and socially" by the "cousinry."[20]

Other states, especially the more settled ones, were even more exclusive in the management of government positions, especially on the local level. Kentucky neighborhoods, according to a recent account, provided abundant evidence of this. In Franklin County, for instance, the family of McKee had "preponderating influence in the county court." Family members obtained nearly all the coveted posts. Nor was North Carolina immune. The Pooles of Pasquotank and the Riddicks of Perquimans were firmly entrenched in county offices throughout the antebellum period. Virginia's Princess Anne County was in the hands of the interconnected Cornicks, Kellams, and Calverts. The Taliaferro family of Amherst County, Virginia, so monopolized the magistracy there that a young officeseeker complained to Governor William G. Giles in 1827. He wrote that there were almost no justices of the peace three miles beyond the county seat, an inconvenience to residents farther away, because the Taliaferro in-laws, cousins, and nephews all lived within that vicinity. These examples are by no means idiosyncratic. Even when formerly appointive positions were opened to election, family connections often continued to hinder the young aspirant for county office from challenging old and well-affiliated incumbents. Politics, of course, did offer an alternative to planting, particularly to young lawyers, but the tendency was to elect men either well fixed in the planter hierarchy or with every sign that they would take up the business of farming once their political and legal career was underway.[21]

To some degree, politics in the rural North followed similar patterns, with family ties a significant factor in the launching of a career. The historian Ronald P. Formisano has noted that in Michigan, for instance, people "described 'heredity in politics' as 'stronger even than in religion' and that 'It was expected as a matter of course that partisan politics would descend from sires to sons with unbroken regularity.' " Northern officeseeking, whether under one party label or another, also grew out of those foundations. Yet in a more pluralistic and complex society such expectations were bound to erode more swiftly than in the homogeneous South.[22]

In the North teaching, charity jobs, and sometimes low-paying government posts served as temporary expedients for young men still in search of more lasting and satisfying commitments. Though often transitory, such employment served to give ambitious youths time and experience for planning their futures, while the organizations for which they worked benefited from the services of highly skilled young men. Samuel G. Howe, Horace Mann, and Elizur Wright, all prominent reformers later in life, began their careers in this way. Ofttimes the eager recruits continued in the work of reform or service. Many more, though, went on to other jobs of a conventional nature.[23]

In contrast, posts that could offer a psychological moratorium for the gifted young man were rather scarce in the Old South. Teaching, as in the North, gave temporary occupation. But even in this sphere openings were limited. Chances to be a plantation tutor or academy master were snatched up by Yankee college graduates, whose credentials from Princeton, Yale, and other schools gave them a decided advantage over home-trained rivals. By and large it was the "Old Field" school, with its low pay, that belonged to the native-born. Ordinarily the posts were filled by incompetents, drunk-

ards, and sometimes ignorant bullies. One such specimen was Major
Bouchelle. He had succeeded Miss Betty Turnipseed at the school in
Pickens County, Alabama. She had whipped only the poor children,
a practice that he also adopted. An opium addict and veritable
"sepulchre of rum," the major spent as much time at the grog shop
as at the schoolhouse. He prided himself on his one-time friendship
with S. S. Prentiss, a famous Mississippi orator and gentleman of
leisure. By local standards Bouchelle was a model of "high intelligence" and "profound learning." Once the major, lying drunk in
the road, was spied by some passing matrons. One sighed aloud at
the sight of so intellectual a man in so pitiable a state. Bouchelle,
without getting up, tipped his hat and said, "Yes, Madam, though
covered with dust the jewel yet shines."[24]

Government and charity posts were few and far between. The
struggling institutions that did exist attracted few qualified native
young men. The Rev. P. Lane, superintendent of the Mississippi
Institute for the Blind, reported in 1852 on his labors in a way that
cast doubt on his capabilities. Typical of the state of Southern bu-
reaucracy, Lane complained that parents refused to send him their
children out of a "senseless indulgence and mistaken tenderness,"
and instead kept them at home. But all he had to offer the eleven
inmates in his charge was a single course in basket-making. Even he
had to admit that the products were "tolerable at best." Though the
South made some progress in mental institutional care (in Virginia
and Kentucky especially), the standards for the custodianship of the
handicapped and indigent were abysmal.[25]

The ministry might have been an obvious field for the aspiring
poor youth. In the North it functioned chiefly for the advancement
of those without much capital. Unlike merchandising or doctoring,
the ministerial calling required no capital or purchased clientage,
but only an investment in education. In the South, however, the
ministry lacked social standing unless it was coupled with plantation ownership. Some gentlefolk did combine the duties. The Pettigrew, Polk, Elliott, Gailor, Bratton, Green, Barnwell, Tucker, and
DuBose families produced a succession of Episcopal luminaries.
Most of them married well. Presbyterians not only had similar

dynasties but even the beginnings of a string of seminaries in the region. Nevertheless, even in these faiths a surprising number of the best appointments went to Northerners, better trained and in full supply. As one scholar has recently pointed out, a large number of proslavery tracts and sermons came from these imported divines, who were usually situated in the more affluent parishes. They salved both their Yankee consciences and their wealthy congregations with fantasies about the perfections of slavery. Thus, even when it came to defending the "home institution" the Southern-born young clergy-man could boast no monopoly of insight or erudition to entitle him to perference as a pastor to slaveholders.[26]

Nor was his occupation a very attractive one once a Southern-born cleric was installed in his first church. Presbyterian and Epis-copalian ministers could at least justly claim to reach the planter elite; if lucky, they could marry into wealth. Otherwise, though, the pay was low, commensurate with the poor attendance. A young Episcopal clergyman from Maryland wrote home in 1839 from his first parish in Demopolis, Alabama, that his wealthy parishioners showed "much coldness and indifference, particularly among the gentlemen" when the plate was passed. Without the donations of a handful of ladies, "I do not know what we should do."[27]

These problems were even more severe in the Methodist and Baptist churches. Although some city churches provided profes-sional standing and decent conditions for their pastors, young men on circuit or in rural missions could not manage on the pittance offered. By and large, what was given was by way of charity and done purely "from friendship" and not as "compensation for valu-able services," according to a New England observer.[28] Needless to say, these denominations looked for qualities other than education and gentle upbringing in the selection of preachers, and only in the larger cities could one accurately refer to a professional class of Baptist and Methodist ministers.

In the 1820s a younger breed of clergymen started agitating for regular salaries and full-time employment. National voluntary asso-ciations, chiefly based in the Northeast, were urging churches every-where to establish chapters for the spread of tracts, Bibles, Sunday schools, for foreign evangelism and other aims. The evangelical movement that stimulated these goals also stressed the building of seminaries and the establishment of religious newspapers, and national, regional, and state clerical associations to coordinate the programs. Such activities provided justifications for making the clerical office a full-time and more prestigious profession.[29]

Older Baptist and Methodist clergymen grew restive about these attempts to erode the church as they knew it. Perceiving the church as a family and community gathering, they disdained the *"money-making factoried"* priesthood with its collection of "Mite Societies, Children Societies, and even Negro Societies." They all smelled, said one Kentucky planter-preacher, "of the *New England Rat*." The antimodernist movement pitted the farmer-preachers against the generally more youthful newcomers to the calling, sometimes seminary trained, but poor as young men usually were. In a recent study a scholar has discovered that 34 percent of the Missionary Baptists at a key North Carolina convention were between twenty and thirty years old. Their anti-Mission opponents mustered only 12 percent in that age category.[30] Complicated as the conflict was, with its wide theological, sectional, and racial overtones, the struggle also concerned professionalization and generational conflicts. Largely because they represented a trend running through all of Western Christendom, the supporters of "associationism" soon outdistanced their reactionary opponents, who adhered to familial, part-time church management. But truculence toward learned "eastern men" and benevolent society agents—"well-dressed beggars"—lingered even in Missionary Baptist and Methodist ranks.[31]

In the newer vocations of engineering, factory and railroad construction and management, and specialized commerce, Southern young men with economic and technical abilities were also at a disadvantage. What was accomplished in the slave states in these areas owed little to the native-born young. For instance, in Mobile, Alabama, according to a recent study, most positions of an innovative character were held by foreigners and Northerners. Even in such fields as law, journalism, and merchandising, a third of the lawyers, editors, and factors were newcomers from the Northern states or were foreigners. Two-thirds of carpenters and 100 percent of bank officers, bricklayers, brokers, blacksmiths, builders, and auctioneers were recent arrivals. On the other hand, 100 percent of the planters with Mobile townhouses were native Southerners. Though they had not been quickly welcomed to the inner circles of power, almost 40 percent of the municipal leaders (from 1820 to 1860) had Yankee backgrounds, with foreigners providing another 16.3 percent of the total.[32] The situation was rather parallel with that of developing nations where the innovative fields become the preserve of outsiders from the advanced sector. No doubt Southern unrest over Yankee criticisms of slavery owed much to the fears that an imbalanced dependence on outside experts in lucrative fields had left the region politically and culturally vulnerable. But it was also an indication of the limits of Southern career choices. The tendency was to fall back upon the comforts of family ties rather than meet the competition that these specialists from elsewhere provided. A satirical verse about the city of Charleston's style bore much validity: " 'I thank thee, Lord on bended knee I'm half Porcher and half Huger . . . For other blessings thank thee too—My grandpa was a Petigru. . . ."[33]

Perhaps the mathematically inclined young man had even fewer means of testing his capabilities in Southern society than the literary young aspirant. His best opportunity was attendance at West Point, where civil engineering was taught. Even so, appointments generally went to those with family connections in the United States Congress, whose members made the nominations. Robert E. Lee, Albert Sidney Johnston, and others with special talents of this kind gained admitttance. Yet, more than Northerners of similar inclinations—George McClellan, for instance—they tended to remain in service or enter politics or planting rather than take up careers in civil engineering, banking, or the railroad. In the academic sciences, the story of Lewis Gibbes of Charleston illustrates a typical situation. He owed his appointment to a professorship of mathematics at the college in Columbia as much to family patronage as to his qualifications for the post. To ensure his appointment, Henry De-Saussure, a wealthy Charleston aristocrat, urged Gibbes to cultivate the wider network of his kinspeople, the Gibbes family having declined somewhat in wealth because of too many subdivisions in their once extensive holdings. "You are connected by blood with the Miss Pinckneys. Allow me to say that you ought to present yourself to them," DeSaussure advised. Gibbes did obtain the job, largely through family connections. Yet Yankees and foreigners were much more likely to have the necessary skills for such positions, and thereby obtained a healthy share of them. Once again the Southerner was ill-equipped, by the cultural order of the South, to make his way in professions requiring specialized, technical knowledge.[34]

The only occupation that enjoyed the same prestige accorded planting and the planter-professions of medicine and law was military service. So much has been said about the Southern inclination to war and military honors that the point need not be dwelt on here. Veneration of warrior virtue owed very little to the "cavalier" tradition as it appeared in the literary tastes of the antebellum Southerner. Instead it reflected the more primitive concern with courage as a social value; tastes in fiction and occasional mock tournaments serviced that more basic notion. James C. Bonner and Wilbur Cash have insisted that frontier conditions, slavery, and race repression were the bases of martial ardor. These factors certainly gave immediacy to the usefulness of soldiering, but actually the occupation was held up to popular acclaim because it was the most efficacious means of exhibiting and defending personal, family, regional, and national honor. Long after the frontier had disappeared, long after slavery ended, and even long after the black proportion of the Southern population began its decline in the twentieth century, that martial spirit has steadfastly remained a Southern characteristic.

Yet in terms of opportunities, Southern youth found that the professional life of the soldier entailed serious disadvantages. It may be true, as the historian James C. Bonner observed, that antebellum "Southerners occupied nearly every important position in the United States Army, and Southern statesmen had filled the office of Secretary of War since 1849." Moreover, there is no gainsaying that the best families of the South contributed many more general officers than equally prominent Yankee households. Whereas the leading Massachusetts families, the Channings, Cabots, Lowells and others, furnished only nine officers from their midst, the Lees of Virginia alone offered ten, with four achieving the rank of major general. The Randolphs also supplied ten in the prewar years. It must be remembered, however, that the American army was too small and the turnover too slow to make military service a promising occupation for very many. Moreover, if a young officer had hopes of marrying well, his assignments often carried him far from the best hunting fields for courtship. When resignations were on the increase, as they were in the Seminole War period of the 1830s, for instance, promotions came faster, but the resignations themselves testified to poor army morale. Moreover, unconnected young officers discovered to their dismay that choice postings and advancements often went to those with political influence, the same situation that afflicted their brothers and cousins in the legal and academic professions in the South. "I presume I shall remain in the army, and perhaps be a captain by the time I am sixty," lamented a friend of Jubal Early in 1838. "It seems like a joke, but d——n me if I don't think there is a good deal of truth in it." His estimation was not far from the mark. During the decade 1824 to 1834, the ordinary second lieutenant of twenty upon graduation from West Point could expect to reach captain at age fifty-four. His chances of making major before retirement were practically nil. The circumstances in the United States Navy, a branch of service not especially appealing in the South, which lacked New England's seaward tradition, was not much better. How much easier it was to obtain a repute for warrior spirit *and* the honors of rank through the militia, which could be combined with planting and the other traditional professions. As James Bonner points out, even as recently as 1955 as many as twenty-five hundred rural Georgia lawyers gave themselves the title of "Colonel," an honorary appellation derived from the militia heritage.[35]

At the heart of the problem of career choices was the primitive state of Southern education. The field was itself grimly unprofessional in all its aspects. So demoralized and undersupported was the system in Kentucky that only 20,402 children attended school in 1852, out of a population of 173,988 eligible youngsters. In 1830, 73 percent of school-age children in Massachusetts were enrolled; in New York, 74 percent; in Georgia, only 25 percent; in South Carolina, a mere 9 percent (paupers only); and in Virginia, 9 percent (paupers only).[36]

For those who did attend, the experience was not always promising, in light of the woeful deficiencies in instruction. J. H. Baker, an Alabama county school superintendent, reported in 1855 that some of his teachers could not "add ½ and ¼ together" and knew nothing about spelling "or the seat of the accent" in words. To correct such problems, it occurred to some Southern state governors that normal schools should be established. Stiff legislative opposition brought such ideas to a sharp halt. Governor John H. Adams of South Carolina almost apologized for even introducing the possibility, conceding that teacher training schools were "too exclusively professional" for Carolinian tastes. Despite the wealth that Southern agriculture was creating, little of it was diverted to education, although an increasing proportion of meager state budgets was devoted to it in the 1850s.[37]

Even though Southern efforts to expand education became more determined in the last decade before the war, the number of days spent in the classroom varied dramatically: 157 days for the mid-Atlantic states; 116 days for those of the Northwest; and only 80 days for the Southern states. "At an age when the youth of the North are confined at hard lessons for six hours a day from one season to another, these children," remarked a Yankee teacher in rural Georgia, "are wasting the spring time of their lives, in the fields and woods, climbing trees or breaking up the haunts of squirrels. . . ."[38] Actually, most were at work with their fathers, but the results were the same: the failure to gain the sort of education that could be preparation for nonfarming careers.

Illiteracy and poor education had wide effects upon the quality of Southern life in general, however well they served to keep Southern white youth within the confines of family life. In New England, illiterate adults comprised less than 1 percent of the population, but in the South 20 to 25 percent of all whites were unable to sign their names in 1850. In Breckinridge County, Kentucky, on the Ohio River, for example, out of 279 wills registered between 1802 and 1862, 100 were signed only with a cross. A few were perhaps too ill to sign, but most did not wait until the final moment. (The cross signatures included witnesses as well.) This indicates that a rather significant proportion of Southerners were unable to master the simple art of writing. At a guess, another 15 or 20 percent in Breckinridge and elsewhere were only marginally literate. The cause was not hard to locate: weak educational systems, from primary school through college. Governor James Hammond of South Carolina admitted in 1843 that the state's private academies were below their former state, for retrogression there had accompanied the agricultural malaise of the state. "There are comparatively few [private schools] where young men can be well prepared to enter the higher classes," he said. Nor were the many colleges of the South worthy of the name, except for the University of Virginia, Chapel Hill, Columbia (South Carolina), and a few others.[39]

Although Southerners claimed a deep concern with literary progress, parents were not in fact so keen as regional polemicists claimed. Among the poor, education had a low priority. "Jus' 'cause a boy's been to school," declared one mountaineer, "don't mean he's legible [i.e., eligible for respect]." For a yeoman laboring in field and wood from dawn to dusk, the necessity of solid study for his sons seemed very remote. "Their pride revolts," said Governor Hammond of South Carolina, "at the idea of sending their children to school as *'poor scholars'* and besides, they need them at home to work." Hammond's solution was to close the pauper schools altogether and use the state's meager funds to support the flagging private academies for richer citizens.[40]

Even among planters there was no consensus about the value of higher education. "Many planters," declared a college instructor in Mississippi, "are opposed to give their sons, whom they destine to succeed them as farmers, a classical education." For the very rich and refined, of course, such sentiments did not apply; their boys had to be schooled for leadership. But newcomers to planter ranks retained some of the old suspicions about the college dandy (a stereo-type that had some truth to it). Two reasons were offered for not encouraging college attendance: the dangers of debauchery and over-intellectuality. "A Parcell of Dam'd fools," exclaimed an alumnus of William and Mary, "are afraid their children will learn to Dance or game or drink &c &c," as if they did not learn those vices at home. But equally worrisome was the risk of a youth becoming bookish. Sidney Bumpas's father, for instance, opposed his son's going to col-lege for fear he might become too learned to follow his father into planting. The youth took up an apprenticeship as a "Mechanick" to escape the role of planter. Eventually, though, his father relented and allowed him to advance his education and become a minister. Only the most determined appeals from Jefferson Franklin Jack-son's schoolmasters at Irwinton Academy in southern Alabama con-vinced the boy's father Jacinth to let him attend Yale. "The princi-pal reason" was not money, the gifted boy wrote a teacher, but "is (to be plain with you Dr.) he does not *want* to do it." Ill-educated and self-made, the father would have preferred his son to settle on some new lands he had just bought in Mississippi.[41]

Educational advancement threatened the patriarch's authority. Boys might come back with high notions of themselves. Also a sire might well feel discomfited by the reminders of his own aging pro-vided by a son's plans for career and marriage. These were natural and perhaps unexceptionable strains. But in a patriarchy, oedipal feelings were bound to be acutely felt, especially if the boy unduti-fully marked out his own path to follow without bowing to his fa-ther's wishes.

These familiar strains in father-son relations did not, however, mean that such conflicts undermined the patriarchal system; rather they were simply part of the life cycle as Southerners experienced it. Besides, fathers and sons did have common aims. In the course of time seniors had to accord the next generation grudging respect at some point, postpone it though they might. At this stage of young manhood three things, so well depicted in Faulkner's works, drew son and father together. They were a passion for the hunt, a loyalty to family honor, and a mistrust of women. More than labor in the field, more than consultations about family policies, sport welcomed the young adult son to the fraternity of manhood. Sport, most especially hunting, introduced the youth to his father's friends, a fellowship of men with its special vocabulary, nourished with the bottle passed hand to hand, the ritual gossip of dogs, guns, and obstacles overcome to kill game—"the best of all breathing and forever the best of all listening," as Faulkner described it in "The Bear." The experience of the hunt signified dominance over nature, just as the claim to honor, in fistfight, verbal assault, and sometimes duel, meant dominance over men. It was remarkable how many duels grew out of father-son defenses of each other's honor. Like the hunt, such episodes were exhilarating moments of clear danger, sweat, and conquest, one over the wilderness, the other over the wildness of man. But the third component, a passing on from father to son of the ancient mistrust of women, was binding too. About some things mothers and wives were to be obeyed, but on the muster field and in hunting camp, never. Paternal advice rarely excluded warnings about feminine wiles.[42]

In this truncated, restrictive world of men and honor, a father did not relinquish power easily, no matter how harmonious the communion in duck blind or skiff might be. The chances for misunderstanding and hostility were enormous, although hidden beneath the deferential words of sons and the condescension of fathers. Paternal advice was often much more ambivalent than the givers realized. "I have always apprehended that you would prove incapable of handling money," wrote James H. Hammond to a son at Harvard; he almost seemed to ask the collegian to prove him right. By still having the power to be bountiful, fathers convinced themselves of their virility and indispensability. "I have lived for many years," Hammond continued, "& have hoped to devote the remainder of my life to accumulate for my children the means of starting in the world & pursuing at least an independent career." If they fail, however, "my labour will be thrown away & my life will be as useless as I will be miserable," he insisted. Edmund Ruffin had also provided his son with a start in life, a well-stocked plantation on the eastern shore of Maryland. But he was so distressed by the young man's failure that he hoped for "his honorable death" in the early years of the Civil War. Battle heroics, he mused, were "preferable to a useless & inglorious life extended to old age. . . ." Like Hammond, he was worried less for the son's good name than for his own. The honor of the patriarch outweighed, at least at times, love of the prodigal son. "Good God," cried Landon Carter in reference to his son Robert Wormeley Carter, "that such a monster should have descended from my loins." Carter competed with his son on the size of their crops, a contest that the senior invariably won. Not one to show much discretion, the older man drove home the lesson of his son's inferiority. The constant rivalry gave the Virginia squire both pleasure and pain. At times he realized that matters got nearly out of hand and worried that, but for laws to "Prevent Parricide," Robert Wormeley might put him "out of the way."[43]

Indeed, so powerful was the grip of the father that the rarest of all crimes in the South was patricide. Aggressions moved toward outsiders rather than toward one's own tormentor at home, if such was the perception. If there was fatherly worry about the prodigal son, there was sometimes filial distress about the violent father. When tragedy did strike, the son was much more likely to direct his anger against anyone, even himself, rather than the head of the household. For instance, in 1814, near Williamsburg, Virginia, a sixteen-year-old boy could not prevent his drunken father from once again beating his mother unmercifully. Just as he was choking her nearly to death, the youth picked up a musket and put the muzzle in his own mouth. With his toe he pulled the trigger and, said a horrified neighbor, the blast "laid him a breathless corpse at his fathers feet."[44]

It would be wrong to convey the impression that in every family fathers and sons were engaged in perpetual, destructive oedipal warfare. Nevertheless, the characterization rather well resembles the rural life of the Irish peasantry as Conrad Arensberg, the anthropologist, described it. "Nothing prevents the development of great mutual pride, the boy in his experienced and skillful mentor, tutor, and captain in work, and the man in a worthy and skillful successor and fellow-man, but on the other hand everything within the behavior developed in the relationship militates against the growth of close mutual sympathy," he wrote. "As a result, the antagonisms inherent in such a situation often break through very strongly when conflicts arise."[45]

Paternal egocentrism was chiefly responsible for fatherly ventures to western lands, a common antebellum phenomenon. Family honor required the maintenance of wealth and, to large degree, perpetuation of the planting occupation. As old lands gave out new acres had to be bought and cleared. A grizzled frontier planter wrote from Alabama in 1818 to friends in South Carolina, "Old people lives [*sic*] for their children & not themselves" when, as aging parents, they started afresh on virgin soil.[46] Nevertheless, selflessness was often a less significant motive than the demonstration of continued paternal power and largess that relocation in the wilderness represented. Indeed, such strenuous undertakings late in life held sons in the bondage of gratitude. For them to select some vocation other than planting would have been a rejection of the father's self-sacrifice as well as of the occupation that the patriarch had specified as a family duty.

Even when father urged son to improve upon his own record, though it might mean breaking family tradition, there was not much to beckon the youth toward new enterprise. Neither education nor family life nor economic structure prepared him well for such a mission. In any case, honor was itself a constraint against experimentation. What would kin and neighbors say? To escape parental control, the young man could do as others did: prove himself a man and convert family heritage into patrimony. Another possibility had community approval, too: a comfortable marriage.

8

Strategies of Courtship and Marriage

Men controlled the economy, and as part of that power they controlled matrimony as well. No less than career and education, marriage was a means for securing livelihood and social position. It was preferable, though, to get a start with a sound education and a promising career, then use them for high marital ambitions. "A good marriage," James H. Hammond remarked, "is the *result* of success in one's career—very rarely the beginning of it."[1] Yet Hammond, like many others rising from indifferent economic status, did not follow the precept. He had married wealth before making it, but he had prepared for the situation with a college degree and the beginnings of a law practice in the early 1830s. It was the desperate need to make a place in the world for oneself that drove the ambitious young man to self-justifications such as Hammond expressed.

A rather dim appreciation of womankind seemed to accompany such exercises. "Women were meant to breed—Men to do the work of the world," Hammond intoned for the benefit of his younger brother Marcus Claudius Marcellus. They were ornaments or playthings, in his view, but "one soon tires" of the game and returns to the important doings of marketplace and battlefield, courthouse, and cotton plantation. As conveyers of their fathers' property, prestige, and power, women were certainly worth courting and marrying, Hammond explained to his son Harry. But, he warned, expect nothing from feminine initiatives, since "one woman in ten thousand—not one more—has mind enough to be a true '*help-meet*' to a man of mind." A chap could be poor, but if he were willful and intelligent enough he would be more valuable to her than all her riches, charms, and rank. "With these words, I shall when my girls are to marry look solely to the man, & pay little regard to his means or origin." Harry Hammond, his father thought, should be like the up-and-coming men whom the father sought for his daughters' partners. Do not be misled into romantic fancies, the patriarch warned, but aim for "a large dower not only in virtues" but in those tangible possessions and riches that Hammond called "*palpabilities.*" Speaking of his own experiences, he remarked, "Somehow—God forgive me—I never could bear poor *girls*. When pretty & pure spirited I pitied but nevertheless avoided them. Even the sweetest pill of that kind should be gilded."[2] To Dr. John Hammond, another younger brother then considering marriage to an ostensibly well-placed girl, Hammond advised a fast retreat from the altar. Her father had remarried, complicating her future; worse, he "is one of those who would let a child starve before his eyes sooner than dividing his estate." It would be nothing short of "insanity" to "marry a girl with less than $20,000 in *personal possession.*" Hammond expected so much "common sense" from him that he had resolved to "say nothing of that rigmarole *love.*"[3]

Hammond's view of womanhood was more cynical than that of most Southern males, but the desire to keep forever distinct the two spheres of labor for men and women, the sharp division between work and home, pervaded the culture of the antebellum South. Young men were supposed to fall in love, honor and cherish their mates, and live upright, Christian lives in conventional fashion. Nevertheless, in meeting these unexceptional goals, it would never do for men to assume domestic chores that women ordinarily performed, or for women to step out of customary roles unless circumstances, such as necessity in widowhood or spinsterhood, required that they become self-supporting. As a result, the suitor on the scent of good marital prospects looked for signs that reassured him of traditional compatibilities. The younger the girl was, the more likely her malleability and the weaker her self-assertiveness was presumed to be. Quick learners simply were not much in demand. According to a Tennessee paper, "There is an unaccountable antipathy to clever women. Almost all men profess to be afraid of blue stockings—that is, of women who have cultivated their minds; and hold up as a maxim, that there is no safety in matrimony; or even in the ordinary intercourse of society, except with females of plain understanding." The preference was not so "unaccountable." Men often lacked confidence in their own intellectuality. Writing a close female friend, Anna Hayes Johnson of Charleston warned her to suppress an interest in books. Failure to do so would damage one's standing with the "runagate beaux of this most enlightened city. . . ." Literary topics, she said, "make them run from you as if you had the plague," but if escape was impossible the male victim at once assumed a lugubrious "gravity" in order "to conceal the defects of the mind."[4]

Unfortunately for the ill-prepared suitor, Southern girls were fast becoming better educated, more dissatisfied with the limitations of men, and more unhappy with the lack of respect accorded their own talents. One belle remarked to a male cousin that "the time is fast approaching when the beauties and excellence of [women's] minds, will no longer lie dormant," and "the Lords of Creation"— a constant, sardonic phrase in female correspondence—will have to take notice. Aware of the changes, advisers of young girls such as Mrs. Virginia Cary of Richmond tried to reconcile the old custom of complete womanly submissiveness which "enveloped the female mind" in ignorance with the new "age of intellectual improvement" abroad in refined sectors of the South. Mrs. Cary rejoiced that women's "minds are no longer cramped by rigid, domestic discipline, but soar above the narrow limits of family avocations, and catch a glimpse of those lights hitherto reserved for their master spirits." Yet, she quickly warned in 1830, matters should not get out of hand. With alarm she noted that some women "aim at equality of rights; in other words, at absolute dominion," whereas they should be satis-

fied to "continue in contented subordination to [man's] authority."
After all, "it is no derogation from the dignity or utility of woman,
to declare that she is inferior to man in moral as well as in physical
strength." As a result, she claimed, the wise female sought "meek-
ness" and "retirement" from the "unchecked gaze of the world"
which "tarnishes, like the meridian beam of a summer sun. . . ."
Throughout her account, as well as in the advice that Professor
Thomas Roderick Dew provided, men were pictured as "tigers in
the desert," subject to a "characteristic moodiness of humour."
Womankind was expected to lighten the burden of man fleeing to
hearthside "from the troubled scenes of life, with a cloud gathered
over his soul" by offering him "a cheerful greeting." To accomplish
this soothing task, the supreme duty of her gender, the woman had
to be aware "that men are jealous of literary and scientific ladies,
and not without cause; for though they have little chance of being
surpassed in these attainments, they have a pretty strong one of
finding no one to superintend their domestic establishments with
skill" in "the household department." Therefore, women should
strive not for "elaborate accomplishments" but instead for a simple
"taste for music or drawing," if "moderately cultivated and made
subservient to purposes of rational amusement."[5]

The advice was eminently sound, given the social criteria of the
region. The ambitious young professional, no less than the well-
situated planter's son, preferred the uninitiated, simple-hearted
young virgin. There was likewise considerable wisdom in John
Randolph's advice to his nephew, bachelor though Randolph was,
that "few love-matches are happy ones. . . . After all, 'suitability'
is the true foundation for marriage. If the parties be suited to one
another, in age, situation in life . . . temper, and constitution,
these are the ingredients of a happy marriage—or at least, a convenient one—which is all that people of experience expect." Suitability all too often involved a common commonness of mind,
though the language of love suggested something grander and
the Southern advice literature something more ennobling. Hardy
Wooten, a young and unmarried physician of pioneer Lowndesboro, Alabama, condemned the young bloods in his neighborhood

because they made their distrust of feminine brains all too plain. Lacking any ability to carry on "intellectual discourse," he said, they could only consort with women through the *"sensual* gratifications" of perpetual dancing. Yet Wooten himself was scarcely immune from the convention of seeking out a wife with less education and intelligence than he possessed. Stung by local gossip, he abandoned a friendship with a woman separated from her husband and married Ermassenda Rochelle, an eighteen-year-old girl of little education. He had been looking, he reasoned, for "unsuspecting innocence—a native jewel, unpolished by art." Such heavenly virgins made the more agreeable companions (and certainly they did not often stir up unpleasant rumors damaging to a struggling young physician's prospects). James Norcom of North Carolina, another physician, took the same view of the matter. He wrote his sixteen-year-old fiancée Maria Horniblow that it was "her *innocence, modesty,* simplicity and good nature" that had won his heart.[6]

Contrary to legend, Southern women did not invariably marry as young as Maria Horniblow. Nonetheless, they did tend to marry at an earlier age than Northern women of comparable social and economic standing. Jane Turner Censer, who has studied the wealthiest planter-merchant families of North Carolina in the antebellum period, shows that the average age for brides at first marriage was 20.5 (median age 20) in her rather large sample. But in the Southwest teenage brides were more common, even among the wealthy. Ann W. Boucher, a student of Alabama history, has discovered that among the thirty-five richest planter families in Forkland District (near Demopolis), the average age for brides was 18.8 years during the period from 1800 to 1819. In 1860, for some thirty-nine marriages the average age was 18.5 years. Similarly early bridal ages have been recorded by James McReynolds for east Texas throughout the first half of the nineteenth century. By contrast, in antebellum New England upper-class Boston women wedded for the first time at the average age of 24.9 years (1820–39) according to Peter Hall, a full four years later than even the most cosmopolitan and well-educated Southern belles, such as those whose statistics Censer has computed.[7]

Southern upper-class males, including those with professional aspirations, tended to marry late while choosing young brides, in the fashion of Dr. Hardy Wooten. According to Ann Boucher's careful work, the Forkland District husband on his first stroll to the altar was most likely to be two years older than his bride if he married between nineteen and twenty-nine years of age, 6.8 years older if thirty to thirty-nine, ten years older if forty to forty-nine, and 13.55 years older if fifty to fifty-nine. Using a wealthy Bostonian sample, Peter Hall finds that grooms on first nuptials were 26.8 years of age, about the same age as Southern males of the same social class under the same circumstances. But the Bostonians' choices were usually women well into their twenties, in contrast to Southern habit. Obviously many social and economic factors determined these patterns. Geography, class position, occupation, ethnicity, birth order, and other variables have all been cited in family studies both in this country and abroad. Certainly age at marriage tells us little about degrees of patriarchy and companionability in married life. Some of the most patriarchal societies, such as those of the Mediterranean and Adriatic, encourage early marriages for both genders, but the pairings are often arranged by parents. Late marriage ages in Ireland reflect economic conditions as well as ethnic and religious customs, but male domination of households was probably no less pronounced in Irish life than in colonial Plymouth, for instance, where couples married when both partners were in their early twenties. One can build no case for Southern patriarchy upon wide age disparities alone. Jane Censer argues, for instance, that "planters' daughters neither married extremely young nor extremely late." The point is well taken: underage brides (fifteen or sixteen) were rather infrequent. On the other hand, the later the marriage date, the longer the daughter was under her father's roof and command; the earlier the ceremony in her life, the sooner she was under her husband's charge. It would seem, however, that if husbands were older by significant degrees than their mates, age would help to replicate in married life the father-daughter relationship. Ann Boucher finds, for instance, a gap of 6.8 years between partners in her Alabama sample, a difference that could affect family polity.

Since so many marriages resulted in an early death for the first wife, owing to childbirth complications (puerperal fever and other causes), ages at second marriage for men evinced a patriarchal aspect to Southern styles perhaps more clearly than ages at first marriage. Ann Boucher, for instance, has compiled figures on second marriages and discovers an *average* discrepancy of sixteen years for her group in the wealthy Forkland District. No doubt the sample is too small, and exceptional in some way. But it suggests that Southern widowers selected girls with many years of childbearing ahead rather than widows encumbered with offspring and fewer years for raising a second family. Because of high mortality rates for small children, Southern fathers had to assure themselves of surviving progeny. Large, healthy families enhanced paternal prestige by displaying power, will, and wealth in the rearing of so many dependents. As in developing countries today, an abundance of children supplied parents with providers for old age, for one never knew what fortune the future would bring. Philemon Hawkins, a North Carolina planter, for instance, wrote one of his thirteen children congratulations upon the arrival of the latest grandson: "Tell [the mother] that I give you and her Joy with him and that . . . you and she will be rewarded . . . in the next world . . . the more she brings the greater will be the reward." Fecundity in women was also a matter of high commendation among some Southern matrons. Rachel O'Connor of Louisiana remarked with much satisfaction that her neighbor Mrs. Rhea, wife of an elderly judge, "has lately been delivered of twins, a son & daughter[;] they have at this period fifteen children alive and only one Dead, and two sons in law and soon expect a grandchild. They say that the old man is highly pleased at his good luck. Mrs. Rhea is not more than 37 years of age—her family may yet be much larger."[8]

Sometimes second marriages furthered such cheerful prospects for fathers. For instance, Joseph Davis, wealthy brother of the future Confederate president, though over forty, married a sixteen-year-old New Orleans belle twenty-six years his junior. (This marriage, however, was unfruitful.) Mary Chesnut's mother was nineteen when she was born, her father then being thirty-four. Having lost his first wife, as well as two sons, her father, like Joseph Davis, sought to replace the young wife with an equally young one who could bear him a long line of heirs.[9]

Unfortunately, we know too little about eighteenth-century Southern marriages. Certainly youthful ages for brides were not uncommon in colonial Chesapeake planter households. In 1728, for instance, William Byrd fretted that his daughter was a "most antick Virgin" at age twenty.[10] While all the illustrations and computations presented by careful scholars have neither proven nor disproven the influence of patriarchal habit in Southern marital plans, yet it is fair to say that, as common sense and circumstantial evidence suggest, there was a slower rate of change from premodern styles in the South compared with Northern evolutions.

Age at wedding date was not, of course, the sole consideration for people embarking upon so momentous a change in status. Class position mattered as much or more, for both male and female. For example, Dr. James Norcom advised a young relative to beware marrying out of his social stratum in the neighborhood, for it would be viewed unfavorably. By and large, "poverty," he continued, "subjects a man to the evil of vulgar connections and is too apt to vitiate his manners and corrupt his character." While a man could sometimes marry a woman "below him, [in] birth, education and accomplishments" and raise her to "his own rank and consequence in society," a woman could not perform the same miracle for her husband. Women shared these sentiments. Referring to an overseer's wife, Kate Stone of Louisiana remarked, "She seems entirely too nice a woman, and her fashion is evidently from the planter class. I wonder why she married him. She does not look like a contented woman."[11]

To avoid such class indiscretions, parents, especially fathers, expected to have final say about the fitness of a betrothal. Yet threats of disownment were rare, if only because young people in possessing families were already used to conforming to family mores. Brothers and sisters often reinforced parental opinions about their siblings' marital plans. Writing his younger, much better educated brother, then at an Alabama boarding school, an Alabama overseer

advised, "Do not think of marriaing until you complete your Education in fact you are too young to marrie." When John Bryan courted
a dowerless girl, his sister echoed their father's disapproval. In rebellion, Bryan took to gambling, drinking, and profligate spending.
"Oh when I think of how Brother conducts himself towards the
best of parents," sighed his sister Maria, "it makes me tremble for
him."[12]

In a new study, Carl Degler argues that paternal control over
marital decisions disappeared by 1800 in the United States. Indeed,
Jane Censer's study of 100 upper-class North Carolina wills between
1790 and 1860 strongly indicates that no sons and daughters were
denied legacies for failure to choose appropriate mates. Surely the
threat of disinheritance was a weapon used in some households,
though even in the most patriarchal families it was bound to be rare
enough. In any event, fathers could command formidable resources
by marshaling kinfolk sentiment against controversial pairings.
Censer, who disputes the existence of Southern patriarchy altogether, herself quotes Sophia Deveaux, a North Carolina belle in
1855, whose independence took this typical form: "I would marry,"
against paternal wishes, Sophia said, "but it should be in [my father's] house." In other words, she could not attempt an elopement.
For all the talk of romance, undying passion, and self-fulfilling independence, sons and daughters no less than parents expected elders
to have a strong, even final voice on marital choices. James Norcom
of Edenton, North Carolina, was glad that his dutiful son was "willing to endure in cheerful submission . . . to my will . . . in all
such cases." He was less lucky with his daughter Mary Matilda,
whose union with a Yankee lawyer he opposed. The pair were not
welcome in Norcom's house. When the otherwise happy couple lost
their four-year-old child, Mary Matilda asked her mother to inter-
cede: "Ask Pa to forgive and forget all. . . . If you could turn aside
your prejudice—forget the past, and know him [her husband] *as he
now is,* and *has been* since I married, your feelings I'm sure would
change, for no one ever had a kinder or better husband." The break
was not mended.[13]

In contrast, however, fathers could be most helpful when filial and parental views coincided. Alfred Howell, a young lawyer in Texas, asked his father for aid in courting a belle near home in his native Virginia. He wondered "if she is actually worth $40,000." Whether his father could verify the sum or not, plans fell through. Later he married a rich planter's daughter from nearby Fort Worth.[14] At all events, the father was seldom indifferent in any of these transactions.

Fathers of wealthy boys had to be sure that the girls were not fortune hunters. After all, marriage was the only way for daughters to advance the prestige and security of their parents as well as themselves. "Those Miss Stuarts of whom I have heard you tell are on Sullivan's Island," James L. Petigru of Charleston wrote his sister. "It puzzles me that I hear of them as belonging to a *very* high family, yet they brought no letters [of introduction]. Tell me what you know, and particularly . . . how Tom came to be introduced to them and who they represent themselves to be."[15] Satisfactory explanations might be forthcoming. Yet it was always wise to obtain some verification.

For young men trapped by relative poverty the prospect of a good match was also not only tempting but possibly the only way upward. On one level Southern society was fairly charitable about the efforts of such suitors. Everyone recognized the actualities of limited capital and restricted opportunities, even for professional men. Moreover, the relatively small supply of genuinely eligible males had to be taken into account. Marriage was by far the most convenient way to status and wealth. Writing a son at college, Joel Lyle, a newspaper editor and planter of Paris, Kentucky, revealed in 1826 the dominant mood of the marital game there: "It seems probable to me that E. S. and Henry Duncan are engaged. The old mother is violently opposed to the match and has threatened to scald the squire the next time she can get. . . . I think it probable that old Sam is also opposed to the match. In about a month, if consent be not obtained you may calculate on hearing of a runaway expedition! It is reported that Hugh Ines Brent and Garret Davis are each of them about to marry into the associate Judge Bob Brimble family. A salary of $4500 in hard dollars is very alluring to the aspiring young men of this place. Money, money is the object, and a wife a secondary one." Actually "E. S." and Henry Duncan did not elope, but bowed to parental disapproval and married other partners whom the parents accepted. Garret Davis, on the other hand, won Judge Brimble's favor and went on to become a leading Kentucky politician.[16]

Within limits, finding a woman of potential wealth was acceptable, even recommended behavior. But fear of outright fortune hunters was universal, for their numbers were as great as other means of getting ahead were few. A young Georgia matron fumed that one Mr. Hollinbec, a local Baptist preacher of questionable morals, was "inquiring for ladies of fortune, says he rates his education at fifty thousand dollars. . . ." If slaves had prices on them, so too did gentlemen with bachelor's degrees. Apparently one desperate young lady took Hollinbec's advances seriously, until her friends put the matter in the proper light. In 1811, John Randolph had to acknowledge that a child "with about 6000 dollars to her portion" had married "a ruffian of my own name" who was "beggaring her as fast as possible."[17] Nearly every family of means had to contend with such problems, because laws that restricted women's property rights and all but denied divorces presented the unscrupulous with grave temptations.

Fear of the male fortune hunter and insistent family inquiry into the backgrounds of a daughter's suitors not only pervaded matrimonial negotiations but also had an effect upon the girls themselves. Southern men spoke of the beguiling timidity of their belles, and indeed the girls had ample reason to be so. The risks of being swept away by some youth of doubtful character forced maidens to be tough, practical, and cool. A chipper Boston girl who married Henry Burgwyn of New Bern, North Carolina, in 1838 was surprised to discover that "the girls here are not so easily flirted with as with us [in New England]. They expect far more attention from Gentlemen than our ladies, and are more reserved with them at the same time." The restraint was not only a wise precaution to prevent misunderstandings but also a refutation of the standard myth of Southern belle frivolity. Partly, too, it was fear of displaying either too much ignorance or too much intellectuality, either of which was a social danger.[18]

Northern courting patterns, particularly in the first half of the nineteenth century, were rather liberal, reflecting parental trust in the girls' discretion and conscience. To be sure, the occasions were very often quite decorous affairs—church suppers, picnics, and outings in large groups with adults not present or in the distant background. In the South gatherings for young people also were popular, but only in the lower classes was there very little strict supervision by parents or chaperones. In the eighteenth century, upper-class parents had been rather informal about such matters. For instance, Jane Carson, a historian of Virginian society, cites the frolic of one Lucinda Lee. She and her girl friends slipped down to the plantation kitchen and had a late night snack when "in came Mr. [Corbin] Washington, dressed in Hannah's short gown and petticoat, and squeezed me and kissed me twenty times, in spite of all the resistance I could make. . . ." After further play, the girls sent the young man off and went up to their hostess's room to report the doings and "she sat laughing fit to kill herself at us."[19]

Matrons of the antebellum South, however, would have taken a much dimmer view of such goings-on. The rising tide of evangelicalism and a loosening sense of hierarchy made mothers wary. In the better houses of the Old South, girlish jollity was not at all in vogue. J. H. Ingraham, a Yankee teacher at Jefferson College, near Natchez, noticed the differences between the "license given to daughters" in Northern homes and the restraints placed on Southern girls. "In the South it is deemed indecorous for them to be left alone" with their beaux, and if a mother or maiden aunt was unavailable, a female slave was assigned to sit "on the rug at the door." A married gentleman told Ingraham that in the upper strata of society couples seldom walked by themselves and kissed even more rarely: "I know several young ladies in this vicinity who have told me that they were never for two hours out of sight of their mammas."[20]

As Ingraham observed, "This watchfulness, by and by," defeated its own aim; there were occasional elopements. Hasty and unapproved marriages were, he said, usually disastrous because of the inexperience and vulnerability of sixteen-year-old girls thrust so early upon the matrimonial stage. Yet the only way to escape the verbal pushes and shoves of parents and relations was to leap into marriage with the nearest unattached male. This was the choice a desperate planter's daughter of Mobile, Alabama, made in 1824. Mourned Mrs. Shephard in a letter to another gentry matron: "Mary Sawyer, the beautiful and accomplished, is no more. She married a few days ago a man named Thompson near fifty years old, and a bankrupt, not worth one cent. Every body is in amazement at her folly and most unheard of sacrifice, nearly all her relatives were opposed to the match, but she appeared determined to marry somebody. Her exit," warned Mrs. Shephard, "ought to be an awful lesson to all fine ladies who sport with fortune." She worried that the impulse might be catching; Miss Mary Jones might next fall victim "to some advanced cockfighter I suppose."[21] Yet the reason for Mary Sawyer's seemingly irrational decision, which led to social burial, was partly a rebellious if imprudent response to severe parental and family pressures to get on with the business of life by fleeing spinsterhood. Trapped between bondage to parents and subjection to a husband, the Southern belle sometimes exchanged one dependency for the other in an ill-advised search for relief, if not freedom.

When a daughter or son was ready for the rituals of courting, mothers naturally played important roles. "Be cautious in making your choice," wrote a mother in typical style, "be well acquainted with the disposition of the man you marry & do not involve yourself in difficulties by giving yourself to one in needy circumstances." Relatives near and far also took an interest, because so much depended upon judicious unions. Although everyone expected love to be the basis of a union, a good match also provided the chance for a soft touch for loans in time of need. An entire community could become aroused when some marital action broke all precedent. For instance, in 1830 in De Kalb County, Georgia, a lawyer married a ten-year-old ward to secure her "handsome property." The neighbors intervened, though the mother had approved the match. The

Augusta, Georgia, *Courier* explained that twelve should be the earliest possible marriage age, even with parental consent. Apparently the lawyer surrendered to community opinion.[22]

As this odd case suggested, local gossip was highly influential. Marriage of young people was public and family business, not just that of the couple involved. In reporting the engagement of a kinswoman, Selina Deveaux remarked that nearly all the cousins, however distant, had immersed themselves in "all the transactions, and little occurrences which transpire" in regard to it, "so fond are some folks of Gossipping. . . ." When James L. Petigru, for instance, was courting a girl, she abruptly broke with the struggling young lawyer to engage herself to an old squire with three plantations. "The relatives," concluded William J. Grayson, Petigru's biographer, had influenced her, thinking "the match too good to be refused." Yet the ultimate power even if it was rarely invoked, rested with the father in question, or, if the father was dead, the widow or guardian; seldom were rich Carolinian young people allowed to make these choices themselves without recriminations.[23]

Once married, the young couple was still under the ever-watchful eyes of fathers, mothers, and elderly kinfolk. The strategy then became the cultivation of in-law relationships for the sake of economic self-sufficiency or advancement. The economic side of family life is conspicuously revealed in the plantation correspondence and personal diaries preserved in Southern repositories. Quite remarkably, the pervasiveness of family financial preoccupation extended beyond the planter circle. Southern merchants, storekeepers, druggists and other town dwellers were no less affected than their kinspeople in the country. The point is significant. It suggests that even as the Old South entered more fully into the main currents of nineteenth-century economic and social life, old styles did not entirely disappear. Besides, many Southern enterpeneurs were only temporarily engaged in trade. Whereas his Yankee counterpart might have laid aside his grocer's apron to start a small manufacturing firm, the Southern storekeeper—a planter's son perhaps—locked the grocery door in order to return to the land upon the old man's death. Information about the nonrural South is most readily accessible through the early records of the Mercantile Agency, a credit-rating company founded in the 1840s. As a rule, Northern credit-rating agents seldom mentioned anything about wives or in-laws; they thought men ought to stand on their own merits. Southern reporters, on the other hand, usually country lawyers, showed the same customary domestic inquisitiveness that their male clients and friends displayed.

Through the agency's thousands of semiannual entries, one finds that the source of capital for most Southern businesses was family based. Banks were available, of course, in larger communities, but, naturally, family resources were preferred. Quite often it was a father-in-law rather than a father who put up the money for a young man's entry into Southern trade. O. G. Dennis, a twenty-year-old newlywed, for instance, opened a dry goods store in 1850 in Macon, Fayette County, Tennessee. The reporter noted that Dennis's "father in law is rich," and had advanced the funds. In 1858 Dennis was still flourishing and, the reporter emphasized, "will inherit a good Property at his father in law's *death*." In some cases the capital invested came not from the bride's father but from another kinsman, related either by blood or marriage. Miguel Jamison, for example, had come over from either Scotland or Ireland (the reporter was uncertain) with his sister and their father, with whom he formed a partnership. In 1845 their trading house failed. Matters changed dramatically, however, when the sister married a building contractor "worth over $100,000." Soon Jamison's dry goods store on Chartres Street in New Orleans was handling accounts totaling $60,000 a year. The capital came from the brother-in-law, as Jamison's father was a man "of limited means only." By 1853 the reporter declared, "They are regular Creoles & are generally considered to be well off." Socially and economically, these immigrants were among the lucky few to break into the closed familial circles of New Orleans society—owing to a fortuitous marriage. Other typical comments along these lines were: "has married a rich widow"; "appears to have the support of his wife's family"; "is a Yankee who came here worth 00 & married $20,000"; "made some property & married a good deal more"; "just married to the daughter of a wealthy planter"; "is backed by his father in law, who is worth $10,000"; "future prospect by marriage [is] good." Scarcely a single entry of this character can be found in comparable Northern ledgers.[24]

The usefulness of a wife for the economic success of a plantation has long been established. What is less commonly recognized is that the familial pattern had its utility in small business firms as well. Contrary to the region's stereotypes of feminine fastidiousness, members of the Southern middle class in village and town did not hesitate to make use of their wives' commercial talents, if any. The tradesmen's style, reaching far back in the American and European past, permitted such activity, although the wealthier bourgeoisie in the North and well-established plantation owners of the South kept their women closer to the hearth and away from the counter. Southern reporters for the Mercantile Agency quickly sensed if the wife was actually the force behind whatever success a firm enjoyed. H. J. Weddils, a bachelor druggist of Baton Rouge, for instance, in 1849 was "reported to be lazy & fond of fishing." When he began the business he knew "00 of it," but in 1852 he married and, observed the reporter, "his wife has property." Soon the store was prospering, under her supervision. Likewise, Abraham Schlenker's wife in Clinton, Louisiana, not only managed one of his two stores but was credited with holding the entire operation together. Her husband "is addicted to the very common vices here of tippling & gambling," declared the resident agent. She died; he remarried. The second wife had the good sense to draw up a marriage contract protecting her properties and all "revenues are secured to herself." Apparently the arrangement had a sobering effect. Schlenker went off to the Civil War a rather well-secured entrepeneur, though all was lost by 1865.[25]

A wife with some talents, it seemed, could work remarkable cures. Nimrod W. Stewart of Cow Grove, South Carolina, started with funds of his own and, with many local relatives as customers, he made money, "but what he has done with it is something of a mystery. . . ." The reporter suspected "gambling" and *"intemperance."* By 1857 Stewart had straightened out his affairs, having married a girl with property. R. A. Taylor of Whippy Swamp, South Carolina, owner of a general store, "drinks & has no property, worth 00. Would recommend caution," advised the reporter. A year later, like Nimrod Stewart, Taylor had "married a lady who after the death of parents will be very well off." Sober or not, Taylor watched his credit rating rise on the strength of his wife's fortune. Seldom were Yankee reporters willing to give a man a completely clean record if he was a drinker, no matter how well fixed his wife might be. But even keepers of taverns and ninepin alleys could improve their rather shady reputations with a successful match. Occasionally, even schoolteachers could overcome local prejudices by the same means. In 1850 schoolteacher Thomas Dillard of Pontoloc, Mississippi, added to his meager pay by running a country store on a very close margin. Then he married the daughter of Captain John Boulard, "who is worth $100,000 & has but three children." Soon Dillard was handling a farm of 350 acres with his wife's slaves, as well as operating the store. The reporter noted, "Tom is a teaching chap but has thus far succeeded well."[26] The qualifier was called for because schoolkeepers in the South were often thought to be lazy dreamers.

The collective history of many small establishments, especially at the villages and crossroads, was rather along the following lines. A young man would obtain money from his father, a planter of moderate wealth. With this $2,000 to $5,000 of working capital he would join another young planter's son who had perhaps an equal sum. After a few years in trade one or the other would marry, permitting him either to buy out the partner, or, more likely, leave the business and work the lands of his wife until his own paternal inheritance could be added. So it was with the Wardlow brothers in Abbeville, South Carolina. Likewise at nearby Church Hill John Cothran dissolved his storekeeping with Franklin Stephens to start "planting as good as anybody," after an advantageous marriage.[27]

In Northern business communities, the pattern was quite different. Very seldom does one encounter references to marital ties that could enhance an entrepeneur's credit standing. Jacob Brunn of Springfield, Illinois, for instance, in 1847 was worth "30m$," with a "Splendid 4 storey Brick store." The reporter noted in 1851 that he was the "Best man here. Wor[th] say 30 to 50m$. Sells 100m$ pr annum & makes prob. 8 or 10m$ yearly. Sagacious prompt bus. man." By 1867 Brunn had become a leading banker, with assets of $1.5 million, and his brother had assumed direction of the grocery business, then worth $100,000. Throughout the various entries not a word was said about Brunn's wife or in-laws. In the assessment of the firm of Hurst & Taylor, another large grocery house, however, it was mentioned that Taylor, a young venturesome man "without Cap[ital]," had married the sister of the more cautious Hurst, for whom Taylor had clerked for several years. What was more important, though, in the reporter's opinion, was Taylor's intemperance, about which he had much to say. In explaining the status of an auction and commission house, the Sangamon County, Illinois, reporter noted that Isaac Keyes, the owner, had originally invested $2,000 from a farm sale to start the enterprise. In 1847, however, Keyes "came into possession of 4 or 5m not long since"—whether from wife, father, or another source the reporter failed to mention. A Southern agent, on the other hand, would not have been likely to omit such crucial information, because of the importance given to family ties and marriage arrangements.[28]

In Ohio, as in Illinois, sales of farm lands were used to finance the establishment of general stores and other activities, and the entrepeneur seldom returned to the cultivation of land if his business prospered—the opposite order of investment from slave-state custom. In commenting on the sales for business purposes, reporters seldom mentioned how the land had been acquired. Nor did they indicate what sums wives or in-laws contributed to the new enterprises. Of course there was some motion back to farms, when a tannery or woolen mill failed, for example, and often enough the failure of kinfolk to rescue a firm in trouble had to be mentioned. Nevertheless, the impression given by a sampling of entries is that Northern credit agents in antebellum times felt more comfortable describing the moral character and business prospects of commercial men than in delineating their fortuitous or inopportune marriages. The difference reflected the fact that Southern lawyers, upon whom the Mercantile Agency relied, were not so often avid church-goers as their Northern counterparts were. The company, especially during the evangelical Lewis Tappan's tenure as head of the firm, preferred to hire religious professional men wherever they could be found, and the Northern pool of that type of individual was much larger than the Southern one.[29]

In view of the intense Southern desire to increase the bonds of fam-ily reliance and to enhance both career and marital success by con-centrating wealth, intermarriage among cousins (first cousins in-cluded) was relatively common. Unfortunately, historians have only started to calculate exactly how common. The pattern was not at all unknown in the eighteenth-century North, especially among wealthy merchant dynasts. Whereas, as one able scholar explains, nonkin marriages diluted the holdings of a family, the marriage of first cousins reconcentrated the portions, the supply of socially pre-sentable mates being often so very small. But as New England mer-chants grew wealthier and economic opportunities expanded to embrace more families and lines of endeavor, parents could en-courage and support college education and professional training for sons rather than require them to cement merchandising partner-ships and holdings through cousinly marriages. In the decades 1740 to 1759, 66.6 percent of marriages in a birth cohort of wealthy mer-chant families (Cabots, Lowells, and others) joined first cousins. A hundred years later the percentage had dropped to 20.6 percent, still a high proportion that was certainly atypical of Yankee families with lesser wealth.[30]

In the Old South it would be surprising to discover an equally dramatic change during those years in old, eastern, and wealthy neighborhoods. Probably the decline was gradual. In fact, Ann Boucher has found that cousin marriages actually increased in the Forkland District of Alabama, where 10 percent of a wealthy slave-holding group in 1860 were married cousins and 38 percent were so connected in the period 1861 to 1880. No doubt the strategy re-flected the concentration of wealth in an ever-narrowing circle at the top under the duress of war, slave sequestration, and a static postwar economy. This sort of defensive policy in the face of declining prospects certainly had precedent in antebellum Virginia. Thomas Nelson Page, the famous post–Civil War romantic novelist, for instance, served as an example. Lorraine Holland points out that "his parents were first cousins, his maternal grandparents were first cousins, and his maternal great-grandparents were first cousins. Six of his fourth generation ancestors were fathered by the same man, King Carter."[31]

Sometimes, though probably most infrequently, a will even stipulated that the disposition of plantation property was to rest upon cousinly unions. For instance, William King of Abingdon, Virginia, bequeathed all his real estate, including a salt works and store, "at the death of my wife to William King son of my brother James King on condition of his marrying a daughter of William Trigg and my niece Rachel his wife. . . ." If that arrangement failed, then the estate would devolve upon "any child giving preference to age of said William and Rachel Trigg that will marry a child of my brother James King or Sister Elizabeth wife to John Mitchell and to their Issue. . . ." William Porcher DuBose's uncle William Deveaux, for whom he was named, urged him to marry one of his two nieces, declaring, "If you marry one of these girls here is a plantation I'll give you, so look out now." DuBose, later an Episcopal theologian, refused to comply. Other young men were more obliging when presented with temptations subtly or overtly offered. Silk Hope, one of the Manigault holdings in South Carolina, passed from Gabriel Manigault's hands by sale to John Heyward, his sister's husband. Twenty years later, in 1825, Heyward's daughter married her first cousin Charles, Gabriel's son, whereupon Heyward presented his son-in-law and nephew with Silk Hope and 126 slaves as dowry. Thus the Manigaults once more acquired a handsome property and thereafter held it for over one hundred years.[32]

Besides the marriage of first cousins, another common pattern was the pairing of sisters in one family with the brothers in another, a parallel arrangement (called sibling exchange by behavioral scientists) that seemed as frequent among the yeomanry as among the very wealthy. In a later chapter the Foster clan of Adams County,

Mississippi, will receive ample attention. It was founded by three obscure brothers who settled in the Spanish Territory in the 1780s, grew to planter status, and married three sisters of an equally unpretentious clan, the Smiths. It was customary practice for brothers to share implements as well as chores and social life. If they married sisters they were likely to continue these convenient arrangements. Moreover, marrying into the same family meant avoiding many of the uncertainties about the eligibility of strangers. Also, inheritances of land might well be contiguous, so that the family bonds already well established would continue, even to the point that the next generation in turn would intermarry. How unexceptional such patterns were, and how different from Northern ones, remains to be studied. Nevertheless, it would be safe to guess that, except for the Brahmins of Boston and a few other wealthy families in the North, Yankees were less likely to intermarry than Southerners were, especially in the lower ranks.[33]

In addition, men did not hesitate to wed their deceased wife's sisters, although the American Anglican church had once condemned such unions. As a result of these arrangements there was often a doubling of connections amongst the offspring. If similar patterns persisted into the next generation, the confusions defied even the most dedicated family genealogist. So complicated was the Randolph family that William Cabell Bruce, John Randolph's biographer, likened it to "a tangle of fishhooks" because it was "impossible to pick up one without drawing three or four with it." By 1879 the children of Dr. Robert C. Randolph, he said, had "in their veins the united blood of five of the seven sons of William Randolph," founder of the clan's American branch.[34]

In the aristocratic Jefferson and Lewis genealogy, according to the biographer of Thomas Jefferson's roguish nephews, there were thirty-five marriages between 1750 and 1810. Seven involved the pairing of cousins—five first cousins and two second cousins—20 percent of the total. According to a Middle Eastern anthropologist, Professor Khuri, even a 10 percent ratio of cousinly unions represents a startling proportion in Lebanon, where the practice has always been considered especially prominent. Moreover, in one instance Peter Field Jefferson married Jane W. Lewis, a pairing that united two young people who were first cousins by two separate reckonings.[35] Nor was this simply a matter of preserving lofty familial status and alleged blood purity, a motive that compelled the royal families of Europe to seek partners from within a confined circle of relations. At least as important was the fact that it tended to concentrate plantation inheritances and preserve the capital held in the form of slaves.

In the backlands of the South the pattern also persisted. According to a rural sociologist, 22 percent of 77 marriages in a sampling of one Kentucky community brought together second or closer cousins (6.5 percent were first-cousin marriages; 1.3 percent, first cousins once removed; 14.3 percent, second cousins; and 5.2 percent, second cousins once removed). In only 54.5 percent was there no relationship at all between the spouses. In another rural community, Flat Rock, 22.7 percent of the familial relations were first cousins, creating obvious and inevitable tendencies toward close intermarriages. Some families in the hills were more prone to the practice than others, and the figures vary. Thus in one household close to a quarter of all the marriages were with first and second cousins and nearly 60 percent involved blood kin. In another no first cousins had wedded; only first cousins who were once removed had paired off (6.7 percent), though a third of the total marriages were with second cousins, and an additional 20 percent were with second cousins once removed. In other communities cousinly unions were as rare as anywhere else in the country. However, when full historical figures are available the prevalence of Southern intermarriages will no doubt be more evident than at present.[36]

Curiously, these marital patterns received no bold defense. In fact, family members themselves sometimes grumbled about the practice. Frederick Blount complained to John H. Bryan, his half-brother, about a cousin named Gains Whitfield. He had made "considerable acquisition to his estate" in wedlock to a first cousin, but, said Blount, "at the sacrifice of some very proper scruples, which any man of refinement must acknowledge, who marries a lady so nearly related to him. They are rather a strange set for intermarrying—resembling very much the colony of Isocks in your neighbour-hood in that particular." Obviously Blount thought it a "tackey" thing to do. But high or low, such marriages took place with the same regularity with which they were mildly criticized. When queried about the matter, one mountain woman told an inter-viewer, "I'd rather they wouldn't marry their kin, but I couldn't help it. . . . We told 'em everything, and they quit writing. But the first thing we knowed they's married." Yet she clearly had been only half-hearted in her opposition.[37]

Worries there might have been, but the advantages seemed evi-dent to those whose relatives intermarried. Sighed one Tennessee mother, "My three daughters married Ed's three sons; ain't nothin' that brings a family together like that." She and Ed were already related, so that each set of their grandchildren were blessed with being not only brothers and sisters but also each other's cousins as well, a double-bond relation offering special security. The purpose, as Elmora Matthews, an anthropologist, has explained, was to pre-vent property dispersals that could throw these marginal folk into abject poverty. At the other end of the social spectrum, there was the enhancement of status and influence through close ties. The Virginia families concerned, for instance, took enormous pride in the fact that the venerable Edmund Pendleton, by a series of cous-inly unions, was both the uncle and the first cousin once removed of John Taylor of Caroline, the state's rights philosopher.[38]

By permitting such intricate marriage patterns, families not only reinforced positions of honor and wealth but also ensured con-tinuations of custom and demands for conformity. After all, the hardiest of rebels might think well about challenging a father-in-law who was also an uncle, and possibly cousin too. Yet the effect was to create chains of duty and rationales for intrusiveness too chafing for easy resolution. The result could sometimes be most compli-cated, even gothic. For instance, excessive cousinly intimacy in the Randolph circle helped to bring on the famous tragedy of the 1790s. Nancy Randolph, a headstrong woman, had left the Tuckahoe plantation of her father Thomas Mann Randolph to escape grow-ing discord with her parents. She joined the household of her sister

Judith, who had married their second cousin, Richard Randolph. For a time Nancy had been engaged to marry Archibald Randolph, another close kinsman, but then had fallen madly in love with Theodorick, yet another cousin and the brother of the famous Jeffersonian leader John Randolph, of Bizarre. When Theodorick suddenly died in 1792, Nancy was so grieved that her affair with her sister's husband Richard could well have been an emotional reaction. During an overnight visit to Glenlyva, belonging to cousin Randolph Harrison, Richard and Judith had to assist Nancy, who was in labor, unbeknownst to their host. (Even sister Judith had not known of the pregnancy until that night.) Several weeks later, however, the slaves showed Harrison where a fetus had been hidden among the shingles in the woodshed. Richard faced charges of murder, but John Marshall and Patrick Henry (at a fee of 500 guineas) gained him an acquittal.[39]

Consanguinity, some claim, led to genetic difficulties in the Old South. It seems most unlikely. Certainly cousinly marriage was no more prevalent than in the ranks of the British nobility or, as mentioned earlier, among the merchant princes of Massachusetts. What made the situation more deadly in the South was not the pattern itself but the intensity of all social relationships, especially those within the patriarchal household. An isolated, tedious existence, financial difficulties in a credit-poor region, an inadequate educational system, and limited career opportunities—all these made family intertwinings both necessary and sometimes very chaotic.

The advantages, however, were thought to outweigh the dangers. Blood kinship through marriage offered the promise of stability, both financial and psychological. The claim to cousinship provided easier access to a family circle for courting, and it signified a socially commendable desire for familiarity and equality of social rank. Among the poor, more than among the rich, marriage of cousins helped to confine family horizons to the known terrain and to exclude the different and dangerous. When asked why there was so much coupling of cousins, a poor white Kentuckian explained, "I just felt practically every body *not* related to us, all those that wasn't related to us and mixed up with us, was *against* us." When a poor white farmer's niece married Tom, a hunchback, her uncle "wondered," he confessed, "if I ought to tell her about Tom bein' so helpless and all. But since she had been knowin' him all her life I thought she" could figure out the matter herself. After all, they were first cousins "even if it didn't look right"—and she was healthy enough to meet the burden, he concluded. In the *Western Weekly Review* of Franklin, Tennessee, an editorial explained that in the South young unmarried female "cousins . . . are so near sisters [to their male cousins] that they think they can treat one as they please, and . . . take great liberties," saying " 'Oh, it's only my cousin. . . .' " The girl felt safer; the boy saw advantages, for under these circumstances she did the courting and entertaining. The "poor fellow" had no chance, the editor mused, but willingly took her to dances until "the next thing that is heard of them is the announcement."[40] In addition, ambitious yeomen who married above themselves ran the risk of alienation from their kinfolk and neighbors. Cousin marriages were a means of reducing risks of incompatibility and of economic and social discrepancies that could lead to trouble.[41]

It must be recognized that most Southern men and women found great satisfaction in marriage. At least it was better than the single life. "The cares," said James Norcom of North Carolina, "are certainly numerous & various; but many of them are animating & exciting in a high degree and not a few of them delightful!" He argued that marriage heightened "the faculties and affections of human beings," providing also a welcome chance to exercise moral duties and responsibilities. A life of celibacy, on the other hand, "is a cold and comfortless condition, in which our moral nature is neglected."[42]

These abstractions, though typical of his time, class, and region, received enthusiastic confirmation in the endearing words of husbands and wives from colonial times through the Civil War. In fact, so affectionate—outspokenly affectionate—were Southern couples that the strains and strategies that have been emphasized here might seem inconsequential. It is not the purpose here to deny or belittle the domestic attachments of these long-dead Americans. Yet one must be careful to judge less by appearances and kind words than by the whole situation that may have been masked in courtly gesture and pleasantries. There can be no doubt at all that Frances Peters genuinely yearned for the return of her husband when she wrote, "You have just been gone one week today but I believe it is one of the longest I have ever spent." Even though all was well, *"nothing* can fill your place here," she wrote at the beginning of a series of ever-longer absences. Discomfited by her growing irritation, Robert Peters a year later decided to "please my wife and smoke fewer cigars—drink less wine and indulge less in other expensive luxuries. . . ." Also, Peters vowed to buy her a piano for their Lexington, Kentucky, house. Nevertheless, his absences made her cross. Unmollified, she burst out, "I must recollect that I belong to that degraded race called woman—who whether her lot be cast among Jew, or Turk, heathen or Christian is yet a *Slave*."[43] It was a common matronly reaction.

No aspect of marital life was quite so fraught with distress as the tendency of men to escape home, on long trips for either business reasons or pleasure. Furthermore, kind words, presents, and promises of reform, such as those that Robert Peters offered, did not always appease the women left behind. A Virginia plantation wife of Fairfax County humorously complained in the *Turf Register*, a hunting and racing journal, that every time her husband returned from sport in the woods, he would reply to her complaints: "Mrs. Rosebud, you are the very pink of perfection. I declare, my love, there is an infallibility about you, not to be found in any other woman." She admitted, though, that the children were not always in good order and may have contributed to his frequent disappearances. She had to box the ears of her husband's hunting companion for mocking her with a quatrain:

> "Two or three girls and two or three boys,
> All ragged and dirty, making a noise;
> One bawling for this, and one squalling for that;
> One kicking the dog, and one scalding the cat."

She urged the editor to advise her husband to "give up his fishing boats and his hounds, persuade him to drop his hunting acquaintances, and frequent the society of clergymen, except that old fox-hunting parson, Mr. Broders," and send his son Robin to theological seminary, and the daughter to dancing school.[44] The letter was not, of course, a genuine account, but beneath the humor there was much truth. Southern men were well versed in the art of flattery—it was a social necessity for courting and for domestic tranquility. The relations between husband and wife were customarily more cordial and companionable than the stress given in this discussion to economic factors and male prerogatives might suggest. Nevertheless, women had to be long-suffering and men blissfully insensitive toward their wives' feelings if the unions that gave them nourishment and mutual dependence were to survive.

9

Women in a Man's World:
Role and Self-Image

The encounter of antebellum Southern male and female was intense, competitive, and almost antagonistic. Intense, because all exchanges were, in a society that placed so much value upon personal contact and close relationships. Competitive, since independence was a social goal that women, despite the contrary requirement of subordination, shared with men. The struggle, however, had to be subterranean and devious, for men alone were given the privilege of expressing their feelings openly. Antagonisms grew out of the conflict, but also out of the misogyny that arose from male fear of female power.

It should not be supposed that these attitudes were peculiar to the Old South alone. They had always existed. Nevertheless, antebellum Yankee women, at least those in the upper and middle classes, had begun to question, with increasing insistence, their age-old subjection. In response, Southern spokesmen reacted to the threat of unfamiliar notions of feminine rights by articulating long-held assumptions. Southern men were not, as one authority recently claimed, "would-be patriarchs." They were the genuine article, and intended to remain so eternally. One writer, for instance, declared in 1845 that "the husband acquires from the union increased capacity and power," but that the wife simply brought a "feebleness that solicits protection—a singleness that requires support."[1] These prescriptions were not the product of Victorian sentiment. Rather they expressed ancient convictions in contemporaneous terms.

Southern male honor required that women be burdened with a multitude of negatives, a not very subtle way to preserve male initiative in the never-ending battle of the sexes. Female honor had always been the exercise of restraint and abstinence. "She cannot [that is, ought never to] give utterance to her passions like a man," commanded T. R. Dew of William and Mary College. She must "suppress the most violent feelings," yet show a "contentment and ease which may impose upon an inquisitive and scrutinizing world." The advice that planter Bolling Hall of Alabama gave his daughter in 1813 was typical of the social ideas of womanhood that had been handed down for generations. "If you learn to restrain every thought, action and word by virtue and religion, you will become an ornament," he promised. To be sure, Yankee parents had made the same sort of prediction in prior years; many still did so, although the winds of change were abroad during antebellum times.[2]

Of course, everyone knew forceful women, stern in rectitude, commanding in personality, but by no means were such formidable matrons recognized as part of a formal matriarchy. They held power by virtue of willfulness, not prescriptive right. Aunt Rosa Mallard in Faulkner's *The Unvanquished* exemplified the type. She did what she deemed necessary to preserve family fortune, but always in the name of the owner, Colonel John Sartoris, who was away at war. The same type appeared often in real life. "Grandmother" James, recalled Emily Semple of Alabama, "was looked upon as a severe old lady whom everybody feared, even her sons and grandsons." Yet even she could not get her "jovial" husband to attend Methodist camp meeting, although later she did successfully use her powers of purse, as his widow, to ensure the occasional appearance of her sons at services. Among the lower classes, too, some women possessed the necessary grit. " 'Granny,' " said Vance Randolph in reference to an old farm woman, "was regarded as a chimney-oracle, and her grown sons and grandsons consulted her about many matters which they did not mention to their wives. Illiterate and superstitious she was, and filthy and disgusting in her personal habits, but [with] magnificence about her, a sort of couraged pessimism. . . ."[3]

Reversals of role—the hen-pecked husband, the scolding wife—offered a deviance that supported the prevailing view by negative example. How such individuals were handled by gossip and sometimes public humiliation will become evident in the course of these pages. Enforcement of gender and family conventions was community business, at least among the common folk of the Old South. All ranks of men agreed that women, like other dependents upon male leadership and livelihood, should be subordinate, docile. As Dr. James Norcom of North Carolina put it, "God in his inscrutable wisdom, has appointed a place & a duty for females, *out of which* they can neither accomplish their destiny nor secure their happiness!!"[4]

The ideals that men defined for women were to a considerable degree reenforced by women themselves. First, they found in matrimony their *raison d'être,* just as they were supposed to do. According to Mrs. Sarah Hale, a New England widow and editor of *Godey's Lady Book,* women everywhere—South *and* North—were "confined to *one* pursuit." With some exaggeration, at least in regard to Northern life, she declared, "It is in the marriage establishment only that woman seeks her happiness and expects her importance. . . ." A telling exchange on this topic appeared in Sarah Wadley's youthful diary. Her mother had playfully asked the father by letter if he would approve a minister for son-in-law. Sarah was then only fifteen. She recorded that he replied in earnest: "Whenever Sarah marries, which I hope may not be before she is twenty years old, I should prefer that her husband be engaged in some active out of doors business, not that I object to a parson, except that I suppose she will take an interest in her husband's profession and I think it best that her mind should be turned *from* metaphysics to which I think she is rather too much inclined." The social assumptions of what constituted a good husband and a good helpmeet were evident, but so was Sarah's own acceptance of her father's judgment. Depressed during the next six months, she often felt that she was

simply not up to the standards of intellectual vacuity her father set
and that she would have to remain single.[5]

The difficulty was that if one did not marry, there were no appropriate alternatives. Women's money-making occupations were chiefly
confined to doing the work of other women in the home—sewing,
managing a house as landlady or paid housekeeper, supervising
children as governess or teacher. It was acceptable for widows to
manage the business in which their husbands had been engaged,
but spinsters, unless milliners or dressmakers, seldom started a firm
on their own. Unlike their Northern sisters of comparable education, Southern women could not even teach school without feelings
of guilt and self-consciousness. Leaving Alabama for Georgia, Margaret Gillis, for instance, thought that her employment as a plantation music teacher would provide new fulfillment as well as a way
to survive the Civil War. "Well I have braved all opposition, and
the displeasure of those who love me, and come here to teach," she
wrote in her diary. "I thought I never could be contented without
teaching," but "how my heart aches," she discovered, as homesick-
ness and a sense of social declension overwhelmed her. Her worries
were justified. Dr. James Norcom of North Carolina, gossiping about
a physician's widow named Mrs. Sawyer who had to take up music
teaching to earn her living, admitted that her occupation was respectable, but barely so. Few ladies wanted to know the musical
arts, he claimed, and those few were all that stood between Mrs.
Sawyer and "starvation."[6]

With the alternatives nonexistent or demeaning, Southern women
strained for security in marriage. Margaret Wilson, a Mississippi
governess, dreamed of escape from the snubs of planters' ladies. "I
know I would make a faithful, obedient wife," she sighed, "loving
with all my heart, yielding entire trust in my husband." When prospects dimmed, then and only then was she prepared to rue her fate.
Woman, she bitterly remarked, must suffer in silence, foreseeing but
unable to "avert or repel" her doom, forced to rely "on beings" over
whom "she has no control excepting the mockery submission of the
hour when she is marked out by her tyrant for a still deeper slav-

ery," yet must go on "smiling, cheering" her tormentor.[7] Margaret Wilson's miseries were as conventional as her fancies of bliss.

Second, women undertook their own inner policing to avoid unseemly rebelliousness. They stifled in themselves alien thoughts, cynicism, misanthropy. When Caroline Merrick and her cousin Antoinette of East Feliciana Parish, Louisiana, received word that Caroline's father had refused permission for their early-morning rides, "we were obliged to submit to his authority without protest," Caroline recalled. She was, however, prepared to inform him that "there is a word sweeter than 'mother, home, or heaven,' and that word is 'liberty.' "[8] But in actual fact she did not have the nerve.

Feminine dependency was woman's fate, no matter how much she secretly wished that it were otherwise. When brides were much younger than their husbands, the latter held the initiative, even in regard to planning the household. Fifteen when her father literally gave her to Thomas Merrick, Caroline had nominal charge of nursery and kitchen, but her husband interfered whenever it suited him. For instance, he abruptly moved the family to New Orleans when she was twenty and already burdened with three babies. Without any consultation, he purchased a house that she had never seen. Suppressing her disappointment, she only admitted later that "the home chosen was not such as I should have selected," being miles from the busy city life. Yet she lived there for fifty years, long after her husband had died. James H. Hammond's wife Catherine also had to hide her resentment when he went to New York from South Carolina to buy all the china, glass, tableware, curtains, sofas, and bedsteads for a new mansion in Columbia. Catherine had only the pleasure of reading his letter about the trials of shopping. "It takes so long to look all around," he complained in hopes of sympathy, "and even after one finds the right place it requires several visits to get what you want." Henry Burgwyn's wife was so young and eager a bride (Yankee though she was) that she delighted in her furnishings and possessions, which, she rejoiced, were "all Henry's taste." Soon she found, however, that there was little left to do. She undertook excursions by foot, accompanied by roving hogs, until the neighboring ladies in New Bern made fun of her Yankee energy. Walking, especially alone, was thought indelicate.[9]

Marital squabbles were inevitable. Yet the wise woman tried to loyally suppress her misgivings as she had been commanded by parents, teachers, ministers, and friends. Chafing under some criticism from her husband, Mary Louisa Williamson of Alabama's Black Belt confessed that his arbitrariness had added to "the cares that devolve upon a wife." But "in the evening" she once more *"vowed to love, honor, and obey my husband."* The local preacher stressed the obligation that Mary Williamson felt in surmounting her anger. "Listening to the Minister," she wrote, who assured her "that 'those were *ties,* that neither angels nor men could render void,' I felt perfect confidence in the strength and vitality of my *love"*—although "once or twice since the fervor and steadfastness of my faith has wavered." Like the slaves who often heard in the white people's church about the necessity to obey, women were commanded to defer to male authority. The spiritual message had its effect.[10] Out of necessity women adjusted to the pattern and took situations as they came. The process made them sometimes a trifle hard.

Toughness beneath the soft exterior had its origins in childhood. Girls, it will be recalled, were raised without much sexual differentiation from their male peers from birth to the boys' "clothing" stage. During that first period of childhood they too were indulged, fretted over, and given every opportunity to make demands, and even allowed the sort of wild outdoor activity that led to easily preventable accidents. In frontier Alabama, Colonel Semple's aristocratic daughter Emily Virginia Semple remembered that she was accustomed to bruising herself by running in the yard, age four, with a sunbonnet drooping over her eyes. Finally her father ordered the inconvenient article removed, to prevent her from "butting my brains out." Her mother, fearful of the ill effects of sunlight on a girl's white complexion, refused, and won the dispute. At an earlier time in Southern history mothers were not so solicitous about ladylike appearance and behavior. In 1769, for instance, Agan Blair of Maryland reported that for several days past "Betsy and her Cousin

Jenny had been fighting," to the vexation of all, and after repeated threats of whippings had failed to restore order she had finally intervened, although neither child was her own. Southern colonial women were averse to strict regulation of young girls. An Englishwoman visited the Blair plantation on the eastern shore and brought along a "little girl," who was much "to be pitied," declared Agan Blair. "This poor thing is stuck up in a chair all day long with a Coller on, nor dare she even to taste Tea fruit Cake or any little Triffle offer'd her by ye company. . . ." Fathers like William Byrd II often preferred their girls over sons, not because of some loosening of patriarchal requirements, but because, at least in part, daughters were often less aggressive and more easily handled than boys.[11]

Although stricter controls became more fashionable in the antebellum era, a degree of indulgence often continued for girls into the next period of their moral and physical development after the age of four. J. G. Clinkscales remembered that in his pre–Civil War childhood, "many of the young ladies could ride as well as their brothers, and not a few of them could handle firearms with great accuracy and skill." Fathers took their girls fishing. Sometimes they went on hunting trips, too. In Mississippi, John J. Pettus's sisters accompanied the boys on their sporting forays in the forests. Thomas Page of Virginia recalled that girls ran about the plantation yard "wishing they were boys, and getting half scoldings from mammy for being tomboys and tearing their aprons and dresses." Half-scoldings were also half-approvals. Just as boys showed courage in the killing of animal bullies, like Wade Hampton's drake, so too did girls sometimes prove very brave souls. J. G. Clinkscales's sister Barbara, for instance, went after an old sow, a dangerous beast, that had been devouring baby chicks. She took her father's muzzle-loading shotgun and "emptied a load of bird-shot into the anatomy of the notorious chicken-eater." Needless to say, however, mothers insisted that the girls learn womanly chores, feeding the farm animals, sewing, and mending. Like the boys, they also learned the lessons of tyrannizing slaves, sometimes in very unladylike fashion.[12]

Early and late, Southern critics complained that girls were taught to be just as aggressive and difficult to manage as boys. Colonel

Landon Carter hardly ever had a good word to say about the manner in which his son and daughter-in-law raised his grandson and granddaughter. From his point of view both children were excessively indulged. Little Lucy imitated the gross manners of her mother, to the old colonel's distress. Carter, however, believed (correctly or not) that "the first she has entirely ruined by storming at me whenever I would have corrected him a child; and the other has already got to be as sawsy a Minx as ever sat at my table." In 1831 Moses Curtis, the North Carolina schoolmaster, had trouble with a girl of thirteen who refused to answer a question, for which offense he thrashed her with thirty blows over a three-hour morning session. Obstinately, she did not submit with proper deference until mid-afternoon. Family and personal pride could be as powerful a force in girls as in boys. Teachers, parents felt, had little right to punish girls severely, if at all. Even James Norcom, a stern believer in parental corrections, thought that schoolmen should not be allowed to use physical force upon either girls or boys, for it degraded their sense of personal integrity and honor, particularly so after the age of twelve or thirteen.[13]

Family pride and sense of honor were important attributes for girls to share with their brothers, for two main reasons. First, they encouraged resistance to matches based largely on sexual attraction. Although tomboy behavior was acceptable at an early stage, as soon as they reached menarche girls abruptly had to recognize their vulnerability to male aggression. Sexual experiment had to be forbidden, not for reasons of morality alone but also to prevent unwanted young men from violating girls' chastity. Illicit pregnancy forced marriage on the one hand or social ostracism on the other. It was hard for Southerners, like the Irish folk from whom so many of them sprang, to imagine that illicit sex was merely a search for pleasure; the ulterior motive had to be greed for lands and social advance. Or else it was simple gallantry—a licentious expression of masculinity that motivated the rogue. Hence, young girls were warned to remember their parentage as well as their self-respect. Second, the development of family honor in the young virgin served the purpose of reinforcing courage. Bravery in woman, as in ancient

Germany or in eighteenth-century Celtic lands, was still honored in the Old South. Women's expression of valor, however, was to be in the form of stoical acceptance of fate or, if their protectors were unavailable, fierce defense of hearth. As a result, some fathers even trained their daughters in the use of guns. Though the boys often objected, their sisters sometimes went on hunts, and most Southern women had learned to ride horseback when they were still young.

The familiar stereotyping of Southern ladyhood—the glorification of motherhood, the sanctity of virginity, and the noble self-sacrifice of the matron—had a very important social purpose. Such concepts ensured at least outward submission to male will. They incorporated the ideals of inner constraint and hardihood within the framework of the softer feminine values of modesty, reserve toward outsiders, and warmth of affection toward the men who were significant in women's lives. Moreover, the hymns of praise to virtuous womanhood made the ascriptive disadvantages of the gender more bearable. They elevated the negative features into admirable qualities. Some scholars have argued, however, that these idealizations were mischievously self-deluding. The myths failed in their purpose, leaving misery in their path. Mythology pretended that every woman could think herself a belle, and at the same time offered no inkling of the distresses of motherhood that awaited most belles. So the legend of ladyhood might seem from our perspective today. But all societies have their conventional illusions, which are designed to make the unbearable somewhat less frightening. Besides, no one knew of any alternatives. Companionate marriage would have to await changes in women's property rights, prospects of decent employment for wives and mothers, and a culture devoted to egalitarian principles generally. Until then, the feminine ethic had to encourage submission to reality.[14]

It is sometimes argued that Southern young women suffered needlessly in silence, that worries were voiced only in private, not in public as they should have been.[15] Yet the reason for reticence was not anxiety lest the myth of the ladyhood be shattered. Instead, the injunction to hold the tongue was a demand for stalwartness against adversity. That mattered much more than delicacy. The latter was a luxury thrown aside when women had to meet difficult times—agrarian disasters; sudden changes in fortune, whether from bad luck or male inadequacy; epidemics; or, most especially, military catastrophes and losses during the Civil War. Women were expected to nurture a capacity to bear burdens with grace, courage, and silence. That social ideal far outweighed any girlish dreaming about being a belle, a fancy to be indulged only in the brief sojourn from paternal control to husbandly dominion. Thus to appear poised, forbearing, and hopeful, especially when things went wrong, was to please friends and relations. In fact, it signified inner stamina. Having lost her mother just before the Civil War, Margaret Gillis, a rich planter's daughter of Alabama, could not quite overcome her grief, for she had needed her mother's prenuptial advice and support as she reached late adolescence. With remarkable courage and resilience, she endured the war and early Reconstruction with only a pittance from her circuit-riding Methodist husband. Her diary was her solace: "Mother, come back from the echoless shore./ Take me again to your heart as of yore/ . . . Over my slumbers your loving watch keep,/ Rock me to sleep, mother; rock me to sleep." She died during childbirth, largely because of malnourishment, according to a close relation.[16] Yet for all the depression that she felt within, she, like most Southern women, met these disasters with the kind of gallantry that the Southern ethic instilled. Southern antebellum and Civil War women bore their fate admirably.

Before the Civil War this emphasis upon feminine grit perhaps had been more muted, but it was implicit not only in the way girls were raised but also in literature. No doubt it accounted for the popularity of *The Heart of Midlothian*, Scott's novel of Effie Dean's endurance for the sake of her wayward sister. In reviewing a book on Southern women's role in the American Revolution, an antebellum literary critic voiced similar ideals. The plantation wife in that era, he rhapsodized, "exhibits a strength, a courage and a variety of resource, which no one had deemed her to possess," even leaving behind "enjoyment of security and repose" to meet the enemy if necessity required.[17] The ideal of feminine courage and honor almost replicated that of men under such circumstances, and certainly it found expression in legends of female heroism in Civil War recollections and novels. But these values were still traditional ones; they did not at all point toward a modern feminism. Rather, they reflected the ancient view that mothers of brave men had to be brave themselves. By and large, many of them were. The aspiration and actuality were conjoined, particularly under the bitter duress of war.

In happier, more settled circumstances women were supposed to be uncomplaining and docile. When Mrs. Gildersleeve, a Georgia physician's wife, found herself pregnant once again, she took herself promptly to bed, "so great," friends gossiped, was her "disappointment." It was a quietly emphatic way to respond to bad news, but somewhat too transparent and self-indulgent to win her much sympathy from the other matrons.[18]

Mrs. Gildersleeve's unhappiness about facing the ordeal of childbirth was no sign of a present-minded spirit at work in the womanly conscience. Childbearing was an ancient and sacred calling of the gender. Few in the Old South disputed so self-evident a proposition as that. For instance, Mrs. Chesnut stood by a wife, a newcomer in the community, who was thought to be barren. She told her circle of friends that the woman had actually had three babies but lost them all. "Women have such contempt for a childless wife," Mrs. Chesnut commented. "Now they will be all sympathy and kindness. I took away her 'reproach among women.' "[19] Mrs. Chesnut knew whereof she spoke: she was exceedingly conscious of her own unfruitfulness.

Barrenness in women, like kinlessness, which was discussed earlier, had always been a point of shame, and sufferers were contemptible or at best pitiable in the eyes of others. To be sure, Southerners were not so primitive and brutal about the matter as archaic peoples had once been. Nevertheless, family continuity was highly prized and childlessness was a sore grievance. The married woman who disappointed her husband and relations in this respect could scarcely help having feelings of incompleteness. Moreover, it cut her off from a source of personal power—the duties of nurture—and from sense of fulfillment as a woman. C. Vann Woodward and Elisabeth

Muhlenfeld, students of Mary Chesnut's literary diary and of her sad, dramatic life, speculate that one of her many trips north away from the dull plantation routine in the 1840s was prompted by a nervous depression, the cause of which was related to her infertility. Indeed, her antislavery convictions might well have been connected with the problem. Mrs. Chesnut, reared to slaveholding wealth and enjoying all its privileges and responsibilities, had fewer political than domestically moral objections to the institution. A major component of her assault upon the system was the thought that "we live surrounded by prostitutes" whose offspring populated the quarters. "Thank God for my countrywomen—alas for the men! No worse than men everywhere, but the lower their mistresses, the more degraded they must be."[20]

What drove home the point was her attitude toward her lusty father-in-law, James Chesnut, Sr. and his attitude toward her. How bitter it was for her to record that "these people take the old Hebrew pride in the number of children they have. . . . Old Mr. C. said today, 'Wife, you must feel that you have not been useless in your day and generation. You have now twenty-seven great-grandchildren . . . «Me a childless wretch. . . . Colonel Chesnut, a man who rarely wounds me . . . And what of me! God help me—no good have I done myself or anyone else, with this I boast so of, the power to make myself loved. Where am I now, where are my friends? I am allowed to have none. (*He did not count his children!!*)»'" An autocrat—like the Russian czar or the emperor of Austria, as Mary Chesnut described him—the old planter earned her deep respect and even admiration and affection. But he was father, she suspected, of a mulatto line. Practical, jealous of his property, and completely unsentimental, Chesnut, Sr., she mused on more than one occasion, "was born when it was not the fashion for a gentleman to be a saint." The wonder was, she thought, that he had not been "a greater tyrant." The sins of slaveholding which her husband's father so regrettably exemplified in her mind were not unconnected with her own sense of blameworthiness for not providing him with grandchildren, a task that the blackest "wench" in a slave harem could do.[21]

Mary Chesnut was, however, luckier than many women in the

Old South. She had wit, style, and, above all, a loving husband, whom she believed faithful to her despite her barrenness. Wealth and marriage gave her status in the tight South Carolinian world. Some were much less graced. In the eyes of neighbors and kin, there was nothing more pitiful among women than the spinster who was deprived of both husband and children, a double curse. Her "sin" was the failure to please a man, by being either overly aggressive or too "sensible" (that is, intellectual). Caroline Merrick's father, for instance, intensely disliked any young girl who flirted too much. She was destined, he thought, "to become a lonely old maid and hold a pet dog in her arms, with never a child of her own because she had turned away from her highest vocation, and all for mere vanity and folly." In ridicule, a bachelor in western North Carolina claimed that the girls there were so desperate that they paraded the streets of Salisbury staring at strangers "with a fixed and intent gaze." He made it a habit to place his hat "on one side when about to pass in review before them." In earlier days, he claimed, girls had been less forward and better prepared for marriage by working at home instead of "giggling and gazing on the side walk." Husband hunting was thought a contemptible occupation, less shameless than prostitution but disgraceful anyhow. Twenty-five years later, attitudes toward unmarried women had not much improved. Another Carolinian observed that "hardly can half a dozen persons spend an evening together without the manoeuvres of some (alleged) husband hunting spinster becoming the subject of discussion." (Very old spinsters, of course, gained something from the ascriptive prestige of age, and eccentricity then became an endearing characteristic rather than a sign of "unnatural" compulsions.)[22]

As the single woman reached her mid-twenties, spinsterhood became a form of social death. Better to have a husband who ran off with one's inheritance or drank away the cash from a year's farming than to be without a husband at all. At least the neighbors pitied rather than condemned the woman with a roguish husband. In any case, the spinster usually faced an uncertain future as an economic dependent upon father, brother, or married sister. For a small number there was the occasional chance to serve as a plantation governess. The pay was poor, the employers often pretentious and mean-spirited, and the chance to meet single men rather slim. Worst of all was the condescension toward the working woman, which even the children quickly sensed and exploited, and the boredom of country living without sufficient duties. Margaret Wilson's diary on a plantation near Washington, Mississippi, a hamlet outside Natchez, offers glimpses of the misery of genteel singleness. As far as the young woman could tell, the ladies of the household spent their hours driving "little negroes in the yard and their mothers in the kitchen." Even that activity was closed to the governess. "I positively have nothing to say this evening," she informed herself, "really it is impossible to lead a more uneventful life." Sarcastically, she added, "Oh! what I was forgetting: have I not just before Tea followed Mrs. S—— into the garden intent upon robbing a nest of mocking Birds. . . ."[23]

Margaret Wilson may have been the spinster-governess whom J. H. Ingraham mentioned in one of his several books on the Southwest. Ingraham, a Yankee immigrant, taught at the Jefferson Academy in Washington, Mississippi, a school for boys. He reported that they held a few words in her room while the family and guests were at dinner. "I prefer dining in my room," she said, "though to tell you the truth, I am never invited at the dinner parties; nor when invitations are sent for the family am I included. . . . Teaching here is by some families looked upon as beneath 'position,' as the phrase is." As Ingraham observed, her chances for marriage to a gentleman were slim because her occupation disqualified her, and she was too refined to suit plainer men. In further illustration Ingraham described how, though forced to open a school for her own support, a Vicksburg widow refused to allow her two daughters to assist her "lest it should be an obstacle in the way of their marrying *en regle*." In the free states, however, the schoolteacher belonged to the local intelligentsia. As Ingraham concluded, "A New England mind can scarcely comprehend how teaching youth can be looked upon as a lowering vocation."[24]

The middle-aged bachelor could take a much more sanguine view of life. He had the solace of his higher standing as a male. Early in the nineteenth century there had been talk in North Carolina of penalizing unmarried men by imposing special taxes on them. Like spinsters, they were not fulfilling the universal obligation to procreate. But by the Jacksonian era there was nothing scandalous or wholly pathetic about the aging bachelor as such. At least he could afford condescension about women in the same position as he. T. W. Peyre, a Carolinian bachelor, remarked about a landlady's daughter who was "a maid . . . approximating the antique, but of what degree I know not, whether a voluntary old maid, or an involuntary, or an old maid by accident, an explicable old maid, or a literary old maid."[25]

Being a widow was considerably less shameful than spinsterhood. Yet the widow was also subject to disparaging glances and opinions. For instance, Hardy Wooten, the physician of Lowndesboro, Alabama, complained that his mother Jerusha Wooten, a Georgia matron, was "a widow who could not suppose that anyone could manage her affairs so well as herself," a very arrogant position for her to take. As a result, she had given "herself an abundance of unnecessary trouble and inconvenience." Nevertheless, from the inadvertent evidence that Wooten supplied in his diary it is clear that Jerusha had made a success of the same farm that her deceased husband had burdened with heavy debts. She even managed to retire his obligations.[26]

In fact, a surprising number of widows seemed to get along quite well in the single state, that is, if their husbands had left them sufficient wealth to manage on their own. Even so, the widow had to struggle keenly against the presumption that she would be the loser in any sort of transaction. Such was the source of troubles for Rachel O'Connor of St. Francisville, Louisiana, who faced a number of difficulties with her grasping brothers-in-law. They involved her in the alien toils of the law, a harsh reminder that men ruled not only at home but at the courthouse, too. The latter was as degrading an arena for a respectable woman as a cockfight pit or tavern. First widowed at eighteen, Rachel had remarried at twenty-three, in 1797. Her second husband, Hercules O'Connor, bought and developed a thriving plantation in West Feliciana. In 1820 he died from overdrinking, a not uncommon fate in that malarial, stultifying region, and Rachel had to manage by herself. Her brother and sister lived in St. Mary Parish, a hundred miles away. Like most widows, she knew nothing of her husband's affairs until creditors and lawyers appeared by the score after the funeral. Horrified at the sums owed, she hired an agent to collect monies on loan and pay off the notes due. Unfortunately, the agent embezzled the funds, then died; the creditors reappeared, pockets still empty. In the suit that followed, the court ruled that though "her agent had abused her confidence and had defrauded her, she had trusted him and must bear the consequences of her indescretion [*sic*]. The rule is, who trusts, must lose." Southern chivalry did not take precedence over the rights of property.[27]

Unexpected problems with a husband's debt were common in the period. Other difficulties also arose. Widows had to deal, for instance, with sons who felt released from paternal pressures and free to make use of the vacancy in family leadership. Rachel O'Connor had two such specimens on her hands, her husband's inebriated son by a previous marriage and their own boy, Stephen, who ran up enormous debts in New Orleans, hoping to make a killing in merchandise. Feeling somehow guilty about their father's sudden death, she indulged the boys with loans, cash, and endorsed notes. Luckily for her, they both soon died of alcoholism, but Stephen left two orphans and a tangle of debts that Rachel felt she was obliged to cover for the sake of the family's reputation. Chief holder of Stephen's notes was William Flower, whose brother Henry had married Pamela, Mrs. O'Connor's half-sister. Somehow the two women remained on affectionate terms. Blood ties prevailed over marital loyalty in this instance. William and Henry Flower, however, did not let family sentiments interfere with a chance to exploit a widow's fear of lawsuits and sense of shame over her son's irresponsibility. Foolishly, Rachel agreed to meet some $3,100 worth of Stephen's promissory notes in William Flower's hands. When he raised the claims to over $10,000, she at last felt compelled to get advice from her brother.[28]

Rachel's brother David Weeks, a rising planter of St. Mary Parish, intervened by "buying" the greater part of his sister's plantation for a nominal sum. In effect, he established a trust so that Flower would have to deal with Weeks himself and his lawyers, not with an easily bullied widow. He was to lease her the plantation and slaves, thus affording her male protection at the cost of her own legal control of the property.

Proprietorship, however, was one of the few rewards of widowhood. Nonetheless, Rachel's decision to retain some land and slaves in her own name provided Flowers with excuses for mounting more legal assaults and attachments. Matters finally came to a head in 1832, ten years after the fight began. The sheriff arrived to serve her with eviction orders, frightening the old lady, as she put it, "out of my wits," while the slaves fled "like wild hogs" into the woods.[29] A jury trial ended the business in the widow's favor, but it was Weeks's interventions that actually led to that result.

As the history of Rachel O'Connor's troubles demonstrates, male protections were indeed requisite, because the inequalities of conditions made them so. Since women often outlived their husbands and since planters so frequently died heavily in debt in that credit-short region, single Southern women of the upper class, like Mrs. O'Connor, were particularly vulnerable to legal exploitation. Lawsuits, like the glass of brandy, the barroom scuffle, the meetinghouse revival, were just a part of life in those very litigious days. But for women they were a special agony. Most women had too little social preparation, power, or experience to handle the ordeal at the courthouse with much assurance.

As mothers, antebellum Southern women might be expected to have enjoyed commanding influence, however subordinate the status of spinsters, widows, and childless wives might have been. Such was not the case. In the naming of newborns, for instance, fathers had preeminent right if they wished to exercise it. The issue was not a petty concern, given the importance attached to naming and the emphasis placed on remembering patrons and beloved friends, usually members of the family. Robert F. W. Allston, for instance, decided to name his infant girl Charlotte, after his mother. His wife, however, called the baby Frances, after a favorite relative, Aunt Blythe. The aunt in question had ideas of her own. She called the child Elizabeth Waties, after the sister of a first cousin whom Aunt Blythe's father had not allowed her to marry. Nevertheless, Allston eventually had his way: the girl was christened Charlotte. Varina Davis, wife of the Confederate president, had an unusually deep relationship with her husband, who was a good family man, whatever his faults as father of his aborted nation might have been. She wished to name their fourth child William, in veneration of her father William Howell. But Jefferson Davis sought to honor his brother Joe, who had served him well in advancing his political and plantation careers. Varina was outraged—she disliked the austere, unbending brother—but eventually she acknowledged her husband's right to make the choice.[30]

Despite all the worship that mothers garnered from men during most of the antebellum years, they did not have first claim to their own offspring. Law and custom gave priority of possession to the father. Declared one Mississippi judge in a child custody case, "We are informed by the first elementary books we read that the authority of the father is superior to that of the mother. It is the doctrine of all civilized nations." Paternal discipline, he said, not the "superior affection" of mothers, determined the matter. Very young children were not separated from their mothers, at least not until they were six or so, and sometimes girls were allowed to remain with their mother, whereas boys went to the father. But by common-law tradition in regard to male property rights, children were considered to be possessions of the head of household. Thus, in law, fathers had the better case for child custody. As late as 1858, the Alabama Supreme Court stated "as a general principle" that "the father is entitled to custody and control of minor children because he is bound for their maintenance and support."[31]

At least on the appellate level in nineteenth-century Southern courts, a gradual shift away from common-law precedents can be detected. In the same 1858 Alabama case mentioned above, the high court sustained a lower tribunal's award of a child to the father, finding no reason "to disturb what has properly been done." The justices, however, insisted upon proof of the demonstrated fitness of the parent before the father could obtain full custody rights. A husband could forfeit his respectability by gross and shameless "misconduct" or "misfortune" and thereby lose such a suit, the Alabama jurists proclaimed. The child's emotional welfare ought to be considered, too, so the court implied. In this regard, Southern justices at the appellate level were in line with the rulings of their Northern colleagues. It would be hard to prove that one section moved more quickly to new ground than the other. Being the most conservative repository of traditional ethics, the American bench and bar were seldom in the vanguard of social change when family sanctities and gender roles were involved. But whether they were the same as or different from their counterparts in the free states, Southern courts departed from old ways with great reluctance. In *Goodrich* v. *Goodrich*, for instance, the Alabama Supreme Court in 1870 granted a mother custody despite the still recognized "general principle" of male priority. (The husband's misconduct, the jurists declared, was sufficiently "cruel and shameful" to disqualify him for custody of his offspring. The mother, on the other hand, had acted throughout her ordeal with propriety and evident concern for her children.)[32] By then Alabama law, under Reconstruction statute, permitted juridical discretion in child awards under divorce decree.

As was stressed in earlier chapters, honor was not a system of values that had entirely disappeared from Northern usage, certainly not in the eighteenth century and not in all instances in the nineteenth. In regard to divorce law, there was considerable variation from one state to the next about the numbers granted, the percentage awarded to one sex or the other, and the grounds for successful pleas. Nevertheless, the prevalence of male favoritism in divorce actions in the Southern states is most striking. Lawrence M. Friedman and Robert V. Percival have compiled statistics that underline the point, though their figures cover only the second half of the nineteenth century. The south Atlantic, east south central, and west south central states all gave about one-half of all divorce decrees to wives, whereas for the same period, 1867 to 1906, the Northern states registered two-thirds to wives and the western states presented three-fourths to the distaff side. Mississippi, Louisiana, Alabama, Virginia, and North Carolina granted husbands well over half the judgments (with a range of 41.6 percent to at most 47.9 percent for wives). The authors do not speculate upon the reasons for the disparities between North, South, and West, but the figures reveal a not surprising depth of conservatism about family life in the South.[33] Yankee women had reason to expect a favorable verdict, whereas Southern matrons had to be pessimistic.

In light of the generally uniform antipathy toward divorcées in the antebellum period, regardless of regional location, it is instructive to examine a divorce and child custody case of the time that was not strictly a Southern affair but one with a most unprovincial character. The circumstances were largely Northern, but not at all untypical of the vulnerabilities of Southern women in relation to law and male prerogative and their effects upon feminine self-image. Fanny Kemble, an English actress, had impulsively married a Philadelphia aristocrat with a large plantation on St. Simon's Island, Georgia. Pierce Butler took his bride there and for years the sensitive young woman experienced the drab and sometimes horrifying life of plantation mistress. Later she published her opinions, to Butler's anguish and the abolitionists' delight. Fanny's outspokenness at the time—"suddenness," she called it—was too much for the small-minded planter she had married. After a decade of acrimonious struggle, parting, and reconciliation, Fanny gained a legal separation, but only when she had agreed to see her two daughters only at hours and places that their father specified. There was no question but that he should have custody. When he further restricted her visiting privileges, she gave up and sailed for England, to renew her stage and literary careers.[34]

Fanny Kemble was far in advance of most women on either side of the Atlantic. Women, wrote Kemble to her friend Harriet Martineau, should be "dealt with, not mercifully, not compassionately, nor affectionately, but *justly*," for the sake of both themselves and men. (Quite accurately, Butler accused her of holding that "marriage should be a companionship on equal terms," a novelty so astonishing that he advertised it as justification for his distress with her. Anyone "not morally astray" could see "the heedlessness" of such claims, he wrote.) In addition, she had a long heritage of personal confidence derived from her career, though not in regard to motherhood, to give her emotional support in breaking convention. Her aunt was Mrs. Siddons, the eighteenth-century actress, and Fanny's English education and stage career gave her much more sophistication and self-possession than the ordinary planter's wife could imagine. Yet even Fanny could not overcome the pervasive demand for feminine deference, and she showed deep uncertainty about her role as wife and mother. Writing Butler in pleasanter days, she had often referred to "your child" instead of "ours." But most of all she failed to fight cold-bloodedly for the custody of little Sarah and Frances, her daughters. Proving Butler's adulterous conduct would have been an easy matter—he had even fought a farcical duel with an outraged husband—but she shrank from the unpleasantness. Had she permitted her lawyers to pursue the matter, she could have gained court-appointed guardianship, the surest means of winning custody. Instead she allowed herself to be put before the public as "a monster of iniquity," and Butler as a figure of some "glamor."[35] But despite these problems, some of them a result of an inner worry about her fitness as a mother, she agreed at once to accept Butler's compromise—two months out of the year of unrestricted custody of the girls. Perhaps Fanny Kemble was psychologically more withdrawn and intimidated than her correspondence reveals. In any case, the law and the conventions of the day conspired against her sense of maternal competence. She won the divorce but not Sarah and Frances.

If someone as intelligent and sensitive as Fanny Kemble suffered under psychic burdens of enforced dependency, how much more subject to similar feelings were Southern women of less education, experience, and opportunity. Time and again women's selfhood was seriously assaulted, not just by the actions, hostilities, or indifferences of men but by the institutions of law, invested as they were with the majesty of the state, the formidability of the male jurists and lawyers, and the unbroken faith of the public. One reason, of course, for the reluctance of respectable women to obtain divorces, sue in civil actions, or bring criminal charges against men was the sense that the court and attorney's office were alien, frightening, grim places of last resort. Legal proceedings exposed them to male scrutiny and thus defeated the feminine claim to privacy and protection from public gaze. Too often historians have emphasized the obstacles confronting women, but not women's inner acceptance of those obstacles as they contemplated the risk of disgrace.[36]

In what has become a classic among feminist studies, Carroll Smith-Rosenberg has offered a sensitive explanation of how nineteenth-century American women responded to their status in a very masculine world. They developed, she says, intimate relationships with other women. The feminist historian observes that close bondings between mother and daughter, sister and sister, aunt and niece, and friend and friend "were frequently supported and paralleled by severe social restrictions on intimacy between young men and women. Within such a world of emotional richness and complexity, devotion to and love of other women became a plausible and socially accepted form of human interaction." Certainly the evidence from Southern sources supports her interpretation. In addition, the traditional world of colonial America, as Mary Beth Norton explains, furnishes similar examples, both Northern and Southern, especially between mothers and daughters. Emotional deprivations in the paternal household of father and husband contrasted with the possibilities for highly intense female friendships.[37]

Other reasons for their development included, first, the recurring cycles of confinement owing to disease and childbirth, bodily concerns that modest women could not so easily share with members of the opposite sex. Women frequently had occasion to fear for the lives of their mother or daughter, friend or cousin, and many opportunities to commiserate over the loss of children and grandchildren. As nurses and confidantes ministering to each other's health, they were in touch with other matters of heart and head as well. In ways only women could appreciate, death in the family and among those nearby tended to bring survivors together. Like the rituals of the wedding, the rites of the funeral were times when women could express themselves in public without restraint. The occasion represented a contrast with the decorum expected of them in male company. In fact, for those who sought privacy and disliked emotional outpourings, the pressure to show grief even when none was felt inwardly could prove irksome. "If you don't 'show feeling,' 'indignation awaits the delinquent," fumed Mary Chesnut, just back from a burial.[38]

A second factor was the importance of religious work, most especially in the upper reaches of society. (Among the lower classes worship, while often segregated by sex within the church, was largely confined to services and revivals, the paraphernalia of female-oriented activities being rather rare.) Sewing societies and Sunday schools, where they existed, brought women together and gave them a sense of special purpose outside the home. (After 1860, war work—knitting for Confederate soldiers, for instance—had the same advantage.) Men objected that religion in women was a danger. Such "studies and pursuits," asserted one suitor of a North Carolina girl, "that qualify women to *shine* in the Society of the learned tend essentially to rob them of the attractions which are most fascinating in the eyes of men—the softening, refining, humanizing influence which nothing that is not wholly feminine has the power to exert." Yet what gave discomfort to the secular male provided companionship for the woman. With others of her sex, she could enjoy the fellowship that charity duties, prayer meetings, and other activities encouraged.[39]

A third contribution was applicable to all the social classes, high and low: common domestic tasks that could be performed while the women gossiped and shared experiences, gatherings much more practical than those of men at a crossroads tavern, muster ground, or sporting event. Among poorer rural folk in the South even today, married sisters and cousins, mothers and married daughters make a practice of getting together and maintaining close relations, in contradistinction to the "togetherness" of modern urban and middle-class couples. "My cousin spent the day with me a few days ago," reported a Tennessee farm woman. "We had fun making hominy in the black lard kettle. Then my daughter spent the day with me to-

day, and we worked like mad to get the beans picked and canned."
In the "Applecross-Millstone" community of Tennessee, according
to Elmora Matthews' study, married sisters spent almost as much
time in each other's kitchen as at home. (The married brothers
meantime shared field work in similar fashion.) Certainly the patterns still extant in the 1960s had existed a hundred and fifty or
more years before, since the economic and social conditions underlying them remained unchanged.[40]

These and other factors formed the sexually differentiated sphere
of "love and ritual" of which Carroll Smith-Rosenberg has written.
Yet it would be a mistake to consider the womanly connection
without reference to the disabilities that women endured in marriage, even though they often expressed a preference for men who
were real breadwinners over ones who were merely "warm and
loving," as a farm wife put it. Loneliness also encouraged the pattern. When her husband Robert left Marion Deveaux and undertook a long trip in 1835, she pursued him with a letter defending
her "remaining *so long standing in the door* the morning of your
departure." He had criticized her for it; it made him feel "uneasy." Southern husbands could be most formidable, especially in
the early years of marriage and sometimes longer. The mature
Mrs. John C. Breckinridge dared approach her husband, a Confederate general, about a matter of military business during the Civil
War, but she framed her advice in this deferential ritual: "I have
no right to say anything except privately and as you advocate free
speech I may venture an opinion." She could not intrude very far
upon his sense of male propriety. Female friendships were bound
to develop under such circumstances as compensation, as well as for
companionship in its own right. They were safe from tensions of
the kind that arose in marriage. In contrast, men were often un-
confiding, even vaguely hostile. Mary Chesnut, for instance, once
remarked, "It is the habit of all men to fancy that in some inscrutable way their wives are the cause of all evil in their lives." Naturally, women turned to each other.[41]

Perhaps the South Carolina diarist was being overly cynical, but
women were expected to show affection toward each other, perhaps

to compensate for the cold reserve of their husbands. "There is a custom," wrote a Yankee observer of Southern antebellum custom, "of kissing when ladies meet. . . . You might see in Boston the meeting of one hundred pair of young ladies during the day, and not seven couples would salute each other on the lips." Schoolgirls in Tennessee and elsewhere likewise expressed their affection openly, imitating older sisters. "At church doors of a Sunday there is quite a *fusilade* of this small arms." However, such shows of emotion may have been more for show than for real affection, particularly in light of the fierce rivalries of women, like their men, over issues of place in society.[42]

No doubt if American marriages had been companionate instead of partiarchal, gentlewomen, North and South, would still have enjoyed each other's company. But ancient sexual divisions of labor almost enforced same-sex closeness out of necessity. On this score, Southern and Northern patterns rather coincided, even though the Yankee style was becoming more "modern." For those women in the antebellum North who felt themselves repressed by social conventions of this kind, intense female friendships were a desperate, rather poignant refuge. Well educated but enslaved to a meaningless existence and male condescension, the "bluestocking" of the big city found expression for her feelings in what was called a "Boston marriage." The label hinted slyly at lesbianism, fairly or not. In the South, nonmarital friendships took a somewhat different form, but in the North nonrelated women sometimes found close ties with one another an untaxing comfort. An example was Sarah Butler Wister, mother of the novelist Owen Wister. In her adolescence she formed a very intense relationship with Jeannie Field Musgrove, in which the two Philadelphia maidens adopted male and female noms de plume respectively. Sarah and Jeannie continued to use these nicknames into their declining years, long after Sarah's eventual marriage. It is worth mentioning that Sarah was one of Fanny Kemble's two daughters, and that her close relationship with Jeannie flowered during the unhappy, indeed traumatic period of the separation and divorce of her mother and her father, Pierce Butler. The fact that Fanny Kemble in effect deserted her and her sister—

not wholly voluntarily, but partially because of her ambivalence about fighting for child custody—had some bearing on Sarah's connection with Jeannie Musgrove. She had need of someone to trust. A brutish father and a career-absorbed mother did not suffice. "If the day should come," Sarah wrote Jeannie, "when you fail me either through your fault or my own, I would foreswear all human friendship thenceforth." It is interesting that Sarah took the male part in their secret games and fancied names. Jeannie was also a child "abandoned," in her case by the death of a parent.[43] Few mothers then were as modern in their career aims and confusions about domestic life as Fanny Kemble. Likewise, few women were as modern in their reactions as her daughter Sarah. Although generalizations about the intricacies of mother-daughter relations, particularly as expressions of sectional cultures, are necessarily risky, the pattern of "Boston marriages" was probably more a Northern than a Southern one. There was no comparable term in the South, no "Charleston marriages" of paired female friends.

Much more common in the Old South was the close association of brother and sister. This may have stemmed from the general character of isolated, family-bound plantation life. The paradigm in schematic form was along the following lines: Mothers were confined at home, resentful of their immobility, whether they knew it or not. Fathers were often abroad, to escape the monotony and the control that their wives sought to impose upon them. As a result, the mother lavished attention upon the children. They saw to it that their daughters replicated themselves. With sons, however, they were more ambivalent. Boys filled them with pride and wonder, but also with hidden resentment of their unmanageability. With unusual zeal, a mother often protected her son from the wrath of his father, but her intense concern threatened the lad, who frequently feared that her "leading strings" would unman him. Time and again fathers complained of this interference by mothers, because it would shame them to raise effeminate sons. Caught between the competition of the parents, the son could only turn to his sister, who then served as surrogate mother in imitation of her own mother's impulses. Naturally the girl, knowing few other men besides her father and brother, responded to her brother's need for affection. To him she was the only woman who could be trusted. Thus misogyny and manliness were entangled in a sometimes emotionally destructive way. Upon his marriage, the son repeated the same style his father had set before him—pursuing his own interests and leaving his wife to her own devices. The cycle then started anew. Thus the intensity of the brother-sister relation in the Old South was born of the deep antinomies in patriarchal family life, as an island of comfort in a sea of misapprehension and dread of dependency upon mother's love and father's good favor, both often withheld. This analysis is admittedly speculative, but the childrearing practices of the gentry class in the Old South point in that direction.

The theme of sibling intimacies is one that Edgar Allan Poe and William Faulkner both explored. Their fiction reflected a nineteenth-century Southern reality, though they carried the tendency to its ultimate (and certainly rare) expression: incest. Just as Sarah Butler Wister's experiment with female homoeroticism was exceptional, so too was brother-sister sexual contact. Yet sibling ties were encouraged by families that put strong emphasis upon all intrafamilial loyalties. Also, brothers and sisters often shared fears of a formidable father or grief for an absent or deceased one. Sometimes sisters felt a severe tug of jealousy when their brothers married their most intimate friends, a situation that was very often built into the ubiquitous network of cousinry. Both siblings were drawn, it might happen, toward the same girl, though not, of course, for the same reasons of passionate infatuation. So it was in the life of Kate Stone of Brokenburn. She was a Louisiana belle whose brother William was not just her beau ideal, but also the substitute for her father, long since dead. She mourned, fumed, and rejoiced in a few hurried lines of her youthful diary:

Also a letter from Kate Nailor. From her main message to My Brother, they must be betrothed lovers again. I am glad for his sake and hers. And Kate is my dearest friend, but it is hard to give up the first place in the heart of my darling Brother

even to this other Kate. . . . Truly I shall never love a stranger
as I love him who has been my heart's desire since babyhood.[44]

Kate Stone was no "neurasthenic," no aberration. Nor was her attitude solely a reflection of Southern cultural patterns entirely different from Northern ones. On this score, as in regard to many others
in this study, familial relations in both sections were very similar, particularly among those of comparable economic and social
position, North and South. But these traditional characteristics,
ones that joined brother and sister in deep but also partially competitive affection, arose from the common ethic. The system of
honor or, to use the more familiar terms, patriarchy and womanly
subordination, engendered these emotions as a way to cope with
the process of maturing. Wherever fathers exercised their right to
rule—and to be free—children were likely to see in each other idealizations that were a comfort to them both. To be sure, most siblings
gradually weaned themselves from immature attachments to each
other. They lost the earlier yearning for safe and androgynous passion. Nevertheless, the less taxing patterns often retained a special
place in their lives, adding romance and a sense of sharing. That
arrangement was a way to compensate for a lack of power, particularly for the sister. When a girl married, particularly in the still
highly patriarchal South, she was to discover that the man she
vowed to obey was more like her father than like the brother whom
she adored. The husband naturally assumed the patriarchal role,
being master of her property and the source of her honor and power
as well as of his own. The wheel of life turned in the next generation in the same way as in the previous one. One girl's brother had
become another's master. The wife, in time, became the nurturing
possessor, the figure that her mother once had been.

10

Law, Property, and Male Dominance

The foundation of woman's status in marriage was her legal unity with her husband, as defined in common law. It is a curious but not unexpected fact that whereas woman's social existence largely depended upon her being married, her legal identity ended the moment the ceremony was performed. Sir William Blackstone, whom American jurists of both sections cited as often as they did the Constitution, bluntly put the issue in perspective in his *Commentaries* in 1765: "By marriage, the husband and wife are one person in law," so much so that her "legal existence" was "suspended" for the duration of the marriage. This heavy and complacent dictum was slightly mitigated in Chancellor Kent's *Commentaries on the American Law*, published 1826 to 1830. Whereas Blackstone stressed the consolidation of the wife's interest with that of her husband, "under whose wing, protection, and cover, she performs every thing," Kent boasted that a new "Christian" era had begun to provide "equality and dignity" for women. It had all been done, he thought, in a manner flattering to "the female character," a distinctly different order of being. Kent was not altogether misleading. There had been a number of significant changes in legal policy: the simplifying of procedures to construct separate estates through prenuptial trusts, marriage settlements, and other means. Also, a legislative trend had gradually conferred upon married women control of their earnings by individual application for "free trader" status. Finally, some states in both sections had transferred divorce actions from state lawmakers to judges on circuit in one court or another.[1]

Within a few years after Kent's monumental work appeared, other innovations also emerged: the routine acceptance of feminine breach-of-promise claims, humane views of common-law obligations, and the hesitantly growing tendency to award child custody to mothers instead of to fathers, though the preference, as mentioned before, was by no means uniform in the Old South. Nevertheless, male honor required masculine headship of the family. Judges and attorneys, guided by common-law assumptions of male primacy, helped immeasurably to perpetuate the old ethic—and not in the South alone. Even in New England and Pennsylvania, the fundamental principle of gender hierarchy found vindication in law and therefore in social expectation.[2]

For most of the early half of the nineteenth century, the vital issue of property rights for American women was still very circumscribed. Following common-law precedent, Kent pointed out that "the disability of the wife to contract so as to bind herself, arises not from want of discretion but because she had entered into an indissoluble connection" in which her husband, not herself, administered property, including "all personal property in possession" at the moment of marriage. Not only could a husband treat his wife's property as his own, but her assets could be seized to meet his debts. His control over her "chattels personal" (slaves in particular, in the South) was absolute. There were various refinements about "chattels real," or real estate, but for our purposes here it is no exaggeration to claim that the husband's use of his wife's lands was virtually untrammeled. In addition, his responsibilities to her were minimal: he was held accountable for her debts incurred before and during the marriage, and he had to meet a rather low standard of support. Needless to say, not many women were free enough to run up heavy obligations. Furthermore, married women could not make contracts in their own name, initiate suits at law (or be sued separately), make separate wills, conduct sales, or have legal right to their own earnings, rents, profits, or compensations.[3] These distinctions were based upon the old division of labor.

So long as the law made it close to impossible for women to control their own property and have first claim to children, even the happiest of unions were affected to a degree. The law may have changed much slower than custom, and men may well have consulted their wives on a growing range of topics. They may have even granted them rule at home on most subjects. But in the South companionate marriages remained the exception, at least until the Civil War. "The law is a ass," as Dickens's hen-pecked Mr. Bumble asserted, but it was one with a powerful kick.[4]

Surprisingly, however, the American states, especially the Southern ones, enjoyed a high reputation for equitable laws regarding women. Harriet Martineau, Kemble's friend and a very observant English traveler, explained that American women benefited from the "entire prosperity of the country," the "greater freedom of divorce, and consequent discouragement of swindling, and other vicious marriages," a higher degree of reciprocity in marital relations, "the arrangements about property being generally more favorable to the wife than in England," and the gradual elimination in America of the legal concept that a wife was "to all intents and purposes the property of her husband." In the South Martineau found still more striking advantages. She discovered that single women managed their own property in a way unknown in England itself. "It would be a rare sight elsewhere to see a woman of twenty-one in her second widowhood, managing her own farm or plantation; and managing it well, because it had been in her own hands during her marriage." Martineau doubtless exaggerated the American legal situation in order to prompt British reform. There was much truth in what she said, but the legal position of women in both countries after marriage was scarcely an invitation for them to insist upon marital equality.[5]

In the South, for instance, slavery, not some special attitude toward women, made possible the kind of independence of which Martineau spoke so glowingly. Women, unmarried or widowed, could operate a farm or plantation with a ready work force of slaves. In the North the single woman would have had to hire scarce and expensive labor, men who might well quit on the grounds that they would not have a woman for a boss. Apprentices assigned by orphan's courts or nearly fully grown sons not yet independent were also sometimes available, but slaves, where the law allowed, were obviously a much more satisfactory and universal resource for a single woman's prosperity. As Thomas R. Dew, the proslavery apologist, observed, women of the South owed a special debt to slavery for their relative freedom. But this autonomy came at a high price. Besides, slaves, being "chattels personal," were particularly subject to seizure for payment of a husband's debts, more so than lands, by common law. In addition, slaves in a wife's possession immediately became her husband's throughout her coverture. In fact Eleanor Boatwright, a Georgia historian, cites a case in which two men sued each other for possession of a slave girl belonging to an estate in the distribution of which their wives—a mother and daughter—were named as beneficiaries. Neither of these Georgians had original claims to the property; only by grace of matrimony had they any interest in the matter.[6]

While Martineau was correct that married women in the South did gain some mastery of their own property during the pre–Civil War and Reconstruction eras, they did so chiefly when fathers or guardians went to the expense of filing elaborate marriage settlements to create separate estates completely free of husbandly interference. In time the courts were to relax the rules of equity so that the settlor need only indicate his desires by some phrase such as "her husband to have no control" or "for her sole use and benefit." In the earlier part of the century, however, such informalities were not allowed in the making of trusts. Fathers had to be exceedingly meticulous when conveying property after their daughters had married. It was presumed that *femmes coverts* (married women) required either a husband or some male surrogate to bear the unfeminine responsibility of handling property. The creation of a trust with trustees nominally to administer the property offered an alternative in equity to the strictures of common law. Though adopted by rich fathers as early as the eighteenth century, this approach to saving paternal holdings for upcoming generations was not well known. Moreover, it was expensive in a cash- and credit-poor region like the slave states.[7] Poor whites had neither the knowledge nor the faith in lawyers to make trusts.

What often occurred may be illustrated by a South Carolina case of 1802, *Stockton* v. *Martin,* in which a father's clear intentions were thwarted by a conservative regard for common law. William Harden, a planter, had drawn up a deed of gift by which he "lent" some slaves to Mrs. David Stockton, his daughter. The interest was to last *"only during her life,"* after which time they were to be divided equally among her descendants. Harden had not thereby created a "dynastic trust," as the designation should be. Instead, he simply conveyed the slaves to her directly, with no male trustees appointed. Two years later David Stockton went bankrupt. The slaves were sold at sheriff's auction to another planter named Martin. Then Stockton died. At last the widow, free of coverture, was able to appeal to a court. She did so at once. When the case reached South Carolina's highest bench, it was not at all legally significant. Nevertheless, it is worth examination because the judges' opinions on the technical errors reveal some of the legal rationales for resolving ascriptive difficulties and contradictions—the rights of the father and the husband, and their property claims versus the claims of creditors, appealing to the sacred obligations of contract. Justice Elihu Bay, known as a genial soul, took an appropriately benign view. He maintained that the father's deed should be honored. The husband had then merely shared in the life interest in the slaves that his wife was given, so that when he died their possession "reverted to her." Justice Waties was no less patriarchal in his approach, stating that "the deed ought to be construed with the same liberality as if it were the last will and testament of the donor." The rights of the father to convey property stood paramount over other considerations. He was even willing to overlook the failure to establish a trust. A wife's right to separate estate did not, of course, even occur to any of the justices.[8]

Waties and Bay's colleagues were not so willing to forego the traditions of common law, even in so venerable a cause as the maintenance of patriarchal discretion. Justice Brevard took a constrictive view, pointing out that by South Carolina statute and ancient precedent the "chattel personal" (slaves in this case) could not be lent to a *femme covert* free of husbandly possession, whereas lands could be so bestowed. As a result, the slaves were liable to sale to meet his debts, just as slaves given to him would have had to be sold to meet her debts. Likewise Justice Trezevant worried that her father had not made a proper trust, so that she, as *femme covert*, "had no right to recover [the slaves] . . . in her own right."[9] What these opinions demonstrated was that in South Carolina and in other states of the South the law and its administrators were not very conscious of woman as a legal personality with guaranteed rights. In this case, the widow lost the suit. More often than not, when the scales of justice were tipped in the woman's favor it was because it pleased the court to show magnanimity and "condescension," in the eighteenth-century sense of gentility, as well as to take judicial responsibility for dependents.

Slowly, sometimes imperceptibly, the status of women did improve, even in so conservative a state as South Carolina. Christopher Dew of Marion willed his daughter Marina Hays 574 acres of land, by which terms she was to have interest in it "on loan" until she died. Thereupon the land was to succeed to her children or be divided among kinsmen of the donor. No phrase eliminated the husband's claim, as it should have, but clearly Dew wanted Marina to have sole use and her descendants the eventual ownership. As so often happened in disputes over married women's property, Henry Hays, the husband, was an alcoholic and bankrupt. In 1850 the sheriff seized the 574 acres to relieve Hays's creditors. C. D. Evans, the husband's obliging brother-in-law, bought the land at auction. At once he ordered the family off the property. Marina was a stubborn woman and she refused to leave. Destitute and bitter, she plowed the fields herself. Meanwhile her husband swilled down booze on the front porch.[10]

Evans threatened her with insults, court battles, eviction notices. In his stupor, Marina's husband took his brother-in-law's part, beating her several times. Finally Evans proposed a compromise whereby he would occupy the bottom lands and she would receive 127 acres, unimproved and not generally arable. But the smaller upland patch at least included the old slave cabin where the Hayses lived. She acquiesced and Hairgrove, the clerk of court, appeared to take her statement renouncing the inheritance of the acreage that Evans would gain. Hairgrove complied with common-law practice, made statutory in the South Carolina Act of 1795, by meeting with the *femme covert* privately—out of the hearing of Marina's disagreeable husband and of Evans. Some days later, upon being questioned, Hairgrove acknowledged that probably Marina Hays had been under some coercion, but he filed the release anyhow.

At a later point Henry Hays, the husband, died of the obvious. causes. At once Marina, free of coverture, hired a lawyer to retrieve all her property. In her behalf the attorney claimed that the land had been granted by common law in fee simple; it could not be divided in the manner Evans had insisted. Marina had complied with her husband and Evan's demands, the attorney argued, only because of physical and mental abuse. In 1851 the case was tried before a jury in the court of Thomas Jefferson Withers. He was an able, conscientious, and influential judge, who controlled his juries with a biting wit and superb legal knowledge. In this case Withers clearly was sympathetic to the widow's plight; the jury found in her favor. Southern judges were reluctant to allow married women to dispossess themselves of their inheritances, and backed by common-law precedent and very specific, exacting statutory rules, they insisted upon strict observance of every technicality, almost as if a capital offense were involved—and quite rightly so. The Hays case offered a classic example of the masculine arrogance that the laws were designed to prevent, though not wholly for humanitarian reasons. It was hard enough that a woman might lose what her father intended to be hers and her posterity's alone, but she might also become a dependent upon county charity. That was a matter of some consequence in rural and none-too-wealthy communities.[11]

Evans appealed to the state Supreme Court on the grounds that

Withers had prejudiced the jury. The renunciation before Hairgrove met all the legal requirements, Evans claimed, being a strictly
voluntary, uncoerced transaction. Chief Justice John Belton O'Neall
upheld the lower court decision, concluding that Marina Hays's
signed release had been "wrung" from her by force, imprecations,
and "the paramount necessity" that she felt to provide a home for
her family and "her drunken husband." O'Neall was a stalwart
evangelical and temperance man, well known for his assumption
of benevolent guardianship over slaves caught in the hands of irresponsible masters or even in the regular toils of criminal justice.
The concept of paternalistic justice sometimes assumed almost a
liberal cast in the hands of men of Judge O'Neall's character and
professional persuasion. His decisions have been so interpreted. Yet
it would be wrong to attribute either very modern or very feudal
ideas to the Carolina jurist. As a Victorian and as a common-law
disciple, he interpreted the relation of women to property in ac-
cordance with two propositions: first, the strict adherence to the detailed regulations regarding *femme covert* renunciations; second,
the dependency of women, especially widows, that called forth the
protective mantle of the law, an ancient but also very Victorian
duty, born of community, not individualistic needs. Thus he construed the Act of 1795 to mean that there could be no division of
an inheritance transferred in fee simple. Moreover, he asserted the
impropriety of Hairgrove in filing a document obtained under such
patently doubtful circumstances. In a ringing declaration that did,
however, go beyond the ministering of common law, the judge concluded, "*Such a release, so obtained, never, with my consent, shall
bar the rights of the wife.*"[12]

Judge Joseph Brevard who sat on the case of *Stockton* v. *Martin*
in 1802 would not have felt obliged to make such a pledge. Like
William Byrd II of Westover or any other eighteenth-century
squire, on or off the bench, Brevard was not given to hand-wringing
about the plight of orphan, widow, slave or servant, not when it
came to matters of property and law. The sacred precepts of common-law jurisprudence was a sufficient basis for decision making. In

contrast, O'Neall's paternalism, for all its inherent conservatism, humanized the situation. He gave expression to a growing latitude in Southern justice, a secular thrust that reflected the larger trends of law in this country and abroad. Southern wives and daughters were gradually being treated with equity by fathers and husbands who sought to provide them with security. Prior generations of patriarchs would not have been eager to dispense property at expense to sons. According to one historian, thirty-five of ninety wills written by rich Alabama planters in Dallas and Marengo Counties, transferred property in "either *fee simple* or *fee tail*" to their wives. Such generosity would have been considerably rarer a half-century earlier in such a state as South Carolina from whence Alabamians so often hailed.[13] Nonetheless, the slow erosion of common law and ascriptive tradition—the two went hand in hand—came about through largely unrecognized cultural and social transformations, rather than through the institutional dynamics of the law itself.

A reason for the slowness of the process, as Robert Gordon, a legal historian, has observed, was that the common-law heritage "gave a significant elite of the American bar its sense of identity as a mandarinate of masters of an ancient technique; the tradition associated law with both science and high culture. . . ." These were factors most appealing in a South that honored tradition, loved the forms of deference that the law and courts exemplified, and, with other intellectual avenues closed, used the law to combine intellectuality and social utility in a conservative setting. For these reasons, as well as worry that innovation of any kind might have implications for race control and stability, the common law in family cases was slow to change. For instance, in regard to widows' dowers, the law had customarily been protective, a virtue with new uses when social attitudes about feminine individuality as mother or property holder moved somewhat faster than statutory changes in family law. Therefore, it was not surprising that patriarchal right and dynastic principle, as in the Hays case of South Carolina, should have been used to enhance a widow's claims against her husband. Mrs. Hays gained the award, but with a distinct bow to her father as well as to her from the learned judge.[14]

Curiously, the South has enjoyed some reputation for being for-
ward-thinking about women's legal rights. By selective use of high-
court cases from particularly noteworthy, high-minded jurists—such
magnanimous gentlemen as Nathan Green of Tennessee and John
Belton O'Neall of South Carolina—one could make a convincing argument for Southern liberality about women's place under law.[15]
Indeed, the Southern bar and bench would have been a credit to
any state or national system. Nevertheless, statutory and judicial alterations for safeguarding married women's property, for instance,
must be seen as an outgrowth of old traditions rather than a whole-
hearted break with the past. Suzanne Dee Lebsock, in a study of
Virginian women during the post-Revolutionary years, correctly
points out that "in inspiration and in operation the early statutory
reforms in the law of married women's property were very much
like separate estates under equity," a form long recognized in common law. To be sure, the laws passed in the late Jacksonian era,
both North and South, were protective, as intended, so that wives
were enabled to retain title to property and have it exempted from
liability for husbands' debts. But they did not enjoy full powers for
its disposition. As a result, Lebsock says, "the stage was set for a
riot of interpretations and complications capable of scrambling the
wits of the most experienced attorney." Marriages were becoming
more and more like partnerships (on the junior-senior pattern),
but when it came to property matters women did not have equal
rights set down by legislation. Antebellum and Reconstruction politicians would have been horrified if their laws had been so construed. Thus Mississippi, though first to pass a married women's
property act, in 1839, was by no means intentionally radical and
feminist. Ascriptive principles of male honor continued to guide
both judge and lawmaker in the making of decisions.[16]

The plight of women—and sometimes of slaves—might bring down
the gavel of righteousness in O'Neall's court, but almost everywhere
else, in state capitol or county courthouse, the misfortunes of men
and creditors far outweighed any legitimate concern for the weak
and helpless. For instance, the Mississippi Act of 1839 grew out of
the same concerns that led other states to pass such laws through-

out the century: economic setbacks, not libertarian zeal. In good times the gentry and upcoming farmers of the South were all too willing to speculate with their wives' dowries and inheritances. But in adversity they had to scramble hard to escape creditors by transferring property from themselves to other family members until the personal crisis passed. To transmit ownership to wives rather than to trusted brothers or uncles was certainly the most convenient and reliable method. By 1839 sheriffs' sales, bank failures, and foreclosures were commonplace, an economic collapse not to be equaled until the Reconstruction era. Under these circumstances one T. B. J. Hadley, a Democratic state senator, introduced a bill to grant wives new rights over property in their names. Hadley's wife was the owner of a well-paying boardinghouse for politicians gathering for sessions at Jackson, located in Hadley's constituency. Himself heavily overcommitted, he had ample reason to see the measure through.[17]

When Hadley presented the bill to the legislature, the Whigs were incensed. The state had already defaulted on bonds, a humiliating betrayal of state honor, they claimed. The new measure compounded the sin. Leading the Whig opposition was state senator Spence Monroe Grayson, a lawyer originally from Natchez but lately a plantation owner in the Yazoo country not far from Vicksburg. On the floor of the upper chamber, Grayson and others insisted that the proposal was just a novel way for men to escape honest demands. Hadley retorted that the proposal merely strove to "secure to man's dearest idol the possession of the property which they have required [*sic*, acquired] by their own exertion, or the liberty [*sic*, liberality] of a fond father." In minority protest, the Whigs countered that "female delicacy forbids their participation in the turmoils and strife of business." Besides, the state's financial reputation was "in all conscience, low enough already." Grayson became so heated during the exchanges that the journalist could not catch his torrent of words. The state senator's concluding statement, however, was recorded: "If you would degrade and disgrace all that is lovely in woman, pass this bill; but if you would sustain them firmly in the high and exalted eminence which they now occupy in the eyes of the world of men, spurn and reject this bill, as one of the most unholy and fraudulent devices ever presented."[18]

Eloquence of this kind, or else uneasiness about the practical effects of this debtor-relief law (for that was its basic purpose), defeated the Hadley bill momentarily. Perhaps Grayson's idea that women should not be sullied by the sordid business of buying and selling slaves had some influence, too. In the long run, though Grayson's triumph was fleeting. The bill had some tempting provisions. Wives, for instance, might "own" slaves directly, but their management and "the receipt" of the slaves' "productions" remained strictly in husbandly control. But most important, the bill provided the debtor with an opportunity to avoid seizure of property for debts by transferring it to his wife's name. After some further votes, the bill went to the Democratic governor, who signed it at once as a party measure. Mrs. Hadley retained her boardinghouse. According to legend, she had cut the provisions set before the legislators who lodged there until the bill was passed. Afterwards they once more enjoyed full rations at the common board when the landlady celebrated the good news.[19]

For all the deficiencies of the Mississippi Act and similar laws in Texas, Arkansas, Florida, and Alabama, they were much more advanced than the laws of the older, more tradition-bound states of the southeast. In South Carolina, repeated efforts to guarantee women these minimal protections failed. A rather conservative bill, for instance, was introduced in 1855 to prevent husbands from taking possession of property in the wife's hands "at the time of her marriage" only, thus excluding later acquisitions by inheritance, gift, or personal endeavor. Introducing the measure, Senator Dudley of Marlborough pointed out that by Carolina law a husband had every right to "strip" his wife of all her personal holdings. If she owned real estate, he had full use of it during her life and even after her death. On the other hand, he noted, upon the husband's death "the wife has no part of the personal property" of her husband and "only the use of one-third of the estate during her life." Yet the bill was not nearly so generous or so useful as the Mississippi law. Dudley only sought to prevent men from selling their wives' estates to their own private advantage. As one would expect, the dynastic consideration—protecting paternal gifts to daughters— was uppermost in Carolinian thoughts. The wife could not sell even "a milch cow" or chicken coop without first obtaining permission from a court of equity. "We want the cool, calm, and clear judgment of the court, as to the necessity of the sale," he assured the assembly. "I am opposed, generally, to all innovation," the Carolinian legislator pledged, but he did feel that daughters of Carolinian fathers needed some legal recourse from the blunders, greed, "whims, caprices, and prejudices" of wayward husbands. In opposition, Senator Brockman recalled that "our forefathers" had decreed that "the husband was to be the ruling power," and he saw no reason to repudiate so wise a system. He admitted, "It may be true," as Senator Dudley had suggested, that "young men are pointed out all over the country as seeking to obtain a fortune by matrimonial connection rather than by working for it." Nevertheless, the bill did more harm than good by giving the wife a "separate estate" and making her "accountable for her own contracts," a violation of common law and good sense. Beneath Dudley's concern for patriarchal integrity Brockman detected the siren call of women's equality. Likewise Senator Mazyck of St. James Santee, in the low country, spoke darkly of the "revolutionary" implications of the bill. He complained that by common law a husband would have to pay his bride's debts out of his own resources, since hers would be exempted from sale; such a burden was quite unthinkable. Dudley replied rather warmly, "Why sir, what debts did he ever know a blushing young maiden of seventeen to owe to any one in the world? . . . Are we [to] turn the cold shoulder to this law for such an extraordinary reason?" The tally was 21 to 16 for its passage. Yet the lower house was uncooperative, and the measure never reached the governor's desk.[20]

In 1868 the South Carolina constitutional convention finally was able to get a more comprehensive measure passed. The rationale was as revealing as the results were ambiguous and piecemeal. From the debate one would have guessed that South Carolina's womenfolk were in imminent danger, less from carpetbaggers or freedmen than from "plausible villains" eager to plunder the helpless maiden, spinster, and widow. War, emancipation, and poverty had intervened, but fortune hunters were allegedly as pestilent as they had ever been in the old days. In fact B. F. Randolph, the presiding officer, relinquished the gavel to take the floor in order to claim that all members voting nay could be presumed to be bachelors "looking for rich wives" to "squander their property" in debauchery and drink. A proviso was added to prevent fraudulent transfers from husband to wife in order to escape creditors. Nonetheless, economics and male dominion were combined to provide the debtor as well as the "weaker sex" with the protection of the law. The purpose was indeed to help women. Yet in the drastically confused state of the Carolina economy after the war the husband was a beneficiary, too. He could at least enjoy the proceeds of his wife's property once it was no longer subject to seizure for his debts.[21]

Nineteenth-century lawmakers generally tended toward brevity and vagueness in drawing up statutes, but, as Lebsock notes, the habit was anything but beneficial to female litigants.[22] Jurists could decide cases rather as they pleased in the absence of explicit directions. Granting women any powers at all was fearsome enough that judges were inclined to be as restrictive as possible. By the Mississippi Act of 1839, for instance, it was not clear whether a wife could mortgage her real estate without her husband's consent. Even that Galahad of the upper chamber, Spence Monroe Grayson, missed the glaring omission when heaping ridicule upon the "dishonorable" law, as he viewed it. He need not have worried: Mississippi courts were unlikely to reduce husbandly authority on property matters.

Whether well or poorly drafted, laws of this kind meant very little in practical terms for most women. In the first place, judges were not always as liberal as the legislators, even though the latter's casual lawmaking provided ample opportunities for jurists to circumvent the lawmakers' intentions. Second, conservative reactions set in. Governor John C. Edwards warned the Missouri legislature in 1852 against following the fashion of other states in providing women with new-fangled property rights. "No general good" could come of it, he insisted. Bachelors are constantly warned, Edwards explained, to get themselves married off to obtain good "household managers." With separate estates, the advantage would be lost, as each partner became preoccupied with personal holdings to the neglect of the children. Besides, "a separate property would change the character of the wife. . . . She would lose the woman and become in character a man. All that was soft and tender and endearing would vanish, and she would grow sturdy, obstinate and masculine, as is the case where affeminate [*sic*] husbands surrender the reins of government to their wives."[23] The politicians heeded his plea for statesmanship that consisted of doing nothing.

Women's difficulties about property, and thus about their freedom of choice in so many other ways, did not wholly depend upon the attitudes and labors of state politicians and judges. Instead they were located at the seat of Southern life: the home itself. When so inclined, husbands did what they liked with their wives' property regardless of the law. No doubt some women were able to withstand husbandly pressures to relinquish control over their holdings, after legal reforms made it possible. Even under common-law restriction, a few, like Mrs. Mary Sharpe Jones, wife of the Rev. Charles C. Jones, were so competent as plantation managers and investors that they virtually ran the household economy, from kitchen order to bankbook entry. Such exceptions aside, women had to do what their menfolk wished, if only to keep peace at home.

The evidence of male control of women's property was especially dramatic in the civil actions of one Louisiana family, the Fosters. Because of the Napoleonic tradition of the state, wives had formal possession of separate estates. Though prior consent of husbands was required, wives could sell, mortgage, donate, and will their holdings, both real and personal, as they desired. In the American experience, North and South, Louisiana was exceptional in this respect. Some men, such as the Fosters of Bayou Teche, found ways to make use of female property possession for their own, not their wives' advantage.[24]

Levi Foster, originally from Natchez, Mississippi, had settled in southern Louisiana at the beginning of the second war with England. As eldest son of an enormously wealthy Natchez planter, Levi had the advantage of some education at law. A dynamic and enterprising businessman, he had dabbled in legal work, but mostly he busied himself as a plantation supplier, horse, cattle, and slave dealer, and sugar planter. His marriage to Zeide DeMaret introduced him to greater wealth and to social prominence. Zeide's maternal grandfather was Don Martin Navarro, the eighteenth-century Spanish treasurer and acting governor of the province.[25]

Zeide's father had willed her an eighth of a fifty-five-arpent tract of land on both sides of Bayou Teche. At Levi's instigation, she sold the share to her brother Louis DeMaret in 1824. The following year DeMaret sold the land to Levi. In 1829 Levi then sold to a planter named Kaigler a parcel of the tract as well as adjacent land of his own, for a total of $12,450.[26] Like so many planters and speculators in that region of the South, Levi found himself overextended in the early 1830s. With his creditors impatient for repayment, Levi sought to deny his ownership of his wife's former holdings. The means was a suit that he had his wife Zeide initiate against him. Judge John Moore, a friend of the family who was married to Zeide's sister, obligingly compelled Levi to turn over $9,800 to his wife as her share of the sale to Kaigler. Levi's creditors, particularly the firms of W. A. Gasquet & Co., New Orleans suppliers, and Goble & Thomas, a New York firm, recognized the subterfuge at once. They intervened to carry the case to the Louisiana Supreme Court. Justice John Martin delivered the court's opinion. Quite clearly, he argued, the transactions were disingenuous; he kindly refrained from calling them a fraud, no doubt to save Judge Moore embarrassment. Both husband and wife had originally sought to preserve the means of disposing of the tract because the state legislature was then entertaining a measure to prevent married women from selling their real estate. The sale to Louis DeMaret, Zeide's brother, was undertaken for that purpose. When the bill failed to pass, the brother had reconveyed the tract to Zeide's husband Levi, who then sold it. Since, however, Kaigler had bought solely on credit, with no evidence brought forward that he had ever made any payments, "the husband's liability and the consequent right of mortgage of the wife" could not really be ascertained. The judge had erred in his decision, the justice concluded, and at the cost of the appellee, Zeide, a new trial was ordered. Levi Foster's manipulations had been in vain. Not until 1847, however, were the creditors able to extract any money from the heirs of Levi Foster. (He had died in 1834.)[27]

Certainly there was nothing unusual in the manner by which Levi had sought to escape just debts. Southerners were often short of cash and long on paying up. At the same time, it was quite evident that Zeide's suit against her husband by no means indicated free agency on her part. She was merely a pawn in her husband's schemes, even though her father had no doubt intended the lands for her sole benefit. Thus even when women did hold rights to their own property, it did not avail them very much. Levi was a hard man of uncertain integrity, his wife a compliant woman. That was the essence of the matter.[28]

The point of these cases is crucial to an understanding of the burdens that Southern women bore, affecting not only their livelihood but also their sense of themselves. So little has been said about these transactions and the effect of law upon gender relations that the hard economic and legal reasons for women's passivity have been hidden from historical view. Too often advances in church life, opening new vistas for usefulness, have obscured the implications of restraints in law. Women were often just observers, rejoicing or grieving over the good or ill fortunes that their husbands experienced with family fortunes, their own or their wives'.[29]

Out of the legal situation may be traced the deep-seated Southern ambivalence that men and women held toward each other. The situation was not uniquely Southern, as Northern wives suffered under the same inequities. Yet the circumstances underscored Southern habits of male honor. It would be a mistake to think that these disabilities made Southern women whimpering souls incapable of inner strength. "These timid Southern women!" Mrs. Chesnut exclaimed in her diary. "And under the guns they can be brave enough." After all, their idea of what a man could be came from their fathers, men who felt all the pressures to live up to ideals of honor and valor. "There is nothing a woman so dreads as to lose respect for the manhood around her, so sweet to trust, to look up— we are willing to be second, but second only to the first," declared Martha DeSaussure, a member of an old Carolinian clan. "How would the women and men look each other in the face if the men failed or compromised!"[30] Even the acidulous Mary Chesnut would have agreed. Women thought their own bravery derivative. It was not.

The absence of power in law and convention provided women a compensation. They could use that vaunted masculinity as a weapon to turn against the men themselves. Their lovers very well knew it, too. And they also knew their dependence upon their wives' dowries and settlements. As a result, the tendency was to judge women not as worthy recipients of male respect so much as servants to male needs. "My wife," wrote Henry Wise, a late antebellum Virginia governor, "is not competent to advise the statesman or the politician—her knowledge, her advice, her ministry is in a kindlier sphere." She was a true helpmeet by being one to hear "my griefs, know of my troubles, understand the cause of my perplexities, be the confidant of my secret feelings and sympathize with me in them all."[31] The role was inert, uncritical, and flattering to the self-regarding male. Most women found that service a happy occupation, yet its limitations were bound to create feelings that all but the most mature, self-knowing matron could neither articulate nor fully understand.

11

Male Custom in Family Life

If historians have until recently neglected the legal basis upon which family ethics and behavior functioned, they have also said too little about the customary habits of married men, particularly in traditional households, as opposed to pious ones. Here again the law favored the man no less than social convention did. At least according to their aggrieved husbands, women could be and sometimes were difficult partners. A special cause of complaint in that regard was the problem of making a smooth transition from affection for a father to that appropriate for a husband. Daughters of particularly notable men like Thomas Jefferson, for instance, sometimes idealized the parent and thereby exacerbated the ordinary tensions that arose in the early years of marriage. Speaking of Jefferson's daughters Martha and Mary, two historians remark that "to deserve and retain their father's love had been the aim implanted in both daughters from their early youth." Martha, the eldest and the most intimate with her father, eventually married but did not give her husband the love that she showered upon the parent whom she almost worshiped. Jefferson, in turn, could not restrain his feelings for her. "No body in this world can make me so happy, or so miserable as you," he once wrote. Such ties could interfere with the relationship of husbands and wives.[1]

Overattachment to "papa" was a small issue, however, in comparison with male license within marriage itself, as so many women soon discovered. Mary Boykin Chesnut once observed: "To men— glory, honor, praise, and power—if they are patriots. To women— daughters of Eve—punishment comes still in some shape, do what they will." She later elaborated with considerable bitterness, "So we whimper and whine, do we? Always we speak in a deprecating voice, do we? And sigh gently at the end of every sentence—why? Plain enough . . . When a man does wrong, does not his wife have to excuse herself if he finds out she knows it? Now, if a man drinks too much and his wife shows that she sees it, what a storm she brings about her ears. She is disrespectful, unwifelike. Does she set up for strong-minded? So unwomanly—*so unlike his mother.*"[2] The termagant's response might be that he, likewise, did not live up to the perfection of her father. The battle would then be fully engaged. Adding to these woes, born of male pride and female deference to illustrious parentage, as it might be, was the Southern male's reticence about his affairs, even his thoughts. Mary Chesnut's husband, whom she dearly loved, was one among many who kept his feelings to himself. "Sometimes," she wrote in her journal, "I *feel* that we understand each other a little—then up goes the iron wall once more. Not that for a moment he ever gives you the impression of an *insincere* . . . person. Reticent—like the Indian too proud to let the world know how he feels."[3]

Infatuated with the notion that alienation is a modern ordeal growing from capitalistic and industrial sources, historians sometimes romanticize the allegedly generous exchanges of premodern society and family life. Such a view ignores the evidence of traditional male habit, the congregating of men at tavern, courthouse, auction sale, racetrack, brothel, and churchyard—with the women safely busy with the preacher inside singing hymns. The emotional chasm between husband and wife was then much greater than today. Men feared domestication, not simply because it inhibited their business and pleasure but also because of male ribbing about a too-uxorious manner. No one approved of overt philandering and heedless fun-making, but the *media res* of gentlemen left ample room for a married man to do as he pleased. To be faithful to male ascriptions was sometimes a first order of business, and there was precious little a woman could do about it, by law or custom. In the eighteenth century, according to an English friend of William Byrd III, "a reasonable Man would have thought his character forfeited for ever had it been known that he spent six evenings in a week in the company of women." That standard applied, to some degree, in male planter society of South Carolina and the Tidewater well into the nineteenth century.[4]

Dinner parties in the upper circles of the South, for instance, were sexually segregated in the early years of the Republic. In 1805 Margaret I. Manigault of Charleston reported to her daughter that she had just entertained a large party of gentlemen at dinner. As a special treat, the wives were allowed to come over later. Politics and power lay behind these social forms. Common male duties led naturally to common male entertainments. Having finished their business as jurymen, John Grimball of South Carolina and his colleagues, "the Planters on the river," dined in 1832 on "turtle soup, pie, turtle steaks, vegetables, potatoes, beans, beets, soups, fish, broiled mutton and haunch of venison, Sauterne, Madeira, Champagne, stilton cheese, bread and butter, Chamertin wine, and then fruit, bananas, oranges, pineapple, Sherbert, and then Chateau Margaux & Madeira." His judicious summary was: "The party went off very well." No ladies were present, or missed.[5]

Customs changed; women were often present at formal banquets held to entertain friends, not just kinspeople. In 1847, for instance, Grimball noted that supper began at ten for both ladies and gentlemen, with an outlay of meats, fowls, shellfish, and desserts. "After the ladies retired the Gentlemen sat down—three other hot ducks were brought in . . . and when the Turkey was sufficiently eaten, it gave place to a hot oyster pie—We had champagne—using two bottles—and four decanters of Madeira which proved an ample supply" for the eight husbands. But the best wines, the choicest china ("White with a very deep border of green, richly gilt") were used for the male-only banquets. "The Agricultural Society met yesterday—I was one of the finders, and sent my Dinner," Grimball noted in a typical reference to a Charleston gentleman's obligation.[6]

To be sure, single men and women had always assembled for purposes of entertainment and courtship, in both the upper classes and the yeomanry: balls for the rich, corn-husking and drinking parties for the farming people. Yet high or low, men and women already married often gathered separately. These affairs were, of course, pleasantly social, but the exchange of gossip was a significant order of business at such affairs. Who was invited and who was not established the boundaries of acceptability. Everybody who belonged to a social circle attended weddings, regardless of gender. But sometimes special rooms were set aside for the older men so that they could gamble or gossip without interference. Funerals too might draw acquaintances and relatives of both sexes together. In earlier days, though, men ordinarily attended the coffin in procession to the grave site, leaving the women to prepare the feast at home. Regular Sunday services were also likely to be segregated. "When we reached the [Presbyterian] church, everyone had gone in," Lida Robertson of Sumterville, South Carolina, wrote in her diary in 1851. She added, "([I]t is the custome [*sic*] in all this part of the world, for the gentlemen to stand out, until the minister & ladies begin to sing.)" Some men never came in at all—unless it was raining.[7]

Physical distance meant emotional distance as well. Women frequently did not know what their husbands were doing when abroad. Many did not wish to know. And it would scarcely have been honorable to bring candid reports home. Caroline Gilman was one of those who had to acquiesce to her planter-husband's departures. "The club-engagement," she noted, "brought on others. I was not selfish, and even urged Arthur to go to hunt and to dinner parties. . . ." Soon she discovered that she was growing annoyed. She hid her feelings from herself, though, by calling her discontent "undefined forebodings." The fault, she believed, must be hers, for yielding to "an irritable temperament!" Dutifully, she tried love, patience, and silence, and claimed that eventually her forbearance paid off handsomely in a renewed intimacy. That, at least, was the way she supposed to respond to the trials of married life.[8]

Certainly one reason for the elaborate weddings that plantation matrons insisted be provided their slaves was that they required the presence of the master to perform the ceremony. These ceremonies were not only reminders of the white people's own marital vows, but also helped to make the black marriage rites dignified and sacred enough to throw some cold water on biracial temptations. Certainly from the white woman's point of view, formality in slave marriages had benefits beyond a pleasant orderliness in the quarters. After all, the more seriously blacks took the vows, the more incumbent it was for masters to do likewise.

The constant mingling of kinsfolk served as another means to get the husband home. Familial obligation required his attendance. Emily Barrow, wife of a racetrack enthusiast and planter of East Feliciana, Louisiana, across the river from Woodville, Mississippi, was forever bringing relatives over to the plantation or arranging visits to other connections. Nevertheless, Barrow was often away on unknown business in New Orleans and elsewhere. Moreover, women, especially sisters, were forced by necessity, if no other reason, to be dependent upon each other, because husbands were so often inadequate in that regard and so frequently away with their male cohorts. For instance, when Emily Barrow was dying she urged her husband to marry her sister Mrs. Haile, a widow. She recognized that she could count on her sister to do right as a stepmother for the six children left behind. Thus, in a curious way, the very importance of the kin network was built upon the disparities that rigid sex differentiation imposed upon husband and wife. The strength of the family, as it were, helped to make up for the strains of married life.[9]

Ordinary home-loving planters found themselves enjoined to family duties to give the wife company and pleasure, but the boyish desire to cut away, to "break the apron-strings" that seemed a threat to autonomy, haunted them still. Escape from mother could become escape from wife and children—and curiously, dread of shame pushed the husband to seek male pleasures, for otherwise he might be a mamma's boy, a hen-pecked milktoast, a disappointment to himself and his father. Gossiping about Governor Allston of South Carolina, Benjamin Whitner recalled his alleged effeminacy as a young man: "A most superlative fop and ladies' man, dangling after his mother, carrying her fan or reticule bowing simpering and silly as any exquisite I ever met with." It was a characterization, however unjust, to be avoided at all costs.[10]

Yet then came some crisis, and the husband discovered that time had slipped by, that he did not know his wife or understand his children, and that he had squandered away precious hours and money better spent at home than in entertainments and sport abroad. So it was with Bennet Barrow. From the close of 1844 until the spring of 1845, Emily, his wife, was dying during her last, most difficult pregnancy. Barrow was an earthy, unintellectual sort, not given to infidelities (so far as his diary reveals) or to callous disregard to his wife's feelings. By planter standards, Barrow was hardworking and shrewd at business and management. Until those last months of helpless attendance on his wife, he occupied himself with routine male duties and entertainments and seldom referred to her at all, not even on birthdays or Christmas. As soon as she was sick, he began to recall happier times. "Emily's feelings and situation at this time makes me reflect on the past and think there are many things neglected that might have been done," he moaned. The same attitude of penance for past neglect had marked Southern childrearing—a diffidence until the dread moment of crisis, when regrets and soul-searchings poured out as if they had been dammed up for years before. In his distress, Barrow displayed the familiar traits of remorse. He even pledged to "quit Fox hunting—and study amusements with my wife & children, God speed an end to all my troubles." A prayer for his wife might have been more in order, rather than a supplication in his own behalf, but at any rate he promised God to take Emily and the six children on a long holiday as soon as she recovered.[11]

Likewise, Thomas Chaplin, even more immersed in "pleasuring" himself, as the phrase went, felt the pangs of guilt as his wife grew weaker. "Oh! *Remorse, Remorse* I am *thy Slave now & Forever,*" he wept in 1851. All those evenings spent drinking with Dr. Jenkins and then racing gigs until one or the other took a spill—of what use were such follies now? he asked himself. The agricultural dinners that he had had to "find" were expensive, and left him feeling very "groggy" the next morning. He even forgave her for pouring "all the brandy out the window" one New Year's Eve, for his own good. (Later, however, Chaplin noted in his diary that it was a pretty "costly good," as the liquor had been worth $500, but he had been too drunk to make a fuss at the time.) The fact was that Chaplin had consumed his way through his own fortune and partially through hers as well. From thirty slaves he was reduced to eight, having sold the rest off to pay for parties, "frolics," militia uniforms, liquor, and gambling debts. "Had it not been for my wife's legacy thank God" he mused, he would have had to declare bankruptcy long before.[12]

In the struggle over which would be the greater commitment, the husband's loyalty to male friends or to his wife, nothing played so decisive a role as alcohol. Its importance in American male habits has not been fully appreciated until very recently, in studies just now appearing. Unfortunately few regional statistics were compiled at the time, so that a careful reading of the custom, especially in the South, is hard for historians to make today. According to one scholar, using gross national estimates, the consumption of absolute alcohol reached the astonishing rate of 7.1 gallons per year for all those Americans over fifteen years of age in 1830. The most recent calculation (1970) is only 2.5 gallons. Cheap whiskey could cost as low as 25 cents a gallon, brandy a mere $1.25. Southern figures, if any were gathered, would have revealed a higher level of consumption per capita, if only because of the relative slowness of the temperance crusade to cut the rate there as it did in the Northern states after 1830.[13]

Although drinking could be a domestic pastime, even then it was usually enjoyed with other males present and the women left out. Like smoking, drinking was a function of masculinity, and upper-class women who partook of anything stronger than a sweet wine risked loss of respectability. Consumption of hard liquor signified virility. Convivial male drinking was intended to show affection and group solidarity in permissible fashion, perhaps in lieu of the kinds of tenderness that women alone were allowed to exhibit toward each other. An anthropologist has declared, "Why the ingestion of a mild poison should be regarded as a test of manly virtues is curious," but, he concludes, it serves to validate friendships and incorporation into the male tribe, so to speak, particularly in Celtic regions, of which the South was one.[14] College initiation rites almost always involved displays of superhuman capacities, deeds of alcoholic derring-do among friends that sometimes continued not only through the youthful years but into full manhood as well. In 1802 Nathaniel Beverley Tucker wrote John Randolph about the typical habits of his classmates at William and Mary College. "The dissipation which at present prevails accedes [*sic*] that of your day. . . . Mint juleps in the morning, Gin Twist in the middle of the Day, & wine at dinner, and at night to the accompaniment of cards." At Charlottesville, the "University" had already become renowned for its students' whiskey consumption. Matthew Singleton reported in 1836 that there were no "manly sports" to speak of, "but the greatest pleasure they have is to get drunk." What began as a youthful display of virility often led to the dangers of heavy and solitary drinking. Another Virginian, one Carter Branton, Esq., admitted that until he was thirty years old it had been a "daily practice to drink from two to four glasses of julep, and toddy, and sometimes 'spirit water.' This was considered a temperate and moderate use of the article."[15] Quite naturally, drinking was a detriment to stable marriage, a point that teetotalers, North and South, accurately if self-righteously proclaimed in song, verse, drama, and moral fiction.

One cannot read through the correspondence of any Southern family, except teetotal ones, without being struck by the number of incidents of alcoholic illness and deaths. The writers were not just prudish temperance folk gloating over the fallen, but concerned relatives made uneasy by a regional problem coming so close to home. Just as modern man shrinks from tales of lung cancer, the antebellum Southerners were overawed by news of alcoholic disease. "Cousin Mott has destroyed himself by a life of dissapation [*sic*], this is a living sorrow and grievous to hear," wrote one Louisiana matron. Outsiders echoed a refrain often heard from the lips of native Southerners. "The highest & lowest Classes," reported a Yankee visitor to Alabama in 1821, "are much adicted [*sic*] to excessive drinking." Statistics gave credence to casual impressions: in Charleston between 1822 and 1837 135 deaths were attributed to alcohol. Much of the blame fell on the young, not without reason. In 1833 Dr. James Norcom complained that the only apparent way to prevent his son John from overdrinking "of which he is unhappily too fond" was to buy him a plantation to divert his attention from the local "tippling house." The problem was a common one, the solution likewise, though unfortunately it did not always work.[16]

An unusual perspective on the matter was offered in the diary of William L. Brown, the twelve-year-old son of a Kentucky iron maker. He had to share his bed with his father's companions after their all-day, all-night carousing; they were too drunk to get home. "Last night," ran a typical entry, "pappa sat up very late and William B. Ross came to bed to me about 4 o'clock. . . . I think he was groggy." When father Brown got restless from his drinking, he used to kick the smaller brother out of the parents' bed, and the mother had to bring the toddler up to his older brother's room. Brown treated strangers well not so much for their own sake but to provide an occasion for special conviviality. One night three brothers named Outlaw arrived and old man Brown had them stay over for three days. "I slept with one of them Outlaws, the biggest one. The morning was clear and cool and pappa sent for some brandy by Uncle Will and sat down a . . . quart of brandy at first." The Outlaws had their share. Not surprisingly, the father did not look forward to the time when young William would leave to study the law; he wanted him home to keep things going. When the lad complained, the old man threatened to disinherit him, and drunkenly furious, showed the youngster who was boss; he called in Squire Wells and the local deacon to help him write his son out of his will and enjoy a round or two of drinks. Luckily Squire Wells, a lawyer, refused to assist his host in the work of disowning his son by changing Brown's will, believing that Brown was too incapacitated to make a rational decision. A few days later, Governor Isaac Shelby and Colonel Samuel Craft came by, another good time was soon in progress, and they "staid all night." With such illustrious company around, Brown let the quarrel blow over and did not cut the boy out of his will. But, the lad sighed, "Oh, think of me sometimes."[17]

As a son, William Brown perceived only part of the difficulty that a drinking man presented his family. Mrs. Brown had a much more difficult time, but other women had still more agony to face. Alcoholics were often wife-beaters as well, and given the kind of society that the Old South was, one must conclude that physical abuse had to be a much greater problem than any statistical or legal record could demonstrate.[18] In its general strategy temperance propaganda had a great deal to say about the viciousness of the alcoholic husband, but for all the drama the teetotalers invested in the topic, they could not really match the reality. To be sure, Southerners were not unique in these failings, but in light of the general level of violence in the region, the number of assaults carried out in the home under the stimulation of drinking probably exceeded the numbers elsewhere in the country, and extended through a wider range of the social classes.

In light of these unhappy circumstances, women's recourses were minimal. The legal system was of little practical use. Common-law precedent permitted men to chastise their wives with a stick less than a thumb's width (hence "rule of thumb" as rough measure). Women's chief advantage was growing social discomfiture about wife-beaters, a worry that affected other traditional societies during the late eighteenth and early nineteenth centuries, too. Not until 1857, for instance, did Georgia make wife-beating a penal offense. A millhand in Augusta two years afterwards received the penalty of a $5.00 fine for whipping his wife, though the statute had provided for six months in jail. Juries were loath to convict, judges to sentence harshly.[19] Twenty years earlier matters had been much worse. In 1821, for instance, a Natchez, Mississippi, editor boasted that the crime was at last recognized and considered socially disrespectable. The examples cited, however, came from the very lowest jurisdictional bench: the magistracy of one Henry Tooley. Almost all of them resulted in very minor penalties, if any. One case did proceed to a higher level. Cornelius Stranahan, thoroughly drunk, had beaten his wife and she had fled to Tooley for help. For the first time, declared the *Ariel,* a Mississippi jury had ruled "that *a husband had no right to whip his wife in any case*" and that the marriage bond "did not deprive the wife of any personal right that she possessed, some few small matters excepted." Tooley recorded five other cases of a similar kind in less than six months. These examples suggest that the wife-beater was no more uncommon in the Old South than in contemporary Europe. According to Edward Shorter, wife-beaters were subject to village mock parades or charivaris during the "woman's month" of May in parts of France, but the remaining eleven months were more or less open season, so long as the husband was no sadist and exercised discretion in giving his wife moral correction. In the South, too, it remained a private matter.[20]

Drunken assaults of this kind were not at all confined to husbands in the lower classes. In 1855 David Gavin listed four local wife-beaters in a very small radius of his plantation. Two of the husbands were physicians, all four belonged to the gentry set, and their wives all had excellent pedigrees. Dr. Moses West, who was married to a "Miss Rumph," had not only beaten her in a drunken fury but had taken the children to another district and returned periodically to beat her again when the "spirits" moved him, as it were. At last she went to equity court to restrain him under a $5,000 bond and require the forfeiting of the children. As soon as the judge complied, however, "she took his arm and I hear," gossiped David Gavin, "went back to live with him." Christopher Rumph, her father, had spent $1,200 in legal fees to Benjamin Perry, and "she upset the whole in less than a week," the planter remarked.[21]

Gavin's comment provoked a further observation: that most women submitted to their husbands regardless of the cruelties they had to endure. In fact, the pattern "has almost convinced me that the more a man abuses and ill treats his wife the closer she will cling to and the more she will undergo and bear for him." His insight was not remarkable, for Southern males sometimes believed that a little home violence went a long way to ensure loyalty and inspire healthy respect. If it worked with blacks, it surely would help with meddlesome women. Likewise in Tooley's records for 1821 in Natchez, the women rarely prosecuted their abusive husbands, who claimed that they had apologized once arrest had sobered them. Besides, they were the women's sole support in so many cases. The real reason, though, for the women's acquiescence was the same then as it is today: the woman's feeling of inferiority, no matter how addicted her husband was to alcohol, no matter how violent he became in self-despisement and anger. Not surprisingly, the Southern cultural emphasis upon total masculinity, total femininity encouraged male abuse and female submission that stimulated even more violence. Constantly urged to prove his manhood as he was growing up, the male used alcohol and physical violence to overawe his wife with a male superiority that he did not altogether feel. Convinced from childhood that she was always to defer, being less worthy of attention than her brothers, and dependent first on father, then on husband, the woman felt duly chastened by a beating, but remained resentful of it anyhow. Modern studies show that wife-beaters and wives unable to break with abusive husbands are overwhelmingly likely to have been physically maltreated as children themselves—by fathers ordinarily, but sometimes by mothers, too. A heavy use of alcohol and a male tendency to find male company preferable to domesticity further accentuated these patterns in Southern marital living.[22]

Charging a husband with assault and battery was a poor remedy, but divorce was scarcely a more satisfactory one, for a single reason. For women abused, the outcome of a petition to court or legislature (laws varied) was very problematic. Even when life itself was in jeopardy, divorce pleas initiated in a woman's behalf gained only rare sympathy or success. The official explanation, generally accepted by historians, was the worry lest easy divorce, separation, or annulment undermine the stability of the home. If that were so, then husbands should have had as much difficulty freeing themselves as wives did, but they did not. In fact, the chief obstacle to liberalization was dread of alterations in male prerogatives, the erosion of male honor, not an anxiety about sundering God's union of man and wife. Although the origins of divorce restrictiveness lay deep in the common law and ecclesiastical polity, the continuing conservatism of marital practice should be seen as a defense of male ascriptiveness in all sections of the country. It would be a travesty to claim that Southern attitudes toward divorce widely differed from Northern ones. In both sections, the oath taken at marriage was considered a pledge of sacred honor, for both parties. If some falling-out later occurred, the general rule of both law and common opinion was *caveat emptor*—let the buyer beware. As was explained earlier, oath-taking in the formation of a family was a rite no less serious than that which was supposed to link subject with ruler, citizen with country. Maintenance of the sanctity of the home was a means of curbing, to some degree, individual will; to let a couple dissolve the tie, no matter how justified their reasons, threw into doubt the legitimacy of the institution upon which human society was organized. But a man's honor (less often a woman's) might at times require vindication by means of divorce, a latitude to which adult Americans, North and South, could make claim on the basis of their equality in honor over the honorless, shameless black, whose presumed state of mind kept him or her from understanding the value and duty of indissoluble union.

In no other way can the rationale of state policy be understood when pleas for divorce were presented than by the rubrics governing male honor. Northern divorce actions were decided upon that basis, but perhaps even more were the decisions rendered in the slave states. Consider, for example, some cases from early nineteenth-century Tennessee. In that state, as in most others of the South during the early years of the Republic, the state legislature granted divorces through committee oversight and recommendation. Margaret Ramsay of Sumner County sought a divorce in 1821. For four years, she complained, she had submitted to her husband

Shewbridge's cruelties. With his friends helping to hold her down, he had whipped her during drunken sprees. Once he drew a knife across her throat, and frequently he brought in prostitutes for his evening entertainment. But he refused to let her visit friends. To ensure that she stayed at home, he gave her only one dress. In addition, Shewbridge had taken up with a mulatto woman, from whom he had caught a venereal disease, "& is at the time under Doctors Jepson & Milikin to be cured." Likewise, Elizabeth Martin discovered that she had married a wife-beater as well as a Methodist minister when she had wedded Richard Webb. In the space of three years, he had moved her thirteen times, his ecclesiastical inspirations having vanished along with her modest dowry upon their getting married. Sometimes he left her "in a state of starvation and intolerable slavery." When he took up with another woman, he forced his wife to watch their fornication. Hannah Stone of Haywood County also had a physically abusive husband, who finally deserted her altogether to live with another woman in Mississippi or Louisiana. None of these three women won divorces. The grounds were deemed "insufficient." Margaret Sitz from McMinn County had a husband as intemperate in manners as in drinking habits. He beat her repeatedly and eventually deserted her. Three years later she sued for divorce because she had inherited a rather sizable estate and, quite understandably, worried that he might suddenly learn of it and return to despoil her and flee once again. Her suit for divorce was thought "unreasonable."[23]

Much more conservative on divorce than the newer states of the Southwest was Virginia. Lucy B. Dabney of Fredericksburg sought to dissolve her marriage with William Dabney in 1819. He had beaten her with fire tongs, attacked her mother, sister, and younger brother, a child, and finally grew so threatening that he had to be thrown into jail. One witness testified that he had once seen William strike Lucy "with his fist, attempted to choak her & threw her against a Barrell" and then forced her out in the cold. Moreover, he was reputed to have a wife and two children in Pittsburgh. Another witness claimed that he had heard Dabney confess that he married "for convenience here" while he straightened out some affairs before returning to his new home in Pittsburgh. The petition was rejected.[24]

The problem lay not with the grounds but rather with the gender of the plaintiff. After all, in the Dabney case the legislators might have given credence to Lucy's charge that her husband was already married. By common law, bigamy was not only a criminal offense but also one of the few grounds for divorce (along with impotence and lengthy desertion), whereas cruelty was not. In fact, there was little of an aggressive nature that a man could do that might win sympathy for a wife's suit. The problem was not just the protection of women, but of male self-image and reputation before the world: honor. The matter was much more obvious in cases where a husband resorted to murder to defend his honor against the seduction or adultery of his wife, an issue that will be examined later. But it also underlay women's powerlessness before the bench or assembly overseeing divorces. Descriptions of misbehavior inevitably forced men to consider the consequences to patriarchal authority should they take the wife's part in such disputes. A North Carolina case in 1822 provided a typical example. In this instance, the husband had not only contracted venereal disease from a prostitute but also had transmitted the illness to his wife. The high court refused to grant the wife a divorce. Only when a "husband abandons his family, or turns his wife out of doors, or by cruel and barbarous treatment endangers her life" was the state authorized to intervene, ruled the justices. In this instance, they could find no evidence that the husband had done anything hurtful, and therefore his misdeeds—appropriately deplored—were not covered by "positive law." Besides, upon learning of his wife's illness he had commendably "expressed his sorrow in tones of unfeigned remorse." Enjoining friends of the alienated couple to bend all efforts toward their reconciliation, the court censured "her relations" in particular for fomenting a separation "which might have been avoided" but for their "whispers" and "intrusion." The court refused to grant a divorce. The prerogatives of men were thus given priority once more.[25]

The inequity of early nineteenth-century divorce rulings was somewhat altered during the Jacksonian period. State after state, particularly in the Southwest, expanded the grounds for divorce to include cruelty, for which formerly only the remedy of legal separation had been provided, if life itself was endangered. The purpose, in the South as in the North, was to protect the virtuous wife, for husbands, needless to say, were more likely to be physically and even verbally barbarous than matrons were. Public opinion had much to do with the legal reform, but jurists were not always eager to utilize the wide discretionary powers that the new laws provided. In 1827 Justice Thomas Ruffin of North Carolina viewed a new divorce statute with skepticism: "I cannot suppose, however, that the discretion conferred is a mere personal one, whether wild or sober, but must from the nature of things be confined to those cases for which provision was before made by law, or for those of a like nature." Even after the liberal statutory provisions were incorporated in appellate court precedents, the wife had not only to prove the maliciousness of her husband but also her own submissiveness, chasteness, tender affection toward him, and motherly protectiveness toward the sometimes abused children. Such polarities in behavior lessened the natural reluctance of jurists to break with common-law custom and thereby seemingly weakened authoritarian domesticity, without which the family institution itself was thought to be endangered.[26]

Besides displaying an unblemished character, the female litigant had to show, at times, an uncommon persistence to win her suit. Cases sometimes dragged on interminably. So it was for two female members of the Foster clan in Mississippi (which will later be examined in detail); death of one partner or the other preceded a final ruling that came years after the suits were introduced. Nancy Wilson of North Carolina, however, was not so lucky as to have her husband die before the court made up its mind. Her pleas began in the early 1860s and languished for years in equity. Already estranged and intermittently separated from her before the war, De-Witt Wilson, her husband, left her permanently in 1861 to live with Moll Whittaker, a "lewd" woman of the neighborhood. Tiring of Moll, Wilson then discovered a handsome "bright Mulatto" named June, belonging to a neighboring farmer. He offered the astonishing price of $1,900 for June, $800 of it in pure gold, and most of it from his wife's dowry. Wilson brought the girl back to his wife's place, and thereafter, despite her protests, he took June and his eldest daughter to church in the carriage, leaving Nancy at home. The atmosphere grew unbearable, so Wilson threw his wife out of her own house and she found shelter with some distant relatives not far away. Once she was gone, Wilson then seized her plantation, then her slaves and all movable property, and sold the entire estate for $18,000, allegedly to pay his debts, but really to despoil his wife. Repeated efforts to prevent his actions through lawsuits failed. Nor could Nancy Wilson obtain a divorce. The turmoil of the Civil War and the conservative operations of the courts left matters unresolved until in 1867 the Reconstruction court granted the divorce and forced Wilson to return the possessions and deeds and provide her with corn and hay as well.[27]

In earlier days the woman's chances of getting a divorce were much less promising, but special circumstances such as social prominence and mental incapacity, or both, were of some help. In Virginia, Anne Roane, daughter of Spencer Roane, a former justice of the state supreme court, was the owner of a 1,000-acre plantation. The aging spinster suffered long spells of insanity. Bentley Woolfolk was her overseer for some two years. Uncouth though he was, he managed to entice her into marriage, for his own purposes. On the day after the wedding in 1849, Woolfolk made love to a slave woman and saw to it that his wife discovered the philandering shortly afterward. In addition, he struck up a liaison with his own niece, the daughter of his sister, both of whom moved into the main house the day after the ceremony. Anna was already a hysteric, but these were especially unsettling events. As Woolfolk anticipated, she could no longer bear the shock, and departed. The neighbors kindly took her in, as she had no kinfolk to assist her. At once Woolfolk assumed full control of the plantation, though he mostly neglected the farm chores and repairs and instead gave parties for friends, selling off his wife's possessions and dwindling crops to meet tavern bills. When Anna sued for divorce two years later, witnesses came forward to prove that years before Woolfolk had worked for a grocer, stolen his supplies, and fled with his female slave, with whom Woolfolk had struck up relations. Eventually recaptured, Woolfolk had set fire to the jailhouse before the trial and had escaped in the confusion, only to reappear as Anna Roane's overseer several counties away. Miscegenation was the least of Woolfolk's offences, and was given scant notice in the catalog of his wrongdoings. So it was in many divorce cases. In this instance, villainy did have limits, however, and the long-abused Anna, still unclear of mind, was granted release from the marriage. Woolfolk obviously was so thoroughly roguish and had so offended the gentry class by marrying a woman of superior family that the court took pity. Her connection with the late presiding judge of the same court no doubt helped her case enormously.[28]

There was, however, one sure way for a woman to gain male sympathy for her plight—when her husband failed in his marital duty. In fact, a reputation for impotence, made public by mob ridicule or through what in Europe was called the charivari, could be soul-destroying. The offense was thought to be a sin against nature itself, a departure from normality so humiliating that men would go to considerable lengths to throw the burden of guilt away from themselves. No doubt drinking to excess was itself sometimes both an excuse and a denial of the inner failing. But few men were so imaginative as one Peter Miller, eighty years of age, who sued his wife Polly, fifty, for divorce in a North Carolina court. He complained that her organs were so malformed that she could not comply with his very masculine needs. Polly, however, told the court that her husband "has likely been unable to accomplish his desires" for quite a different circumstance than the one he gave, for he had "some physical defect in himself": on the wedding night and thereafter, he could not make a "proper erection, nor was there emission," since he had to "get up every few minutes" to relieve himself. Another Carolinian complained that her husband had been a "fraud" for nearly a year, and had once even confessed that "he was not a *man.*" He slept with a knife under his pillow, and when she accused him of being impotent, he threatened to use it on her. The divorce was granted, as in most such (rare) cases.[29]

For men there could be no greater humiliation than an admission of impotence, a state of affairs hardly unique to the pre–Civil War South, but in a society in which there was so much pressure upon the male to live up to the ideals of his sex, even the presumption of failure could be disastrous. A most intriguing and puzzling incident of this kind was the abrupt separation of Sam Houston, governor of Tennessee, and Eliza Allen, his bride, who was just over twenty. John Allen, Eliza's father, was a major political force in east Tennessee, and doubtless he saw advantages for himself in having a daughter united with President Andrew Jackson's Tennessee protégé. The couple was married on January 22, 1829. On April 11, just as Houston's campaign for reelection was gathering strength, she suddenly departed for her parents' house in Gallatin. The whole affair is shrouded in rumor and innuendo, but it seems likely that from the very start Eliza had not shared her father's enthusiasm for the governor, fifteen years her senior. In light of Houston's unsatisfactory and almost incoherent correspondence with his father-in-law, and Eliza's silence and determined resistance to conciliation, it may safely be guessed that the marriage had not been consummated. Family rumors had it that she had been repelled by the sight of a pussy groin her husband suffered as the result of an Indian skirmish. Or it could have been that she had deliberately rejected him in ways that undermined his confidence. The truth cannot be known, nor does it matter much. (Both Eliza and Houston later married others and raised families.) What was significant was the public effect of rumors about Houston's impotence.

At the state capital a mob gathered in the streets and howled for several nights. News came from Gallatin that partisans of the Allen clan had burned the governor in effigy in front of the courthouse. One night Governor Houston could see from the executive mansion a rowdy group unfurling a banner lettered "Purity—in Defense of Woman's Honor—Purity." There was talk of lynching him, but the militia dispersed the rioters. When Houston asked Dr. William Hume, a Presbyterian clergyman, to baptize him, the divine refused. After all, "the respectable connections of the lady in Sumner County are much offended," he replied. The ethic of honor was more powerful than the authority of the Christian church. Unable to offer any explanation that would not further deepen the shame of impotence, Houston had no choice but to bow to popular will. The people of Tennessee were not to be ruled by a man incapable of meeting the prime duty of his gender. Only a dozen days elapsed between Eliza's flight and Houston's departure, in disguise, on a steamboat. He went into Indian country, often the refuge of the shamed, the deviant, the unwanted. When sacred principles were violated, the community will was not to be thwarted.[30]

To be sure, few Southern men experienced Houston's sexual difficulties, at least in so public a fashion, and few women were subjected to more than the usual distresses of married life. But the certainty of communal watchfulness as well as the physical and psychological power of men were bound to fetter women to conventional responses and reticences. As in so many aspects of Southern ethical life, the result was to create a successfully stable order—within the confines of regional culture. At least everybody knew what was expected of him or her. The community as well as the legal apparatus assigned every married couple duties and rules of behavior that they had to meet, with men given the wider options on the traditional grounds of their moral superiority. Most lived up to minimal expectations. Some were loving, even adoring husbands; some were worshipful wives. But others suffered in loneliness and pain, without, by and large, a protective shield of law to alleviate their travail.

12

Status, Law, and Sexual Misconduct

In reply to Yankee criticism, Southern proslavery apologists claimed that their region was far from being the Sodom the abolitionists depicted. In 1844, James Henry Hammond boasted that "there are fewer cases of divorce, separation, crim[inal] con[versation], seduction, rape and bastardy, than among any other five millions of people on the civilized earth."[1] Hammond exaggerated. Low rates of divorce, separation, and "criminal conversation" proved nothing about the stability or morality of married life. The compilation only revealed the capacity of ethics and custom to compel men and women to endure misery or find remedies outside the law. Bastardy, for example, has not been examined as a regional phenomenon. Doubtless the problem abated with the spread of preachers and religious attitudes, but legislative bills to legitimize bastards and petitions demanding stricter penalties against marital irregularity did reach the Southern legislatures. Rape constituted only one-half of one percent of all arraignments in antebellum South Carolina, according to a recent estimate. Yet the figure means little. Shame, guilt, and family pride certainly held down the number of reportings in the pre–Civil War South, as they still do in modern times. Later in the same essay, Hammond also claimed that white prostitution was a rarity in the slaveholding states, particularly in comparison with London and New York. (Indeed, 1841 London with its 3,325 licensed brothels was hard to rival.) But in 1858 the mayor of Savannah reported one courtesan for every thirty-nine men. In Norfolk the ratio was one to twenty-six. By contrast, New York's rate was one to fifty-seven, and New Haven's one to seventy-six.[2] And even if many of the Southern streetwalkers were black, their customers were not necessarily so.

The point is not to condemn the South for its sexual sins, particularly the wrong-doing that slaveholding so greatly encouraged. Enough has been said of those problems by others. Rather it is to ascertain how the issues of sexual misconduct were handled and what the means for their control reveal about the culture as a whole. As one would expect, the same inequalities in other aspects of Southern life naturally applied to breaches of the sexual code. Unlike the pious Northern middle classes, who adopted a new doctrine of feminine "passionlessness," Southerners presumed that women were subject to sexual feelings no less than men. Women were thought to be childlike—easily manipulated—and their immature emotions allegedly resulted in moral weakness. Therefore society decreed that women should be circumspect to a fault. Social rules aided the repression: gentlemen had to guard their language, literature had to avoid unmentionable topics, prudery reigned. When a Charleston iron-worker placed nude male figures on the corners of his new building, residents were aghast, and insisted that he fashion iron aprons for each of them. As one critic reported, the figures were larger than life, and "nearly as large . . . or larger at *some points.*"[3]

In maintaining what appears to us as a "double standard" of sexual behavior, Southerners were not very self-conscious, most especially in the early years of the Republic. Differences in the very physiques of the genders properly signified inequalities in "points of honor," declared Thomas R. Dew of Virginia, basing his arguments upon such eighteenth-century English authors as Addison and Burke. Thus, he continued, men could retrieve "a lost character" by a simple "reformation" of former promiscuity (though their wives should not provoke them with tears but entice them back with winning ways). On the other hand, a woman ought not be touched "even by the breath of suspicion," and could never fully recover her good name once it was blemished. Honor and interest combined to repress feminine lustfulness, but basically the sanction was external: fear of social ostracism. As proprietors and protectors of female virtue, fathers, brothers, and husbands were brought to public shame by the tarnished woman. Needless to say, Southern churchmen sought to impose a higher ideal of chasteness upon men, but they, like Dew, could not repudiate the ethic that condemned womanly sin and excused male vice. As a result, hard custom, undergirded by common-law jurisprudence, held the South to the traditional "double standard." In contrast, middle-class Northerners were gradually forsaking that view, and instead deeming women by nature morally superior and more self-controlled than men.[4]

Three broad categories in the realm of sexual ill-conduct reflected the general structure of Southern ethics: simple male fornication, which, under some conditions, was not even disapproved but almost sanctified; second, adultery, particularly female adultery, for which the remedies of the aggrieved husband were sometimes violent; and finally, certain (but not all) varieties of miscegenation. In each of these situations public response depended upon broad, customary expectations, but in practice these were modified by perceptions of how the principals conducted themselves.

Simple male fornication hardly requires much elaborate analysis. Yet it is worth mentioning that middle-class evangelical and Yankee ideals on this score were different from the mainstream of Southern mores. Although most Northern males doubtless had sexual experience before marriage, physicians and clergymen urged the duty and the healthiness of male continence. Ralph Waldo Emerson shocked his English friends Thomas Carlyle and Charles Dickens by observing that in his homeland "young men of good standing and good education . . . go virgins to their nuptial bed, as truly as their brides." After witnessing scenes of vice in Paris in

1848, he resisted carnal temptations by recalling "the dear and comely forms of honour and genius and piety in my distant home," who "touch me with chaste palms moist and cold, and say to me, You are ours." It was all very well to exhibit manliness in self-denial, as Victorian advisers like Emerson declaimed, but cold, chaste palms were not much in favor in the South. Neither the economy, the system of race control, the concepts of family life, nor even the understanding of gentlemanliness and social status stimulated the kind of repressive psychology that male continence involved.[5]

Attitudes toward male fornication were permissive. Male lust was simply a recognized fact of life. To repress natural impulse was to defy nature itself, leading to prissiness and effeminacy. Outright libertinism also suggested unmanly self-indulgence and inner weaknesses. But a healthy sex life without regard to marriage was quite in order. Fathers and mothers tacitly expected their boys to be adequately prepared for marriage. After all, the virgin male could too easily make the first wedding night a veritable disaster, hardly an auspicious beginning for a lifetime union. Young men made sexual experience a point of honor and boasting among themselves. Older men found that a masculine odor of mild indiscretion enhanced their respectability—if certain rules were followed. In his diary, Hammond defended his own inclinations, noting that "Casar [sic] spared no woman—that in all ages & countries down to the present day & nation the very greatest men . . . have been addicted to loose indulgences with women. . . . Webster & Clay are notorious for it & President Harrison got his wife's niece by child."[6] Hammond gave more credence to these stories than they probably deserved; he had committed similar blunders, and his misery at having been caught led him to find solace in the misadventures of others. Yet Hammond's remarks were fairly representative of the male perspective. In 1852, James L. Petigru gave an account of a dashing Carolinian and the young wife of an aged physician at a Virginia vacation hotel. On a midnight call, the doctor discovered the half-clothed couple leaving a neighboring room and chased them about the corridors, waving a shotgun. To the amusement of the other Southern guests, the lover managed to slip away undetected on the morning train. Such matters were delicious fare for the Carolinians.[7]

In the normal course of things, young members of the gentry set could do rather as they pleased—to the exasperation of the more religious residents in their community. Probably there was more bragging than doing. "Southeasterly breezes" from a nearby outhouse that some local belle frequented "doth make my cock stand as furious as a stud's, *sed non masculavi vestens!"* exclaimed Thomas Jefferson Withers, a frail but peppery Carolinian straight out of college at the state capital. He was writing from the security of his boardinghouse room, contemplating all the sex that apparently was somewhat beyond his power to obtain. Having failed to interest the fair visitor to the neighboring outhouse, he turned to a girl of darker color, musing, "My tool is made out of the same material as her's, and if 'tisn't in the very same shape—I believe it stinks as little, and I would as soon have it." That, too, was not a sexual adventure that materialized. After an initial meeting with the girl at a cockfight, Withers returned disappointed. In reference to the alleged smell of negritude, the immature young man remarked, "May I stink like a Pole Cat if I ever notice her again." Though later a South Carolina Supreme Court justice and husband of a gentle blueblood (Mary Chesnut's aunt), Withers as a youth was more bluster than performance. After all, no college student would wish to be known as a virgin. It led to suspicion and ridicule.[8]

In the American South, as in England and France, sleeping with a woman was an informal rite of virilization. The obvious way was to pursue a black partner. If the initial effort were clumsy or brutal no one would object, in view of the woman's race and status. Moreover, black girls were infinitely more accessible and experienced than the white daughters of vigilant, wealthy families. On a visit to Charleston in 1809, Alexander Wilson of Philadelphia observed the contrast between the "frigid insipidity" of "melancholy" upper-class "females" and the "negro wenches" who were "all sprightliness and gayety." A young white virgin male had only to down a few jiggers, light a "segar" to steady his nerves, and ask a passing black to "find him a girl."[9]

Chancellor Harper of South Carolina scoffed at abolitionist objections to such carnal pairings. He said that after the "warm passions of youth" had cooled, the ordinary planter's son realized that he was "connecting himself with one of an inferior and servile caste." He then invariably turned to court "the female of his own race," who offered "greater allurements." The essay by Harper in which these remarks appeared implied that a class of enslaved black women performed a useful service: their availability made possible the sexual license of men without jeopardizing the purity of white women. Prostitutes performed that convenient service in free societies; fallen women, it was thought, kept the rest of the world in good moral order. Slave companions did the same in the Old South.[10]

Unrestrained promiscuity by men was by no means uniformly condoned, but discretion was the mark of a gentleman. One should not flagrantly presume upon another man's territory, in home or quarters. If the "Lothario" lacked repute, woe betide him. For instance, if a poor boy or man "stole" another's slave girl, the penalties were stiff, even though the intention was strictly temporary cohabitation. Though a rich but wayward youth might beat the charge with a good lawyer or an appeal to the outraged master, men of low standing faced serious problems. In South Carolina, when John L. Brown, already known for "dissolute habits," ran off with another man's slave, he was caught, tried, and sentenced to hang for "negro-stealing." Judge John Belton O'Neall recommended commutation and Governor James H. Hammond complied. Brown received thirty-nine lashes on the back instead.[11] Obviously the master and the community sought to set a stern public example, a warning to those without slaves to keep their hands off the valuable possessions of the better element.

Overseers who took liberties in the quarters were a constant cause of complaint. Their activities disrupted life among the slaves and led to demoralized work habits. But at least they did not "steal" their prizes away. When a yeoman boy—eighteen-year-old Levin Johnson of Mississippi, for instance—ran off with a "handsome mulatto" girl, lawyers pleaded the client's immaturity, nonfelonious intent, and remorse. He and the girl had spent the night on a wharf-side steamboat, and for this Johnson was almost sent to the gallows. His sentence was commuted to life in prison. Masters did not invariably go to law for redress, however. J. J. Lyons of up-country South Carolina discovered that the female slave clerk of his store had been sleeping with one of the Perry clan. Since Perry belonged to a leading family, legal action would probably have failed before a jury. At their next meeting Lyons horsewhipped the young blade unmercifully. Many such examples could be given. The main lesson was not "thou shalt not fornicate with black women," but rather "thou shalt take care to do so at no other man's expense."[12]

The second and much more serious issue of sexual misbehavior, the infidelity of a married woman, could no more be separated from questions of status than could male improprieties of the kind just mentioned. By and large women of planter rank were too strictly supervised to have much experience with infidelity, though the "flirt" was a constant source of scandal and fascination among the ladies. Certainly the kind of feminine license that prevailed in the upper classes of seventeenth- and eighteenth-century England and France had no Southern parallel even in the aristocracy of the colonial and early national South. But if grand jury presentments, foreign travelers, and itinerant clergymen are to be given any credence at all, the lower classes of the hinterland South were fairly casual about marital arrangements in general and adultery in particular. Conditions of moral informality gradually diminished under the auspices of revival enthusiasms and church discipline. In fact, a major and unstudied reason for the rise of evangelical churchmanship throughout the South after 1800 was that it provided an effective means for more orderly, sober folk to demarcate and insulate themselves from an element with roistering traditions stretching back to British origins. So little work has been done to describe the ethical and cultural structure of the yeomanry outside the churchgoing crowd that historians are caught between the romantic and bourgeois presentation of Frank Owsley on the one hand and the familiar stereotypes of poor-white depravity on the other. Nevertheless, the backwoods Southern yeomanry, particularly in the early antebellum years, was no more morally refined than the pre-Wesleyan working classes of England. Therefore, most examples of feminine adultery—and of responses to it—involved the middle and lower orders of the white South, not the wealthy, churchgoing matrons of Charleston and Richmond.

The attitude toward feminine adultery was scarcely casual, but it was not a matter of criminal violation. Although grand juries and remonstrating citizens urgently requested that antebellum state legislatures punish adulterers (particularly female ones), lawmakers steadfastly refused. In South Carolina, for instance, bills to provide penalties for adultery were introduced in 1844, 1856, and 1860. None passed. By common law, sexual offenses of this kind had been under ecclesiastical jurisdiction, but when the church was disestablished in Revolutionary times, sexual policing duties were not transferred to other tribunals. In New England, by contrast, adultery had initially been a statutory felony, punishable by death and later by less sanguinary but quite humiliating penalties. Southerners did not believe that the machinery of the state should intervene in matters of local morality. After all, common law provided a husband with the necessary legal right to seize his wife from a seducer by force and to apply to her whatever physical chastisement he felt suitable—within limits. Citizens could band themselves against a local malefactor, with appropriate results, but state intervention on a comprehensive scale, it was thought, would have overtaxed the limited resources of central power.

Nevertheless, for the individual husband two alternatives for handling an adulterous wife did exist within the law itself. Neither was socially approved, and both therefore were seldom used. The first was criminal conversation, a tort action. Only men could sue under this ancient theory of trespass. The common-law rationale was that men, having proprietary claims upon a wife's property, should not be obliged to support children by another man and have their own offspring's legitimacy questioned. Samuel Johnson claimed that "confusion of progeny" was the central problem in a woman's unfaithfulness and accounted for the universal disapprobation of it, but the real problem was, of course, protection of male ego, honor, *and* purity of bloodline. James Hammond thought the absence of criminal-conversation actions from the routine judicial calendar was a mark of Southern moral superiority. It was not. The action was rare simply because it was not well known, and that circumstance was a function of its embarrassing connotations. Criminal conversation was a suit for damages against an adulterer for the loss of a wife's labor, affections, and good name. Who wanted to admit that he was a cuckold? An example of the ambivalent feelings involved arose in a South Carolina case before Justice Elihu Bay in 1820. The husband sought $5,000 in damages from his wife's seducer, but the husband then had to admit that his wife was utterly promiscuous before she had run off with her lover. Bay thoroughly denounced the wife's seducer as "the villain *spider of society*" who had heaped "dishonour" upon the husband. Five thousand dollars was not an excessive compensation, he declared. Nevertheless Bay ruled that condonation (the husband's toleration of his wife's earlier concupiscence) had to be presented to a jury before the court could assess the extent of punitive damages to be awarded.[13]

Thus filing a criminal-conversation action ran counter to notions of how a man should act under trying circumstances. "Mortification of mind" and "depression of a husband's happiness," as Justice Daniel Huger of South Carolina declared, constituted the basis of such suits, not the medieval notion of a poor man with no other recourse available to him seeking redress against a lecherous overlord.[14] In America each man was to defend his own honor as a freeholding citizen. Money damages were unsuitable.[15]

Divorce, though always a more familiar way to gain freedom from an unfaithful wife, presented similar difficulties. In South Carolina neither husband nor wife had access to that remedy; even legal separations were forbidden. Judge O'Neall boasted that "the *Legislature never has, and never will act*" to validate divorce. From time to time, he said, "the most distressing cases, justifying divorce even on scriptural grounds," such as adultery by a wife, reached the legis-latures, but they "nobly adhered to the injunction" of the New Testament never to sunder bonds sanctified by God. It was a "stern policy," but one intended for the good of all "in every respect." Even when South Carolina did briefly have a divorce statute during Reconstruction, only one litigant (in *Grant* v. *Grant*) had the temer-ity to apply, and he was peremptorily denied the suit on the grounds that the final settlement reached the state Supreme Court after the law's repeal under the Redeemers.[16]

Even in states more secular than South Carolina the outcome of a divorce plea was at best problematical for distressed husbands. First of all, divorce for any cause was seldom granted, either by state legislatures or by equity or chancery courts. Hoping to reduce, not increase, the number of applications, some Southern state legisla-tures began in the 1820s to relinquish the power to grant private bills of divorce and confer the jurisdiction upon the bench, where stern common-law jurists were supposed to stand impervious to political, democratic demands. But under pressure of changing no-tions the lawmakers did liberalize the grounds, reflecting a curious conflict of motives that deserves further investigation. Nevertheless, the number of requests was always slight relative to population size. In 1821 fifty-five divorce petitions reached the Tennessee legislature. Ten years later the number of pleas had risen to sixty-six, hardly an impressive increase. In Alabama the number hovered around 63 per year from 1849 to 1854, then leapt to 105 in 1855, a rate sus-tained until the Civil War. In Georgia, 291 legislative divorces were submitted between 1798 and 1835, but the acceleration was really confined to the last two years. How many were actually granted remains unascertained, but the number was not high. In North Caro-lina, according to one estimate, only one in twenty pleas was hon-ored in 1810, four in twenty-two in 1813. No doubt the ratio grad-ually improved over the next forty years. Yet careful work with county and state records still remains to be done to discover the pat-terns of the average state assembly and trial judge.[17]

In seeking release from a wayward wife—the most usual and most often successful grounds—the Southern husband faced serious obstacles whether he approached the bench or state assembly. Social hierarchy mattered, especially so in the less democratic early years of the Republic. Thus at the turn of the century John Hutchins, a member of the Adams County, Mississippi, gentry, sued for divorce on the grounds of his wife's repeated infidelities. He had "whiped [*sic*]" Elizabeth's lover each time he had caught the couple together. Then he had discovered (he claimed) that she had taken up with his own brother Samuel. It was beyond endurance. As often happened in such scandals, factions developed around each of the parties' causes, almost exploding into a full-scale political confrontation. In 1805 the wealthy James Norcom, physician of Edenton, prevailed upon his gentry friends in the North Carolina legislature and gained release from a woman whom he regarded—probably unfairly—as unfaithful and "turbulent." The protestations of both young gentlemen included long harangues on how much they feared loss of face if compelled to remain united to such "treacherous" creatures. To them, temporary declensions in their standing because of divorce action was worth the risk. Nevertheless, it took five years for Norcom to find a woman of suitable wealth and rank who would marry him. Like Mary Miller when she married James Chesnut, Norcom's second wife was only in her mid-teens.[18]

Since divorce pleas early in the century ordinarily arose from members of the poorer classes, gentry legislators had little difficulty in withholding the privilege, as common-law tradition enjoined. An example was the 1813 case of John O'Quin of Wayne County, North Carolina. He and his friends, among whom was a magistrate, caroused at a village house of prostitution one evening. When he woke up the next morning he found himself bedded with "a *Huge Mass of Creation*, purporting to be of the Female Sex, who called herself MARY JACKSON." She announced that the drunken magistrate had married them the night before. Shortly thereafter Mary Jackson joined the troops going to the Canadian front in the war with Great Britain. O'Quin pled for release. The lower chamber rejected the bill, no doubt with much guffawing about how young men should not mix pleasure with the serious business of matrimony. Yet, as always, there was a rationale behind seemingly arbitrary decision making. A fool and his honor, it might have been said, were soon parted. O'Quin's misfortune, in a sense, made more valuable a wiser man's respectability. One's moral reputation was supposed to conform with one's social position, which, as we know, was a very ancient concept. Rich men were imputed to be wise, poor to be foolish. Therefore, examples of folly should be presented to the public in the form of clownish folk like O'Quin. Judge Eugenius A. Nisbet of Georgia admitted that in the handling of divorce cases, legislators were most often influenced by such factors as who the parties were, rather than the circumstances of the case. "The wealth and standing of the parties," he said in 1835, "their political and social relations, or perhaps, the personal beauty and address of the female litigant, controlled in many cases the action of the legislature." Negative decisions, then, meant the very opposite: a disapproval of petitions from the stupid, ugly, and poor, regardless of the inherent merits of the plea. With clear consciences, the politicians thus reaffirmed the sacred character of marriage and male honor by rejecting socially unimportant litigants, the class that overwhelmingly dominated registries of divorce actions.[19]

No less significant than the class status of the plaintiff was evidence of his manliness in the handling of his travails. Without it, chances of winning a divorce from an adulterous wife were slim. In 1833, for instance, John R. Sexton, an illiterate yeoman of Blount County, Tennessee, sought freedom from a most incorrigible wife. Not only was Elizabeth Sexton unfaithful, but, said one deponent, she used her husband's bed to entertain two men at a time. By another deposition, she had sex "three times in broad day light with one David Hammontree," whom she called "much of a man." Finding her rutting under a bush with a stranger to the neighborhood, the local deacon reproached her. Elizabeth retorted, "My ass is my own and I will do as I please with it." The divorce committee was unimpressed and rejected Sexton's plea as "unreasonable." He had observed these goings-on without taking appropriately manly action. Even when a wife deserted a yeoman husband to turn up as a prostitute somewhere else, the husband's chances of winning a suit depended less on the wife's shamelessness than on the manner in

which the husband managed the situation. In the minds of legislators—men of the world—the hidden requirement was a confrontation
with the lover(s) and, one may safely guess, administration of some
firm corrective to the erring wife. If the husband could not control
her, he was not to be awarded community approval in the form of
divorce. In North Carolina in 1813, Peter Riley argued that he had
had to leave his sluttish wife "to protect his reputation." But from
depositions there was no sign of his chastising his rivals or his wife.
The petition was denied. In the same year, before the same committee, Frederick Ward of Lincoln County, North Carolina, was not
freed from marriage, even though his wife had repeatedly cuckolded
him, left the state for "New Spain" (Louisiana), and there remarried. He, too, had not fulfilled the unwritten demand.[20]

If, however, a poor man could demonstrate that his wife had
been moved by the enticements of a rich seducer, then he stood a
decent chance of winning his case. After all, the reasoning went, any
man might be deceived by a daughter of Eve who proved too easily
swayed by pretty promises and fine clothes of a gentleman. In divorce cases, as in criminal-conversation actions in English settings,
the higher the standing of the adulterer the greater the sympathy
for the husband upon whom he supposedly preyed. Thus Thomas
Taylor, husbandman of Bedford County, Tennessee, gained a total
divorce from Nancy Nuzum in 1821. She had threatened to pile up
fifty-dollar debts upon the yeoman, ridiculed his poverty, and boasted
that the child she bore belonged to "a gentleman and she wold take
it to him that he wold Dress it." Just how accurate the accusations
were could scarcely come to light now, but they apparently impressed the committee. Indications of a clandestine unfaithfulness,
cleverly hidden even from neighbors, also gave the unsuspecting
husband a winning hand. James Trotter, for instance, had witnesses
to testify that his wife had deceived everyone for years. Her misdeeds came to notice only after she had abruptly admitted her
promiscuity and departed for Petersburg to become a streetwalker.
He, too, gained freedom at the hands of a legislature that was generally niggardly about handing out divorces to poor folk, or indeed
anyone at all.[21]

On the surface, these decisions appeared whimsical. Yet they were judgments based upon the principles of a traditional ethic. The courts and lawmakers never put honor into statutory or judicial form because it was commonly understood that there should be a division between the workings of the law and the stalwart defense of a man's sense of self. As Joel P. Bishop, a nineteenth-century legal specialist, explained, "The government does not take cognizance of all the laws of human association existing in a community." Breaches in "the law of honor," he said, belonged in that category.[22] The young or foolish fellow who bound himself to a notoriously brazen woman such as Mary Jackson, or one under suspicion of wantonness, such as Betsey Sexton, had to pay the price of his folly or ineffectuality.

The personal interests of the legislators themselves sometimes affected the way they voted, regardless of any abstractions about social values and ascriptions. An unusual example was a petition in 1831 to the Tennessee legislature in behalf of the Rev. Robert Baker of Carroll County. He sued on the grounds that his bride turned out to be two or three months pregnant at the time of the ceremony. "We cannot believe," declared the Presbyterian divine, "that the solemnity of the marriage tie, was ever intended to bind a virtuous and Honorable man, to a loathsome woman, who had concealed from him the fact that before their marriage she had prostituted herself to the embraces of her own uncle who was a married man." One might have expected a favorable verdict. After all, a clergyman's reputation, like that of a woman's, had to be as spotless as his clerical collar. So too should his wife's virtue be unquestioned. On the other hand, a single instance of fornication before marriage, under common law, was no offense. Bastardy, especially by incest, a felony, certainly was criminally punishable. Yet should it be allowed to affect the validity of a subsequent marriage? By common law, the husband of a woman in such condition had no option but to remain wed and support the child. In addition, the Tennessee legislature had recently received complaints about an alleged rise in bastardy cases with too many sworn denials of paternity by knavish fathers, and the consequent addition of new child support burdens on the limited resources of rural taxpayers. Legal precedent and the desire to set an example both counted against Baker's plea. In addition, one other factor may have tipped the scales. The misbehaving uncle in the case had the same name as Warham Easley, chairman of the lower chamber's divorce committee. Chairman Warham Easley was at the very least a close relative of the corespondent, unless by improbable coincidence two unrelated Easley families had happened to settle in the same county. The divorce plea was denied.[23]

Unpleasant though violence was, the most socially approved course for a husband with a wayward mate was to take the law into his own hands. Even judicial experts all but suggested that physical retort was the proper means of retrieving lost honor. On matters of sexual honor the law took account of community opinion. Tapping Reeve, in reference to common-law precedent about adultery, conceded that "where a man finds another in the act of adultery with his wife, which is the greatest possible injury, yet the husband is not justified . . . to avenge his own wrongs." Nevertheless, he continued, the husband was only guilty of manslaughter, to the lowest degree, and liable to suffer "burning in the hand to be inflicted gently," probably with a cold iron. Texas law on this issue was much more straightforward than even common law. According to Article 1220, still on the books, a killing under circumstances in *flagrante delicto* is justifiable homicide. Other states were less bloodthirsty, but juries were loath to convict on even the mildest charges of manslaughter under provocation.[24]

Murderers and their lawyers played upon popular notions about how such situations should be handled, appealing to the sacred principles of masculinity. "It is vain," said Jereboam Beauchamp, killer of his wife's alleged lover, to think that "the laws of society" were sufficient guardians. Beauchamp justified himself on the grounds that any husband, brother, or father "of any sensibility or honorable feelings" would rather have their beloved "silently put out of the world" than have her seduced and left "to drag out a wretched degraded existence tenfold more painful" to her male protector "than her death." (In this instance, however, the killer was hanged because his wife, a woman of bitter fantasies and questionable reputation, had induced him to kill the Kentucky state's attorney, whom she had falsely accused of seducing her.)[25]

Beauchamp's sentiments did not merely express the romance of nineteenth-century love, but reflected a much more ancient, primordial code of male possessiveness that was still very much alive. The language in which these primitive ideals were couched posed the eternal dichotomies of right and wrong, innocence and evil, honesty and deception, without the slightest hint of ambiguity or introspection. A Tennessee lawyer defending a husband who had dispatched his wife's seducer declared before a jury, "Whose presence will you encourage in your midst, the man who does his duty, works hard, accomplishes good, and blesses every one with whom he comes in contact, or the slimy wretch, besotted with lust, the hoary lecher, the practiced seducer, the aged debauchee, the common enemy of social purity, the outlaw from Christian civilization?" Every juryman knew his responsibility and felt a kinship with the accused. Yet as George Bishop, a nineteenth-century commentator on family law, observed, the husband who hurled charges indiscriminately at a wife or alleged lover without sufficient reason was the most despised of men. "What sort of shield to innocence were the law, if it permitted a husband's spleen or suspicion" or common gossip "to destroy" a woman's "fair fame" and cast her "adrift upon a pitiless world?"[26] Though men were often prepared to believe the worst, false claims upon honor, as in the Beauchamp case, only blackened the reputation of the accuser. Such incidents arose in the turbulence of Southern family life once in a while. In a society in which man had to play a formal role of virility or lose all reputation, jealousy could all too easily arise when men, many of them bowed down by alcohol and poverty, felt inadequate to meet the circumstances. Yet false accusations could underline a man's weakness and thereby diminish his esteem in the eyes of other men.

Miscegenation between a white male and black female posed almost no ethical problems for the antebellum Southern community, so long as the rules, which were fairly easy to follow, were discreetly observed. First, the relationship, even if long-standing, had to seem to be a casual one in which the disparity of rank and race between the partners was quite clear to any observer. Second, the concubine had to be sexually attractive in white men's eyes. The lighter the skin, the more comely the shape, the more satisfactory the arrangement appeared to be. Third, the pairing could not be part of a general pattern of dissoluteness. If the wayward white was alcoholic, unsociable, and derelict about civic duty or work, then his keeping a mistress became a subject of general complaint. But gentlemen of discretion and local standing were able to master these simple conventions and suffer very little public disapproval.

Moreover, a man should by all means never acknowledge in mixed company his illicit liaison with a woman, black *or* white. Whispers among members of the same sex did not constitute public exposure. In a conversation among the ladies, Mary Chesnut referred to a genteel old reprobate and how his family reacted to his midnight doings in the quarters. "His wife and daughters in the might of their purity and innocence are supposed never to dream of what is as plain before their eyes as the sunlight," she observed. "They prefer to adore their father as model of all earthly goodness."[27] If someone had violated good taste and brought up the matter in their hearing, however, then all family members, the "sinner" included, would have been disgraced. Transcendent silence was the proper policy.

An example that readily springs to mind is the case of Thomas Jefferson and his slave Sally Hemings, his deceased wife's half-sister by a mulatto slave and Jefferson's father-in-law, a Virginia squire. The controversy surrounding the matter, raised anew by Fawn Brodie's recent biography of Thomas Jefferson, requires only brief comment here. Brodie argues that Jefferson carried on a lengthy liaison with his handsome houseservant at Monticello, a relationship marked by romantic love and deep sexual passion. Her critics, chiefly historians of Virginia's past, have roundly condemned not only Brodie's interpretation but also the very thought that Jefferson's character and stature could have been so imperfect as to permit such an illicit affair. Brodie is preoccupied with sentimental notions of love across the racial barrier, with all sorts of heavy breathing about long-standing national hypocrisies and the plight of two lovers caught in a poignant human dilemma worthy of Hollywood treatment. Her critics, with equal intensity, are determined to preserve Jefferson's reputation from such cheapening. But neither she nor they have fully grasped the social and psychological context of sexuality in that pre-Freudian, pre-Victorian era.

Eighteenth-century gentlemen seldom identified themselves in terms of their sexual proclivities. Sex was too casual for that kind of intense involvement. Eighteenth-century men who lost their composure in love were more likely to be held in contempt than celebrated. Sexual intercourse was viewed as a natural biological function. For reasons of health, it was simply thought good policy for men to have a reasonably active sex life within marriage or, if necessary, outside it. "Wenching" (as occasion permitted) or having a mistress was strictly a private matter. Illicit male heterosexual activity involved notions of guilt and shame only when it affected reputation or when it resulted in personal complications or illness. In modern culture, by contrast, sexuality holds a much greater place in the hierarchy of personal values, so that who and how one loves has come to be considered a valid form of self-expression. (Even homosexuality, thoroughly condemned in prior ages, has shed some of its former shamefulness.) In any event, we are more obsessed with the sex drive than our forefathers ever were.

From the perspective of the eighteenth century, rather than our own, Jefferson was perfectly capable of having a liaison with Sally Hemings, but a full-blown love affair? Never. Someone as self-aware and self-controlled as Thomas Jefferson would not have lost his heart to a slave mistress. Besides, the evidence for any sort of relationship between Sally and her master, as Brodie's critics insist, is simply too insubstantial and probably will remain so.[28]

For purposes at hand, though, it is not at all important what Jefferson's sexual practices were. What was significant was the way in which Jefferson and his kinfolk handled the rumors of sexual misconduct. Whether the gossip was accurate or not, the veil of privacy that ordinarily surrounded a gentleman's sexual habits had been torn away. Then—as now—Americans delighted in hearing about misconduct among the great. It helped to cut leaders down to comprehensible, very human size.

As for the parentage of mulattoes born at Monticello, the most likely candidates were Peter and Samuel Carr, Jefferson's young nephews. In 1868 Henry S. Randall, an early biographer of Jefferson, reported in confidence to James Parton, another writer, that Colonel Thomas Jefferson Randolph, the president's grandson, had once given him the family's version of what had occurred. On a tour of Monticello, Randolph had pointed to one slave cabin where, he said, Peter Carr and Sally Hemings had slept together. Next to it was another small house once occupied by Samuel Carr and Betsey, another Monticello slave. At the time of this exchange, the colonel had enjoined Randall not to make public the family's defense of Thomas Jefferson's virtue. Randall recalled in his letter to Parton, "When I rather pressed [Colonel Randolph] on the point, he said, pointing to the family graveyard, 'You are not bound to prove a negation. If I should allow you to take Peter Carr's corpse into Court and plead guilty over it to shelter Mr. Jefferson, I should not dare again to walk by his [Jefferson's] grave; he would rise and spurn me.' " Randall himself agreed that if he had done so "I should have made a *shameful* mistake." Indeed, by the standards of traditional society, no defense of Jefferson was necessary. One could hardly imagine a better illustration of the Stoic-humanistic tradition in practice: the whole-souled man who would not deign to answer scurrility and misrepresentation. Honor as expressed in gentility demanded family reticence, not to conceal anyone's wrongdoing but to shield honor itself. The Carr boys might have volunteered to come forward, but Jefferson himself would never have requested public confession. They were not made of the same stuff as he. Instead, according to another family member, Peter Carr laughed "that 'the old gentleman had to bear the blame for his and Sam's (Col. Carr) misdeeds.' " No doubt the pair of mediocrities took some pleasure in reducing their distinguished kinsman's reputation, knowing that the rules of gentility forbade the president from ever mentioning the business to them.[29]

Needless to say, rules of silence were not always so scrupulously observed in Aristotelian fashion. Deathbed contrition occasionally led to breaches of the taboo against personal, public confession. Lieutenant-Governor Winston of Mississippi, for instance, freed his slave mistress and their son by will in 1834. As he had no wife or heirs to bear the disgrace, however, there was no public outcry in that frontier state. David Dickson of Georgia bequeathed an estate of half-a-million dollars to his concubine when he died in 1885. A North Carolina planter required that a mulatto should share equally in an estate with the legitimate line. A Virginia planter freed his lifetime mistress, then over sixty years old. In all such cases, public reaction—as well as the outrage of heirs—was intense. Usually, however, the law upheld the validity of wills. What was most galling to survivors about these incidents was not just the loss of estate that they entailed but also the exposure to public criticism.[30]

Beyond these obvious difficulties was a further complication: the danger that the illicit pattern of the father would be perpetuated in the next generation. Lillian Smith, in *Killers of the Dream,* speculates that the early association of children with black mammies led to male adult longings for a love earlier denied them by their white mother. White miscegenators, she argues, feared that sons and daughters would be attracted to mulatto offspring "and should continue the blending of races to which they and their forefathers had made such lavish contributions."[31]

For obvious reasons, a mulatto girl posed less danger to a family's well-being than a mulatto male, unless, as Southerners sometimes fancied, an unsuspecting white male tried to marry her in the mistaken belief that she was white. Ella Thomas, a plantation matron, read a novel in which a bewitching girl who turns out to be the daughter of a mulatto slave and a "Col. Bell" becomes engaged to a young slaveholding gentleman. "I must say I was sufficiently *Southern,*" the Carolinian diarist declared, "to think him justifiable in breaking off the engagement after a great deal of suffering." After all, there were the future generations to think of. Richard Mentor Johnson had little trouble over his concubinage with Julia Chinn, a well-brought-up mulatto. A Jacksonian congressman and senator, he kept her in safe seclusion on his Kentucky plantation until her death in 1834. But Johnson tried to introduce their two attractive daughters to Washington society, and the effort made his love life a matter of notoriety. When he ran on Van Buren's ticket, he became the only vice-president in American history to gain the office by narrow Senate election, having failed, by reason of his domestic unorthodoxy, in the electoral college. Had he left his daughters on the Kentucky estate the issue might never have become a scandal, although by the mid-1830s marital regularity had become an evangelical prescription for public office.[32]

The real difficulty was the mulatto male who was the offspring of a planter's union with a mulatto slave. The "bleaching" process, as Southerners perceived it, enhanced his attractiveness to white women and also provided him with a pride in blood hardly suited to the black race and its place in society. Bennet H. Barrow, for instance, became highly incensed when some young mulatto sons of a neighboring planter came riding through his slave quarters in their fine clothes, accompanied by mulatto girls imported from New Orleans. "As I rode up to them," Barrow gloated, "I never saw any thing humble as quick as they did, forgot all their *high breeding* and self greatness." He scared them off with hard talk and whip-cracking. When he complained that "people submit to Amalgamation in its worse Form in this Parish," he was not so much referring to the sin of biracial intercourse as to the impropriety of raising mulatto males to levels that encouraged "impudence."[33]

There was always the chance of a drastic mistake. Since white girls were often quite intimate with their brothers, it followed that their fathers' mulatto offspring would hold a special attraction for them. In the catalog of Southern nightmares, none loomed more ominously than the notion of a pairing of sister with black male. "Would you have your sister marry one?" was not just a cliché. It exposed a taboo that the possibility of incest further strengthened. Henry Hughes, a young intellectual of Port Gibson, Mississippi, declared in a proslavery treatise, "Hybridism is heinous. Impurity of races is against the law of nature. Mulattoes are monsters. . . . The same law which forbids consanguinous amalgamation forbids ethnical amalgamation. Both are incestuous. Amalgamation is incest."

The chain of logic was an expression of Southern ascriptive sanctities: family, blood, gender, race. The myth of Orestes had its Southern parallel. As one Kentucky clergyman argued, "Many mulattoes know that the best blood of the south runs in their veins, they feel its proud, impatient and spirit-stirring pulsation; and see themselves cast off and oppressed by those that gave them being." A white man would surely resent such displacement; therefore the white man's mulatto son might well seek vengeance, too, in "treason, stratagem, and spoil."[34]

The probability of incestuous amalgamation was exceedingly low, but once in a while incidents did occur. For instance, in South Carolina's Union District one Colonel William Farr, a bachelor, took as his "bright mulatto" mistress the daughter of his half-brother. Fan, as she was called, bore him a son named Henry. Farr did not openly admit to being either the father or the uncle of the boy, and his wealth and reclusive habits helped to prevent a community outcry. As he said, he did not "wish to make a blowing horn of everything he did." Moreover, he cultivated a friendship with Judge John Belton O'Neall. Nevertheless, Farr and his mistress were an unhappy pair, sometimes seriously hurting each other in furious alcoholic battles. As his health and disposition deteriorated, Farr prepared for the future by sending his son, named Henry, to boarding school. The boy was expelled as soon as his origins were known, however, and he had to finish his education in Indiana. To assure mother and son a competence, Farr bequeathed them half of his $60,000 estate, the other portion being assigned to Judge O'Neall as a precaution against a challenge. Shortly before dying, however, Farr replaced O'Neall as beneficiary with Dr. William Thompson, his physician. Presumably the judge had lectured him on debauchery once too often. Upon his death in 1837, the colonel's white kinsmen by his half-brother disputed their mulatto relatives' rights to the inheritance. As Farr had anticipated, however, Thompson stoutly defended the original settlement through various trials and appeals. The plaintiffs claimed that Fan's African magic was the only possible explanation for Farr's perversity: he must have been somehow poisoned or mesmerized into mental incompetence, the lawyers argued. With Judge O'Neall abstaining, the final court ruling upheld the will by a verdict of two to two (a majority would have been necessary to overturn it). However distasteful the circumstances were, the jurists really had no choice. South Carolina probate law, bowing to common social practice, decreed the proportion that a concubine should receive, a singular fact that Hammond and others were loath to mention when defending slaveholders' virtue from abolitionist attack. Farr's will met the stipulations, and his mental competence was never in doubt.[35]

What was genuinely significant about the case was not the decision of the bench. Rather, community toleration of Farr's living arrangements was noteworthy. That toleration was based on the fact that Farr had not advertised his deviation. He did not take his concubine to public places or impose her presence upon relatives. She acted as his servant. Moreover, his kinsmen had a vested interest in checking any public outcry, so long as Farr kept them uninformed about the contents of the will. Under conditions so bizarre, it was best not to make a fuss. And it must be remembered that the mulattoes involved were so light-skinned that driving them out by charivari or some other coercive community action would have been morally confusing.

There was already enough confusion about miscegenation as it was. Moreover, there were some regional as well as class variations in attitudes. Professor Joel Williamson, the leading authority on the topic, argues that in the Chesapeake area and other parts of the upper South the planter class "early set an adamant face against miscegenation," but yeomen and poor whites were more tolerant. "In the lower South," he says, a "Latin pattern prevailed." Yet, judging by divorce proceedings already mentioned and from other sources, it would seem that miscegenation nowhere was sufficient grounds to ostracize the unrepentant white lover unless he compounded his sin with other vices and deliberately sought to affront local "respectability." Whether a "Latin" liberality or a Protestant restrictiveness marked local attitudes, white Southerners were always ambivalent, watchful, and intense regarding unions of white men and black women. Out of these materials that the ethical scheme of the Old South created, William Faulkner fashioned his masterpiece *Absalom, Absalom!* with its themes of human insensitivity, patriarchy, incest, self-love, and racial complications. It is no gothic tale, but bears out the moral and social dilemmas that in real life the Farr family confronted.[36]

Just as the wellborn mulatto, like Faulkner's Charles Bon or Colonel Farr's son, could threaten social order with their white man's pridefulness, the white female who copulated with a black slave posed problems of a similar kind: the encouragement of white pride in a black man and an implied rejection of white men's claims to exclusive sexual possession. The number of white women so inclined was always very small. Women with a consciousness of their social place were scarcely likely to throw themselves into the arms of men not of their class, education, and color. As one eighteenth-century matron recalled, she and other children were "from infancy in habits of familiarity with these humble friends, yet being early taught that nature had placed between them a barrier, which it was in a high degree criminal and disgraceful to pass, they considered a mixture of such distinct races with abhorrence, as a violation of her laws."[37]

Nearly all examples of female intercourse with black men from the antebellum period involved women with defective notions of their social position—hardly surprising in view of the deep horror the violation of this taboo inspired in the community. Sexual attraction, fascination with the exotic, and most of all a sense of gratification in submitting to the dark lover were all involved. One may also be sure that the blacks in question were unusually gifted— and bold—lovers, whom a white man might well envy. No doubt black vengeance through white jealousy was much of the attraction that the black lovers found in these poor-white girls. Some of the slave lovers were conjure-men whose tricks promised the adolescent girls their hearts' desire. Elizabeth Pettus of Fluvanna, Virginia, for instance, was intrigued with a conjure-man named Bob, who seduced her with the threat that he would use magic to break off her match with Dabney Pettus "if she did not conform to his humours." She gave in. Likewise, Lydia Bright of Norfolk in 1803 went to bed with slave Robin because he had promised "that he would conger for to get Benjamin Butt, Jr. to be her husband." In Anson County, North Carolina, Mary Dunn, a serving girl, watched with fascination as a slave named Warwick used a ball of twine and a pan handle to fashion some sort of zodiac in the farmyard dirt. She whispered to a neighbor that what his magic had revealed to her was "so ugly she would not tell." The secret was not hard to guess: he came to her that night.[38]

Placed in close proximity to slaves and themselves enjoying very little standing in the community, girls like Mary Dunn, Elizabeth Pettus, and Lydia Bright heard much about black sexual prowess, but also about their own duty never to touch the forbidden fruit. Even for these adolescents, poor as they were, there was much self-respect to lose. Yet the temptation was great to see for themselves what it was like to bed with a virile slave. No doubt there was much truth in Edward Long's comment that lower-class women in England were "remarkably fond of the blacks, for reasons too brutal to mention. . . ." Likewise, in the colonial and early Republic eras some American women of wayward disposition made no color distinctions. Needless to say, husbands of such prostitutes or "debauched" girls, as one witness called Mary Dunn, easily won divorces. If their spouses had only white bedmates, however, husbands did not automatically gain freedom.[39]

Judging from women's responses to accusations of unnatural amalgamation, one might safely argue that they were often mentally retarded or else had a very poor self-image. An exception, however, was Betsey Mosley, mother of a black baby. In reply to her outraged husband, she said "that she had not been the first nor would she be the last guilty of such an act and that she saw no more harm in a white woman's having a black child than in a white man's having one, though the latter was more frequent."[40] Usually the woman either felt deep remorse over her indiscretion or brazenly prostituted herself in defiance of husband and family.

One avenue of escape did exist: a claim of having been raped, a claim that Southern whites have continued to prefer to believe even into the recent past. (The Scottsboro case of 1931 and incidents arising during the same period in rural Alabama are among the more famous illustrations.) Thus Governor Hutchins Burton of North Carolina was called upon to review a Davidson County case in 1826, one in which a girl's poor-white family sought to salvage some respectability by insisting that she had been coerced by a wealthy planter's handsome slave Jim. Like Mary Dunn, Polly Lane was a serving girl—bored, lonely, overworked, and fascinated by her lover. Fantasizing about fleeing to Cherokee country in Georgia where they could escape notice, the pair stole money from Jim Palmer, the overseer. Palmer caught slave Jim, however, and threatened to have him hanged. Jim fled to the woods where Polly, whose complicity had not yet been discovered, brought him food and comfort. Weeks later another slave overheard her wailing in the woods about her upcoming pregnancy. To escape humiliation, Polly had to claim that she had been brutally assaulted that very morning. She denied pregnancy, and the jury, true to racial custom, ignored the evidence of her swollen belly. Jim was sentenced to hang. Jim's owner, however, hired a young lawyer named J. J. Daniel, who beseeched the governor to delay execution until the color of the child could be ascertained. It was a fact backed by "the highest *authority* of Medical Jurisprudence," declared Governor Burton's Raleigh medical consultants on the case, that rape victims could not become pregnant. Conception depended upon "excitation" or "enjoyment of pleasure in the venereal act." Since Polly was clearly pregnant, Jim's defense was probably true, they reasoned. The governor granted the respite, and the Davidson County community undoubtedly spent the winter wagering about the complexion of Polly Lane's forthcoming baby.[41]

Jonathan M. Smith, a semiliterate member of the clan to which Polly Lane belonged, fumed that "trifling white people all ways" had "purtected" Jim from the punishments he deserved. In every way possible, he sought to hurry Jim to his appointment on the gallows. But to Smith's chagrin the child arrived thirty-nine days too early to conform with the date of the supposed rape, and only the most prejudiced observers in the Lane faction could deny that the child was mulatto. In this instance, the community concluded

that Polly Lane was so depraved and her family's status so problematical that Jim should be granted his life. Petitions to that effect,
organized by the planter elite and signed by the presiding judge,
sheriff, county militia general, clerk of court, and half the jurors,
provided Governor Burton with ample grounds to proclaim a reprieve, with transportation out of state. The latter was a sad necessity, since the Lane faction would not have permitted Jim to survive
otherwise.[42] To Jonathan Smith's mortification, Polly was charged
with bastardy, but it is doubtful that the infant lived very long. It
was so easy to allow an unwanted child to die of neglect.

Miscegenation of this kind suggested a weakness in the moral and
social sense of the white female by the standards of a primitive culture. Likewise, white men who showed a disregard for consequences
displayed similar problems of self-identity. Although upstanding
men indulged themselves in concubinage without incurring community wrath, others with less inner confidence and savoir faire
could find themselves ostracized from respectable society. A telling
illustration of both forms of miscegenation—the acceptable variety
and the improper—involved the same woman, Mary, mistress of
Colonel Thomas Hart Benton. The young Nashville attorney lived
for years with Mary, a beautiful, well-educated quadroon from
Louisiana. So careful was Andrew Jackson's companion that even
his most recent biographers have not mentioned the liaison. When
the time came to marry into the gentry class and pursue his upward
climb, Benton, who later became a prominent senator from Missouri, relinquished Mary to fellow militia officer Major Marcus
Winchester. The pair at once set off for Memphis, where Winchester supervised his father's vast landholdings and became the frontier
river port's first mayor. Winchester, however, fell in love with his
mistress, and made the unforgivable mistake of wedding her in
Louisiana, which was at the time the only slave state to permit
mixed-blood marriages. (The Louisiana law was later changed.)
Public feeling against Winchester ran high. The town merchants
objected, particularly because Mary had more cultural attainments
than any other woman in Memphis. The river men also became
abusive; Winchester had compounded his unpopularity by periodic

raids on their disorderly taverns. Under these pressures, Winchester became the alcoholic and caricatured "dissolute" that his enemies claimed him to be. Eventually he and his family had to flee Memphis under threat of a charivari. He died shortly afterwards.[43]

What prompted Winchester's unrealistic defiance of race decorum cannot be discovered from the historical record. A fair number of men involved in such situations, however, did show signs of immaturity before their break with sexual and race conventions. Keith Thomas has discussed the similar phenomenon of seventeenth- and eighteenth-century Englishmen who had liaisons with socially inferior mates. Their motives, he says, may have had Freudian roots. Such men, as Freud interpreted them, could not direct both their sexual drive and their affections toward the same woman. Instead, they divided their women into the double image of ancient tradition—the madonna and the harlot. This dichotomy, Thomas explains in Freudian terms, arose because the philanderer feared his own feelings of jealousy of his father's role in the marriage bed. The son idolizes his mother, but finds these feelings no less overwhelming and dangerous than his attitudes toward his father. In repressing his fantasies, he splits the sexual and the affectional impulses in his relations with women. Sex becomes associated with an inferior, an expendable woman whom, outside of wedlock, he both enjoys and socially despises. But the wife whom he should love and protect, Thomas suggests, becomes a source of resentment. He blames her for his confusion and accuses her of coldness. Driven to indecision and self-hatred, the adulterous husband cannot have a complete relationship with either his mistress or his wife.[44]

Thomas's insights, drawn from psychoanalytic sources, also suggest that the difficulty often had incestuous overtones. There may be in such situations an unresolved oedipal frustration resulting from a fixation upon a sister—seen as a reflection of the self and a replacement for the mother whom the son could not possess. In the realm of psychology, such paradigms, even when offered by so astute a scholar as Keith Thomas, are always risky. Human beings too often defy the labels given them. Yet the pattern he described conformed with what has been discerned about Southern childrearing

and patriarchy and the problems of personal identity that the regional culture created. The mores of the society, with its notions of
unequal sexual obligations and of deferences due the head of household, established the framework in which cross-class, cross-race sexuality could not help but arise. It was almost as if the temptation to
leap the racial barrier in the South served to strengthen the boundary line of respectability. The possibility of deviation made more
hallowed the precepts of conjugal purity, or rather its outward appearance, by warning those tempted to be wise as serpents, quiet as
doves. When James H. Hammond remarked that "the white man
who takes a colored mistress loses caste at once," he did not mean
the casual dabbler but the fool who defied conventional rules about
how such matters ought to be conducted. As Mary Chesnut bitterly
remarked, "Who thinks any worse of a negro or mulatto woman
for being a thing we can't name? God forgive us but ours is a
monstrous system and wrong and iniquity." But she saw it differ-
ently from a gentleman like Hammond.[45]

Whether the problem was psychological, cultural, or both, these
factors of filial rebellion and moral dissolution played true to form
in the marriage of Thomas Foster, Jr., and Susannah Carson, a
young couple living in Adams County, Mississippi, in the 1820s.
Foster, the son of the twentieth wealthiest planter in the richest
county in late Jeffersonian America, was a representative "dissolute."
His father had carved out a $100,000 estate near Natchez, and at
Foster Fields, center of his many plantations, he and his wife Sarah
raised a large brood of children. New to wealth and unsupported
by religious faith or intellectual aspirations, Thomas Foster, Sr.,
thought material benefits would suffice to sustain the next generation. Son Thomas, upon his marriage, received two plantations and
the requisite number of slaves. He was simply to carry on his father's career. A college education would have been superfluous,
Thomas, Sr., and his wife Sarah believed.

Thomas's sixteen-year-old wife, whom his parents had selected,
was the daughter of James Carson, an Irish refugee from the 1798
Rebellion, land speculator and part-time Methodist preacher. She
was supposed to bring to a close the young Thomas's already worri-

some profligacy. But two years of married life and the prospect of a second child led to his rebellion against domesticity and parental surveillance. The late months of pregnancy were commonly referred to as the "gander months," because during that period husbands traditionally found outlets other than their wives for their sexual interests. Thomas was no exception; like the barnyard creature, he had gone prowling. Shortly after his wife Susannah returned from her confinement at her parents' house in Natchez, bringing with her a newborn son, she discovered her spouse lying naked in a slave cabin with Susy, the couple's cook, a handsome slave who had been a gift from his father.

Faced with Susannah's tears and anger, Thomas Foster, Jr., was dutifully remorseful for a day or so. Two years of chaos, tears, and threats of blows followed. Finally Susannah went to her husband's parents to explain why she had to have a divorce. By then Susy had displaced her in the master bedroom and was wearing her mistress's bonnets. The pattern that Susannah Foster recounted in her petition for divorce scarcely deviated from the scenario that most Southern women so humiliated described in their marital histories: threats against the children's lives, verbal abuse of the wife, declared preferences for the mistress as companion and bedmate, occasional vows to reform, self-pity followed by defiance once more, increasing alcoholism, and rejection of respectable company and association with low tavern friends.

In 1826 Thomas fell ill. With thoughts of impending death on his mind, he even agreed that his father could shackle Susy and prepare to have her sold. General William Barnard, a son-in-law, assisted Thomas Foster, Sr., in arranging Susy's sale. Before the transaction was completed, however, Thomas recovered. Secretly he met Susy at the tollbridge tavern outside Natchez where he and his racetrack friends had often gathered. Crossing the ravine at the western edge of town, the pair fled to his second plantation. There they lived until, in 1830, Thomas sold Susy and other slaves to his eldest brother Levi for half their worth. Depressed and half dazed from alcohol, Thomas was convinced by Levi and another brother, James Foster, Jr., that this was the only solution to his habitual indebtedness. In the following year Thomas Foster, Jr., died, before Chancellor John A. Quitman had rendered a decision on the divorce petition Susannah Foster had initiated some four years earlier.[46]

Though one might be tempted to cite such examples as Thomas Foster, Jr.'s, or Colonel Farr's as signs of a Southern egalitarianism in the midst of monolithic racism, that view would be sentimental and wholly inaccurate. Thomas's motives were not so admirable. He had no more quarrel with "the home institution" than Colonel Richard Mentor Johnson had. Nor was he simply more honest than the surreptitious "gallant" who slipped off to the quarters when his wife was pregnant or refused him to prevent an unwanted pregnancy. The very opposite was true. Thomas Foster's difficulty was an inability to know himself. His transactions were unconsciously calculated to express self-disgust and mistrust of his family, for reasons that no one who knew him could fathom.

In the cultural matrix in which Thomas and so many other failed young men were caught, miscegenation was a weapon of social and familial suicide, a product of anger, despair, and resented dependence. Pauli Murray in *Proud Shoes* discusses in detail a similar and no less grim account of miscegenation in her family's history, told in brilliant fashion. Like most families caught up in the storms surrounding biracial sex, the senior Fosters cursed the "base wretch, Susy" for driving Thomas from "decent society." After all, they and others reasoned, what had black women to lose? All was gain—in prestige, material comforts, and freedom from the usual drudgery and chastisements that were a black woman's fate. Yet the Foster family's own uncertainty about morals, the proper dispensing of riches, and the purposes of their lives had helped to bring on the tragedy. Perhaps Thomas Foster, Sr., patriarch though he was, showed remarkable sympathy for his daughter-in-law in permitting her to scandalize the clan by registering for divorce from his own namesake; many a father-in-law would not have been so considerate in those times. But unintentionally, the Fosters' troubles did have its social uses to others: it offered an example to be avoided. Moreover, the incident was one of many that confirmed once more that man was born to sin and not much could be done about it.[47]

What happened to Susy, the rejected paramour, after her sale to Levi, then a plantation owner in Franklin, Louisiana, is not known. She had been a daughter of Abd al-Rahman Ibrahima, a "prince" in the House of Timbo (located in present-day Nigeria). Misfortunes in war had led to Ibrahima's sale to black traders, and in the 1780s Thomas Foster, Sr., then a struggling planter in Spanish Mississippi, had purchased him and appointed him his chief driver. The daughter shared her father's aristocratic bearing, and no doubt Thomas found her an exotic partner. In his old age Ibrahima wished to see his homeland once more, and Thomas, Sr., perhaps embarrassed about his son's misbehavior, at last agreed. The two old men, master and driver, had a mutual grief to bear in their final days. At least, however, Ibrahima never learned that Thomas had forsaken his daughter. New York philanthropists made possible his return to Africa; he died within sixty miles of Timbo in 1829, the same year and month that Thomas Foster, Sr., passed away. Susy's sale did not occur until the following year. The denouement would have pleased the senior Foster, who had placed such hopes upon his son's eventual repentance. It would have been another blow to Susy's father, however, a Muslim whose sense of honor and dignity far outdistanced that of his master and his master's sons.[48]

As these illustrations suggest, Southern sexual mores were evaluated not in the haphazard fashion that scholars have often claimed, but by rules of specific moral force. The hypocrisy of the casual miscegenator was built into the ethical structure itself. Mary Chesnut of South Carolina and others were bitterly aware of the burden that slavery placed upon their shoulders, particularly in the form of rivalries between women in the quarters and in the house. "Honor thy father and mother" was a commandment that Mary Chesnut found difficult to obey. Her father-in-law's dalliance with a slave woman was notorious but, of course, at the same time unmentionable. "*Rachel* and her brood," she said, "make this place a horrid nightmare to me—I believe in nothing, with this before me." But, like everything else, it had to be borne.[49] When, however, husbands or young men openly flaunted their liaisons the white matrons were the very first to cry shame—blaming, as Mary Chesnut often did, the black "wenches" for the men's fall from grace.

Despite this unhappy state of affairs, it is only fair to add that even in the rough world of the Southwest, sexual misconduct probably declined during the antebellum decades. In the wilderness regions where white women had been in short supply in earlier days, ratios of men and women started to even out. Men could find marriageable partners and resorted less to irregular arrangements. Churches and church discipline encouraged domestic honesty. Education and prosperity helped to reduce the disorders, sexual and otherwise, that accompanied depressing struggles against disaster. It would carry matters too far to call Thomas Foster, Jr., a member of an endangered species. "Black sheep" were a ubiquitous curse. But new, rather Victorian social attitudes were reaching the gentry class and, through revivals and clapboard churches, the yeomanry as well.[50] Nevertheless, in the persistent war between "civilization" and primal ethics the principles of honor, shame, and pride still had enormous strength. Certainly the guns that blasted the walls of Fort Sumter did not destroy the ancient code as well. Instead they expressed the determination to keep it holy.

Part Three

·

Structures of Rivalry and Social Control

BLANK PAGE

13

Personal Strategies and Community Life: Hospitality, Gambling, and Combat

Welcoming strangers, taking risks at cards or sport, and defending personal honor were all characteristics that Southerners eagerly seized on to identify themselves. Although Southerners boasted loudly enough about these inclinations before the Civil War, afterward they became articles of sacred memory. In the 1880s, for instance, to illustrate the hospitable and gentlemanly ways of fellow Virginians in the old days, George W. Bagby, a Richmond journalist, described how "Colonel Tidewater had come half the length of the State to try a little more of Judge Piedmont's Madeira, to know what on earth induced Piedmont to influence the governor in making that appointment, and to inquire if it were possible that Piedmont intended to bring out Jimson—of all human beings—Jimson!— for Congress?"[1] Leisure, graciousness, and quaint concerns, Bagby and others of his kind fancied, had been more or less the rule until the Civil War.

Indeed, it is not at all hard to be seduced by the image. Although some recent historians would claim that Colonel Tidewater was really Mr. Moneycrop, an avaricious profit maker rather than a gentle soul, countless diaries and letters suggest that Bagby's portrayal, despite its wistful romanticism, caught something of the ambience of Southern life. Take for instance the hunting expedition of Dr. Thomas Ravenel and T. W. Peyre, his neighbor in Pineville, South Carolina. Peyre arrived early to get a fine start, but Ravenel first had to visit a distant field for a word with a driver and overseer there. After the delay, Ravenel and company returned home so that he could change horses. This gave Ravenel the opportunity to while away another half-hour in the outhouse. The party mustered once more and headed for the woods. By the time the hunters reached the scent, the dogs, tired and thirsty, could not be roused from a convenient pool. The lunch hour approached, and all went home. On the second day, the hunt finally took place, and ended in triumph, though Peyre had had to prevent several side excursions beforehand. Peyre had enjoyed the human spectacle, Ravenel the chance to make a common business into an elaborate two-day ritual. What else was there to do in the July heat in the country anyhow, except to fashion something out of the materials at hand—the doings of wildcats, hounds, and people?[2]

Yet behind the agreeably slow pace of Southern gentry life, the friendships joyfully affirmed by hunting, the barbecues, the wild nights at cards and drink, and even the fights, there often lay cheerless anxieties and unmanageable furies. Minor doings, pointless trips, and complaints about the "wuthless" hands merely punctuated the boredom that greeted nearly every rising sun. As Thomas Chaplin of St. Helena's Island noted in his diary, "Christmas Day— DULL, DULL, DULL." In the summer, moist, unrelieved heat sank the most sanguine spirits. "Bitten by fleas, buzzed by mosquitoes, poisoned by wild flowers, tired of drinking warm water . . . and so sleepy as to be almost in a state of id[i]ocy, I 'take my pen in hand' to write you about our exciting Sunday," sighed one Virginia resident to another. Duels also served to enliven routine. "Our city," wrote a planter of Franklin, Louisiana, "is becoming as usual at this season exceedingly dull" and "our good citizens are diverting themselves in performing feats of arms, there have been four or five duels within the last week. . . ."[3]

Gregariousness and conviviality were a way to give drama to life. No one can stand too much reality, particularly if one day is very

much like yesterday and tomorrow. The comings and goings of relatives and friends, the thin excuses to go up to the courthouse, the
interminable "friendly" games, and the personal contests of arms
and fists attested not only to Southerners' desperate need to conquer
ennui but also their compulsion to find social place in the midst of
gatherings. That was the great charm of the South, the willingness
to create good times with others, but behind that trait was fear of
being left alone, bored, and depressed.

Thomas Carlyle, the reactionary Scottish-reared author whom
the Southern literati so much admired, put into words a feeling
that bedeviled the Southern white: "Isolation is the sum-total of
wretchedness to man. To be cut off, to be left solitary: to have a
world alien, not your world, all a hostile camp for you; not a home
at all, of hearts and faces who are yours, whose you are! . . . To
have neither superior, nor inferior, nor equal, united manlike to
you. Without father, without child, without brother. Man knows
no sadder destiny." Harriet Martineau, one of the most sensitive
students of nineteenth-century American character, recognized the
importance of honor as originating from fear of solitariness. "Where
honour is to be derived from the present human opinion," rather
than from loftier notions of "truth and justice," she said, "there
must be fear, ever present, and perpetually exciting to or withholding from action. In such a case, as painful a bondage is incurred as
in the pursuit of wealth." Especially was this so, she believed, in the
South. The more "American" or Yankeefied the white Southerner
was, the more he feared losses as a moneymaker. The more Southern
he was, the more honor icily gripped his thoughts. The two pre-
occupations, to greater or lesser degree, functioned together, mocking Southern claims to leisure, individualism, and stability superior
to other cultures. "Fear of imputation is here the panic, under
which men relinquish their freedom of action and speech," Martineau observed.[4]

Under these circumstances, the most pressing Southern fear was
not death so much as dying alone. That was a veritable nightmare.
Corydon Fuller, a Yankee itinerant in Arkansas, walked into a tavern and found a group of drinkers poking fun at an old alcoholic's

dying twitches on the barroom floor. Contempt masked their own worries; laughter covered fright. Dread of aloneness helps to explain why sometimes even refined folk, as well as less educated ones, feared so much the night, graveyards, ghosts of dead kinspeople, and nameless "ha'nts," hidden emblems of one's own uncomfortable memories of wrongs and omissions. "Do you remember the conversation we had with your Aunt Wales?" asked Henry Cumming of his wife in 1825. The old lady had been startled by a "bird that flew in at the window and again out towards the Church yard." Not two weeks had passed before Aunt Wales's husband died, he reminded her. "Her unreasonable apprehensions have certainly been realized in a most remarkable manner. . . ." The bird signified, however, her forlornness, not her husband's doom. Indeed, some years later, Maria Bryan, another relative, remarked that Aunt Wales was "one of the most unhappy persons I know, lonesome & disconsolate, & [thinks?] herself forsaken by the world & her friends."[5]

The lack of privacy, the hostility toward those who wished to be alone to read or think, the overabundance of alcohol to nurse self-pitying male egos, the scarcity of lending libraries, books, and literary societies, the low state of education, the distances between people of similar intellectual interests, the temptations of hunting, fishing, and just aimless wandering in search of company—all these characteristics of Southern social life gave special meaning to special gatherings. People came together nòt just to celebrate a holiday, mourn the dead, pay respect to the sick and dying, join the wedding party, go to camp meeting, muster the militia, attend the election poll, or entertain the visiting relative. They came to escape solitude as well. In an oral society, where words and gestures counted so much, the opportunity to exchange ritual words or hear them eloquently pronounced was deeply cherished. "The man who wished to lead or to teach," the late-nineteenth-century Georgia historian William Garrott Brown recalled, "must be able to speak . . . [and] charm . . . with voice and gesture." Those like William L. Yancey of Alabama earned special authority with their amazing oratorical gifts. "How such a great man mounted the rostrum, with what demeanor he endured an interruption, with what gesture he silenced a murmur,—such things were remembered and talked about when his reasoning was perhaps forgotten," Brown wrote. What mattered was the sense of community and reconfirmed loyalties that such occasions aroused.[6]

Three kinds of events in which the personal strategy of the principals gave meaning to life and strength to reputation seemed particularly suited to the Southern ethos. The first was the host-guest relation, a frequent transaction despite (or else because of) the great distances separating one farmhouse or plantation from another. The second was strictly a male encounter (with clergymen uninvited): gambling and horse racing (with women present in the more sophisticated settings). The third was supposedly a rather private affair, the duel. But here no less than in the barroom brawl or fistfight, the whole male community was involved. Each ritual encounter in this sequence was more antagonistic than the previous one, but all three helped Southerners determine community standing and reaffirm their membership in the immediate circle to which they belonged. In all of them honor and pursuit of place muted the threat of being alone and provided the chance to enjoy power in fellowship.

The first of these strategies has been the least well understood. Scholars have treated hospitality largely in terms of the Southern economy: was there much or little conspicuous consumption? Undoubtedly the purchase of grand estates, exquisite furnishings, coaches, and thoroughbreds was confined to a much smaller proportion of the planter class than legend and popular tour excursions today might suggest. The building of Melrose, Gunston Hall, and similar lordly sites served to substantiate the claims of their planter-owners to rule. Some Marxist historians like Eugene Genovese and Raimondo Luraghi have emphasized that obvious function, and they have taken to celebrating the "prebourgeois" spending habits of the slaveholding elite. Others have blamed Southern backwardness partly on such misuse of capital. Gaudy display, they reason, solidified planter control over awestruck yeomen, but drained off funds that might have been spent to improve general economic conditions. But it is really doubtful that fancy improvidences really had an adverse effect upon the Southern economy as a whole. More serious inhibiting factors were ubiquitous habits of familial defensiveness and whites' suspicion of collective and governmental enterprises. The slave system certainly encouraged white labor inefficiency, for reasons too well explained elsewhere to need amplification here. These were more important causes of economic backwardness than the occasional appearance of a columned palace in the wilderness. Besides, the Old South's exhibitions of enormous household wealth could have been easily matched by the homes of Boston merchants and Philadelphia bankers, individuals seldom accused of frivolous investment. In any case, as Jane Pease wisely says, "it would be hazardous," at this point of historical study, "to rest any significant part of an argument about Southern failure to develop economically on assumptions about the impact of Southern planters' consumption patterns."[7] The argument is a dead end.

To understand the social meaning of hospitality—the relationship of an individual and family to outsiders on home turf—it must be treated in its constituent parts. The individuals involved, the circumstances of the moment, the relative standing of host and guest made all the difference. It should be no surprise that outward appearance, ascriptive signals, and prior relationships gave context and meaning to the encounter between host and guest.

First and foremost, hospitality in its broadest definition was family-centered. The planter of means was obliged to share good fortune with less well-fixed kinfolk or be severely criticized for Yankeefied tightfistedness. When no other agency existed to care for the weak, the family was the first and often sole resort. Northerners likewise felt obliged to extend the helping hand, and did so with no less and no more willingness than Southerners. However, there was, one may speculate, a sense of deeper obligation in the South, if only because the slaveholding states were slow to find public means to house the dependent and indigent—asylums, hospitals, poorhouses, or rooming houses. Moreover, it was much more dignified for a widowed distant cousin, like Edmund Ruffin's relative Mrs. Lorraine, to accept an invitation for a visit that lasted over a year than to request a handout. One never knew when misfortune might descend. Helping kinsfolk was both more personal and more consoling than other means.[8]

Yet even within the family circle, hospitality was often exploited by one or the other party as a means of exercising personal power. Although keeping a fine house or throwing barbecues for the neighbors did have many social purposes in a community, in some instances the prime reason for lavishness of expenditure was strictly familial. J. Motte Alston, for instance, recalled that his wealthy grandfather, nicknamed "King William," used sumptuous dinners to keep his Charleston family under surveillance. Every Saturday night the table was set with the best china, silver, and linens. All sons and daughters, their spouses and children had to attend. "Only a valid excuse was received for not so doing." Guests, too, could make use of the seeming friendliness of the custom. "Grandmother" James of Livingston, Alabama, had lent a cousin a thousand dollars, which he postponed repaying. She packed her trunk and arrived by coach for an unannounced visit. After the typical effusions of welcome, she stated her business and her intention to stay indefinitely until the bill was met. An order on the planter's Mobile factor was in her hands the next morning, and "the old lady returned home in great good humor."[9]

The dependency of relatives upon the good will, good humor, and generosity of those better off was a mortification only exceeded by being thrust onto the public charge. We have already seen the contempt in which traditional societies held individuals who lost the ability to manage for themselves or never had it in the first place, particularly orphans, spinsters, and poor widows. No writer has caught the desperation and pathos of such circumstances better than Tennessee Williams, whose plays, especially *The Glass Menagerie, A Streetcar Named Desire,* and *The Eccentricities of a Nightingale,* explore the theme of unavoidable dependency in once proud families. In *The Glass Menagerie* Amanda Wingfield, an East Tennessean and former Mississippi "belle," dreams of entertaining a "gentleman caller" for her daughter Laura, who is crippled both physically and emotionally, as if the chance to do domestic honors for a marriageable man would itself transform their sad existence. Laura's ineffectuality and passive refusal to imitate her mother's coquetry of earlier days drives Amanda to say, "What is there left but dependency all our lives?" She had seen the fate of women unfit "to occupy a position." They were "barely tolerated spinsters living upon the grudging patronage of sister's husband or brother's wife!—stuck away in some little mousetrap of a room— encouraged by one in-law to visit another—little birdlike women without any nest—eating the crust of humility all their life!" To be sure, some families surmounted the strains, making dependents feel needed and loved. But the role of kinfolk host, though it offered the chance to give succor disguised as hospitality, was scarcely any more enviable than that of recipient. Both parties to the transaction felt coerced by custom and duty, and at the least the danger of mis- apprehension and resentment was ever-present. More fundamentally, permanent dependency contradicted tacit expectations that help in time of family need would later be returned under similar exigency.[10]

With strangers, however, the rules of hospitality were consider- ably more discretionary than with relatives, who could not be cast aside without loss of family repute and guilt-laden recriminations. Not many planters lived grandly enough to live up to the regional self-acclaim about lavish entertainment. First of all, the living quar- ters were often exceedingly uncomfortable for permanent residents, let alone for visitors. Heat, dust, and ever-worrisome insects some- times undermined household resolve to make even spacious dwell- ings presentable. Neither slave nor mistress took pride in keeping good order. Cultural ideals that stressed male good times over do- mesticity, special occasion over routine habit made for a haphazard struggle against dirt and disrepair. An anonymous Virginia diarist reported that at one small farmer's house in Louisiana, he and his companions literally had to strip off their clothes, but still found themselves "a la cooty," so full of fleas was the house. Mrs. Sarah Hicks Williams, a Northern woman, blamed the disorder of her North Carolina neighbors' houses upon "the want of system." The cause, however, lay more in the depression of will that semitropical climate and unspecialized work habits engendered. Not willful laziness, as outsiders imagined, but a sense of paralysis gripped even the well-bred planter's matron. There was too much to do and little to show for the effort once things were done. Instead it was easier to immunize oneself with the distractions of talk and drink for the men, seeing friends for the women. Cornelia Spencer, from the long-settled town of Chapel Hill, North Carolina, where order was a source of community pride, found conditions all but intolerable among kinsfolk in frontier Alabama. They had "solid silver castors" and delicate china, but had not bothered to plaster the walls. As a result of inattention, there were "holes in the walls—holes under the doors[,] holes in the windows—." The cousins nervously fretted about her obvious discomfort, but she did nothing to relieve their embarrassment.[11] If, at times, inquisitive strangers were greeted with less cordiality than they anticipated, the reasons should not be hard to imagine.

As far as one can tell, the wayfarer who stopped for the night was treated with considerable suspicion, particularly if the request for lodgings came unexpectedly, without the accompaniment of a special claim to hospitality—a letter of introduction, or a blood relationship quickly ascertained between the visitor and host. If such conditions were met, the visit could become a celebration, a welcoming into the family circle. If the newcomer could produce proper introductions, he or she was ordinarily recognized. When John Bernard, Harriet Martineau, Frederika Bremer, John F. D. Smyth, James K. Paulding, and many other writers of travel accounts appeared on the doorstep, their presence could be a great source of gratification, about which the host could brag for months thereafter. A Mrs. Matilda Houston rhapsodized that through Virginia and the Carolinas, she and her party spent not a "sixpence," so welcome was her presence, at least so she claimed.[12] Others who bitterly complained that Southern hospitality was more legend than reality often reflected the indifference that their standing elicited. "Of such hospitality the traveller will find nothing," declared Francis Hall, "except indeed, his rank or character would be such, as to give eclat to his entertainers." Charles Latrobe said that the guest who came unrecommended was made to feel himself "the party obliged, and that obligation could never be repaid." A poor appearance certainly was construed as beggary, a powerlessness and dependence that incited contempt, not sympathy. Elkanah Watson, for instance, discovered that he could not obtain lodgings at the same isolated North Carolina household where some years earlier he had been handsomely treated. The sole difference was the state of his clothing after a harrowing ride through dust and storm. John Cornish, a young Northern clergyman in low-country South Carolina, feasted royally one evening at Squire Wistal's plantation, where his letters of introduction commanded the host's respect. The next night, however, a less well-to-do planter turned him away on a stormy December night because he was without horse, money, and decent, dry attire. A slave put him up in the master's corn crib in exchange for half a "segar." Even if he was admitted to the inner premises and greeted warmly, the weary traveler was more than likely to sleep "in a room with others, in a bed which stank, supplied with but one sheet, if with any," Frederick Olmsted reported, and offered no "fruit, no tea, no cream, no sugar, no bread" (except corn pone), because these and most other amenities were not to be had. Yet by local standards these houses and their residents were supposed to be above the ordinary level of hospitality and refinement.[13]

Strangers to the South were often surprised to discover that money was at times accepted, to defray the costs of the host and even to make him a profit. Such travelers' anticipations of largess led to immediate disenchantment. Yet their hosts did not thereby violate the concept of hospitality, at least not in every instance. The charges were a means to make a distinction between family-centered obligation and the treatment of an alien. The cash transaction signified the termination of obligation, and was sometimes even used when fellow Southerners arrived on the scene without invitation. For instance, Mrs. Elizabeth McCall Perry found herself and her party far from their destination, Laurens, South Carolina, as a heavy storm and sundown were approaching. They took shelter at the home of a Mr. Barksdale, brother, it turned out, of her husband's chief antagonist in an upcoming law dispute and election.

Aware of the delicacy of the situation, Barksdale was welcoming but formal. Only at loss of his own reputation could he have refused her altogether. Sensitive to his feelings, Mrs. Perry volunteered to pay for the horse feed, meals, and inconvenience. With perfect understanding, he suggested she pay $2.00. The sum was far less than a hotel would have charged, but if he had graciously refused any payment he would have put the Perrys under an obligation inappropriate to the circumstances. Two dollars was exactly the right sum to charge.[14]

As this example reflects, hospitality could not be divorced from honor, nor honor separated from the coercions of public opinion. To refuse an offer of magnanimity—even if only a drink in a grog shop—was to insult the donor, by throwing doubt on his claim to worthiness as a companion. At all levels of society, even the lowest, hospitality could often signify a test of status, a means of discovering who a stranger thought himself to be and what he thought of those urging him to join their pleasures. Corydon Fuller, who had observed the dying drunkard in Arkansas, felt sufficiently intimidated to accept a glass from the merrymakers dancing about the corpse. But just as guests had to meet the situation demanded by their entertainers, so too was the host under firm obligation. Drink-treating at election times, for instance, was by no means simple bribery but rather the demand of male constitutents that the office-seeker thereby prove his manhood, indifference to heavy financial loss, and claim to the respect of those accepting his bounty. The title of office for the one, the grog for the others seemed a fair exchange. On a somewhat grander plane, Thomas Jefferson "felt bound in honor" to entertain any and all worthies who passed Monticello during and after his presidency. Wellborn folk swarmed there in the summer months on their way to spas, and each gentleman was certain that his support of president and party entitled him to the personal gratitude of the host. Meeting that expectation was a major factor in Jefferson's financial troubles in his declining years.[15]

In all the coercions and obligations that surrounded the custom of hospitality there ran an undercurrent of deep mistrust, anxiety, and personal competition. Thus, for instance, James Hammond gloomed that his career had been destroyed by the jealousy of rivals: "Manning could not conceal it. He built his fine home in Clarendon to beat me"; nevertheless, "I beat them in their own line—furniture, balls, & dinner parties." When men gathered at each other's houses, the appointments were as much on display for their benefit as for the comfort of the inhabitants. Although the dwelling might impress the yeomanry, it mattered much more if the house and furnishings awed the neighboring planters. The necessity of pleasing equals aroused some grumbling: it was expensive and often unappreciated. Thomas Chaplin "found dinner" for his fellow huntsmen on the Sea Islands, providing "five times as much as the men could eat" because the example of others had made him "afraid there would not be enough." Apparently Chaplin's associates thought that the competition had grown too keen and that everyone was spending too much. Therefore they voted to fine those offering more than "six dishes of meat for dinner" in order "to prevent competition." The fifty-cent penalty, however, was not likely to have the sobering effect Chaplin anticipated. Edmund Ruffin objected less to the competitive aspects than to the wastefulness of encouraging "loungers and spongers" in the name of " 'the hospitality of old Virginia.' " Ironically, he hoped that Yankee ways of thrift would find a Southern home the better to whip the North in the struggle for sectional preeminence.[16] But for better or worse, hospitality, like slavery, was an intrinsic part of the antebellum scheme of things.

The strain of hostility that these illustrations evince, if seen in the context of the Revolutionary and post-Revolutionary eras, might appear to be the result of the infant country's political uncertainties about democracy, slavery, and republicanism, the dislocating effects of economic and territorial expansion, and the growth of centralized institutions and industries. These abrupt transformations, early republican historians are accustomed to say, invoked deep-seated frustrations, worries about present and future, and nostalgia for a simpler past. No doubt the equivocal response to a stranger at the gate was in part a function of these anxieties, particularly as the Civil War approached and Northern and foreign strangers came under general suspicion. Nevertheless, host-guest antagonisms long preceded the era of dynamic growth and continued long afterward, when the South, sunk in defeat and poverty, experienced too little change, unless for the worse.

Ambivalence had in fact always been the underlying factor in traditional hospitality. Guest and host were supposed to show respect for each other, and failure to do so sundered the transaction of honor in which they were engaged. For the moment they were to set aside their struggles for supremacy, but the reciprocity could not obscure the distinction between the roles. The stranger in a tavern, for instance, was invited to be the first to drink or at least be the first to receive the gift of a glass from the rest. But he was under obligation to play host to the next round—thereby making equal all parties present, each in turn serving as guest and host. The coercion implicit in that situation should be evident, but so should the brittleness of the feelings under the restraint of the hospitable code. As the tongues grew looser, the jokes broader, the sly remarks more cutting, the same conventions that compelled outward friendliness then turned to anger, and the fists and oaths flew thick. Hospitality was meant to be a ritualized truce in the rivalries of men, but instead it was sometimes prelude to violence, particularly among the less gentle planters and the yeomanry. Certainly the top echelons of society seldom indulged themselves in this fashion, but as Dickson Bruce points out, violent behavior was part of the general culture of the region. Whether men competed gracefully under the formal rules of hospitality or furiously in the violence that sometimes resulted, the drama of these strategies was their appeal, and status their prize.[17]

Gaming, the second kind of ritual occasion for the muting of rivalries, was related to hospitality and often appeared, along with alcohol, in male society. Southerners, like their Scots-Irish and English forebears, loved sports, hunting, games of chance and skill—in fact, any event that promised the excitement of deciding the inequalities of prowess among men, or among men and beasts. Whatever the uncertainties and daily risks of life might be, for a moment or two at least, games dramatized vicarious triumph and misfortune within a structure of set rules. As in the case of hospitality, money could and did change hands. But unlike its role in the host-guest relation, money in the context of the game or sport served as a means to ratify obligation and deference, not to terminate them, no matter how cheerily the winnings jangled in the pockets of the bettor. The point of play was the distribution of honor and status. Although men invariably expressed an indifference to the outcome, the depth of their involvement belied the outward show. Once the play was joined, it engaged all participants in a special, enclosed world. All-night sessions over cards were a proverbial custom early and late in Southern history. John B. Nevitt, a Natchez planter, reported in his diary in 1828 that he entertained forty guests and "sat up all night" over "brag." In 1765 a visiting Frenchman recounted that there was not a "publick house" without "tables all baterd [*sic*] with the [faro] boxes." Gaming had universal appeal throughout the slave region and among all social ranks almost from the start of settlement in the seventeenth century. Although Mississippi, Louisiana, and Texas were best known for the habit, residents of the Carolinas, Georgia, Tennessee, Kentucky, and Arkansas were also devoted to cards, dice, horse racing, and cockfights. Such diversions had to involve more than simply a chance to turn a profit. The practice had to have social meaning for those participating.[18]

Three aspects of gaming in the South were especially significant in terms of social structure and ethics: its coercive and consensual pervasiveness, its distinctions between the "sporting gentleman" and the professional, and finally its pathological aspects in a patriarchal society. The first feature should be no surprise in light of other factors in the all-male world of planter and yeoman life. Partially at least, the rationale for gambling was the camaraderie it afforded, especially since other forms of entertainment or civic enterprise aroused little interest. One Mississippian summed up his idea of a grand time: "Last Sunday we took 42 people aboard, one sheep and one shoat, two cases of whiskey, hung up two lanterns on cypress snags . . . and had a barbecue. Good fun, poker and crap game, one fight." What more could any man ask of such an outing? he implied.[19]

T. H. Breen, historian of the colonial South, has persuasively
argued that betting sports had the function of reducing other kinds
of "dangerous, but often inevitable social tensions." Aware of the
swift rise and fall of fortunes, the ubiquity of sudden death, the
dangers of slave unrest, early colonial Virginia planters solidified
their loyalty to each other with cards and quarterhorse racing. So
serious was the business that "race covenants" were drawn up ahead
of an important event, so that if the outcome was questionable, the
injured party had a legal right to sue. "By wagering on cards and
horses," Breen says, planters "openly expressed their extreme competitiveness, winning temporary emblematic victories over their
rivals without thereby threatening the social tranquility of Virginia."[20]

Certainly the same benefits were enjoyed by the antebellum
gaming set, although by then some changes had developed. Love of
sport had not declined but instead had become open to more individuals. Men of the same social rank continued to play chiefly
among themselves, but there were no longer laws prohibiting lesser
folk from betting at public tracks. The larger population of Jacksonian times supported commercial gaming operations of considerable size, whereas before they had been confined to major centers
like Richmond or limited to a tavern billiard table. Moreover, cockfighting had become increasingly popular, especially after the new
republic began. In 1797, for instance, twenty-one cocks were pitted
at Halifax, North Carolina. In fact, state rivalries encouraged large
meets. In 1806 gentlemen of several counties of Virginia and North
Carolina proposed to organize a cockfight with Maryland planters,
meeting at Norfolk, with a $10,000 "main" and fifty cockers par-
ticipating. Laws had always existed to prevent Sunday sport and
even weekday gambling, but they were seldom enforced. It would
be difficult to guess the number of gamblers and horse race and
cockfight watchers, but one may be sure that they vastly outnum-
bered male churchgoers.[21] Yet Southern scholars have devoted considerably less interpretive effort to this body of ritualists than to
the more easily studied churchmen of the South.

The excitement of the game or race, the crowds that special

events could draw, the absence of other forms of amusement, the ineffectuality of the clergy in suppressing such activities, and the determination of fathers that sons should know manly arts of all kinds—these elements all conspired to make gaming an accepted diversion. Not to play implied cowardice, differentness, unwholesome and even antisocial behavior. To be sure, some men, such as Landon Carter of Sabine Hall, despised the gaming set, never indulged, and sought to immunize the young against the preoccupation. Complaining that his grandson had gone off for a race on one of his fastest horses, Carter ranted that his neighbors, fearful that other planters' sons would get ahead too fast, lured them away "from Duty."[22]

As the Northern middle classes turned against such excitements, pious Southerners also began to lodge complaints and even make serious conversions in the gaming ranks. Samuel Townes of Abbeville, South Carolina, for instance, reported in 1831 that revival enthusiasm at the Mt. Moriah Church just about equaled the jubilance at a racetrack. In fact, since the church was nearby, "every racer, groom and steward, has been converted or seriously impressed." Sadly, "Col. G——" was so overwhelmed with religious zeal that he had sold his training horses "and let out his face as long as a yard-stick." It is hardly a wonder that revivals were popular in the South, more so than religious formalism, since revivals offered the converted something of what they were leaving behind. Even though many in the respectable portion of the population frowned upon gaming functions, the old ways died hard.[23]

Antigambling polemics aroused the sportsmen to defend their practices. In 1862, for instance, "Erskine" replied to "Botetourt," a religious planter, in a Richmond pamphlet. At its worst, he said, gaming was only a small vice, "and all vices are small when the culprit is socially popular and intellectually great." After all, he argued, Southerners were not much inclined to study "Raphael's cartoons" or "Cicero's orations," and gaming provided mental fare in place of such contemplations. Besides, the great men of past and present ages had sometimes been devout gamblers: Charles James Fox; Horace Walpole; Seargent S. Prentiss, the Mississippi Whig;

Henry Clay; and Andrew Jackson, owner of both cockers and race-horses. In addition, gamblers had their place in the political order, and formed an interest group that few presidents had been willing to alienate. Jackson had freed a notorious professional from a Washington jail, disputing that the antigambling law under which he had been tried was in the community's best interest. (James Madison had released Robert Bailey, a faro-box keeper, from the District's prison on similar grounds.) Clergymen "might rant and rave," claimed "Erskine," but men would continue to do as they pleased. Echoing these sentiments from the vantage point of the 1880s, W. H. Sparks, a Georgia memorialist, asked rhetorically if such "rude sports" as quarter race, cockfight, and gander pull had not been "more innocent outlets to the excessive energies of a mercurial and fun-loving people than the . . . shooting-gallery of to-day?"[24]

The very fact that betting was almost a social obligation when men gathered at barbecues, taverns, musters, supper and jockey clubs, racetracks, and on steamboats suggests that Breen's thesis has validity beyond the colonial period about which he wrote. Community loyalties have always found vivid expression in cheering on sportsmen and bettors. There was always a huge turnout in any neighborhood when such occasions arose, crowds that included men and sometimes women of all ranks and conditions. Even slaves could join in the public exhibitions. "Doing-together precipitates a sense of interdependence which is manifest in the ramifying exchanges of services," says Fred W. Voget in regard to such activities. Exchanging money as bets was such a service, with the money almost considered identical with the personalities of winner and loser. As Rhys Isaac, a colonial historian, has perceptively observed, "an intensely shared interest" in a gaming and sporting event, "crossing but not leveling social distinctions, has powerful effects in transmitting style and reinforcing the leadership of the elite that controls the proceedings and excels in the display." In this case, the planters were the priests of the occasion, as it were, and the affair enlisted all the fervor of a religious exercise. In Charleston's race week, for instance, courts, schools, and shops all closed, as if the Sabbath had been extended for seven days. Litanies of oaths, prayers, and other demands for divine or profane intercession were part of the rites of the games. The Southerner was well known for the eloquence of his swearing, and a gaming event provided the opportunity to demonstrate. But most of all, the union of the individual with the instrument of his prowess—the horse, cocker, cards, marksman's gun, or dice—took on a sacred character. That oneness seemed magical, and gave the participant and his supporters the feeling of potential omnipotence in striving for the prize.[25]

Under such circumstances, as Johann Huizinga has observed, games of chance were no less efficacious than ones of skill. By either method, whether by personal ability or sheer luck, "the good powers" triumphed "over the bad." In fact, luck had "a sacred significance; the fall of the dice may signify and determine divine workings; by it we may move the gods as efficiently as by any other form of contest." The emblem of victory—the money won, in most cases—conferred status. It *was* the status, palpable, real, yet supernatural, in the sense that the profane and sacred were joined together. The same exaltation was true for the cockfighter and horseman. The Marquis de Chastellux was struck by the nearly trancelike state of a young man at a cockfight in Virginia who kept repeating, as if in incantation, "Oh, it's a charming diversion!" Others, too, observed the ecstasy that games seemed to arouse. On a tour of South Carolina, Josiah Quincy remarked, "He who won the last match, the last main, or last horse-race assumed the airs of a hero or German potentate. The ingenuity of a Locke or the discoveries of a Newton were considered as infinitely inferior to the accomplishments of him who knew when to shoulder a blind cock or start a fleet horse."[26] The sense of power, heightened by the chance for public admiration, was the appeal of gaming: the congruence of belief and action, symbol and reality, group and individual, outward appearance of moral efficacy and its inner feeling. All these factors inspired allegiance to male ideals of friendly rivalry and good fellowship.

Gambling, no less than hospitality, brought the code of honor into very serious play because of its intimate connection with both personal and group status, which depended so largely upon public perceptions. To abuse the trust of others by cheating was the height of disgrace. For instance, Robert Potter, a state legislator in North Carolina, having lost all his money in a card game, had pulled a gun, seized the winnings, and fled. Indignantly, his fellow politicians waited not a moment to expel him from the state assembly. The investment of honor in games of chance and skill was related to the ephemerality of the glory attached to winning. To delay payment robbed the winner of the immediate gratification of his trophy, the emblematic value of which lasted only as long as public memory of the occasion. As William J. Grayson of South Carolina remarked, echoing traditional English sentiment, "A gambling debt is a debt of honour, but a debt due a tradesman is not."[27]

The distinction deserves some scrutiny. In a cash- and credit-poor economy, ordinary indebtedness was not only unavoidable; it was a means to cement long-standing social connections. In fact, it could be said that the gentry ranks, even more than the yeomanry, were meshed together through intertwined promissory notes, indentures, and other forms of financial entanglements, all duly recorded at the county clerk's office. It would not do to turn down a friend's request for a loan or a signature to stand liable for someone else, a favored kinsman or boon companion. Repayments were, of course, expected, but sometimes, as court records attest, notes were carried for months, even years beyond the date due. A man of wealth gained authority as well as accrued interest by allowing the number of those owing him to increase. Not paying tradesmen and others of lesser social standing was no violation of the code, because honor was very much tied to hierarchy; to manipulate the weak (within some bounds) was no detraction from a man's reputation, and in fact it made the lowly creditor obliged to the nonpaying client in hopes of eventual satisfaction of the debt. In a sense, it was antisocial neither to borrow nor lend. The whole economic and social structure was thus a source of security, of mingled fealties and deferences as well as of anxiety and possible disruption. Of course, not all Southern communities were quite so primitive about finance as this interpretation suggests. Nevertheless, the tendency was to look upon debt as a permanent condition of life and therefore something that should be made to serve other ends than just financial transaction. No doubt a reason for the hostility toward banks in the Jeffersonian and Jacksonian South was the fear that these quasi-political obligations that complemented the economic ones would give way to more impersonal, distant, and invulnerable ways of conducting business. The gaming debt, however, was ordinarily one that could not draw upon these social ties of deference and condescension or sheer friendship; rather it was an arrangement between equals, with triumph and defeat at wager the sole bond. The obligation had to be paid so that the relationship between the players could be terminated.[28]

The place of the professional gambler in relation to the issue of honor and obligation was somewhat problematical and much more complicated than riverboat and frontier historians of an earlier generation once assumed. On the one hand, as legend has long insisted, the professional belonged to the lower orders, outside the social pale. Such clever operators as Jonathan Green, John Morris, George DeVol, and others who plied the Mississippi could scarcely lay claim to high rank. As a Southerner told Harriet Martineau, a man "may game, but not keep a gaming house," just as he might be shabby in money deals "but may not steal." A distinction was drawn between the "high minded liberal gentleman, attached to amusements regardless of loss or gain," as a Virginia gambler explained, and a socially despised "cheating gamester."[29] As a result, laws piled up in the statute books of every state setting high penalties for professional gambling. South Carolina, for instance, banished gamesters, after penalizing them with heavy fines. The punishments had little more than a temporary effect. The tribe was needed to gratify the pleasures of those who did belong to the gentry ranks, sometimes including the legislators themselves. Professionals often arranged the races and matches, set the odds, bought and sold the cocks and horses, furnished the billiard tables, organized the pools, and played with those who would otherwise lack partners.

These sometimes profitable services to the gentry offered a means for ill-educated but shrewd young men to advance in livelihood, if not altogether in respectability.[30] An example was Robert Bailey of the Shenandoah Valley. He came from poor half-Irish folk and never properly learned to read or write. Yet he sent one son to college and law school and a daughter married into the gentry set of Botetourt County, where Bailey's winnings had furnished him with a fine plantation. Nevertheless, his career illustrated the social chasm that sometimes opened up to swallow those who serviced the needs of sporting gentlemen, men "whose motto," Bailey declared, "is honour." On one crucial occasion at the turn of the century, Bailey arrogantly refused some women the use of a hall for a dance at Sweet Springs, near Staunton, Virginia; he had made arrangements for an all-night gaming session there that evening. The next night, at the rescheduled ball, the ladies refused him even a cool greeting, but whispered that he was a "gamester."

Prior to the incident his profession had scarcely been hidden from public view. Bailey held membership in the local Masonic lodge, he had nearly won a congressional seat not long before, and he had just been promoted to captain in the Virginia "Light Blues." These attainments, as well as his efficiency as a gaming impresario, had earned him what might be called a brevet rank of gentleman.

But the incident at Sweet Springs was his undoing, at least temporarily. Once the label of "gamester" was affixed the sporting gentry shunned him; then the authorities felt bold enough to have him arrested for faro dealing. Judge St. George Tucker, then a candidate for a seat on a higher court, sentenced Bailey to three months' labor, the wages to be given to the poor. Mortified, Bailey fled the county, sure that public prejudices, as he later said, "emanated from the name" of "gamester" more than from any of his alleged misdeeds, so long tolerated before the Sweet Springs confrontation. Lamely he tried to ruin Tucker's election plans by charging Tucker with attempted bribery, an accusation so clumsy that even state legislators who had been accustomed to gambling with him refused to investigate. The gamester was forced to move on to Washington. (There his ups and downs—levees at the White House one day and jail the next—continued.)[31]

The labeling process was essential to Bailey's downfall: it clarified at once how the public was to view the fallen gamester, and it was significant that it was women, not men, who exposed him to public contempt. When sufficiently aroused, women could exercise considerable power in determining who belonged in polite company, who was unacceptable, and their husbands had to go along.

Two forces operated on the professional gamester at once. The first was Christian opinion, a growing force throughout the era, especially in the late antebellum years. The Southern clergy, even as early as the 1770s, had begun to speak out forcefully against the whole cluster of male indulgences, although they met with opposition, particularly in the earlier years and always in the newly settled areas of the west. "Fighting parsons," as they were called, proved their manliness by battling sin and sinners. Peter Cartwright of Kentucky was a famous example of the type.[32] No less important, however, was the secular authority of the gentry sportsmen and men of social refinement, not necessarily connected with pious interests. A new sense of gentility was speedily arising.

Even as early as the mid-eighteenth century, those concerned with the orderliness of Southern life recognized that traditional male habits, especially in their own ranks, set a bad example for the rest of society. Aside from admonitions such as Landon Carter's to his grandson and John Randolph's to his nephew, the gentry luminaries had little to offer as social remedy for the violence and corruption that accompanied gaming and other pleasures. Laws were passed. Even in the boisterous river port of Natchez arrests mounted. Out of 249 criminal arraignments between 1829 and 1841, 76, or 30 percent, were for gambling offenses. Yet proportional to the problem the number was very small, Natchez being the headquarters for gamesters, especially after the Vicksburg riots drove the tribe to other locations in 1835. The use of law, however, ill suited gentry notions of how men should be coerced into meeting obligations. Besides, the purpose was not to banish sin entirely but to keep it within proper bounds. As a result, reformation of manners was scarcely an entire success.

Fines, short sentences, social stigmatizing—the penalties Bailey had received—were usually thought sufficient to limit gambling without making such diversions inconvenient by enforced legal prohibition. But when gamblers grew "obnoxious" sterner measures were needed, and the gentry was well prepared to oblige. The most celebrated example, the outbreak of warfare between militiamen and Vicksburg gamblers in 1835, need not be recounted here. Suffice it to say that a military banquet ended up in a general riot in which five gamblers were whipped and hanged, with a wheel of fortune pinned to one of the dangling corpses. Such events were linked in the public mind with rumors of a black insurrection, still more frightening. But these grim events, more complicated than historical studies have so far shown, did finally run their course. Restoration of public morals included the revival of regular gamesmanship, not its expulsion from decent society, the forming of an Anti-Gambling Society in Vicksburg notwithstanding.[33]

Finally, there was the social attitude toward the fallen amateur, the man of substance who despoiled his inheritance in gaming, whether his property was large or small. In the militia set and among those who considered gaming a manly and generous vice, not to play was, like the refusal to share drink-treating, an insult, a denial of equality of standing. Attending a large party of gaming gentlemen, Philip Fithian, the Yankee tutor in Virginia, wrote in his diary, "In my room by half after twelve, & exceeding happy that I could break away with Reputation." Before retiring to bed, a French visitor to early republican Virginia felt likewise under obligation to play a few hands with the insatiable gambler William Byrd III and his company.[34]

Ironically, though, the compulsion to gamble was thought just as unmanly as failure to play. Among modern psychologists, controversies rage about the nature of the gaming obsession, but most agree that the modern victim of this serious addiction is ordinarily someone with feelings of dependence upon the good favor of a father, living or dead, whom he believes deprived him of affection or assistance. The narcissism involved in gambling and the frequently related sexual problems and inability to establish mature relationships all seem part of the magical thinking in which the gambler is engaged, especially when caught up in the passion of play. For some, the greater the loss, the greater the thrill of playing becomes. The punishment of losing provides an autoerotic satisfaction along with the pain and anger of defeat. As in cases of flaunted miscegenation and alcoholism, the antebellum compulsions of the gaming table perhaps had their sources in the rivalries and recriminations between fathers and sons. According to psychoanalytic specialists, the self-destruction involved in compulsive gambling punishes the rebel as well as the parent, though the prodigals seldom recognize that hidden agenda in a conscious way. Richard Minster, a seventeenth-century aristocrat, was among the few to reveal his own anguished delight in self-inflicted shame and humiliation. He declared that when he was winning, "in my recollections there lurked the feeling of a beast, a fornicator suffering a virgin to take his whim," a sense of guilt that mounted with each successful hand. But at last he lost, and a "feeling of relief" overcame him: "It was like a solvent to the harsh world to which I must now return." No doubt pathological gambling was a deviancy to which only a few Southerners were subject. But as with drinking, the occasions for indulgence were everywhere condoned, except among the very pious, very upright male minority. For the individual at war with himself and, most likely, with his family, the addictive world of gambling, in which time, ordinary work, and expectations were all suspended, was both a refuge from reality and a means of acting out resentments. This turmoil and psychic frustration were things that neither the gambler nor Southern society fully understood.[35]

The duel, no less than hospitality and gaming, was inseparable from community evaluation of the individual, although dueling, the most antagonistic of the three strategies for self-enhancement, was alleged to be a defense of personal honor. Actually, that honor was little more than the reflection of what the community judged a man to be. Three ironies emerged from the dueling custom. First, though confined to a segment of the upper classes, dueling served essentially the same purpose as the lowliest eye-gouging battle among Tennessee hog-drivers. Second, because of this congruence between upper- and lower-class concepts of honor, dueling was not at all undemocratic. It enabled lesser men to enter, however imperfectly, the ranks of leaders, and allowed followers to manipulate leaders to their taste. Third, the promise of esteem and status that beckoned men to the field of honor did not always match the expectation, but often enough dueling served as a form of scapegoating for unresolved personal problems.

Southerners themselves recognized that dueling too much resembled the ways of a boisterous, ill-educated society. Not surprisingly, the greatest internal opposition to the practice came from the ranks of the gentry itself. "It is the product of a barbarous age and flourishes in proportion as the manners of the people are coarse and brutal," admonished William J. Grayson of South Carolina. At an 1844 meeting of the Anti-Dueling Society of Mississippi, Judge John F. Bodley disapproved "the anti-moral, anti-legal and anti-ecclesiastical custom," a sentiment which Jefferson Davis and other state dignitaries applauded. Of all the customs of the Old South, dueling was the most vulnerable to the onslaughts of secular and religious nineteenth-century reforms. Yet the proliferation of societies to prevent the tradition had no more impact than the numerous laws that state legislators—duelists included—passed to prohibit the practice.[36]

A recent historian of the *code duello,* Dickson Bruce, follows the earlier lead of Daniel Boorstin in observing that it differed markedly from the combative style of the lower orders. According to Bruce's analysis the duel, institutionalized with "boards" and "courts of honor," carefully orchestrated events prior to the climax. Rules governing the classical fight served to check passion and transform it under the rubric of honor. The crossroads melee, on the other hand, represented a surrender to the passions "which in general Southerners deprecated."[37]

The distinction provides some useful insights. For one thing, there is the relationship between duels and feuds. Bloodthirsty, lengthy feuds—revenge fights among families that were so prevalent in early Celtic and Germanic tribes—were also likely consequences of brawls and killings among American hill-country yeomen in the South. Even among upcoming slaveholders they were not unknown on the frontier. William Faulkner's great-grandfather, Colonel William C. Falkner, for instance, was involved in a family feud that resulted in the killing of two men. The trouble arose over the blackballing of Robert Hindman, applicant for admission to a Tippah

County temperance society. Hindman blamed Falkner, although the young Mississippi attorney claimed to have been Hindman's sponsor. The fight started when Hindman called Falkner "a damned liar" and ended when Falkner drove a knife into his armed opponent. A year later, in 1850, Falkner shot to death Erasmus W. Morris, a Hindman partisan, in an argument over a house rental. He was tried for murder. After the jury rendered a verdict of not guilty Robert Hindman's father Thomas tried to shoot him, but the gun misfired. In 1855 the dispute flared again. This time Hindman and Falkner agreed to a duel, but a third party managed to resolve the conflict without bloodshed. The families did not confront each other again. Like Colonel John Sartoris, a character in *The Unvanquished* based on Falkner, the novelist's great-grandfather stepped out of the Oxford courthouse one day in 1889 and was shot in the throat and mortally wounded by a business and political rival. The jury acquitted the murderer (there were hints of bribery) and the possibility of a new blood feud arose. Colonel Falkner's son, however (like Bayard Sartoris in *The Unvanquished*), decided to end the train of bloodshed. He let the matter rest.[38]

As this story indicates, the duel and the feud were somewhat connected, especially in the socially unstable world of the Southwest. Feuds were generally much deplored, particularly among the gentry, because quite obviously they disrupted community life grievously, and incited conflicts of loyalty among related family members and their friends. Duels, in contrast, provided structure and ritual. Referees assured the fairness of the fight and witnesses reported back to the public on the impartiality of the proceedings. Moreover, the rites of challenge and response afforded time and means for adjustment of differences through third parties. Intermediaries, as in the Falkner-Hindman encounter, were more often successful in peaceably satisfying the injured pride of the principals than legends of duels would lead one to expect. In addition, the duel set the boundaries of the upper circle of honor. They excluded the allegedly unworthy and therefore made ordinary brawling appear ungentlemanly, vulgar, and immoral. In a hierarchical society, all these factors were socially significant. They made violence a part of the social order even in the upper ranks, but at least duels helped to restrict the bloodletting, which otherwise would have been much more chaotic and endlessly vindictive.

It would be a mistake, however, to argue that duels were as much deplored as Southern hand-wringing would lead an observer to believe. Hardly more than a handful genuinely considered duels socially beneficial, although some apologists claimed that the prospect of dueling forced gentlemen to be careful of their language and cautious in their actions. The criticism of outsiders, the clear opposition of the church, the recognition that valuable members of the community sometimes fell for reasons that retrospectively seemed petty—these attitudes placed duelists on the defensive. As a result, most of them explained their general opposition to the *code duello* in almost ritual words, but in the next breath gave reason for its continuation. For instance, Seargent S. Prentiss of Mississippi declared, "I am no advocate of duelling, and always shall from principle avoid such a thing . . . but when a man is placed in a situation where if he does not fight, life will be rendered valueless to him, both in his eyes and those of the community," then the only option was to fight. In fact, men took pride in such vices. All the words against dueling as well as other manly activities made them more appealing. It was a childish but nonetheless powerful motive.[39]

Although duels were confined to the upper ranks of Southern society, the practice cannot be seen as purely exclusionary. The general public was intimately involved (unless the duel occurred on a college campus, a world unto itself). Ordinarily, honor under the dueling test called for public recognition of a man's claim to power, whatever social level he or his immediate circle of friends might belong to. A street fight could and often did accomplish the same thing for the victor. Murder, or at least manslaughter, inspired the same public approval in some instances. Just as lesser folk spoke ungrammatically, so too they fought ungrammatically, but their actions were expressions of the same desire for prestige. Even planters were not above assaulting one another with fists, and sometimes with firearms and dirks. "The violent planter was a deviant," Bruce asserts. "The violent yeoman was not." But in actuality violence pervaded all the white social classes. Whether the combat took a prescribed form or consisted of sheer unchecked fury did not make too much difference, if one or both of the contestants died.[40]

Of course, among Christians and older men who were not expected to show youthful passions excessive violence was considered inappropriate. As Henry Foote noted, devout churchmen could forgo duels or, in fact, any other form of physical redress without incurring public censure. For other men a different standard prevailed. Prestige was the reward for the successful fighter of planter status. After thoroughly beating up a low-class "brawler," James L. Petigru, a young but dignified Carolinian lawyer, "became," as a friend declared, "a favorite with the people, who readily appreciated a strong arm and resolute spirit." Though the forms for defending it differed, the basic concept of personal valor, however displayed, bound the male ranks together even as the distinctions of class remained.[41]

The second irony was related to the first: the effect of general democratic tendencies within the dueling scheme itself. That this should be so, even in rank-conscious Southern society, should come as no surprise, given the origins of the duel. Although introduced to America by British and French aristocrats serving in America during the Revolution, the duel was adopted by regular United States Army officers and, more especially, by the state militia officer corps. The latter was not only democratic in its election of officers but also increasingly so in the kind of men selected from the ranks to be officers. The process of change began even before the Revolution and grew apace. As Colonel John Lewis of Gloucester County, Virginia, reported in 1802 to Governor James Monroe, no "men of the first respectability" were among the officers of his regiment. Yet he had no discretionary power, "as they were the choice of the majority of the company."[42]

In the absence of enormous wealth perpetually held under primogeniture, men in slaveholding states were prone to designate status by titles, and militia rankings were an obvious and useful signification of esteem. Many men, once having gained an elective title, as one Virginia officer complained "care but little about" it and promptly resigned. But once a major or colonel, always one—making these titles especially coveted by those whose property holdings might not otherwise have provided them with status. As one Carolinian wrote his brother in Alabama, "You are right in wishing to get rid of the infernal and eternal title of *Captain*" and become instead "Col. Townes," as "Col. is the prettiest title belonging to the military profession in my opinion." The democratic character of the militia was bound to affect the dueling custom. The duel was not an aristocratic custom that was learned at "mother's knee," contrary to Daniel Boorstin. Instead, dueling was a means to demonstrate status and manliness among those calling themselves gentlemen, whether born of noble blood or not.[43]

Thus it would be a mistake to consider dueling confined to the bluebloods. Aristocracy, as William J. Grayson explained in the 1850s, was far from being an exclusive caste. "We are all *parvenus,* pretenders, or snobs," he admitted. For instance, nothing pleased Robert Bailey, Virginia gambler and captain in the "Light Blues," more than a challenge that he received from a fellow militia officer: the confrontation assured him reception into the world of gentlemen. Yet he knew little about the ritual that lay ahead. (Very few first-time duelists, outside Charleston and New Orleans, probably ever did, and some duels were so poorly conducted that they hardly qualified.) After half an hour of futile instruction, Major Thomas Lewis, his second, advised him simply to feint when his opponent fired, then take careful aim. His opponent was indeed so surprised by his unorthodox motions that Bailey wounded him without receiving a scratch himself.[44]

Not many men of the first rank in society would have deigned to trade shots with an illiterate cockfighter like Bailey, whatever his militia title might be. Yet more duels of that proximate level probably took place than of the more celebrated variety between politicians and editors. In addition, the challenger could always appeal to his peers for vindication if turned down on the grounds that he was socially inferior. Haughtiness was not admired, and the challenger might gain sympathy. Quite clearly, someone like Andrew Jackson could refuse a young civilian like Thomas Swann of Philadelphia without incurring criticism. Less formidable gentlemen often had to fight, because peers had determined that the plea of inequality did not apply and was merely an excuse. Pleas of age difference were generally accepted. Thomas Lesesne of South Carolina noted that a planter had refused to duel a younger man on the grounds that "it would be a degradation of his character to put his life on the footing with so young a Boy." But with social distinctions often difficult to measure, especially in the Southwest, a man was more or less compelled to meet the challenge.[45]

Finally, principals and their seconds were not the only ones involved in disputes leading toward a formal reckoning. Often men of various positions in the local hierarchy acted as a Greek chorus in the Sophoclean drama. For instance, in the famous Jackson–Charles Dickinson duel of 1806, over a dozen men, some of them at the fringes of male society, helped to create a consensus for a lethal settlement that the principals could not ignore. It took nearly six months for the affair to play its course, owing to Jackson and Dickinson's reluctance. Various gossip-mongers, as Jackson himself recognized, had more to do with staging the event than either of the duelists.[46]

A further irony was the role of the "mobbish inferiors," whom the gentry were supposed to ignore when engaged in affairs of honor. Although duels were to be staged away from prying onlookers, the larger male community sometimes determined who should fight and why, particularly so in the less socially rigid Southwest. Militia officers, politicians, and journalists were obliged to prove manhood in order to demonstrate their worthiness as community leaders. Militia officers were most particularly called upon to exhibit prowess with firearms before their troops.

A telling illustration of such pressures from below was the duel between General Felix Huston of the Texan Army and Albert Sidney Johnston, whom President Sam Houston had ordered to command Huston's regiments. A tall, rowdy, and shrewd lawyer from Natchez, Felix Huston had recruited men from Natchez-under-the Hill and brought them to Texas. They proceeded to kill each other, not Mexicans, in Saturday-night brawls. President Houston had decided to replace their commander with a stricter disciplinarian. When Johnston arrived, Huston challenged him to a duel, claiming that his assumption of command had been the result of intrigue and had inflicted "stigma" upon Huston's "prospects in the Texan Army." The charge was false, and Huston knew it full well. But he felt obliged to defend the honor of his troops, who otherwise would have to accept the change in command as criticism of their conduct. Johnston, who had sworn never to participate in a duel and had no experience with small arms, was compelled by circumstance to accept. For six rounds the pair blasted away. (Huston had evened the odds by firing a defective pistol.) Finally, Johnston fell with a ball in his thigh that he carried to his death at Shiloh. According to one officer present, if Johnston had killed Huston or if he had failed to fight, he would have been killed by the soldiers themselves. As it was, Johnston had gained "the moral preeminence" over Huston and the troops that was so necessary for his successful command.[47] The point should be clear. Tyranny of the community, whether simply the participants' peers or the large male fraternity of various social classes, governed Southern society. Leaders, as duelists, orators, and politicians, had to bear that Tocquevillian fact in mind. It was democracy perhaps, but a kind of democracy that placed primary stress on white, manly virtue. Those who failed to set the appropriate standard were soon unseated. Duels were a method for ascertaining who should exercise the power that the community of men was willing to accord the winners.

The final irony was the curious effect that dueling had upon survivors. Most duels were fought by young men (some of them with deceptively senior titles). Quite often their arrogance masked an uncertainty about their place in society and, indeed, about their manhood as well. The inexperienced youth was very likely to take his own measure from public opinion of himself, an inclination that forced a good number to fight—and die—when peers demanded it. Harriet Martineau and William J. Grayson, among others, cited poignant examples to show how young men were compelled to fight each other largely because their equally young peers (and sometimes their seniors as well) insisted that to do otherwise would be construed as cowardice, ruining their future prospects. (Indeed, duels did open up positions in society that young men sought to fill.)[48]

Southerners themselves were sometimes uneasily aware that some duelists seemed driven to violence by inner furies. Such an individual was labeled as "bully," but the term was most often directed toward an unpopular victor, rather than seen as a general problem. For instance, William Cumming, who had gravely wounded George McDuffie in a celebrated duel, was criticized for showing "a Hyena thirst for blood which has lowered him in the estimation of all good men." Partisans of the defeated rival were very likely to take that position when a favorite fell. Nevertheless, the number of fighters who seem to have been harshly driven toward gambles with death is striking—a propensity that puzzled more than disturbed the public at the time. Figures such as William L. Yancey were drawn to this method of acting out bitter feelings because dueling promised not just moral vindication against the "calumniator" who ruined "reputation," but the wonder of all who heard of it. Even though death might ensue, there was supposed to be glory for the defeated as well as the winner. When excoriated for fighting Thomas L. Clingman, a Whig congressman of North Carolina, Yancey replied to the highly critical editors of the *Alabama Baptist* that the laws of God and state and the "obligations" to wife and children all had to bow, "as they have ever done from the earliest times to the present, to those laws which public opinion had formed, and which no one, however exalted his station, violates with impunity."[49]

The appeal of dueling to the restless spirit was exactly that public appproval, a reassurance of self-esteem instantly gratified in victory. Even the victim, declared the Virginia belleletrist George Tucker in 1823, "touches our sympathy and excites our honor," and while, as in a play, the spectators applauded the survivor, they also celebrated the fallen, who "excites more than ordinary regret, and the recollection that his conduct was rash, illegal, impious, and immoral, is lost in the warm and generous feelings of pity and admiration." These Aristotelian emotions of pity and fear were supposed to be aroused and satisfied in the catharsis of the outcome.[50] But the aftermath was not as unambiguous, structured, and glorious as the dedicated duelist presumed.

Although most Southern duelists managed to live through the experience with scarcely a twinge of regret, some both entered and left the dueling ground with their anxieties unresolved. One may speculate that a patriarchal order that left young men desperate for purpose in life was bound to create a scheme whereby self-vindication could be achieved in killing one another. Like gaming, drink-treating, and overt miscegenation, dueling was sometimes the recourse of a failed spirit, or at least of men who feared that consequence. Louis T. Wigfall, for instance, who fought or threatened to fight a number of duels, suffered deeply from "dissipation," remorse, uncontrollable ambition, and total incapacity to reconcile himself to the insolvency that his own aspirations brought down upon him. "Had I been studious & sober instead of idle & dissipated what an immensely high position would I now have inspired in the public estimation," mourned Wigfall. His self-esteem was too low to be retrieved, even through duels. Impatience drove Wigfall from Carolina to try his luck in Texas. Though he there became a secessionist leader and senator, he never matched his hopes.[51]

Other duelists with equal if not greater emotional distresses included William L. Yancey, whose restlessness and alcoholism all but disqualified him from significant participation in the Confederate cause that his eloquence did so much to promote. Seargent S. Prentiss, though popular as an orator, cardplayer, and drinking companion, shared similar states of depression, anguish, and inner rages. Senator Prentiss, declared his friend Joseph Shields, constantly sought the "wild excitement" of alcohol and gaming, a "mysterious and singular infatuation" that he could not overcome.[52] Colonel Alexander K. McClung, age twenty-three when promoted to that title, had already fought one duel as a midshipman. He killed General Allen, about the same age, and fought several others in the course of his life. A man of strange disposition, he was subject to severe depressions that alcohol only made worse. When he was in a drunken state others had to avoid him for fear of arousing his belligerent temper. Alienated from the public he sought to impress, he killed himself. Similarly, General John McGrath, reminiscing about famous encounters in Baton Rouge, remarked that the survivor of one affair "became despondent" in the following years and died "a dissolute character" in his youth. James Stith, another duelist whom McGrath remembered, "also grew morose" and avoided "former associates."[53] Obviously the field of honor was a repository of self-pity.

Although the occasions for duels differed somewhat, almost all arose because one antagonist cast doubt on the manliness and bearing of the other, usually through the recitation of ritual words—liar, poltroon, coward. The stigma had to be dealt with or the labels would haunt the bearer forever. In making such charges or returning them with similar words, the principals might well have been acting out private dramas of their own and asking the public to bear witness that their inner sense of worthlessness applied better to the opponent than to themselves. The parties sought to kill personal anxieties along with the scapegoat who stood ten or twenty paces away. But many discovered, as one Major William F. Pope of Arkansas did, that the duelist carried the mark of death, a kind of evil eye. The promise of immortality that George Tucker made the loser was not always fulfilled. Though he was "pit[t]ed twice," like a cock in the ring, Pope's "sunshine friends" deserted him as he lay in agony from the wounds. He had fought for the sake of family reputation, but even his uncle failed to visit him or pay his medical expenses. Death and abandonment were all too often the outcome for the losers, and even some victors found themselves without the companionship that the duel was supposed to bring them.[54]

These circumstances belied the cult of chivalry. The Southern ethical scheme's personal strategies did not and could not provide the happiness, permanency of status, and degree of authority demanded of them. Hospitality, gaming, and arranging duels to the death all created worlds of adventure in the midst of rural monotony, and the oppressive spirit of rivalry among those who were master to slaves, wives, and fellow men. As George Tucker, the Virginia philosopher, said, if these diversions had been replaced with "literary pursuits" or motions to improve the social and religious order, men of leisure and sensitive pride would have been "spared the necessity of flying from themselves" in search of pleasure and reputation.[55] Whether they really banished fear of apartness and alienation depended upon the resilience of individuals, not upon the society that gave these strategies their romance and appeal.

14

Honor, Shame, and Justice
in a Slavocracy

For many years historians have argued that "justice" for Southern antebellum whites "was mixed at best." The whiter the skin, it seemed, the better matters stood for the felon, especially when the fate awaiting the black criminal, slave or free, was compared with that of the white. "The combination of archaic laws, penalties far in excess of popular values, and the lack of facilities for the long term confinement were easily turned to a defendant's benefit," a recent critic of Southern justice has suggested. As a result, the argument runs, personal violence, public disorder, and crimes against property were all but encouraged, so inefficient, incompetent, and casual the apparatus. The whole machinery of criminal justice either promoted the interests of the slaveholding elite, who used it "to shape the world in its own image," as another historian has said, or suited the needs of a frontier individualism that gave all whites freedom from Old World restraints, as the disciples of the great historian Frederick Jackson Turner once averred.[1] By either interpretation, white society was allegedly ill served by a legal structure both unjust and ineffective.

Unfortunately, the immorality and ineptitude for which Southern criminal jurisprudence has had a long-standing reputation do not explain much about the system. Southern attorneys and judges were no less knowledgeable about common and statutory law than their Northern brethren. The intriguing questions therefore become: Why was the law so readily manipulated? Why was English common-law severity so often and so completely cast aside by judges, juries, and governors? Why were some crimes, such as murder and petty theft, lightly pursued and others, such as grand larceny, rigorously penalized? Why, in sum, were so many "abuses" condoned? The presence of slaves and the determination of whites to control their behavior played a role in such decisions. In addition, there was the ethic of honor, which itself figured in race as well as in class relations and tensions.

As reflected in law, the ethic of honor required the unfeigned willingness of slaves to bestow honor on all whites. For instance, if slaves merely pretended to offer respect, the essence of honor would be dissolved; only the appearance, shabby and suspect, would remain. Hence it was important that blacks show obedience with apparently heartfelt sincerity. Grudging submission to physical coercion would not suffice. In part the slave codes were designed to that end. They heavily penalized the slave for infractions to deference. By the nineteenth century they also punished the master who used excessive coercions to obtain compliance. Criminal justice had other black-white connections with honor and shame as well. Among whites, there were disputes about rights of personal discretion regarding slave management, privileges that might conflict with community needs for safety against a potentially unruly work force. Such issues sometimes had to be resolved at law.

Moreover, honor, as a matter of hierarchy, was related to the distribution of powers along class lines. The operation of criminal justice gave the upper ranks the titles and authorities for administering justice and at the same time presented the lower orders with the chance to participate on juries and in other functions of the law. Also, the law was intimately connected with family honor, serving as the court of last resort in kinfolk disputes, sometimes including charges of murder. The tensions of brothers and brothers-in-law led to fatalities more often than struggles among blood relations did.

All these matters before the bench were judged less by abstract principles than by the exigencies of the hour—as perceived locally. How could it have been otherwise? Law is a cultural artifact; the more personal, oral, and small-scale the community in which it is administered, the more certain it is that the law will reflect the neighborhood will.[2]

By this reading, honor was a medium or filter through which specific cases were often decided. As has been stressed throughout this study, local opinion, not individualism in either a modern or a "pioneer" sense, was the dominant force in Southern public life, even in instances of public violence. Naturally, the law had to be interpreted with that in mind. It could sometimes be molded to fit circumstances, in ways that will be demonstrated. Honor was not so tractable. At the moment of its conferment upon an individual or a community, honor alone was absolute and indivisible. Statutory and common law, on the other hand, were subordinated to the needs of the community, and therefore were applied with the utmost severity or indifference, depending upon the consensus of the public. When, perhaps, the law could not be so readily bent without jeopardizing its credibility, then the resort was to community appeals for mercy at the next tribunal—the state executive with its pardoning power. Another, darker and retributive alternative to perceived injustice at law was lynching. Although Blackstone would not have recognized the legitimacy of American mob actions, the general orientation of criminal justice in the Old South would hardly have shocked him. He was the Southern legal profession's patron saint because his *Commentaries* supported the traditions of a rural, hierarchical society that paid respect to communal feelings.[3]

By placing the power of the state at the disposal of the community, Southerners scarcely resolved all dilemmas. Indeed, the seeming whimsicality of Southern justice demonstrated that deep ambiguities lay at the heart of the ethic itself. Ambivalence was inseparable from honor, as Bacon's Rebellion illustrated. For honor to thrive there must be room to jockey for position—an invitation to rebelliousness, though it might be duly suppressed. Were it otherwise, honor could not survive. It cannot exist under absolute despotism because the tyrant assumes all honor, leaving none for others. And too much groveling, obsequiousness, and slavishness demeans not only the subjects but also the object of such unmanly worship. The planter surrounded simply by Sambos was like a king in a court of fools. The more dignified the owner, the more incongruous it was for him to be served by comical servility—an emperor unclothed, subject to subtle mockery. (Herman Melville's Babo and shipmaster Don Benito Cereno offer a menacing example.) Likewise, if there had been a rankless democracy in the Old South, honor would soon have become irrelevant, its ubiquity cheapening its value. Between these two poles, then, there was a gray area of ambiguity and potential explosiveness that accompanied the bestowal and receipt of deference and honor among whites and among whites in regard to blacks. The criminal justice system supplied a framework for rituals mediating between the givers and receivers of honor by adjusting the penalties of shame to meet community demands. It was intended to clarify the moral and social ordering of things. Sometimes it did so even if rigid adherence to the law was set aside. Sometimes, though, the ambiguities were not resolved.

The rites of criminal justice were taken deadly seriously. Trials dramatized the moments when community customs and written laws were tested and celebrated anew. Jealously, all white males wanted a voice in that spectacle of decision making. Aggrieved parties— whether they were judges outraged at a wayward jury or defendants convicted by doubtful means—had to bow to that communal will. The consensus itself, though, was reached by much talk and deliberation—in the courthouse yard, and the taverns, parlors, and cabins of the district. The public had to weigh the ascriptions of those involved—their race, age, repute and so on—the frequency or rarity of the offense, and the local circumstances. Nor was the consensus itself permanently fixed. What men felt at the time of the felon's arrest might differ completely from sentiments at the moment of the jury report. Moreover, class differences as well as familial interests strained the attempts to preserve white solidarity. These factors enhanced the drama. But the most cherished aspect of the system was that it sustained local autonomy. Criminal justice was a neighborhood, not metropolitan affair. The courthouse, more than the church, was the center for local ethical considerations. This orientation had once existed throughout the country, but Northern cities, to a degree, had become too large, too secular for such parochial, personal, and sacral community values to be served.

Although the subject has many aspects, it may be conveniently treated along these four lines: first, the centrality of violence, as opposed to other forms of criminal behavior, for the maintenance of personal honor; second, the individual white's discretionary right to rule over blacks, a prerogative about which slaveholders and non-slaveholders were not always agreed; third, the family quarrel that became a community and legal matter, to the consternation of all; and fourth, the fabric of common-law traditions as they were used to preserve racial order and the distinctions between honor and shamelessness.

Historians of Southern mores are agreed that violence as an aspect of Southern life clearly distinguished the region from the rest of the country. To be sure, the West had an unenviable record too, but high rates of murder and mayhem in mining camps and cattle depots were largely due to the age and status of the predominant class of residents. Young male adults, unmarried, transient, and often menially and irregularly employed, were those most likely to be violent, especially on a Saturday night. This state of affairs among marginal young males (with some ethnic variations) would also apply to the nineteenth-century inner city, as Roger Lane has recently pointed out. But violence in the South, while including such individuals, also had its unique source in slavery and the strictures of black subordination. In addition, notions about personal honor naturally provided another element in the equation, one that existed in the North, too, but surely to a less intense degree. Yet the levels of physical attack varied greatly within the region. Chapel Hill, North Carolina, for instance, slumbered with only occasional college pranks to break the monotony. Occasionally small towns and communities in the Southwest also escaped unpleasantries, particularly so if churchmen and settled family men managed to set the moral tone. But in the boisterous river port of St. Francisville, Louisiana, a town comparable in size to Chapel Hill, Rachel O'Connor reported these disorders in the course of one month in 1830: a senseless mortal stabbing of a widow at a country dance; an insurrectionary scare in which two slaves were hanged without trial; one murder by gunfire (no suspects); and fatal dirk-knife attack for which the murderer was to hang.[4]

Crimes, as Emile Durkheim observed long ago, reflect the culture of a people. In the North, men—apart from the group Lane has identified—generally found means other than physical assault for expressing themselves. Repute could be found in learnedness, in professional skills, but most especially in wealth. In Massachusetts, for instance, between 1833 and 1838 personal violence was a relatively low 17.4 percent of all offenses brought to justice. Reflecting the social orientation toward acquisition of money, antebellum Massachusetts burglars, on the other hand, rang up a healthy 30.4 percent of the criminal indictments. In South Carolina, as Michael Hindus has carefully demonstrated, the thieving element was most anemic, making up a meager 16.2 percent of all criminals brought to justice. On the other hand, Carolinians maimed, murdered, slayed, and assaulted to the point that such felonies constituted 61.5 percent of the total registered (1800–60). In Ohio County, Virginia, the ratios were even more startling: for the opening decade of the nineteenth century there were ninety-one indictments for assault and battery and three murders, but only one robbery and two breaking-and-enterings. In the Southwest the same pattern prevailed. Between 1829 and 1841 in Adams County, Mississippi, one of the richest districts in the South, clerks of court entered 175 assaults of varying degrees on the docket, but only 45 prosecutions for property crimes.[5]

Murder rates North and South were equally distinct, at least according to the few quantitative studies so far undertaken. In 1878 three southern states, South Carolina, Kentucky, and Texas, counted between 12.2 and 28.8 murders per hundred thousand inhabitants, whereas in Massachusetts the rate was only 1.4. In Boston no murders were recorded for any of the years between 1826 and 1830. The rate scarcely became alarming when, for the next fifteen years, there

was one each year per one hundred thousand.[6] Obviously Southerners worried much more about their status in the eyes of neighbors
and their own sense of physical power than about the acquisition of
goods, lawful or not. In the Northeast, the opposite preferences commanded human aspirations.

These fugitive numbers scarcely convey the depth of the phenomenon. Not only were fistfights, eye gougings, duels, and other
forms of violence less likely to be reported in the Southern court
docket books than they would be in the North, but convictions were
considerably less frequent in the South as well. After examining reports from twenty-seven counties, the Rt. Rev. B. B. Smith, an Episcopal bishop, concluded that in Kentucky from 1835 to 1838 there
were thirty-five murders but only eight convictions. In a larger sample of eighty-four counties, only eleven persons had been committed
to the state penitentiary and there was *"not one instance of capital
punishment,"* not because of popular, secular sentiment against that
form of retribution but simply because of indifference toward violence itself. Malicious assaults upon dependents and possessions—
wives, children, and especially slaves, not to mention domestic animals and livestock—whether by family members or outsiders, did
not necessarily induce officials to investigate, unless someone in the
neighborhood had the temerity to report suspicions. The bishop
and others thought slavery, drink, illiteracy, and other evils explained the unhappy record. The list of causes could be expanded
to include rural isolation and anxiety fed by boredom, tight family
loyalties, the permissibility of harsh levels of domestic "correction,"
a reticence on the part of witnesses that encouraged malefactors to
persist, and a degree of fatalism about the world and its risks.[7] In
addition, ancient Celtic patterns of life and violence, yet to be fully
studied, made a contribution.[8] Much of the danger to life and limb
never surfaced in the written record, sometimes because it was not
even considered worthy of notice.

The use of physical force flourished at all levels of society. As always, though, the lower ranks, burdened with economic and social
anxieties that the rich escaped, committed the greater share of violent offenses. A reason more fundamental than some vague "frontier

spirit" or an American penchant for violence was the social necessity for men of all ranks to preserve white manhood and personal status in the fraternity of the male tribe to which all belonged. Through violence a degree of proximate stability was created, the balance wheel of race, order, and rank was maintained, and the values of what Victor Turner has called *communitas* were upheld.[9] By the latter term is meant the idealized social whole to which individual loyalty was pledged and from which ethical consensus could be drawn. Some have preferred to call this social phenomenon a "fantasy," "myth," or "romance," an artifact of imagination in which illusory views of life prevailed over actualities. These labels are useful chiefly as reference points to modern, or at least contrary moralities and concepts of acceptable behavior. But for those who lived within the boundaries of Southern white *communitas* there was no alternative social plan about which even to dream. With some exceptions, white Southerners were not given to conjuring up utopias; they resigned themselves to what was and assumed that it approached what ought to be. (Needless to say, blacks, with lively traditions of their own, did not share this vision of society.)

When dissenters or deviants called into question the premises of the social order, they had to be rendered powerless. Either by extermination or public humiliation, they were used to cleanse the community of the dangers they allegedly posed. The procedures, whether undertaken by personal initiative, legal process, or mob action, might have been barbaric by the standards of another place or time. Yet they were grimly effective in preserving the sense of white solidarity. First, the resort to personal, physical force preserved a man's self-estimation, property, and family from injury and disgrace. Second, the law served to distinguish the righteous from the roguish and, to some degree, the rich from the poor. Finally, the community, the final arbiter of morals and justice, acted to invest its worthy members with collective power in the name of tradition and order. The community functioned as the sanctifier of deeds committed on grounds of personal or group honor. The power of the community, which included the lower ranks, did not lie simply in jury panels. The views of the underprivileged classes influenced the way judges and governors adjudicated cases brought before them. When regular procedures seemed inappropriate or inadequate, the community, not always under planter control, acted through lynch law. Mob reprisal should not invariably be seen as a violation of statuary law, but sometimes as its complement. In all three areas—personal honor, criminal proceedings, and mob retaliation—there was much overlapping of jurisdictions. Resentments springing from the crossing of the rather loose boundaries of specialization did arise in particular situations, but not as issues requiring social or legal reformation. There was no state law specifically against lynching. How could there be, when the mode was intimately affiliated with the law?

Because white society was small, homogeneous, and cohesive about fundamental values, lawlessness, as outsiders saw it, was seldom a major internal worry, though it made a fitting topic for editorials, sermons, and speeches about the general sins of man. Stability prevailed. Class consciousness was only beginning to arise. Ordinarily each criminal case was seen discretely, judged not as part of a conspiracy of rich against poor or vice versa but on the basis of honor vindicated or abused.

In keeping with that line of reasoning, individuals had the authority to patrol their own social and ethical space. The law and community punished severely only when the offender made false claims to a status that his actions belied. The criminal law not only functioned as it always has—to punish violators—but also to mediate between the classes, to provide an intellectual "priesthood" of lawyers and jurists possessing the ancient mysteries of common law, and to offer a setting in which the community could celebrate in high drama the momentary triumph of good, the temporary eradication of evil. Although the community was already an active force in the functioning of law and personal autonomy, public action was the most irreversible—and most economical—way to police the racial and moral boundaries. It took several forms: insurrectionary scares, lynchings, vigilante warnings, and the charivari (most easily pronounced *shivaree*), a nonfatal but still fearsome way of shaming. All these devices, from personal honor to legal and extralegal action, shared a major objective: the maintenance of white masculine values as the rightful means to achieve order and fundamental safety. Popular justice in its several guises will be treated in the subsequent chapters, but it must be mentioned here because social control involved a weaving together of all forms of moral activity.

Policing one's own ethical sphere was the natural complement of the patriarchal order. When Southerners spoke of liberty, they generally meant the birthright to self-determination of one's place in society, not the freedom to defy sacred conventions, challenge long-held assumptions, or propose another scheme of moral or political order. If someone, especially a slave, spoke or acted in a way that invaded that territory or challenged that right, the white man so confronted had the inalienable right to meet the lie and punish the opponent. Without such a concept of white liberty, slavery would have scarcely lasted a moment. There was little paradox or irony in this juxtaposition from the cultural perspective. Power, liberty, and honor were all based upon community sanction, law, and traditional hierarchy as described in the opening section.

The purpose of unchecked freedom to be one's own final authority went quite beyond the needs of the slaveholding system. It was a matter of personal reputation to prove oneself a master of events to one's family and household, as well as to the world at large. For instance, when Robert E. Lee of Arlington, Virginia, discovered that two young slaves had run away to Pennsylvania, he had them sought after and returned. An anonymous critic informed the Northern public, through the New York *Tribune,* that Lee had personally supervised their flogging. Lee was responsible for some sixty-three slaves, not all of whom could be usefully employed at the Arlington plantation. He sent some to eastern Virginia, particularly the rebellious ones, who would have less opportunity there to flee northward. Perhaps, as Douglas Southall Freeman claims, that was the extent of his reaction to the runaways' offense. Wesley Norris, one of the pair, gave a grim account of the whipping, however. He said that Lee had watched the proceedings with eyes black with fury and had ordered brine poured into the wounds. Whether this and like reports are to be believed, it must be remembered that even the gentlest masters—and Lee was reputedly one of them—found occasion when there seemed to them very little choice about the use of coercion. It would not do for any slave to take flagrant advantage of a master's delicacy of conscience. To push too hard against the institution or against an owner's sense of self-esteem was to threaten the social order as it was then understood. Failure to react appropriately could be misinterpreted, not only by the compliant slaves but by the white community, too. The moral problem was itself built into the Southern ethic. One simply could not be made to look inept, powerless, or squeamish. For these reasons, in a case about which there can be no doubts, the Rev. Charles Colcock Jones of Liberty County, Georgia, had a slave girl flogged until she revealed the name of the individual who had fathered a mulatto child she had given birth to. The gentleman in question had been the elderly clergyman's secretary, a member, temporarily, of the household. Jones was incensed at this breach of the rules regarding hospitality, and his torture of the mother to confirm his suspicions was the consequence.[10]

Neither Lee nor Jones, it must be stressed, used the lash with any regularity. Far from it. One doubtful incident and a singular break with custom, one in northern Virginia, the other in southern Georgia, scarcely prove these gentlemen recreant to the traditions of Christian honor to which they both subscribed. In response to the newspaper report, Lee acted with customary prudence—hallmark of the chivalric code. His only surviving words about the matter appeared in a letter to his son Custis. "The *N.Y. Tribune,*" Lee wrote, "has attacked me for my treatment of your grandfather's slaves, but I shall not reply. He had left me an unpleasant legacy."[11]

Yet, most planters (those without severe mental or character disorders) used the ultimate weapon of the rod with some selectivity, at least when sober. The reasons were not necessarily humanitarian, or utilitarian—fear of damaging valuable goods, as it were. Rather it was the danger of cheapening the deterrent itself. Just as there could be an "inflation of honors," as Lawrence Stone described the seventeenth-century proliferation of titles, so too there could be an inflation of humiliations. "The punishment of infamy should not be too frequent," warned Cesare Beccaria, the Enlightenment philosopher, "for the power of opinion grows weaker by repetition, nor should it be inflicted on a number of persons at the same time, for the infamy of many resolves itself into the infamy of none."[12] Southern planters knew little about criminological theory. Common sense sufficed. Besides, there was always honor in *caritas,* the pre-Christian idea that the exercise of mercy honored the bestower. Christian benevolence reinforced the policy, at least among some masters.

Although nearly every historian of slavery has regarded the apparent whimsies of generosity and cruelty as signs that the system defied easy categorization, the ethical scheme accounted for the variation. By law and custom the master was his own policeman, jury, judge, and jailkeep. He was also the dispenser of good things— teacher, father, priest, confessor, arbitrator, provider, and agent of relief. Frederick L. Olmsted, for instance, came upon a Mississippi master whose fondness for his "black family" partly rested upon pride in their literacy. When told that by encouraging their reading he was violating state law, he claimed ignorance of the prohibition.[13] After all, should he not run his place as he saw fit? So long as the slaves did not boast about their accomplishments or show imprudent pride, the master's indulgence would be thought harmless enough in the community. Nearly everyone enjoyed some latitude in slave management.

Any signs of impudence or insurrection, however, made planters feel threatened and betrayed. Retaliation, even to the point of killing, was thought to be rightfully within the master's power. In 1845, for instance, a Mr. Harley of Louisiana discovered that his driver Isaac, a leading churchman and exhorter, had become a Millerite, a believer in the imminent destruction of the world. Isaac persuaded fellow slaves to place their bedding on the roofs of the cabins, pray, and sing, assuring them that true believers were immune from white men's whips and guns. Hearing the uproar in the quarters, Harley waited on his front porch, shotgun across his knees. Armed with a stick, Isaac approached and announced the end of bondage. When he was ten paces away, Harley fired both barrels. Then he had all the hands whipped.[14]

At no point did Harley have to worry that any legal complications would arise from his murder of Isaac. Both his honor and his life had been endangered, and threats to either one or the other would have been a sufficient defense. Of course, most slave challenges and most responses were considerably less drastic, but white honor, on plantation or in court, had to be vindicated. Corydon Fuller, the Ohio book salesman, reported in 1858 from Claiborne Parish, Louisiana, that a slave who had struck his mistress, a Mrs. Hepp, with a bridle was awaiting punishment in the jail. She had struck him first, but in warding off the blows he had hit her back. "His sentence is one thousand lashes, to be inflicted 100 each day for ten days. Many think he will die; several in the jury were for hanging him; and I think it would have been more humane to have done so. . . ." It was honor—a white "lady's"—that had been assaulted; the penalty expressed local views about how to handle the affront.[15]

White honor was also at stake in judging the guilt of masters who had killed their slaves. When Colonel Joseph Ivey's Jim died after a severe paddling, the Mississippi slaveholder himself at once called for a coroner's jury. Jim had "sassed" him and started to run off from a timber-cutting crew in the woods. Ivey often employed hired hands, and it would not do for him to have a reputation for recklessness. But also the colonel wanted to prove that he was a good master. Gross inhumanitarianism signified to many a character weakness, "white trash" origins, and other disagreeable imputations. When his neighbors met as a coroner's panel, Colonel Ivey wanted to know, he said, if he had killed Jim "by accident," or if the slave "died naturally or if God had killed him" for purposes of His own retribution against slave rebelliousness. Ivey was relieved to learn that the wound at the base of Jim's skull caused by a piece of metal was not the cause of death. Inquests often resulted in such convenient decisions. Slave Aggy in South Carolina, in 1848, underwent a severe lashing which so dehydrated her system that she kept drinking buckets of water. Her master importuned the neighbors to look kindly on the sad business. Her death was duly attributed to a "cramp in the Stomack."[16]

Those who excessively beat slaves were not necessarily brutes. Punishments of fatal or nearly fatal proportions were too common to be explained by that kind of aberration. Actually masters oft-times acted out of genuine fear, either for their lives or for plantation command. Momentarily they felt helpless, shamed, and driven to inarticulate fury. Stubborn children, as slaves were thought to be, only learned at the end of the lash, according to conventional wisdom. Legal punishments, administered in the courthouse yard or jail, were often as much as a thousand stripes, sometimes administered over days, in the fashion Fuller described. To do less than that on the plantation itself would have seemed insufficient to an enraged master. Servants, sailors, and soldiers had always been subjected to the whip in the British tradition; Southerners kept that heritage very much alive.

Fellow whites—as well as blacks themselves—would have despised a squeamish slaveholder who was unable to make his will felt. For instance, Harry Hammond, son of the hardheaded master Governor James H. Hammond, felt acutely his inadequacy as a leader of his work force. "The negroes in the yard & on the plantation will tell you that I failed," he confessed abjectly to his father. "If I spoke to a negro, I saw he knew it and pitied me for they liked me. I let them fool me and was amiable." He thought of suicide. Far better it was to earn a reputation for "firmness" than one for cowardly permissiveness, not just in order to discipline slaves but also to win approval from other masters. One had to prove manliness in this vital situation, as in so many other circumstances of Southern life.[17] Even kindly masters were not to be thought weak-hearted.

When the laws against murder and manslaughter collided with the right of personal autonomy in slave management, the community, not an abstract system of justice, determined the outcome. Some legal historians have tended to treat appeals cases as typical instead of exceptional, thus giving a benign cast to slave jurisprudence that simply distorts the picture.[18] Nevertheless, statutes and sometimes court decisions did aver that a slave's right to life and

members, as a Mississippi high court declared, was inviolable. By
the middle of the nineteenth century all Southern states had strict
penalties for convicted slave molesters and killers. But the social
position of the violator often affected the outcome, as in Colonel
Ivey's case. For example, a locally prominent Sea Island planter
named James H. Sandiford ordered Roger, a crippled slave, to
brave a winter gale to collect marsh grass and oysters. The slave's
efforts failed to please Sandiford, and then he overheard Roger
complain to the kitchen help. Furious, he had Roger trussed up in
an abandoned meat house. During the night the slave died of exposure. Thomas Chaplin, Sandiford's bibulous neighbor, served on
the jury of inquest that ruled the death accidental. Privately Chaplin fumed about Sandiford's "inhuman treatment," which he regarded as especially deplorable because Sandiford was a leading
member of the "Babtist" church. The jury, though, was scarcely
prepared to recommend a grand jury indictment. Frederick Olmsted once heard a Louisiana Creole explain such circumstances as
those that Chaplin faced: "Suppose you are my neighbor; if you
maltreat your negroes . . . am I going to prefer charges?" The law
might punish the offender (or at least embarrass him until he obtained a jury acquittal), but "I should have you, and your family
and friends. far and near, for my mortal enemies." Chaplin, with
his debts and drinking problems, had enemies enough already without earning another over a mistreated slave.[19]

Slaveholders without much local standing, however, were more
likely to get caught in the toils of criminal justice than better-placed
masters, hardly surprising in the rank-conscious South. A poor
North Carolina yeoman named Emett was convicted of castrating
his only slave, a boy of seventeen, and ordered to serve twenty days
in jail and pay a $20 fine. In 1846 a coroner's jury in Edgefield Dis-
trict returned a verdict of murder upon "Oliver Simpson, a sort of
simpleton," when they examined the body of his slave Lewis, dead
from starvation, cold, and exhaustion. A one-eyed drifter, Henry
Sides, along with his inebriated brother-in-law named Jonas Bradshaw, picked up Sides's slave Dick at the Wilkesboro, North Carolina, jailhouse, where the runaway was being held. They kicked,

beat, and choked the slave to death. Townspeople watched but did nothing. An enterprising prosecuting attorney indicted the strangers for the "heinous crime" and urged the governor to have the fleeing pair retrieved. These are among many indictments of masters that could be cited. Unfortunately, they do not prove the even-handedness of Southern justice, but rather the power of local opinion. In most cases the owners so accused were men of little reputation. Not every owner of a slave was automatically elevated to planter status. But even those without rank or money usually received acquittals, pardons, or light sentences. If Simpson could prove that he had killed "in suddent [sic] heat and passion," such a fatality became only a misdemeanor in South Carolina. In North Carolina, Sides and Bradshaw were not even returned to stand trial: the legislature overruled the governor's proclamation against the fugitives. Outraged by the supposed severity of Emett's penalty, the county jailkeeper refused to let him in to serve the twenty-day sentence, and the local militia general urged the governor to remit the $20 fine on the grounds that the slave had "a notorious bad character" and that the master was "under the mistaken opinion that he had a right" to castrate the boy, whose value had thereby risen in any case.[20]

Personal discretion also extended to those who killed, maimed, or assaulted slaves belonging to someone else, but both the law and community opinion did establish limits because of the value of the property, the customary disapproval of outsiders' acting *in loco parentis,* and the restiveness and demoralization that outrageous antiblack crimes caused among slaves themselves. Overseers were the most likely candidates for relatively harsh applications of the law. It was deemed that they had betrayed the trust given them by employers when they administered excessive punishments. General C. C. Pinckney of South Carolina grumbled, "I put overseers on my Plantations to protect my negroes, not to kill them." The sentiment was heartfelt.[21]

Although men possessed the right to do as they pleased in regard to race control, what they pleased to do had to conform to the guide-

lines that local society provided. The basic rule was that neither
the rich masters nor the poor nonslaveholders had the authority to
identify their interests with that of the slave or free black. One of
the temptations of slave ownership was to make the plantation the
prime center of group loyalty. In exchange for obedience, masters
boasted that they shielded their slaves from cold, want, and outside
depredations—the castle under siege. As Justice Charles Colcock of
South Carolina intoned, "It is the duty as well as the interest of
every master to protect his slave from unnecessary punishment and
to resist the abuse of legal authority" that slave patrols or citizens
making civilian arrests were sometimes guilty of. If "every unprin-
cipled and unfeeling man" assuming "this brief authority" should
have license to kill, law and justice would suffer, he reasoned. Yet
in most cases a master's ability to avenge abuse against slaves was
severely handicapped, first by law, second by community surveillance. In South Carolina, the master who sued a patroller for injuring his slave had to pay three times the sum demanded and all
court costs if the suit failed. Even so, such suits occasionally arose.
In 1819 Thomas Lang of Kershaw District registered a prosecution
against two yeomen, Zach Johnson and Elijah Payne. He later
dropped the charges for reasons unrecorded, but possibly because
the beating of another's slave was too often regarded sympatheti-
cally by juries. Also retaliation for a conviction was no idle threat.[22]

Increasingly, planters spoke of slaves as members of their "family," rather than as mere chattel, an evolution that reflected a growing concern with humanitarian welfare but also with rationalizing
a traditional institution under attack from progressive and religious
sources. Planters like the Rev. Charles C. Jones of Liberty County
prided themselves upon their interest in improving the habits, morals, and well-being of those whom God had allegedly placed under
their tutelage. The effort at "domesticating" the "domestic institution" created a conflict with those who opposed any significant advance for slaves that could jeopardize black subservience. Community members both high and low needed reassurance that white
hegemony was not being breached under the sanction of masterly
discretion. Worry about white disunity no less than about slave re-

bellion was a fundamental anxiety in the slave regions. The use of slaves as skilled workmen also threatened to erode white consensus by providing blacks with money and marketable talents greater than those that lesser whites enjoyed.[23] Too close identification between master and slave, therefore, was a social danger.

Benevolent planters sometimes found themselves at risk when they protested slave patrol incursions or court decisions against their slaves. For instance, Robert F. W. Allston, a former governor of South Carolina, was exceedingly circumspect when one of his slaves was charged with disturbing the peace by assaulting another black at a Methodist camp meeting. To the applause of spectators, the judge sentenced the young black to a hundred lashes. Allston, however, was unwilling, as he later said, "to interpose to arrest the punishment which my neighbours thought should be inflicted on him." He hurriedly left the scene before the blows fell.[24]

Masters less pusillanimous than Allston, however, sometimes stood by their slaves, justifying themselves on the grounds of personal discretion and denying others the right to interfere. After all, a man's honor was compromised when outsiders questioned his style of business. One such individual was Colonel Joseph Bryan of Georgia. As his daughter explained, slave patrollers were entering "the cellar at all times of the night, waking up the family and making an uproar." After they struck one house servant, "Pa went out to protect him and they became dreadfully angry with him; said he 'upheld his negroes in their rascality.' 'You are a liar,' said Pa." The retort proved costly. The man whom Bryan had so characterized did not challenge him to a duel or strike him then and there. The colonel was too prominent and the patroller too aware of his place for that kind of response. He gained his revenge in another way. Later in the week, someone led a valuable riding horse out of the colonel's stable in the middle of the night and "knocked him in the head." A more serious mode of retaliation would have been to burn down the stable, barn, or gin house, a tactic rather frequently employed by the poor to teach rich men that the right of personal responsibility had to surrender to community notions of security and a common front against the slave populace. Planters grumbled about the maliciousness of their less fortunate neighbors, but the complaints led nowhere.[25]

At the same time that planters found themselves occasionally hemmed in by lesser folk around them, so too poorer folk were never supposed to identify their personal interests with those of the black underclass. Time and again members of the yeomanry appeared before judges on charges of trading in stolen goods obtained by slaves from their plantations. It was a vexing issue, though the thefts were generally cheap items—whiskey, tools, harnesses, "watter millions" (as one indictment read), and other kinds of provender for man or beast. (Property of greater value would have been hard to fence in the countryside.) Such "unnatural" conspiracies against the wealthy had to be stopped with as much firmness as planter tendencies toward indulgence of slaves. Communities became incensed when slaves acted as wild as white men—high-spirited drunkenness, disturbing the peace, and getting into fights among themselves. Planters were blamed for laxity in discipline, patrollers for inattention to duty, and tavern-keepers for "trading with slaves," a very common offense on the courts' books.[26] Pursuit of individual interests rather than concern for civic order was deemed a public menace.

The license that flourished in regard to control of slaves also applied, to a lesser extent, to white relations with each other, except in one particular. There was no latitude permitted in the way men treated their own white household dependents. Although women and children, within the boundaries already discussed, could be given supposedly gentle "correction," their rights to life and limb were absolute, even more than another man's. Killers of dependents could not expect communal sympathy. James McQuirk of Washington County, Virginia, for instance, not only axed his wife but also choked to death the twins she had delivered two weeks before. What outraged the judge most of all was McQuirk's utter indifference in court. It was generally expected that murderers stand penitent and offer a warning to the throng about the dangers of drink, unwarranted sexual jealousy, or evil companions, as the case might warrant. McQuirk did none of these things. Dumbfounded, the judge could only fulminate that the wife "ought rather to have received protection at his hand, than such barbarous treatment."[27]

Unlike violence in contemporary American society, both North and South, startlingly few antebellum Southern murders occurred among people closely related by blood or matrimony, at least according to the sources surveyed for this study. Statistically, it would be hard to prove beyond doubt that intrafamilial violence was rare, so scattered and incomplete are antebellum records. But mothers, fathers, sons, daughters, husbands, and wives seldom took out frustrations by assaulting one another with deadly weapons. Infanticide was also rare, judging solely from impressions. Much more usual was the style of a Virginia yeoman named Goode who, at the mercy of "the care drowning Bowl," rushed out of his cabin and stabbed a passerby to death. His daughter, the killer learned not long before, had run off with "an aged, penniless man, already married."[28] The crime was attributed to his distress.

In contrast, modern Southern violence, at least in cities, has followed national trends. In Houston, Texas, in 1969, out of a total murder count, 7.17 percent was the work of wives against their husbands (many of the cases being in response to wife-beatings). Men were somewhat less bloodthirsty, killing their wives at the rate of 4.30 percent of all reported slayings for that year. The total percentage of deadly assaults among blood-related kinspeople in Houston was 17.22 percent, a rather sizable proportion.[29] In the antebellum South, a fair guess would be not more than 5 to 6 percent, perhaps much less. (No figures currently exist to decide the matter.)

Certainly white Southerners prided themselves on their selectivity about choice of victims. As one postwar Atlanta newsman declared, the Southern killer was inclined to wreak vengeance upon some stranger or acquaintance who insulted him, "while in New England the murderer moves quietly, even humbly . . . and usually plies his vocation in the bosom of his family."[30] In traditional societies, ascriptive hierarchies and relationships, such as father and son, husband and wife, elder brother and younger brother, blood-related uncle and nephew, were powerful deterrents to family violence. There was no justification for torturing or killing within the domestic walls, and only utter disgrace for any who dared do so. Even the life of an adulterous wife was ordinarily sacrosanct (though her lover's was not). In the never-ceasing battle against a harsh environment and an ugly, often malicious world, there had to be taboos against internecine warfare among blood relatives, sometimes as sole protection against disaster. Under circumstances of foul play within a family, the immunity that clans ordinarily enjoyed in pursuing their own affairs and serving their own notions of honor was speedily revoked. Sometimes wives who killed their husbands or husbands who killed their wives, for instance, were subjected to lynch law.[31] Intrafamilial crimes were truly remarkable for their rarity in the South, but they touched areas of grim sensitivity.

In light of the sanctity surrounding the patriarchal household and its blood intimates, it should not be surprising that conflict between brothers and brothers-in-law, when they were not otherwise related, was a major factor in familial tension and violence. The marital tie was supposed to unite two families in friendship and love, but very often enmity arose instead, complete with suits at law, assaults, murders, and celebrated feuds, especially in the hill country. (The doings of the Hatfields and McCoys and other clans in the Southern highlands, though germane, must be excluded from this account.) The causes of such tensions were, first, the ambivalence of the brother-outsider relationship; second, the problems of partible but inequitable inheritances; third, rivalries for power within the family structure, sometimes in the political arena as well; and fourth, inequalities of age and community status between the newcomer and those already established in the inner circle. Oftentimes men who married sisters struggled for preeminence in the families of their wives, particularly so in fatherless households and in the absence of a willful brother competing for power.

In light of these family rivalries and woes, it might be speculated that the Southern inclination to marry cousins was partially to ease strains by pairing off those already accustomed to familial styles of compromise and concession. The intimacy of brothers and sisters, the collaboration of brothers (though competitors themselves) against the rest of the world, the fear of the patriarch all conspired to make the blood-related members of the family unite in suspicion of the nonrelated male who married into the group. Because of the vitality that honor retained in Southern mores, the rivalry between the brothers and the newcomer could sometimes lead to fatal conclusions. Patricide, on the other hand, was the rarest of crimes in the Old South. In fact, affinal murders of any sort were well below the Yankee numbers. The South's other forms of aggression and lethal mayhem probably represented a displacement for troubles at home. As Mrs. Chesnut complained during a struggle in her family circle, "Wrangling rows, heart burnings, bitterness, envy, hatred, malice, unbrotherly love, family snarls, neighborhood strife, and ill blood" were common woes. "Everybody knows exactly where to put the knife," she concluded. But her language was entirely figurative. The real knives went into strangers' flesh.[32]

The right of personal discretion enabled a family to maintain an outward show of pride and reticence in the aftermath of intrafamily violence, even when everyone in the community knew about the incident. Most such violence centered around disputes between those within the blood-kin circle and nonrelatives who married into the group. In reporting such affairs, newspapers were very circumspect. Ofttimes the relationships of the parties were not even mentioned. When they were, the circumstances were treated gingerly. A duel, for instance, was fought between John G. Burton of Newberry District and Major John Partlow. The local South Carolina paper declared that "both these gentlemen married each other's sisters, and the difficulty which led to this fatal result is said to have originated in private affairs, of which the public should know nothing." Indeed, such was often the case. For instance, in the Townes family of Alabama there was constant trouble between Eliza's husband General John Blassingame and Sam Townes, who assaulted him with a cowhide whip because of alleged abuse of his sister. What really lay behind the fighting is not at all clear from the letters remaining. Likewise, Enoch Jackson of North Carolina undertook to whip his sister's husband. The intended victim and another brother, however, stood their ground and drew guns to drive him off. He killed them both. Again, the reasons for the dispute have not survived.[33]

Fortunately, criminal court records provide some insight into the patterns of intrafamilial violence and the moral confusions that arose in the community and in law because of the latitude given personal discretion. Men were expected to handle family matters without interference, but when a family war broke out the community itself was likely to be embroiled because it sometimes happened that many in the locale were related to one faction or the other, or both.

The case of Daniel Allen and Howell Huston of Greene County, Tennessee, indicates the problems of honor and status that were involved in brother-in-law confrontations. Allen, a supplier of feed for the seasonal hog-drives, had grown enormously prosperous by local standards. His barn and its contents at harvest were valued at $2,500 to $3,000. Well placed socially, Allen was suspected of having once killed a slave, but the crime was excused because, it was said, he was a man of "hasty and overruling passions"—something of a compliment among the Scots-Irish pioneers.

His brother-in-law Howell Houston, a poorer and much younger farmer, could not restrain his envy. Somehow he wheedled their alcoholic, widowed mother-in-law, Mrs. Baker, into transferring all her property to her daughter Polly, Houston's wife. Outraged, Allen went to court and had his mother-in-law declared "incompetent"; he then enlisted Mrs. Baker's only son to challenge in court another of Houston's manipulations. In retaliation Houston recruited his father's slave Edd, a professional arsonist. (Houston had previously lent him out to others with grudges in the area.) On the night of November 1, 1825, Allen's barn was ripped by gunpowder explosions. The flames shot up so high that they could be seen "for many miles around," in fact, all the way to Houston's place, where he and Edd, upon the slave's return, danced in glee at a riotous, hard-drinking corn-husking party. Allen and a posse of relatives approached the Houston house in the dark. Howell, drunk, yelled out, "Are you there you negro murdering son of a bitch?" Allen re-

plied with gunfire, but missed his target and instead struck Howell's brother James as he stepped out of the door. To avoid a family
feud from developing, Allen made his peace with the dying James,
who "put his arms" around his killer's "neck in a most affectionate
manner."[34]

Nevertheless, the Houstons were a powerful tribe. The jury
reached a verdict of guilty of manslaughter. The judge assigned
Allen the penalty of a branded *M* on "the Brawn of the thumb"
as well as six months in jail. The disgrace of incarceration and dis-
figurement, however minor, was unendurable to the Allen clan.
Their forces rallied, and petitions from his friends and kinspeople
reached Governor Sam Houston. Various prominent East Tennes-
seeans, including a former governor's son, added their weight to
Allen's cause. Sam Houston, though, refused to act. He said it was
a matter of principle—he had to be true to the Houston clan. By the
ordinary course of things Allen should have gained his reprieve,
since even the trial judge supported it. Within the community,
jurymen belonging to the Houston faction had voted guilty and
the others had deferred to them, expecting that a pardon would
eventually serve the same end as a verdict of innocent. Unhappily
for them, Houston's fortuitous occupancy of the governor's chair
had thrown the issue into confusion.

It was common opinion that family affairs of this kind did not
belong in court. When circumstances dictated that the community
should intervene as part of the legal system, there was consternation. Cousins and neighbors would have preferred not to entangle
themselves in family violence. Reluctance to become involved when
feuds of this kind developed was evident in another Tennessee case
between brothers-in-law. Peyton Randolph of Rutherford County
spread the word "much more than fifty times," said a neighbor, that
he would kill his brother-in-law Albert Keeble, Keeble's father, or
General William Brady, another brother-in-law in the Keeble family. Both Albert and his father were on the best of terms with Brady
but disliked Randolph's bullying manners. Randolph had come
from the famous Randolph line but had fared poorly, especially in
comparison with the prospering Keeble and Brady families. Brady

in particular deeply aroused his jealousy because Brady had a promising political career, having just been appointed inspector general of the state militia.

Catching Albert Keeble alone at his grocery one night, Randolph drunkenly rushed at him with a small knife. Keeble was prepared: he shot Randolph as the inebriated man plunged forward. When Randolph died after a few days, Keeble had to stand trial, and was found guilty of manslaughter.

Behind the affair was the same layer of unrecognized self-hatred that one often finds in the failed sons of the plantation South. Peyton Randolph, of course, would have denied it. As he lay dying, surrounded by watchful neighbors, he had told his son, then four years old, that like Hamilcar, son of Hannibal, he should "make war upon Rome, until Carthage, or Rome, should cease to exist." Nevertheless, the appeal to honor before the community could not hide the emptiness and incompleteness that the dying Randolph felt within. The community was being asked to judge status rivalries within a family as well as a case at law. But as in the Houston case, the result was ambiguity. The jury would have acquitted Keeble. The judge was probably a new, professionally minded jurist, eager to control juries long accustomed to wide discretion. Based on a narrow reading of the law, the judge refused to allow the jury to accept a plea of self-defense. As a result, citizens resorted to the customary means of redress: appeal to the governor. A petition of 394 signatures, the longest this writer has ever seen in such a case, attested to the Keeble faction's strength. Once again Governor Sam Houston refused a pardon, perhaps for the sake of his own consistency, in light of his position on the Houston-Allen case.[35]

Howell Houston and Peyton Randolph had sought to use force and community applause to hide their own anxieties about social declension inside and outside the family. But the jurors and others who were called upon to set matters aright failed to meet the situations boldly, first rendering a guilty verdict, then urging the governor to undo their handiwork. Family violence of this kind left neighbors and cousins very discomfited. It reminded them too much of their own family disputes. When personal honor was pitted against clan loyalty, the conflict endangered community consensus and exposed the dangers of relying on the right of self-assertiveness.

The final mode of policing the moral landscape was through the structure of English criminal justice, modified to some degree by American and Southern circumstances. First, criminal justice was useful as a means of formalizing punishments for blacks whose crimes were neither so petty that individual masters could handle punishment nor so threatening to the social order that the community felt obliged to act on its own. Second, the legal apparatus functioned to mediate between rich and poor, usually to the benefit of property holders but not so much so as to put at a permanent risk the credibility of justice itself.

Whites were ordinarily willing to place slave criminals in the hands of the law because the outcome was predictable: the protection of white order. Why, though, one slave was given a jury trial whereas another was mobbed—when they were charged with similar crimes—was probably a matter of chance, if that is the right term.

Sometimes slaves charged with crimes of atrocity received unusually fair trials, very often because the judges, prosecuting attorneys, and masters—sometimes men of singular independence—sought to strengthen the machinery of justice itself. The more cases that a court tried, the better served were its practitioners, struggling for place, profit, or higher professional standards. For instance, young attorney Charles C. Jones, Jr., of Liberty County, Georgia, applauded his father for having turned over a case of slave theft to the county circuit court rather than try the matter at the family plantation, Montevideo. As it happened, the senior Jones's slave Lucy was acquitted. "The power of the law is brought to bear," his son declared, "the slaves made to realize the fact of a misdemeanor committed, and a new element of mercy and forbearance impressed upon them."[36] He might have added that the example should have a salutary effect upon masters and also enlarge the scope of business for struggling, penurious attorneys in need of experience, public exposure, and the small but important fees.

Slave law was sanguinary in the extreme to begin with, but lucky was the slave who was given the privilege of a trial instead of the still more arbitrary vengeance of the community. In Southampton County, Virginia, in 1808, Charles Briggs's slave Dick raped his master's four-year-old daughter Sally, a barbarity that somehow ended up being dealt with in the courtroom rather than a lynching site. Sally's older sister Polly opened the kitchen door to see Dick holding the child, who was bleeding profusely down her legs. Polly cried out, "Good Lord mama Sally is ruin'd." The mother ran to the weeping child, who put her arms around her mother's neck and said that Dick had nearly killed her with a "chunk" of a log. Sixteen-year-old slave Davy had known beforehand of Dick's sexual interest in Sally and tried to appeal to Dick's common sense, saying that the child was too small for him. Dick had replied, "She is big enough." Davy, though, did not warn the parents, probably because he thought Dick was just talking. Dick was found guilty and hanged. In many such rape cases, though, masters took matters into their hands, for according to the ethic of honor there was no greater offense to white authority than the black spoliation of white womanhood, especially when the deed was done against a member of a proud household. As Polly had screamed in horror, her sister was ruined for life. Who would ever marry her—if Sally even recovered from the assault to live to maturity? In a North Carolina case of a black, aged fourteen, who raped a four-year-old, Thomas Maxwell, one of the prosecutor's witnesses and the owner of the defendant, swore that the child's mother had pronounced her daughter "ruined."[37] The term did not just mean physically and emotionally wounded, but socially as well. By no means were such cynical thoughts what was on the minds of parents who found their daughters in such distress. Even the cold phrasings of courtroom testimony convey the parents' grief. But the language of that day carried the weight of social as well as personal meaning when a word like "ruined" was used.

All too often, slaves believed guilty of malicious crimes—rape, murder, poisoning, sedition, and insurrection—were denied even the most perfunctory of trials. Castration and burning alive were common tortures. Bennett Barrow, in Louisiana, described how two runaways killed an old man, raped and whipped his "Daughter ('simple minded')," killed another owner, and kidnapped his wife and young child. The woman managed to leave a trail of cloth strips, and eventually rescuers tracked the fugitives down. The murderers were "Burned alive," but Barrow thought that "burning was even too good for them." When a similar incident took place in Chicot County, Arkansas, in 1857, Mr. May, a leading planter in the neighborhood, led a search party and found the gang of rapists and killers. The blacks in the gang were burned alive, but the posse merely shot the white man who was the ringleader in the tragic business.[38]

Slaves found guilty of horrifying felonies could sometimes find the paths of justice relatively fair, but only by contrast to mob action. Lawyers ordinarily did the best they could for their clients. They were thus faithful to the code of gentility whereby, as Robert E. Lee asserted (in a reference mentioned earlier), the weak enjoyed the largess and protection of the strong, against the popular will if need be. But in addition a stout defense, utilizing every option available under the law, assured the lawyer of notice, even if the outcome was foreordained. For instance, slave Elijah of Wilson County, Tennessee, had an attorney who sought a new trial on the grounds of a juryman's pretrial prejudice, the incompetence of several witnesses, and other motions typical of regular defense procedure. Such efforts showed considerable legal expertise, sound argument, and clever tactics.[39] But, as one would expect, attorneys for slaves were usually overruled and their clients hanged.

When passions cooled, communities frequently were divided after the trial of a slave facing death. Like people in any country, no matter how authoritarian, Southern whites, when they felt unthreatened, were not eager witnesses at another's execution. Elizabeth Kelly's Sam had raped her neighbor Elizabeth Swint, or so the latter claimed. The trial ran true to form, but before he was to hang, Elizabeth Swint, the accuser, died, and some members of the community remembered that years earlier she had charged another of Mrs. Kelly's slaves with the same offense, which had proved false and had been thrown out of court. The pair of women had had a long-standing feud. On this basis, petitioners urged clemency for Sam. The governor of North Carolina, however, refused to exercise his prerogative, and Sam died on the gallows. In Patrick County, Virginia, seventy residents pled for the life of slave Gabriel, doomed for an attempted rape of a fourteen-year-old girl who managed to escape him. The memorialists were, they said, "ignorant of the rigors of the law," and thought "the offense punishable by castration" alone, for which reasons they sought commutation from hanging to a severe whipping. In one instance, however, a judge on a slave rape case urged clemency, apparently so that the community could take the place of the orphan girl's "natural protector" to wreak "vengeance due such an offense in the blood of the perpetrator." Public feelings about horrific racial crimes could not easily be constrained within the formal structure of criminal justice, but the legal system did provide some defense for accused slaves against the more primitive emotions of the moment.[40]

In regard to whites, the administering of criminal law was much milder in effect and more flexible in response than when the exigencies of race control were at issue. Every element in white society was well represented: the rich, as judges and sometimes jury foremen; the middling ranks, as sheriffs, constables, magistrates, and younger attorneys; the yeomanry, as freeholding jurors and patrol leaders; and the poor, at times, as members of patrols, witnesses, informers, and active spectators at the trials. This arrangement was faithful to the nature of Southern life generally: a rigid rank-conscious placement of individuals, but a communal sense that provided for wide participation in rendering the final verdict. Eighteenth- and nineteenth-century England's correlation between a flexible but technically sanguinary legal tradition and a rural, hierarchical order resembled the Southern situation. "Let the civil authority learn," cautioned William Paley, the English philosopher and exponent of conservative sanctions, "that general opinion . . . ought always to be treated with deference, and managed with delicacy and circumspection." Every unexpected act of repression or reform by the ruling powers, he warned, "diminishes the stability of government" by undermining loyalty to custom. "Hence some absurdities are to be retained, and many small inconveniences endured" on behalf of making changelessness a sacred obligation.[41] What was true for Great Britain was also valid for the white South. The jury system was a poor man's "vote," his service on patrol was his passport to white fellowship, his presence at the courthouse spectacle was a contribution to civic improvement.

If the jury "ballot" was delivered with bias, that was the small inconvenience that richer folk had to pay for diffusion of class resentment. If the nonslaveholder on patrol abused slaves unjustly, the master had to hold his peace, for having patrols on duty was thought less cumbersome than calling out the militia, and was much thriftier than a paid constabulary. Moreover, the administration of criminal justice offered chances for the wealthier classes to exercise mercy on behalf of the lower, a cheaper and more gratifying mode than the dispensing of condescending charity, which reduced a poor white's honor. There was the fortuitous coupling of outrageously sanguinary laws on the books, derived from common law, with bountiful opportunities not to make use of them. Long before, Sir William Blackstone had boasted of the dual nature of English criminal law that provided lessons in "practical humanity." As a result of statutory severity, the "injured," he said, "through compassion, will often forbear to prosecute; juries, through compassion, will sometimes forget their oaths, and either acquit the guilty or mitigate the nature of the offence; and judges, through compassion, will respite one half of the convicts, and recommend them to royal mercy." Southern justice rested on the same principles, and largely for the same reasons: the retention of power in local hands, by which means the community and the grades of society could work out their own compromises and distributions of power without the interference of external and abstract principles of justice.[42] Loose construction of criminal law was quite compatible with strict construction of national law. Both preserved power at home.

The system worked well, given its social purpose. It took account of local circumstances. Also, it offered means to provide stern justice when excesses required severe suppression and enabled some crimes thought unthreatening—depradations against slaves, personal grudges, affrays, and the like—to go virtually unpunished. If the system made violence a personal more than a state concern, the result placed a premium upon male virtues, a gratification to all.

Appropriately, the Southern practitioners of law were the intelligentsia of community life, especially in the more isolated, rural settings. Conservative by its very nature, the law was much less unsettling than the church, which could, in "fanatical" hands, provoke all sorts of passionate disputes and unseemly radicalisms. Besides, everyone was subjected to legal discipline, whereas the various church denominations were not only divided among themselves but comprised a minority of Southern white people, at least until after the Civil War.

Judges usually enjoyed the highest respect—like Judge Thatcher in Mark Twain's *Tom Sawyer,* whose self-importance was only matched by the deference he commanded from those who admired him. By and large, the Southern jurist was exempted from the communal requirement to duel under provocation. Given the volatility of courtroom personalities, the fear of being shamed at court, this immunity was not to be lightly dismissed. Judge Shattuck of Mississippi, for instance, had the temerity to criticize a juror's impartiality in a bank case. The offended party called upon his friends and rushed the judge after the session ended. Luckily, several lawyers, led by state senator Spence Monroe Grayson, prevented Shattuck from "being lynched, by the very men who had called upon him to preside over them as their high judicial officer."[43] Such effronteries to the bench did not have public approval by any means.

Nevertheless, Southern judges had to be keenly aware of their mediating role. By and large, they adjusted sentences to fit the local mood—often toward mercy. After all, they too belonged to the community and could not ignore public feeling. "Judge O'Neal [*sic*] is very severe in his sentences . . . and is no favourite with the sessions folks," sighed Benjamin Perry, a young attorney of western South Carolina. O'Neall rendered decisions according to principle, not expediency. Perry liked Judge Gantt much better: "We always

make the point to try criminal cases before Gannt [*sic*] if possible."
There were three-score Gantts on the bench for every O'Neall.[44]

However, this does not for a moment signify that the law was
purely an exercise in futility, broken arbitrarily as village ruffians
or irate citizens deemed fit. Attorneys and judges functioned very
much as the keepers of a tradition. It was a tradition that was venerated by all ranks, but if one belonged to the ruling class of educated and wealthy men, one had to know something of its mysteries.
"Every citizen, who expects to take any position ought to know the
general principles of the laws," a Carolinian father advised his son,
for without such expertise "he will often find himself compelled to
sit and listen to conversation in which he can take no part."[45] It
must be remembered that judges and the attorneys who followed
them on circuit formed a fraternity of their own, and took enormous satisfaction in performing feats of erudition and finely turned
decision-making before the often awe-struck spectators at various
isolated courthouses.

Most circuits were dull affairs. Assault and battery made up the
bulk of criminal cases, with mayhem to enliven the scene once in a
while. But even minor fracases (minor at least to all but the principals) offered their moments of drama and dissent. In Davidson
County, North Carolina, a drunken young mountaineer named
William Tippett had bitten off a large piece of old Arthur Newsome's chin, almost plucked out his left eye, and grasped Newsome's
right eye with his other hand. A witness at the tavern scene reported that Tippett "felt the eyeball slip around his fingers," and
said with a laugh before the crowd watching that "he reckoned the
fire flew mightily" out of that eye. Indeed, the old man was left with
just one, badly injured, eye when the right one popped out some
days later. The little community was in an uproar when the judge
sentenced Tippett to lose his ears as punishment for the mayhem.
A long, half-literate petition from Tippett's kinsmen for remission
of the penalty quickly circulated. Newsome, they argued, was an
old rogue whom nobody liked. Tippett, on the other hand, was a
man in the prime of life. The governor, recognizing that the will of

the people should be heard, showed becoming mercy, writing on the back of the memorial, "Allowed to keep his Ears, 1827." The incident and the manner of its adjudication represented a grand exercise in the exchange of upper-class patronage for lower-class acceptance of a simple system of public order. The law was upheld, the judge's authority was not injured in the overturn, and the governor's elective chances in the neighborhood were considerably enhanced. The law was kept malleable and personal, more to accommodate the needs of consensus than to reform public morals. At the same time, something of the awesomeness of sanguinary penalties persisted. With governors' pardons to reconcile the factions in a community, the balance of order was reconfirmed.[46]

In the operation of the courts, criminal procedures led to the same result: the mitigation of harsh penalties and the expression of a family-centered community will. Ancient custom had always helped to ameliorate the severity of criminal statutes in Anglo-American law by permitting curious legal imperfections to impede and even reverse the wheels of court transactions. Only the *cognoscenti* were conversant in the lore of common law, ensuring that the upper classes and the ambitious parvenus welcomed to their midst retained control. Attorneys who knew their business could not only rescue the palpably guilty but also appear to observers as the most impressive of men, who had the best interests of their clients and their families at heart.

Reuben Davis of the Mississippi bar, a poor farmer's son who made good, explained how he rose to eminence on the basis of legal expertise. He recalled years later that "scarcely a case occurred in which the bill of indictment could not be quashed on account of some error in the organization of the court or action of the grand jury. I remember quashing more than eighty bills of indictment at one term of the court in Tishomingo County, by one motion." Davis, however, was not at all unique. In July 1834 lawyers of the caliber of Henry Foote, Felix Huston, or Seargent S. Prentiss would have noticed that a recent (1830) statute had confused Mississippi clerks of court, leading them to draw up improper jury lists. For six to nine months thereafter, lawyers throughout the state displayed unaccustomed genius by making motions to "challenge the array" or to "quash the *venire*" on the basis of the failures of tax assessors, sheriffs, and clerks to perform the complicated new rituals required for impaneling juries. More often than not, the judges presiding had no choice but to dismiss entire dockets, free prisoners, and require officials to straighten matters out before the following quarter's session. In some instances, prosecuting attorneys simply dropped charges; in others witnesses disappeared and a true bill could not be reintroduced.[47]

Such motions had always been legitimate, and enjoyed the full approval of Sir William Blackstone. His influence was felt not only by the Southern bench and bar but also by such legislative authors as those who drew up the original 1830 statute that had offered defense attorneys their moment to shine.

In the first such case to reach the Mississippi High Court of Errors and Appeals, the charge against Mercer Byrd, a free black, was dismissed in a celebrated trial for killing a white man. (Later he was reindicted, convicted, and hanged.) "The right of trial by jury," proclaimed the author of the high-court opinion, "stands so conspicuous in the Bill of Rights, and its value is so directly instrumental in the protection of life, liberty, and prosperity of the citizen, that I could not regard any legislation tending to impair it, as judicious."[48] Common law and American constitutional law were wholly compatible, in the view of Southern courts.

The Mississippi judgment, like most such readings of procedure, was a sophisticated, thorough, and well-presented document. This kind of legal exactitude and the seriousness with which common law was treated should not be dismissed as a sign of Southern legal incompetence or obsolescence. So long as the South was functioning on the basis of slavery, so long as its culture remained chiefly rural and ascriptive in orientation, the legal system was obliged to mirror stability. Within that framework there was much room for judicial mediocrity or worse, a mindless reliance upon old formularies, rather than innovation and efficiency. But exemplary judges like Thomas Ruffin of North Carolina and John Belton O'Neall of South Carolina found it possible to exhibit their considerable mental talents in much the way that Jonathan Edwards had done in defense of Calvinistic principles, sometimes transforming the old ways to suit current conditions. The law was brutal, the readings of it very often equally so. But if the "one-hoss shay" of Southern jurisprudence was about to collapse, it was not because of inner contradictions. Instead the old forms fell victim to the external forces of war, defeat, and, above all, the reforming measures of Yankees and freedmen in Reconstruction legislatures.

All the same, occasional rumblings of discontent did arise to remind prewar Southerners that the world was not static or backward-glancing. With some ease the western slave states adopted the use of penitentiaries. Virginia was an early seaboard model that legitimized this basically Northern reform. Such changes were possible because to Southerners everywhere it seemed wrong to administer corporal punishment to whites and so reduce them to the level of the disciplined slave. By the mid-1840s the transformation was virtually complete: prisons sprang up in the countryside to replace the stocks.[49] The new system had its own defects, quite apart from whether it could deliver the "rehabilitation" and conscience-stricken repentance that its advocates promised. Locking felons away meant that their wives and children were deprived of economic support. With the old ways, by contrast, a man with a cropped ear or a brand on his cheek could still plow a furrow. Moreover, he wore the sign of his disgrace for a lifetime, warning anyone who saw him what kind of fellow he was.

Yet the voice of a new era of conscience could even be heard in the Carolinas, though not so loudly that those states relinquished the older forms. In 1825 Nathaniel Green Cleary, sheriff of Charleston District, made an unusually forthright assault upon the old system. "Our Criminal Code," he wrote the South Carolina legislature, "stands before a patched, rusty and uncouth edifice," in which "feudal tyranny, superstitious cruelty, and sombrous ignorance of its remote origin" have free rein. He wondered if it was really necessary to require death for over fifty crimes. Branding and other "cruel" modes should be abolished, especially in an age "when the voice of religion and philanthropy has gone forth" to "denounce" such barbarisms, he argued. But Carolinian legislators, jurists, and other authorities made only minor changes in the sanguinary code during the antebellum years. In Delaware and North Carolina the same conservatism prevailed. In those states white men were still made to stand in the stocks and receive lashes, brandings, and other scarifications of the flesh until the latter third of the century.[50]

On occasion, the ancient prescriptions that allowed the indicted to escape any penalty, sanguinary or otherwise, came under community fire. Recourse to lynch law was the favored method of criminal code reform. The preference continued in force even after the penitentiary mode was made law—and in part precisely because it had been. Lynch law did informally what common law had once officially stipulated. Individual jury decisions also aroused popular resentment from time to time, but few were willing to tamper very much with the sacred authority of trial by peers (white, adult, male freeholders or taxpayers). In addition, jails were so notoriously cheap in construction and unrepaired that prisoners could often find their own means to escape and avoid penalty. But few relished the thought of paying higher taxes and subsidizing better pay for officials to assure a more efficient order of things. Poor surveillance of prisoners and old common-law devices helped to keep the lynch-law spirit alive. That spirit represented the voice of the community.

The appeal of the traditional system of criminal justice was simply its moral basis: the easily drawn distinctions between right and wrong. Each actor in the courtroom drama fitted himself to the appropriate role of righteousness or villainy. The criminal in the dock, as often as not, gratified all present by appearing as evil in countenance as the deed for which he was being tried. Ellis Thomas, a murderer in McMinn County, Tennessee, a jailkeeper reported, "has a scar on his throat occasioned by a Cut with a Knife from a man whom he assaulted beginning under the left ear & extending across the throat and . . . also a scar on the left cheek a piece having been let out and one on the Right cheek" from "the bursting of a gun" and "a halt in his walk" from a broken leg "which bulges considerably." Uriah Medlock, burglar, who escaped the gallows by breaking out of a Tennessee jail, and William Cobbs, murderer, both of Virginia, had a "down look." Horse-stealing Aaron Gladden's "downcast villainous look" was another typical example.[51]

Also, those who belonged to what might be called the roguish element often had speech difficulties: "speaks slow," "stutters," "Hectick Cough & a Whining voice Speaks through his nose and is fond of drinking." The latter reference was to a squat Mississippi killer named Solomon Morgan. (One historian has argued that stuttering was a frequently advertised mark of identification for runaway slaves. The defect was also often ascribed to white fugitives from justice.)[52] How gratifying it was that there should be so close a resemblance between shamelessness of character and the outward appearance of evil. Like one possessed of a black skin, the one-eyed, scar-pocked, inarticulate poor white did not have much of a chance. (The exceptions were those lucky enough to have juries packed with their kinsfolk.)

When a criminal's demeanor failed to match the nature of his offense, there was a tendency, familiar to all societies, to romanticize him. As a result, a handsome, manly countenance on an offender provoked considerable moral confusion. For instance, Alonzo Phelps, who had killed eight men, some of them fellow brigands, and robbed citizens on at least sixty occasions in a spree through Mississippi, was a most prepossessing candidate for the gallows. Henry S. Foote, his defense attorney, reported later that "his hair was blood-red," his complexion fair, unmarked, and bronzed from the outdoor life. He stood almost six feet tall and "was a muscular well-shaped man . . . evidently possessed of great vigor and activity." A lover of poetry (when caught he was reading Horace), Phelps thought of himself as something of a wilderness intellectual. He "admired the works of nature" and befriended "the widow and orphan," as he wrote Governor Hiram Runnels in 1834. Seargent S. Prentiss, for the prosecution, however, ably turned Phelps's outward appearance against him by describing the cowardliness of the defendant's midnight massacre of his colleagues in crime as they slept. Suddenly Phelps, as if feeling a need to betray himself, quivered "with convulsive agony" and muttered foul curses at the prosecutor reciting the litany of his crimes. Phelps's agitation excited the jury as much as Prentiss's speech. The verdict was guilty, and Judge Alexander Montgomery (whom we shall meet again) sentenced him to hang. Cheating the hangman, Phelps died in an attempted escape from prison.[53]

Such scenarios did more than reassure the populace that morality and justice dwelt in harmony. They reaffirmed the values of masculinity. Phelps, as Prentiss portrayed him, was renowned as the "Rob Roy" of Mississippi, an appellation that reflected the ambiguity of popular admiration for and fear of a villainous hero, as it were. Foote himself "could not help loving and admiring" his vicious client, he admitted. Nobility was possible in the worst of criminals; the charismatic appeal of virility was hard to deny. Nevertheless, the attorney destroyed the sixty-page autobiography that Phelps turned over to him for publication: Foote worried that Phelps's unabashed delight in murder might have an unhealthy impact upon young readers. Traditional morality, violations of which stirred fears of disaster, had to be vindicated, even if the attitude toward the criminal was sometimes deliciously ambivalent.[54]

Thus criminal justice served several social ends. First, it established the customary ground rules of public behavior, drawing and redrawing the uncertain boundaries between personal license and community need for order. Second, through the penal code (especially before 1830) it set the styles of physical punishment that men informally inflicted upon one another. Whether because of direct or indirect influence, mayhem by knife, fingers, and teeth declined as corporal legal punishments gave way to the penitentiary model.

As the formularies of honor in the way whites encountered whites declined, so too did legal penalties become more impersonal, less bloody. But these alterations were still rather minor compared with the power of the virile code. Mutilating punishments at law were quite compatible with Southern notions of sin and shame. Thomas Jefferson, for instance, required by his reformation of the Virginia laws that a husband who murdered "his wife, a parent his child, or a child his parent" be hanged and the body given to "Anatomists to be dissected." The humiliation of a corpse (like that attempted on Nathaniel Bacon's) assured the living that the culprit's remains would not rise whole on the Last Day of Judgment. Once a label was attached to the criminal, dead or alive, it could not be withdrawn, even on that final Day. Men engaged in personal assaults replicated that primitive rationale. They humiliated each other more often than they killed impersonally with bullets—the formality of a duel being a way to legitimize that gentry-class exception. Just as the corporal techniques of the constable were exercised upon the guilty one's back, so men used whips to avenge a personal wrong. Just as the courts decreed a facial mutilation, so men in personal conflict or in lynch action scarified the face and head—crown of honor and symbol, too, of shame. For instance, one of John Randolph's cousins who bore the same name sought to dishonor the Virginia senator by gouging his left eye out over some political dispute. (Randolph recovered.) Normally, however, it was the less educated ranks who took more delight in such insults to the head—from scalping Indians to knocking off hats. But they, after all, were also most often the objects of the ear-cropping criminal code.[55]

Third, Southern criminal practices ensured the dependence of local justice on neighborhood opinion. That consensus was ordinarily led by the gentry ranks, but all had the right to be heard. Planters occasionally found themselves at odds with the poor, but reconciliations were always possible through judicial permissiveness and executive pardon or commutation. More often, however, communities divided along ethical rather than strictly economic lines, especially in criminal slave cases. The benevolent element in the planter class sometimes sought amelioration of harsh punishments against slaves, but other planters, more sanguinary, and lesser slaveholders and poorer folk frequently demanded no weakening of white resolve to rule. Through the legal mechanisms that Southern justice provided, such divisions could be harmonized, or else time alone would heal the social scars.[56]

Whatever the outcome might be in any particular case, the moral focus was honor, and the reprisal for its violation was the opposite: the stigma of shame. As a result, there could not be much distinction between the legal and community forms of retribution. Common law and lynch law were ethically compatible. The first enabled the legal profession to represent traditional order, and the second conferred upon ordinary men the prerogative of ensuring that community values held ultimate sovereignty. The consequence was a fragile social equilibrium.

15

Policing Slave Society:
Insurrectionary Scares

Lynch law, vigilantism, and charivaris were the ultimate expressions of community will. They established the coercive lines between acceptable and unacceptable behavior for all members of the Southern social order. Most especially, these ancient rituals demarcated the separate spheres of racial life, but they also imposed upon the entire spectrum of Southern white ranks the ethical principles to which the consensus of a locale was dedicated: the integrity of family life and the rule of men over women, of "respectability" over the shameless, sometimes of the honor-conscious poor over the rich deviant. Within the rubric of lynch law the slave insurrectionary scare must be most carefully considered—a phenomenon that outlasted, under modification, the "domestic institution" itself. It may seem perverse to categorize the prosecution of the white South's most dreaded crime, black insurgency, as a facet of community action. But the standards of evidence used in court trials were so low, the means of obtaining damaging testimony so dubious, the impotence of constituted authority so evident, that insurrectionary prosecutions at law must be seen as a religious more than a normal criminal process. By such means individual slaves, and sometimes whites affiliated with them, were made sacrifices to a sacred concept of white supremacy. The rite was a celebration of white solidarity, the maintenance of which was reconfirmed by the very disorders and agitations accompanying these exercises in social control.

The issue here is not to decide once and for all whether insurrectionary panics were based upon authentic black conspiracies. The topic cannot be wholly set aside, but it is less relevant to the purposes at hand here than the use whites made of such affairs, real or imagined. For instance, there is no question that Nat Turner's bloody trail across Southampton County, Virginia, 1831, was not a figment of popular hysteria. Outside that southeastern corner of the state, however, scores and possibly hundreds of slaves were whipped, maimed, and killed by one form of justice or another, innocent though all of them were of complicity in the lonely undertaking of Turner and his small number of religiously guided associates.

Nor can there be any doubt that "maroons" or bands of runaways roamed the more isolated reaches of the South, proudly independent of white authority. However, they seldom hoped for more than survival in liberty for themselves, and were not engaged in enlisting others to general rebellion. No condescension is intended in calling them brigands. To endure they had to make forays against solitary plantations, rob travelers, and collaborate, even intermarry, with Indians. They were thought a menace, but Southerners did not consider them guerrillas at war with slavery as such. Their aims were not so lofty. Mrs. Rachel O'Connor reported, for instance, that some runaways robbed Mrs. Pierre's house in 1829. The neighbors in the St. Francisville, Louisiana, vicinity were incensed, and a planter recruited the help of a young slave, who gave information about who the thieves were. Learning of the arrangement, the runaways returned, caught the boy, and "cut his legs and arms off and then pulled out his eyes." He died from loss of blood. The band, it turned out, consisted of twenty-four men, but within a few days a posse of a hundred mounted whites killed eight or ten and dispersed the rest. Incipient revolts could well have sprung from such groups, but trial records do not reveal much connection between outlaw slaves and blacks charged with insurrectionary conspiracies, who were almost always free blacks, black artisans, and domestic slaves.[1]

Under these circumstances slave rebellions, as whites perceived the threat, were much more significant as an abstract, awesome danger from within than an ever-present reality of small parties of runaways and outlaws. Eugene D. Genovese has explained the dynamics of white-black relations generally and has argued that most blacks realistically appraised their situation. Successful insurgency, they knew, was problematic because of the ubiquity of white observers, on and off the plantation; the unfavorable geography, which limited places of refuge and defense to inhospitable swamps and wilderness; the relative inaccessibility of firearms; the lack of a common tongue among imported Africans in which to communicate without risk of white comprehension; and the fear of reprisals against families and friends. These and other factors distinguished North American slave life from the much more volatile situations in the West Indies, Brazil, and Spanish America.[2]

Instead, slave resistance ordinarily took a much more personal and subtly orchestrated form, a mingling of resistance and reluctant, self-protective accommodation that was suited to survival and even a degree of limited autonomy, as Genovese has skillfully demonstrated.[3] Of course, the predominance of one form of resistance scarcely precluded others from taking root as well. Free blacks were more likely to have reading skills, knowledge of the larger world, and a degree of privacy and autonomy, all meaning that thoughts of insurgency could more easily mature into action. Such possibilities did not escape white notice. With every insurrectionary panic the cry went up that something drastic, including deportation, should be done about the free blacks, many of whom, it was noted, had white folks' blood running in their veins and quickening their resolve.[4]

In light of these factors, it may seem paradoxical that the ruling race did not live in constant dread of revolt from below. Instead, masters both early and late boasted of their freedom from such intolerable nightmares. William Byrd, for instance, wrote to an English correspondent in 1735, "Our negroes are not so numerous, or so enterprizing as to give us any apprehension or uneasiness," whereas those who presided over the "poor People of other countrys" had to live in fear. As antislavery criticism mounted in the nineteenth century, Southerners contrasted their lackadaisical habits with those of the wealthy up North. "New York," wrote Judge Thomas Jefferson Withers of South Carolina while on a visit there, "is vehemently exercised in devising laws to hobble the multitude" and provide "locks and bolts to secure the plunder of the few from daily nightly spoliation." He was sure that only in the South was there genuine security from revolution.[5]

Southern plantation dwellers did not live in fear of robbery, rape, or massacre. They left doors unlatched, windows open, gates ajar. Slaves freely roamed in and out of the "Big House" day and night, much to the wonderment of visiting Yankees and foreigners. Her first night in the slaveholding states, wrote Sarah Hicks Williams of New York, a young bride, "we slept in a room without a lock. Twice before we were up a waiting girl came into the room, and while I was dressing, she came to look at me," she said. The slaves "are in the parlor, in your room, and all over." Edmund Ruffin would have found her discomfiture amusing. Said he, "We all feel so secure, & are so free from all suspicion . . . that no care is taken for self-protection," a defiance of fate "incredible to northerners, who have to use every precaution to guard their houses from robberies, & who suppose that every slave in the South wants nothing but a safe opportunity to kill his master." Murder, he admitted, could not be ruled out. But it was rare enough "that no fear is entertained by the most timid of the whites." The consequence was, however, a "blameable & general neglect of all police regulations, & of means for defence against possible violence."[6]

How then was it possible for large-scale, well-educated planters, not ordinarily given to wild fancies, to forsake their usual equanimity and succumb to panic at the prospect, real or imagined, of black-led bloodbaths and the upturning of the social order, with the slaves the new masters, the masters the new slaves? The answer was that two alternating states of mind—apathy and horror—each provided the context for the other. In that fairly institutionless society there was no feeling of permanent mastery of events; instead there were periodic, almost cyclical rallies of white solidarity quickly organized to reassert traditional values, then a lapsing back into somnolence as the fears faded. The slave insurrection scares were analogous to the heresy trials of the Reformation era, the anti-peasant outbreaks that produced the English Black Laws, or the "great fear of 1789," when France was convulsed with worries about vagabonds and rogues. Whether real or not (in Europe the upheavals often were authentic), these perceptions of social imbalance led to frantic demands for group conformity to the traditional moral values.[7] In the Southern situation, the obvious purpose was the allegiance demanded of all to white-race superiority and the obligation of all to ferret out those who threatened the social structure through secret malevolence. Whether there by self-selection, as rebel leaders, or by white scapegoating of innocents, blacks in the dock for conspiracy and treason were despised as symbols of all that was evil. Labeled deviants, they embodied what the community thought to be satanic design.

Obedience and even the semblance of affection were the first requirements of slave conduct; impudence was thought a prelude to insurgency. The method of testing these attributes in a public way was to create what one social scientist has called "degradation ceremonies," a term that has lately been applied to the corporal styles of early American legal punishment. By this means the black rebel became a visible and punishable sacrificial victim. He was the archetypal reverse image of the self-effacing "uncle" that whites liked to think was the ideal servant. Whatever the malefactor's former character might have been, he was thereafter the personification of unreliability, disorder, and nameless horror.[8]

The process took the form of mass ritual: the initial discovery of the plot, the arousal of public opinion to the danger, the naming of conspirators through informers and trials, the setting of penalties, sometimes reviews by state authorities, the final disposition of the prisoners, and the relaxation of agitation. The causes of the periodic explosions may be divided into three categories: general economic, social, and political conditions; the encroachments of slaves and free blacks into forbidden areas of autonomy; and the struggle for community preeminence between two factions within the white world—

a better-educated benevolent element and the more traditionalistic and hard-minded group, which was aided and sometimes controlled by the ordinarily less powerful yeomanry and small planters. One is easily tempted to reduce these rival groups to a simple dichotomy between rich and poor, but economic position alone did not make one man a friend to blacks and another an implacable enemy of the race.

The first set of conditions has been well explored in the historical literature and need only be sketched here. Downturns in the plantation economy often affected the degree of anxiety about the black populace. In 1802 Tidewater Virginia, southern Maryland, and eastern North Carolina, all with large slave populations, suffered from the disruptions of overseas trade arising out of the Napoleonic wars, a state of affairs repeated during the scares of 1808, 1811, and 1812. At the time of the Denmark Vesey plot in South Carolina in 1822, similar economic difficulties appeared. A depression that began in 1819 grew worse in the early 1820s as cotton yields declined precipitously from soil exhaustion. Thousands of planters and farmers migrated west, successfully competing on world markets with their eastern relatives. On a more local level, in 1835 Madison County, Mississippi, was peculiarly aroused to slave dangers, owing in part to the fragile state of the local economy, which was lagging behind more prosperous nearby counties.

Political problems at home and abroad also vexed whites, leading to panics, especially in heavily slave-populated areas. In 1800, 1802, 1808, 1811, and 1812, fears of possible invasion by English and French marauders along the coast and disturbing news of racial struggles in Santo Domingo, Gaudeloupe, and Domenica; in 1822 and 1831, the rise of Northern abolitionist sentiment during the Vesey and Turner tragedies; in 1835, the abolitionists' postal campaign, with widespread anti-insurrectionary reactions. When the Republicans fielded their first national candidate in the 1856 elections, their campaign provoked rumors of an upcoming Christmas rebellion. There was an obvious connection between antislave panics and John Brown's Raid in 1859, and Lincoln's campaign and election in 1860.[9]

The connection of politics and economic and social frustrations to antiblack hysteria continued strong in the postwar era. Insurrectionary plots were uncovered even after emancipation, most notably at Christmas 1865. The last judicial "lynching" for alleged plans for rebellion occurred in Choctaw County, Alabama, in 1881. The paraphernalia of forged documents, a frequent prop in these affairs, helped to convict Jack Turner, a courageous black Republican leader. He was hanged immediately after the trial judge pronounced sentence. But ordinarily, postwar anti-insurgent activity had to adapt to new conditions: the less sanguinary criminal code meant the transference of repressive justice from the courts to lynch law, and the substitution of such charges as rape or impudence for the older one of conspiracy. Nevertheless, the patterns were otherwise similar and devoted to the same ends: the political repression of blacks and the prevention of other whites, at home or elsewhere, from allying with them. Hence in the 1890s lynching activity rose and fell in various localities with the success or decline of Populist party biracial campaigning, most notably in Louisiana.[10]

The second and much less historically visible factor leading to white frenzy was the advance of slaves in ways difficult to halt either by law or everyday custom. Black and white struggles over slave autonomy never ceased. Masters often wearied of trying to impose their will on every occasion that reached their notice. As Genovese and others have shown, slaves in field and kitchen were shrewd observers of "ole massa" and knew how to exploit his grave weaknesses, largely in answer to their grim exploitation at "ole massa's" hands. The irate owner, in helpless fury, could use the whip unmercifully—but mostly with counterproductive results. As John Blassingame has observed, under such conditions slaves became indifferent and worked less effectively than ever before, and some even risked their lives in open confrontations.[11]

On the other hand, tolerant masters watched impotently as each new privilege begged for and granted, at once became plantation tradition and the precedent for further requests. Moses Ashley Curtis of Wilmington, North Carolina, posed these thoughts in his diary as the Nat Turner uprising and subsequent scare unfolded: "No class of beings I ever heard of take such vile advantage of favors as blacks. . . . The faithfulness of a servant who at first brushed my boots as regularly as I took them off was rewarded by occasional donations," for example. But when Curtis tired of offering the gratuity, he discovered that "now I cannot get my boots brushed once a month without issuing an order to that purpose." To neglect strict, undeviating discipline, he advised himself, led directly to poor performance, then to resentment upon correction, and finally to insurrection. Curtis was not at all surprised to hear that Turner had had an indulgent master.[12]

But what Curtis described was a relatively minor infraction, the sort of thing slaveholders took endless pleasure in complaining about to their friends. Far more serious were the perceived signs of a different spirit among blacks. Just as a plantation owner or manager could not hope to regulate every movement and habit of every slave, so much less was white society able to govern the social demeanor of so large a portion of the population. Acts of personal deference—the doffing of the cap, the intoning of the right greeting, the required downward glance, the appropriately modest attire, the lively gait in response to a patroller's order—these were the signals that all was well in the best of worlds. But a glum stare, a brusque reply to a question, a reluctant move—such gestures in face-to-face encounter raised instant worries. Frank Carr of Williamsburg, Virginia, during one scare, wrote a friend that the inhabitants were sure of an incipient revolt. A suspected conspirator, Carr explained, had "addressed Thomas W. Maury in the street yesterday evening" in so rude a fashion that there was "not the smallest grounds for doubting that an insurrection was in agitation." The problem was not, of course, the bad manners per se, but the feeling that whites were helpless to prevent blacks from moving out of accustomed patterns of behavior.[13]

The way slaves dressed could also induce suspicions of the direst sort. According to a black observer writing in New York in 1850 about the Vesey plot of 1822, one young master brought two slaves into court on suspicion of being conspirators. The pair were dressed in their "country rags" and exhibited manners befitting field hands.

The magistrates dismissed them as obviously innocent. Later the same hands, washed and dressed in city clothes, were again brought before the magistrates, who at once "pronounced these very men participants in a scheme of the contemplated conspiracy." However, this sort of protest against kangaroo-court proceedings—for that was the master's purpose in reclothing the two—usually occurred much later in the panic cycle. To have done the trick when fears ran highest would have jeopardized the master himself; he might have been accused of complicity in the slave plot. But as the scare ran its course, detection of false witnesses and other ways of slowing down the slaughter became important. At some point whites had to recognize that the machinery of persecution was beginning to injure the economy.[14]

Black religious advances aroused considerable resentment, too, especially among nonchurchgoing planter and yeoman elements. The intrusion of Christian principles among whites was bad enough. In an attempt at satire Bennet Barrow of Louisiana had painted the "nick Bone of a horse" (the rear end) to look like "a Priest or Preacher praying." He placed the object in the parlor, but kinsfolk did not approve because, he scoffed, they and others had come to "think that a man can't be honest unless a professor of Religion—in other words a church goer, Bah!" Dismayed by the rise of Bible-toting planters, men like Barrow had little sympathy for neighboring do-gooders who sought to advance black religious interests. Thus a planter told Frederick L. Olmsted how a controversy had broken out between a local churchgoing group and those who worked their hands on Sunday. The benevolent faction had started a church at the Louisiana schoolhouse and "made their negroes go to meeting." At the next gathering of the school trustees, the majority voted to deny the facilities to the church. Otherwise, the hardliners maintained, rebelliousness might spring up among the slaves who had to work on Sundays instead of sitting all day hearing sermons and singing hymns. Almost every insurrectionary scare featured complaints about black preachers, especially free ones. "I am convinced that the negro preachers are more dangerous than any other description of blacks," wrote Richard W. Byrd of Smithfield to Virginia Governor John Tyler during the 1810 panic.[15]

In retaliation pious slaveholders would point to the liquor-law violations encouraged by drink-treating masters. "The Saturnalia of the Christmas and other holidays should be suppressed," wrote Calvin Jones to Governor Montfort Stokes of North Carolina in 1830. "Selling spiritous liquors to negroes and permitting their assemblys at musters, elections and other places where they acquire insolence and audacity, should be provided against." But owners had the right to run their places as they liked, and even black tavern-going was hard to stop in a routine way.

Sometimes efforts to control black leisure time figured directly in the insurrection panic itself. In 1810 or 1811 a group of slaves in Georgia bought "a can of grog" and drank it in a garret. As a mounted militia detachment approached on an anti-insurgent mission, one of the hidden slaves drunkenly sounded a bugle, with "electrical effect" upon the troops, who were riding past the site where the slaves were drinking. They caught and whipped a member of the group until he confessed to being part of an insurrectionary plot and named as its leader Billy, a slave belonging to a Captain Key. (His captors probably demanded Billy's name from the frightened prisoner.) At the time, Key was hosting William Johnson, a United States Supreme Court justice. (He recalled the incident for the edification of the panic-stricken citizens of Charleston during the Vesey plot.) Not only was slave Billy in dire trouble but so, though to a much lesser degree, were his owner and the tavern-keeper who had dispensed the whiskey. Billy was hurriedly hanged as the ringleader of an insurrection that was allegedly to be launched by the horn-blowing. The magistrates feared that if they delayed the execution Billy's master and his distinguished guest would gain a pardon for Billy from the Georgia governor. Key's slaves were known to be independent-minded because of their master's deviantly kind treatment, and Billy, "a very worthy fellow," as William Johnson later said, was a prime target for punishment: he was a blacksmith, earning extra money with his skill. The "evidence" in the trial was a bugle, dusty and full of cobwebs, that had been found in Billy's cabin where he and his family lay asleep until he was abruptly awakened to answer the charges. Once the "culprit" was found and punished the community returned to its ordinary repose. Thus, slackness of race discipline, whether in the form of unsupervised tavern-going or permissiveness about black autonomy at work, was part of the anti-insurrection ritual. (Needless to say, Johnson's story, published in 1822, did not have the effect that the justice desired. He had publicized his skepticism too soon in the cycle.)[16]

The white men's objectives in such instances were probably gained for the time being. No doubt for several weeks after Billy's hanging, slaves did not turn up at the local grog shops on Saturday afternoons. Likewise, there was a noticeable change in black habits during and after the Vesey plot frenzy. Following the execution of six Vesey conspirators in the summer of 1822, there was "a wonderful degree of politeness shown to us," a white Charlestonian boasted, "bows and politeness, and—give way for the gentlemen and ladies, met you at every turn and corner." For the citizens of Charleston it was a great relief to see blacks smile deferentially and laugh softly. The world was once again as it should be.[17]

Perhaps the repression of potential revolt was really aimed at achieving just this: the outward appearance of black submissiveness and the restored sense of security arising from white consensus. In addition, the process of repression served to break up any motions toward black unity under a body of leaders like Nat Turner and potentially dangerous figures like Billy, whose self-possession had been interpreted as an unmistakable sign of incorrigibility and "impudence." Several facets of the insurrectionary pattern suggest this reading: first, the curiously self-conscious actions and reports made by those seeking out the guilty parties, and the mixture of skepticism and belief that both slaves and masters exhibited; second, the clear distinction made between the supposed crimes of rebellion and actual offenses committed by slaves, so that seldom was a slave's killing of a master seen as a conspiratorial act but rather as merely a discrete felony; and third, the way in which antiblack zeal would eventually begin to decline so that everyone in the slaveholding society could return to their normal pursuits without further disruptions.

The initial alarm aroused almost universal fright. The rallying of whites extended from the governor to the lowliest woodchopper. Rumors flew about that black bands, numbering in the scores, even hundreds, were fanning out in all directions. Messengers galloped hither and yon to warn villages of approaching rebels. Invariably the rumors proved false—but no matter, an explanation was ready to hand. Black informers, it always turned out, had luckily alerted the white people to their impending doom, days or just hours beforehand, and the ringleaders were now safely in jail, the others having melted into the shadows. Yet everyone was warned to stay vigilant, no matter how normally the slaves were behaving in the quarters and fields. As one militia officer wrote Benjamin Williams of North Carolina, the neighborhood was particularly quiet, but "we still keep a strick patrole [*sic*]." During the same scare in Virginia, a militia general informed James Monroe that those in his district "can give no good reason for their fears" but "they appear fully satisfied that some attempt will be made by the Blacks."[18] Actually, of course, the situation was the reverse, with whites the first to attack.

Complicating the situation was the fact that slaves themselves both hoped the white fears were justified and also feared that they might be mistaken for conspirators. As a result, rumors spread as quickly through the plantation slave quarters as they did at the courthouse and in the parlors of white residents. Fired by whiskey as well as by the rumors of slave conspiracy, Toney, a slave of Halifax County, North Carolina, for instance, muttered a few slurs against the whites and was promptly hustled off to jail for conspiracy. He was sentenced to hang. (A juryman admitted that only during "such a clammer [*sic*]" would Toney's offense have warranted so severe a punishment.) Likewise, a slave called Leggett's Sam in nearby Bertie County, North Carolina, heard talk of how Virginia slaves had begun to rise. Though fellow slaves warned him of the dangers, Sam spread the news, thinking, said one slave witness, that "them guns we heard was in Virginia"; actually the sound was the firing of Carolina patrollers, not of slave insurgents. Sam grew so excited by all the drama around him that he told the slaves that he would raise up a band himself: "If I can git a great many to join me which I will try to do then I will let you all know I have a gun. . . ." But if Sam could not find a gun, he said, then he would "try clubs & if theay [sic] wont do I will try to lay stuff at the Doors." His actual rebellion, sadly, turned out to consist of nothing more than the spreading of conjure powders, a sure sign of impotence compared with the military superiority of the enemy. Fellow slaves turned Sam over to the authorities—to save themselves from the magistrates who soon sent him to the grave.[19]

More often than not, the initiating factor in the majority of panics was the work of whites who claimed to have overheard blacks cursing whites and making plots or who had slaves whipped into making such confession because of their apparent insolence or misdeeds. Women, boys, poor whites—people at every level of white society, rich or poor, eminent or obscure—were involved. In 1830, for instance, Mrs. Lewis, the wife of a jailkeeper in Edenton, North Carolina, reported to John Burgwyn, a prominent planter and magistrate, that she had heard black prisoners talking of reprisals upon the white race. Burgwyn, however, discounted the rumor, and the local panic it had provoked subsided. In 1821 Mrs. Frances McDougle reported that she had heard an old white man with "red whiskers" talking to a vegetable seller, an "old tall black negroe man who walked lame," and that the pair had been muttering about the basic equality of the races, before dispersing at three in the morning outside her hotel-room window in Richmond. She admitted to being hard of hearing, and nothing much came of the matter.[20]

In Mississippi, however, Mrs. Latham, a wealthy widow of Beattie's Bluff, Madison County, had tragic success with her alarm. For weeks before the Fourth of July, 1835, rumors of a revolt sputtered and died out. Then several days before the holiday "gentlemen" of the county traced the stories to Mrs. Latham. In an interview she said that the clue was the unaccustomed disobedience and impudence of her house servants. She said she had heard one of the girls say "that she was tired of waiting on the *white folks* and wanted to be her own mistress the balance of her days, and clean up her own house." A genuine, full-scale frenzy was soon underway. It quickly became entangled with the antigambling crusade across the state at Vicksburg and Natchez and with the fright over John A. Murrell's imagined gang of horse and Negro stealers, "abolitionists" in the guise of Thompsonian "steam-doctors" (medical quacks), and other itinerants and transient strangers. On the other hand, in 1829 two white Virginia blacksmith apprentices claimed to have overheard a conversation about insurrection among slave workers at the forge. The neighbors, however, were not in the right spirit for an antislave witchhunt and decided that the trouble lay in a personal controversy between the white and black crews at the forge. No one was tortured or hanged, in stark contrast to the events that Mrs. Latham helped to spark in Mississippi.[21]

There can be no question but that slaves were constantly seeking ways to expand their horizons and, in frustration, risking their lives by talking about insurrections. They well knew, especially after the Santo Domingo revolution and the Turner affair, that not only was freedom a possibility some time in the future but whites elsewhere in the world were protesting their thralldom. White patrols, panics, and intrusions all suggested to them the vulnerability of the Southern scheme of things, but were also the short-term obstacles against internal revolt. Talk was easy, action militarily impossible. Some intrepid spirits—Gabriel and Denmark Vesey, and, of course, Nat Turner—did initiate plots, but even so, these attempts only fed into the massive witchhunts that whites organized. The situation was much more complex, much more subtle than historians, with some exceptions, have so far realized.

Slaves and free blacks hoped that the rumors were true. So obvious was the connection between black excitability about the prospect of liberty and white fear of it that sometimes slaveholders themselves recognized the circumstances. In Hanover County, Virginia, in 1802, slaves Glasgow and Tom came to trial on the strength of an alleged conversation: James, a mulatto slave belonging to Benjamin Oliver, testified that he had heard Tom declare, "You know our masters are very bad to us," and had urged James to join in a fight against the oppressors. Testimony at the trial indicated that Colonel Bathhurst Jones and others on militia patrol had caught James out without a pass. To escape punishment, James had explained that he had just left Glasgow and Tom at the tavern kitchen (Tom belonged to Mrs. Paul Thilman, a widow who ran the neighborhood tavern) because they were planning revolt and he was off to report it to the authorities. Although Tom and Glasgow were at most only guilty of making some casual remarks, thanks to James's quick-witted alibi for his own infraction the two were sentenced to hang. The Thilman family had a curiously unfortunate record; they had already lost slaves in the Gabriel frenzy two years before. In the meantime the husband had died, and his wife was struggling hard to pay off old debts. The loss of Tom would have been especially disastrous, since he was an excellent cook and brought the tavern lots of business. The better element prayed that Governor Monroe would pardon the pair on the grounds that James, the informer, was a "notorious bad character" anyhow, forever running off when it suited him. A petition for Tom read:

> We are convinced from recent circumstances that when a meeting hap[p]ens among this description of people that they hold conversation relative to what hath not only already happened, but what may hereafter come to pass, without having a real intention of put[t]ing the same into Execution. This has lately been the case in the County of King William, where a number were taken up & tried, though nothing could be made to appear sufficient to affect their lives. We have no doubt but a conversation was had among those two slaves [Tom & Glasgow] and the Witness [James] relating to something about an insurrection; but the Witness being also a slave, not without his faults, and perhaps the first who mentioned the subject which might lead to their conversation.

In this case, special circumstances worked in favor of the accused. The petitioners, one may surmise, were Mrs. Thilman's friends and creditors, concerned lest she be bankrupted by the troubles. Their pleas were heard, largely because the whole community had cooled off by the time the petitioners launched their efforts. Had there been much opposition to clemency, however, Tom and Glasgow would have hanged. As it was, the community took pity on the slaves and on a woman who might have added to the tax bill if forced to go on the county.[22]

Even at the height of an insurrectionary scare there were occasional doubting Thomases whose voices of complaint about the kangaroo-court proceedings nettled the inquisitors. During the Turner uprising John C. Cabell and John Hartwell Cocke, a retired militia general, earnest evangelical temperance leader, and friend of Thomas Jefferson, bluntly denounced the uproar that the episode had inflamed throughout the state. "We have frequent & no doubt exaggerated reports about discoveries of hostile designs among the negroes, in so much that the white females in this neighborhood, can scarcely sleep at all at night," Cabell wrote Cocke. As a precaution, however, he advised that white ferrymen take the posts of the slave boatmen, to reduce the means of transcounty communication. Cocke, on the other hand, was even more disbelieving, replying to Cabell that an attorney from Petersburg and another friend in Surry County had told him that slaves executed there for conspiracy were totally "innocent," and had known nothing of events farther to the southeast. As for Cabell's plan, "how would it answer to provide by law" that a white should occupy every boat, Cocke asked, in light of "the present State of our miserable navigation" of the rivers? Whites simply would not take the jobs. Cocke advised another course: the education of the public to ignore false, malicious rumors.[23]

The Rev. Moses Ashley Curtis also found the situation much exaggerated near Wilmington, North Carolina, far from the scenes at Southampton. His wife's younger sister, he said, returned from a neighbor's house "sat down, rose—sighed—clasped her hands behind her neck—went out & called to me." She reported that "an express has come" from Wilmington "saying that 200 blacks are within 20 miles," but Curtis dismissed the news and told her to go to bed. Soon, however, he watched as women carrying "trinkets & mattresses" headed for the garrison. Within an hour a hundred and twenty screaming children and hysterical women were sweltering in the tiny, odiferous guardhouse and "under the muzzles of the great cannon in the fort." The next morning, after nothing happened, they all trooped back, somewhat the happier for the fine gathering, though they had had to soothe "their noses with cologne, honey & lavender waters." The whole business was the "silliest" sight he had ever seen, Curtis concluded. Likewise, a wealthy planter in Tennessee exclaimed in 1856, "We are trying our best in Davidson County to produce a negro insurrection, without the slighest aid from the negroes themselves. . . . There is in sober seriousness no shadow of foundation for any belief of domestic plot in insurrection."[24]

For those in official positions the uproar presented the opportunity to display heroism, civic activity, and bureaucratic efficiency. At first militia generals were delighted to have a reason to call out the troops, inspect their military polish, and count the arsenal weaponry. All too often, the militia armaments turned out to have been lost or to have fallen into thorough disrepair, and governors found themselves overwhelmed with requests for fresh supplies of muskets. Thus insurrection scares served the needs of many in a material way, as the clamor itself attested. In fact, in 1856 General Cocke of Virginia was sure that the uproar in that year was owing to the designs of "petty politicians" and others who found some advantage in creating havoc among the slaves. In 1800, the same circumstances took shape around the panic of that year, with officers and politicians lamenting the poor state of defense against insurgency and the need for greater expenditures and new promotions in the military to meet the crisis. Governor James Monroe, a parsimonious executive in ordinary times, reported to the legislature that $10,000 had been expended on new armaments during the Gabriel insurrectionary repression.[25]

The distribution of supplies afforded militia officers and state authorities the chance to solidify political patronage with judicious, selective handouts. In addition, demands accelerated for the formation of new militia units, meaning that whites of uncertain social standing could have the chance to become officers. Such requests challenged the existing regimental commanders. In 1831, for instance, Captain John Price of Danville urged Virginia's Governor John Floyd not to commision Robert W. Williams to form a new company because Williams had just lost an election in the existing unit and was seeking the title through this other means. His troops, said Price, would be composed of the local scoundrels who thought the excitement would gain them free muskets. At the same time, Price himself asked for "75 stand of arms" for the "better informed and more respectable portion of the Town." During the same panic a citizen of Portsmouth, near Norfolk, Virginia, warned the governor that a "Mobb," both "inexperienced" and "undril[l]ed," sought commissions as a new unit, to be called the "Portsmouth grenadiers." Not only was the town already well equipped with regulars, the citizen confided, but the petitioners "would be pritty [*sic*] grenadiers" indeed: most of them "are scarcely five feet high."[26]

Despite these dramatic, if contentious, circumstances, officials felt the winds of contrary forces as the crisis extended from hours to weeks. James Monroe of Virginia (1800 and 1802), Benjamin Williams of North Carolina (1802), and Thomas Bennett of South Carolina (1822), for instance, all became aware during episodes in their respective states that the resources of government were being sorely stretched. Knowing that they would be held responsible for raising taxes after the frenzies subsided, they had a natural tendency to raise doubts about the panics as soon as it seemed feasible to do so without political risk. After several weeks of excitement, Monroe confided to President Thomas Jefferson that "the spirit of revolt" had become so subterranean that it could not be discovered, or else "the symptoms which we see are attributable to some other cause." Like all others involved, Monroe did not understand exactly what the social purposes of the panics were, but nevertheless suspected that something profound was shaking the society: "After all the attention which I have paid to the subject my mind still rests in suspense upon it."[27] Nevertheless, he, like other slave-state governors in such situations, urged his legislature to reform the militia and patrol systems, ponder the future of free blacks, and pass such measures as would eliminate or restrict black preaching, reading, and writing, and other supposed sources of risk. A more important part of the hidden agenda of the insurrectionary scares was the justification of existing race relations and the advancement of white institutional controls.

Although they were a significant part of the rationale behind the scares, mobilizations were costly. In North Carolina, Governor Williams met the needs of the hour with the customary recommendations for reform, but worried lest expenditures outrun the existing budget. When asked to supply arms to Camden County, he argued that all counties "should rest their safety on their own exertions and patriotism," instead of relying upon the state militia, which would necessarily burden all with "the great expence of taxation." In South Carolina, Thomas Bennett also followed the usual pattern in proposing new and harsher laws and improved constabulary efforts. But in contrary spirit he questioned the court procedures of the Vesey plot investigators. In a special message to the state legislature Bennett pointed out these departures from customary rules: star chamber secrecy at the Vesey trials; lack of rights of the accused to confront prosecution witnesses; mingling of prisoners together so that alibis and accusations were harmonized among the parties; and the ready acceptance of testimony of such slaves as Charles Drayton, whose "chilling depravity," Governor Bennett asserted, was obvious. Bennett, however, did sanction the use of torture and other means to "eviscerate the plot." Moreover, he had no doubts that the emergency was real enough. He alerted the federal authorities to the dangers. Though attempting to combine his scruples with stern measures for community defense, Bennett did not by any means escape severe public censure. Both he and Supreme Court Justice William Johnson, his brother-in-law, also a critic of the local inquisition, were suspected of dangerous tendencies. Once his gubernatorial term had ended several years were to pass before Bennett felt that his standing had improved enough that he could reenter political life in a serious way.[28]

Planters often agreed that "no doubt many innocent ones would suffer," as one of them wrote Justice Thomas Ruffin of North Carolina during the Nat Turner fright. Any forthright animadversions about a particular case, however, threw doubt on the critic's loyalty to community values. Politicians were most circumspect, but prudent men of all ranks held their tongues. Some self-assured individuals boldly spoke out regardless of consequences, a credit to their high sense of honor. For instance, Ruel Blake, owner of the slaves whom Mrs. Latham of Madison County, Mississippi, accused of evil designs, strenuously objected to the torture of one of his own blacksmith slaves. Suspicion turned at once on him, and he was accused of being a ringleader. He fled, but was caught and hanged, slaveholder though he was.[29]

In the Nat Turner tragedy young Edmund Ruffin, later a violent secessionist, nearly wrecked his own career by boldly defending an accused slave against local opinion. Some "fellows of the baser sort, who in times like these always rise to power & influence" had instigated false charges, and "community insanity" had pressed them forward, he fumed. The evidence "at any sober time would not have been deemed sufficient to convict a dog suspected of killing a sheep." Yet Ruffin was branded, for a time, a "favorer . . . of . . . midnight slayers of sleeping men, women and children." Likewise, in 1835, Patrick Sharkey of Hinds County, a leading slaveholder and cousin of Mississippi's Chief Justice William L. Sharkey, freed two whites who had been charged with conspiracy for lack of evidence. Madison County vigilantes were incensed and demanded that Sharkey be delivered to them for punishment. Even Chief Justice Sharkey had to concede the helplessness of the courts. Governor Runnels refused to act at all. Eventually, however, Patrick Sharkey escaped the lynch mob's noose.[30]

Less fortunate was James Allen, near Petersburg, Virginia, who was accused of harboring a suspected slave conspirator during the 1802 panic. Several low-class young men lashed him so relentlessly that "his body[,] his head[,] his legs[,] nay even his very feet" no longer were covered by enough skin to match "a nine pence." The culprits fled to Georgia and never appeared to stand trial for murder.[31]

These demands for conformity to community will were not the work of a planter class in control of events. If there was a slave-holders' hegemony, as some historians have claimed, these elaborate degradation ceremonies cast it temporarily aside. It did not serve rich men's interests to have mischief-makers take advantage of the uproar to make war on the propertied by destroying their most valuable possessions, their slaves, many of them highly trained. The high compensations given to masters for most slaves executed in the scares in Virginia and elsewhere attest to the slaves' economic worth. But wealthy masters, including governors, judges, and militia generals, were often impotent to prevent the losses. Sometimes as many as a score in a county were killed or maimed through lynch action and judicial process. For instance, during the Turner tragedy James Wright, a wealthy planter of Duplin County, North Carolina, found that a cavalry unit had crossed the state line from nearby Southampton County, Virginia, and was about to torture his slaves in order to obtain "confessions." Secretly, Wright urged the slaves to postpone the lashings by admitting complicity and thereby get themselves transferred into the custody of understanding local authorities. The plan worked for all except young Jerry, who told such a good story of a rebel plot that he alone was sentenced to hang. Some weeks later the defense attorney came to believe Jerry's explanation for his false confession, and managed to secure verification from the owner, then on a sickbed. The presiding judge, who was "no friend of the negro," supported the petition for pardon, and the governor agreed.[32] Jerry was quite lucky; few masters would have jeopardized their standing or their lives to save a slave. John H. Cocke, young Edmund Ruffin, and a few others had sufficient honor to meet the danger of public passion. Most planters did not.

Further evidence of the special character of the insurrection scare can be found in the disposition of regular slave criminal cases. If there were genuine revolts one would expect that in most instances the authorities would have regarded any murder or assault on a white as part of the current conspiracy or conspiracies under investigation. Such was not at all the case. In the midst of the frenzies the usual pattern of slave crime persisted. Although offenses included murders of malicious owners, all the careful preparations of evidence and common-law technicalities were observed, or challenged—quite in contrast to the slipshod, hasty insurrection trials. Also, memorials for convicted slaves on whom the community took pity arrived as usual at the governor's desk—at least in states with executive review of capital crimes, notably Virginia, Kentucky, North Carolina, and Tennessee. (Georgia, South Carolina, and Mississippi, however, had no such mandatory provision.) In Caroline County, Virginia, at the height of the panic in 1802, for example, neighbors petitioned for the reprieve of a slave named Cato. His elder brother Patrick had slain their master; Cato had merely helped to place the body under a fallen tree to make the axing appear accidental. The governor and executive council commuted Cato's sentence to life at the new state penitentiary.[33]

More curious was the case of Randall and Cudge of Isle of Wight County. They had quarreled with Reddick Godwin, their master, fired his gun at him, and then pelted with stones the upstairs bedroom in which Godwin locked himself. The governor and council reprieved them both from hanging, changing the sentence to sale and deportation. No doubt the spokesmen for the slaves conveyed orally some scandalous information about Godwin to the Richmond authorities, for the written record does not reveal why such rebellious behavior, in the midst of a supposed rebellion, should be treated so magnanimously. The show of mercy, though, was not unusual, suggesting that the insurrectionary scares were seen as something with a separate and quite deliberate rationale.[34]

The exception, however, was poisoning. Slaves accused of this crime were usually thought to be involved in a widespread scheme of insurgency because, like arson, poisoning was a crime of stealth which whites could neither control nor understand. Herb and conjure doctors, like preachers, were extremely suspect. Yet at the same time they were much in demand, not only for the customary love potions and vengeful tricks that members of both races sometimes sought to obtain, but also for medical healing. During a Kentucky scare in 1824, for instance, Sam, reputedly "skilled in 'necromancy, conjuration, and poisoning,' " was accused of murdering his master (who had been dead for seventeen years) and, more recently, "his two promising & lamented young masters," even though the local physician could explain the natural causes for all three fatalities. "Perhaps," observed a petitioner for Sam's life, "in no part of the world does so great prejudice prevail on the subject of negro poison as in this county. Every disease at all obscure & uncommon in its symptoms & fatal in its termination is immediately decided to be a case of negro-poison." Likewise, during the 1802 Virginia "witch-hunt" a slave named John belonging to John Hopson of Halifax County was accused of poisoning a Mrs. Lewis Ragsdale, one of his patients who had momentarily taken a turn for the worse. The "evidence" consisted of "palma-christal seeds, dirt-dauber nests, with dead spiders and snail shells" found in John's box of conjuring items. (The medicine had a double purpose, John professed. It could ease sore joints, and also was to be used by Mrs. Ragsdale's houseservant "to keep peace with" Mr. Ragsdale by blowing it at him and sprinkling it around the house.) Contrary to all rules of evidence, General Carrington, a physician named Dr. Walter Bennett, and others mixed these ingredients with powders from another source and fed it to a cat. The animal promptly died. After John was convicted and sentenced to die, William Faulkner, the county sheriff, and others were appalled to learn that John Hopson, the herb doctor's master, had pled for a gubernatorial reprieve for John. He had signed the affidavit in a neighboring county, whence he had had to flee because of the uproar. If the governor was bold enough to affront the community in this fashion, Faulkner wrote, he could not answer for the consequences, so determined was the prejudice of the people against poisoners. Passions, however, did eventually cool, and Monroe and colleagues, more courageous in this case than in many others, waived the death penalty and John was sold and deported. Dr. Bennett, the local white physician, however, was no doubt gratified to have his competition reduced by one conjure-man.[35]

The final aspect of the insurrectionary panic that suggested specific community purposes rather than authentic warfare between the races was the general pattern of the trials and the gradual emergence of a consensus in favor of a return to normality. Almost all cases of conspiracy shared common features. First, chief prosecution witnesses were predominantly fellow slaves, although whites participated in a secondary way, having initiated the proceedings. The reason was that by such means blacks were implicated in the destruction of their own leadership, sowing distrust, perplexity, and fear in the quarters. Second, prosecuting attorneys were seldom able to produce any paraphernalia attributable to planned revolt— firearm, pike, sword, incriminating letter, or coded message—directly associated with the accused. Such items were occasionally introduced. Some if not all of the letters were obviously forged, bearing spelling that conformed to white rather than black phonetics. "No weapons," declared Thomas Bennett, South Carolina governor during the Vesey episode, "(if we except thirteen hoop-poles) have been discovered; nor any testimony received but of six pikes, that such preparations were actually made." Six pikes for 5,000 alleged conspirators in South Carolina stretches modern credulity; even for sixty men it would not constitute much of an arsenal. Surely slave brigands or "maroons" ordinarily did better than these conspirators, if such they were.[36]

In this writer's opinion, no substantial evidence presentable in a modern court has appeared to show large stockpiles of arms in any aborted rebellion before the Civil War. Without such weaponry, how could plots have been put into execution? Yet in all these emergencies the exposers of conspiracy claimed to have acted just hours or days before the rising. With so many informers telling on fellow slaves, why would not at least one informer in the scores of uprisings have led his captors to such a hidden arsenal? The absence of evidence is always hard to prove. But surely, even given the crude quality of detective work in that era, the nonappearance of armaments would ordinarily have thrown doubt on whether there was intent to use any.[37]

Third, the damaging testimony was ordinarily an alleged conversation between the informer and the accused, usually without corroboration and often with contrary evidence offered by other slaves who testified to more plausible exchanges. These exchanges were generally so vague that prosecuting attorneys would have been laughed out of court under less compelling circumstances, just as Ruffin attested in his own experience. Fourth, the individual who named the conspirators was usually either severely tortured prior to the revelations or else imprisoned, isolated, demoralized, and deliberately drained emotionally to the point that he would comply with any suggestion offered. (The curious identification of the captive with menacing captors has become a psychological commonplace in recent years.) The slave "medium" who named the victims whom the inquisitors had preselected or who conjured up individuals from his own past to gratify the captors' wishes was the most pitiful victim of all in the degradation ceremony. Once the name was on the confessor's lips, it could not be retracted. Fifth, the confessors were almost always granted the reprieves they begged for as reward. Some received pensions. For such men, perjury was a small price to pay, especially after torture, for rewards ahead.

The most active "medium" for the 1802 rebellion was one Lewis, a runaway caught with a forged pass of his own making. Ability to read and write and a job as a ferryboatman made him a prime suspect. Twenty-four hours of unremitting scourging in the Nottoway County jail elicited from Lewis a detailed and far-reaching story of clandestine doings, though it bore suspicious resemblance to the public accounts of the Gabriel plot of two years before. For the next few months he traveled around the circuit with the judges and attorneys to help the prosecution of those already named. As ringleader he chose an old carpenter from Richmond named Arthur, whom he had not actually seen for nine years. The story that Lewis told of Arthur's plan to burn down Richmond was riddled with contradictions, but it impressed the Henrico court of magistrates. Arthur was to hang. Two white debtors and the warden of the penitentiary where Arthur was temporarily housed before execution were certain of his innocence, and other whites came forward, too. Eventually Arthur was pardoned by Governor Monroe and council, though some whom Lewis named were not so fortunate. Meantime, Lewis received travel expenses to return to his master.[38]

In response to this reading of the slave panic, it could be argued that a prejudiced selection of facts, quotations, and trial verdicts, taken out of context, has unjustly cast doubt upon what in fact was a genuine series of incipient rebellions. Prominent historians such as Herbert Aptheker and Eugene Genovese have approached the matter from quite an opposite point of view.[39] Ideological disagreements are bound to color any such discussion and in any case could not be resolved here. Nevertheless, it may help to offer a more detailed single example of the typical methods employed to convict an innocent slave, one whom Aptheker and others have named as one of the authentic plotters of the 1802 Virginia rebellion.

In this case, Will, a slave of Princess Anne County, accused three others of conspiracy, though only one of them, Jeremiah Cornick, a slave of Norfolk Borough, became the focus of popular tumult. The story Will told was a classic of brevity. On April 11, 1802, he claimed, Jerry Cornick and Walker's Ned, another Norfolk slave, had hailed him on a country road. As they walked, Jerry had turned to Will: "Wont you join us Will? in what said I, in Burning the [Norfolk] town on Easter Monday night, to which I reply'd I will have nothing to do with it in case worse befal[l] me, and Immediately left him and Ned together." Later on the same day, Will explained, he happened on another Ned, belonging to a Col. James Ingraham, and the same exchange took place.[40]

This singularly barren account, a contrast to Lewis's much more fulsome embroideries, triggered an unusual pattern of events: the pursuit of the true circumstances, undertaken by a gentleman of considerable integrity and boldness. The trial and conviction of Walker's Ned, but more especially the proceedings against Jerry

Cornick, aroused the skepticism of George McIntosh, a Scottish immigrant who had married into the powerful Walke and Cornick families of Princess Anne and had a sizable plantation near Lynnhaven on Cape Henry. He had known Jerry for many years as the slave of John Cornick, deceased, one of his wife's relatives. There is no indication that he had any pecuniary interest in Jerry's fate. Respected as a community leader, with his wife's uncle, Cornelius Calvert, on Monroe's executive council, McIntosh was a life-long Jeffersonian. As late as 1848 he was still true to the faith, lamenting the 1848 defeat of the Democratic nominee Lewis Cass and the victory of Zachary Taylor, the Whig candidate. McIntosh not only followed President Jefferson's political credo but also his concern for the precepts of gentility, the ones that insisted on due attention to the protection of the weak by those who had the means and morals to undertake the mission. McIntosh (like Faulkner's Gavin Stevens) understood the responsibilities of gentry rule and, judging from the quality of his thought and prose, he also had the requisite education and good sense to fulfill the old Stoic-humanist tradition regardless of popular opinion. Certainly, as a slaveholder himself and the proprietor of a gun and grocery store in Norfolk he had no quarrel with the institution of slavery as such. But loyalty to the institution had to be accompanied, he thought, by a solicitude for the defenseless. As a result, he undertook an exhaustive search for evidence of what actually occurred, retracing Jerry's steps on April 11, the date of the supposed rendezvous in the country. In every respect Jerry's alibi checked out, with whites and blacks alike verifying the account, though the whites refused to be placed on the witness stand or sign depositions. At no time had Jerry left the town, nor was he ever in the company of Will or Walker's Ned on that day.[41] According to other slaves, Ned and Will had not crossed paths for many months, though, by Jerry's admission, they had known each other for at least twenty-five years. (Jerry claimed that Will had always been a liar and villain.)

Some ten days after Jerry's quick conviction, McIntosh attended the trial of Ingraham's Ned, whom Will had claimed he had met alone later on April 11. McIntosh was surprised that Will's testi-

mony against the slave was word for word the same as that which he
had supplied against Jerry and Walker's Ned. Was it likely that
conversations held miles apart could be so curiously identical?
When asked about the matter after the trial, Will refused to reply.
When they had urged him to fire the town, McIntosh asked, did
Jerry or the others warn him to silence? No, Will replied. Surely
during a scare, with patrols everywhere, an insurrectionist would
demand such a pledge. McIntosh realized that something was very
much amiss. Moreover, Ingraham's Ned was acquitted. Six justices
of the peace were on the bench. Four voted guilty, but James Holt,
in handwriting to rival John Hancock's on the Declaration, declared him innocent. The presiding officer refused to vote at all,
since a single nay was sufficient to acquit. After the trial McIntosh
asked Holt why he had defied the majority. His reply was that Will
clearly was "a rogue" and Ned a victim of lies. Even the presiding
magistrate, who had refrained from voting, whispered that he
thought Will a liar, too. But he had spared himself the frowns, or
worse, of neighbors. To Monroe and council, McIntosh reported
the discrepancies between Jerry's conviction and Ned's acquittal,
both based on the very same testimony.[42]

In addition, McIntosh investigated the character and possible
motives of the confessor Will. In the Scotsman's opinion, the key to
the episode was Will's capture on April 17. Through interviews
with sundry people, he reconstructed events. Two whites, William
Boush (owner of twenty slaves) and a man named Jarvis, who had
been drinking very heavily, were walking along a road in Princess
Anne. They spied Will ahead of them. Jarvis observed that Will was
probably running away from John Floyd, a small farmer who had
hired him. Jarvis grabbed Will, calling him a "great rascal," in fact
"one of the sons of bitches" who had recently assembled near Norfolk for evil designs. Apparently there had been a black revival outside the town. Perhaps Jarvis had heard the unfamiliar sound of
Afro-American chanting and assumed that insurrection, not worship, was the purpose. In any event, Boush told his neighbor Mc-
Intosh later, Will had denied any wrongdoing, saying "I am shure
[*sic*] Mr. Jarvis you would not have me tell lies. . . ." Jarvis drunk-

enly kept saying, "You *must tell better than that*." Boush departed, and Jarvis escorted Will back to John Floyd's farm. There the two whites spent the rest of the afternoon drinking. Alternating threats of torture with promises to "let him loose," the pair wore down the slave's resistance as he stood tied to a tree nearby. Finally, by Floyd's admission to McIntosh, Will "sweat large drops for 15 minutes," and then told the story used for the prosecutions.[43]

Further inquiries revealed to McIntosh a clearer picture of what Jarvis was: an unskilled laborer who swilled down as much rum before breakfast as his supply of money could buy. According to the Norfolk court records, he loitered about the courthouse, where, one may be sure, he heard all the exciting news of insurrections and trials. The accounts fired his imagination. Otherwise, Jarvis had no means of making a mark in community life. A former employer thought him no more trustworthy than the lowliest slave in the county. Well might such a man seize the chance to swagger on the public stage. By identifying a plotter Jarvis could not only enhance his own soiled reputation but also contribute to community welfare. After all, society offered him no higher duty than slave patrolling, no chance for acclaim except the discovery of slave wrongdoing. McIntosh discovered that Jarvis had earlier tried to induce another slave to find out "something about the conspiracy," for which testimony the slave "ought to be [set] free." The master overheard the conversation and ordered Jarvis off his place.

Still more remarkable was the disposition of the case. First, McIntosh suffered the inconveniences that too often snuffed out the lantern of reason in such cases. Former friends shunned him in the street. Witnesses who had given him valuable information refused to cooperate in the slightest way. McIntosh complained that "men are afraid to speak or act as they ought, and at this moment I am told a petition is going about for Signatures praying the negroes to be hung, as if examples without public *conviction* of their *guilt* could tend in any way to the Public Good. . . ."[44]

At first Monroe and his council were inclined to accept McIntosh's reconstruction of events. They observed that, "even admitting the perfect credibility of Will," the death penalty was too sanguinary since "the guilt of the said slaves [Jerry and Walker's Ned] does not by any means appear to have been established." The council ordered temporary respites. John Cowper, mayor of Norfolk and presiding justice of the freeholders' court, received a demand for more proof. Cowper was outraged. "I am very much mortified to . . . state that" the executive's intercession "has produced much discontent," in fact, "almost universal discontent." The trial had been a model of equity, he said. Jerry's lawyer "made a most ingenious defence," and the prosecutor "barely expounded the law and summed up the evidence." Despite that advantage, Cowper continued, neither Jerry nor Walker's Ned had convinced a single justice or one citizen among the three hundred spectators that they were uninvolved in an Easter revolt. Furthermore, few were willing to sign McIntosh's petition for clemency for Jerry. Cowper proposed a reprieve for Walker's Ned as consolation, however, since he was "a character of simple cast" duped by his coconspirator. Monroe at once gave the second Ned the reprieve of sale and transportation.[45] For the Norfolk citizens, Ned was an insufficient symbol of the chaos that the social exigencies required.

The outcome was tragically predictable, given the nature of the Southern executive pardon as a ratification of community will. Lacking that public sympathy, Jerry had to die. Monroe did as the mayor insisted and no more respites were forthcoming. The convicted insurrectionary was hanged on June 1, 1802. Until the final hour he had protested his guiltlessness. When asked at the last moment about his crime, he said nothing. Presumably thoughts of his pain and agony over the previous days, of his wife and children, of the kindnesses received from McIntosh and his wife, who had comforted the grieving black family, occupied his last hours. Norfolk residents took his final silence as an admission of guilt. Yet as far as they were concerned he had contributed to the common welfare more in death than ever he had in life. "I have no doubt," exulted Cowper, "but this example will produce the effect that is wished."[46]

An anthropologist examining the insurrectionary phenomenon might well conclude that the purpose of the exercise was the restoration of order through the venting of the society's worst fears. By proclaiming that catastrophe was about to descend, the whites rallied to the banner of white supremacy and sought out victims over whom they could unmistakably triumph. Indeed, the chief result of the scares was the prevention of insurrections. By primitive but effective means, the frenzy reestablished proper race relationships, as whites defined them. In a sense, even the genuine cases of rebellion achieved this end, none being more helpful than Nat Turner's. Authentic and imagined uprisings provided the chance to display the power at white disposal. The subduing of potential rebels (real or not) reassured the dominant race that forcible, concerted means could handle any emergency. The paraphernalia of a judicial system—the county tribunals, the executive review, the sheriff's rope—were the stage props for a performance illustrating that sense of mastery. They were not the essence of the tragedy, but rather the liturgy by which slave society expressed the vitality, racial hierarchy, and oneness of white determination. Instead of signifying the strains of instability, insurrectionary upheavals demonstrated the unity of one race against the perpetually enforced disunity of another. Black was posed against black in these courtroom dramas, forced into betrayals that whites themselves manipulated.

Common interpretations of the ceremony were likewise imposed upon all whites, regardless of class or official position, forcing benevolent and indulgent masters and leaders to remember their duty to the community. By and large, those officials who carried out the will of the white constituency were, by the standards of the time, decent, honorable men. Governor Monroe, as respectable a gentleman as Virginia could produce, was an honest, humane member of the gentry class. If he had had his way, not a slave would have hanged at any time in the course of the 1802 rebellion. (The Gabriel revolt, however, may have had more serious origins in actual sedition and conspiracy.) As governor, and thus as representative of popular will, however, he had no options in the case of Jeremiah Cornick. If because of political misjudgment or a greater sense of integrity—neither of which the review process was designed to encourage—Monroe and the council had granted Jerry a reprieve, the citizens of Norfolk would have responded with a lynching, destroying not only Jerry but also the credibility and authority of the governor himself. In other words, executive defiance of local objectives would have led to instability, and to unsettling results—white perplexity and doubt.

These periodic, seemingly irrational explosions enabled masters and their families, and nonslaveholders and theirs, to express and then master their dread. Moreover, the scares offered a cheap means of public enforcement, one designed for a rural people underpoliced and fearful of taxation. After such an exhibition of white power there was no need to mount expensive guards, constabularies, and standing armies. Policing, like the legal system as a whole, remained rooted in the community. Thus the panics were "fire-bells in the night," as Jefferson once said of antislavery agitation. They were drills to test the whites' mettle and dedication. At the height of the scare, everyone became civic-minded—or else. Patrol captains meticulously followed regulations. Militiamen mustered without straggling. Even the county arsenal, for a while, was stocked with working muskets and shining sabers. It was all very reassuring and impressive to the unsophisticated. Once more the voice of inner terror was stilled.

Almost within days after the last black conspirator had been whipped or hanged, normal routines resumed. Established authorities seized the reins of power again. To them the loss of control of events had been disturbing, especially since the crisis seemed to implicate slaves of high value and loyalty. Planters gradually noticed that the white accusers often belonged to the class without slaves of their own. It was therefore good, most large planters felt, to see slaves returning quietly to the fields to harvest or plow instead of hiding in the woods to escape patrollers foraging for trouble. Even the common folk grew weary of long, dull patrol vigils. A young immigrant barkeeper in Norfolk, Virginia, complained to his father in Scotland at the close of the 1802 panic that he had had "to go out there and wait with my gun" from eight in the evening to five in the morning, before regular work, all during April and May. No wonder he missed muster roll in the summer, costing him a $40 fine. Besides, after Jerry hanged, he said, things had quieted down.[47]

Soon enough, as the Virginia experience between 1800 and 1802 suggested, the same old problems reappeared: quarrels on the muster field, sloppy patrol rounds, broken or misplaced firearms, and other signs of mischief and public lassitude that critics had thought the recent emergency would permanently cure. A resurgence of black encroachments on white regulations (inattentiveness, tavern-going, wearing of fancy clothes, Saturday afternoon horseplay in the village square), increases in masters' largess (indiscriminate pass privileges, unsupervised black church worship), and new symptoms of economic and political woes set the stage for the next panic. Then as the cycle began again the rich and poor, the townsman and countryman, the soldier and civilian, the drunk and sober rallied to the racial banner.

For such occasions, Southern society had to have its ready supply of victims, individuals who were deviants by choice or by public decree. They provided the standard of unacceptable conduct, making clear what rules could not be broken without reprisal. As the insurrectionary ceremonies attested, the powerless and guiltless were most often the subjects of popular sacrifice. In a letter to McIntosh, Jerry spoke to the issue himself: "I have only to imploy [sic] my time in the most earnest manner in endeavouring to make peace with my God whom I call this day to witness my innocence. . . . Perhaps I may never see you more. Therefore Gratitude binds me to return to you my most sincere thanks for the many favours received at your hands. Pray Sir take care of my wife and the dear little ones . . . —and I hope that you and yours may be happy hear [sic] and hereafter[.] [It] is the sincere wish of the innocent but unfortunate Jeremiah."[48] Yet given the passions swirling about the merchant and the slave, McIntosh had reason to be grateful, too. If Governor Monroe had not overruled Jeremiah's defender, McIntosh could also have suffered at the hands of those who were determined to make an example of anyone with discountenanced opinions. In that sense, Jeremiah was put to death, in a manner of speaking, so that McIntosh might live in peace with his neighbors and racial supremacy might prosper.

16

Charivari and Lynch Law

In a remarkable scene in *Huckleberry Finn* (1885), set before the Civil War, Mark Twain has Colonel Sherburn heap scorn on a mob gathered to lynch him. Sherburn has just killed the unarmed Boggs, a drunken old man whose reckless insults Sherburn had repaid with two shots in the chest. The crowd rages in front of Sherburn's house until he steps out, shotgun in hand, and coolly says, "The idea of *your* lynching anybody! It's amusing. . . . Because you're brave enough to tar and feather poor friendless cast-out women . . . did that make you think you had grit enough to lay your hands on a *man?*" Empty praise from Southern journalists, Sherburn continues, could not hide the fact that lynchers were cowards, no better, no worse than other men, but cowards nonetheless. Otherwise, why do juries acquit murderers? "Because they're afraid the man's friends will shoot them in the back . . . so they always acquit; and then a *man* goes in the night, with a hundred masked cowards at his back, and lynches the rascal. . . . The pitifulest thing out is a mob." The crowd dissolves, each villager slinking off to protect his own skin.[1]

Twain gave his outrage against a common nineteenth-century phenomenon a fictional voice. In reality not many Sherburns materialized in actual history to put a community to shame. Between 1885 and 1903 there were 3,337 mob killings in the United States. (Only Utah and three New England states reported none.) Of these, 2,585 took place in the South, approximately three-fourths of the total. Most of the victims were black. In Mississippi, for instance, between 1882 and 1903 only 40 of 324 lynching deaths were of whites. The statistics reveal the continuing strength of community control of custom against the tides of social change. No single individual, however courageous, could have done much to alter the record.

Three factors ensured the permanence of popular white rule by means of charivari and lynch law. The first of these was the acquiescence, and sometimes the leadership, of those with social and official power. Second, rituals to shame or kill deviants involved the most sacred, ethical rules of the white populace. Third, the lynching rite was socially efficacious. Like the insurrectionary panic, it satisfied participants and spectators that their intent and the result of their actions were one. With no uncertainty, the social and racial values upon which white order rested were thought to be well guarded by such means. Because family purity—in lineage and reputation—was the bedrock of personal and group honor, lynchings and charivari both before and after the Civil War were concerned with misconduct, real or imagined, that threatened familial security and status. Even politically motivated lynchings—to prevent slaves from developing leadership for rebellions or, later, freedmen from voting the Republican or Populist ballots—were ultimately a means to protect white family integrity. Black advances in any aspect of life meant departure from accustomed servitude, endangering the white man's honor. Just as before the war insurrectionary panics provided mechanisms for dividing the blacks and uniting the whites, so postemancipation lynch law set the boundaries beyond which blacks were not to go. For the most part neither mode of social control was a routine occurrence, casually undertaken. By word of mouth the news of a grim summary execution traveled far and wide. A warning was conveyed. No doubt it deterred crime or "impudence," but at a price for both races—in mutual re-

spect, compassion, and economic well-being. For lesser offenses, usually ones committed by whites, the charivari was sufficient. Though
different in their levels of violence, both were ceremonies of moral
purification through the sacrifice of one or more victims, polluted
and profaned. As the antigambling lynchers of Vicksburg put it in
1835, respectable "heads of families, members of all classes, professions, and pursuits" were convinced that " 'order' is the 'first law' "
of society, but that society "can sometimes be purified only by a
storm." The hanging of numbers of riotous gamesters, averred a
chronicler of the events, "will ever reflect honour on the insulted
citizens" of that community. It was a common justification for
lynchings.

Lynchings, like the quasi-judicial trials and executions in insurrectionary scares, differed from charivaris in the degree of violence
attending them. Lynchings consciously defied the law and abstract
justice and could result in an explosion of hatred, rage, and anarchy. Certainly such was the case in the aftermath of the Nat Turner Rebellion in 1831. But charivaris and sometimes the firmly controlled extralegal killings of individual (usually black) deviants
were often stylized affairs. As anthropologist Victor Turner argues,
the use of ritual tends to anticipate deviations and conflicts by
channeling crowd actions into long-practiced forms. Ritual only
half-loosens social controls; it circumscribes just how far the participants should go, thus upholding stability and order. The last chapter of this book will illustrate how the role of ritual functioned to
save the life of a (fallen) member of the planter class. Although the
fully unleashed mob and the ritualized charivari aroused strongly
hostile feelings, both were ecstatic events. The mingling of justice
with bacchanalia, centering about the scapegoat, whether a lowly
black or an unpopular member of the ruling class, released social
tensions in spectacle. Either the one or other form could sometimes
lead to anarchy or rebellion. Most often, though, the ritual itself
served to maintain order. The allegedly omnipotent forces of evil
existing *within* the society were externalized in bloody reprisal or,
more mildly, in the costuming of victims and participants. A recent
literary exposition of this theme is John Kennedy Toole's *A Con-*

federacy of Dunces, a story of a madly comic, perversely intellectual and bedeviled protagonist. His rage against himself and his intrusive mother is expressed in wild masquerade and androgynous costume, as if Mardi Gras license characterized the everyday world of policemen, businessmen, tavern-keepers, and whites and blacks in New Orleans.[2]

Whether collective behavior was to culminate in simple ritual or in chaos largely depended on the first issue—official leadership or the lack of it. A festival of misrule such as Mardi Gras was generally contained within bounds because its social leaders provided the authority and ceremonies to ensure a degree of public peace. Lynch law, on the other hand, often lacked these stabilizing components. Officials frequently looked the other way. In 1880, for instance, when four Yankee bank robbers were arrested in Anderson, Indiana, a crowd of over a hundred gathered to storm the jail. The sheriff gave the prisoners advice on how to use their wits to turn away the mob's wrath, but offered them no more substantial aid. As always, particularly in rural and unsophisticated American (not just Southern) communities, the officers of the law saw themselves as mediators between the populace and the institution that they represented. Neither the sheriff nor the lynchers were exceptionally cowardly. So it had always been, ever since Bacon's Rebellion: each man sought his own interests and feared, like Sherburn's mob in Twain's story, to be caught isolated and vulnerable outside the bonds of "brave" men. Honor was thus locally defined as conformity, not individuality.

Sometimes a victim's bold demeanor, a willingness to die game, could modify crowd resolve, precisely because such behavior exemplified conventional ideals. Langdon W. Moore, the leader of the Indiana bank robbers, managed to save himself and his friends with a clever mixture of feigned innocence, generous respect for the mob, and bravado. The sheriff was much relieved that a showdown did not occur. As a later observer of such police behavior noted, it was "less a matter of the individual policeman than of the [community] sanctions behind it."[3]

Sometimes too, a figure of local prominence tried to save the victim, but not always with much success. In the Mississippi insurrectionary scare of 1835, despite his long-practiced courtroom eloquence Henry S. Foote was unable to rescue a young Kentucky boatman from summary execution as a supposed member of the mythical Murrell gang. Not long afterward, at Clinton, Mississippi, he also tried to protect a slave boy falsely accused of rebellion. "I am not willing," he told the excited throng, "that a few generous-minded young men" should have to bear the blame for a wrongful death, once the frenzy subsided. Only eight or ten took the attorney's side. "I left the spot with feelings of sorrow and disgust," Foote recalled. "The boy was swung into eternity in less than fifteen minutes." He warned the slave's owner, a wealthy, respected widow, not to prosecute, but "to bow to the imperious necessity of the hour"—to save her own life.[4]

Although nearly every Southern community had leaders no less capable of firm principles than Henry Foote, those who held local power ofttimes shared the convictions of the neighborhood. For instance, in 1911 Joshua W. Ashleigh, a state legislator of South Carolina, headed a crowd of Greenville residents that dismembered a black accused of raping a white girl. His son, editor of the local paper, not only assisted but announced in print that he "went out to see the fun without the least objection to being a party to help lynch the brute." Though scarcely one who would have participated in such gruesome rites, U.S. Senator John Sharp Williams, a patrician from Mississippi, argued in the same era that "race is greater than law now and then, and protection of woman transcends all law, human and divine." Most political leaders could not for a moment question the general legitimacy of lynchings. A famous twentieth-century example was the struggle between Tom Watson, former Populist leader and editor of the Atlanta *Jeffersonian*, and Governor John Slaton of Georgia. Watson whipped up an impassioned mob to ensure the conviction of Leo Frank, a Jewish factory superintendent who allegedly raped and killed Mary Phagan, a white working girl. Under duress from milling crowds outside, the jury convicted Frank on the slimmest of evidence, to the outrage of the entire Western world. "THE VOICE OF THE PEOPLE IS THE VOICE OF GOD," declared Watson; by Frank's hanging, *"Wom-*

anhood is made safer, everywhere." Then in 1915 the governor commuted Frank's sentence to life imprisonment. Not long afterward a
lynch mob seized Frank at the penitentiary and hanged him in
the dark of night. Like Governor William Berkeley of Virginia, who had also faced public anger and demand for scapegoats,
Governor Slaton had underestimated the power that common folk
held. To be sure, ten thousand Georgians as well as the presiding
judge at the trial had bid the governor to act with mercy, a showing
unimaginable twenty years before. Judging from the enthusiastic
response to Watson's flaming editorials, however, it must be concluded that the subsequent lynching had widespread approval. On
the other hand, Governor Slaton was disgraced. Only the Georgia
National Guard stood between him and a raging mob, and he had
to flee the state. In this case it was Tom Watson, aging warhorse of
a failed Populist crusade, who cackled in glee over the humiliated
governor's flight, in a manner reminiscent of Governor Berkeley's
mockery of Nathaniel Bacon's fate.[5]

The second type of Southern mob action, the charivari, being
a less bloodthirsty, more festive occasion, was more parallel with
church ritual and custom than was lynch law, which was more a
complement to ordinary judicial procedure. (Fine distinctions are
nonetheless hard to draw, and lynchings, at least in the hands of
Ku Kluxers, also had their liturgical aspect, as will be explained
later.) The charivari included a range of crowd activity, from wedding-day jest to public whipping and tar-and-feathering. It was a
means of community policing stretching back to Neolithic Europe.
Examples can be drawn from Portugal to the Balkans, the Levant
to the Hebrides, from Plutarch's *Moralia* in the first century A.D.
and the Old Testament book of Leviticus to news reports from
present-day Belfast and Londonderry. (Not long ago, an Ulster
Catholic girl who fraternized with an English officer was treated to
a dousing in tar and feathers.)

In some cases the crowd prepared effigies or simply made noises
imitating howling wolves, cackling geese, and clucking chickens
while ringing cowbells and beating on pots and drums. In its more
serious form, the victim was not just serenaded in this fashion, but

whipped and forced to wear a disfiguring guise, reducing the individual from human to animal order. The goat or ass was often associated with the rite. "And the goat shall bear upon him all their iniquities," reads Leviticus 16:22. On the Day of Atonement, the priest laid hands on a live goat selected by lot, transferring by ritual words the sins of the people to the beast, which "a fit man" would then release in the wilderness. "Scapegoating" was the literal meaning of the rite. It continued to be the essence of charivari—as well as lynchings—through the millennia.

Thus the figure of shame was made to ride a goat or ass. In America or England the one ridiculed was placed on a ladder, pole, or rail. In England this unpleasant means of transportation was called "stang-riding," or "riding the skimmington." Meantime a crowd gathered about, and the marchers were accompanied by "rough music" or, in Germany, *Katzenmusik*. In America, the noisy procession was called a "rogue's march."[6] Tar and feathers were often, although not always, smeared on the offender. As early as in post-Homeric Greece, if not much earlier, tar or pitch was mentioned in connection with the ridiculing of homosexuals, though the emphasis was on their effeminacy rather than on public ceremonies of befouling.[7] In any event, tar was associated with charivari in those locations where the ugly substance was used in quantity for ship caulking—places such as European ports, colonial Boston, or the river towns of the Mississippi Valley. In all these folk customs there was no insistence on particular devices or materials. What mattered was symbolic intent, not punctilious regularity. The prehistoric origin of the ritual may have been connected with Indo-European human sacrifice. The Iron Age European, Celt, or Teuton, apparently pulled a victim, carefully fed and freed from labor, about the countryside in a decorated cart. Then this human votive offering to Nerthus (Fertility), this Scapegoat King as it were, was strangled and thrown in a bog.[8]

Because of the religious significance attached to the rites, the early Christian church tried to eliminate pagan meaning from the custom. In A.D. 1133, for instance, the Monk of St. Trond complained bitterly that villagers still accompanied the Ship of Wheels

(*Narrenschiff*, ship of fools) out of its hiding place in the Germanic forest. Human sacrifice had no doubt ceased, but the enterprise disturbed the early church fathers nevertheless. The Statute of Beziers of 1368 denounced such activity as the *ludum iniquitatis*, the evil game. The Edict of Avignon, some years earlier, declared it "obnoxious sport." Nevertheless, the custom endured, chiefly as a young men's frolic. It lived on vigorously as a way for them to enforce community values, whatever the church might do to curb it. To this day, *el vito* (mocking dance), *la pandorga* (the mobbing-up), or *cencerrada* (cowbell-ringing) persists as a means of ridiculing violators of local morality in Spanish rural provinces. Despite centuries of sporadic attempts at suppression, the church as well as civil authorities in Spain have not wholly repressed the folk tradition. It retains, to some degree, its sacred heritage as a scapegoating rite for community evils. When confronted with the opposition of regular authorities, the reply of those engaged has ever been—in America as in present-day Basque districts—"We have given this Charivari because it is our right."[9]

For hundreds of years, ecclesiastical precept and attempts to impose outsiders' law on community life but failed to halt such proceedings, in either the Old World or the New. Only as society became more secular in character, more impersonal in its dealings, and more institutional in its forms of exchange and control did the ancient ideal of community justice erode. In the American South that transformation was somewhat slower than in the rest of the country. There, where a form of primal honor continued to flourish, one could find the same attitudes about aliens, deviants, and social underlings as once existed in very ancient times.

Because of its persistence as a festive as well as shaming rite, the church and even the state adjusted their practices to accommodate the popular mode. For instance, common-law punishments prior to the great reformation of penal policies in the late eighteenth century consisted largely of folk tradition carried out under the aegis of the law, itself a ritualistic and supposedly divine institution. The penalty for thievery on Richard I's crusade in 1189 was, by royal edict, the tar-and-feathering of the felon before he was set upon land and abandoned. In England as late as 1722, Eleanor Elson, who had killed her husband, was first covered in tar, with "a tarred bonnet put on her head," then hanged before she was enveloped in flames. In 1779 a fourteen-year-old girl, a member of a counterfeiting ring, was to be burned after being covered with tar, but a nobleman prevented the ritual from being carried out.[10]

In America many of the common-law customs were allowed to die out or were never introduced. Yet as late as 1796, to take one example, South Carolinian statute still provided that a woman illicitly with child was to be not only fined for bastardy but also forced to walk behind the "cart's tail," as the phrase went, as it was drawn through the streets of Charleston. The objective was to encourage citizens to join in the customary charivari, pelting the woman with stones and sticks and accompanying the procession with the requisite "rough music."[11]

Just as the law found ways to incorporate community rites, so the church adopted the rituals. Many of them made their way into morality plays in comic, cuckold characterizations. In A.D. 837 Pope Gregory transformed the Druids' rites of the dead on November 1 to All Souls' Day, or Hallowe'en. Most popular of all was the Feast of Fools, derived from the Roman Kalends, one day of which has come down to us as the New Year's celebration. In the slave South, as in ancient times, it was a time of holiday, with much drinking, dancing, and even some loosening of the bonds of slavery. The mummeries of the Old World were continued particularly in Catholic Louisiana, where whites and blacks fashioned the decorated carts (the modern-day floats) and paraded with music through the streets of New Orleans. A "Rex" was chosen and honored in mock deference. In Scotland the figure was called the Abbot of Unreason, in England the Lord of Misrule, but the object was the same: the brief throwing off of the ordinary monotonies and restrictions of institutional life, customarily corrupt and unpredictable even in the best of times.[12] The participants were chiefly young people, especially unmarried young men. (In New Orleans, however, old aristocrats took the coveted masked role of "Rex.") In Mobile, leaders of the Mardi Gras, mostly young militia officers and planters' sons, called themselves "the Cowbellions." In revels, as in lynchings, male youths served, with their elders' blessing, as the "conscience of the community by making" themselves "the raucous voice of that conscience"—and of pleasure, as an early modern European scholar has pointed out.[13]

Although the religious-festive aspects of Mardi Gras in the Catholic Deep South are too well known to require examination, it is possible to find similar traditions in Protestant sections of the Old South. Slaves sometimes acted out fantasies of power by wearing masks, dancing nimbly in the streets, and subtly ridiculing their masters. In 1830 the Rev. Moses Ashley Curtis described a saturnalia in Wilmington, North Carolina:

> The negroes have a singular custom here . . . of dressing out in rags & masks, presenting a most ludicrous appearance imaginable. They are accompanied by a troop of boys singing, bellowing, beating sticks, dancing & begging. Three or four of these John Cooners as they are ycleped [called] made their appearance to day. One of them was completely enveloped in strips of cloth of every color which depended in the most ragged confusion from every part of his ebony hip. Over his face was drawn the nether part of a raccoon skin from the center of which hung the tail signifying that "nasal attributes are meant here." On each side of the tail appeared two holes through which shone the whites of his eyes. . . . Then dancing & his rags flying & his flexible nose gamboling about his face, singing with a gruff voice in concert with his satellites, I was ready to burst with laughter.

Curtis thought that the custom had been introduced by visiting Frenchmen some years before. African origins were more likely. But in traditional societies the world over mask and revelry, religion and entertainment were universal combinations, though the specific forms differed from one society to another. What mattered to the Episcopal clergyman, however, was the eventual disappearance of such heathenish practices as the saturnalia, especially since he observed that some of the young blacks involved had ended their revel with a session around a jug that left them insensible.[14]

Special religious events aside from the seasonal occasions were also subject to the boisterous jest of charivari, most particularly a marriage celebration. Vance Randolph, for instance, described the "shivaree" as practiced in the twentieth-century Ozarks. The day of a wedding a company of bachelors first selected a captain who led the way to the newlyweds' home and removed the obstacles—hidden wires and the like—placed in the young bachelors' path by the bridegroom. The new husband was supposed to treat the visitors for as long as they wished to make merry—all night if need be. (The newly married couple was not supposed to have intercourse the first night; marriages were as much public as private events in Southern folk society.) If his hospitality fell short of expectations, a mock shivaree with a riding to a nearby creek and dunking usually followed. In 1830, at St. Louis, a thousand to twelve hundred ruffians *"charivaried"* the wealthy Colonel John O'Fallon on the evening of his second marriage. In customary fashion, the colonel sent word to the cowbell-ringing, chicken-crowing throng that he considered them a "respectable company of gentlemen" who were his "friends," and promised to pay for all their entertainment that night. The pledge cost him a thousand dollars but, said a city chronicler, he had no choice; "such was the honor and respect" that had to be "paid to power" of the "loafers and rabble."[15]

The significance of this kind of charivari, even in its most jocular vein, was its mixture of fun and hostility, an ambivalence about the marital event itself. In rural backwaters where these games were prevalent as late as the early twentieth century, the bridal couple celebrated not only love but also freedom from the yoke of parents and the beginning of independence. For the bachelor friends of the groom, however, there was joy, jealousy, and a sense of comradely loss. Moreover, for the small neighborhood itself the new status of the nuptial pair meant a change in family arrangements and alliances, perhaps for the better, possibly for the worse. The purpose of the tricks and jokes was to act out these mixed emotions in a structured though unruly way, without serious jeopardy to the marriage. In small-scale societies, anything that required abrupt readjustment in community relations entailed uncertainty. The charivari helped assuage that anxiety. It also provided a way to resolve it: the groom and bride eventually regained privacy, and the revelers had to go home to solitary beds.

As the benign form of "shivaree" in the example of wedding jollity suggests, the central concern among the common folk of the South was to preserve family reputation and inviolability. By and large, the social impact of gossip sufficed to keep family members true to communal values. In some honor-shame cultures, most notably in Spain, North Africa, and the Levant, women were held in close confinement. Men, indeed all members of society, dreaded the possibility of sexual misbehavior and maintained strict means of guarding against it. In the Old South, although chaperones in the upper ranks were common, young girls and women generally enjoyed much greater latitude in this regard. Anglo-American tradition permitted women a wide range of acquaintances, associations, and even occupations, at least by comparison with the Mediterranean mode. As a consequence, gossip was the mechanism used to enforce restraint and hold everyone in the grip of public scrutiny. Also, it gave meaning to the lives of those who had little standing themselves. In 1622, for instance, William Gouge, an English writer on manners, remarked, "When servants of divers houses men or maids meet together, all their talke for the most part is of their masters and mistresses, whereby it cometh to pass that all the secrets of the house are soone knowne about the whole towne or city."[16] So it was, too, in rural America, where democracy opened all to the public gaze, and most especially in the slaveholding South. Despite the isolation, slaves in field and house soon spread the word of goings-on among the whites, conveying information faster, sometimes, than masters thought possible.

As a result, talebearing was not an "idle" pastime, though the gossipers in fact may have had little better to do. The exchange of speculations and opinions among the whites served to guide all members of the community toward a common set of standards for sexual and marital behavior. True, in church circles, of which there was a growing number throughout the antebellum years, church members and elders in rural settings did not hesitate to warn malefactors publicly or even to expel them if they were impenitent. Gossip, however, was used by churchgoers and nonchurchgoers alike as the least disruptive and most effective way to impose social sanctions. It helped to name who belonged and who should be excluded. The power of rumor may be seen in the fact that there were so many suits for defamation, particularly in the early years of American settlement. False reports from unbridled tongues had to be regarded as a social and certainly a personal menace. Such irresponsible behavior threw doubt on legitimate gossip. Sometimes charivari or, in colonial times, the "cucking" or "ducking" stool of ancient folk and common-law custom was the remedy for excessive and divisive rumormongering. Despite constant complaints about the danger of idle speculations, especially women's, Southern folk society was accustomed to use gossip as the first line of community defense against individual waywardness. When that resource or church admonition failed, then, it was thought, more stringent measures should be invoked.[17]

A grim destiny awaited the serious violator of family and gender ethics. Among the deviants singled out for charivari were promiscuous unmarried women—prostitutes or otherwise; wives adulterous or violent toward their husbands; and both women and men who made marriages deemed incongruous. The charivari was also used for certain kinds of male offenses, from chronic inebriation to political or religious unconventionality. By no means were these rough exercises confined to the South. Charivaris, usually for sexual offenses, could be found in late nineteenth-century New York, New Hampshire, and other New England states, but they had all but disappeared from the more populous and sophisticated Yankee areas. The punitive "shivaree" flourished most widely in the Mississippi Valley, from Iowa to New Orleans. The reason was not the inadequacy of frontier justice, but rather the continuation of primal modes of social control that farming and pastoral folk still found useful as their ancestors had before them. Primitive conditions, not simply the dislocating process of settlement alone, held men and women true to these customs. In new settlements of sophisticated planters in the West one was unlikely to find these ancient traditions, but among common folk, whatever their location might be, there the old heritage lived on.

Not surprisingly, charivaris were very popular among the Creoles and Cajuns of the coastal Southwest, from the late seventeenth century to the 1940s. Probably the most celebrated one—over an incongruous marital union—took place in New Orleans about midway between those dates. In 1798 the young widow of the enormously wealthy Don Andres Almonster y Roxas remarried too soon. The bridegroom did not suit the New Orleans populace. For three days large crowds surrounded the house of the bridal pair. "Many were in disguise dresses and masks," wrote a foreign observer, "and hundreds were on horseback; and all had some kind of noisy musical instrument, as old kettles, shovels and tongs, and clanging metals." The masqueraders drew carts containing effigies of the former husband in a coffin and the second lover, while another mummer impersonated the widow. Refusing to respond in the required spirit of gracious submission, the widow found herself ostracized and rudely treated in the streets for weeks thereafter. Finally, she gave three thousand dollars "in solid coin" for an outdoor mass to mollify opinion. In the 1940s it was still customary in isolated bayou country to carry out this relatively harmless but hostile sort of charivari, with nightly appearances lasting as long as thirty days.[18]

High on the list for still more serious doses of community ridicule were girls who violated the code of chastity. The evidence was the appearance of an illegitimate child. Charivaris in Europe most often centered on such unwelcome events. The shaming rite was also used for this purpose in the South, Old and New. Vance Randolph recalled from his Ozark experiences in the 1920s that in one Arkansas settlement a girl had caused so much trouble for other men's wives that the neighbors "decided to 'drum her out.' About thirty men and women appeared at her cabin one morning, firing pistols, beating on tin pans, and yelling at the top of their voices." Without a word she ran out the door and was not seen in those parts again.

Her relations were utterly "humiliated rather than belligerent." They made no attempt to protect or avenge her. In fact, they accepted the community verdict and acted as if she had never belonged to the family. Yet exceptions should be noted. In the far backlands, according to another investigator as well as to Vance Randolph, mountain girls were allowed to produce a child before wedlock. In this way a girl's fecundity would be assured. (Herbert G. Gutman, a leading authority on the black family, has discovered the same phenomenon among slave girls and in modern black culture as well.) Ely Green, a mulatto from Sewanee, Tennessee, recalled a most unusual example of sexual practice and family reaction in the isolated Lost Cove valley near there sometime in the 1890s. A daughter in the Cannon clan, a large "covite" family, was living with a black partner, Alf Cannon, her father's former slave. When whites from Sherwood came to drive the couple out, her brothers took up arms. The mob wheeled off. "The Cannons were a tough sort. They made them scram," Ely Green concluded admiringly. However, in most parts of the Southern hill country, as elsewhere, the "shameless" woman was a local byword, one who risked public humiliation.[19]

Women who beat their husbands or entertained gallants at the expense of their husband's reputation were another category of miscreants. At Turkey Hills, Massachusetts, in 1761 a Mrs. Phelps was seized for both offenses. A crowd of young people "carried her on a rail, blowing horns and ringing cow bells" in the traditional fashion. In the American South such customs persisted well beyond the more disorderly eighteenth century. Following the First World War, believers in traditional ethics, whether they were city dwellers or countrymen, were horrified at the secular ways of the new America. They undertook organized missions to repress an upsurge of age-old vices, as well as new ones such as gangsterism and bootlegging. In Muskogee, Oklahoma, for instance, a defender of old-fashioned community retribution in all its forms declared, "I have not seen a case . . . that all the leading good people of the town have not said, 'It's a good thing, push it along.' It moves out the gangster, bootlegger . . . fast and loose females, and the man who abuses and neglects his wife and children." Moral offenses—adultery and fornication among them—were part of the repertoire of the post–World War I Ku Klux Klan, with whippings, tar-and-feathering, and sometimes branding the usual penalties during that era of community anxiety and dread of a sort of social change that was beyond popular comprehension.[20]

Defense of womanly virtue and family standing was always a prominent motive for community action, one that sometimes involved the victimizing of adulterous, abusive, or philandering men. For instance, in 1730 a visitor to North Carolina found that the last Anglican clergyman in the region was known for his sexual proclivities. He "Importun'd a Woman to give him a Nights Lodging but no sooner had the parson his Cloths off" than a party of irate women came with horsewhips "& Chastized the poor naked Parson to that Degree that He took his Horse next Morning & has never been seen since. . . ." (The notion that women could act in this way, in violation of their submissive role toward any male, moral or immoral, surprised the observer. In 1707 a similar incident took place in Boston, where an assembly of both sexes hauled a man from his house, tore off his clothes, and beat him with rods for harsh treatment of his wife. The local magistrate was so alarmed that he had the women in the crowd whipped in retaliation.) Likewise, both an adulterous wife and a cuckolded husband might be given mob punishment, on the grounds that he was as recreant as she in meeting the duties of gender. Moreover, townsmen did not take lightly affronts to their virgins. In Charlotte, North Carolina, in 1845, for instance, three young men had made up enormous posters directing obscenities against "some of the respected young ladies of the community," the local editor said, and had nailed the signs to the courthouse door. Early the next morning the villagers were highly agitated. The town's young men found the culprits out, gained confessions, and rode all three on a rail, each covered in the customary feathery garb. The newspaper piously denounced the rough work, but excused it on the grounds that all townsfolk had agreed about the imperative for "summary punishment." After all,

the pranksters had defamed their own sex by casting unjust asper-
sions on the good name of the girls and their families.[21]

Punishments on behalf of family regularity and social control of
female behavior were always prominent in American as well as in
foreign charivaris. Yet in this country there was a second category
of offenses that were not to be tolerated and for which popular justice was the favored remedy. These were, first, the fairly petty infractions that the law overlooked or punished more lightly than the
community judged proper, and second, misdemeanors that only became a public nuisance because of their number, not their character. An example of the first was the irritant of small thievery and
trading with slaves—two offenses that were almost synonymous in
parts of the South. Ofttimes the malefactor was thought to be a
Yankee peddler, a figure usually regarded with deep suspicion. (He
might be an abolitionist spy "tampering" with the slaves.) Even if
an outbreak of purloining might actually have been traceable to
some local poor white who was trading whiskey for a master's stolen
provender, nevertheless the peddler was a convenient scapegoat. In
1839 in Elizabeth City, North Carolina, for instance, one Charles
Fife from Connecticut was suspected of trading with blacks. The
offense could not be proved in court, so some young men of the
village gave him a pole ride through town, followed by the tar-and-
feather ritual. When the peddler, claiming innocence, refused to
leave town, the rowdies repeated the ceremony the next Sunday.
Fife then sued his enemies before Judge John L. Bailey, a young
planter, but in the midst of the proceedings the ruffians leaped on
the plaintiff and his lawyer and beat them up before the bench.
Judge Bailey acquitted the defendants and fined Fife $100—without
evidence or prior indictment—for trading with Negroes. Fife, at last,
left town.[22]

Sometimes poor whites actually were caught at "Negro-trading."
In 1829 Mrs. Rachel O'Connor's slaves stole some corn and sold it to
a yeoman near Jackson, Louisiana. The young village braves gathered and, she reported, made the suspected tradesman ride a pine
pole all through the town. "His wife clamored all the while for

them to stop," but instead "they put her on the same pole, and gave them a ride together." The slaves meantime fled homeward.[23]

An illustration of a minor infraction that required "shivaree" was a rash of riotous drinking. Towns and crossroads were sometimes plagued by yeomen and laborers who came to grog shops on Saturday and ended up in the jailhouse for the night, paying only a light fine. Residents wearied of the noise and stench. In 1838 matters were so out of hand in Windsor, North Carolina, that young villagers seized those "staggering about the streets" and gave them due warning "by blacking and painting their faces and putting them in boxes." As in many such charivaris, the perpetrators had disguised themselves. Although fear of retaliation from the abused parties was a factor, as Twain's Sherburn had observed, anonymity served to give the impression of complete community solidarity—making the ritual a more sobering experience than punishment at the hands of particular individuals would be. William D. Valentine of Windsor, who recorded these proceedings, was delighted with the results. Lawyer though he was, he considered "wretches" all those who demeaned "their family's standing" by public drunkenness. They had committed "an unpardonable sin," he believed, for which the shaming penalties were almost insufficient.[24]

Finally, the shame ritual was appropriate for the political or religious deviant. "Rough music" had accompanied the departures of Tories in many of the colonies during the American Revolution. Many years later, in the 1880s, when Mormons began their missionary efforts in the South they were often subjected to tar-and-feathering, even mob shootings. Needless to say, they had previously suffered such persecutions in the North and West in the days before the Civil War. Efforts to prosecute the mobsters through the law failed utterly. A Georgia court reminded the complainants from Utah that the state "recognized no law for Mormons"; their polygamy was thought to be a particularly heinous sin.[25]

Defense of sacred notions of family purity was even more applicable to advocates of abolitionism. The Southern *cordon sanitaire* descended on all forms of public antislavery agitation after the Missouri Debates in Congress (1819–21), and even more so after Turner's Rebellion and the appearance of William Lloyd Garrison's *Liberator* in 1831. Nor was the initial popular hostility confined solely to the slaveholding states. Although tar-and-feathering had diminished since the triumph of the Patriot cause in 1781, the practice revived in Yankee political affairs over the slavery issue, which proved no less divisive than the Revolution. For instance, in 1837 the Rev. Marius Robinson, a youthful Ohio member of Theodore Weld's antislavery band, was kidnapped by a dozen or so men, stripped naked, tarred, and feathered. At dawn a Trumbull County, Ohio, farmer found him in a nearly incoherent state, lying in a ditch.

Needless to say, such incidents occurred with greater frequency in the South. A one-legged Yankee clock mender in Dothan, Alabama, for instance, talked too openly about the merits of "free soil." His penalty was a session of repeated duckings in a nearby waterhole and a boisterous escort to the edge of town, riding a rail and accompanied with the usual "rogue's march" of cacophonous music. Native Southerners also had to be very circumspect about airing their feelings on the touchy subject of race emancipation. At Columbia, South Carolina, recalled an old-timer, a stonemason named Powell had spoken up for the freedom of blacks. His fellow workers and others seized him, ran him to "Fisher's Pond," and removed his clothes; then "he was well smeared with tar, then a pillow-case was opened and he was feathered."[26]

In essence, lynching was a charivari with deadly as well as shaming intent. Like the charivari, it was often associated with community efforts to protect family security and conventions, but the perceived menace was not as manageable as a girl's wandering affections, a mistake in marital choice, or an oversupply of local drunks. Instead, the problem was often regarded as a gross violation of race custom or rule. Frequently, a black victim was alleged to have raped a white woman. The charge was often patently fraudulent and other motives, such as fears provoked by black tendencies to independence, refusal to be servile, or signs of economic advance, were involved. Particularly after the Civil War these "violations" were a hidden factor beneath the more sensational accusation. In any case, the two were linked: black economic parity with whites would, many believed, encourage "amalgamation." From the point of view of the lynchers it scarcely mattered whether the sexual offense was real or not. Family defense and white racial supremacy were so inextricably mingled in the public mind that the victim's "crime" boiled down to the sheer effrontery of remaining alive after he had been accused of whatever it was that aroused popular fury.

In proceeding with a lynching, the Southern white mob did not necessarily show much sense of ritual. Rumors circulated about a crime and its perpetrator, and then the accused was seized from his home or place of work or the jail and tortured, humiliated, and hanged or burned. But even that simple, grim rite had overtones of religious meaning. It was carried out in the name of Christian rule—the maintenance of divine as well as human order, which decreed the separation of black from white, the honored from the forever honorless.

At times of unusual social and racial stress, however, lynchings were carried out with some attention to liturgy and magical paraphernalia. The Ku Klux Klans and other secret fraternal orders (chiefly made up of young men) arose after both the Civil War and the First World War. The commercialism of the second Klan was based on the impulse for pomp, masquerade, and religious ceremony. The Klan of the 1860s and 1870s, however, indulged in such fantasies in a less artificial, moneymaking way than the manufactured machinery that "Doc" Simmons and Hiram Evans hawked throughout the country in the 1920s. With post–Civil War Emancipation and then congressional intervention in Southern "home rule," all the most horrible nightmares of Southern whites, rich and poor, suddenly seemed to burst upon their society in satanic retribution. The supernaturalism of the Klan rituals, dress, and language deserves more attention as windows into the Southern white soul than historians, preoccupied with the political aspects of racism, have been willing to give.

The early robes of the Klan, reminisced the chroniclers of the Klan's founding at Pulaski, Tennessee, in 1866, were white, "the

emblem of purity for the preservation of the home and for the protection of the women and children. . . ." The trimmings, sewed by
Pulaski matrons, were red, "emblem of the blood which Klansmen
were ready to shed in defense of the helpless." But there was no
uniformity. Some Klansmen of that era wore robes of black trimmed
with white, with a red cloth to mark the mouth. Some robes were
entirely red. Hawthorne's bizarrely costumed militia leader would
have been properly attired for a Klan rally. The headgear varied as
well, but the customary symbols of charivari were certainly unmistakable. Caps were tall and conical or crowned with horns, a phallic
representation as old as the charivari itself. The cowbird's or cuckold's horns, the horns of the Devil, were chosen for the Klansman's
headpiece with no self-conscious or contrived intent: such gear was
simply a tradition.[27]

In the early Reconstruction Klan rituals, after the usual oaths of
allegiance the blindfolded initiate was covered in a "royal robe"
and had a "royal crown" placed on his head and a "sacred sword-
belt" strapped to his side, recalled William B. Romine of Tennessee. Then the blindfold was removed and the new recruit saw "in
the altar (a mirror) that his robe was a donkey skin, his crown an
old torn hat bedecked with donkey ears, and his sword-belt a common saddle-belt." The horseplay mingled the customary seriousness
of fraternal ritual with a mocking spirit. So it had always been in
the *ludum iniquitatis* so typical of young men's games since prehistoric times. To be sure, the eclectic nature of the Klan's title for
the organization (from *kuklos*, the Greek word for circle) and for
officers—Grand Cyclops, Grand Exchequer, Lictor, "Hydras, Furies,
Gobbins [*sic*, Goblins?], and Night Hawks"—indicated borrowings
from Masonry and college Greek-letter fraternity usages. In turn,
these clubs, too, in many respects, reflected honor-shame traditions.[28]

No doubt for many members of the post-Emancipation Klan and
its revived successor these were mere trappings, with little inherent
meaning. The main objective was to frighten the allegedly gullible
blacks who, whites thought, were subject to unsophisticated fears of
ghosts, monsters, and other apparitions of the night. Costuming,
then, was secondary to putting the black in his place by whippings

or worse. Nevertheless, we must remember that the common white folk were themselves not immune from dread of supernatural manifestations. The impulse to overcome the evils of the world by donning a fantastic mask and other regalia was indeed still thought to be a way to master events and drive off evils, seen and unseen. The Klan "magic" made men feel unconquerable, with purposes blessed by God.

At a revival service in Blount County, Alabama, in 1870, the relationship between supernaturalism and Klan activity was particularly evident. During the service the wife of the presiding preacher gave birth to a stillborn, deformed baby, at her home near the campground. A witness before a congressional hearing into antiblack atrocities later declared that the malformed baby "was a perfect representation and facsimile of a disguised Ku Klux": the infant's forehead was square and flat and about "three times the height of an ordinary child"; near the temples two small horns appeared; "around the neck was a scarlet red band; and from the point of the shoulder, extending down each side to about the center of the abdomen, was all scarlet red." Displayed before the fifteen hundred worshippers at the revival, the chimera created a great sensation. It was regarded as a judgment on the preacher, a white who had twice been beaten for failing to join the Klan and for preaching against it. During the congressional hearing the congressmen asked for a description of Klan attire and witnesses described it in terms resembling the child's appearance. Indeed, the violent mummers often claimed supernatural powers for themselves. One North Carolina witness at the hearings said that the Klansmen boasted "in my county that a man could not kill a Ku-Klux; they said that they could not be hit; that if they were the ball would bounce back and kill you. I thought though that I would try it. . . ." He had in fact wounded a Ku-Kluxer.[29]

Blacks knew better than to be as fearful of Klansmen's supposed magical powers as they were of the Klan's real power to inflict immediate, ghastly pain. For all the Klansmen's bragging that they had "come from the moon," ridden with ghosts on the wind, and consumed gallons of water without a swallow, their truly fearsome aspect was the ethical certitude of divine command with which they meted out the Klan's punishments. Half-belief in magic gave the Ku-Kluxer all the assurance he needed to treat violators of his sacred principles as if they were less than animals. In this spirit, Klan work included all the humiliating rites against sexual offenders—whites guilty of common-law mating with black women, supposed black rapists, prostitutes of both colors—and petty thieves (mostly hog stealers), plus unnumbered punishments and killings of political activists in the Republican parties of the Southern states.[30]

The work was quasi-judicial and quasi-religious at the same time, at least by the standards of the primal ethic. Yet as in Hawthorne's story, the grimmest of lynchings, whether carried out by Klansmen or by an aroused throng, had its celebratory side. At Maysville, Kentucky, in 1899, for instance, Robert Coleman, a black who confessed to having killed his employer's wife, was marched to the outskirts of town by a crowd numbering in the thousands. Tied to a tree and surrounded by a pile of dry brush, the victim screamed for mercy. His pleas only increased the will of the mob that he should die as painfully and slowly as possible. The murdered woman's husband was given the honor of applying the first match. Her brother lit the second. Then a third relative gouged Coleman's chest with a knife. His eyes had already been burned when an onlooker threw acid in an eggshell into them. Somehow he lived through these ordeals for at least three hours, while the fire, deliberately made to burn slowly, consumed him. The newspaper account declared that "all the leaders of the mob were well known and . . . some are the leading citizens in all lines of business and many are members of churches. . . ." To visit upon the sinner the fires of hell was simply to carry out on earth the fate awaiting him on the other side. Such a rite of complete exorcism—the total obliteration of the victim's remains—was seldom if ever performed on a white, but a member of the alien race was not even to be allowed the burial of a dog. For those outside the sacred white circle no absolution, no opportunity to live, even in disgrace, was considered fitting if the crime supposedly committed was judged fiendish. But mockery and amusement were still part of the ritual. For all its inhumanity, it was—sad to say—a very human event. The community rejoiced that an evil had been avenged. There was no wrenching sense of guilt. The tortures and death expelled guilt; they did not incur it. The festivities signaled that feature. Even children were allowed to share the pleasure. "All afternoon," noted the *New York Times* report of the Coleman murder, "children, some of them not more than six years old, kept the fire blazing around the blackened body by throwing grass, brush, bits of boards, and everything combustible that they could get together. This they kept up until dark," when mothers called them home for supper.[31]

The festive character of the Southern charivari and lynching suggests the efficacy of these tragic rites. The chief aim was the protection of traditional values and conventions against forces outside as well as within the community. They were simple group dramas in which evil was defeated, good was reinstated. By that means virtues were reconfirmed, boundaries of conduct set, and allegiances to the *deme* revitalized. The execution of lawful sentences could do the same, so long as spectators were present to see that the will of court and community was carried out. But particularly after Reconstruction governments abolished public hangings and whippings, that sort of popular participation in the enforcement of decisions was no longer possible. Yet the ethic of honor and shame lived on for another half-century, through the system of summary justice. People thought they needed to see the actual triumph of right over wrong, not just be told about it in a newspaper summary of how the felon looked and acted in his final moments.

Like Robin Molineux, the witness to an official hanging or a popular action felt the alternations of "pity and terror," the twin Aristotelian responses to tragedy, feelings often followed by hilarity. This primal psychology had begun to disturb the sensibilities of some thoughtful reformers in England and America early in the nineteenth century. A movement to abolish public hangings, if not the penalty itself, gradually won victories in the Northern states and finally, in 1867, in Great Britain. It was thought preferable to make the death penalty a private business, behind walls, impersonal, no longer a public drama, or carnival, of savagery and death. In the Southern states the end of public executions did not come until Reconstruction. Until then, however, the practice excited common folk, whites and blacks alike, who streamed to the site. William Faulkner's great-grandfather, William C. Falkner, upon first arriving in Mississippi, wrote up a condemned murderer's confession in 1845 and sold it to the thousands attending the execution at Ripley. Similarly, hawking penny sheets and broadsides, "last confessions" and doggerel verse was in the best of English tradition at Tyburn and later at Newgate. Public displays, of course, did little to deter crime, but they brought home to spectators—most often men and women who were at the edge of the law themselves—their luck in being alive. The misery of another made life a little sweeter.

George J. Holyoake, a British observer in the 1860s, explained the crowd's feelings at Newgate—emotions no different from those of the spectators at an American hanging or lynching. "The wretch," he said, "stands face to face with inevitable pitiless premeditated death. Not the scythe, but the strange cold cord of death strikes against his ear, and the crowd knows he knows it. They see the neck. The noose is adjusted, the click of the drop is heard . . . and the wretch descends still in sight; and then the rain, the cold, the damp, the struggling of the night is all forgotten in the coveted gratification of that . . . moment."[32]

For the American writer Mark Twain, however, justice of this kind was hard to comprehend, particularly if the community will, not the law, was being served. He could not bring himself, skeptic though he was, to think that "people at a lynching enjoy the spectacle and are glad of a chance to see it. It cannot be true; all experience is against it." In reaction to the atrocities that blacks suffered at the turn of the nineteenth cenury, Twain declared, "We are out of moral-courage material; we are in a condition of profound poverty."[33]

The problem was still more tragic than that. Moral courage is always in short supply, and it could scarcely be expected that some cavalier would try to prevent even the most palpable injustice against the powerful consensus that usually set these rites in motion.

Hawthorne understood the issue better than Twain. For the heart of the matter was the primal ethic. Until the code of honor was itself destroyed, such practices were bound to persist as the means of moral enforcement. Under such circumstances there was no difference between the legal public hanging and the communal rite of lynching. Both were the same insofar as they exercised the spectators. For them the violence of the gallows was just retribution for the prisoner's misdeeds, but it had to be witnessed, not hidden away, brutally explicit, not antiseptic.

The malefactor not only suffered for his crime in such rituals, legal or otherwise; he also served as an offering to the primal, sacred values of common folk. This is evident from the trophies seized on such occasions—for instance, swatches from Leo Frank's clothes and bits of the rope that hanged him. Like the Indians' scalp locks, these mementos signified triumph over villainy and deception, and gave proof that the once live enemy was no more a threat. The humiliation and death of perceived miscreants served as a "suppurating device," as one scholar has called it. It was a means of bringing evil to a head so that it could be lanced like a boil, purifying the ailing social body. If the rites of charivari and lynching seemed profane to outsiders, that profanation, if such it should be called, also had its purposes. As Mary Douglas, the English anthropologist says, pollution is often used to provide atonement and rededication to traditional ideals. The punishment of transgressions and the separation of the villainous from the virtuous community members "have as their main function to impose order on an untidy experience." Life itself was untidy, unclean; to smear tar, blood, and feathers or to employ flame or scaffold purified those who belonged. They rested easier for having eliminated fellow men who had been transformed in their eyes into beasts.[34]

Like the Germans whom Tacitus observed, like the milling throngs of Englishmen outside the Debtor's Door at Newgate, American whites took satisfaction in the wretchedness of others because the shaming rituals dispelled abiding fears of their own loneliness, vulnerability, and inevitable demise. Every society has its own forms of insensitivity, of communal practices and strategies for dealing with the unwanted, the powerless, and the damned. In later life Sigmund Freud was struck by the intractability of primal traits in man, a conviction made the more poignant by his flight in old age from Hitler's Teutonic Reich. "Psychoanalysis," he wrote after World War I, "has concluded from a study of the dreams and mental slips of normal people, as well as from the symptoms of neurotics, that the primitive, the savage and evil impulses of mankind have not vanished in any individual, but continue their existence. . . . They merely wait for opportunities to display their activity."[35]

The good that primal honor could arouse in men was equally matched by the tragic horrors that it produced. But sinister as those very personal rituals of degradation were, it is not enough simply to take comfort in the fact that they are gone. Remember that in modern times murders, rapes, and crimes of terrorism have far outpaced the number killed earlier by lynching or unfair legal judgment, even when differences in size of populations are taken into account. Today a gun, rather than a flimsy sheet, makes men, criminals and policemen alike, feel omnipotent. The moral boundaries are much wider today than then, in deference to personal liberty and in condemnation of ascriptive and communal prejudices. Yet, with impersonal means of destruction more available than ever before, the impulses of which Freud spoke still abide, with tragic consequences. Though none would wish to reinvoke the Iron Age sanctions that once flourished in this and other lands, the exchange of old for new ways of judging men and character has had its ironical costs.

17

The Anatomy of a Wife-Killing

The end of this study, like the beginning, concerns violence, family expectations and disappointments, male-centered community life, and elemental popular traditions. The killing of Susan Foster near Natchez, Mississippi, in March, 1834, was not a notable crime. Neither the deed itself nor its aftermath was well publicized nationally, regionally, or even locally. Unlike Lilburne and Isham Lewis, Thomas Jefferson's feckless nephews and literal butchers of a slave boy in Kentucky in 1811, the Fosters, husband and wife, had no famous connections to lend their lives notoriety. Folklorists will recover no ballads, broadsheets, or ghost stories commemorating the tragedy. Moreover, in contrast to a parricide in France of the same period (1835), the Foster affair aroused no public stirrings about the insanity plea. Unlike the celebrated Manning case in 1849 London, the Natchez killing did not attract a writer of Charles Dickens's stature seeking to use it as material for a novel (*Bleak House*) and as an argument against public punishments that simply indulged the popular taste for blood. Even Yankee abolitionists missed the chance to savor the incident as yet another example of Southern atrocity.[1] Yet although the Fosters were not famous and their troubles lacked both political and literary significance, the events surrounding Susan Foster's death and the public reaction to it function as illustration. Many of the themes that have arisen in these pages were woven into the circumstances, a tapestry that brought together real emotions, mythic qualities, and grievous results.

Here the case will be used as the people of Natchez used it—as text, a moral scenario in which actions spoke a language that revealed inner passions and intensely felt social values. The "deep play" of the drama reproduced, on a small, manageable scale, the ageless contradictions of honor when disorder was paradoxically employed to reconfirm collective order. And on an individual level, the rites of humiliation to which Susan Foster's killer was subjected gave the individual participants a momentary sense of mastery over death, as if the bloody shaming of their victim extended and gave rich meaning to the lives of his tormentors. In that exercise, the Natchez participants in the charivari mocked human mortality, just as Hawthorne's symbol of Authority gloated over his own survival by means of Molineux's disgrace, and just as Corydon Fuller's Arkansas tavern associates danced drunkenly around the dying inebriate.

What occurred in Natchez could, of course, have happened elsewhere—in the semirural North or even in some other part of the Western world. Nineteenth-century Southern whites were not unique in upholding the ancient ethic, but they did so with a primal spirit that elsewhere in the transatlantic community was under steady attack. This was a consequence, in part, of their reliance on the institution of slavery and race-based caste proscriptions. In 1834 Natchez, Mississippi, was ethically not very distant from the world that Hawthorne described in his classic story "My Kinsman, Major Molineux."

At seven in the evening on Friday, March 14, 1834, James Foster, Jr. took his wife Susan for a walk near his widowed mother Sarah's house at Foster Fields. The large plantation stretched almost a mile along the winding St. Catherine's Creek, a treacherous stream that eventually runs into the Mississippi River a few miles below the town of Natchez. Though it was only three miles from the Adams

County courthouse, those living at Foster Fields considered themselves residents of Pine Ridge, a neighborhood on the Natchez Trace. At ten o'clock Foster ran back to the homestead in a state of agitation. There were twelve adults and a number of small children asleep at the house. But the planter roused only his sister, Nancy A. Wood, a woman old enough to have been his mother, and his niece, Nancy Ligon.* Hastily they put on wraps as he stammered out his story. (When under stress, Foster had a tendency to stutter.) He and his wife, he told them, had been down by the bayou, about a thousand feet from the house. There he had "switched" his wife for being "unchaste," and she had confessed her guilt. Somehow, though, the inflictions had "frightened her into a fit." Grabbing Mrs. Wood by the arm, Foster led the women to the slave quarters. He had carried Susan to one of the cabins.

Inside, Mrs. Wood and Mrs. Ligon found the body laid out on a low bed. Prince, Will, and Bridget, slaves belonging to the widow Sarah, stood by. Prince was a son of Abd al-Rahman Ibrahima, the African ruler whom Thomas Foster, Sr., late owner of Foster Fields, had finally allowed New York colonizationists to transport home to Africa. Both the senior Foster and his aged black servant Ibrahima had been dead some five years. They had not escaped the misery that Thomas Foster, Jr.'s liaison with Ibrahima's daughter Susy had caused, but at least death spared them the disgrace into which the family was plunging in 1834.

Frightened and confused, Mrs. Wood and Mrs. Ligon glanced quickly at Susan's body. Foster excitedly begged the women to apply camphor to her face. But resuscitation was impossible. The body still felt warm, but the hands, Mrs. Wood recalled later, had already turned cold. Susan's dress had been removed, and she was covered only with an underdress that had no bodice. The body had been washed; her hair was still damp. The slave Bridget, Prince's wife, had done her task tenderly, and so well that the women did not notice much evidence of violence. They could only see a small bruise near the temple—or so they later claimed. On Mrs. Wood's

---

* Because the family was so large and the relationships so crucial to understanding the case, a genealogical table has been appended at the end of this chapter.

orders, Prince and Will, another slave, carried Susan Foster to the
main house. They placed her on the bed in the couple's bedroom.[2]

The following day Sarah Foster, Thomas Foster Sr.'s invalid
widow, summoned William Foster from his neighboring plantation.
William was her husband Thomas's elder brother. A childless but
long-married kinsman, he had always taken a special interest in his
brother's thirteen children at Foster Fields. Aged though he was,
William recognized more signs of violence on Susan's body than a
flickering lamp in a slave hovel had revealed the night before. As
far as he could tell, "the neck and shoulders from one point to another were all black and blue." On later inspection, he noticed "a
grip" on her neck and blood and froth "oozing . . . slowly . . .
out of her left nostril."[3] Meanwhile David McIntosh, the husband
of Caroline, one of James Foster's nine sisters, hastened over. The
McIntosh place was on the opposite bank of the creek, not far
away. With Susan lying dead in his own room, James Foster had
spent the night at David and Caroline's house. At breakfast on
Saturday Foster had told the pair that his wife had died, but had
not elaborated on the circumstances. McIntosh came to Foster Fields
seeking more information, but could not seem to get a straight story
from anybody. The women were too shocked and distracted from
the sight they had seen the night before. When Mrs. Ligon and her
mother Nancy Wood asked him if Susan should be buried "publickly or privately," McIntosh answered, "Publickly of course as she
had died with a Fit there could be no danger." For the first time the
two women faced up to the truth, at least partially: they replied,
"She did not die in a Fit." Mrs. Frances Ann Wells, another Foster
sister in residence, and Mrs. Wood admitted to McIntosh that the
night before they had "advised James Foster to escape." Yet they
denied having any suspicions of wrongdoing when they were informally questioned later by Woodson Wren, the Adams County
clerk of court.[4] Captain Samuel K. Sorsby, husband of Elizabeth,
another sister, who had died in 1831, was present in the house on
the fatal weekend, but apparently neither took command nor even
volunteered advice. The women had had to face the situation as
best they could.

At four o'clock on Saturday afternoon, as soon as a coffin could be hammered together and a hole dug, a small retinue of whites and a pair of slaves accompanied the remains to the Foster burial site, about a hundred feet or so from the bayou where she had fallen. One can only guess who attended the burial: Mother Sarah, if her health or inclinations so directed, Mrs. Wood, Mrs. Ligon, Mrs. Wells, and old William Foster. James was not present. Being a religious man, Uncle William may have said a few appropriate words. The Rev. James Smylie, a well-known Presbyterian clergyman and the author of an early apology for Christian slaveholding, lived within easy reach; he was not, however, asked to preside or attend.

David McIntosh left Foster Fields for home before the interment, to keep an eye on James Foster. He found his guest fast asleep; James did not awaken until long after the burial had been completed. As the sun disappeared, Foster expressed his regret over losing his wife so early in their marriage. Uneasily, he inquired if any "suspicions" had been voiced at the house. McIntosh, his best friend, had collaborated with James on many a business deal; four years earlier the pair of them and Levi Foster, the family's first son, had tried to gain control of slaves belonging to James's alcoholic brother Thomas Foster, Jr. McIntosh would not let his old drinking companion down now. He lied that he knew of no "suspicions."[5] The family was not much given to facing matters straight on.

After breakfast at the McIntosh place on Sunday morning, Foster saddled his horse, put fifty-two dollars of McIntosh's money in his pocket, and left. His host accompanied him as far as the Pine Ridge meetinghouse where the Reverend Smylie held forth. Upon parting, McIntosh suggested that Foster not go through Natchez as he intended. Rumors might have traveled there already, he implied. But McIntosh may have known that Foster was in bad odor in town for other reasons, too. In any event, Foster did as his partner advised, following a back route into Wilkinson County, where the family owned another plantation.[6] At Foster Fields the family rested easier upon hearing of Foster's flight.

Rumors originating from the slaves or some talkative family member circulated quickly. Yet not until the next Wednesday did the wheels of Southern justice begin to turn. Ferdinand L. Claiborne, a leading squire, magistrate, and militia officer—he had captured Aaron Burr many years before—presided over a jury of inquest at the gravesite. (A coroner's jury could convene even though a physician was not present.) Claiborne's examination was thorough. He failed to confirm William Foster's report of fingermarks at the throat, but even so, other reasons for death besides strangulation were evident. Lifting the body out of the coffin, the jurors discovered that "on the back of the neck and shoulders, and on the small of the back there were marks of great violence, so that the skin was sloughing off of these parts. That there were many whip marks over her back and her thighs red, suposed [sic] to be produced by whipping. That her left arm was broken near the shoulder and that every part of her body had blisters . . . produced by a whip." Moreover, the bottom of the coffin was covered by a thick film of blood, and "the clothing [was] bloody." Claiborne surmised that "the blood seemed to have terminated very much to the head, and the clothes that were laid under the head to raise it were saturated with blood."[7] Susan's agony had been prolonged.

Judging from the report of the coroner's jury and William Foster's deposition, one may conclude that Susan Foster's killer had acted in a frenzy, probably without deliberation and possibly without any premeditation. Though no one at Foster Fields mentioned James's condition the evening Susan died, he was probably thoroughly drunk. Foster was a "stout, athletic" man, over six feet tall; he did not know his own strength. Although a complete description of Susan Foster cannot be found in any record, she, in contrast, was likely to have been small. In any event she was barely full grown, being still three months short of her sixteenth birthday at the time of her death.[8]

Two days after the exhumation, Woodson Wren, neighbor, justice of the peace, and county clerk, came by the Foster house to interview witnesses. Mrs. Ligon, Mrs. Wood, and David McIntosh recited some of the bare facts informally, but generally were tight-lipped. Wren ordered them to appear at the courthouse for fuller, sworn statements on Monday, March 28, before himself and state

prosecutor Daniel Greenleaf. Joining them there were William
Foster and the family lawyer, Felix Huston, a neighbor on Pine
Ridge. Under more searching scrutiny, the witnesses expanded their
testimony somewhat. Yet they shed no light on why Foster had
acted as he did. They did not say that he was insensibly drunk that
night, nor, curiously, did the interrogators ask them. The witnesses
simply noted that the couple had arrived sometime before Christmas 1833, but said nothing of the way Foster supported his wife. He
was not, however, gainfully employed. Winter was a slack time on
the plantation anyhow. Probably he and McIntosh occupied themselves with hunting by day, drinking by night. The unhappy group
facing Wren and Greenleaf divulged none of these particulars. Reticence came naturally to these country folk. Their chief loyalty was
not to some abstraction of duty or justice, nor were they really concerned to protect James, a family disgrace the sooner forgotten the
better. Instead, it was the family itself that was under threat of un-
raveling. Only William Foster fully cooperated with the investigation. But the old man knew little of affairs at Foster Fields, much
less than when his brother Thomas had still been in charge there.

If there was something furtive about the Fosters' behavior
throughout the episode, the reason was not hard to find. In a society
where patriarchal leadership was so greatly needed and usually
forthcoming, they sorely felt its absence. How the Fosters' difficulty—one seldom treated historically—came about deserves some
explanation.

The Foster clan had not always been as demoralized as it was in the
early spring of 1834. In fact, for some forty years Thomas Foster, Sr.,
and his brothers had fared extremely well. Like so many Southwestern settlers of their generation, they had struggled from obscurity to
local prominence and wealth. Yet the substantial claims for reputation laid by the first generation were squandered away by the next—
a pattern we have encountered before. The original Foster settlers
arrived in Natchez about 1783. They were so undistinguished that
recent efforts to trace them in South Carolina, their point of departure, have been unavailing.[9] The immigrants—an aged mother

named Mary, four brothers, their wives, one sister, and some neighbors, probably from South Carolina's Abbeville ("Old Ninety-Six") District—arrived in Mississippi and took out Spanish land patents. Without slaves (or at most only one or two among them all) at first, they began to clear the forest along St. Catherine's Creek. John Foster, who was either the eldest or second eldest of the brothers, not only prospered over the next two-score years, but following American annexation of the region in 1798 he took public philanthropy seriously as an expression of his republican zeal. He helped to found the village of Washington a few miles from Pine Ridge. The little center for a short time rivaled Natchez in growth, and the Mississippi territorial legislature met there briefly. John Foster also provided some of the land and set in motion the plans for Jefferson College, housed in a federal-style structure, now a state monument and park site. Of all the brothers he was the most civic-minded; he had even served as a constable during the Spanish period. John Foster was one of the three brothers (James and Thomas being the other two) who all married into the Zachariah Smith family. The Smiths were the Fosters' Pine Ridge neighbors, and may have been from the same South Carolina district whence the Fosters had come in 1783. This pattern of brothers marrying sisters was a common occurrence among Southern yeomen families. Unfortunately the genealogical and court records do not reveal much information about John Foster, aside from his philanthropies and land transactions. However, he may have been the John Foster who in 1822 left the overcropped soils of St. Catherine's Creek for Texas. Possibly this John Foster was the pioneer's son, but in either case the decision to emigrate was a wise one if the upcoming generations were to flourish as well as the first settlers did. In any event, John Foster (father or son) was one of Stephen Austin's famous "Three Hundred" when he settled at Fort Bend, Texas, on the Brazos, near the future city of Houston. There the clan thrived, in contrast to the cousins left behind at Foster Fields.[10]

James Foster, who was perhaps the eldest brother, also succeeded in tobacco farming and later in cotton growing on the alluvial lands of Pine Ridge. Unlike Foster Fields, which has long since been abandoned and obliterated, Foster's Mound, James, Sr.'s, homestead, still stands on the site of an ancient Indian barrow. Joseph Ingraham, a teacher at Jefferson College on Pine Ridge and prolific writer on the Southwest, thought Foster's choice of site was tasteless: "A strange dwelling-place for the living, over the sepulchres of the dead!" But even a slight elevation made life a little more comfortable in that insect-infested region. Although a man with little education, James Foster, like John, dispensed charity, giving liberally to the institution where Ingraham taught. Perhaps James was Thomas's favorite brother, for he christened James Foster, Jr., for him, the only brother so honored. At the time of Susan's death, James Foster, Sr., was still alive, but had recently sunk into apathy, and possibly into senility. Not much guidance or command could be expected from Foster's Mound.

William Foster, the next in line, was the only male member of the first generation to assist widow Sarah and her family in the crisis. His interest showed a fidelity to family and Christian precept that his brothers either lacked or confined strictly to their immediate kin. William put little faith in things of this world. He had a comfortable property and twenty-four slaves, but he made no pretense of wanting or working for more. In fact, in wry comment on his brothers' vast holdings on Pine Ridge, William called his place Poverty Hill. He was different in other ways, too. He loved the Bible and the Methodist order, serving the faith throughout the region. He entertained circuit riders, organized new churches, and healed factional wounds. Though not as rich or distinguished as the nabobs in Natchez, William was honored with a seat on the board of trustees of the Mississippi Bible Society and led the subscription list for the building of the first charity hospital in Natchez. In 1834 the kind of devout, mission-minded, and benevolent planter that William Foster represented was not very easy to find in the Southwest. Such folk were in greater supply in the east. And William differed from most planters in the region in another respect. Unlike his brothers, he entertained doubts about the morality of slaveholding. He willed his slaves their freedom, on condition that they emigrate to Liberia. A church historian and beneficiary of his kindnesses later recorded that "Mr. Foster was taciturn, and not much gifted in exhortation . . . but he had important and useful talents as a financier, and they were solemnly dedicated to God and the good of the Church." In fact, his loans to preachers accounted for his relatively sparse resources. Not all of them were paid back. William and Rachel, his wife, were just as generous toward the family as toward the church. Though illiterate, Rachel raised a number of orphans in the clan, and William faithfully protected their inheritances. Yet despite his useful characteristics, William did not serve as example to the younger males of the Foster clan. Besides, he too was old and worn. He died before the ordeal of 1834 had fully run its course.[12]

If Thomas Foster, Sr., the youngest in the first generation, had come west alone instead of in so large a family, one would be tempted to imagine him as the inspiration for Faulkner's Thomas Sutpen. They shared some characteristics. Like Faulkner's character, Thomas was highly ambitious and ruthless in his drive to found a dynasty. Moreover, like Sutpen he had to witness family commotions over which he had little control. Nor was he, any more than Sutpen, able to set the family securely on an upward course. But Faulkner's figure was much larger than life, while Thomas Foster, Sr., was something less grand than either hero or villain: he was a conventional farmer who did well and hoped to see his sons and daughters do likewise. As was noted in an earlier chapter, though, he did not much believe in learning. His boys were simply to get along as he had. Not even Levi, the eldest, was sent off to college.[13]

Unlike William, Thomas Foster, Sr., hardly ever went to church. His wife Sarah could not even persuade him to read her the Bible, which she could not read for herself. William and Rachel sometimes took her to their Methodist meetings at the Presbyterian church on Pine Ridge. But whatever his failings as a Christian might have been, Thomas Foster was certainly an ample provider for his family. On some occasions, especially after the War of 1812, he deposited as much as $9,000 in the Bank of Mississippi at one time—a fund of cash that freed him from the expense of high interest rates. Before his death, his slave work force grew to 102, despite various disbursements to sons and dowry gifts to daughters. He even owned a coach, mostly for his daughters to parade up and down the streets of Natchez in. (Mother Sarah was not much interested in such pleasures.) In addition, Foster owned a large number of horses, necessary for his overseers and young sons on the 16,000-acre properties that he owned. Money was useful for family needs and luxuries but little else, according to Thomas's philosophy. He failed to contribute to Jefferson College, though the struggling school was almost a family fiefdom. Certainly he wasted nothing on a library. In contrast, his brother William owned twenty books of sermons and history. When Thomas Foster, Sr., died, he still owed eight years' subscriptions to the *National Intelligencer,* a Washington paper. Thomas Foster, close-mouthed, rugged, and commanding, did not bequeath his strengths to the next generation, nor did he give his progeny the educational means to find other inner resources.[14]

At one time Sarah Smith Foster, his widow, might have ably filled her husband's shoes. Widows often rose to such occasions, and she was as hardy as most. According to family tradition, she was a young girl in Revolutionary South Carolina when British troops swarmed over the farm where she was then living. They were hunting for loot that the family had hidden away. Young Sarah knew where the cache was but refused to tell the soldiers. The commander of the unit ordered her to be hanged by the neck until she talked. As historian Terry Alford tells the story, "Sarah had no more to say dangling above the floor than she had had standing on it." Choking and only half-conscious, she was finally cut free from the noose, and the troops left no richer than they had come. Another story also gave insight into her character. Early in Ibrahima's life at Foster's place, the proud slave had run away in response to a beating by his master for refusing to work with his hands. (He was born of royal blood and in his own land had been exempt from menial toil.) Several months passed, but then one night Ibrahima returned, gaunt from his failed effort to reach his homeland. Sarah was alone in the earth-floor hut that later became the large house on St. Catherine's Creek. Though startled as the ragged apparition emerged from the shadows, she held out her hand in welcome and smiled.[15]

In keeping with this determined temperament, Sarah fulfilled the wishes of her husband. She had borne him four daughters in succession (Ellen, Cassandra, Sarah, and Nancy), then a son, Levi. Three more girls followed—Mary, Frances Ann, and Elizabeth. The ninth child was another son—Thomas Foster, Jr.—and then came a daughter, Barbara. James Foster, Jr., born in 1804, stood eleventh. Caroline, David McIntosh's wife, completed the roster of daughters.[16] Isaac, child of Sarah's old age, was the last of the sons, though he scarcely fulfilled the biblical hopes that his mother had in mind at the christening. Scattered as they were through an overwhelmingly female family, the three sons must have felt at times quite alone in the midst of so many women. What Sarah was able to do to counteract the effect upon her boys cannot be known. With thirteen children to handle, no doubt she found the burden increasingly wearisome over the years. After Thomas, Jr.'s, escapades with Susy, she might have greeted the scandal of Susan Foster's killing with some apathy. She was herself not far from death.

Failing even a single fragment of family papers, we can only speculate why no one in the second generation of Foster men measured up to the role of patriarch. Only Levi, the eldest, had much talent and self-confidence and, unwilling to wait for his father to retire, he had left Natchez and established himself in Franklin, Louisiana, as a planter, lawyer, and speculator. In June 1834 he too died, quite unexpectedly, thus depriving the clan of his counsel in its time of need over the next several months. Thomas and James were both family black sheep; Thomas had died a drunkard in 1831. Isaac, it seems, was either totally unreliable or mentally defective. By her will of 1835, mother Sarah had to place Foster Fields under a trustee; Isaac was apparently incapable of managing the plantation by himself.[17]

It sometimes happened that a daughter filled the role of family leader in the absence of a male with the necessary qualities. Traditional societies seldom acknowledged such deviations openly, but widows with sufficient property, for example, could inspire enough awe and hope for future reward to work their will. Such, however, was not the case in the Foster household. Thomas Foster, Sr.'s, daughters lacked the requisite drive. Perhaps Mary (Carson) Foster, Uncle James's daughter-in-law, set the tone for her young cousins by marriage. There was not much social life at Foster Fields; old Sarah had a fine pioneer spirit but was hardly a woman to relish a fast social pace. Mary Foster, however, did her fluttery best. Margaret Wilson, a Yankee governess who met her at Foster Fields a few years later, reported that Mary looked "like a jolly milk maid" but, aware of her own lack of polish, compensated with "as many fine airs as she could manage, but without any effect but that of disgusting me." The Yankee observer may have been unfair. But certainly there was nothing very commanding about any of the women in this Foster generation.[18] Their Southern, half-genteel upbringing freed them from the milk pail perhaps, but they were not comfortable issuing orders to menfolk from the parlor.

Cassandra, alone among the nine daughters, might have been able to assume the headship. She most resembled her father Thomas; she had always been his favorite. As her name suggests, Cassandra was not born to happiness, despite her father's special regard. First she married a wastrel named Ephraim Foster, possibly a cousin. Not only was he a poor plantation manager on Pine Ridge but he was a very abusive husband as well. Cassandra, an independent soul, returned to her father's house and, in 1824, sued her husband for divorce to escape his "severe, cruel and dangerous blows." Before the matter could be adjudicated, Ephraim died in a Natchez boardinghouse. Within days of his passing, Cassandra, wasting no time on bereavement, married John Speed in early 1825. The family was delighted that Cassandra, thirty-seven years old and childless, had so quickly rescued herself from the solitude of a single life. Six years later, in 1831, she too died. At Cassandra's request, mother Sarah relinquished her burial spot next to her husband Thomas so that Cassandra could once more be close to her father. Almost at once the family, including James Foster, Jr., sued Speed as Cassandra's heir. The litigants claimed that Speed was a bigamist and argued that therefore Chancellor John A. Quitman should restore Cassandra's sizable holdings to the Foster survivors. No doubt one reason for James Foster, Jr.'s, lengthy stay at Foster Fields the winter of 1833–34 was the expectation of a ruling on the case. Quitman, however, took his time. The following year he dismissed the suit, on the grounds that Speed's prior marriage had never been proved. Rather than helping matters, Cassandra, even after death, had helped stir up a bitter dispute over an outsider's possession of property once belonging to the clan.[19]

In the absence of direct kin able or willing to assume patriarchal burdens, sons-in-law sometimes filled the role. Once again, the Foster family was hapless. Either the best of the number, like General William Barnard, Barbara's husband, had already died, or they lived too far away. The most likely candidate was David McIntosh, but he was not the kind to take on extra responsibilities. He was known as a "bottle man and proud of the fact." He had encouraged James Foster's unfortunate habits, so much so that widow Sarah had little use for him. Some years after this family crisis, McIntosh crossed St. Catherine's Creek at high water. Drunk, he stumbled and began to drown. A slave woman heard his cries and struck him on the head with a plank, which split his skull. He went down for good. She claimed that she had only meant to save him; there was no way to prove otherwise.[20]

Quite clearly the Fosters were the antithesis of the model patriarchal family, which was well ordered, with a clear purpose and clean lines of authority. As this recounting suggests, however, death as well as the vagaries of gender order and number could sometimes play havoc with the usual expectations. The conditions of life often showed the vulnerability of patriarchy, but for centuries there seemed no other way to organize matters. The Foster clan represented that sometimes-overlooked historical factor—family failure—even as its members also typified the dilemmas of the planter nouveaux riches. There was a desperation in the Fosters' battle to retain wealth that they had not become wholly accustomed to having. No doubt pressures over money, his place in the family counsels, and his own wretched failings led James Foster, Jr., to make a scapegoat of his wife. Just a week before the murder, Sarah had made clear her feelings about him. She had distributed some additional lands to her favorite, widowed daughters, including Nancy Wood, whom Foster called upon to help resuscitate his dead wife. But the aged widow had not given James a single acre.[21] Without land and capital, Foster could hardly support himself, much less a wife as well.

James Foster, Jr., had no way out. His fury, for a time, was out of control. Perhaps the tragedy would not have occurred if Thomas Foster, Sr., had still been alive. But in the absence of some formidable or calming authority, James had let his resentments and self-hatred take command. For all of the recently deceased Thomas Foster, Jr.'s, alcoholic and sexual compulsions, he had only threatened to destroy Susannah, his wife, and their children, but he had never actually harmed them. In a sense, the old patriarch had stood in the way. Perhaps he had somehow stunted his sons, but once he was dead Thomas Foster, Sr.'s, presence seemed more necessary than ever. Despite their bravado, Thomas, Jr., and James were not complete men, but quivering bundles of contrary feelings. Like so many young planters' sons caught under the patriarchal yoke, they threw their aggression outward from a garrison that had no walls.[22]

The killing and the family's ineffectual reaction to it illustrated the anarchy that threatened a traditional household when the patriarch had no successor. It also pointed to issues of honor and shame. Had Foster simply been a wife killer, the public response might have been milder than it proved to be. But in the community's view he was not just a wife beater who had let his feelings get the better of him. To the epithet "murderer" the people added the label "blackleg," that is, professional gambler. It was therefore a matter of public satisfaction when Constable Norwood found Foster passively waiting, like Faulkner's Wash Jones, for the arrival of the law at the plantation doorstep in neighboring Wilkinson County. Quite probably James was apathetic because he was not fully conscious of what he had done that night. It was almost as if he half-sought a public judgment to ascertain who he was. The tendency to find one's reflection in the mirror of public praise or blame was much a part of the old ethic.

The prisoner returned with his captor sometime in the early summer of 1834. For six months or more he was to languish in the Adams County jail awaiting trial for murder.[23] Sheriff Gridley, a good Methodist and a friend of Uncle William Foster, would not have permitted Foster's gaming friends from Natchez-under-the-Hill to help him idle away the hours. In fact, they too were currently subject to heavy public criticism, which Foster's crime only made more severe.

James Foster, Jr., had not been a gambling addict at the start of his adult life. Like his eldest brother Levi, who had left years before to make a fortune in the Attakapas District, James had been impatient for the old man to die. What was a young fellow to do while waiting for his father to distribute his properties? Tiring of the slow pace of the declining port of Natchez, James left town in 1825 and headed for Franklin, Louisiana, where brother Levi and his in-laws, the DeMarets, had established themselves as land, cattle, slave, and cotton dealers.[24] James was a welcome addition to society in St. Mary. Black-haired and wild—like Nathaniel Bacon—he led no cause but his own claim to glory. Some called him the best-looking man in the Southwest. Certainly he was popular with the men, thanks to high animal spirits and a willingness to open his purse for another round of whiskey. When old Thomas Foster, Sr., finally died of a stroke in 1829, James bought some land from Levi, next to Levi's plantation on Bayou Teche. He raised "pretty fair crops," young Daniel Lacy, Levi's overseer, declared. One year he brought in enough cane to make over sixty hogsheads of sugar. Generous as always, he grandly lent the widow Lacy, Daniel's mother, over $500.[25]

From the moment of his arrival in Franklin, James was willing to take risks that Levi, his elder by ten years or so, ordinarily passed by. In those very litigious times, Levi had only found occasion to sue seven individuals from his arrival in 1812 to 1824. After brother James appeared in 1825, he and Levi, his new partner, were plaintiffs in forty-three cases between 1825 and 1832. (After that date, matters grew worse.) By 1833, Levi discovered that he had lent over $5,000 to various people.[26] The collateral that they offered was no more valuable than the borrowers' reputations.

Levi had always been one to speculate without too much regard for business proprieties. The evidence is in the records of his manipulation of his wife's estate, an inheritance from her father, the aristocratic head of the DeMaret family. But the frenetic activity that Louisiana court records reveal suggests that James Foster, Jr., had inveigled his brother into lending money to gaming friends. With capital in short supply, Levi fell behind in debts he owed suppliers for his store and other enterprises. Sometimes the gamblers, usually cowpokes, also appeared in the suits, making claims that they had been plied with liquor and then forced to sign notes to cover losses at the table. James, a master card player, easily assumed the role of the genial planter at leisure. He owned a handsome faro box and bet sums as great as one hundred dollars at a time. (Few of these devices were not rigged.) Games made him feel omnipotent, an arbiter of destiny. Neither the ordinary routines of planting nor even money itself offered comparable excitement. Besides, the other big men in Franklin often cut the decks with him—Judge John Moore, planter Edgar DeMaret, Helair Carlin, attorney Benjamin R. Gant, Attorney Alexander Splane, and Captain Winfrey Lockett. It was a fast society, and James Foster, Jr., moved with the best.[27]

Levi Foster also played hard, and he admired James for being much like himself. But in 1832 the press of lawsuits and James's increasingly erratic behavior, noticeable ever since Thomas Foster, Sr.'s, death in 1829, threatened to break up their close relationship. They quarreled over who owned which of Thomas Foster, Jr.'s, slaves. But the crop of 1832 was so enormous that James Foster, Jr., saw still greater vistas for making a name for himself and outdistancing his elder brother. Instead of paying off outstanding debts, he bought himself an eighty-foot schooner, the *St. Mary*, sported "fine clothes," traded for "fine horses," and even found time for a trip to Texas to look over a half-league of land that he had bought with money borrowed against his father's bequest. In early January

1833 he grandly announced a special trip to New Orleans to sell his remaining crop. Widow Susan Lacey, the mother of Levi's overseer, entrusted her crop to his care.[28] That excursion proved to be James Foster, Jr.'s undoing. At a later trial for fraud, initirted by his creditors, evidence about his habits during this period came to light. As several witnesses remarked, Foster boasted of picking up five to six thousand dollars for the cane sold in New Orleans. He would produce a bankroll "as big as your wrist" to prove the point.[29] After a visit to a theater, declared Edgar DeMaret, a Franklin planter, James Foster, Jr., entered a New Orleans "gaming house where they had rolette and Farrow [sic]." DeMaret watched him bet and drink until Foster went off and "frolicked" (whored) for a while. Later DeMaret came upon Foster at a coffee house, and Foster boasted that he had been betting "fifty dollars at a time" and that he was only pretending to be as drunk as he appeared. DeMaret's testimony was particularly impressive; he was one of Levi Foster's brothers-in-law and belonged to one of the oldest families in the district.[30] However, other witnesses claimed that Foster was not so penniless as DeMaret and several other witnesses claimed. William B. Lewis, a Franklin resident, implied that Foster was very successful at cards throughout the time he was in New Orleans, and had even won at "veint-un" on the way back to Franklin. The issue was important; creditors suspected that Foster had hidden away his profits to escape their demands. Helair Carlin, a well-regarded planter, maintained that Foster was "verry [sic] much addicted to gamboling [sic] . . . drank a good deal . . . and had become more and more embarrassed until the time he left" for Mississippi in November 1833. Carlin's opinion seemed to be the common view in Franklin, however much Foster's creditors hoped that he had not completely "busted."[31]

When James Foster, Jr. returned to Franklin from New Orleans in January 1833, he certainly acted as if he had no cash at all. He put off an emissary from Susan Lacy, eager to have her crop money. Loading up his schooner with cargo, still unpaid for, Foster set sail for the Gulf. He was spotted, however, and the sheriff of St. Landry Parish seized him on behalf of creditors in the Opelousas area.

Though he was forced to walk from Franklin to Opelousas on a leash attached to the sheriff's saddle, James Foster, Jr., had not yet run out of luck. Brother Levi hastened to the Opelousas courthouse and stood bond for him, whereupon he was released from jail.[32]

In March James was to be found aboard the *Calcasieu,* a vessel about which there is no information at all. Witnesses reported seeing James Foster, Jr., aboard with Captain Bundick, the master, playing cards and drinking. The vessel was apparently a floating casino, although it carried flour and other kinds of cargo, too. It was during the sojourn on the *Calcasieu* that Foster met and perhaps solemnized the union with Susan. (No marriage record can be found.)[33]

The honeymoon was not long. In September the sheriff of St. Mary Parish arrested James Foster, Jr., for fraud. This time all his creditors, some eighteen of them, joined their suits together. While Alexander Splane, the prosecutor, prepared his case, James spent the fall in the Franklin jail. Meantime, Susan lived at Levi Foster's place. She had come in June "decently dressed," but by fall her husband, "shabby and ragged" himself, had gambled away her clothing, too. She did not even have a bonnet left, making her look "common," said the Foster brothers' cousin John Smith of Franklin. Nothing could have been more mortifying for the bride, or indeed for the family as a whole. At James's urgent request from jail Levi supplied a new bonnet.[34]

With the always pliable Judge John Moore to help, Levi arranged Foster's bail in November, with gaming friends Lockett, Boyce, and Hungerford posting bond. Wheedling money from cousin John Smith, Foster and Susan fled to Natchez, much to the outrage of Prosecutor Splane and the planters who had forfeited the bond money. Ironically, when the trial was held in James Foster, Jr.'s, absence the following year the jurors found him innocent of fraud. But all his assets, including the schooner, a dirk, a pistol, a cowhide whip, card decks ($1.38), saddles, and horses, were sold. The total came to $10,895.75, far short of the sums owed.[35] From being a "sporting gentleman" James had become a mere "blackleg," a status among men equivalent to that of a prostitute among women. For a young wife, he was not much of a figure to admire.

Nothing is known about Susan, his bride. Her maiden name may have been Alphin, Alphari, or possibly Alpha. Since neither the people of Franklin nor those of Natchez knew her or her family, she remains, from the historical vantage point, a wraith. All efforts to trace her have failed. But one fact is readily clear: whoever she was, she had no kinfolk to avenge her death or to hire an attorney to help the prosecutor, a common and welcome addition to state cases in those days. The lack of curiosity of those in Franklin and Natchez said something about the attitude of Southern society toward kinless womankind.

As a rule, a young married girl preferred to be within reasonable proximity of kinspeople. Susan was not given that option, probably because she came from poor or unsettled people. She brought nothing to the marriage but herself. Like Susannah, Thomas Foster, Jr.'s, young wife, she was particularly vulnerable to her husband's whims. Married before her fifteenth birthday, she was hardly mature enough to judge her handsome spouse in a critical light, at least at first. Mrs. Wood, Mrs. Ligon, and Mrs. Wells, the widows at Foster Fields, befriended the young girl, but she certainly made few acquaintances on Pine Ridge—not enough to give any substance to Foster's charge of unfaithfulness. Had there really been some liaison or flirtation, the Fosters would have quickly pointed it out to county officials.[36]

The Pine Ridge neighborhood was shocked that one of its residents had so cruelly killed his wife, a friendless, kinless waif, a mere child. The gentleman who took it upon himself to serve as her guardian *post mortem* was Spence Monroe Grayson, a thirty-one-year-old lawyer just gaining local prominence. In 1839 he was to oppose the passage of the Mississippi Women's Property Act in the state senate, arguing eloquently that woman's purity had to be kept free from the corruption of business transactions. In keeping with these chivalrous views, he volunteered to assist the state's attorney, Daniel

Greenleaf. In fact, Grayson had himself listed as the prosecutor of record in the court docket.[37] Known for his speaking abilities, Grayson no doubt expected to make the chief plea to the jury, leaving to Greenleaf the paperwork and investigation of the circumstances.

Grayson's associations with Pine Ridge ran deep. His uncle and guardian, Beverley R. Grayson, had raised him. William Grayson, congressman, planter, and Revolutionary hero of Prince William County, Virginia, was the head of the clan. Spence Monroe Grayson had lost both parents in 1803 when he was an infant. His uncle Beverley removed to Mississippi, where he hoped to reduplicate the glories and prestige of the family's Virginia forefathers. Beverley Grayson raised his nephew as his own son, and set his young charge a very high example, in the best Southern tradition. Beverley Grayson was long active in civic affairs in Natchez and on the Ridge. With the Foster brothers, James and John, he had helped establish Jefferson College and Elizabeth Female Academy on Pine Ridge. Far from what Southwesterners regarded as the typical Virginia gentleman, impractical and overcivilized, Beverley Grayson operated sawmills, cotton gins, and stores as well as the requisite plantation. Spence Monroe Grayson followed suit. Though just about the same age as James Foster, Jr., whom he must have known since boyhood, Grayson had long before charted his course and knew his mind. He had studied well in school and at Jefferson College, and at age twenty-three he had already joined the Natchez bar through the sponsorship of Senator Thomas Read, his mentor. In 1830, unlike James Foster, Jr., he married a woman with unimpeachable Virginia and Philadelphia connections, Sarah R. Chew, whose father was a leading Natchez nabob. The couple settled down not far from the Fosters' district. It would be interesting to know if there had been bad blood between James Foster, Jr., and his prosecutor when they were growing up together. In any case, Spence Monroe Grayson, as his obituaries in 1839 later attested, was a flower of Southern gentility.[38] Susan Alpha (?) Foster was to have a bold knight after all, though only as avenger of her death.

If Grayson was to serve as representative of Southern civilization, Felix Huston, Foster's attorney, epitomized Southern tradition. Scots-Irish by extraction, Huston was as tall as an ancient Frankish king; the troops in Texas whom he led a few months after Foster's ordeal called him "General Long-Shanks." He and Seargent S. Prentiss, his partner for a time, had the most lucrative practice in Natchez, and Huston's wife, Mary E. Daingerfield, had a plantation directly adjacent to Foster Fields. There Huston entertained lavishly—hunting parties, balls, picnics, shooting matches—but whether the Fosters were ever invited is not known. Sophisticated though he was, Huston was much less genteel than Grayson. Proud of his marksmanship, he fought more than one duel, although his encounter with Albert Sidney Johnston during the Texas Revolution was the most celebrated.

Felix Huston had no second thoughts about taking up the defense of James Foster, Jr. He was already representing him—and many other Foster relations—in the dispute with John Speed over Cassandra's will. Fortunately for Huston's legal strategy, the confusions over the impaneling of Mississippi juries under common law were still obstructing judicial procedures. Therefore, Prosecutor Greenleaf quickly responded with a brief upholding the methods by which Woodson Wren, the clerk of court, had established the array. Since no other attorney had utilized the same challenge in that court session, Judge Alexander Montgomery (who had presided over the Alonzo Phelps case) decided to postpone the Foster trial. In the October term Montgomery had felt obliged to throw out all jury cases on the same grounds—that the grand jury that presented the indictments had been improperly convened—and did not wish that to happen again. Therefore he set Foster's trial for the very last day of the term, so that the Foster indicment could be dismissed without cleaning out the docket for the entire term. Although Montgomery did not announce his intentions regarding the Foster trial, its postponement gave a hint that the townspeople did not at all like. It suggested that Huston's motion to quash the venire would probably be accepted. However, they would have to wait until January 2, 1835, the final sitting, to learn whether the wife-killer was to be tried or not.

By the time Montgomery was ready to give his opinion, the Natchez public had been entertained with a full session of cases—four Negro-stealings, an embezzlement, thirteen assault and battery charges, two fornications, and other assorted crimes.[39] Excitement mounted as the only murder trial that term approached. Moreover, there were other tensions in Natchez, indeed in Mississippi and in the nation at large. Devastating cholera attacks had already shocked the region and the country as a whole. Poor weather conditions had unsettled expectations in the Mississippi Valley. In national politics, partisan warfare over President Jackson's determination to destroy the Bank of the United States had grown increasingly bitter. In prior months both Felix Huston and Spence Monroe Grayson had been in fist fights at local rallies of Jacksonians and their opponents, soon to be called Whigs. Still more alarming to friends of the Union was the appearance of organized abolitionism. In October 1833 Northern evangelicals and Quakers had formed the American Anti-Slavery Society in New York, with a local riot to give their efforts national notoriety. At that time, Felix Huston had written to the New York *Courier and National Enquirer,* a fiercely anti-abolitionist paper, saying that if, as a result of the new organization's agitation among slaves, "one female had been violated by that unhallowed union of white and black desperadoes, no man in the State" with antislavery sentiments "would have escaped—they would have perished to a man."[40]

In broad terms, some kind of public sense that moral boundaries and expectations were no longer so precise and sturdy as they once had been seemed to afflict the nation at large. In New York City there were sudden outbreaks of riots, not only against abolitionists and free blacks, but also among political factions. Mobs from Boston burned the Ursuline convent and school at Charlestown, the first of many attacks throughout the northeast in protest against Irish immigration. The epidemic of civil disorders was to grow still worse in 1835. Particularly was this so after the abolitionist postal campaign, which aroused much indignation, North and South, when antislavery pamphlets reached their destinations. Even in 1834, Mississippians feared for public safety when Alonzo Phelps, brigand and murderer, escaped from jail, though he was killed when cornered. The dramatic revelations of Virgil Stewart about a widespread conspiracy of similar highwaymen, "steam doctors," and professional gamblers under John A. Murrell was to reinforce those worries in 1835. White Mississippians readily believed that abolitionists had joined with these villainous elements to overthrow the social order and pillage, murder, and tyrannize law-abiding citizens. There was not a word of truth in the public fantasy. The terror, however, served a customary purpose, notifying all whites of the need for solidarity.

All these eruptions, North and South, were directed toward the reestablishment of traditional popular morality: the supremacy of the Protestant "good" over the Catholic "menace," the white man over the rebellious black, the gentleman of leisure over the lying gamester, the patriot over the subversive abolitionist, the honest citizen over robbers, medical frauds, and anyone else who sought to snatch away the citizen's hard-won cash. These simple themes of alien menace reduced complex circumstances to masterable proportions, so that even the most illiterate yeoman or worker could understand and participate in the rites of exorcism, expulsion, and purification.

James Foster, Jr., it might be said, was one of the early victims in this recurrent but variously motivated "inflammation of the popular mind," as Hawthorne called it. The rituals of sacrifice, by shaming one individual, thereby "proved" the worth, purity of purpose, and security of those beset with evils not so readily apprehended. Such actions thrust the pain of self-recognition upon the victim and what he or she represents. In a sense Foster was to be punished not for his crime alone, but for the anxieties of the citizenry.

There was nothing class-conscious or very modern about any of the mobs of the 1830s, particularly the one that milled about Natchez's handsome, porticoed courthouse on January 2, 1835. The crowd was there to participate in a ritual no less stylized and mythic than that which Hawthorne depicted in his story. Believing that Foster's indictment was likely to be quashed, the citizens told each other, as people had in similar situations in America since the seventeenth century, that the system of justice was defective, unreliable, that technicalities conjured up by the wizards of the law protected rich clients like Foster, leaving the public at the mercy of fiends. The waiting crowd, one of its members later recalled, expected that the judge would soon let the prisoner "loose upon an outraged community, unscathed, unwhipped of justice." Foster's hands would be "reeking with the blood of his virtuous and butchered wife," and he would be free "to exult and gloat over his infamy, and, like a wild beast *once* fed on human flesh and blood, acquiring an insatiable love for such food, to hunt for other victims." Colonel James Creecy, who later wrote these words, expressed the less grandly articulated feelings of the mob. The ceremony of degradation itself would translate those visceral sentiments into symbolic actions.[41]

Yet, as in all such enterprises, anger was not the sole emotion to sweep that assembly in Natchez. There was also the sense of joy and celebration that a charivari ordinarily elicited. After all, it was January 2, a Saturday in the New Year's holiday. It was a time when, traditionally, bells were rung and noisemakers twirled to scare off a community's old sins and spirits and to welcome in a new beginning, pure and innocent—when ancient Authority, Father Time, was deposed and the new-crowned child was exalted.

Sheriff Gridley and his deputies marched the accused the short distance to the courtroom. Pale and faltering after months of close confinement in shackles, Foster met Felix Huston before the bench. Judge Montgomery, the first native Mississippian to serve as a state common pleas judge, wasted no time. It was his last case before retirement. The venire was quashed, he ruled. Foster was free, at least momentarily.

The crowd outside swelled to three hundred or more as word of Montgomery's decision spread. It was as diverse a throng as could be imagined—planters' sons in town to promenade and carouse, Choctaw Indians and their squaws, riverboat men, steamboat passengers, prostitutes, gamblers, town urchins and apprentices, slaves and ordinary white folk visiting on court day. None were dressed for outlandish masquerade. Their regular attire was motley enough, however, according to "Thimblerig," an observer and participant. Thimblerig, who was a professional shell-game artist, later told his story to Colonel David Crockett, whom he joined on a steamboat bound for New Orleans not long afterward. Crockett, on his way to Texas, included the account in his famous autobiography.[42]

Officials of the court and the better sort of folk were not visible. However, they certainly were aware—and tacitly approving—of the events that would ensue. Judge Montgomery, prosecutor Greenleaf, and Sheriff Horace Gridley were nowhere in sight. The Duncans, Holmeses, Quitmans, and others of high station would never have led the rites. The task belonged to upcoming young men not yet weighed down with honors and dignities. Grayson, the prosecutor of record, and Huston, Foster's attorney, remained to accompany him as he stepped into the light of the winter noonday sun. At once "two gentlemen" seized Foster, who fell in the ensuing scuffle. Huston intervened. Urging the pressing throng to move back, Huston helped Foster up and gained permission for them both to pass up the street a hundred yards or so. As they walked away from the catcalls and angry fists, Foster, sobbing abjectly, begged Huston to save him. There was not much the attorney could have done, even if he had wished to do so; by acting like a wheedling coward Foster merely aroused mob disgust all the more. Then, as Huston and the mob had arranged, Huston gave Foster the signal to run. If Foster could have outrun the crowd, he would have gained his freedom. But the prisoner was paralyzed. Depression, shame, and dread sapped his will. The mob grabbed him once again.[43]

According to one account, a line then formed in near silence. "The word 'march' was pronounced finally by the tall man in front," Colonel James Creecy later remembered. He was referring to Felix Huston, who was no longer the prisoner's lawyer but now his chief tormentor. Grayson also joined the head of the procession as it moved toward the ravine near the toll bridge. It was the place where Thomas Foster, Jr., and the slave Susy had met to make their escape together a few years before. The hollow was the customary site for community rituals of this kind in Natchez. The leaders lashed Foster to a tree. For the next several hours—from about noon to sundown—the citizens laid on the strokes with a cowhide whip, "until," said Thimblerig, "the flesh rung in ribands from his body."[44] Each lash was a reminder of the agony that Foster had perpetrated upon Susan, a biblical retribution indeed.

As the sun began to set, the lynchers heated up the tar, while debating whether Foster should be branded on both cheeks, have his ears slit, or be scalped. (The first two choices were penalties current on the state's statute books. Not for another decade did the penitentiary mode replace corporal exactions in Mississippi.) The decision was for a partial scalping; a complete one would have been fatal. After this was done, tar was poured over Foster's head, shoulders, and back, followed by a dousing with the traditional feathers. Dressed in this manner and otherwise wearing only "a miserable pair of breeches," Foster was led back to town. On the way he fainted several times. As he lay groaning, no one attended him. He was, recalled Thimblerig simply, "an object of universal detestation." After Foster was seated backwards to the cart's tail, the lynchers accompanied the "common dray" with the sounds of pots banging, lids clashing, boys whistling, and drummers beating unrhythmically—the "rough music" of the antique "rogue's march."[45]

By this time the crowd was a happy thoroughly drunken New Year's throng. As Sheriff Gridley helped Foster climb the jail steps, a howl went up. "Take him to the river, tie him to a log, and set him adrift," some yelled. "Hang the villain!" "Never turn such a fellow loose to butcher another wife," cried others. These bowdlerized threats from Colonel Creecy's account do not capture the gutter language that was no doubt really used. But Grayson, who addressed the mob from the steps, was probably accurately quoted. He was said to have replied, "My friends, we have *done* our duty as good citizens, and I now propose that we all go quietly to our homes!" The "common dray" was rolled off. The bulk of the mob dispersed. Gridley took Foster inside, for Foster's own protection. Only a few stragglers remained, but they had murderous intentions. Some were muttering that Foster should have been branded and his ears cut off, back at the hollow. They were waiting for a chance to act on their own.[46]

James Creecy, in his memoir, claimed that he had not seen Foster clearly until the victim was led up the steps. In awe and fear, he exclaimed, "Almighty Father, what a picture! He was more like a huge shapeless fowl, covered with masses of feathers, all turned the wrong way, than anything else." Thimblerig also described him: "The blood oozing from his stripes had become mixed with masses of feathers and tar, and rendered his aspect still more horrible and loathsome." Finally, the editor of the Natchez *Courier* aptly remarked, "So far from recognizing Foster" as he had appeared in court that morning, "we could scarcely realize that he was a man. The mob believed he was a monster at heart, and were determined that his external appearance should correspond with the inner man."[47]

The mob had sought to purge the community of a deviant judged so beneath human attribute that tar—a kind of representational excrement—was fitting apparel. Instead of acting as the protector of his wife (who was also a child), he had had no "fear of God before his eyes" and, as the common-law indictment read, had been "moved and seduced by the instigation of the Devil" to slay her maliciously. In a patriarchal world, one might chastise a loved one, but few crimes were worse than intrafamilial killings. In addition, Foster was a gamester—in debt, accused of fraud, and so addicted to gambling that his habits aroused contempt even in that gambling-obsessed age and region. Like an alcoholic who could not hold his liquor, Foster repelled other men who were drinkers and gamblers themselves. His excesses caricatured their own inclinations in frightening ways. He was the mirror of what they might become. For these reasons Foster had to be transformed from what he was, an ordinary, even physically attractive young man, into a creature with whom no one needed to identify himself. Clad in feathers, he became the male-turned-female, a humiliated cowbird, the symbol of the cuckoldry that he had sought to escape in his furious assault upon his wife. From a superhuman beast "hunting for other victims," to borrow from Creecy, Foster was translated into a puny-brained, two-legged, feather-covered capon, as harmless as the bird whose neck was habitually wrung for Sunday dinner.[48]

One may be sure that such humiliations had the desired psychological effect on the victim. Hawthorne's description of Major Molineux's reaction was very accurate. Foster's state of mind was even more abject. His agony can best be compared with the violation felt by a man or woman subjected to unremitting gang rape. Later that night, at about two in the morning, two men on horseback led an unmounted horse to the jail. Thimblerig, who watched, recalled that "Foster was with difficulty placed astride." The mob's lookouts tried to grab him, but Foster found strength enough to shake them loose. One fired a pistol, but the shot only grazed Foster's hat, and the three rode off into the night. The party stopped at Foster Fields, only a few miles away.[49]

One of the two men who rescued Foster was one of his brothers-in-law, Daniel MacMillan of neighboring Franklin County, Mississippi, a justice of the peace and a hard-driving man. Perhaps the other horseman was MacMillan's son. On May 21, 1835, almost five months later, Foster had sufficiently recovered to assign his share of whatever remained of Thomas Foster, Sr.'s, estate to that son, Calvin MacMillan, his nephew. No doubt this was the reward for the rescue. The Foster clan of James, Jr.'s, generation, it would seem, seldom did much for each other without some monetary exchange. Once his signature was on that indenture, Foster disappeared.[50]

The Fosters seldom spoke of him again, but one member of the clan thought that he had gone to Texas. Allegedly, he never remarried and died at the close of the century. According to the same unsubstantiated report, he left a large estate in Houston town lots to his grandnephew, Governor Murphy Foster, the grandson of James's former partner in Franklin, Louisiana, Levi Foster. The legacy, so the story goes, would have been a public embarrassment during the reform governor's reelection campaign against the infamous Louisiana Lottery gang, then a powerful political machine, and so Murphy Foster, fearing that the ancient murder would hurt his election chances, refused the inheritance. The whole tale seems implausible.[51]

Nevertheless, it appears that Foster did survive, as Grayson and Huston had intended. Certainly recuperation from some 150 lashes required a strong constitution, but Foster owed his life to the attorneys who had allowed his humiliation but had prevented a sentence of death. The reasons for this mercy were several. First, Grayson was a gentleman who took the title seriously. It would have been barbarous for a Virginian and Christian to let him die after a court had rendered a contrary verdict. Second, both Grayson and Huston were lawyers sworn to uphold the sanctity of the court with which they were affiliated. Third, they were members of the planter class, and Foster had once been so regarded, too. Though his rank had been lost, it could not be forgotten. To let a mob of the poor and powerless kill someone of superior original standing would violate convention and order. The ordinary cheating gamester, the rebellious slave, the lowly ne'er-do-well were fit objects for a death sentence under lynch law. But a planter, even a wife-killer, was not to be hanged summarily. The second generation of Fosters might have forfeited their place in local estimation with two divorce cases, adulterous miscegenation, and then murder. Nevertheless James Foster, Jr., reasoned Huston and Grayson, should be allowed to survive.

Yet these factors do not explain why the crowd so promptly obeyed Grayson's call for a return to order. All but the handful who lingered in hopes of more excitement accepted his plea and left the scene. The reason they did so was that Grayson and Huston had also served another purpose. As leaders of the mob, they had given sanction to what was done. For the duration of the charivari they were exploited by the crowd as much as they used it for their own ends: the punishing of a planter who had violated the class code and the code of honor attached to it. The attorneys lent legitimacy to deeds that were clearly illegal, even reprehensible if undertaken by a single actor. Through them the rite became "holy aggression," in contrast to Foster's distinctly unholy offense. Someone had to initiate the action in the name of all, and at once such an individual became more than a leader: he was regarded as a hero by those following him, as one whose strength of will and sense of rightfulness could set aside all doubts and fears. The crowd shared in his glory even as they were the instruments by which the hero acquired it. If the individual who instigated the first acts against the scapegoat had no prior prestige but arose from the mob itself, matters could quickly get out of hand. But leaders like Huston and Grayson were men already held in respect. They had the authority to control both the beginning and the ending of the episode, so that studied "misrule" did not degenerate into wild disorder. If that had occurred, Foster would doubtless have perished. To folk ill equipped for deeds of special courage, the power of the respected leader assumed almost a magical character. He made possible, as Ernest Becker put it, "the expression of forbidden impulses, secret wishes, and fantasies." As father and elder brother in the phalanx of honor and heroics, individuals such as the two attorneys condoned and supervised the appetites of conventional men for power, or rather the semblance of it. If anything went wrong, the leaders, not the anonymous participants, would have to bear the burden.[52]

Yet it was important for the leaders' own self- and group esteem to restrict the action, much as a father would in dealing with a child dangerously close to a frightening loss of control. Too much power makes men afraid. It opens floodgates of passion not easy to shut. It destroys the crowd's unanimity, beneath which hide the ever-present anxieties of life and of death. Grayson thus demanded what the crowd really wanted: release from their own dreams of omnipotence, dreams too intense to sustain for very long. At the same time, his words of restraint implicitly reminded the listeners that those who initiated such awesome proceedings had the authority, derived from the crowd and from their own local prominence, to end them. The fantasy of heroism that fellowship evoked had to cease. The squeaks of Foster's empty cart, receding into the night, signaled the return to mundane human concerns and transciencies.

It was therefore hardly surprising that the Foster affair led to no reexamination of public policy. No journalist or judge called for the strengthening of the police and judicial systems. No preachers—Adams County boasted very few anyhow—climbed the rostrum to denounce the charivari or the ethic that made it so serviceable a device. The very opposite occurred: the launching of lynch law crusades throughout the state to hunt down other deviants from conventional standards of behavior. Even the Fosters may have thought it all had turned out for the best. The wastrel son relinquished his legal claims to Cassandra's fortune and whatever else might come to him from his father and mother's estates in future. The succeeding generations buried the memory of his disgrace as they had Susan, who still lies in the sod of Foster Fields, without a marker. People who rely upon oral tradition have very selective memories.

What was true of the clan's amnesia about James was also true for the South as a whole. The darker aspects of honor were seldom to be questioned, then or for many years to come. Individuals and sometimes groups spoke out against popular forms of injustice and honor—duels, summary hangings, mob whippings. These efforts at reform seldom received public acclamation and support. Even historians, whether native to the South or not, have not seen these expressions of public will and private esteem as part of a total cultural pattern. Instead they have been labeled tragic aberrations, or techniques by which the planter class manipulated lesser, more virtuous folk. Gentility, the nobler, brighter feature of Southern ethics, has been a more congenial topic. Certainly it was the model that Southerners have publicly revered and exalted. The selectivity was natural. Nonetheless, the higher claims of chivalry, Stoic and Christian, were put to the service of primal honor. Gentlemen like Spence Monroe Grayson often found themselves carried along on the tides of multitudes, or were driven to silent acquiescence with no chance of guiding the public into calmer moods. The choice that Grayson made in standing at the head of Foster's enemies was exactly the same one that many others would later make when "honor" cried out for secession. The prudent man was wise to stand aside, saving doubts for afterthoughts when passions died away. Thus the "innocence" of primal values, as Faulkner made clear, was an imperfect shield against misperceptions, contradictions, and thoughtless cruelty. It could even be their very source. As Hawthorne had observed, men had many voices, and more than one mask. Honor had always had many faces.

THE FOSTER FAMILY GENEALOGY*

Mary Foster of Abbeville, S.C.?
b. ?
m. ? (husband d. before 1784)
d. 1819

John of Old Oaklands	James of Foster's Mound	William of Poverty Hill
b. ?	b. Aug. 2, 1752	b. 1759
m. Rachel Gibson	m. Charlotte Brown	m. Rachel?
m. Sarah Gibson (sister)	m. Elizabeth Smith	d. 1834
m. Mary Smith	d. Nov. 14, 1835	no issue
d. Fort Bend, Texas, 1836 (?)	c. 8	
c. 4		

Ellen (Elinor)		Levi		Frances Ann
b. mid-1780s		b. 1790?		b. 1795
m. Isaac Nierson		m. Zeide DeMaret		m. Samuel W.
(1802)		(1816) of Franklin,		Wells (1814) of
m. Joseph Carr		La. (d. 1852)		Opelousas, La.
(1815)		d. June 13, 1834		d. Dec. 1837
		c. 4 (incl. Gov.		
		Murphy J.		
		Foster's		
		father)		

	Cassandra		Nancy	
	b. 1787?		b. 1791?	
	m. Ephraim		m. Ethan Wood	
	Foster (1807)		(1810)	
	m. John Speed		d. ?	
	(1825)		dau. Mrs. Ligon	
	d. March 21, 1831			
	no issue			

	Sarah (Sally)		Mary	
	b. Feb. 1787		b. ?	
	m. Daniel MacMillan (1810)		m. William K. Collins	
	of Franklin County, Miss.		d. (1814)	
	d. 1852		c. 1?	
	c. Calvin MacMillan			
	(James Foster left property			
	claims to him, 1835)			

* The names of the family members important in reference to this account are italicized.

This genealogy is partly an adaptation from a table in Alford, *Prince among Slaves*, pp. 194–95; it is reprinted by permission of Terry Alford and Harcourt Brace Jovanovich.

Thomas of Foster Fields
b. Sept. 19, 1762
m. *Sarah Smith* (1768?–1837)
d. Sept. 1, 1829
c. 13

Nancy
b. ?
m. Wm. Gilbert
d. 1796
issue raised by
William and Rachel

Barbara
b. Oct. 1800
m. William
   Barnard (1818)
   (d. Dec. 1833)
d. ?
c. 6

Isaac H.
b. ?
m. ?
d. ?
no issue

Elizabeth
b. ?
m. Samuel K.
   Sorsby (1816)
d. Jan. 1831 (?)
c. 5

James, Jr.
b. 1804?
m. *Susan* ? (June 1833)
   (d. March 14, 1834)
d. ?

Thomas, Jr.
b. ?
m. *Susan Carson* (1820)
   of Natchez
   b. 1807 (?)
   (remarried to Adelard
   DeMaret of Franklin, La.,
   in 1831)
d. June? 1831
c. 3

Caroline
b. 1806?
m. *David S.*
   McIntosh (1824)
   of Adams County
   (d. July 12, 1845)
d. ?
c. 5

BLANK PAGE

List of Abbreviations and Short Titles

AdCC	Circuit Court Clerk's Office, County Courthouse of Adams County, Natchez, Mississippi
AgH	*Agricultural History*
AHR	*American Historical Review*
AHQ	*Alabama Historical Quarterly*
AJLH	*American Journal of Legal History*
AJS	*American Journal of Sociology*
AlaDAH	Alabama State Department of Archives and History
AlaHQ	*Alabama Historical Quarterly*
AQ	*American Quarterly*
AR	*Alabama Review*
ArkHQ	*Arkansas Historical Quarterly*
ASR	*American Sociological Review*
ChanCo	Chancery Court
CVSP	*Calendar of Virginia State Papers,* 10 vols. (Richmond: James E. Goode, 1890)
CWH	*Civil War History*
DB, Baker	Dun & Bradstreet MSS, Baker Library, Harvard School of Business, Cambridge, Massachusetts
DUL	Duke University Library, Durham, North Carolina
GHQ	*Georgia Historical Quarterly*
GR	*Georgia Review*
HBC MSS	Hammond-Bryan-Cumming MSS, South Caroliniana Library (see USC)
JAH	*Journal of American History*
JHI	*Journal of the History of Ideas*

JIH	*Journal of Interdisciplinary History*
JMH	*Journal of Mississippi History*
JNH	*Journal of Negro History*
JSH	*Journal of Southern History*
JSocH	*Journal of Social History*
KyHS	Kentucky Historical Society, Frankfort, Kentucky
L&SR	*Law & Society Review*
LC	Library of Congress, Washington, D.C.
LH	*Louisiana History*
LHQ	*Louisiana Historical Quarterly*
LP	Clerk's Office, Lafayette Parish Courthouse, Lafayette, Louisiana
LSU	Library, Louisiana State University, Baton Rouge, Louisiana
MMH	*Maryland Magazine of History*
MissDAH	Mississippi State Department of Archives and History, Jackson, Mississippi
MLR	*Michigan Law Review*
MQ	*Mississippi Quarterly*
MVHR	*Mississippi Valley Historical Review*
NCDAH	North Carolina State Department of Archives and History, Raleigh, North Carolina
NCGSJ	*North Carolina Genealogical Society Journal*
NCHR	*North Carolina Historical Review*
NEQ	*New England Quarterly*
NULR	*Northwestern University Law Review*
NYRB	*New York Review of Books*
NYULR	*New York University Law Review*
OAHQ	*Ohio Archeological and Historical Quarterly*
O.C.	Original Conveyances
O.S.	Original Suits
PR	*Psychohistory Review*
RS	*Rural Sociology*
SAQ	*South Atlantic Quarterly*
SC	South Caroliniana Library (see USC)
SCDAH	South Carolina State Department of Archives and History, Columbia, South Carolina
SCHGM	*South Carolina Historical and Genealogical Magazine*
SCHS	South Carolina Historical Society, Charleston, South Carolina
SF	*Social Forces*
SHC	Southern Historical Collections (see UNC)
SHR	*Southern Humanities Review*
SLM	*Southern Literary Messenger*
SMP	Clerk's Office, Courthouse, St. Mary Parish, Franklin, Louisiana
SQR	*Southern Quarterly Review*
SSH	*Social Science History*
SwHQ	*Southwestern Historical Quarterly*
THQ	*Tennessee Historical Quarterly*

TSA	Tennessee State Archives, Nashville, Tennessee
UKL	University of Kentucky Library, Lexington, Kentucky
UNC	University of North Carolina, Chapel Hill, North Carolina
USC	University of South Carolina, Columbia, South Carolina
UVa	Alderman Library, University of Virginia, Charlottesville, Virginia
VHS	Virginia Historical Society, Richmond, Virginia
VLR	*Vanderbilt Law Review*
VMHB	*Virginia Magazine of History and Biography*
VSL	Virginia State Library, Richmond, Virginia
WLCL	William L. Clements Library, Ann Arbor, Michigan
WMC	Swemm Library, William and Mary College, Williamsburg, Virginia
WMQ	*William and Mary Quarterly*

BLANK PAGE

Notes

Chapter One: Honor in Literary Perspective

1. I do not mean to suggest that historians have been totally present-minded. Edmund S. Morgan's *American Slavery/American Freedom: The Ordeal of Colonial Virginia* (New York: W. W. Norton, 1975) and the writings of C. Vann Woodward, William Freehling, Charles Sellers, and many others use the themes of irony, paradox, and guilt with considerably more sophistication and enlightenment than this introductory sketch can convey. It should be added, however, that Eugene D. Genovese has been among the few to challenge these themes in his numerous writings, usually to great effect.

2. Nathaniel Hawthorne, *Complete Works*, 12 vols. (Boston: Houghton Mifflin, 1899) 3: 617.

3. Ibid., p. 634. On inheritance and careers, see John Demos, *A Little Commonwealth: Family Life in Plymouth Colony* (New York: Oxford University Press, 1970), pp. 120, 123–25; Philip J. Greven, Jr., *Four Generations: Population, Land and Family in Colonial Andover, Massachusetts* (Ithaca: Cornell University Press, 1970), pp. 82–99.

4. Hawthorne, *Works* 3: 631, 632 (quotation).

5. Ibid., pp. 637 (quotation), 638.

6. Ibid. pp. 638–39.

7. Ibid., pp. 639–41.

8. The most useful interpretations of Hawthorne's story are Peter Shaw, "Fathers, Sons and the Ambiguities of Revolution in 'My Kinsman, Major Molineux,'" *NEQ* 49 (December 1976): 559–76; Roy Harvey Pearce, "Hawthorne and the Sense of the Past; or, The Immortality of Major Molineux," *ELH* 21 (September 1954): 327–49; Julian Smith, "Historical Ambiguity in 'My Kinsman, Major Molineux," *English Language Notes* 8 (December 1970): 115–20; and Seymour

L. Gross, "Hawthorne's 'My Kinsman, Major Molineux': History as Moral Adventure," *Nineteenth-Century Fiction* 12 (September 1957): 97–109. Taking a Freudian approach, Frederick Crews sees Molineux as a surrogate father figure. He inaccurately makes him Robin's uncle, rather than Robin's father's first cousin by a brother—thus drawing the tie closer than it was. Robin's failure, then, to achieve his goal stimulates "latent rebelliousness," expressed in his laughing mockery of Molineux's agony. The proposition is plausible, but we should remember that Robin passively observes the shaming ritual. It is forced to his attention. There is no sign whatsoever that Hawthorne intentionally or unconsciously projected such thoughts in Robin's head. There is nothing at all in the pastoral tableau to indicate "unresolved, unformulated feelings" toward Robin's father and family. Nor are the crowd members "father figures," for many of them are Robin's own age; certainly the prostitute is not much older. See Frederick Crews, *The Sins of the Fathers: Hawthorne's Psychological Themes* (New York: Oxford University Press, 1966), pp. 74–75, passim. Taking a similar line are Simon O. Lesser, "The Image of the Father: A Reading of 'My Kinsman, Major Molineux' and 'I Want to Know Why,'" *Partisan Review* 22 (Summer 1955): 372–390; Louis Paul, "A Psychoanalytic Reading of Hawthorne's 'Major Molineuy' [*sic*]: The Father Manqué and the Protégé Manqué," *American Imago* 18 (Fall 1961): 79–88; and George B. Forgie, *Patricide in the House Divided: A Psychological Interpretation of Lincoln and His Age* (New York: W. W. Norton, 1979), pp. 110–15.

9. Cited in Lionel Trilling, *Sincerity and Authenticity* (Cambridge: Harvard University Press, 1972), p. 5.

10. I have been much influenced by Julian Pitt-Rivers's essay on "Honor" in David L. Sills, ed., *International Encyclopedia of the Social Sciences* (New York: Macmillan, 1968) 6: 503–11. In contrast, see *Encyclopedia of the Social Sciences*, Edwin R. A. Seligman, ed. (New York: Macmillan, 1932), pp. 456–58. I have also benefited from John Ladd, *The Structure of a Moral Code: A Philosophical Analysis of Ethical Discourse Applied to the Ethics of the Navaho Indians* (Cambridge: Harvard University Press, 1957).

11. See Clement Eaton, "The Role of Honor in Southern Society," *SHR* 10 (suppl. 1976): 47–58. Eaton offers a thoughtful summation of the conventional historical understanding of honor in the Old South, but wisely perceives the topic, "elusive and difficult" though it is (p. 47), as a major distinguishing feature of Southern life rather than as "myth." Phyllis Vine, "Preparation for Republicanism: Honor and Shame in the Eighteenth-Century College," in Barbara Finkelstein, ed., *Regulated Children/Liberated Children: Education in Psychohistorical Perspective* (New York: Psychohistory Press, 1979), pp. 44–62, offers an anthropological interpretation in line with the approach taken in this study. Though her theme is confined to a number of Northern college student and faculty practices, she demonstrates in the process the common American ethic that once prevailed in all sections of the country and that continued, outside the evangelical and increasingly secular circles of national society, well into the antebellum era. Like Eaton and Vine, Lewis O. Saum, "Schlesinger and 'The State Rights Fetish': A Note," *CWH* 24 (December 1978): 351–59, challenges the notion of Southern artifice, in this case in regard to a political expression of honor: states' rights.

12. David B. Davis, *The Problem of Slavery in Western Culture* (Ithaca: Cornell University Press, 1966), pp. 341–48.

13. See Sumner C. Powell, *Puritan Village: The Formation of a New England Town* (Middletown: Wesleyan University Press, 1963); David G. Allen, *In English Ways: The Movement of Societies and the Transferral of English Local Law and Custom to Massachusetts Bay in the Seventeenth Century* (Chapel Hill: University of North Carolina Press, 1980); Timothy H. Breen, *Puritans and Adventurers: Change and Persistence in Early America* (New York: Oxford University Press, 1980); Edward Pessen, "How Different from Each Other Were the Antebellum North and South?" *AHR* 85 (December 1980): 1119–49, with replies by Thomas B. Alexander, Stanley L. Engerman, Forrest MacDonald, Grady Mc-Whiney, and rebuttal by Pessen, pp. 1150–66.

14. Gary B. Nash, *The Urban Crucible: Social Change, Political Consciousness and the Origins of the American Revolution* (Cambridge: Harvard University Press, 1979) is a useful exposition of Boston's surprisingly elemental character throughout much of its early history. It should also be mentioned that Peter Shaw's *American Patriots and the Rituals of Revolution* (Cambridge: Harvard University Press, 1981), which also uses the Molineux story as an initial reference point, throws highly suggestive light on honor and popular and elite ambivalences toward authority during the American Revolutionary era. Shaw's work appeared months after I had written this interpretation, but his findings and mine are remarkably compatible, even though he restricts his study to Boston's crowds and leaders and the Old World tradition of charivari as it applied in that setting.

15. C. Duncan Rice, "Literary Sources and the Revolution in British Attitudes to Slavery," in Christine Bolt and Seymour Drescher, eds., *Anti-Slavery, Religion, and Reform: Essays in Honor of Roger Anstey* (Folkstone and New York: Dawson and Archon, 1980), pp. 319, 320.

16. E. Anthony Rotundo, dissertation on New England manhood under preparation at Brandeis University, chap. 1, p. 2 (draft). I am grateful to the author for permission to use this quotation.

17. *Henry IV*, pt. 1, act 5, sc. 1, lines 135–43; *Richard II*, act 1, sc. 1, lines 182–83; George F. Jones, "Lov'd I Not Honour More: The Durability of a Literary Motif," *Comparative Literature* 11 (Spring 1959): 131–43; *Antony and Cleopatra*, act 2, sc. 4, lines 22–23.

18. Chaucer, *Complete Works*, F. N. Robinson, ed. (Boston and New York: Houghton Mifflin, 1933), p. 19.

19. William J. Grayson, "The Character of a Gentleman," *SQR*, n. s. 8 (January 1853): 58.

Chapter Two: Primal Honor

1. Mervyn E. James, "The Concept of Order and the Northern Rising, 1569," *Past and Present*, no. 60 (August 1973), pp. 56–57; see also pp. 49–53; idem, "English Politics and the Concept of Honour, 1485–1642," *Past and Present*, suppl. no. 3 (1978), p. 27; and idem, "Obedience and Dissent in Henrician England:

The Lincolnshire Rebellion, 1536," *Past and Present*, no. 48 (August 1970), pp. 3–78. I am grateful to G. R. Elton for bringing the work of James and other early modern English historians to my attention.

2. Quotation from Elisabeth Muhlenfeld, *Mary Boykin Chesnut: A Biography* (Baton Rouge: Louisiana State University Press, 1981), p. 15. See, on the ethical ideals of Tudor-Stuart England, E. W. Talbert, *The Problem of Order* (Chapel Hill: University of North Carolina Press, 1962), pp. 1–117; J. H. Hexter, "The Education of the Aristocracy in the Renaissance," *Journal of Modern History* 22 (March 1950): 1–20; Lawrence Stone, "The Educational Revolution in England, 1560–1640," *Past and Present*, no. 28 (July 1964), pp. 41–80; Elizabeth T. Pochoda, *Arthurian Propaganda: Le Morte Darthur as an Historical Ideal of Life* (Chapel Hill: University of North Carolina Press, 1971), pp. 102–40; John Darrah, *The Real Camelot: Paganism and the Arthurian Romance* (New York: Thames and Hudson, 1981); Robert Hoopes, *Right Reason in the English Renaissance* (Cambridge: Harvard University Press, 1962).

3. Ethelinda Eagleton in Alden B. Pearson, Jr., "A Middle-Class Border-State Family during the Civil War," in Edward Magdol and Jon L. Wakelyn, eds., *The Southern Common People: Studies in Nineteenth-Century Social History* (Westport, Conn.: Greenwood, 1980), p. 164; Phillips Russell, *The Woman Who Rang the Bell: The Story of Cornelia Phillips Spencer* (Chapel Hill: University of North Carolina Press, 1949), p. 85. See also John F. Marszalek, ed., *The Diary of Miss Emma Holmes, 1861–1866* (Baton Rouge: Louisiana State University Press, 1979), June 15, 1865, p. 456; June 22, 1865, p. 459.

4. Peter Gay, *The Enlightenment: An Interpretation—The Rise of Modern Paganism* (New York: Knopf, 1966), ch. 1; Keith Thomas, *Religion and the Decline of Magic* (New York: Charles Scribner's Sons, 1971), pp. 3–24; Peter Laslett, *The World We Have Lost* (New York: Charles Scribner's Sons, 1965); Darrett B. and Anita H. Rutman " 'Now-Wives and Sons-in-Law': Parental Death in a Seventeenth-Century Virginia County," in Thad W. Tate and David L. Ammerman, eds., *The Chesapeake in the Seventeenth Century: Essays on Anglo-American Society* (Chapel Hill: University of North Carolina Press, 1979), pp. 156 (Rutmans quoted); 159 (on family death statistics); 168 (Fitzhugh quoted); 172, table 2 (comparisons of regional rates of mortality). See also Lois G. Carr and Russell R. Menard, "Immigration and Opportunity: The Freedman in Early Colonial Maryland," ibid., pp. 206–9; Julius Rubin, "The Limits of Agricultural Progress in the Nineteenth-Century South," *AgH* 49 (April 1975): 362–70.

5. Quotations from Russell L. Blake, "Ties of Intimacy: Social Values and Personal Relationships of Antebellum Slaveholders," Ph.D. diss., University of Michigan, 1978, pp. 10, 14, passim. On fatalism, see Dickson D. Bruce, Jr., *Violence and Culture in the Antebellum South* (Austin: University of Texas Press, 1979), pp. 15–16; Stow Persons, "The Cyclical Theory of History in Eighteenth Century America," *AQ* 6 (Summer 1954): 147–63; Guy A. Cardwell, "North and South: 1860," *GR* 11 (Fall 1957): 271–78.

6. Hugh A. Garland, *The Life of John Randolph of Roanoke* (New York: Appleton, 1856) 2: 345–46. On the fatalism of common people in antebellum America, see Lewis O. Saum, *The Popular Mood of Pre-Civil War America* (Westport, Conn.: Greenwood, 1980).

7. See Lorraine E. Holland, "Rise and Fall of the Ante-Bellum Virginia Aristocracy: A Generational Analysis," Ph.D. diss., University of California, Irvine, 1980.
8. C. Vann Woodward, "The Irony of Southern History," in *The Burden of Southern History* (New York: Vintage, 1962), pp. 167–91; idem, "The Search for Southern Identity," in ibid., pp. 3–25.
9. Herbert B. Adams, *The Germanic Origin of New England Towns in Local Institutions* (Baltimore: Johns Hopkins University Press, 1883), vol. 1; idem, *Saxon Tithing-Men in America*, ibid.; James K. Hosmer, *Samuel Adams, Man of the Town Meeting*, "The Folk Mote," ibid., 6: 1–17.
10. Ray Billington, *America's Frontier Culture: Three Essays* (College Station, Tex.: Texas A & M University Press, 1977), pp. 20–21.
11. Richard B. Onians, *The Origins of European Thought about the Body, the Mind, the Soul, the World, Time, and Fate* (Cambridge: Cambridge University Press, 1954), p. xvii. See also Lionel Rothkrug, *Religious Practices and Collective Perceptions: Hidden Homologies in the Renaissance and Reformation*, in *Historical Reflections/Réflexions Historiques* 7 (Spring 1980), a fascinating study of cultural continuities.
12. Walker Percy, "Mississippi: The Fallen Paradise," *Harper's* 230 (April 1965): 170, 171.
13. *Sumter Banner* (Sumterville, S.C.), July 19, 1854; C. Vann Woodward, ed., *Mary Chesnut's Civil War* (New Haven: Yale University Press, 1981), June 29, 1861, p. 86; Ruffin quoted in Kenneth S. Lynn, *Mark Twain and Southwestern Humor* (Boston: Little, Brown, 1959), p. 22. See also Daniel R. Hundley, *Social Relations in Our Southern States*, William J. Cooper, Jr., ed. (Baton Rouge: Louisiana State University Press, 1979 [1860]), p. 224; and T. R. Dew, in *SLM* 2 (November 1836): 765.
14. Sanders quoted in James L. Roark, *Masters without Slaves: Southern Planters in the Civil War and Reconstruction* (New York: W. W. Norton, 1977), p. 26; see also N. W. E. Long to his wife, April 28, 1863, Harrold Family MSS, Georgia Historical Society, ref. kindly supplied by Prof. Frances Harrold, Georgia State University. Woodward, *Chesnut's Civil War*, May 10, 1865, p. 811. Moses I. Finley, *The World of Odysseus* (New York: Penguin, rev. ed., 1979), p. 117; Xenophon, in K. J. Dover, *Greek Popular Morality in the Time of Plato and Aristotle* (Berkeley: University of California Press, 1974), p. 229.
15. This section is greatly influenced by the work of Grady McWhiney and Forrest McDonald. See McDonald and McWhiney, "The South from Self-Sufficiency to Peonage: An Interpretation," *AHR* 85 (December 1980): 1095–1118, but note the criticisms by Stanley L. Engerman and Thomas B. Alexander in the same issue, pp. 1150–54, 1154–60, and the authors' reply, pp. 1154–63. See also McDonald and McWhiney, "The Antebellum Southern Herdsmen: A Reinterpretation," *JSH* 41 (May 1975): 147–66; and Forrest McDonald and Ellen S. McDonald, "The Ethnic Origins of the American People, 1790," *WMQ*, 3d ser. 37 (April 1980): 177–99.
16. See Gerhard Herm, *The Celts: The People Who Came out of the Darkness* (New York: St. Martin's, 1977); Alwyn Rees and Brinley Rees, *Celtic Heritage: Ancient Tradition in Ireland and Wales* (New York: Grove Press, 1961). William

F. Claiborne, "A Trip through the Piney Woods," in *Publications of the Missis-sippi Historical Society* (Oxford: Mississippi Historical Society, 1906) 9: 530.

17. Sir Walter Scott, *The Heart of Midlothian*, 2 vols. (New York: Harper & Row, 1900) 2: 227; *SQR* 3 (July 1843): 217; G. M. Young, "Scott and the Historians," in *Sir Walter Scott Lectures, 1940–1948* (Edinburgh: University Press, 1950), pp. 81–107; *SLM* 22 (April 1856): 293; John Hope Franklin, *The Militant South, 1800–1860* (Cambridge: Harvard University Press, 1956), pp. 193–96. On Scots-Irish migrations and customs, see James G. Leyburn, *The Scotch-Irish: A Social History* (Chapel Hill: University of North Carolina Press, 1962); Charles A. Hanna, *The Scotch-Irish, or the Scot in North Britain, North Ireland, and North America*, 2 vols. (New York: G. P. Putnam's Sons, 1902); Barry Levy, "Radical Family Formation in Early America," Paper presented at Armington Seminar, Case Western Reserve University, February 26, 1981, which demonstrates con-clusively the migration of "honorless" folk from barren sites in Wales, Cheshire, and other Celtic Fringe areas to Pennsylvania (but by implication to Southern colonies, too). On migrations, see also Wayland F. Dunaway, *The Scotch-Irish of Colonial Pennsylvania* (Chapel Hill: University of North Carolina Press, 1957); and Forrest McDonald, "The Ethnic Factor in Alabama History: A Neglected Dimension," *AR* 36 (October 1978): 256–65. McDonald argues that the Celtic heritage can be traced back to the era of Strabo, Julius Caesar, and Diodorus's descriptions. The primeval hypothesis advanced here, however, does not require evidence of direct genealogical roots to a single group, since our concern is with primitive values that, though not unrelated to specific economic and social forms, nevertheless persisted owing to general conditions of hard living.

18. Mrs. Varina Jefferson Davis, *Jefferson Davis: Ex-President of the Confederate States*, 2 vols. (New York: Belford Company, 1890) 2:302–5; Hudson Strode, *Jefferson Davis: American Patriot, 1808–1861* (New York: Harcourt Brace, 1955), pp. 4–5; Charles M. Wiltse, *John C. Calhoun* (Indianapolis: Bobbs Merrill, 1944), pp. 11–24; William M. Meigs, *The Life of John Caldwell Calhoun*, 2 vols. (New York: G. E. Stechert, 1917) 1: 27–47; Charles G. Sellers, *James K. Polk: Jacksonian, 1795–1843* (Princeton: Princeton University Press, 1957), pp. 7–16.

19. George Tucker, *The Valley of the Shenandoah; or, Memoirs of the Graysons* (Chapel Hill: University of North Carolina Press, 1970 [1824]), pp. 47–58.

20. "On the Second Resolution of the Committee on Foreign Relations, Decem-ber 12, 1811," John M. Anderson, ed., *Calhoun: Basic Documents* (State College, Pa.: Bald Eagle Press, 1952), p. 105; Finley, *World of Odysseus*, p. 116. Yancey quoted in Bruce, *Violence and Culture*, p. 192.

21. On Boston housewives see Nash, *Urban Crucible*, p. 59.

22. Rhett quoted in Ulrich B. Phillips, *The Course of the South to Secession* (Gloucester: Peter Smith, 1964, [1939]), p. 132; Brown in the Jackson *Mississip-pian*, November 9, 1860. See also David M. Potter, *The Impending Crisis, 1848–1861* (New York: Harper, 1976), p. 92, fn. 3; William J. Cooper, Jr., *The South and the Politics of Slavery, 1828–1856* (Baton Rouge: Louisiana State University Press, pp. 69–74, 272–73, 358–59, 361–62, 370–74—the first study in many years to take Southern honor seriously.

23. Quincy quoted by Shaw, *American Patriots and Rituals of Revolution*, p. 160.

24. Geoffrey of Monmouth, *History of the Kings of Britain*, Lewis Thorpe, trans.

(New York: Penguin, 1979), pp. 23–32; see also H. P. R. Finberg, *The Formation of England, 550–1042* (London: Hart-Davis, MacGibbon, 1974), pp. 17–18; Finley, *World of Odysseus*, p. 113. Tacitus, *Germania*, H. Mattingly and S. A. Handford, trans. (New York: Penguin, 1948), pp. 114 (quotation), 117, 119, 121; see also Timothy H. Breen, "Horses and Gentlemen: The Cultural Significance of Gambling among the Gentry of Virginia," *WMQ*, 3d ser. 34 (April 1977): 239–57; and David Bertelson, *The Lazy South* (New York: Braziller, 1963).

25. Jackson quoted in Michael P. Rogin, *Fathers and Children: Andrew Jackson and the Subjugation of the American Indian* (New York: Knopf, 1975), p. 147; for parallel attitudes in the ancient world see Finley, *World of Odysseus*, p. 118. *Beowulf*, lines 1384–89, in John R. Clark Hall, C. L. Wrenn, and J. R. R. Tolkien, eds., trans. (London: George Allen & Unwin, 1940 rev. ed.), p. 90.

26. See John M. Wallace-Hadrill, *Early Germanic Kingship in England and on the Continent* (Oxford: Clarendon Press, 1971), p. 4; idem, *The Long-Haired Kings and Other Frankish Studies* (New York: Barnes and Noble, 1961), p. 124; Tacitus, *Germania*, p. 113. Tacitus, of course, cannot be treated as if his report were wholly objective or accurate, as Wallace-Hadrill notes in *Early Germanic Kingship* (ch. 1). Nevertheless, in many essentials, especially those selected here, his views conform with other sources, particularly the notion that a warrior disgraced himself if he outlived his chief on the battlefield. Quotation from Finley, *World of Odysseus*, p. 118.

27. William H. Masterson, *William Blount* (New York: Greenwood Press, 1969 [1954]), p. 3. On Southern acquittals, see Chapter Ten of the present study.

28. Dover, *Greek Popular Morality*, p. 229; George Fenwick Jones, *Honor in German Literature* (New York: AMS Press, 1970 [1959]), pp. 33–34. Frederick R. Bryson, *The Sixteenth-Century Italian Duel: A Study in Renaissance Social History* (Chicago: University of Chicago Press, 1938), p. xiii, traces the duel to the Lombard Germans of the sixth century. Tacitus, *Germania*, p. 120.

29. James T. Flexner, *The Young Alexander Hamilton: A Biography* (Boston: Little, Brown, 1978), pp. 8–27; Eugen Weber, *Peasants into Frenchmen: The Modernization of Rural France, 1870–1914* (Stanford: University Press, 1978), p. 19 (quotation); Wallace-Hadrill, *Early Germanic Kingship*, pp. 40–42; Wallace-Hadrill, *Long-Haired Kings*, pp. 121–47; Tacitus, *Germania*, p. 119. For similar attitudes about Andrew Jackson's climb to power from orphan status, see also John William Ward, *Andrew Jackson: Symbol for an Age* (New York: Oxford University Press, 1966), pp. 175–76.

30. Ralph B. Draughon, Jr., "The Young Manhood of William L. Yancey," *AR* 19 (January 1966): 28–40; Malcolm C. McMillan, "William L. Yancey and the Historians: One Hundred Years," *AR* 20 (July 1967): 163–86; Alvey L. King, *Southern Fire-Eater: Louis T. Wigfall* (Baton Rouge: Louisiana State University Press, 1971), pp. 3–10, 18–24; Robert V. Remini, *Andrew Jackson and the Course of American Empire, 1767–1821* (New York: Harper & Row, 1977), pp. 1–29. Remini sees young Jackson's spiritedness as "fun-loving," but more desperate feelings may have been involved, ones not necessarily psychological but social, arising from the stigma of being an orphan that had to be overcome. See Jones, *Honor in German Literature*, pp. 21–22, on meaning of "wretch."

31. Polybius, *The Histories*, W. R. Paton, trans. (Loeb), 7: 53, 54; Tacitus,

Germania, p. 123. See also *SLM* 9 (October 1843): 588; Dover, *Greek Popular Morality,* p. 229. Donald Day and Harry H. Ullom, eds., *The Autobiography of Sam Houston* (Norman: University of Oklahoma Press, 1954), p. 6; see also Susan F. Wiltshire, "Sam Houston and the *Iliad,*" *THQ* 32, no. 3 (1973): 249–54; William Faulkner, *Light in August* (New York: Modern Library, 1950), pp. 65, 418, 430. The title of the work, it is interesting to note, refers to ancient Greece: "In August," Faulkner said at the University of Virginia, "in Mississippi there's a few days when . . . there's a lambence, a luminous quality to the light, as though it came . . . from back in the old classic times . . . from Greece, from Olympus. . . ." See Cleanth Brooks, *William Faulkner: The Yoknapatawpha County* (New Haven: Yale University Press, 1963), p. 375.

32. Dover, *Greek Popular Morality,* p. 226; Randolph in Henry Adams, *John Randolph* (New York: Fawcett, 1961), pp. 192–93; Brown in M. W. Cluskey, ed., *Speeches, Messages, and Other Writings of the Hon. Albert G. Brown* . . . (Philadelphia: Jas. B. Smith, 1859), pp. 336–37; see also John Witherspoon DuBose, *Life and Times of William L. Yancey,* 2 vols. (New York: Peter Smith, 1942) 1: 40; Cooper, *South and Politics of Slavery,* pp. 70–71. Casey quoted in Kenneth R. Wesson, "Travelers' Accounts of the Southern Character: Antebellum and Early Postbellum Period," *Southern Studies* 17 (Fall 1978): 311.

33. Winthrop D. Jordan, *White over Black: American Attitudes toward the Negro, 1550–1812* (Baltimore: Penguin, 1969 [1968]), pp. 232–33. Perkins quoted by J. H. Plumb, "Slavery, Race, and the Poor," *NYRB,* March 13, 1969, p. 4; see also Jones, *Honor in German Literature,* p. 63; and Weber, *Peasants into Frenchmen,* p. 4.

Hundley, *Social Relations,* p. 252; Frances A. Kemble Butler, *Journal of a Residence on a Georgia Plantation, in 1838–1839* (New York: Harper Brothers, 1863), p. 146; Shields McIlwaine, *The Southern Poor-White from Lubberland to Tobacco Road* (Norman: University of Oklahoma Press, 1939), pp. 16–32; John E. Cairnes, *The Slave Power* (New York: Negro Universities Press, 1969), app. D, pp. 368–76; *The Mountain Whites of the South* (Pittsburgh: Presbyterian Banner, 1893); John Fiske, *Old Virginia and Her Neighbours,* 2 vols. (Boston: Houghton Mifflin, 1897), p. 321.

34. Onians, *Origins of European Thought,* pp. 13–14, quoting from W. Stern, *Psychology of Early Childhood* (1924), p. 384.

35. E. Fisher in *DeBow's Review* 7 (October 1849): 312; William G. Brown, *The Lower South in American History* (New York: Macmillan, 1902), p. 127.

36. Donald Bullough, *The Age of Charlemagne* (London: Paul Elik, 1973), pp. 41–42; Tacitus, *Germania,* p. 104; Geoffrey Ashe et al., *The Quest for Arthur's Britain* (New York: Praeger, 1968), pp. 126–28; Wallace-Hadrill, *Early Germanic Kingship,* p. 2; Jones, *Honor in German Literature,* p. 22.

37. E. Ramsay Richardson, *Little Aleck: A Life of Alexander H. Stephens, The Fighting Vice-President of the Confederacy* (Indianapolis: Bobbs-Merrill, 1952), p. 324; A. L. Rouse, *The Cousin Jacks: The Cornish in America* (New York: Charles Scribner's Sons, 1969), p. 121; A. W. H. Adkins, *Moral Values and Political Behaviour in Ancient Greece: From Homer to the End of the Fifth Century* (New York: W. W. Norton, 1972), pp. 14–15.

38. This section is largely derived from Julian Pitt-Rivers's "Honor," Sills, *International Encyclopedia of the Social Sciences* 6: 505.

39. James Curtis, *Andrew Jackson and the Search for Vindication* (Boston: Little, Brown, 1976), pp. 5–6; James Axtell and William C. Sturtevant, "The Unkindest Cut, or Who Invented Scalping?" *WMQ*, 3d ser. 37 (July 1980): 451–72; Wallace-Hadrill, *Long-Haired Kings*, pp. 246–47; Tacitus, *Germania*, pp. 127–28; James Lal Penick, Jr., *The Great Western Land Pirate: John A. Murrell in Legend and History* (Columbia: University of Missouri Press, 1981), p. 31. Murrell, it should be said, died years after the supposed insurrectionary scare of 1835, from tuberculosis; his legend, however, led to this unfortunate incident.

40. The powerful legend of Ham later served as explanation for enslaving Africans, a notion that antebellum Southerners retained. Its original purpose, however, is explained in William McKee Evans, "From the Land of Canaan to the Land of Guinea: The Strange Odyssey of the Sons of Ham," *AHR* 85 (February 1980): 15–43; see also Jordan, *White over Black*, pp. 17–20, 35–37, 60, 62n, 200–201, 308; and Thomas V. Peterson, *Ham and Jepheth: The Mythic Worlds of Whites in the Antebellum South* (Methuen, N.J.: Scarecrow Press, 1978). Montaigne, *Complete Works*, Donald M. Frame, trans. (Stanford: Stanford University Press, 1957), p. 534.

41. See William C. Bruce, *John Randolph of Roanoke, 1773–1833*, 2 vols. (New York: Putnam's Sons, 1922) 2: 318–22; Robert Dawidoff, *The Education of John Randolph* (New York: W. W. Norton, 1979), pp. 98–100; Marshall Smelser, *The Democratic Republic, 1801–1825* (New York: Harper & Row, 1968), p. 51. Castration was also used to punish runaway slaves, on the grounds that it deterred further such manly spiritedness. For most but not all such offenses, castration was largely repealed by the mid-eighteenth-century American provinces. The penalty lacked English precedent and by then was recognized as barbaric. See Jordan, *White over Black*, pp. 154–63. See also James E. Cutler, *Lynch-Law: An Investigation into the History of Lynching in the United States* (New York: Longmans, Green, 1905), pp. 211 ff. On Neal's lynching, see James R. McGovern and Walter T. Howard, "Private Justice and National Concern: The Lynching of Claud Neal," *The Historian* 43 (August 1981): 546–59, esp. 551–52. The psychology and ethical rationale for lynch law is discussed in Chapter Sixteen.

42. "Ellet's Women of the Revolution," *SQR* 1 (July 1850): 326–27; Day and Ullom, *Autobiography of Sam Houston*, p. 9; see also Rogin, *Fathers and Children*, pp. 43, 44.

43. Tacitus, *Germania*, pp. 107–8; Jones, *Honor in German Literature*, pp. 22–23, 29, 98.

44. Virginia legislature quoted by Clara A. Bowler, "Carted Whores and White Shrouded Apologies: Slander in the County Courts of Seventeenth-Century Virginia," *VMHB* 85 (October 1977): 413; George L. Chumbley, *Colonial Justice in Virginia: The Development of a Judicial System* (Richmond: Dietz Press, 1938), pp. 130–31; Colin R. Lovell, "The Reception of Defamation by the Common Law," *VLR* 15 (October 1962): 1051–58; W. S. Holdsworth, *A History of English Law*, 17 vols. (London: Methuen, 1923) 2: 382–83, 7: 334–35; R. H. Helmholz, "Canonical Defamation in Medieval England," *AJLH* 15 (October 1971): 255;

Wyard quoted in Susie M. Ames, ed., *County Court Records of Accomack-Northampton, Virginia, 1632–1640* (Washington: American Historical Association, 1954), pp. 235–36. New England attitudes toward women were little different; see Lyle Koehler, *A Search for Power: The "Weaker Sex" in Seventeenth-Century New England* (Urbana: University of Illinois Press, 1980).

45. *Much Ado About Nothing*, act 6, scene 1, lines 133–37.

46. J. A. Sharpe, "Defamation and Sexual Slander in Early Modern England: The Church Courts at York," *Borthwick Papers*, no. 58 (York: University of York, 1981). Tacitus, *Germania*, p. 291.

47. Quoted in Bert E. Bradley and Jerry L. Tarver, "John C. Calhoun's Rhetorical Method in Defense of Slavery," in Waldo W. Braden, ed., *Oratory in the Old South, 1828–1860* (Baton Rouge: Louisiana State University Press, 1970), p. 179.

48. Julian Pitt-Rivers, *The Fate of Sachem; or, The Politics of Sex: Essays in the Anthropology of the Mediterranean* (Cambridge: Cambridge University Press, 1977), pp. 23–29, 78–83, 161–66; K. H. Connell, *Irish Peasant Society: Four Historical Essays* (Oxford: Clarendon Press, 1975), pp. 51–68; R. H. Hilton, *The English Peasantry in the Later Middle Ages* (Oxford: Clarendon Press, 1975), pp. 95–110; Tacitus, *Germania*, pp. 116–17. On the anthropology of misogyny, see Nur Yalman, "On the Purity of Women in the Castes of Ceylon and Malabar," *Journal of the Royal Anthropological Institute*, no. 1 (1963), pp. 25–58; Peter Schneider, "Honor and Conflict in a Sicilian Town," *Anthropological Quarterly* 42 (July 1969): 130–55; Jane Schneider, "Of Vigilance and Virgins: Honor, Shame, and Access to Resources in Mediterranean Societies," *Ethnology* 10 (January 1971): 1–24; Evalyn J. Michaelson and Walter Goldschmidt, "Female Roles and Male Dominance among Peasants," *Southwestern Journal of Anthropology* 27 (Winter 1971): 330–52; Donald Levine, "The Concept of Masculinity in Ethiopian Culture," *International Journal of Social Psychiatry* 12 (Winter 1966): 17–23; Max Gluckman, "The Role of the Sexes in Wiko Circumcision Ceremonies," in Meyer Fortes, ed., *Social Structure: Studies Presented to A. R. Radcliffe-Brown* (London: Clarendon Press, 1949), pp. 146–67. Gluckman notes that both sexes are thought to contribute to the life and fertility of the Wiko, "but only through the resolution of antagonism" (p. 166).

49. A. G. Roeber, *Faithful Magistrates and Republican Lawyers: C₁ ⁱrs of Virginia Legal Culture, 1680–1810* (Chapel Hill: University of North Carolina Press, 1981), p. 78.

50. Quoted in Christopher Hill, "From Oaths to Interest," in *Society and Puritanism in Pre-Revolutionary England* (New York: Schocken, 1964), p. 382. See also Charles Phythian-Adams, "Ceremony and the Communal Year at Coventry 1450–1550," in Peter Clark and Paul Slack, eds., *Crisis and Order in English Towns, 1500–1700: Essays in Urban History* (London: Routledge and Kegan Paul, 1972), pp. 57–85, esp. 61–63.

51. Beth G. Crabtree and James W. Patton, eds., *"Journal of a Secesh Lady": The Diary of Catherine Anne Devereux Edmondston, 1860–1866* (Raleigh: North Carolina Department of Archives and History, 1979), July 28, 1865, p. 716.

52. Cooper quoted in Charles Coleman Wall, Jr., "Students and Student Life at

the University of Virginia, 1825 to 1861," Ph.D. diss., University of Virginia, 1978, pp. 100–101, passim.

53. William W. Freehling, *Prelude to Civil War: The Nullification Controversy in South Carolina, 1816–1836* (New York: Harper & Row, 1965), pp. 274–78; Willie P. Mangum to Seth Jones, August 8, 1823, certificate of H. B. Adams, August [?], 1823, and further correspondence, in Henry T. Shanks, ed., *The Papers of Willie Person Mangum* (Raleigh: State Department of Archives, 1950), pp. 63–79.

54. Edward McCrady, "Slavery in the Province of South Carolina, 1670–1770," in *Annual Report, American Historical Association for the Year 1895* (Washington: Government Printing Office, 1896), p. 659; John S. Bassett, *Slavery in the State of North Carolina* (Baltimore: Johns Hopkins University Press, 1899), pp. 95–96; see also Jeffrey R. Brackett, "The Status of the Slave, 1775–1789," in J. Franklin Jameson, ed., *Essays on the Constitutional History of the United States in the Formative Period, 1775–1789* (Boston: Houghton Mifflin, 1899), p. 269.

55. C. G. Crump, ed., *The History of the Life of Thomas Ellwood* (New York: Putnam's Sons, 1900), pp. 114–15; Leon Radzinowicz, *A History of English Criminal Law and its Administration: The Movement for Reform, 1750–1833* (New York: Macmillan, 1948), pp. 220–23; see also 223, n80. See also Michel Foucault, *Discipline and Punishment: The Birth of Prisons*, Allan Sheridan, trans. (New York: Vintage, 1979), pp. 3–7; R. H. Hilton, "The Origin of Robin Hood," *Past and Present*, no. 14 (November 1958), pp. 30–45; Marcus Rediker, " 'Under the Banner of King Death': The Social World of Anglo-American Pirates, 1716 to 1726," *WMQ*, 3d ser. 38 (April 1981): 203–27, a superb study of "honor among thieves."

56. Cf. C. G. Coulton, *Medieval Panorama: The English Scene from Conquest to Reformation* (New York: Meridian, 1955), p. 53.

57. Jones, *Honor in German Literature*, p. 40.

Chapter Three: Primal Honor

1. William Faulkner, *Absalom, Absalom!* (New York: Random House, 1972), pp. 286–91.

2. Quotations from Cleanth Brooks's "History and the Sense of the Tragic: *Absalom, Absalom!*," in Robert Penn Warren, *Faulkner: A Collection of Critical Essays* (Englewood Cliffs, N.J.: Prentice-Hall, 1966), p. 187. Brooks sees Sutpen as modern man, and in some ways he is, but it is his connection with the universal experiences of man from ancient to modern times that gives his shattered hopes and his meager self-understanding its dramatic and vital quality. Faulkner, *Absalom, Absalom!*, pp. 288–91.

3. Johann Huizinga, *America: A Dutch Historian's Vision, from Afar and Near* (New York: Harpers, 1972), pp. 16–17, 19. For an extended example of the resentments between rich and poor, culminating in murder and jury acquittal, see Paul J. Vanderwood, *Night Riders of Reelfoot Lake* (Memphis: Memphis State University Press, 1969); and Tom E. Terrill, "Murder in Graniteville," in Orville

V. Burton and Robert C. McMath, Jr., eds., *Class, Conflict, and Consensus: Ante-bellum Southern Community Studies* (Westport, Conn.: Greenwood Press, forth-coming), hereafter *Southern Communities*.
4. F. G. Bailey, ed., *Gifts and Poison: The Politics of Reputation* (Oxford: Basil Blackwell, 1971), p. 20, passim.
5. W. J. Cash, *The Mind of the South* (New York: Knopf, 1941), p. 31.
6. Breen, *Puritans and Adventurers*; Lawrence Stone, *The Crisis of the Aris-tocracy, 1558-1641* (New York: Oxford University Press, 1967), pp. 15-36; idem, "The Inflation of Honours, 1558-1651," *Past and Present*, no. 14 (November 1958), p. 45 (quotation). James Henretta summarizes recent findings on the size of the "Great Planter" class of slaveholders in the early Chesapeake as follows (on the basis of 1,000): 1.5% of wills probated in the 1690s; 2.2% in the 1720s, 3.6% in the 1730s, and 3.9% in the 1750s; see Henretta, *The Evolution of American Society, 1700-1815: An Interdisciplinary Analysis* (Lexington, Mass.: D. C. Heath, 1973), p. 91. See also Lorena S. Walsh, "Servitude and Opportunity in Charles County, Maryland, 1658-1705," in Aubrey C. Land, ed., *Law, Society, and Politics in Early Maryland* (Baltimore: Johns Hopkins University Press, 1977), pp. 111-33; Paul G. E. Clemens, "Economy and Society on Maryland's Eastern Shore, 1689-1733," in ibid., pp. 153-70; and David W. Jordan, "Mary-land's Privy Council, 1637-1715," in ibid., pp. 65-87. Also see Aubrey C. Land, "Economic Behavior in a Planting Society: The Eighteenth Century Chesapeake," *JSH* 33 (November 1967): 469-85.

On the older view of "middle-class origins" for Virginia gentlefolk, see Thomas J. Wertenbaker, *Patrician and Plebeian in Virginia; or, The Origin and Development of the Social Classes of the Old Dominion* (New York: Russell & Russell, 1959), esp. p. 19 (on Byrd family); Mildred Campbell, "Social Origins of Some Early Americans," in James M. Smith, ed. *Seventeenth-Century America: Essays in Colonial History* (Chapel Hill: University of North Carolina Press, 1959), pp. 63-89; but see David W. Galenson, " 'Middling People' or 'Common Sort'?: The Social Origins of Some Early Americans Reexamined," *WMQ*, 3d ser. 35 (July 1978): 499-524, with Mildred Campbell's response, 525-40; and John E. Manahan, "The Cavalier Remounted: A Study of the Origins of Virginia's Pop-ulation, 1607-1700," Ph.D. diss., University of Virginia, 1946.
7. George M. Fredrickson, *The Black Image in the White Mind: The Debate on Afro-American Character and Destiny, 1817-1914* (New York: Harper & Row, 1971).
8. Max Farrand, ed., *The Records of the Federal Convention of 1787*, 4 vols. (New Haven: Yale University Press, 1911-37) 2: 203.
9. Eugene D. Genovese, *The World the Slaveholders Made: Two Essays in In-terpretation* (New York: Pantheon, 1969), pp. 137-50; Michael P. Johnson, "Planters and Patriarchy: Charleston, 1800-1860," *JSH* 46 (February 1980): 45-72; Eugene D. Genovese, *The Political Economy of Slavery: Studies in the Economy and Society of the Slave South* (New York: Random House, 1965). Genovese has readopted Cash's view, however, in "Yeoman Farmers in a Slaveholders' De-mocracy," *AgH* 44 (April 1975): 331-42. Cash, *Mind of the South*, p. 54; Wallace-Hadrill, *Early Germanic Kingship*, p. 15.
10. Harry C. Payne, "Elite *versus* Popular Mentality in the Eighteenth Century,"

Roseann Runte, ed., *Studies in Eighteenth-Century Culture* (Madison: University of Wisconsin Press, 1979), 8: 3–32. On the changing perspectives of the Virginia gentry, see Richard R. Beeman and Rhys Isaac, "Cultural Conflict and Social Change in the Revolutionary South: Lunenburg County, Virginia," *JSH* 46 (November 1980): 525–50; Gordon S. Wood, "Rhetoric and Reality in the American Revolution," *WMQ,* 3d ser. 23 (January 1966): 3–32; Rhys Isaac, "Religion and Authority: Problems of the Anglican Establishment in Virginia in the Era of the Great Awakening and the Parsons' Cause," *WMQ,* 3d ser. 30 (January 1973): 3–36; idem, "Evangelical Revolt: The Nature of the Baptists' Challenge to the Traditional Order in Virginia, 1765 to 1775," *WMQ,* 3d ser. 31 (July 1974): 345–68.

11. Clement Eaton, *The Mind of the Old South* (Baton Rouge: Louisiana State University Press, 1967), p. 72; Eugene D. Genovese, "Yeoman Farmers," *AgH* 44 (April 1975): 331–42.

12. Reuben Davis, *Recollections of Mississippi and Mississipians* (Boston: Houghton Mifflin, 1889), p. 112. Bailey, *Gifts and Poison*, p. 78; Cash, *Mind of South*, p. 115.

13. Tacitus, *Germania*, pp. 113–14.

14. William K. Boyd, ed., *William Byrd's Histories of the Dividing Line betwixt Virginia and North Carolina* (New York: Dover, 1967), pp. 96–98; see Julian H. Franklin, ed., *Constitutionalism and Resistance in the Sixteenth Century* (New York: Pegasus, 1969), pp. 11–12, which suggests the early origins of sixteenth-century notions of resistance to "unjust kings." Franklin sees the customary arguments stretching back to Germanic, Anglo-Saxon roots. The gift-giving character of taxation is evident in Thomas Jefferson's "Virginia Resolutions on Lord North's Conciliatory Proposal, [June 10, 1775]," in Julian P. Boyd, ed., *The Papers of Thomas Jefferson* (Princeton: Princeton University Press, 1950), 1: 171–72: "Whereas, we have right to give our money, as the Parliament does theirs, without coercion, from time to time, as public exigencies may require, we conceive that we alone are the judges. . . . *Because* at the very time of requiring from us grants of Money they are making disposition to invade us . . . which is a stile of asking gifts not reconcileable to our freedom." Likewise, the Congress's Resolutions of July 31, 1775, spoke of taxes as "gifts" not to be "wasted among the venal and corrupt for the purpose of undermining the civil rights of the givers" (ibid., p. 231). Bernard Bailyn, although he does not refer specifically to taxes as voluntary gifts, shows how the concept, because of conditions and weak central authority, was linked to medieval understanding of the need for popular consent (within the circle of honor) of the governed. See his *The Ideological Origins of the American Revolution* (Cambridge: Harvard University Press, 1967), pp. 162 ff.

15. J. Mills Thornton, *Politics and Power in a Slave Society: Alabama, 1800–1860* (Baton Rouge: Louisiana State University Press, 1978), pp. 100–105. This dependence upon reputation at home was quite true even in less democratic settings: see Conrad Russell, *Parliaments and English Politics, 1621–1629* (Oxford: Clarendon Press, 1979), p. 18: "To ask an ambitious politician to choose between permanent allegiance to court or to country [that is, influence at Whitehall or on home ground] would have been to ask him to choose between alternative

methods of suicide." On parliamentary subsidies, see ibid., pp. 49–53, 56–57, and 376. "Take heed you open not a new gap, to proceed by degrees to other taxes upon honour, as knights, Esquires etc.," declared a seventeenth-century M.P. outraged that a high subsidy assessment was to be imposed (p. 376). On taxes for those who enjoyed preferments, that is, the planters, and no or few taxes for those lacking power, see Grady McWhiney and Forrest McDonald, "Reply," *AHR* 85 (December 1980): 1161–62. They conclude that the reason for the discrepancy was the planters' commitment to leisure and "profit-maximization." But the argument being put forth here is that the principle was: those with wealth should pay for the privileges of officeholding. Largess, beginning in ancient times, was required of the aristocracy, and the notion was also present in the democratic setting of the antebellum South.

16. Julian Pitt-Rivers, "Honor," in Sills, *International Encyclopedia of Social Sciences*, 6: 509–10.

17. Thornton's study is the best analysis of this intraregional struggle—ambivalent, confused, and geographically divided as it was. See Thornton, *Politics and Power*. Genovese seems to have backed away from his insightful *Political Economy of Slavery*, and even though he sees the planters as more united and cohesive than they were, he presents an effective refutation of the opposite view that would make planters into southern Yankees, one and all.

18. Jack P. Greene, ed., *The Diary of Colonel Landon Carter of Sabine Hall, 1762–1776*, 2 vols. (Charlottesville: University Press of Virginia, 1965) 1: 19. See also Stone, *Crisis of Aristocracy*, pp. 31 ff.

19. Alexis de Tocqueville, *Democracy in America*, Philips Bradley, ed., 2 vols. (New York: Vintage, 1957) 2: 248–49; Persons, "Cyclical Theory of History," 6: 157; on attitudes toward bankruptcy, see Morton J. Horwitz, *The Transformation of American Law, 1780–1860* (Cambridge: Harvard University Press, 1977), pp. 228–32, and McDonald and McWhiney, "Reply," 1162.

20. Greene, *Carter Diary* 1: 19; H. R. Howard [pseud.], *The History of Virgil A. Stewart, and His Adventure in Capturing and Exposing the 'Great Western Land Pirate' and His Gang . . .* (New York: Harper & Bros., 1836), pp. 18–19. On this point I am indebted to James Lal Penick, Jr.'s *The Great Land Pirate*, pp. 88–99. For other examples of bitterly mistrustful men of ambition, see Flexner, *Young Alexander Hamilton*, pp. 436–51; and Carol Bleser, ed., *The Hammonds of Redcliffe* (New York: Oxford University Press, 1981), pp. 3–18.

21. See esp. Gordon J. Schochet, *Patriarchalism in Political Thought: The Authoritarian Family and Political Speculation and Attitudes, Especially in Seventeenth-Century England* (New York: Basic Books, 1975).

22. William Penn quoted in Nash, *Urban Crucible*, p. 34. Richard Vann, *The Social Development of English Quakerism, 1655–1755* (Cambridge: Harvard University Press, 1969), pp. 1–25 (Crook quoted on p. 87). Vann argues that the Friends came from a socially higher sector of the English populace than previous historians have claimed (pp. 49–87), but see also Christopher Hill, *The World Turned Upside Down: Radical Ideas during the English Revolution* (New York: Viking, 1972), pp. 186–207; and Barry Reay, "The Social Origins of Early Quakerism," *JIH* 11 (Summer 1980): 55–72.

Barry Levy, "Tender Plants: Quaker Farmers and Children in the Delaware Valley, 1681–1735," *Journal of Family History* 3 (June 1978): 116–35; Richard Bauman, "Speaking in the Light: the Role of the Quaker Minister," in Richard Bauman and Joel Sherzer, eds., *Explorations in the Ethnography of Speaking* (New York: Cambridge University Press, 1974), pp. 144–62; Thomas Drake, *Quakers and Slavery in America* (New Haven: Yale University Press, 1950); William C. Braithwaite, *The First Period of Quakerism* (Cambridge, England: Cambridge University Press, 1919); Barry Levy, "The Birth of the 'Modern Family' in Early America: Quaker and Anglican Families in Rural Pennsylvania, 1681–1750," in forthcoming collection edited by Michael Zuckerman, to be published by Temple University Press.

23. Crump, *History of Thomas Ellwood*, pp. 33–41.

24. Philip A. Bruce, *Social Life in Old Virginia* (New York: Capricorn, 1965 [1910]), pp. 222–37. David B. Davis, *The Problem of Slavery in the Age of Revolution: 1770–1823* (Ithaca: Cornell University Press, 1975), pp. 213–54. Davis notes that early Quakerism did not lead directly to hostility toward slavery by some inevitable logic. Nevertheless, from the new point of honor, there had to be an obvious tie. See also Drake, *Quakers and Slavery;* and Sydney V. James, *A People among Peoples: Quaker Benevolence in Eighteenth-Century America* (Cambridge: Harvard University Press, 1963).

25. On problems of order in England, see A. L. Bier, "Social Problems in Elizabethan London," *JIH* 11 (Autumn 1978): 203–31; E. P. Thompson, *Whigs and Hunters: The Origins of the Black Act* (New York: Pantheon, 1975); Douglas Hay et al., eds., *Albion's Fatal Tree: Crime and Society in Eighteenth-Century England* (New York: Pantheon, 1975); C. Kirby, "The English Game Law System," *AHR* 38 (January 1933): 240–62. Stone, *Crisis of Aristocracy*, p. 109.

26. "Culpeper's Report on Virginia in 1683," *VMHB* 3 (January 1896): 226–31 (quotation, p. 226); Warren B. Billings, ed., *The Old Dominion in the Seventeenth Century: A Documentary History of Virginia, 1606–1689* (Chapel Hill: University of North Carolina Press, 1975), pp. 236–87, esp. 258–67; "Rebellion of 1674," *WMQ*, 1st ser. 3 (October 1894): 122–23.

27. See Stephen S. Webb, *The Governors-General: The English Army and the Definition of the Empire, 1569–1681* (Chapel Hill: University of North Carolina Press, 1979), pp. 124, 144–45, 330–61.

28. Charles M. Andrews, ed., *Narratives of the Insurrections, 1675–1690* (New York: Charles Scribner's Sons, 1915), p. 110; Wilcomb E. Washburn, *The Governor and the Rebel: A History of Bacon's Rebellion in Virginia* (Chapel Hill: University of North Carolina Press, 1957), p. 18 (quotation). Julia C. Spruill, *Women's Life and Work in the Southern Colonies* (New York: W. W. Norton, 1972 [1938], p. 145. Duke left Elizabeth a bequest for £2,000 provided that "if she marry Bacon, void." When she brought suit after her father and husband's deaths, the Lord Chancellor ruled on her folly, "Such an example of presumptuous disobedience highly meriting such a punishment, she being only prohibited to marry with one man, by name; and nothing in the whole fair Garden of Eden would serve her turn, but this forbidden fruit."

29. Andrews, *Narratives*, p. 49 (quotation); see also pp. 16, 105–6; Robert Bever-

ley, *The History of the Present State of Virginia,* David F. Hawke, ed. (Indianapolis: Bobbs Merrill, 1971), pp. 36–37; "Papers from Surry Court Records," *WMQ* 1st ser. 3 (October 1894): 21–25.

30. William Berkeley to Thomas Ludwell, April 1, 1676, in "Virginia in 1673–1676," *VMHB* 20 (1912): 247–49; William Sherwood, "Virginias Deploured Condition . . . ," *Massachusetts Historical Society, Collections,* 4th ser. 9 (1871): 166; see also Billings, *Old Dominion,* pp. 276–77; Andrews, *Narratives,* pp. 20–21; "The Indian War of 1675," *WMQ,* 1st ser. 4 (July 1895): 86; William Sherwood, June 28, 1676, in "Bacon's Rebellion, *VMHB* 1 (October 1893): 170–71.

31. Wilcomb E. Washburn, ed., "Notes and Documents: Sir William Berkeley's 'A History of Our Miseries,' " *WMQ,* 3d ser. 14 (July 1957): 406, 409; Washburn, *Governor and Rebel,* pp. 51–52; Billings, *Old Dominion,* pp. 269–74; Andrews, *Narratives,* p. 23 (quotation).

32. Quoted in Andrews, *Narratives,* p. 116; see also pp. 28–29.

33. Billings, *Old Dominion,* pp. 277–79; Andrews, *Narratives,* 29 (quotation), 116–18; (quotation), 119; Morgan, *American Slavery/American Freedom,* pp. 266–67; "Bacon's Speech at Green Spring," *WMQ,* 1st ser. 3 (October 1894): 121 (quotation); Washburn, *Governor and Rebel,* pp. 56–57.

34. "Law. Baker and Rob't Spencer," quoted in "Rebellion of 1674," *WMQ,* 1st ser. 3 (October 1894): 122–23; Berkeley to Coventry, February 2, 1677, in Washburn, "Notes and Documents," p. 412; Beverley, *History,* p. 42; Webb, *Governors-General,* pp. 362–64.

35. Quotation from James, "Obedience and Dissent in Henrician England," pp. 73–74, passim; see also idem, "Concept of Order and the Northern Rising," pp. 49–53. On the commoners' role in the English Civil War, see Brian Manning, *The English People and the English Revolution, 1640–1649* (New York: Holmes & Meier, 1976); Shaw, *American Patriots and Rituals of Revolution,* passim. Also see René Girard, *'To Double Business Bound': Essays on Literature, Mimesis, and Anthropology* (Baltimore: Johns Hopkins University Press, 1978), pp. 84–120, esp. pp. 108–9.

36. Andrews, *Narratives,* pp. 15–16, 38, 39, 139. On landholders either spared or executed, see Washburn, *Governor and Rebel,* pp. 160, 237 n. 32.

37. Bernard Bailyn, "Politics and Social Structure in Virginia," in Smith, *Seventeenth-Century America,* pp. 90–115; John C. Rainbolt, *From Prescription to Persuasion: Manipulation of the Seventeenth-Century Virginia Economy* (Port Washington, N.Y.: Kennikat Press, 1974); Carole Shammas, "English-Born and Creole Elites in Turn-of-the-Century Virginia," in Tate and Ammerman, *Chesapeake in Seventeenth Century,* pp. 274–96.

38. Washburn, *Governor and Rebel,* p. 162, reacts against earlier enthusiasm for Bacon's men but still sees "the aggressiveness of the frontiersmen" as the key factor, rather than the search for honor, as suggested here. The two ideas, of course, are not incompatible but, because of F. J. Turner's influence, the latter is too readily seen as an independent variable rathr than one arising from ancient sources that retained meaning in the New World.

Chapter Four: Gentility

1. Byrd quoted in Lynn, *Mark Twain and Southwestern Humor*, p. 11; see also ibid., pp. 3–22.

2. Anne Royall, *Letters from Alabama, 1817–1822*, Lucille Griffith, ed. (University: University of Alabama Press, 1969), pp. 134–36; Corydon Fuller, Diary, March 12, 1858; see also July 21, 1857; August 19, March 11, 1858; WLCL.

3. Quincy, Jr., quoted in Mark A. De Wolfe Howe, ed., "The Journal of Josiah Quincy, Junior, 1773," in *Massachusetts Historical Society Proceedings* 49 (June 1916), March 30, 1773, p. 460; his son quoted by Stow Persons, *The Decline of American Gentility* (New York: Columbia University Press, 1973), p. 61; Emerson quoted from *The Selected Writings of Ralph Waldo Emerson*, Brooks Atkinson, ed. (New York: Modern Library, 1950), pp. 383–84. On President Quincy's difficulties in gaining agreement about the honorary degree that Harvard conferred upon Jackson, see Robert A. McCaughey, *Josiah Quincy, 1772–1864: The Last Federalist* (Cambridge: Harvard University Press, 1974), pp. 157–60.

4. *The Education of Henry Adams*, Ernest Samuels, ed. (Boston: Houghton Mifflin, 1973 [1918]), pp. 56–59. Cf. William R. Taylor, *Cavalier and Yankee: The Old South and American National Character* (New York: Doubleday, 1963) p. 218.

5. Brattle in Samuel E. Morison, *Harvard College in the Seventeenth Century*, 2 vols. (Cambridge: Harvard University Press, 1936) 1: 165; Samuel G. Stoney, ed. "Autobiography of William John Grayson," *SCHGM* 49 (April 1948): 91.

6. Willoughby Newton, *Liberty and Union: An Address Delivered before the Literary Societies of Virginia Military Institute* (Richmond: McFarland & Ferguson, 1858), pp. 5–6; Bailyn, *Ideological Origins of American Revolution*, pp. 24–26. See also Richard B. Davis, *Intellectual Life of Jefferson's Virginia, 1790–1830* (Chapel Hill: University of North Carolina Press, 1964); "Classical Learning," *Southern Review* 1 (February 1828): 1–49; "Ancient Languages—Study in the United States," *SLM* 17 (June 1851): 329–30.

7. Stoney, "Autobiography of Grayson," pp. 91–92.

8. Jefferson to Peter Carr, August 19, 1785, in Boyd, *Papers of Thomas Jefferson*, 8: 406–7.

9. Montaigne quoted in Curtis B. Watson, *Shakespeare and the Renaissance Concept of Honor* (Princeton: Princeton University Press, 1960), p. 98.

10. Charles C. Jones, Jr., to Rev. Charles C. Jones, May 30, 1854, in Robert M. Myers, ed., *The Children of Pride: A True Story of Georgia and the Civil War* (New Haven: Yale University Press, 1972), 37–38.

11. Edward Everett, *Orations and Speeches on Various Occasions*, 4 vols. (Boston: Little, Brown, 1868) 4: 37, 38; for similar examples see "Chief Justice John Marshall," *SLM* 2 (January 1836): 181–91; Rufus Choate, "Speech on the Birthday of Daniel Webster, January 21, 1859," *The Works of Rufus Choate with a Memoir of His Life*, Samuel G. Brown, ed., 2 vols. (Boston: Little, Brown, 1862) 2: 441–50.

12. *Calendar of the University of the South, 1879–1880* (Atlanta: James P. Harrison, 1879), passim.

13. Telfair Hodgson, ed., *University of the South Papers, Series A, No. 1: Re-*

prints of the Documents and Proceedings of the Board of Trustees of the University of the South Prior to 1860 (Sewanee, Tenn.: University Press, 1888), pp. 100, 101; Arthur Ben Chitty, Jr., *Reconstruction at Sewanee: The Founding of the University of the South, 1857–1872* (Sewanee, Tenn.: University Press, 1954), p. 66 (quotation).

14. Simms quoted in Drew G. Faust, *A Sacred Circle: The Dilemma of the Intellectual in the Old South, 1840–1860* (Baltimore: Johns Hopkins University Press, 1977) p. 28, and passim for Tucker and Grayson; Grayson quoted in Stoney, "Autobiography of Grayson." p. 98.

15. Stoney, "Autobiography of Grayson," p. 98; also 98–99.

16. See esp. Faust, *Sacred Circle;* cf. F. N. Boney, "The Southern Aristocrat," *Midwest Quarterly* 15 (April 1974): 228, an example of a popular misreading of Southern tolerance, which depended largely upon the perceived threatlessness of a dissident's eccentricity. See also Bertram Wyatt-Brown, "W. J. Cash and Southern Culture," in Walter J. Fraser, Jr., and Winfred B. Moore, Jr., eds., *From the Old South to the New: Essays on the Transitional South* (Westport, Conn.: Greenwood Press, 1981), pp. 195–214; and idem, "Proslavery and Antislavery Intellectuals: Class Concepts and Polemical Struggles," in Lewis Perry and Michael Fellman, eds., *Antislavery Reconsidered: New Perspectives on the Abolitionists* (Baton Rouge: Louisiana State University Press, 1979), pp. 319–21.

17. Jefferson to Carr, August 19, 1785, in Boyd, *Papers of Thomas Jefferson,* 8: 406–7. Jefferson to Carr, August 6, 1788, ibid., 8: 470.

18. Edmund S. Morgan, ed., *The Diary of Michael Wigglesworth, 1653–1657: The Conscience of a Puritan* (New York: Harper and Row, 1965), p. 5.

19. Greene, *Carter Diary,* May 16, 1772, 2: 684; see also August 14, 18, 1770, pp. 465, 468–69; February 27–28, pp. 543–44; April 29, p. 565; July 15, pp. 391–93; August 18, 1771, p. 615; June 23, p. 684; July 2, p. 704; October 1, p. 713; October 9, 1774, p. 763, passim.

20. Elizur Goodrich, *Principles of Civil Union and Happiness . . .* (Hartford: Hudson & Goodwin, 1787), pp. 20–22; Edwin Cady, *The Gentleman in America: A Literary Study in American Culture* (Syracuse: Syracuse University Press, 1949), p. 40; see also T. H. Breen, *The Character of the Good Ruler: A Study of Puritan Political Ideas in New England, 1630–1730* (New Haven: Yale University Press, 1970).

21. Paul F. Boller, Jr., *George Washington and Religion* (Dallas: Southern Methodist University Press, 1963), pp. 35, 39, 75, 109. Kay quoted in Rhys Isaac, "Religion and Authority: Problems of the Anglican Establishment in Virginia in the Era of the Great Awakening and the Parsons' Cause," *WMQ,* 3d ser. 30 (January 1973): 8–9 ff.

22. Quoted by Bruce, *Randolph,* 1: 630.

23. Clement Eaton, *The Freedom-of-Thought Struggle in the Old South* (New York: Harper & Row, 1964), pp. 300–301.

24. Francis Lieber, *The Character of a Gentleman: An Address to the Students of Miami University, Ohio* (Columbia and Charleston: Allen & McCater, 1847 [1839]), pp. 14–16, 17, 25, 31, 33, 34. Hammond quotation kindly supplied by Professor Drew Faust, from the Hammond Collection, SC, USC. Grayson, "Character of the Gentleman," pp. 53–80; quotation, p. 80.

25. Hugh Blair Grigsby, Diary, May 14, 1830, VHS. On a gentleman's religious duties, see the Columbus, Miss. *Democrat*, March 16 and May 18, 1839.
26. Stoney, "Autobiography of Grayson," pp. 29–31, 32.
27. Grayson, "Character of the Gentleman," p. 80.
28. See Harold B. Simpson, ed., *Robert E. Lee by Jefferson Davis* (Hillsboro, Tex.: Hill Junior College Press, 1966), p. 1. On legend-making, see Thomas L. Connelly, *The Marble Man: Robert E. Lee and His Image in American Society* (Baton Rouge: Louisiana State University Press, 1977).
29. Burton J. Hendrick, *The Lees of Virginia: A Biography of a Family* (Boston: Little, Brown, 1935), p. 336.
30. Lee to Mary Anne Custis Lee, September 17, 1861, in Capt. Robert E. Lee, *Recollections and Letters of General Robert E. Lee* (New York: Doubleday, Page, 1905), pp. 44.
31. Lee, *Recollections*, pp. 8, 9, 13; Lee to Custis Lee, May 4, 1851, in the Rev. J. William Jones, *Life and Letters of Robert E. Lee: Soldier and Man* (New York: Neale, 1906), p. 72.
32. Douglas Southall Freeman, *R. E. Lee: A Biography*, 4 vols. (New York: Charles Scribner's Sons, 1934–35) 1: 332–34; Lee, *Recollections*, pp. 70–71.
33. Quoted in Freeman, *Lee*, 1: 372; see also Jones, *Lee*, p. 84.
34. Lee to Anne Marshall, April 20, 1861, in Lee, *Recollections*, p. 25; Hendrick, *Lees of Virginia*, p. 424; see also Jones, *Lee*, pp. 133–36, 141; Freeman, *Lee* 4: 495.
35. Hendrick, *Lees of Virginia*, p. 435.
36. Freeman, *Lee* 4: 499.
37. William Faulkner, *Intruder in the Dust* (New York: Modern Library, 1948), pp. 194–95.
38. Brown, *Lower South in American History*, p. 124.
39. See Pierre Bourdieu, *Outline of a Theory of Practice*, Richard Nice, trans. (Cambridge: Cambridge University Press, 1977), pp. 17, 61. See also Bourdieu, "Marriage Strategies as Strategies of Social Reproduction," in Robert Forster and Orest Ranum, eds., *Family and Society: Selections from "Annales, Economies, Sociétés, Civilisations,"* Elborg Forster and Patricia M. Ranum, trans. (Baltimore: Johns Hopkins University Press, 1976), pp. 117–44.

Chapter Five: Fathers, Mothers, and Progeny

1. Hundley, *Social Relations*, p. 74. Clifford Geertz, *The Interpretation of Cultures* (New York: Harper & Row, 1973), p. 203; Mary Boykin Chesnut, *A Diary from Dixie*, Ben Ames Williams, ed. (Boston: Houghton Mifflin, 1949), p. 129.
2. Ruth Benedict, "Continuities and Discontinuities in Culture Conditioning," *Psychiatry* 1 (May 1938): 161–67; William L. Barney, *The Secessionist Impulse: Alabama and Mississippi in 1860* (Princeton: Princeton University Press, 1974), pp. 61–88, 91–95, 100; and idem, "Towards the Civil War: The Dynamics of Change in a Black Belt County," in McMath and Burton, *Southern Communities*. William J. Grayson complained that "a dozen sons look forward to the partition of the personal property with exaggerated notions of their future fortunes. Each one of them expects to live on a part of the property as the father lived on the

whole. They are to be planters. But the fragment of the estate fails to support the inheritor"; in Stoney, "Autobiography of Grayson," p. 40.

3. James Simmons to John Manning, January 7, 1859, quoted in Rosser H. Taylor, *Ante-Bellum South Carolina: A Social and Cultural History*, James Sprunt Studies in History and Political Science (Chapel Hill: University of North Carolina Press, 1942), 25: 46; Samuel A. Townes to George F. Townes, August 8, 1836, Townes Family MSS, SC, USC.

4. James H. Hammond to Harry Hammond, November 17, 1861, HBC MSS, SC, USC. John Randolph to Theodore Dudley, December 30, 1821, in John Randolph, *Letters to a Young Relative: Embracing a Series of Years, from Early Youth to Mature Manhood* (Philadelphia: Carey, Lea & Blanchard, 1834), p. 232; Chalmers G. Davidson, *The Last Foray: The South Carolina Planters of 1860: A Sociological Study* (Columbia: University of South Carolina Press, 1971), pp. 15–16.

5. Quoted in "Sketches of the Pioneers in Burke County History," 22h, SHC, UNC.

6. Randolph to Dudley, February 5, 1822, in *Letters to a Young Relative*, pp. 250–51.

7. Bertram E. Brown to "Cousin Eloise," July 8, 1936, in author's possession.

8. John H. Moore, ed., "The Abiel Abbott Journals: A Yankee Preacher in Charleston Society, 1818–1827," *SCHGM* 68 (January 1967), November 18, 1818, 65, 66 (quotation). See also Johnson, "Planters and Patriarchy," pp. 45–72.

9. I have rounded off the percentages. For a precise accounting, see Daniel Scott Smith, "Population, Family, and Society in Hingham, Massachusetts, 1635–1880," Ph.D. diss., 1971, University of California, Berkeley, pp. 342–43. See also idem, "Child-Naming Patterns and Family Structure Change: Hingham, Massachusetts, 1640–1880," 1975, cited in James A. Henretta, "Families and Farms: Mentalité in Pre-Industrial America," *WMQ*, 3d ser. 35 (January 1978): 29 n63; and see Alice Rossi, "Naming Children in Middle Class Families," *ASR* 30 (August 1965): 499–513. Interestingly, in America today sons are "less apt to be named for fathers and paternal uncles, more apt to be named for maternal grandfathers and uncles than they were in the 1920's," a change (in Northern states) attributable, says Rossi, to "diminishing barriers among adult age groups and between the sexes" (p. 513). See also Helen Codere, "A Genealogical Study of Kinship in the United States," *Psychiatry* 18 (February 1955): 65–79.

10. Riley R. Wyatt, *Autobiography of a Little Man* (n.p., n.d.), p. 13 (sole copy is located in the Auburn University Library, Auburn, Ala.); backwoodsman quoted by Horace Kephart, *Our Southern Highlanders: A Narrative of Adventure in the Southern Appalachians and a Study of Life among the Mountaineers* (Knoxville: University of Tennessee Press, 1976), p. 334.

11. Wyatt, *Autobiography*, pp. 8–9; John Hewitt, "Memoirs," typescript, pp. 10–11, passim, SHC, UNC.

12. J. G. M. Ramsey to Lyman Draper, May 26, 1875, in J. G. M. Ramsey, *Autobiography and Letters*, William B. Hesseltine, ed. (Nashville: Tennessee Historical Commission, 1954), pp. 286–87; Harry Legare Watson II, " 'Bitter Combinations of the Neighborhood,' The Second American Party System in Cumberland County, North Carolina," Ph.D. diss., Northwestern University, 1976, p. 71.

13. James S. Brown, *The Family Group in a Kentucky Mountain Farming Community*, Bulletin 588, Kentucky Agricultural Experiment Station (Lexington: University of Kentucky, June 1952), pp. 7–10; Vance Randolph, *The Ozarks: An American Survival of a Primitive Society* (New York: Vanguard Press, 1931), p. 61; Ramsey to Draper, May 26, 1875, in Ramsey, *Autobiography*, pp. 286–87.

14. Cf. Anne F. Scott, *The Southern Lady: From Pedestal to Politics 1830–1930* (Chicago: University of Chicago Press, 1970); idem, "Women's Perspective on the Patriarchy in the 1850s," *JAH* 41 (June 1974): 52–64; William H. Chafe, *Women and Equality: Changing Patterns in American Culture* (New York: Oxford University Press, 1977), pp. 66–68, 118–19.

15. Matron quoted from Spencer B. King, Jr., ed., *Ebb Tide: As Seen through the Diary of Josephine Clay Habersham, 1863* (Athens, Ga.: University of Georgia Press, 1958), July 10, 1863, p. 40. Dedication in William Faulkner, *Go Down, Moses* (New York: Modern Library, 1940); Jean Stein, "An Interview with William Faulkner," in Malcolm Cowley, ed., *William Faulkner* (New York: Viking, 1959), p. 130.

16. J. G. Clinkscales, *On the Old Plantation: Reminiscences of His Childhood* (New York: Negro Universities Press, 1969 [1916]), p. 36; Eugene D. Genovese, *Roll, Jordan, Roll: The World the Slaves Made* (New York: Pantheon, 1974), pp. 343–65.

17. Mrs. Taylor, *Reciprocal Duties of Parents and Children* (Boston: James Loring, 1825), pp. 29, 35–36, 47, 58, 62; see also Bernard Wishy, *The Child and the Republic: The Dawn of Modern American Child Nurture* (Philadelphia: University of Pennsylvania, 1968); Joseph Kett, *Rites of Passage: Adolescence in America, 1790 to the Present* (New York: Basic Books, 1977).

18. Asa Mead, *Memoir of John Mooney Mead, Who Died at East Hartford, April 8, 1831, Aged Four Years, 11 Months, and Four Days* (New York, Sleight, 1831), pp. 7, 9, 10–11; Bertram Wyatt-Brown, "Three Generations of Yankee Parenthood: The Tappan Family, A Case Study of Antebellum Nurture," *Illinois Quarterly* 38 (Fall 1975): 12–28. See also William G. McLoughlin, "Evangelical Child-Rearing in the Age of Jackson: Francis Wayland's Views on When and How to Subdue the Willfulness of Children," *JSocH* 9 (Fall 1975): 20–43; Nancy F. Cott, "Notes toward an Interpretation of Antebellum Childrearing," *PR* 6 (Spring 1978): 4–20; and Charles Strickland, "A Transcendentalist Father: The Child-Rearing Practices of Bronson Alcott," *Perspectives in American History* 3 (1969): 5–76. In addition see Jacqueline R. Reinier, "Attitudes toward and Practices of Child-Rearing: Philadelphia, 1790 to 1830," Ph.D. diss., University of California, Berkeley, 1977.

19. John Weiss, *Life and Correspondence of Theodore Parker . . .*, 2 vols. (London: Longman, Green, 1863) 1: 25; cf. Philip Greven, *The Protestant Temperament: Patterns of Child-Rearing, Religious Experience, and the Self in Early America* (New York: Knopf, 1977), pp. 21–148; Alice M. Earle, *Customs and Fashions in Old New England* (New York: Charles Scribner's Sons, 1896), pp. 13–15; Alice M. Earle, *Child Life in Colonial Days* (New York: Macmillan, 1895).

20. Quoted in Bruce, *Violence and Culture*, pp. 64–65.

21. Freud quoted by Robert Hogan, "Of Rituals, Roles, Cheaters, and Spoilsports," *Johns Hopkins Magazine* 30 (October 1979): 52; Lee, *Recollections of Lee,*

p. 16; Evelyn Scott, *Background in Tennessee* (New York: McBride, 1937), p. 55.

22. Russell L. Blake, "Ties of Intimacy: Social Values and Personal Relationships of Antebellum Slaveholders," Ph.D. diss., University of Michigan, 1978, p. 39.

23. Natchez matron quoted from Michael S. Wayne, "Ante-Bellum Planters in the Post-Bellum South, 1860–1880," Ph.D. diss., Yale University, 1979, p. 16.

24. Jefferson's troubles are well recorded in Dumas Malone, *Jefferson and His Time*, vol. 3, *The Sage of Monticello* (Boston: Little, Brown, 1981), pp. 153–68, 285–300.

25. Davis, *Recollections of Mississippi*, p. 20. Andrew Jackson's recollection of his mother's words quoted from Curtis, *Jackson*, p. 36.

26. George Braxton to "My Dear Life," November 16, 1755, in Frederick Horner, *The History of the Blair, Bannister, and Braxton Families* (Philadelphia: Lippincott, 1898), p. 131; Levin Joynes to Nancy Joynes, November 8, 1788," in "Letters from Colonel Levin Joynes to Ann, His Wife, *February 9, 1780–December 28, 1790*," *VMHB* 56 (April 1948): 151. On black childrearing in Florida, see Molly C. Dougherty, *Becoming a Woman in Rural Black Culture* (New York: Holt, Rinehart & Winston, 1978), pp. 17, 61 (quotation). On plantation fathers' attitudes toward the young, see John F. Walzer, "A Period of Ambivalence: Eighteenth-Century American Childhood," in Lloyd deMause, ed., *A History of Childhood* (New York: Harper & Row, 1974), pp. 358–59; Richard H. Lee to Thomas Lee Shippen, January 17, 1785, in James C. Ballagh, ed., *The Letters of Richard Henry Lee* (New York: DeCapo, 1970), p. 322. See also, on mountaineer children, Marion Pearsall, *Little Smoky Ridge: The Natural History of a Southern Appalachian Neighborhood* (University: University of Alabama Press, 1959), pp. 80–105, esp. p. 99.

27. On northeastern merchant childrearing, see William H. Pease and Jane H. Pease, "Paternal Dilemmas: Education, Property, and Patrician Persistence in Jacksonian Boston," *NEQ* 53 (June 1980): 147–67, 151 (quotation). On the view, challenged here, that "preindustrial" fathers were homebodies, see Peter Laslett, *Family Life and Illicit Love in Earlier Generations* (London and New York: Cambridge University Press, 1977), p. 37, and Michael Katz, "Families: Cycle, Structure, and Economy in Early Industrial America," paper presented to Armington Seminar, Case Western Reserve University, March 21, 1980, pp. 369–70.

28. William Beverley to John Fairchild, March 9, 1742, in Worthington C. Ford, ed., "Some Letters of William Beverley," *WMQ,* 1st ser. 3 (April 1895): 231–32; Beverley to Lord Fairfax, April 20, 1743, and to Richard Bland, May 11, 1743, ibid., pp. 232–33.

29. Michael Zuckerman, "An Amusement in This Silent Country: The Family Life of William Byrd of Eighteenth Century Virginia," Paper before Armington Seminar, Case Western Reserve University, November 14, 1978, printed under the title "William Byrd's Family" in *Perspectives in American History* 12 (1979): 255–311; but see Louis B. Wright and Marion Trinling, eds., *The Secret Diary of William Byrd of Westover, 1709–1712* (Richmond: Dietz Press, 1941), November 30, p. 112; December 3, p. 113; December 10, 1709, p. 117; and entries for May–June 7, 1710, pp. 177–88. John C. Calhoun to Mrs. Floride Calhoun, April 9, 1815, in J. Franklin Jameson, ed., *Correspondence of John C. Calhoun, Fourth Annual Report, American Historical Association, for the Year 1899*, 2 vols. (Wash-

ington: Government Printing Office, 1900) 2: 128–29. On the supposed indifference of early modern parents, see Philippe Ariés, *Centuries of Childhood: A
Social History of Family Life* (New York: W. W. Norton, 1962); Lawrence Stone,
The Family, Sex and Marriage in England, 1500–1800 (New York: Harper & Row,
1977), pp. 58, 105–14, 168–71.
30. *Moreau de St. Mery's American Journey, 1793–1798,* Kenneth Roberts and
Anna M. Roberts, eds. (Garden City: Doubleday, 1947), p. 54; Greene, *Carter
Diary,* September 14, 1772, 2: 728.
31. Frederick L. Olmsted, *Journey through Texas: A Saddle Trip on the Southwestern Frontier,* James Howard, ed. (Austin: von Beekman-Jones Press, 1962
[1857]), pp. 5–7.
32. Israel Pickens to Walter R. Lenoir, August 25, 1823, Lenoir Family MSS,
SHC, UNC.
33. Johnson, "Planters and Patriarchy," *JHS* 46 (February 1980): 46 n5; Agan
Blair to Mrs. Braxton, August 21, 1769, in Horner, *History of Blair, Braxton,
and Bannister Families,* p. 56; Greven, *Protestant Temperament,* p. 270; Molly
Tilghman to Polly Tilghman, 1783 or 1784, in "Letters of Molly and Hetty
Tilghman," quoted by Daniel Blake Smith, "Autonomy and Affection: Parents
and Children in Eighteenth-Century Chesapeake Families," *PR* 6 (Fall–Winter
1977–78): 48. Jones quoted in ibid., p. 46. Greene, *Carter Diary,* June 27, 1766,
1: 310.
34. Greene, *Carter Diary,* December 30, 1774, 2: 907; March 9, 1776, p. 997.
35. Zillah (Haynie) Brandon, "Personal Reminiscences, 1855–1871," I & II,
AlaDAH. Russel W. Benedict described the Wyley tribe as follows: "They had no
knowledge of Letters or Books, and were . . . as full of superstitions as their
feeble minds were capable of, believing in Witches, Ghosts, Hobgoblins Evil eyes,
and all such traditions," though "harmless and perfectly honest." Quoted by
Malcolm J. Rohrbough, *The Trans-Appalachian Frontier: People, Societies, and
Institutions, 1775–1850* (New York: Oxford University Press, 1978), p. 273; Howard
F. Stein, "Envy and the Evil Eye among Slovak-Americans: An Essay in the
Psychological Ontogeny of Belief and Ritual," *Ethos* 2 (Spring 1974): 15–46;
William L. Montell, *Ghosts along the Cumberland: Deathlore in the Kentucky
Foothills* (Knoxville: University of Tennessee Press, 1975).
36. Raleigh *Star and North Carolina Gazette,* January 31, 1844. Gordon B.
Cleveland, "Social Conditions in Alabama as Seen by Travelers, 1840–1850, Part
II," *Alabama Review* 2 (April 1949): 137. See also Roberts and Roberts, *Moreau
de St. Mery's American Journey,* p. 54; Andrew Burnaby, *Travels through the
Middle Settlements in North America in the Years 1759 and 1760,* Rufus R.
Wilson, ed. (New York: Wessels, 1904), p. 58.
37. King, *Ebb Tide,* August 11, 1863, p. 63. Maria Taylor Byrd to William Byrd,
III, September 21, 1757, "Byrd Family Letters," *VMHB* 37 (July 1929): 245;
Franklin, *Militant South,* pp. 18–20; "Self-Portrait, Eliza Custis, 1808," cited in
Smith, "Autonomy and Affection," p. 42, erroneous ref. cited therein; see also
Davis, *Recollections of Mississippi and Mississippians,* p. 2; William B. Lenoir to
William Lenoir, December 27, 1834, Lenoir Family MSS, SHC, UNC.
38. Matron quoted in Walzer, "A Period of Ambivalence," p. 367. Sir Charles
Lyell, *A Second Visit to the United States of North America,* 2 vols. (New York:

Harper & Bros., 1849) 2: 168–69. William K. Scarborough, ed., *The Diary of Edmund Ruffin*, vol. 1. *Toward Independence, October, 1856–April, 1861* (Baton Rouge: Louisiana State University Press, 1972), September 21, 1858, p. 231.

39. Mary Austin Holley to Mrs. Hariette Brand, November 9, 1830, Peters-Dallam-Holley MSS, UKL; see also Molly Tilghman to Hetty Tilghman, January 29, 1789, in J. Hall Pleasants, ed., "Letters of Molly and Hetty Tilghman, Eighteenth Century Gossip of Two Maryland Girls," *MMH* 21 (September 1926): 232.

40. Penton cited in George C. Brauer, *The Education of a Gentleman: Theories of Gentlemanly Education in England, 1660–1775* (New York: Bookman Associates, 1959), p. 141. See also Mary Beth Norton, *Liberty's Daughters: The Revolutionary Experience of American Women, 1750–1800* (Boston: Little, Brown, 1980), pp. 92–93.

41. Rice quoted in H. Peter Pudner, "People not Pedagogy: Education in Old Virginia," *GR* 25 (October 1971): 279. Families of pious demeanor varied much on parental permissiveness about acts of aggression toward peers and underlings; Bruce, *Violence and Culture*, pp. 48–56, presents a case for orderliness in Southern refined families that has merit, but unfortunately not many families met the social ideals of the Pettigrew family, upon which his views are based.

42. Sidney E. Bumpas, "Autobiography," typescript, p. 1, SHC, UNC; William Porcher DuBose, "Autobiography," typescript, p. 29, ibid.; W. P. Strickland, ed., *Autobiography of Peter Cartwright, the Backwoods Preacher* (New York: Carlton & Porter, 1865), pp. 24–25; Ray Holder, *William Winans: Methodist Leader in Antebellum Mississippi* (Jackson: University Press of Mississippi, 1977), p. 4; Mrs. C. G. Alexwhelan to William Lee Alexwhelan, April 2, 1850, W. A. Hoke MSS, SHC, UNC. On childhood aggression, see Leonard Berkowitz, "Control of Aggression," in *Review of Child Development Research*, Bettye M. Caldwell and Henry M. Ricciuti, eds. (Chicago: University of Chicago Press, 1973) 3: 114–15; see also W. C. Becker, "Consequences of Different Kinds of Discipline," in M. L. Hoffman and L. W. Hoffman, eds., ibid. (1964), 1: 169–208.

43. Anthony F. C. Wallace, *The Death and Rebirth of the Seneca* (New York: Vintage, 1972), p. 35; Erik H. Erikson, *Childhood and Society* (New York: Norton, 1963), pp. 135–36; and William F. Nydegger and Corinne Nydegger, "Tarong: The Ilocos Barrio in the Philippines," in Beatrice B. Whiting, ed., *Six Cultures: Studies of Child Rearing* (New York: John Wiley, 1963), p. 815; Leigh Minturn and John T. Hitchcock, "The Rajputs of Khalapur, India," ibid., p. 311.

44. Virginia parent quoted in Smith, "Autonomy and Affection," p. 48; Mrs. P. M. Sumner to Mrs. Salina Lenoir, October 13, 1835, Lenoir Family MSS, SHC, UNC; "Family Account of Mrs. Lucy Ann Page, Dec'd, Late of Gloucester County, Virginia," *WMQ*, 1st ser. 11 (January 1903): 256; James L. Petigru to Mrs. Caroline North, September 13, 1826, James L. Petigru MSS, LC. Greene, *Carter Diary*, September 14, 1772, 2: 728; Walzer, "Period of Ambivalence," pp. 351–82; Thomas Chaplin, Diary, May 12, 1850, SCHS. See also Norton, *Liberty's Daughters*, pp. 93–94.

45. Clinkscales, *Old Plantation*, p. 105; Wright and Tinling, *Byrd Diary*, February 28, 1711, p. 307; King, *Ebb Tide*, July 27, 1863, p. 53; Richard M. Johnston and William H. Browne, *Life of Alexander H. Stephens* (Philadelphia: Lippincott, 1884), p. 30; Robert W. Dubay, *John Jones Pettus, Mississippi Fireater: His Life*

and Times (Jackson: University Press of Mississippi, 1975), p. 5. Henry C. Cumming to Charles Hall, August [?], 1857, HBC MSS. John T. Irwin, *Doubling and Incest/Repetition and Revenge: A Speculative Reading of Faulkner* (Baltimore: Johns Hopkins University Press, 1975).

46. William K. Boyd, ed., "Rev. Brantley York on Early Days in Randolph County and Union Institute," *Historical Papers of the Historical Society of Trinity College* (Durham: Trinity College, 1898–1909) 8: 16; Edward King, *The Great South,* Macgruder Drake and Robert R. Jones, eds. (Baton Rouge: Louisiana State University Press, 1972), p. 774.

47. Lee to Mrs. Mary Custis Lee, October 16, 1837, in Jones, *Lee,* p. 34. See also Lee, *Recollections of Lee,* p. 16.

48. Lee, *Recollections of Lee,* p. 16.

49. Ray Mathis, *John Horry Dent: South Carolina Aristocrat on the Alabama Frontier* (University: University of Alabama Press, 1979), pp. 164–65. The interpretation given in this chapter differs from that of Daniel Blake Smith, *Inside the Great House: Planter Family Life in Eighteenth-Century Chesapeake Society* (Ithaca: Cornell University Press, 1980), which argues that the Southern family was almost modern in character.

50. Mathis, *Dent,* pp. 164–65.

Chapter Six: Male Youth and Honor

1. Johnston and Browne, *Stephens,* p. 42.

2. See Greven, *Protestant Temperament;* Ross Beales, Jr., "Childhood, Religion, and Society in Eighteenth-Century Massachusetts: An Analysis of Ebenezer Parkman's Diary," Paper for Armington Seminar, Case Western Reserve University, September 25, 1979; Nancy F. Cott, *The Bonds of Womanhood: 'Women's Sphere' in New England, 1780–1835* (New Haven: Yale University Press, 1977).

3. Johnston and Browne, *Stephens,* pp. 30–31, 33–36; see also Greene, *Carter Diary,* June 27, 1766, 1: 310.

4. William Penn quoted in Stone, *Family, Sex and Marriage,* p. 433; Barry Levy, "The Birth of the 'Modern Family' in Early America: Quaker and Anglican Families in the Delaware Valley, Pennsylvania, 1681–1750," in Michael Zuckerman, ed., *Friends and Neighbors: Studies of America's First Plural Society* (Philadelphia: Temple University Press, forthcoming). "Corporal Punishment," *SLM* 7 (July 1841): 576.

5. Wright and Tinling, *Byrd Diary, 1709–1712,* December 3, 1709, p. 113; December 10, 1709, p. 117; March 2, 1712, p. 495; Clinkscales, *Old Plantation,* pp. 84–85; see also Greene, *Carter Diary,* June 27, 1766, 1: 310; Robert Bailey, *Life and Adventures . . .* (Richmond: J. & G. Cochran, 1822), p. 11.

6. Chaplin, Diary, August 31, 1845; May 12, 1850; March 18, 1851; September 23, 1856; SCHS. Henry Craft, Diary (typescript), August 23, 1859; July 20, 30, August 19, December 6, 1860, SHC, UNC; Taylor, *Reciprocal Duties,* p. 23; Goodwin Watson, "Some Personality Differences in Children Related to Strict or Permissive Discipline," *Journal of Psychology* 44 (July 1957): 227–49; Brandt F. Steele and

Carl B. Pollack, "A Psychiatric Study of Parents Who Abuse Infants and Small Children," in Ray E. Helfer and C. Henry Kempe, eds., *The Battered Child* (Chicago: University of Chicago Press, 1974), p. 106. See also Bertram Wyatt-Brown, "Child Abuse, Public Policy, and Childrearing in America: An Historical Approach," in Barbara L. Finkelstein, ed., *Governing the Young: Working Papers* (College Park, Md.: University of Maryland College of Education, 1981), pp. 1–29.

7. John Dickinson to his father, August 15, 1754, in Trevor Colburn, ed., "A Pennsylvania Farmer at the Court of King George: John Dickinson's London Letters, 1754–1756," *Pennsylvania Magazine of History and Biography* 86 (July 1962): 278; Thomas Jefferson, *Notes on the State of Virginia*, William Peden, ed. (Chapel Hill: University of North Carolina Press, 1975), p. 162; "Journal of Josiah Quincy, Junior, 1773," *Massachusetts Historical Society Proceedings* 49 (June 1916): 456. Mrs. Virginia Cary, *Letters on Female Character Addressed to a Young Lady on the Death of Her Mother* (Richmond: Ariel, 1830), p. 203.

8. Cary, *Letters on Female Character*, pp. 203–4; M. M. Peachy to Robert Little, January 16, 1804, in Horner, *History of Blair, Bannister, and Braxton Families*, p. 63; Holley to Brand, November 30, 1839, Peters-Dallam-Holley MSS, UKL.

9. Cary, *Letters on Female Character*, pp. 205–7; Frederick Law Olmsted, *The Cotton Kingdom: A Traveller's Observations on Cotton and the Slave States*, A. M. Schlesinger, ed. (New York: Knopf, 1953), pp. 65, 172–73 and n6; idem, *A Journey in the Back Country, 1853–1854* (New York: Schocken, 1970), p. 179.

10. James B. Avirett, *The Old Plantation: How We Lived in Great House and Cabin Before the War* (New York: F. Tennyson Neely, 1901), p. 91.

11. Cook is quoted in Robert M. Calhoon, "Faith and Consciousness in Early Southern Culture," Paper presented at Guilford College, March 28, 1980, kindly lent by the author.

12. Helen B. Lewis, *Shame and Guilt in Neurosis* (New York: International Universities Press, 1971), p. 42. Helen M. Lynd, *On Shame and the Search for Identity* (New York: Harcourt, Brace, 1958), pp. 13–71; Erikson, *Childhood and Society*, p. 224.

13. Quotation on Jefferson's boating from Henry S. Randall, *The Life of Thomas Jefferson* (New York: Derby & Jackson, 1858), p. 15; Dumas Malone, *Thomas Jefferson, The Virginian* (Boston: Little, Brown, 1948), p. 46.

14. George Coleman Osborn, *John Sharp Williams: Planter-Statesman of the Deep South* (Baton Rouge: Louisiana State University Press, 1943), pp. 8–9; William B. Lenoir to William Lenoir, December 27, 1834, Lenoir Family MSS, SHC, UNC; Davis, *Recollections of Mississippi and Mississippians*, p. 2; Betty L. Mitchell, *Edmund Ruffin: A Biography* (Bloomington: Indiana University Press, 1981), pp. 3–4.

15. Manly W. Wellman, *Giant in Gray: A Biography of Wade Hampton of South Carolina* (New York: Charles Scribner's Sons, 1949), pp. 17–18; Clinkscales, *On the Old Plantation*, p. 102.

16. William C. Preston, "Reminiscences," in Stark Young, ed., *Southern Treasury of Life and Literature* (New York: Charles Scribner's Sons, 1937), p. 17, pointed out that Virginians transplanted in the West differed markedly in their notions of gentility from their kinfolk still settled in the East. Captain Robert E. Lee,

Recollections and Letters of General Robert E. Lee (Garden City: Doubleday, 1924 [1905]), p. 9.

17. Mitchell B. Garrett, *Horse and Buggy Days on Hatchet Creek* (University: University of Alabama Press, 1957), p. 22.

18. Sarah N. Randolph, *The Domestic Life of Thomas Jefferson Compiled from Family Letters and Reminiscences* (New York: Harper & Bros. 1939 [1871]), p. 337; Brauer, *Education of a Gentleman*, p. 141; Randolph to Dudley, October 13, 1811, and December 30, 1821, in Randolph, *Letters to a Young Relative*, pp. 109 and 232.

19. Quoted by Robert Bober, "Young Woodrow Wilson: The Search for Immortality," Ph. D. diss., Case Western Reserve University, ch. 2, pp. 16, 20. On Wilson's upbringing, see also Edwin A. Weinstein, *Woodrow Wilson: A Medical and Psychological Biography* (Princeton: Princeton University Press, 1981).

20. Johnston and Browne, *Stephens*, p. 42; Pearsall, *Little Smoky Ridge*, p. 101; quotation from Margaret J. Hagood, *Mothers of the South: Portraitures of the White Tenant Farm Women* (New York: Norton, 1977 [1937]), 142–43; Vance Randolph, *Ozark Mountain Folks* (New York: Vanguard Press, 1932), p. 32.

21. Boyd, ed., "Rev. Brantley York on Early Days in Randolph County," *Historical Papers of Trinity College*, 8: 18–19; Vance Randolph, *The Ozarks: An American Survival of Primitive Society* (New York: Vanguard Press, 1931), pp. 87–137; Pearsall, *Little Smoky Ridge*, p. 101; the Rev. Jethro Rumple, *A History of Rowan County, North Carolina* . . . (Salisbury, N.C.: J. J. Bruner, 1881), pp. 324–32, 355–61; Scott, *Background in Tennessee*, pp. 21–25; Margaret Devereux, *Plantation Sketches* (Cambridge, Mass.: Riverdale Press, 1906), pp. 31–34; Elmora M. Matthews, *Neighbors and Kin: Life in a Tennessee Ridge Community* (Nashville, Tenn.: Vanderbilt University Press, 1965), pp. 103–7.

22. Pearsall, *Little Smoky Ridge*, pp. 101–2; *William Brooks v. Elizabeth Brooks*, 1821; *Catherine Smith v. John Smith*, 1819; *Margaret Sitz v. William Sitz*, 1831, *Hannah Stone v. Thomas Stone*, 1821, Tennessee State Legislative Papers, Divorce Committee, TSA. William Brown, Diary (microfilm), January 13, 1805. UKL, orig. in New York Public Library. Pearsall, *Little Smoky Ridge*, p. 98.

23. Johnston and Browne, *Stephens*, p. 42; James Claiborne, *Seventy-Five Years in Old Virginia* (New York: Neale, 1904), pp. 20, 21.

24. Recollection of school quoted in Raleigh A. Suarez, "Chronicle of a Failure: Public Education in Antebellum Louisiana," *LH* 12 (Spring 1971): 120. Moses Ashley Curtis, Diary, October 21, 1831, passim, and February 6, 1832, SHC, UNC. See also Johnston and Browne, *Stephens*, pp. 42–60.

25. Claiborne, *Seventy-Five Years*, p. 30; see also William D. Lacey to Thomas Butler, June 25, 1847, Ellis-Farrar MSS, LSU. *A Full and Authentic Report of the Testimony on the Trial of Matt F. Ward . . . With Speeches of Gov. Crittenden, Gov. Helm, T. F. Marshall, Esq., Attorney for the Commonwealth* (New York: 1854), pp. 159, 175.

26. Quotation from "Free School System in South Carolina," *SQR*, n. s. 6 (October 1852): 467; see also *SQR* 16 (October 1849): 52–53. Wyatt, *Autobiography*, pp. 17–20; see also Emily Burke, *Reminiscences of Georgia* (Oberlin: J. M. Fitch, 1850), pp. 209, 210.

27. Julien Cumming to Julia A. D. C. Cumming, March 13, 1842, HBC MSS.

28. Quoted in Bertram Wyatt-Brown, "Conscience and Career: Young Abolitionists and Missionaries," in Bolt and Drescher, *Anti-Slavery, Religion, and Reform.*

29. Pease and Pease, "Paternal Dilemmas," *NEQ* 53 (June 1980): 153.

30. Hunter D. Farish, ed., *The Journal and Letters of Philip Vickers Fithian: A Plantation Tutor of the Old Dominion, 1773–1774* (Williamsburg, Va.: Colonial Williamsburg, 1957 [1943, 1945]), September 15, 1774, p. 190.

31. Ibid.

32. Boyd, "Rev. Brantley York on Early Days," p. 21; see also Nathaniel B. Tucker to John Randolph, February 21, 1802, Tucker-Coleman, MSS, WMC; and Clinkscales, *On the Old Plantation*, pp. 74–75. Farish, *Fithian Journal*, September 5, 1774, pp. 184–85.

33. Farish, *Fithian Journal*, September 5, 1774, p. 185.

34. Thomas Jefferson Withers to James H. Hammond, June 8, 1826, James H. Hammond MSS, SC, USC.

35. John Cantry to John Manning, May 19, 24, 1841, Chesnut-Manning MSS, SC, USC.

36. Alfred Huger to General James Hamilton, October 3, 1855; to James Legaré, August 4, 1853, Alfred Huger MSS, DUL; also Huger to Wade Hampton, August 8, 1853, ibid.

37. Grayson, "Character of a Gentleman," pp. 53–54.

38. Elisha Hammond to James H. Hammond, May 23, 1828, Hammond MSS, SC, USC; William S. Pettigrew to Ann B. L. Pettigrew, November 25, 1851, William S. Pettigrew MSS, SHC, UNC; Randolph to Dudley, December 30, 1821, in Randolph, *Letters to a Young Relative*, p. 233.

39. Curtis, Diary, July 14, September 30, 1831, SHC, UNC; Randolph to Dudley January 8, 1807, in E. A. Alderman and J. C. Harris, eds., *Library of Southern Literature* 16 vols. (New Orleans: Martin & Hoyt, 1909) 10: 4352.

40. Greene, *Carter Diary*, April 27, 1777, 2: 1103; January 13, 1772, pp. 645–46.

41. Sharkey in *Foster v. Alston*, 7 Miss. (6 How.) 460 (1842), at 463. See also Jamil S. Zainaldin, "The Emergence of a Modern American Family Law: Child Custody, Adoption, and the Courts, 1796–1851," *NULR* 73 (February 1979): 1038–89.

42. Greene, *Carter Diary*, March 9, 1776, 2: 998; Thomas R. Dew, "Second Lecture . . . on Parental Faults," *SLM* 2 (June 1836): 436.

43. Bober, "Young Woodrow Wilson." Dr. Bober, Ohio State University Library and Archives, kindly supplied me with the Rev. Joseph Wilson's sermon, "Trust in the Lord: Sermon on Psalm 118: 8, 9," Presbyterian Historical Foundation, Montreat, N.C.

44. Sciassia quoted by Gore Vidal, "On the Assassin's Trail," *NYRB*, October 25, 1979, pp. 18–19. Osborn, *Williams* p. 8.

45. William L. Barney, "Towards the Civil War: The Dynamics of Change in a Black Belt County," in Burton and McMath, *Southern Communities*. A prepublication copy was kindly lent by the author.

46. Woodward, *Chesnut's Civil War*, August 27, 1861, p. 166; August 29, 1861, p. 181.

Chapter Seven: A Young Man's Career

1. James H. Hammond to Harry Hammond, July 16, 1859, HBC MSS.

2. Gavin Wright, *The Political Economy of the Cotton South: Households, Markets, and Wealth in the Nineteenth Century* (New York: W. W. Norton, 1978), p. 35. Cf. Stanley L. Engerman, "A Reconsideration of Southern Economic Growth, 1770–1860," *AgH* 49 (April 1975): 343–61. Abundant land, however, gave many settlers a sense of self-sufficiency surely as great as that which Northwesterners attained: see Leo Soltow, "Land Inequality on the Frontier: The Distribution of Land in East Tennessee at the Beginning of the Nineteenth Century," *SSH* 5 (Summer 1981): 275–92.

3. J. E. B. DeBow, comp., *The Seventh Census of the United States (1850)*, pp. lxvii–lxxxix, 438, 455, 481; Randolph B. Campbell and Richard G. Lane, *Wealth and Power in Antebellum Texas* (College Station: Texas A. & M. University Press, 1977), pp. 12, 13, 43–45, 137; Lee Soltow, *Men and Wealth in the United States* (New Haven: Yale University Press, 1975), pp. 66–67, 134; idem, "Land Inequality"; idem, "Inequality amidst Abundance: Land Ownership in Early Nineteenth-Century Ohio," *Ohio History* 88 (Spring 1979): 133–51.

4. Elizabeth McCall Perry to Benjamin Perry, February 14, 1837, Benjamin Perry MSS, SC, USC.

5. The Rt. Rev. Stephen Elliott, "Address on Horticulture," in Herbert B. Owens, ed., *Georgia's Planting Prelate . . .* (Athens, Ga.: University of Georgia Press, 1945), p. 25; Drew G. Faust, "The Rhetoric and Ritual of Agriculture in Antebellum South Carolina," *JSH* 45 (November 1979): 541–68.

6. Langdon quoted in William W. Rogers, Jr., " 'The Husbandman That Laboreth Must Be First Partaker of the Fruits,' (2 Timothy 2:6): Agricultural Reform in Antebellum Alabama," *AHQ* 40 (Spring and Summer 1978): 41. See Thomas L. Haskell, "Were Slaves More Efficient? Some Doubts about 'Time on the Cross,' " *NYRB*, September 19, 1974, pp. 38–42; and idem, "The True and Tragical History of 'Time on the Cross,' " *NYRB*, October 2, 1975, pp. 33–39. The William S. Pettigrew MSS, SHC, UNC, are unusually rich and detailed, as are the John H. Cocke MSS, UVa; and Edmund Ruffin MSS, VHS.

7. Nathaniel Macon to Bolling Hall, June 20, 1823, Bolling Hall MSS, AlaDAH. On slavery and self-sufficiency, see John T. Schlotterbeck, "Plantation and Farm: Social and Economic Change in Orange and Greene Counties, Virginia, 1716 to 1860," Ph.D. diss., Johns Hopkins University, 1980.

8. Wigfall, in Chesnut, *Diary from Dixie*, p. 347. T. W. Peyre to Robert Marion Deveaux, September 9, 1838, Singleton Family MSS, LC. Mitchell, *Edmund Ruffin*, p. 21. George Fitzhugh, *Sociology for the South; or, The Failure of Free Society* (Richmond: A. Morris, 1854), p. 156.

9. Lorraine Eva Holland, "Rise and Fall of the Ante-Bellum Virginia Aristocracy: A Generational Analysis," Ph.D. diss., University of California, Irvine, 1980, pp. 251, 255, 257, 258, 261, 267 (table 22), 287 (Tucker quoted), 289, 297 (table 41 cited in text).

10. Pettigrew quoted in Blake, "Ties of Intimacy," p. 19.

11. David Gavin, Diary, SHC, UNC, May 31, 1856.

12. John L. Hunter, "Address to the Barbour County (Ala.) Agricultural Society," *Southern Cabinet* 1 (April 1840): 203–7; see also Faust, "Rhetoric and Ritual," pp. 548–49.

13. Joseph Ingraham, *The South-West by a Yankee*, 2 vols. (New York: Harper Bros., 1836), 2: 85. In Virginia's Orange and Greene Counties, despite educational advances, the percentage of farmers among all occupations actually increased, from 59.4 percent in the 1856–60 period to 74.3 percent in the 1876–80 period; see Schlotterbeck, "Plantation and Farm," table 3.4, p. 98, and pp. 97–99. On Jefferson's finances, see Malone, *Jefferson and His Time*; 6: 34–42; on Petigru, see William J. Grayson, *James Louis Petigru: A Biographical Sketch* (New York: Harper & Bros., 1866), pp. 82–85, passim.

14. Mary S. Jones to Charles C. Jones, Jr., December 15, 1859; Charles C. Jones, Jr., to Mary S. Jones, December 26, 1859, in Myers, *Children of Pride*, pp. 547, 551.

15. "Autobiographical Sketch of Dr. Armand John DeRosset, in 1847, Twelve Years before His Death, of the DeRosset Family," in Kemp P. Battle, ed., *Letters and Documents Relating to the Early History of Lower Cape Fear*, James Sprunt Historical Monograph no. 4 (Chapel Hill: University of North Carolina Press, 1903), p. 39; William L. Marbury, *The Story of a Maryland Family* (Baltimore: private printing, 1966); Wright, *Political Economy of Cotton South*, pp. 40–42, 45–46.

16. Neal C. Gillespie, *The Collapse of Orthodoxy: The Intellectual Ordeal of George Frederick Holmes* (Charlottesville: University Press of Virginia, 1972), p. 90; and D. F. Jamison to George F. Holmes, December 13, 1846, George F. Holmes MSS, LC.

17. Seabrook quoted in Laurensville (S.C.) *Herald*, November 29, 1850. Genovese, *Political Economy of Slavery*; James H. Hammond, Diary, December 25, 1850; see also Mauldin Lesesne, *The History of the State Bank of South Carolina* (Columbia: University of South Carolina Press, 1970); A. Toomer Porter, *Lead On! Step by Step* (New York: G. P. Putnam's Sons, 1898), pp. 112–13. Edward W. Phifer, "Money, Banking and Burke County in the Antebellum Era," *NCHR* 37 (January 1960): 22–37.

18. William H. Brantley, *Banking in Alabama, 1816–1860* 2 vols. (Birmingham: Birmingham Co., 1961) 1: 3–36; Thornton, *Politics and Power in a Slave Society*, pp. 281–85, 292; Israel Pickens, to Bolling Hall, December 30, 1823, Hall MSS, AlaDAH; see also James R. Sharp, *The Jacksonians versus the Banks: Politics in the States after the Panic of 1837* (New York: Columbia University Press, 1970).

19. Mrs. Elizabeth McCall Perry to Benjamin F. Perry, November 22, 1840, March 9, 1847, Benjamin F. Perry MSS, SC, USC; see also Hext McCall Perry, ed., *Letters of My Father to My Mother* (Philadelphia: Avil Printing, 1889), pp. 70–71, 99.

20. Thornton, *Politics and Power in a Slave Society*, p. 8.

21. S. G. Forbes to John Bragg, February 24, 1852, John Bragg MSS, SHC, UNC; Samuel E. Pierce, "The Formation of Alabama's First Two Party System: Alabama's Politics from 1830–1840," M.A. diss., Auburn University, 1974, pp. 35, 51–56, 102–210; Harold J. Counihan, "North Carolina 1815–1836: State and Local

Perspectives in the Age of Jackson," Ph.D. diss., University of North Carolina, 1971, p. 23, passim; Robert M. Ireland, *The County Courts in Antebellum Kentucky* (Lexington: University of Kentucky Press, 1972), pp. 166–67; Petitions of John Wilson, Bath County, June 11, 1819; Jonathan Brown, Jr., June 12, 1819, to James P. Preston, Box 253; "Fellow Citizen," Amherst County, to William B. Giles, June 20, 1827, Box 299, Governors' Papers, VSL; Sadie G. Kellam, "Cornick Family Genealogy," Kellam Family MSS, VSL. On political inbreeding among poorer folk, see Milton B. Newton, Jr., "The Darlings Creek Peasant Settlement of St. Helena Parish, Louisiana," in J. Kenneth Morland, ed., *The Not So Solid South: Anthropological Studies in a Regional Subculture*, Southern Anthropological Society Proceedings, no. 4 (Athens, Ga.: Southern Anthropological Society, 1971), p. 42.

22. Ronald P. Formisano, *The Birth of Mass Political Parties: Michigan, 1827–1861* (Princeton: Princeton University Press, 1971), pp. 26–27.

23. Donald M. Scott, *From Office to Profession: The New England Ministry, 1750–1850* (Philadelphia: University of Pennsylvania Press, 1978), pp. 78–81; Wyatt-Brown, "Conscience and Career," pp. 183–206. Kett, *Rites of Passage,* pp. 74–75, indicates that, as in the South, professional openings did not expand to meet the needs of college graduates. David F. Allmendinger, *Paupers and Scholars: The Transformations of Student Life in Nineteenth Century New England* (New York: St. Martin's Press, 1975), pp. 54–74; see also Charles S. Rosenberg, *No Other Gods: On Science and American Social Thought* (Baltimore: Johns Hopkins University Press, 1976), pp. 178–79.

24. Wyatt, *Autobiography of a Little Man,* pp. 21–22. On Yankee tutors, see diaries of Moses Ashley Curtis, John Cornish, Jason Niles, all in SHC, UNC; see also Farish, *Fithian's Journal;* Larry Gara, ed., "A New Englander's View of Plantation Life: Letters of Edwin Hall to Cyrus Woodman, 1837," *JSH* 18 (August 1952): 343–54; Elijah Fletcher to Jesse Fletcher, October 1, 1816, in Martha von Briesem, ed., *The Letters of Elijah Fletcher* (Charlottesville: University Press of Virginia, 1965), p. 14; Raleigh A. Suarez, "Chronicle of a Failure: Public Education in Antebellum Louisiana," *LH* 12 (Spring 1971): 119.

25. P. Lane, "Second Biennial Report of the Mississippi Institute for the Instruction of the Blind," 1852, RG 27, No. 35, MissDAH; Norman Dain, *Disordered Minds: The First Century of Eastern State Hospital in Williamsburg, Virginia, 1766–1866* (Charlottesville: University Press of Virginia, 1971); David G. Rothman, *The Discovery of the Asylum: Social Order and Disorder in the New Republic* (Boston: Little, Brown, 1971); Elizabeth Wisner, *Social Welfare in the South: From Colonial Times to World War I* (Baton Rouge: Louisiana State University, 1970), pp. 23–52.

26. Larry E. Tise, "Proslavery Ideology: Social and Intellectual History of the Defense of Slavery in America, 1790–1840," Ph.D. diss., University of North Carolina, 1975, esp. ch. 7, and table 16, p. 270. See also Larry E. Tise, "The Interregional Profile of the Antebellum American Clergy," *Plantation Society* 1 (February 1979): 58–72; Mat Bolls to James Smylie, March 27, 1837, Montgomery Family MSS, MissDAH; Iveson Brookes to William Brookes, October 9, 1823, Iveson Brookes MSS, SHC, UNC.

27. F. R. Hanson to William Marbury, January 29, 1839, in private possession. See also Farish, *Fithian Journal*, July 10, 1774, p. 180; Rev. Walter C. Whittaker, *Richard Hooker Wilmer: Second Bishop of Alabama* (Philadelphia: Geo. W. Jacobs, 1907), pp. 5, 23, 47–48; Lida Bestor Robertson, Diary [Sumterville, Alabama], September 14, 1851 AlaDAH; Dickson D. Bruce, Jr., *And They All Sang Hallelujah: Plain Folk Camp Meeting Religion, 1800–1845* (Knoxville: University of Tennessee Press, 1974), and idem, "Religion, Society, and Culture in the Old South: A Comparative View," *AQ* 26 (October 1974): 399–416; Strickland, *Cartwright Autobiography*, pp. 160–61, 177; James B. Finley, *Autobiography of James B. Finley; or, Pioneer Life in the West*, W. P. Strickland, ed. (Cincinnati: Methodist Book Concern, 1853), pp. 327–29; Clanton W. Williams, "Early Ante-Bellum Montgomery: A Black Belt Constituency," *JSH* 7 (November 1941): 503; Edwin A. Davis, ed. *Plantation Life in the Florida Parishes of Louisiana, 1836–1846, as Reflected in the Diary of Bennett H. Barrow* (New York: Columbia University Press, 1943), January 31, 1842, p. 250.

28. Ebenezer C. Tracy, *Memoir of the Life of Jeremiah Evarts . . .* (Boston: Crocker & Brewster, 1845), p. 196; Raleigh A. Suarez, "Religion in Rural Louisiana, 1850–1860," *LHQ* 38 (July 1955): 62.

29. Charles I. Foster, *An Errand of Mercy . . .* (Chapel Hill: University of North Carolina Press, 1960); Ronald G. Walters, *American Reformers, 1815–1860* (New York: Hill & Wang, 1978).

30. Keith R. Burich, "The Primitive Baptist Schism on North Carolina: A Study of the Professionalization of the Baptist Ministry," M.A. diss., University of North Carolina, 1973, table 6, p. 110, passim; Bertram Wyatt-Brown, "The Antimission Movement in the Jacksonian South: A Study in Regional Folk Culture," *JSH* 36 (November 1970): 501–29 (quotations).

31. Strickland, *Cartwright Autobiography*, p. 81; Joseph Mitchell, "Traveling Preacher and Settled Farmer," *Methodist Quarterly* 5 (July 1967): 3–14. On the familial nature of backwoods churches, see Hepzibah Baptist Church Records, 1817–1833, LSU; Jesse Cox, Diary, passim, TSA; "Ebenezer Primitive Baptist Church, Minutes, from its Organization on February 6, 1836 through December 3, 1859," Samuel W. C. Catts MSS, AlaDAH; "Minutes of Fellowship Baptist Church, Wilcox County, in the Mt. Moriah Community," *AlaHQ* 17 (Fall 1955): 268–97.

32. Harriet E. Ames, " 'Birds of Passage' in a Cotton Port: Northerners and Foreigners among the Urban Leaders of Mobile, 1820–1860," Paper presented to Southern Communities Conference, Newberry Library, Chicago, Ill., October 1978, pp. 5, 10.

33. Don H. Doyle, "Urbanization and Southern Culture: Economic Elites in Four New South Cities (Atlanta, Nashville, Charleston, Mobile), c. 1865–1910," p. 24; Frederick C. Jaher, "Antebellum Charleston: Anatomy of an Economic Failure," Papers at Southern Communities Conference, Newberry Library, Chicago, Ill., October 1978; John C. Clark, "The Antebellum Gulf Coast: A Study of World Views, Traditionalism, and Backwardness," in Lucius F. Ellsworth, ed., *The Americanization of the Gulf Coast, 1803–1850* (Pensacola: Florida State Department of Education, 1972), pp. 1–19.

34. Quotation, Henry DeSaussure to Lewis R. Gibbes, November 14, 1835; Robert N. Gibbes to Gibbes, November 20, 1835, Lewis R. Gibbes MSS, LC; see also John C. Calhoun to George F. Holmes, January 25, 1846, Holmes MSS, LC and James L. Petigru to Philip Porcher, June 21, 1851, Petigru MSS, LC.

35. Early's friend quoted in Marcus Cunliffe, *Soldiers and Civilians: The Martial Spirit in America, 1775–1865* (New York: Free Press, 1968), p. 131, passim, and see also pp. 37–84. Cunliffe errs, however, in belittling the Southern mystique about military virtue. It was real insofar as it was a conventional and therefore operative opinion held in both the North and South. But as a career, military life (as an officer especially) was not a genuine alternative to planting for most young men. James C. Bonner, "The Historical Basis of Southern Military Tradition," *GR* 9 (Spring 1955): 74–85, esp. p. 84. Cf. Rollin G. Osterweiss, *Romanticism and Nationalism in the Old South* (New Haven: Yale University Press, 1949), pp. 42–52; Cash, *Mind of South*, pp. 39, 70–78; Samuel P. Huntington, *The Soldier and the State: The Theory and Politics of Civil Military Relations* (Cambridge: Harvard University Press, 1957), pp. 211–21; and Charles O. Paullin, "Naval Administration, 1842–1861," *U.S. Naval Institute Proceedings* 33 (December 1907): 1435–77.

36. F. Garvin Davenport, *Ante-Bellum Kentucky* (Oxford, O.: Mississippi Valley Press, 1943), p. 71; David H. Fischer, "Socialization," ch. (p. 32), in "Deep Change," MSS kindly lent by author.

37. J. H. Baker to William F. Perry, September 29, 1855 in William F. Perry, *Report of the Superintendent of Education of the State of Alabama, to the Governor* (Montgomery, Ala.: Britton & Blue, 1855), p. 32; see also *Transactions of the Alabama Historical Society, 1897–1898* (Tuscaloosa, Ala., 1898) 2: 17; Adams quoted in Lancaster (S.C.) *Ledger,* December 5, 1855; Frank L. Owsley, Jr., "Albert J. Pickett: Typical Southern Pioneer and State Historian," Ph.D. diss., University of Alabama, 1955, p. 30.

38. Burke, *Reminiscences of Georgia*, p. 209.

39. Albert Fishlow, "The American Common School Revival: Fact or Theory?" in Henry Rosovsky, ed., *Industrialization in Two Systems* (New York: John Wiley, 1966), pp. 40–67, for literacy rates by region; Will Book, 1802–1862, Breckenridge County, Ky., M–617, #25, UKL; DeBow, *Statistical View*, p. 155. See also, Henry K. Schwarzenweller, "Regional Variations in the Education Plans of Rural Youth: Norway, Germany and the United States," *RS* 38 (Summer 1973): 149–53. Typical was the misspelling-ridden report from Montgomery County, Tenn., to the Legislative Committee of Common Schools Commission, June 4, 1831: "This school, near Willie Hogans place commenced from some time in March and will continue for three or four months: there is taught . . . reading, writing and Arithematic: from 15 to 16 students have attended this school," but they "have been verry irregular in their attendance Parents sending one or two days and perhaps keep their children at home a week or more which makes it verry difficult to form a just idea of the benefit the District will derive from this institution. . . ." Leg. Papers, Misc. 1831, TSA. See also James Young et al., Jackson County, September 20, 1831, Robert Wortham et al., Maury County, September 19, 1831, ibid.

40. "Governor Hammond's Message," Charleston *Courier*, November 30, 1843; Calvin H. Wiley, "Report of Superintendent of Public Instruction, 1854," C.S.P.1., 621, NCDAH; Matthews, *Neighbor and Kin*, p. 76 (mountaineer quotation).

41. I. A. Coles to Henry St. George Tucker, July 20, 1799, in *WMQ*, 1st ser. 4 (October 1895): 105; Bumpas, "Autobiography," p. 5, SHC, UNC; O. T. Hammond to Jacinth Jackson, June 21, 1839; A. J. Chaplin to Jackson, September 10, 1839; John Chain to Jackson, September 10; and Jefferson F. Jackson to Dr. Cowan, April 7, 1840 (quotation), Jefferson Franklin Jackson MSS, AlaDAH; B. Fitzpatrick to Phillips Fitzpatrick, August 20, 1849, Benjamin Fitzpatrick MSS, SHC, UNC.

42. William Faulkner, "The Bear," in *Go Down Moses* (New York: Modern Library, 1940); Clarence Gohdes, ed., *Hunting in the Old South* (Baton Rouge: Louisiana State University Press, 1967).

43. James H. Hammond to Harry Hammond, March 14, 1851, HBC MSS; Scarborough, *Ruffin Diary*, October 18, 1857, 1: 114–15; Greene, *Carter Diary*, March 16, 1776, 2: 1004, passim.

44. E. B. Kennon to Rachel Mordecai, March 14, 1814, in "Kennon-Mordecai Letters," *VMHB* 36 (July 1928): 238.

45. Conrad M. Arensberg, with Solon T. Kimball, *Family and Community in Ireland* (Cambridge: Harvard University Press, 1940), pp. 57–58.

46. Quotation from Josiah Foster to Benjamin F. Perry, July 5, 1818, Benjamin F. Perry MSS, AlaDAH; see also David R. Williams to Bolling Hall, January 24, 1824, Hall MSS, AlaDAH; and Mrs. E. A. Bingham to Mrs. Louisa Lenoir, January 3, 1828, Lenoir Family MSS, SHC, UNC; and Tommy W. Rogers, "The Great Population Exodus from South Carolina, 1850–1860," *SCHGM* 68 (January 1967): 14–21.

Chapter Eight: Strategies of Courtship and Marriage

1. Hammond to Dr. John Hammond, November 17, 1844, Hammond MSS, SC, USC. On economically advantageous marriages, see also Morton Rothstein, "The Antebellum South as a Dual Economy: A Tentative Hypothesis," *AgH* 44 (October 1967): 373–82. Rothstein discusses the interconnections of Philadelphia and Natchez families and property arrangements.

2. James Henry Hammond to Marcellus Hammond, September 5, 1847, Hammond MSS, SC, USC; Hammond to Harry Hammond, December 20, 1852, HBC MSS.

3. Hammond to Dr. John Hammond, May 2, 1841, Hammond MSS, SC, USC. Hammond to Harry Hammond, December 20, 1852, HBC MSS. See also William Byrd II to "Sister Otway," June 30, 1736, "Byrd Letters," *VMHB* 36 (July 1928): 216.

4. Franklin (Tenn.) *Western Weekly Review*, May 8, 1835; Anna Hayes Johnson to Elizabeth Haywood, August 17, 1822, Haywood Family MSS, SHC, UNC.

5. Louisa Maria Anderson to "my . . . valued cousin," June 21, 1820, John Clark McDermott MSS, AlaDAH. See also Greenville (S.C.) *Mountaineer*, May 7, 1830. Cary, *Letters on Female Character*, pp. ix, x, 25, 43–44, 46, 47. Norton, *Liberty's*

Daughters, esp. pp. 117–24, explains American women's general self-deprecation throughout the Revolutionary period, continuing with special emphasis in the South up to the Civil War. Dew, "Dissertation on the Characteristic Differences between the Sexes . . . ," *SLM* 1 (May 1835): 493–512.

6. Henry Vickers Wooten, Diary, typescript, passim and July 26, 1839, January 21, 24, 1840, AlaDAH; James Norcom to Mary Horniblow, February 4, 1810, Norcom Family MSS, NCDAH; Randolph to Dudley, February 5, 1822, in Randolph, *Letters to a Young Relative,* p. 252. For other evidence on early marriages for women, see Childs, *Ravenel Journal,* p. 11; Robert Mills, *Statistics of South Carolina* (Charleston: Hurlburt Lloyd, 1826), p. 607.

7. Jane Turner Censer, "Parents and Children: North Carolina Planter Families, 1800–1860," Ph.D. diss., Johns Hopkins University, 1981, pp. 63–64, 137–96; Ann Williams Boucher, "Wealthy Planter Families in Nineteenth-Century Alabama," Ph.D. diss., University of Connecticut, 1978, pp. 41–45; James M. McReynolds, "Family Life in a Borderland Community: Nacogdoches, Texas, 1779–1861," Ph.D. diss., Texas Tech University, 1978, pp. 116, 160, and also 293; Peter Hall, "Family Structure and Class Consolidation among Boston Brahmins," Ph.D. diss., State University of New York at Buffalo, 1973, table 6, p. 170, cited by Boucher, pp. 41–42.

8. Boucher, "Wealthy Planters," p. 41; Hall cited, p. 42; Hawkins quoted in Censer, "Parents and Children," p. 175; Rachel O'Connor to David Weeks, January 11, 1829, Weeks MSS, LSU.

9. On Joseph Davis, Janet S. Hermann, *The Pursuit of a Dream* (New York: Oxford University Press, 1981), p. 6; on Chesnut family history, Muhlenfeld, *Chesnut,* pp. 12–14; on other aspects of marital patterns in a comparative perspective, see Thomas P. Monihan, "One Hundred Years of Marriage in Massachusetts," *AJS* 51 (May 1955): 534–45; Peter Laslett, introduction, in Peter Laslett, ed., *Household and Family in Past Time . . .* (Cambridge: Cambridge University Press, 1972), p. 52; Demos, *A Little Commonwealth,* p. 151.

10. Byrd, quoted in Smith, *Inside the Great House,* p. 128 n3.

11. Norcom to John Norcom, December 3, 1818, Norcom MSS, NCDAH; also Norcom to M. D. Harvey, January 14, 1848; John Q. Anderson, ed., *Brokenburn: The Journal of Kate Stone, 1861–1868* (Baton Rouge: Louisiana State University Press, 1972), May 23, 1861, p. 15.

12. J. C. C. Jackson to Jefferson F. Jackson, December 9, 1834, J. F. Jackson MSS, AlaDAH; Maria Bryan to Julia A. D. Cumming, May 7, 1828, HBC MSS. See also Richard Singleton to John Singleton, January 18, 1812, Singleton MSS, LC; and "Autobiographical Sketch, De Rosset," in Battle, *Letters and Documents,* p. 40.

13. Carl Degler, *At Odds: Women and the Family in America from the Revolution to the Present* (New York: Oxford University Press, 1980), pp. 11, 76; Sophia Deveaux quoted by Censer, "Parents and Children," p. 160; James Norcom to John Norcom, June 22 [1819]; Mary Matilda Messmer to Mrs. Mary Norcom, July 4, 1848, Norcom MSS, NCDAH.

14. Maxwell Bloomfield, "The Texas Bar in the Nineteenth Century," *VLR* 32 (January 1979): 273.

15. James L. Petigru to Jane North, July 19, 1838, Petigru MSS, LC; see also Henry H. Cumming to Julia A. D. Cumming, July 1, 1829, HBC MSS.

16. Joel Lyle to William Lyle [April 5?], 1826 (quotation); September 2, 1826, Lyle Family MSS, UKL.

17. Maria Bryan to Julia A. D. Cumming, June 1, 1829, HBC MSS; John Randolph to James M. Garnett, May 27, 1811, letterbook, John Randolph MSS, LC. On other examples of fortune-hunting, see H. S. Fulkerson, *Random Recollections of Early Days in Mississippi* (Baton Rouge: Otto Claitor, 1937), p. 8; Thomas J. Withers to James H. Hammond, August 28, 1827, Hammond MSS, SC, USC; and Hammond to Dr. John Hammond, April 11, 1843, ibid.

18. Anna Greenough Burgwyn to David Sumner Greenough, December 26, 1838, microfilm, Burgwyn Family MSS, SHC, UNC. See also Larry Gara, ed., "A New Englander's View of Plantation Life: Letters of Edwin Hall to Cyrus Woodman, 1837," *JSH* 18 (August 1952): 348–49.

19. Kett, *Rites of Passage*, p. 42; Degler, *At Odds*, pp. 19–25; Jane Carson, *Colonial Virginians at Play* (Williamsburg: University Press of Virginia, 1965), pp. 6–7 (quotation).

20. Joseph H. Ingraham, *Not a 'Fool's Errand': Life and Experiences of a Northern Governess of the Sunny South* (New York: G. W. Carleton, 1880), pp. 224–25.

21. Mrs. W. B. Shephard to Mrs. Mary Bryan, March 7, 1824, Bryan MSS, NCDAH. See also Miss J. C. Barette to Miss Mira E. Lenoir, August 27, 1827, Lenoir Family MSS, SHC, UNC; Ingraham, *Northern Governess*, p. 225.

22. *Courier* in the Greenville (S.C.) *Mountaineer*, July 23, 1830.

23. Margaret Deschamps, "The Free Agricultural Population in Sumter District, South Carolina, 1850–1860," *NCHR* 32 (January 1955): 84; Selina Deveaux to Robert Deveaux, September 17, 1837, Singleton MSS, LC; Grayson, *Petigru*, p. 76; S. Cary to Agan Blair, October 20, 1781, in Horner, *History of Blair, Bannister, and Braxton Families*, p. 58; Maria Bryan to Julia A. D. Cumming, January 14, 1822, HBC MSS.

24. O. G. Dennis, September 23, 1850, Fayette, Tenn., Vol. 10, p. 23, DB, Baker, (volume pagination is often confusing, but it is supplied when it may help in locating entries). George Robertson, Charleston, March 17, 1853, June 10, 1856, South Carolina, vol. 6 [p. 177]; Bernard S. Baruch, May 9, 1855, ibid. [p. 236]; J. D. Aiken, September 13, 1855, ibid. [p. 251]; Oswell Reeder and John B. DeSaussure, January 3, 1852, ibid. [p. 144]; Miguel Jamison, February 16, 1849, Orleans Parish (New Orleans), Louisiana, vol. 9, pt. 1 [p. 4], DB, Baker.

25. H. J. Weddils, Baton Rouge, n.d., 1849, East Baton Rouge Parish, Louisiana, vol. 5; Abraham Schlenker, Clinton, June [?], 1849, East Feliciana Parish, ibid., DB, Baker. Laslett, *World We Have Lost*, ch. 1.

26. Thomas K. Dillard, Pontoloc, Miss., August 20, 1850, vol. 18; William S. Pike and Samuel M. Hart, and Andrew Matta, Baton Rouge, East Feliciana, La., vol. 5; R. A. Taylor, December 12, 1854, Abbeville, S.C., vol. 3; David Butts and Anthony Foster, June [?], 1855, Panola, Miss., vol. 18, DB, Baker.

27. Milton Coleman and Leo Lipscombe, September [?], 1847, Smithville, Abbeville, S.C., vol. 6; John Cothran and Franklin Stephens, July 30, 1856, ibid., DB, Baker. The relation of banks, families and property is well illustrated in A. Carroll Gautreaux, "Transactions between Families Associated in Marriage, La-Fayette Parish, 1832–1834," *Attakapas Gazette* 9 (Winter 1974): 179–80.

28. The entry for another Springfield resident, Abraham Lincoln, is particularly

interesting: "Abram [sic] Lincoln. Aug 6/56 w. $10m—good. July 1/57 Lawyers are ordinarily imprudent but seldom ask for credit. w. abt $12m principally in R[eal] E[state]. July 1/58. Worth perhaps $15m—prompt, efficient & skillful." Sangamon, Ill., vol. 198 [p. 163]; Jacob Brunn, banker, groceries [entries from 1845 to 1867], ibid.; Hurst and Taylor, March 26, 1849–July 31, 1849, ibid.; Isaac Keyes, auction and comm. merchant, ibid., DB, Baker.

29. Entries for Ashtabula, O., in vol. 71, DB, Baker, for Marvin and Cotton, Andover; Hiram Sutliff, Jefferson; Paul Hyde and George Enos, tanners, Andover; in Ashtabula, O., vol. 5 for A. J. Talcot, tailor; J. B. Hall, iron founders ("Hall is regarded as a vy honest man & is respectably connected being the son of a clergyman"); Gilbert A. Richards, cheese manu., Auburn; Reuben W. Walton, gen. store, Chardon; and in vol. 71; John Ransom, woolen mill, Harpersfield.

30. See Peter D. Hall, "Marital Selection and Business in Massachusetts Merchant Families, 1700–1900," in Michael Gordon, ed., *The American Family in Social-Historical Perspective* (New York: St. Martin's, 1978), p. 104.

31. Boucher, "Wealthy Planter Families," pp. 105–10; her figures refer to a group whose fathers were in the forty to fifty-nine age cohort. Holland, "Rise and Fall of Ante-Bellum Virginia Aristocracy," Ph.D. diss., University of California, Irvine, 1980, p. 1.

32. James M. Cliflan, "A Half Century of a Georgia Rice Plantation," *NCHR* 47 (Autumn 1970); 393–94; DuBose, "Autobiography," pp. 11–12 SHC, UNC; Last Will and Testament of William King, March 3, 1806, Campbell-Preston Family MSS, LC. Cf. Donald J. Mrozek, "Problems of Social History and Patterns of Inheritance in Pre-Revolutionary New Jersey, 1751–1770," *Journal of Rutgers University Library* 36 (December 1972): 1–19; Will of Moses Hutchins, July 22, 1822, Haywood Family MSS, SHC, UNC; Taylor, *Ante-Bellum South Carolina*, p. 45. See also Boucher, "Wealthy Planter Families," pp. 59, 62–69; Censer, "Parents and Children," pp. 166–69.

33. Randolph, *Ozarks*, p. 57; Matthews, *Neighbor and Kin*, pp. 33–34. "Samuel DuBose, my grandfather . . . married a double niece of General Francis Marion. . . . My father married his first cousin, Jane Porcher. . . ." DuBose, "Autobiography," p. 2. Henry Craft, another member of the upper strata in Tennessee, said, "Old Mr. Battle['s] . . . Mother & my grandfather were double cousins, and his wife & Ella's father [Craft's father-in-law] are first cousins . . . we are pretty considerably akin." Henry Craft, Diary, May 4, 1859, SHC, UNC. See also George C. Homans, *The Human Group* (Glencoe: Free Press, 1955), pp. 334–69.

34. Bruce, *Randolph of Roanoke* 1: 10; see also Rachel O'Connor to David Weeks, December 24, 1832; Weeks Family MSS, LSU.

35. Boynton Merrill, Jr., *Jefferson's Nephews: A Frontier Tragedy* (Princeton: Princeton University Press, 1976), p. 344; Censer, "Parents and Children," p. 166. Fuad I. Khuri, "Parallel Cousin Marriage Reconsidered: A Middle Eastern Practice that Nullifies the Effects of Marriage on the Intensity of Family Relationships," *Man*, n. s. 5 (December 1970): 597–618.

36. See the seminal work of James S. Brown, "Social Class, Intermarriage, and Church Membership in a Kentucky Community," *AJS* 57 (November 1951): 232–

42, esp. table 2, p. 235; Brown, *Family Group in Kentucky*, esp. pp. 15, 17–18; idem, *The Farm Family in a Kentucky Mountain Neighborhood*, Bulletin 587, Kentucky Agricultural Experiment Station (Lexington: University of Kentucky, August 1952), table 6, p. 26.

37. Frederick S. Blount to John H. Bryan, September 1, 1834, Bryan Family MSS, NCDAH; Brown, "Social Class," pp. 233–34; Censer, "Parents and Children," pp. 166–67.

38. Matthews, *Neighbor and Kin*, p. 35; Henry H. Sims, *Life of John Taylor: The Story of a Brilliant Leader* . . . (Richmond: William Byrd, 1932), p. 4.

39. Bruce, *Randolph of Roanoke*, 1: 108–110.

40. First quotation from "Poor White Farmer," Pleasant Hill, N.C., March 15, 1939, folder 115, box 9, Federal Writers' Project MSS, SHC, UNC; Franklin (Tenn.) *Western Weekly Review*, December 20, 1850; Brown, "Social Class," p. 237; Martin T. Matthews, *Experience-Worlds of Mountain People: Institutional Efficiency in Appalachian Village and Hinterland Communities* (New York: Teachers College of Columbia, 1937), p. 98; and Suzanne Keller and Marissa Zaralloni, "Ambition and Social Class: A Respecification," *SF* 47 (October 1964): 58–70.

41. *The Diary of Edmund Ruffin: Toward Independence, October 1856–April 1861*, William K. Scarborough, ed. (Baton Rouge: Louisiana State University Press, 1972) 1: 326. (Ruffin disapproved of close kinship marriages.) For further information on antebellum Southern marital patterns, see most especially Guion G. Johnson, "Courtship and Marriage Customs in Antebellum North Carolina," *NCHR* 7 (October 1931): 384–402; also the observations of James S. Buckingham, *The Slave States of America*, 2 vols. (London: Fisher, Son, 1842) 2: 13–15.

42. James Norcom to Mary B. Harvey, January 14, 1848, Norcom MSS, NCDAH.

43. Frances Peters to Robert Peters, January 5, 1850; February 22, 1851; Robert Peters to Frances Peters, July 26, 1851, Dallam-Peters MSS, UKL.

44. "Juliana Rosebud," in *American Turf Register* 11 (March 1831): 339–40, in Ghodes, *Hunting*, pp. 135–36.

Chapter Nine: Women in a Man's World

1. Scott, *Southern Lady*, p. 19 (quotation); idem, "Women's Perspective on the Patriarchy in the 1850s," *JAH* 51 (June 1974): 52–64; *SQR*, n. s. 10 (October 1845): 351 (quotation).

2. T. R. Dew, "On the Characteristic Differences between the Sexes," *SLM* 1 (May 1835): 498. See also Cary, *Letters on Female Character*, which does not recommend female reticence, but otherwise accepts the dominant views of female deference and submission. See, too, *Raleigh Star and North Carolina Gazette*, February 7, 1844; Natchez *Newspaper and Public Advertiser*, October 25, 1826. Bolling Hall to Polly W. Hall, June 22, 1813, Bolling Hall MSS, AlaDAH; Hagood, *Mothers of the South*, pp. 164–65; cf. Mary Ryan, *Womanhood in America: From Colonial Times to the Present* (New York: Franklin Watts, 1975), pp. 139 ff.

3. Emily Virginia Semple, *Reminiscences of My Early Life and Relatives* (n.p.: private printing, 1905), p. 13; Randolph, *Ozarks*, p. 62.

4. James A. Norcom to Mary B. Harvey, May 25, 1848, Norcom MSS, NCDAH.

5. Sarah J. Hale, *Sketches of American Character* (Boston: Freeman Hunt, 1831), p. 255; Sarah L. Wadley, Diary (typescript), October 2, 1860, passim, and April 21, 26, 1861, SHC, UNC.

6. Sarah Morgan, Diary, May 6, 1862, DUL; Margaret Gillis, Diary, December [?], 1861 (quotation), May 30, 1864, AlaDAH; Norcom to John Norcom, April 15, 1840, Norcom MSS, NCDAH.

7. Margaret Wilson, Diary, July 17, 1835; January 14, 1837 (quotation), LSU and MissDAH.

8. Caroline Merrick, *Old Times in Dixie* (New York: Grafton Press, 1901), p. 11.

9. Ibid., pp. 12, 13, 25 (quotation); James H. Hammond to Catherine Hammond, July 30, 1840, Hammond MSS, SC, USC; Anna G. Burgwyn to Maria Sumner, December 7, 1838; January 5, 22, 1839, Burgwyn Family MSS (microfilm), SHC, UNC; James C. Bonner, ed., "Plantation Experiences of a New York Woman," *NCHR* 33 (July 1956): 390.

10. Mary Louise Williamson, Diary, October 7, 1861, AlaDAH; see also Craig Simpson, "Henry Wise," ch. 2 (kindly lent by author). See additionally Anna Hayes Johnson to Elizabeth Haywood, February 9, 1823, Haywood MSS, SHC, UNC; James A. Norcom to Mary B. Harvey, May 25, 1848, Norcom Family MSS, NCDAH; E. J. Wallace to James DuBose, August 16, 1844, James DuBose MSS, DUL; *Southern Cabinet* 1 (March 1840): 316–17.

11. Agan Blair to Mrs. Braxton, August 21, 1769, in Horner, *History of Blair, Bannister, and Braxton Families*, pp. 55, 56; cf. Michael Zuckerman, "William Byrd's Family," *Perspectives in American History* 12 (1979): 255–311.

12. Clinkscales, *Old Plantation*, p. 102; King, *Ebb Tide,* July 19, 1863, p. 49; Dubay, *Pettus*, pp. 6–7; Semple, *Reminiscences,* p. 2; Thomas Nelson Page, *Social Life in Old Virginia Before the War* (New York: Charles Scribner's Sons, 1897), pp. 25–26.

13. Greene, *Carter Diary,* January 13, 1772, 2: 646; Norcom, Address, n.d., Norcom MSS, NCDAH; Curtis, Diary, February 5, 1832, SHC, UNC.

14. Arensberg, *Family and Community in Ireland*, pp. 212–14; Andrew Burnaby, *Travels through the Middle Settlements in North America in the Years 1750 and 1760*, Rufus R. Wilson, ed. (New York: A. Wessels, 1904), pp. 57–58; Gara, "New Englander's View," p. 347.

15. Scott, *Southern Lady*, pp. 23, 37, 44.

16. Gillis, Diary, March 20, 1862, passim, AlaDAH; see also Sally Randle Perry, Diary, November 30, 1867, passim, AlaDAH; and R. M. Ruffin, quoted in Scott, "Women's Perspective," p. 55.

17. "Ellet's *Women of the Revolution*," *SQR* 1 (July 1850): 326. On Scott's influence and popularity, see Grace W. Landrum, "Sir Walter Scott and His Literary Rivals in the Old South," *American Literature* 2 (November 1930): 256–76; idem, "Notes on the Reading of the Old South," *American Literature* 3 (March 1931): 60–71.

18. Maria Bryan to Julie A. D. Cumming, January 14, 1827, HBC MSS.

19. Chesnut, *Diary from Dixie*, March 24, 1861, p. 25 (not to be found in Woodward, *Chesnut's Civil War*, under that entry date.)

20. Quotations from Woodward, *Chesnut's Civil War*, March 18, 1861, pp. 29 and 31.

21. Ibid., March 18, 1861, pp. 32–33, September 9, 1861, p. 191, May 18, 1865, pp. 815–16. See also, on Mary Chesnut's childlessness, Muhlenfeld, *Chesnut*, pp. 62–63, 203.

22. Merrick, *Old Times in Dixie*, p. 7; Salisbury bachelor quoted from *Carolina Watchman* (Salisbury, N.C.), January 25, 1845; "husband hunting spinsters" quotation from *Western Carolinian* (Salisbury), July 25, 1820, as quoted in Guion C. Johnson, *Ante-Bellum North Carolina: A Social History* (Chapel Hill: University of North Carolina Press, 1937), pp. 194–95; on status of spinsters and bachelors see T. W. Peyre to Robert M. Deveaux, August 28, 1835, Singleton MSS, LC; and Will Percy, *Lanterns on the Levee: Recollections of a Planter's Son* (New York: Knopf, 1941), pp. 8, 9.

23. Margaret Wilson, Diary, June 3, July 17, 1835; December 16, 1836; January 14, April 3 (quotation), 1837, LSU. A typescript of this diary in MissDAH identifies it as Margaret Wilson's. Scott, *Southern Lady*, p. 7 (quotation from Wilson Diary); Belle Kearney, *A Slaveholder's Daughter* (New York: Negro Universities Press, 1969 [1900]), pp. 71–73, 74–89.

24. Ingraham, *Northern Governess*, pp. 268–70; see also T. R. Dew, "On Parental Faults," *SLM* 2 (June 1836): 444. And see Catherine Clinton, "Equally Their Due: The Education of the Planter's Daughter following the American Revolution," Seminar paper, Princeton University, September 1978, p. 8.

25. Peyre to Deveaux, August 28, 1835, Singleton MSS, LC. Dew, "On Parental Faults": "Thousands of unfortunate girls marry rather than live single, simply because their parents and other connexions made them believe that to remain *unmarried*, is to become objects of general derision and contempt." (p. 438.)

26. Wooten, Autobiography, vol. 1, 1813–1837 (typescript), pp. 2–8, AlaDAH; see also Anna Holster to Sarah B. Evans, January 7, 1836, Shilg Collection, LSU; St. George Tucker to John Coalter, February 21, 1802, Tucker-Coleman MSS, WMC. Eliza Wilson to Andrew Hynes, December 21, 1827; October 1, 1828; January 5, 1829, Edward Gay and Family MS, LSU.

27. See Avery O. Craven, *Rachel of Old Louisiana* (Baton Rouge: Louisiana State University Press, 1975), pp. 22–27; quotation, p. 27. See also John A. Quitman to Col. Brush, August 23, 1823, in J. F. H. Claiborne, *Life and Correspondence of John A. Quitman*, 2 vols. (New York: Harper Bros., 1860) 1: 84–85; Norton, *Liberty's Daughters*, pp. 6–7, 133–35, 145–51.

28. Rachel O'Connor to David Weeks, September 29, 1832, Weeks Family MSS, LSU; also Rachel O'Connor to David Weeks, October 27, 1822, and other correspondence for 1823–1824; William Flower to O'Connor May 29, 1828. Her deference, becoming to a widow, was evident when she wrote to David, her brother, in reply to Flower's abusive letter: "I feel two [*sic*] small to undertake a letter to a person so high standing in life as Mr. F. although I suppose he wishes me to do so. . . . But he scarcely will ever catch me nap[p]ing again. . . ." April 1, 1828, Weeks Family MSS. See also newspaper clipping, December 14, 1829, *Pamela Weeks* v. *Henry Flower*, ibid.

29. O'Connor to Weeks, October 6, 1832, Weeks Family MSS, LSU.

30. Elizabeth W. A. Pringle, *Chronicles of Chicora Wood* (New York: Charles Scribner's Sons, 1922), pp. 75–76; Bell I. Wiley, *Confederate Women* (Westport, Conn.: Greenwood Press, 1975), p. 95.

31. First quotation from *Foster and Wife* v. *Alston,* 7 Miss. (6 How.) 460 (1842) at 463, and second quotation from *Ex parte Boaz,* 31 Ala. 425 (1858), as rephrased in *Goodrich* v. *Goodrich,* 44 Ala. 670 (1870) at 677. As early as 1803, Mississippi law provided courts with discretionary power to "take such order, touching the care and maintenance of the children of that marriage" without stipulating considerations of parental gender. (Harry Toulmin, *Statutes of the Mississippi Territory* [1807], c. 13, sec. 7, 373.) On child custody, see also Michael C. Grossberg, "Law and the Family in Nineteenth-Century America," Ph.D. diss., Brandeis University, 1979, pp. 231–38, 257, 313, passim, and Boatwright, "Political and Civil Status of Women in Georgia," pp. 316–17.

32. *Goodrich* v. *Goodrich,* 44 Ala. 670 (1870) at 678.

33. Lawrence M. Friedman and Robert V. Percival, "Who Sues for Divorce? From Fault through Fiction to Freedom," *Journal of Legal Studies* 5 (January 1976): 61–82, esp. 74, 80. On child custody evolutions, see also Zainaldin, "Emergence of Modern American Family Law," pp. 1069–70.

34. Leota S. Driver, *Fanny Kemble* (Chapel Hill: University of North Carolina, 1933); Frances A. Kemble Butler, *Journal of a Residence in America* (Philadelphia: Carey, Lea & Blanchard, 1835); Pierce M. Butler, *Mr. Butler's Statement, Originally Prepared with the Aid of His Professional Council* (Philadelphia: J. C. Clarke, 1850), copy available in Rare Book Room, LC.

35. Kemble to Martineau, quoted in Dorothie De Baer Bobbe, *Fanny Kemble* (London: Elkin Mathew & Marrot, 1932), p. 170; Butler, *Statement,* pp. 9–10, 27 (Kemble to Butler, 1838). Kemble to Martineau, September 22, 1846, in Frances A. Kemble, *Records of a Later Life* (London: Richard Bentley & Sons, 1882) 3: 137. On difficulties of women in child custody cases, see Elizabeth C. Stanton et al., *History of Woman Suffrage,* 6 vols. (New York and Rochester: Charles Mann, 1881–1922) 1: 71, 105, 194, 254–55, 260–61, 562–63, 579–89, 776–79.

36. Ryan, *Womanhood in America,* passim; Christopher Lasch, *Haven in a Heartless World: The Family Beseiged* (New York: Basic Books, 1975); and Degler, *At Odds,* are among those studies that say little about the interrelationship of law and family. See, however, Grossberg, "Law and the Family," and Linda K. Kerber, *Women of the Republic: Intellect and Ideology in Revolutionary America* (Chapel Hill: University of North Carolina Press, 1980).

37. Carroll Smith-Rosenberg, "The Female World of Love and Ritual: Relations between Women in Nineteenth-Century America," in Gordon, *American Family,* pp. 334–53; see also Anne L. Hardeman, Diary, June 1, 1860, in Oscar J. E. Stuart MSS, MissDAH; and Mary Beth Norton, "My Mother/My Friend: Mothers and Daughters in Eighteenth-Century America," Harvey Wish Memorial Lecture, Case Western Reserve University, September 1979.

38. Chesnut, *Diary from Dixie,* June 22, 1861, p. 64.

39. Norcom to Mary B. Harvey, April 24, 1848, Norcom Family MSS, NCDAH; on this function in the churches, see Donald G. Mathews, *Religion in the Old South* (Chicago: University of Chicago Press, 1977), pp. 42–46, 100–101; Fred J.

Hood, *Reformed America: The Middle and Southern States, 1783–1837* (University: University of Alabama Press, 1980), pp. 32–47 and passim.
40. Matthews, *Neighbor and Kin*, pp. 33–35.
41. Farm wife ibid., p. 35. Breckenridge quoted by Wiley, *Confederate Women*, p. 174; Woodward, *Chesnut's Civil War*, May 9, 1865, p. 809.
42. Ingraham, *Northern Governess*, pp. 226–27.
43. See Smith-Rosenberg, "Female World," p. 336; see also p. 352 n6. On "Boston marriages," see Jean Strouse, *Alice James: A Biography* (Boston: Houghton Mifflin, 1980), p. 200.
44. Anderson, *Brokenburn*, May 29, 1861, p. 20.

Chapter Ten: Law, Property, and Male Dominance

1. Sir William Blackstone, *Commentaries on the Laws of England*, 4 vols. (Oxford: Clarendon Press, 1765–69) 1: 442; James Kent, *Commentaries on American Law*, Oliver Wendell Holmes, Jr., ed., 2 vols. (Boston: Little, Brown, 1873) 2: 150, 187.
2. See Marylynn Salmon, "Equality or Submission? Femme Covert Status in Early Pennsylvania," in Mary Beth Norton and Carol R. Berkin, eds., *Women of America: A History* (Boston: Houghton Mifflin, 1979), pp. 92–111. The debate on rights of women to property began with Richard D. Morris's assertion of early and radical divergence from common law. See Richard B. Morris, *Studies in the History of American Law with Special References to the Seventeenth and Eighteenth Centuries* (New York: Columbia University Press, 1930), pp. 126–200. Mary Beard, *Woman as Force in History: A Study in Traditions and Realities* (New York: Macmillan, 1946), pp. 134–35, argued that Kent and Joseph Story both were opposed to common law and favored the movement to equity decisions. Yet, as Professor Salmon maintains, it seems that the transition has been somewhat exaggerated. See also Norma Basch, "Invisible Women: The Legal Fiction of Marital Unity in Nineteenth-Century America," *Feminist Studies* 5 (Summer 1979): 346–66; Peggy A. Rabkin, *The Legal Foundations of Female Emancipation* (Westport, Conn.: Greenwood Press, 1980), pp. 3–13, 19–22.
3. Kent, *Commentaries*, vol. 2, #133, p. 159; #144, p. 179, passim; John D. Johnson, "Sex and Property: The Common Law Tradition, the Law School Curriculum, and Developments toward Equality," *NYULR* 47 (December 1972): 1033–92. Georgia was the slowest of all Southern states to affirm a woman's personal earnings as hers and not her husband's: Georgia *Code Ann.* #53-512 (1961), cited ibid., p. 1070 n156.
4. Cf. Stone, *Family, Sex and Marriage*, pp. 325–404; Maxwell Bloomfield, *American Lawyers in a Changing Society* (Cambridge: Harvard University Press, 1976), pp. 97–99; Spruill, *Women's Life and Work*, pp. 340–46; Cott, *Bonds of Womanhood*, pp. 5, 21, 77; Arthur Calhoun, *A Social History of the American Family from Colonial Times to the Present*, 3 vols. (Cleveland: Arthur H. Clark, 1917–19) 1: 77, 255; Tapping Reeve, *Law of Baron and Femme . . .* (Albany: Wm. Gould, 1862 [1816]), p. 431.

5. Harriet Martineau, *Society in America*, 2 vols. (New York: Saunders & Otley, 1837) 2: 236–37.

6. Eleanor M. Boatwright, "The Political and Civil Status of Woman in Georgia, 1783–1860," *GHQ* 25 (December 1941): 306.

7. David Stewart, *The Law of Husband and Wife as Established in England and the United States* (San Francisco: Sumner Whitney, 1885), #200, p. 283.

8. *Stockton* v. *Martin*, 71 S.C. (1 Brev.) 71 (1802) at 73, 74, 75–76.

9. Ibid. Virginia was no less inclined than South Carolina to favor common law over equity throughout the early nineteenth century. Chief Justice Henry St. George Tucker in 1831 took note, for instance, of the trend toward equity over common law in the handling of married women's property or claims to separate estate, but nonetheless he urged that common-law judgment be sustained in the case at hand "to prevent uncertainty and confusion." He saw no reason to overlook the failure of a father (in this instance) to establish a trust with duly appointed trustees, and claimed to know of no case in which such a failure was conveniently excused in a Virginia court. See *Faulkner* v. *Faulkner's exors.*, 30 Va. (3 Leigh) 255 (1831) at 257. Another signal of strict common-law adherence may be found in *Nicholas* v. *Ex'ors of George Nicholas*, 9 Kent. 338 (1804); also *Administrator and Administratrix of John Smith* v. *John C. Pothress et al.*, 11 Fla. 92 (1843). But see a modern trend in *William Poindexter, Adm'r et al.* v. *Winfred Blackburn et al.*, 1 N.C. 283 (1841).

10. *Marina Hays* v. *Wm. Hays and C. D. Evans, landlord*, 5 S.C. (Richardson) 31 (1851–1852).

11. Ibid. See also Act of 1795 (no. 1609), secs. II & III *S.C. Statutes* (1839) v 5, 255–57; see also *Sadler* v. *Bean and Wife*, 9 Ark. 202 (1848). Consider Mrs. Chesnut's remark about her marriage: "We had our share of my father's estate. It came into our possession not long after we were married, and it was spent for debts already contracted." As a result, she had to beg for pin money so that she felt "humiliated and degraded." Chesnut *Diary from Dixie*, p. 186.

12. O'Neall, in *Hays* v. *Hays*, at 40.

13. Boucher, "Wealthy Planters," p. 132.

14. Quotation from Robert W. Gordon, "J. Willard Hurst and the Common Law Tradition in American Legal Historiography," *L&SR* 10 (Fall 1975), pt. 1, p. 30. See also Beard, *Woman as Force*, pp. 134–35; Lawrence M. Friedman, "Patterns of Testation in the 19th Century: A Study of Essex County (New Jersey) Wills," *AJLH* 8 (January 1964): 34, 35. Idem, "The Dynastic Trust," *Yale Law Journal* 73 (March 1964): 547–92; on p. 555 n28 Friedman offers a good example of the dynastic arrangement of the plantation South, Christopher Williman's three-trustee form of 1813. Friedman observes that in the South these trusts were much more likely to involve ancestral lands than were the trusts of Boston or New England, where trusts were even more popular than in the South. See also *Hext* v. *Porcher* S.C. (1 Strob. Eq.) 170 (1846), and Johnston, "Sex and Property," pp. 1061–70.

15. A. Keir Nash, "Reason of Slavery: Understanding the Judicial Role in the Peculiar Institution," *VLR* 32 (January 1979): 7–218, an incredibly long-winded and confusing apologia, but worth examination; Mark Tushnet, "The American

Law of Slavery, 1810–1860: A Study in the Persistence of Legal Autonomy," *L&SR* 10 (Fall 1975), pt. 1, pp. 119–45.

16. Quotation from Suzanne Dee Lebsock, "Women and Economics in Virginia: Petersburg, 1784–1820," Ph.D. diss., University of Virginia, 1977, pp. 121–23; see also her "Radical Reconstruction and the Property Rights of Southern Women," *JSH* 43 (May 1977): 194–216; Kay Ellen Thurman, "The Married Women's Property Acts," M.S. diss., University of Wisconsin, 1966, p. 12; *Alabama. Acts Passed at the Annual Session of the General Assembly* (1849), p. 79; *Alabama, Code of 1852*, ch. 1, art. III, sect. 1994, p. 382; Clement Eaton, "Breaking a Path for the Liberation of Women in the South," *GR* 28 (Summer 1974): 189.

17. *Digest of Laws of Mississippi* (New York: T. J. Fox & J. A. Van Hoessen, 1839), pp. 920–21; Mrs. Helen D. Bell, "Glimpses of the Past," in *Publications of the Mississippi Historical Society* (Oxford, Miss.: Mississippi Historical Society, 1898) 1: 202–3.

18. *Aberdeen Whig and Northern Mississippi Advocate* in Elizabeth G. Brown, "Husband and Wife—Memorandum on the Mississippi Women's Law of 1839," *MLR* 42 (April 1944): 1110–21; Bell, "Glimpses of Past," pp. 202–3; Dunbar Rowland, *Encyclopedia of Mississippi History*, 2 vols. (Madison, Wis.: Selwyn A. Bryant, 1907) 1: 898–99.

19. John F. H. Claiborne, *Mississippi As A Province, Territory and State* (Jackson: Power & Barksdale, 1880), pp. 475–77; Thurman, "Married Women's Property Acts," pp. 15, 39; *The Grand Gulf Bank v. Barnes*, 10 Miss. (2 Smedes and Marshall) 165 (1844), a ruling that distinguished between property (slaves) and profits and products of slaves. By virtue of that distinction it was ruled that a wife's profits were liable to seizure for a husband's debts, but not the property itself, a narrow reading of the Act of 1839. See also *Sessions v. Bacon*, 23 Miss. 272 (1852); *Lowery v. Craig*, 30 Miss. 112 (1855); *Cameron v. Cameron*, 29 Miss. 112 (1855); *Miss. Laws*, 1839 c. 46, 72; *Ratcliffe v. Doughtery*, 24 Miss. 181 (1852); *Lee v. Bennett*, 31 Miss. 119 (1856); *Friley v. White*, 31 Miss. 442 (1856); Friedman, *History of American Law*, pp. 185–96.

20. *The South Carolina Legislative Times, Being the Debates and Proceedings in the South Carolina Legislature at the Session Commencing November, 1855* (Columbia: E. H. Britton, 1856), December 6, pp. 76–78; December 7, p. 88; December 8, pp. 105–6.

21. B. F. Randolph quoted in *South Carolina. Proceedings of the Constitutional Convention of South Carolina . . . 1869*, 2 vols. in 1 (Charleston, S.C., 1868), 2: 786–87. See also remarks of J. M. Allen, pp. 785–86, and of R. B. Elliott, p. 786, ibid.; Johnston, "Sex and Property," p. 1069.

22. Lebsock, "Women's Property," pp. 209–13.

23. Quoted in Thurman, "Married Women's Property," pp. 58–59, n23; see also Joel P. Bishop, *Commentaries on the Law of Marriage and Divorce . . .*, 2 vols. (Boston: Little, Brown, 1881) 2: 591–610, 626–45, 712–18, 786–809.

24. Brown, in "Husband and Wife," p. 1111, notes that in Louisiana the wife did have considerable freedom if she was a "public merchant," but Friedman, in *History of American Law*, p. 155, correctly says that "attitudes toward law . . . one guesses, are more or less the same in Shreveport as in Little Rock or Natchez." See also A. Carroll Gautreaux, "Transactions between Families Associ-

ated in Marriage: Lafayette Parish, 1832–1834," *AtG* 9 (Winter 1976): 179–80; Harriet S. Daggett, *The Community Property System of Louisiana, with Comparative Studies* (Baton Rouge: Louisiana State University Press, 1931). The husband was assumed to control all property, both "community"—joint properties —and "paraphernal," the wife's property at the time of the marriage, but she could obtain rights of control through court action and she could collect on debts that her husband owed her estate, much to the disadvantage of outside creditors.

25. Walter Prichard et al., eds., "Southern Louisiana and Southern Alabama in 1819: The Journal of James Leander Cathcart," *LHQ* 28, no. 4 (1945): 735–67, esp. 767 n136; Allan Johnson and Dumas Malone, eds., *Dictionary of American Biography* 6: 554.

26. *Foster* v. *Her Husband*, 22 La. (Curry) 6 (1833–34).

27. Ibid., at 24.

28. Ibid., at 24–25.

29. *Caroline Foster* v. *David S. McIntosh*, "Civil Suits," #932 (1831), and #1774, SMP. Harriet Martineau argued that "the husband interferes much less with his wife's property in the south, even through her voluntary relinquishment of it, than is at all usual. . . .": Martineau, *Society in America*, 1: 257. But her opinion must be erroneous, judging from the records of transactions in any county court. (I have looked chiefly at Adams County, Miss., and St. Mary Parish, Louisiana). See also Gautreaux, "Transactions," pp. 179–80.

30. Martha DeSaussure in Taylor, *Ante-Bellum South Carolina*, p. 70; Woodward, *Chesnut's Civil War*, September 20, 1863, p. 473.

31. Quoted from Simpson, "Henry Wise," chap. 4.

Chapter Eleven: Male Custom in Family Life

1. Edwin Morris Betts and James Adam Bear, Jr., eds., *The Family Letters of Thomas Jefferson* (Columbia, Mo.: University of Missouri Press, 1966), p. 10, and Jefferson to Martha Jefferson, March 28, 1787, p. 35. Although regrettably read too late to be fully utilized in this work, Steven Mac Stowe, "All the Relations of Life: A Study in Sexuality, Family, and Social Values in the Southern Planter Class," Ph.D. diss., State University of New York at Stony Brook, 1979, contains a fascinating study of father-daughter relations in the William Gaston family of North Carolina.

2. Woodward, *Chesnut's Civil War*, August 29, 1861, p. 172; February 26, 1865, p. 735.

3. Ibid., March 11, 1861, p. 23.

4. Byrd's gaming friend in London quoted by Carson, *Virginians at Play*, p. 57.

5. Mrs. Margaret Izard Manigault to Mrs. Ralph Izard, February 20, 1805, Ralph Izard MSS, LC; John Berkeley Grimball, Diary, June 6, 1832, SHC, UNC.

6. Grimball, Diary, January 29, 1847; February 23, 1853, October 20, 1855, SHC, UNC. See also Hammond Plantation Journal, December 26, 1832, SC, USC. Cf. Ann Douglas, *The Feminization of American Culture* (New York: Knopf, 1978);

see also Michael Katz, "Families: Cycle, Structure, and Economy in Early Industrial America."

7. Lida Bestor Robertson, Diary, September 14, 1851, AlaDAH.

8. Caroline Gilman, *Recollections of a Southern Matron and a New England Bride* (Philadelphia: John E. Potter, 1867), pp. 296–98.

9. Davis, *Barrow Diary*, April 20, 1845, p. 353.

10. Benjamin Whitner to James H. Hammond, December 20, 1844, Hammond MSS, SC, USC; Robert F. Murphy, "Social Structure and Sex Antagonism," *Southwestern Journal of Anthropology* 15 (Spring 1959): 89–90.

11. Davis, *Barrow Diary*, pp. 353–54.

12. Chaplin, Diary, August 15, 1851; see also June 12, December 31, 1845, SCHS.

13. W. J. Rorabaugh, "Estimated U.S. Alcoholic Beverage Consumption, 1790–1860," *Journal of Studies on Alcohol* 37 (March 1976): 357–63.

14. Lionel Tiger, *Men in Groups* (New York: Vintage, 1970), p. 235.

15. Matthew Singleton to Richard Singleton, September 11, 1836, Singleton MSS, LC; Branton, in *American Temperance Society, Ninth Report—1836* (New York: American Temperance Society, 1837), p. 331. Northern colleges, by contrast, were seedbeds of temperance reform. See David R. Huehner, " 'Water is Indeed Best': Temperance and the Pre–Civil War New England College," in John S. Blocker, Jr., ed., *Alcohol, Reform and Society: The Liquor Question in Social Context* (Westport, Conn.: Greenwood Press, 1979), pp. 69–100.

16. Norcom to [?], January 29, 1833, Norcom MSS, NCDAH; Taylor, *Ante-Bellum South Carolina*, p. 96; Anna Holster to Sarah B. Evans, January 7, 1836, Shilg MSS, LSU; W. Stanley Hoole, ed., "Elyton, Alabama and the Connecticut Asylum: Letters of William H. Ely, 1820–1821," *AR* 2 (January 1950): 67; also Eliza MacGruder, Diary, December 15, 1854, LSU; Minnie C. Yarborough, ed., *Reminiscences of William C. Preston* (Chapel Hill: University of North Carolina Press, 1933), pp. 7–8.

17. William L. Brown, Diary (microfilm), entries for January 11–February 24, April 6, 1805, UKL; original diary in New York Public Library.

18. See Bertram Wyatt-Brown, "Child Abuse, Public Policy and Childrearing Patterns: A Historical Perspective," Paper presented at "Governing the Young," National Endowment for the Humanities Conference, College Park, Md., February 23, 1980.

19. Blackstone, *Commentaries*, book 3, sec. 139–40; Boatwright, "Political and Civil Status of Women in Georgia," *GHQ* 25 (December 1941): 314.

20. Edward Shorter, *The Making of the Modern Family* (New York: Basic Books, 1975), pp. 222–25; "Henry Tooley's Docket, October 8, 1821," in Natchez *Ariel*, July 25, 1829; see also Charleston *Courier*, April 19, 20, 1979, for a recent South Carolina case in which the wife killed her tormenter and was acquitted of murder.

21. David Gavin, Diary, November 28, 1855; February 6, 23, 1857, SHC, UNC.

22. Richard J. Gillis, *The Violent Home: A Study of Physical Aggression* (Beverly Hills: Sage, 1972), pp. 170–71; William J. Goode, "Force and Violence in the Family," *Journal of Marriage and the Family* 33 (November 1971): 624–36; Richard S. Makman, "Some Clinical Aspects of Inter-Spousal Violence," in John M. Eekelaar and Sanford N. Katz, eds., *Family Violence: An International and Inter-*

disciplinary Study (Toronto: Butterworths, 1978), p. 52; Susanne K. Steinmetz, "Sibling Violence," in ibid., pp. 460–65, in which she shows that parents may encourage sibling violence, with consequent effects upon marital violence later in life. See also Elizabeth Pleck, "The Old World, New Rights and Limited Rebellion: Challenges to Traditional Authority in Immigrant Families," Paper for Armington Seminar, Case Western Reserve University, October 22, 1981.

23. *Margery Ramsay* v. *Shewbridge Ramsay*, petition, #57–1821–2, Tenn. Leg. MSS, TSA; *Elizabeth Martin* v. *Richard Webb*, #68–1821–2; *Hannah Stone* v. *Thomas Stone*, #329–1821–5; see also *Minerva White* v. *Thomas J. White*, #277–1831–5; *Nancy Morris* v. *Joseph Morris*, #37–1821–1; *Catherine S. Smith* v. *John P. Smith*, #49–1821–1; *Margaret Fickle* v. *Abraham Fickle*, #150–1831–1; *Margaret Sitz* v. *John Sitz*, McMinn, #123–1831–1, Leg. Pet., TSA.

24. *Lucy B. Dabney*, #7360, 1819, Leg. Pet., VSL.

25. *Long* v. *Long*, 9 N.C. 192 (1832) at 192–93.

26. Ruffin quoted in Jane T. Censer, " 'Smiling through Her Tears': Ante-Bellum Southern Women and Divorce," *AJLH* 25 (Spring 1981): 28.

27. *Nancy C. Wilson* v. *DeWitt Clinton Wilson*, Fall term, 1862, Petition; *Dewitt Clinton Wilson*, August 30, 1864, Decree, Spring term, 1867, Superior Court of Equity, Davie County, N.C., Misc. Rec., "Affidavit-Grand Jury, 1834–1927," NCDAH.

28. Anna Roane, Divorce papers, Hanover County, January 9, 1851, Leg. Pet., VSL.

29. *Peter Miller* v. *Polly Miller*, spring term, 1868, Rowan County, Divorce Papers; *Mary Hep* v. *Joseph Hep*, Fall, 1831, Rowan County, County Records, NCDAH.

30. Houston to John Allen, April 9, 1829, in *The Writings of Sam Houston, 1813–1863*, Amelia W. Williams and Eugene C. Barker, eds., 8 vols. (Austin: University of Texas Press 1938) 1: 130; resignation as governor, April 16, 1829, pp. 131–32; Martha Anne Turner, *Sam Houston and His Twelve Women: The Ladies Who Influenced the Life of Texas' Greatest Statesman* (Austin: Pemberton Press, 1966), pp. 12–20; A. W. Terrell, "Recollections of General Samuel Houston," *SwHQ* 16 (1912–1913): 115; Paul Wellman, *Magnificent Destiny* (New York: Doubleday, 1962), pp. 247–52; Josephus C. Guild, *Old Times in Tennessee, with Historical, Personal, and Political Scraps and Sketches* (Nashville: Tavel, Eastman, and Howell, 1878), p. 278; Marion K. Wisehart, *Sam Houston: American Giant* (Washington: Robert B. Luce, 1962), pp. 38–50; Wiltshire, "Houston and *Iliad*," p. 252.

Chapter Twelve: Status, Law, and Sexual Misconduct

1. James H. Hammond, "Letters on Slavery," in *The Pro-Slavery Argument* (New York: Negro University Press, 1968 [1858]), pp. 118–19; see also William Gilmore Simms, "The Morals of Slavery," ibid., pp. 210–11.

2. Jack K. Williams, *Vogues in Villainy: Crime and Retribution in Ante-Bellum South Carolina* (Columbia: University of South Carolina Press, 1959), pp. 33–34; prostitution figures, from William Sanger, *A History of Prostitution* (New York:

Medical, 1858), p. 614; on bastardy, see *Acts of the General Assembly . . . of Georgia* (Milledgeville, 1816), pp. 40, 80, 182; ibid. (1819), pp. 56, 57, 79; ibid., (1820), pp. 49, 60, 75; ibid. (1821), 5, 6, 32, 56. The total of legitimization bills almost equals the number of divorce petitions.

3. C. Werner, ironworker, November 21, 1856, Charleston, S.C., vol. 6, DB, Baker.

4. Keith Thomas, "The Double Standard," *JHI* 20 (January 1959); 195–216; Nancy F. Cott, "Passionlessness: An Interpretation of Victorian Sexual Ideology, 1790–1850," in Nancy F. Cott and Elizabeth H. Pleck, eds., *A Heritage of Her Own: Toward a New Social History of American Women* (New York: Simon & Schuster, 1979), pp. 162–81; Dew, "Dissertation on Characteristic Differences between the Sexes," *SLM* 1 (May 1835): 497, 498; Ronald G. Walters, "The Erotic South," *AQ* 25 (May 1975): 176–201.

5. Charles Rosenberg, "Sexuality, Class and Role in 19th-Century America," *AQ* 25 (May 1975): 131–53; *Journals of Ralph Waldo Emerson*, Edward W. Emerson and Waldo E. Forbes, eds., 10 vols. (Cambridge: Houghton Mifflin, 1912), entries for April 25, 1848, 7: 441, and for May 13, 1848, 7: 459. See also Ralph L. Rush, *The Life of Ralph Waldo Emerson* (New York: Charles Scribner's Sons, 1949), p. 347.

6. Hammond, Diary, December 9, 1846, SC, USC.

7. Petigru to Alfred Huger, September 8, 1852, Petigru MSS, LC.

8. Withers to Hammond, May 4, 1826, Hammond MSS, SC, USC; Chesnut, *Diary from Dixie*, pp. 187–88.

9. Wilson quoted in Jordan, *White over Black*, p. 474; second quotation from Johnson, *Ante-Bellum North Carolina*, p. 591.

10. Harper in Elliott, *Cotton is King*, p. 583; see also Jacques Rossiaud, "Prostitution, Youth, and Society in the Towns of Southeastern France in the Fifteenth Century," in Robert Forster and Orest Ranum, eds., *Deviants and the Abandoned in French Society*, Elborg Forster and Patricia Ranum, trans. (Baltimore: Johns Hopkins University Press, 1978), pp. 1–46.

11. The episode caused an international uproar involving abolitionists on both sides of the Atlantic in controversy with Judge O'Neall and the governor. See Lewis Tappan to O'Neall, April 29, July 19, September 26, 1844; to Hammond, March 25, June 6, July 23, 1845; letterbook, Lewis Tappan MSS, LC; Hammond to Tappan, June 17, 1845, Claude W. Unger Collection, Pennsylvania Historical Society; James W. Walker to Hammond, June 11, 1845, Hammond MSS, LC.

12. R. J. Walker to Hiram G. Runnels, July 6, 1835, RG 21, MissDAH; also see Thomas H. Garret case, January 25, October 18, 1860, RG 27, ibid.; Daniel Greenleaf to Runnels, May 1, 1834, RG 21, ibid.; J. J. Lyons, dry goods, August 7, 1835, Abbeville, S.C., vol. 6, DB, Baker.

13. *Torre v. Summers*, 2 Nott & McCord (S.C.) 267 (1820), at 269; see also Bishop, *Commentaries on the Law of Marriage and Divorce* 1:348, 443, 647; Williams, *Vogues in Villainy*, pp. 55–57.

14. See *Fennell v. Littlejohn*, 240 S.C. 189 (1962); Huger quoted from *Haney v. Townsend*, 1 McCord (S.C.) 206 (1821) at 207. Such suits were sometimes useful to prove a lack of connivance between the estranged parties, but if there was sufficient evidence of a wife's adultery in the first place, it was impractical and expensive to go to court twice, once for tort, then again for divorce.

15. Nathan P. Feinsinger, "Legislative Attack on 'Heart Balm,'" *MLR* 33 (May 1935); 980–92. See also, Reeve, *Law of Baron and Femme*, p. 175 and 175 n1; Reeve noted the legal uncertainty of criminal conversation in American tribunals. And see George A. Howard, *A History of Matrimonial Institutions*, 3 vols. (Chicago: University of Chicago Press, 1904) 2: 114 on English evolutions of criminal conversation; Homer H. Clark, *The Law of Domestic Relations in the United States* (St. Paul, Minn.: West, 1968), pp. 268–69, cites cases from the 1890s to the 1940s regarding criminal conversation.

16. O'Neall quoted in J. Nelson Frierson, "Divorce in South Carolina," *North Carolina Law Review* 9 (February 1931): 269.

17. Johnson, *Ante-Bellum North Carolina*, p. 217; Tenn. Leg. Pet. 1821 and 1831, TSA; Censer, "'Smiling through Her Tears,'" pp. 24–47; Howard, *Matrimonial Institutions* 2: 52–54, 93–98.

18. *Hutchins v. Hutchins*, RG 2, vol. 10, MissDAH; James Norcom, biographical introduction to papers, and Norcom to Edmund Norcom, October 24, 1805, Norcom MSS, NCDAH.

19. Haywood Roebuck, "North Carolina Divorce and Alimony Petitions: 1813," *NCGSJ* 1 (April 1975): 85–96; Johnson, *Ante-Bellum North Carolina*, p. 217; Nisbet quoted in Bloomfield, *American Lawyers*, p. 212.

20. Riley case in Roebuck, "North Carolina Divorce," *NCGSJ* 1 (April 1975): 89–90; *Sexton v. Sexton*, file 236, 1831, no. 4, TSA.

21. *Taylor v. Taylor*, file 64, 1821, no. 2, TSA; *Trotter v. Trotter*, Petersburg, 1809, A5276, Leg. Pet., VSL; see also *Bond v. Bond*, file 20, 1821, no. 1, TSA.

22. Joel P. Bishop, *A Treatise on Criminal Law*, John M. Zane and Carl Zollmann, eds., 2 vols. (Indianapolis: Bobbs-Merrill, 1923 [1865, 1868, 1872 etc.]) 1: 5. See also ibid., n3: "Blackstone says honor is 'a point of a nature so nice and delicate that its wrongs and injuries escape the notice of the common law, and yet are fit to be redressed somewhere.'"

23. *Baker v. Baker*, file 260, 1831, no. 5, TSA; *Journal of the House of Representatives . . . of Tennessee . . .* (Nashville, 1831), p. 23; Reeve, *Law of Baron and Femme*, p. 409; Petition of citizens, file 25, 1831, no. 5, TSA; Williams, *Vogues in Villainy*, pp. 6, 53–55.

24. Henry P. Lundsgaarde, *Murder in Space City: A Cultural Analysis of Houston Homicide Patterns* (New York: Oxford University Press, 1977), p. 162; Reeve, *Law of Baron and Femme*, pp. 300–1, n2.

25. *The Confession of Jereboam O. Beauchamp . . .* (Bloomfield, Ky., 1826), in Loren J. Kallsen, ed., *The Kentucky Tragedy: A Problem in Romantic Attitudes* (Indianapolis: Bobbs Merrill, 1963), pp. 22–23.

26. George Bishop, *Every Woman Her Own Lawyer . . .* (New York: Dick & Fitzgerald, 1858), p. 135; quotation from Lenny Steinhorn, Seminar paper, Johns Hopkins University, 1978, an excellent summary kindly lent by the author.

27. Woodward, *Chesnut's Civil War*, August 26–28, 1861, p. 169.

28. On the debate over Jefferson's liaison, see Fawn M. Brodie, *Thomas Jefferson: An Intimate History* (New York: W. W. Norton, 1974); Winthrop Jordan, *White over Black: American Attitudes toward the Negro, 1550–1812* (Chapel Hill: University of North Carolina Press, 1968), pp. 429–81; William W. Freehling, "The Founding Fathers and Slavery," *AHR* 77 (February 1972): 85;

Maude H. Woodfin, "Contemporary Opinion in Virginia of Thomas Jefferson," in Avery Craven, ed., *Essays in Honor of William E. Dodd* . . . (Chicago: University of Chicago Press, 1935), pp. 62–65; Dumas Malone, *Jefferson the President: First Term, 1801–1805* (Boston: Little, Brown, 1970), pp. 212–14, 494–98; John C. Miller, *The Wolf by the Ears: Thomas Jefferson and Slavery* (New York: Free Press, 1977), pp. 150–59.

29. Randall quoted in Virginius Dabney, *The Jefferson Scandals: A Rebuttal* (New York: Dodd, Mead, 1981), pp. 78–79; Carr quoted ibid., p. 78.

30. Lucy Boomer, slave of John Winn, January 6, 1835, Lunenburg County, Va., Leg. Pet., VSL; Ralph B. Flanders, *Plantation Slavery in Georgia* (Chapel Hill: University of North Carolina Press, 1933), pp. 141–43 and 142 n31; Helen T. Catterall, *Judicial Cases Concerning Slavery and the Negro*, 5 vols. (Washington: Carnegie, 1937) 5: 180–81, 224, 302–3, 307; Rebecca Felton, *Country Life in Georgia in the Days of My Youth* (Atlanta: Index, 1919), p. 45; Julia F. Smith, *Slavery and Plantation Growth in Antebellum Florida, 1821–1860* (Gainesville: University of Florida Press, 1973), pp. 93–94; Orville W. Taylor, *Negro Slavery in Arkansas* (Durham: Duke University Press, 1958), pp. 200–201; Kenneth M. Stampp, *The Peculiar Institution: Slavery in the Ante-Bellum South* (New York: Knopf, 1961), pp. 350–61.

31. William G. Simms, *Slavery in America* . . . (Richmond: T. W. White, 1838), p. 40, reprinted in *Pro-Slavery Argument*, pp. 228–30; Robert B. Toplin, "Between Black and White: Attitudes toward Southern Mulattoes, 1830–1861," *JSH* 65 (May 1979): 185–200. Lillian Smith, *Killers of the Dream* (New York: W. W. Norton, 1949), p. 108.

32. Ella G. C. Thomas, Diary, entry for April 17, 1856, DUL. In regard to the Johnson story, it should be noted that Johnson's political fortunes had always been tied to his hostility toward high-toned Sabbatarians, against whom working-class and nonchurchgoing members of the bourgeoisie in the North were aligned. The two daughters eventually married respectable Northerners, though being illegitimate they could not inherit their father's property, by Kentucky law. See Leland W. Meyer, *Col. Richard M. Johnson of Kentucky* (New York: Columbia University Press, 1932), pp. 20, 21, 290–320. As a young man, Johnson had taken revenge on his snobbish mother for refusing to let him marry a poor girl by swearing that he would never marry at all.

33. Davis, *Barrow Diary*, p. 206.

34. Hughes quoted by Genovese, *Roll, Jordan, Roll*, p. 418. On the primitive associations of incest and doubling, see René Girard, *Violence and the Sacred*, Patrick Gregory, trans. (Baltimore: Johns Hopkins University Press, 1977), pp. 75, 112–15. Clergyman John D. Paxton quoted in James H. Johnston, *Race Relations in Virginia and Miscegenation in the South, 1776–1860* (Amherst: University of Massachusetts Press, 1970), p. 299.

35. See *J. P. Farr et al. v. W. P. Thompson, Executor of W. B. Farr*, 37 Cheves (S.C.) 37 (1839–40); and *Thompson v. Farr*, 1 Speer (S.C.) 97 (1842–43); a poor summary is offered in Catterall, *Judicial Cases* 2: 375–76.

36. Joel Williamson, *New People: Miscegenation and Mulattoes in the United States* (New York: Free Press, 1980), p. 41. William Faulkner, *Absalom, Absalom!* (New York: Random House, 1964) and his *Light in August* (New York: Random

House, 1932). See John T. Irwin, *Doubling and Incest/Repetition and Revenge: A Speculative Reading of Faulkner* (Baltimore: Johns Hopkins University Press, 1975).
37. Quotation from Jordan, *White over Black*, p. 144; see also Smith, *Killers of the Dream*, p. 17; and Catterall, *Judicial Cases*, 1: 357, 2: 63–64, 167.
38. *Pettus* v. *Pettus*, December 12, 1802, Fluvanna County; *Butt* v. *Butt*, December 7, 1803, Norfolk County; *Mosley* v. *Mosley*, December 6, 1815, Powhatan County, Leg. Pet., VSI. See also *Pruden* v. *Pruden*, December 14, 1840, Nansemond County; *Gresham* v. *Gresham*, December 10, 1833, James City County; *Rawls* v. *Rawls*, December 14, 1840, Nansemond County; *Plum* v. *Plum*, December 9, 1841, Preston County; *Rucker* v. *Rucker*, March 5, 1849, Allegheny County, Leg. Pet., VSL. In the last case, however, Mr. Rucker, unlike all the others, did not obtain a divorce, because his wife had given birth to a black child before they were married; hence she was guilty only of fornication (and bastardy), not of adultery. Morgan, *American Slavery/American Freedom*, pp. 332–36, cites some eccentric examples of intermarriages of white women and black men early in colonial history. See also Johnston, *Race Relations*, passim.
39. *State* v. *Warwick*, March, 1825, State ser. 55, Hutchins Bordon Burton, Governors' Papers, and letterbook, April 13, 1825, 12, GP 55, NCDAH; Long quoted in Jordan, *White over Black*, p. 239 n46.
40. *Mosley* v. *Mosley*, December 6, 1815, Powhatan County, Leg. Pet., VSL.
41. *State* v. *Jim*, Davidson County, 1825–26, Burton, GP 55, NCDAH.
42. Ibid.
43. John De Witt, "General James Winchester," *Tennessee Historical Magazine* 1 (September 1915): 201; Samuel C. Williams, *Beginnings of West Tennessee in the Land of the Chickasaws, 1541–1841* (Johnson City, Tenn.: Watauga Press, 1930), p. 130;; Gerald M. Capers, Jr., *The Biography of a River Town: Memphis in Its Heroic Age* (Chapel Hill: University of North Carolina Press, 1939), pp. 52–53; James D. Davis, *History of Memphis and the Old Times Papers* (Memphis: Crumpton & Kelly, 1873), pp. 70–77.
44. Thomas, "Double Standard," pp. 207–9; see also Girard, *Violent and Sacred*, pp. 71–77, 116–18, 208–9; Fred Weinstein and Gerald M. Platt, *The Wish to Be Free: Society, Psyche, and Value Change* (Berkeley: University of California Press, 1969), pp. 144–51.
45. Hammond in Elliott, *Cotton is King*, p. 645; see also Harper, ibid., p. 583. Woodward, *Chesnut's Civil War*, March 18, 1861, p. 29.
46. Henry G. Hawkins, *Methodism in Natchez* (Nashville: Parthenon Press, 1937), 196–97; *Mississippi State Gazette* (Natchez), July 1, 1820; *Susannah Foster* v. *Thomas Foster, Jr.*, February 1, 1827, #683, Drawer 76, Mississippi High Court of Errors and Appeals (hereafter Foster Divorce), MissDAH; indenture, Thomas Foster, Sr., to Thomas Foster, Jr., March 3, 1820, Deed Book N, Adams County Courthouse, Natchez (hereafter AdCC). MissDAH has acquired microfilms of these papers. See Terry Alford, *Prince among Slaves* (New York: Harcourt, Brace Jovanovich, 1977), pp. 94–95. Despite the alcoholism, Thomas did have funds to buy land in Copiah County in 1825, but he sold some of it in 1829; see Deed Book C, pp. 17–18, 210, 372, Copiah County Courthouse, Hazlehurst, Miss. (courtesy of Professor Alford).

47. Pauli Murray, *Proud Shoes: The Story of an American Family* (New York: Harper, 1978), pp. 33–54.

48. On Ibrahima's life, see Alford, *Prince among Slaves.*

49. Woodward, *Chesnut's Civil War*, June 10, 1861, pp. 71–72.

50. Gary B. Mills, "Miscegenation and the Free Negro in Antebellum 'Anglo' Alabama: A Reexamination of Southern Race Relations," *JAH* 68 (June 1981): 16–34, claims "a wide variance in southern attitudes toward miscegenation" and asserts that "startling statistics" which he unearthed "question the alleged double standard whereby white female participation in interracial sex was viciously condemned while males who indulged in the same extralegal pleasures suffered little more than occasional reproof." In one sense, Mills is correct: particularities of any situation might break the monolithic patterns of animosity toward one kind of interracial sex and condonation of another. But none of the examples or statistics that Mills cites overturn the general propositions mentioned herein. It must be remembered that the numbers with which he is dealing are very small, and acknowledged cohabitations very rare. It would be a travesty to claim that miscegenation by either sex was welcomed or even treated with indifference as a general principle. What Mills has proved is not Southern toleration but rather Southern particularism. On the demographics of miscegenation, see also Williamson, *New People*, pp. 33–42.

Chapter Thirteen: Personal Strategies and Community Life

1. George W. Babgy, *The Old Virginia Gentleman and Other Sketches*, Thomas N. Page, ed. (New York: Charles Scribner's Sons, 1910), p. 3.

2. Peyre to Robert M. Deveaux, July 17, 1841, Singleton MSS, LC.

3. Chaplin, Diary, December 25, 1845, SCHS; the Virginia resident quoted in Richard L. Morton, ed., "Life in Virginia by a 'Yankee Teacher': Margaret Newbold Thorpe," *VMHB* 64 (April 1956): 197; Charles M. Conrad to Alfred J. Conrad, April 26, 1818, Weeks MSS, LSU.

4. Thomas Carlyle, "Captains of Industry," in *Past and Present* (Boston: Houghton Mifflin, 1965 [1843]), p. 271; Martineau, *Society in America*, 3: 10–12.

5. Henry B. Cumming to Julia A. D. Cumming, September 29, 1825, and Maria Bryan to Julia A. D. Cumming, October 1, 1838, HBC MSS; Corydon Fuller, Diary, July 27, 1858, WLCL. See also Harriet Martineau, *Retrospect of Western Travel*, 2 vols. (London: Saunders and Otley, 1838) 2: 9; Thomas O'Dwyer, Diary, March 22, 1825, Samuel Jordan Wheeler MSS, SHC, UNC. Widowers had the option of curing solitude by a quick remarriage, though not without mild disapproval from neighbors and kin. See Wooten, Diary, April 1, 1832 (typescript), p. 38. AlaDAH. Religious folk had the consolation of their faith at times of mourning. See Dickson D. Bruce, Jr., "Death as Testimony in the Old South," *SHR* 12 (Spring 1978): 123–32; Jesse Cox (an anti-mission preacher), Diary, passim, TSA. On Southern supernaturalism and death, see Montell, *Ghosts along the Cumberland;* and Ray B. Browne, *Popular Beliefs and Practices from Alabama* (Berkeley: University of California Press, 1955).

6. For quotation on Yancey, see Brown, *Lower South in American History*, pp.

127–28. On the uses of speech for group solidarity in traditional societies, see Maurice Bloch, *Political Language and Oratory in Traditional Society* (London: Academic Press, 1975), p. 17; John J. Gumperz and Dell Hymes, eds., *Directions in Sociolinguistics* (New York: Holt, Rinehart & Winston, 1972), esp. Basil Bernstein, "A Sociolinguistic Approach in Socialization: With Reference to Educability," pp. 465–67; and idem, "Aspects of Language and Learning in the Genesis of the Social Process," in Dell Hymes, ed., *Language in Culture and Society: A Reader in Linguistics and Anthropology* (New York: Harper & Row, 1964), pp. 51–63. See also H. Peter Pudner, "People Not Pedagogy: Education in Old Virginia," *GR* 25 (October 1971): 263–85.

7. Genovese, *Political Economy of Slavery*, pp. 18, 130, 158; Raimondo Luraghi, *The Rise and Fall of the Plantation South* (New York: Franklin Watts, 1978), p. 74, passim; and Jane H. Pease, "A Note on Patterns of Conspicuous Consumption among Seaboard Planters, 1820–1860," *JSH* 35 (August 1969): 381–93 (quotation, p. 393). See also Stampp, *Peculiar Institution*, p. 391; William E. Dodd, *The Cotton Kingdom: A Chronicle of the Old South* (New Haven: Yale University Press, 1919), p. 15; Robert R. Russel, "The General Effects of Slavery upon Southern Economic Progress," JSH 4 (February 1938): 49–50; but see Fogel and Engerman, *Time on the Cross*, pp. 253–54.

8. Mitchell, *Edmund Ruffin*, p. 55. See, for instance, the troubles of Eliza Wilson, a Louisiana plantation widow who had to manage a violent and paranoid father suffering from Alzheimer's condition in old age: Eliza Wilson to Andrew Hymes, December 21, 1827; January 29, 1829, and later correspondence, Edward Gay and Family MSS, LSU. See also Ramsey, *Autobiography and Letters*, p. 13; and Anderson, *Brockenburn*, pp. xxvi–vii, 3.

9. Arney R. Childs, ed., *Rice Planter and Sportsman: The Recollections of J. Motte Alston, 1821–1909* (Columbia: University of South Carolina Press, 1953), p. 16; Semple, *Reminiscences*, p. 16.

10. Tennessee Williams, *The Glass Menagerie* (New York: New Directions, 1970 [1945]), sc. 2, p. 34. As in rural Ireland of not long ago, farm folk sought reciprocations for "friendly cooperation" among kinspeople, but the permanent dependency of one party blasted that reciprocal pattern. See Arensberg, *Irish Countryman*, pp. 72–73; Frank I. Owsley, *Plain Folk of the Old South* (Chicago: Quadrangle, 1965 [1949]), pp. 104–8.

11. Anon. Diary, Rockingham County, Virginia, 1861–1865, p. 90, DUL; Sarah Hicks Williams to Sarah and Samuel Hicks, October 22, 1853, in Bonner, "Plantation Experiences of a New York Woman," *NCHR* 33 (July 1956); 392, see also pp. 384–417 in the same issue and pp. 529–46 in the October 1956 issue. Cornelia A. Spencer to Laura [?], February 2, 1837, Spencer MSS, SHC, UNC and Wilson, Diary, December 9, 1836, MissDAH; Clement Eaton, "Class Differences in the Old South," *Virginia Quarterly Review* 33 (Summer 1957): 362.

12. Mrs. Matilda C. F. Houston, *Hesperos; or, Travels in the West,* 2 vols. (London: J. W. Parker, 1850) 2: 138; Beverley, *History and Present State of Virginia,* p. 167; Michael Chevalier, *Society, Manners, and Politics in the United States: Being a Series of Letters on North America* (Boston: Week, Jordan, 1839), p. 103; John Bernard, *Retrospections of America, 1797–1811,* Mrs. Bayle Bernard, ed. (New York: Benjamin Blom, 1969 [1887]), pp. 152–53; John F. D. Smyth, *A*

Tour of the United States of America, 2 vols. (London: Robinson, 1784) 1: 70–71; [James K. Paulding], *Letters from the South*, 2 vols. (New York: Harper Bros., 1835) 1: 27. For a thorough discussion see Paton Yoder, "Private Hospitality in the South, 1775–1850," *MVHR* 47 (December 1960): 419–33.

13. Francis Hall, *Travels in Canada and the United States in 1816 and 1817* (London: Longman, 1818), p. 413; Charles J. Latrobe, *The Rambler in North America*, 3 vols. (London: Seeley and Burnside, 1836) 2: 13. Elkanah Watson cited in Yoder, "Private Hospitality," p. 429; John Cornish, Diary December 23–26, 1839, 2: 63, SHC, UNC; Olmsted, *Cotton Kingdom*, p. 520.

14. Elizabeth McCall Perry to Benjamin F. Perry, March 8, 1847 (typescript), Perry MSS, SC, USC.

15. On Jefferson's hospitality, see Sydney G. Fisher, *Men, Women and Manners in Colonial Times . . .* , 2 vols. (Philadelphia: Lippincott, 1898) 1: 112–13.

16. Hammond, Diary, December 9, 1846, SC, USC; Chaplin, Diary, January 19, 1846, SCHS; see also May 9, 1848, ibid. Edmund Ruffin in *Farmer's Register* 2: 96, as quoted in Phillips, *Life and Labor*, p. 356. See also Carter's distress with the task of hosting his son's worthless friends in Greene, *Carter Diary*, March 15, 1776, 2: 1001–2.

17. Julian Pitt-Rivers, "The Stranger, the Guest, and the Hostile Host: Introduction to the Study of the Laws of Hospitality," in J. G. Peristiany, ed., *Contributions to Mediterranean Sociology: Mediterranean Rural Communities and Social Change* (Paris: Mouton, 1967), pp. 13–30; Thorstein Veblen, *The Theory of the Leisure Class: An Economic Study of Institutions* (New York: Macmillan, 1917), p. 69; Michael Young, *Fighting with Food: Leadership, Values and Social Control in a Massim Society* (Cambridge: Cambridge University Press, 1971); Arensberg, *Irish Countryman*, pp. 21–47, 73–75.

18. "Journal of a French Traveller in the Colonies, 1765, I" *AHR* 26 (July 1921): 743; John B. Nevitt, Diary, April 3, 1828; January 8, 1829, LSU; Johnson, *Ante-Bellum North Carolina*, p. 498; Olmsted, *Cotton Kingdom*, pp. 77, 213, 219, 275, 328, 413, 414. See also, Clifford Geertz, "Deep Play: Notes on the Balinese Cockfight," *Daedalus* 101 (Winter 1972): 1–38; Taylor, *Ante-Bellum South Carolina*, pp. 51–56; on colonial sportsmanship and gaming, see Carson, *Virginians at Play*, passim; Bernard, *Retrospections*, pp. 146–59; "A Letter from Mr. John Clayton to the Royal Society, May 12, 1688," in Peter Force, ed., *Tracts and Other Parts . . .* , 4 vols. (New York: Peter Smith, 1947) 3: 35; E. D. Cuming, "Sports and Games," in A. S. Turberville, ed., *Johnson's England: An Account of the Life and Manner of His Age*, 2 vols. (Oxford: Clarendon Press, 1930) 1: 363–72; Philip A. Bruce, *Social Life of Virginia in the Seventeenth Century* (Richmond: Whittet & Shepperson, 1907), p. 189; Smyth, *A Tour* 1: 23, 41; Featherstonhaugh, *Excursion through the Slave States*, pp. 98–99; Francis Baily, *Journal of a Tour . . .* , Jack D. L. Holmes, ed. (Carbondale: Southern Illinois University Press, 1968), p. 21.

19. William Faulkner to Eric J. Divine, February 23, 1949, in Joseph Blotner, ed., *Selected Letters of William Faulkner* (New York: Random House, 1977), p. 286. Certainly the comment is not chronologically appropriate to this work, but the sentiment would have well suited the South of prior times.

20. T. H. Breen, "Horses and Gentlemen: The Cultural Significance of Gambling

among the Gentry of Virginia," *WMQ*, 3d ser. 34 (April 1977): 256, 257; Fisher, *Men, Women and Manners* 1: 100–101. See also Raymond Firth, "A Dart Match in Tikopia: A Study in the Sociology of Primitive Sport," *Oceania* 1 (April 1930): 94–95.

21. B. W. C. Roberts, "Cockfighting: An Early Entertainment in North Carolina," *NCHR* 42 (Summer 1965): 311; Johnson, *Ante-Bellum North Carolina*, p. 181; Lizzie W. Montgomery, *Sketches of Old Warrenton, North Carolina* (Raleigh: Edwards and Broughton, 1924), pp. 25–39; John B. Alexander, *Reminiscences of the Past Sixty Years* (Charlotte: Ray Printery, 1908), pp. 189–90; Raleigh *Register*, July 14, 1806; Charles W. Harris to Charles Harris, May 8, 1797, in Henry M. Wagstaff, ed., *The Harris Letters*, James Sprunt Historical Publications (Chapel Hill: University of North Carolina Press, 1916), p. 44. In the 1840s and 1850s there was much fear (perhaps unjustified) in church circles that even pious Christians, quite apart from "infidels," were becoming increasingly addicted to "worldly amusements," including racetrack attendance and dancing. See Anne C. Loveland, *Southern Evangelicals and the Social Order, 1800–1860* (Baton Rouge: Louisiana State University Press, 1980), pp. 97–101.

22. Greene, *Carter Diary*, December 21, 1774, 2: 900; also June 27, 1772, 2: 703.

23. S. A. Townes to G. F. Townes, September 13, 1831, Townes MSS, SC, USC.

24. *A Controversy between "Erskine" and "W. M." on the Practicability of Suppressing Gambling* (Richmond: Whig Book, 1862), pp. 6–7, passim; W. H. Sparks, *Memories of Fifty Years* (Philadelphia: E. Clayton, 1882), p. 106.

25. Fred W. Voget, "The Folk Society: An Anthropological Application," *SF* 33 (December 1954): 106; Rhys Isaac, "Evangelical Revolt: The Nature of the Baptists' Challenge to the Traditional Order in Virginia, 1765 to 1775," *WMQ*, 3d ser. 31 (July 1974): 351. As Mrs. Ravenel put it, Charlestonians in race week shared the conviction of Walter Scott's laird who told his wife, "Let me sleep until next year, for Ailie woman, there's only one day worth living, and that's the day of the Abbotsford hunt." Mrs. St. Julien Ravenel, *Charleston: The Place and the People* (New York: Macmillan, 1906) pp. 385–86; see also pp. 129–30. Farish, *Fithian Journal* (1957 ed.), April 4, 1774, pp. 91; June 18, 1774, pp. 121–22; September 8, 1774, pp. 186–87.

26. Johann Huizinga, *Homo Ludens: A Study of the Play-Element in Culture* (Boston: Beacon Press, 1955), p. 56; "The Journal of Josiah Quincy, Junior, 1773," *Massachusetts Historical Society Proceedings* 49 (June 1916): April 16, 1773, 467; François Jean, Marquis de Chastellux, *Travels in North-America in the Years 1780, 1781, and 1782*, [George Grieve, trans.] 2 vols. (London: G. G. J. & J. Robinson, 1787) 2: 100.

27. Grayson quoted from "The Character of a Gentleman," *SQR* 7 (January 1853), 59; on Potter, the gaming politician, see Johnson, *Ante-Bellum North Carolina*, pp. 186–87.

28. Merrill, *Jefferson's Nephews*, pp. 49, 308–9, describes the interlocking debts in the Virginia squirearchy. On the social-political obligations of debt in traditional societies, see Frederick Barth, *Models of Social Organization*, Occasional Papers no. 23 (London: Royal Anthropological Society, 1966). Arensberg, *Irish Countryman*, p. 159, on "rural credit system" versus commercial debt; on friendships and nonpayment of gaming debts, see Thomas D. Clark, *The Rampaging*

Frontier: Manners and Humors of Pioneer Days in the South and the Middle West (Indianapolis: Bobbs-Merrill, 1939), p. 240. Cf. Solomon F. Smith, *Theatrical Management in the West and South for Thirty Years* (New York: Harper Bros, 1868), p. 112: *"Money bet on a credit* was never paid, nor was it ever expected to be paid."* In such cases the object was the sport, but games on a credit basis obviously lacked the excitement that gaming was intended to provide. C. C. Pinckney to Thomas Pinckney, October 5, 1794, Pinckney Family MSS, LC. On gambling and violence, see Huntsville (Ala.) *Democrat,* September 18, 1829; Williams, *Vogues in Villainy,* p. 48; James L. Petigru to William Elliott, September 7, 1831, Petigru MSS, LC. On friendship and ordinary debts and signed notes, see Grayson, *Petigru,* p. 138, passim. "It is the Devil to be in Debt & still I feel uneasy unless I have some person to [sponsor?] me," wrote A. Thurston of Louisville, Ky., to Edmund H. Taylor, April 12, 1818, Weeks MSS, LSU.

29. Bailey, *Life and Adventures,* p. 67; Martineau, *Society in America,* 1: 157; Frederick L. Olmsted, *A Journey in the Seaboard Slave States . . . ,* 2 vols. (New York: G. P. Putnam's Sons, 1904) 2: 209, 268, 304.

30. Clark, *Rampaging Frontier,* p. 245; George H. Devol, *Forty Years a Gambler on the Mississippi* (New York: H. Holt, 1926 [1887]); Jonathan H. Green, *The Secret Band of Brothers, Or the American Outlaws* (Philadelphia: private printing, 1847).

31. Bailey, *Life and Adventures,* pp. 66–67, passim. See Robert W. Malcolmson, *Popular Recreations in English Society, 1700–1850* (Cambridge: Cambridge University Press, 1973), pp. 75–86. Charles T. Cullen, "St. George Tucker and Law in Virginia," Ph.D. diss., University of Virginia, 1971, pp. 235–61; Williams, *Vogues in Villainy,* pp. 47–50; Johnson, *Ante-Bellum North Carolina,* pp. 117–27.

32. Cartwright, *Autobiography,* pp. 160–61; Boyd, "York on Early Days in Randolph County," pp. 22–24; Holder, *Winans,* p. 4; William P. Strickland, ed., *Autobiography of the Rev. James B. Finley* (Cincinnati: Methodist Book Concern, 1853), p. 164; Farish, *Fithian Journal* March 6, 1774, pp. 72–73; Isaac, "Evangelical Revolt," p. 358; Bruce, *Violence and Southern Culture,* pp. 112–13; Ernest T. Thompson, *Presbyterians in the South,* vol. 1, *1607–1861* (Richmond: John Knox Press, 1963), pp. 313, 319, 321.

33. Criminal Docket Book, 1829–1841, Adams County Courthouse, Circuit Court Clerk's Office, Natchez, Miss. [AdCC]; see also Laurence Shore, "Making Mississippi Safe for Slavery: The Insurrection Panic of 1835," Burton and McMath, *Southern Communities;* Edwin C. Miles, "The Mississippi Slave Insurrection Scare of 1835," *JNH* 42 (January 1957): 48–60; Davidson B. McKibben, "Negro Slave Insurrections in Mississippi, 1800–1865," *JNH* 34 (January 1949): 73–94; Thomas Shackelford, *Proceedings of the Citizens of Madison County, Mississippi at Livingston, in July, 1835 . . .* (Jackson: Mayson & Smoot, 1838); *Yazoo Banner* (Benton, Miss.), May 18, 1839; Vicksburg (Miss.) *Register,* July 16, 30, August 13, 20, 1835; Patrick Sharkey and James B. Kilbourne to Hiram G. Runnels, July 7, 1835, and Petition of Citizens of Vicksburg to Runnels, July 10, 1835, RG 27, MissDAH; Jackson *Mississippian,* July 17, 1835; Henry Chafetz, *Play the Devil: A History of Gambling in the United States from 1429 to 1955* (New York: Clarkson

N. Potter, 1960), pp. 55–63. [H. R. Howard, comp. pseud.], *The History of Virgil A. Stewart*, pp. 263–68.

34. A. A. Parker, *Trip to the West and Texas* . . . (Concord, N.H.: White & Fisher, 1835), p. 107; Farish, *Fithian Journal* (1957 ed.), January 18, 1774, p. 57; "Journal of a French Traveller," *AHR* 26 (July 1929), p. 741.

35. Richard Minster quoted in Jon Halliday and Peter Fuller, eds., Introduction, in *The Psychology of Gambling* (New York: Harper & Row, 1974), p. 46; see also pp. 1–114. William H. Boyd, "Excitement: The Gambler's Day," in William K. Eadington, ed., *Gambling and Society: Interdisciplinary Studies on the Subject of Gambling* (Springfield, Ill.: Charles C. Thomas, 1976), pp. 373–74; and see Tomas Martinez, "Compulsive Gambling and the Conscious Mood Perspective," pp. 347–70, ibid. Although superseded to some degree by later researchers, see Sigmund Freud, "Dostoevsky and Parricide," in *The Standard Edition of the Complete Psychological Works of Sigmund Freud*, James Strachey, trans. and ed., 23 vols. (London: Hogarth Press, 1953–) 21: 177–94.

36. Stoney, "Autobiography of Grayson," p. 28; James T. McIntosh, ed., *The Papers of Jefferson Davis, June 1841–July 1846* (Baton Rouge: Louisiana State University Press, 1974) 2: 153; Dennis F. Burge, "Louisiana under Governor André Bienvenu Roman, 1831–1835, 1839–1843," M.A. diss., Louisiana State University, 1937), p. 109; Grand Gulf (Miss.) *Advertiser*, March 5, 29, 1839; Baltimore *American & Daily Advertiser*, July 18, 1804; Moses Waddell, Diary, November 18, 1831, LC.

37. Bruce, *Violence and Culture*, p. 73; Daniel Boorstin, *The Americans: The National Experience* (New York: Random House, 1965), pp. 199–212. Nonritual contests were more frequent among planters than duels were: the Greenville (S.C.) *Mountaineer*, March 27, April 3, 1830; Mobile *Register*, November 15, 1837, and Theodore D. Weld, *Slavery as It Is* . . . (New York: American Anti-Slavery Society, 1839) provide examples. See also Maurice Moore, M.D., "Reminiscences of York District, South Carolina in Yorkville *Enquirer*, York, S.C., 1870," copy, p. 7, LC.

38. Joseph Blotner, *Faulkner: A Biography*, 2 vols. (New York: Random House, 1974) 1: 16–50.

39. [George L. Prentiss], *Memoir of S. S. Prentiss* 2 vols. (New York: Charles Scribner's Sons, 1855), 1: 133–34; Henry S. Foote, *Casket of Reminiscences* (New York: Negro University Press, 1968 [1874]), pp. 39–42.

40. Bruce, *Violence and Culture*, p. 91.

41. Grayson, *Petigru*, p. 85; Lorenzo Sabine, *Notes on Duels and Duellings* . . . (Boston: Crosley, Nichols, 1855), p. iv. On yeoman honor and means of battling, see Farish, *Fithian Journal*, September 3, 1774, p. 183; Jackson *Mississippian*, November 9, 1838; Grand Gulf *Advertiser* (Miss.), June 27, 1837; June 12, July 17, 1839. Boorstin, *Americans: National Experience*, p. 211; John Lyde Wilson, *The Code of Honor* . . . (Charleston, 1838), pp. 3–4, conveniently reprinted in Jack K. Williams, *Dueling in the Old South* (College Station: Texas A & M Press, 1980), pp. 88–99. Foote, *Casket*, pp. 185–86.

42. Col. John Lewis to James Monroe, September 15, 1802, box 20, Militia Pap., VSL; for battles over promotions between parvenus and the old elite, see also

Vincent Redman to Monroe, July 5, 1802 and other letters contesting John Tayloe's appointment to colonelcy; James Hazlegrove Tavern Court-Martial fight, May 6, 1803; and Francis B. Cox to Monroe, April 29, 1802; Captain Bathurst Jones to Monroe, May 1, 1802; Jones to Major Samuel Coleman, July 8, 1802; Charles Atkisson to Monroe, March 25, 1802; in boxes 20 and 21, ibid. On the origins of dueling, see Thomas Gamble, *Savannah Duels and Duellists, 1733–1877* (Savannah: Review, 1923), pp. 9–10.

43. Samuel A. Townes to George Franklin Townes, August 8, 1826, Townes MSS, SC, USC; Boorstin, *Americans: National Experience*, p. 211.

44. Bailey, *Life and Adventures*, pp. 71 ff.; Grayson, "Character of a Gentleman," p. 68. For a less than ideal duel, see Davis, *Barrow Diary*, pp. 150–51.

45. Thomas Lesesne to Robert Brown, August 21, 1804, Singleton MSS, LC.

46. "Certificate Regarding the Duel of Dickinson and Andrew Jackson," Hanson Catlet MSS, LSU; John S. Bassett, ed., *Correspondence of Andrew Jackson*, 6 vols. (Washington: Carnegie Institution, 1926–1933) 1: 122–24, 130. Those involved in the preparations included, besides Dickinson and Joseph Ervin, his father-in-law, the following: Thomas Swann, General John Coffee, Nathaniel McNairy and Robert Prudy, Jonathan Hutchins, Patten Anderson, John Baird, Robert Hays, Robert Butler, Samuel Jackson, Thomas A. Claiborne, and Charles S. Carson, most of them as tale bearers. See also Marquis James, *Andrew Jackson: Border Captain* (Indianapolis: Bobbs Merrill, 1933), p. 114; Ward, *Andrew Jackson*, pp. 163–64; Rogin, *Fathers and Children*, pp. 57–59, 136–38; and Remini, *Jackson and the Course of American Empire*, pp. 136–43. Political and journalistic duelists no doubt were motivated in part by a desire to please large segments of their publics, along with hopes of eradicating the stigma of insult from the opponent. See, for instance, the political overtones of the congressional handling of duels in Vicksburg *Whig*, March 14, 15, 1839.

47. Samuel Asbury, ed., "Extracts from the Reminiscences of George W. Morgan," *SwHQ* 30 (January 1927): 188–93; Amelia W. Williams and Eugene C. Barker, eds., *The Writings of Sam Houston, 1813–1863*, 8 vols. (Austin: University of Texas Press, 1938) 1: 514–17; Felix Huston, "Biography, 1831–1845" (typescript), MissDAH; Charles P. Roland, *Albert Sidney Johnston: Soldier of Three Republics* (Austin: University of Texas Press, 1964), pp. 59–62; Houston, *Autobiography*, p. 141.

48. See Charles M. Conrad to Rachel O'Connor, August 16, 1833, Weeks MSS, LSU; James L. Petigru to William Elliott, September 7, 1831, Petigru MSS, LC; Stoney, "Autobiography of Grayson," *SCHGM* 49 (January 1948): 28–29; Martineau, *Society in America* 3: 12–13. See also Wesley Hoby to Wade Hampton, August 8, 1853, Huger MSS, DUL; Vicksburg *Advertiser*, August 7, 1829; Mrs. Mary Austin Holley to Mrs. William Brand, November 30, 1830, Holley MSS, UKL; Jackson *Mississippian*, March 14, 1834.

49. On the McDuffie-Cumming duel, see Anna H. Johnson to Elizabeth Haywood, August 17, 1822, Haywood MSS, SHC, UNC; William L. Yancey to Editors of the *Alabama Baptist*, February 10, 1845 (typescript), Yancey MSS, AlaDAH. On Yancey's fight with Dr. Robert Earle, see Yancey to Benjamin C. Yancey, September 8, 1838 (typed copy); and Greenville *Mountaineer* (S.C.), November 9, 1838 (copy), Yancey MSS, AlaDAH. In this case the instigator, Yancey thought, was not Earle

himself but his wife, who demanded that her husband show courage. On Yancey's psychology, see Draughon, "Young Manhood of Yancey," *AR* 9 (January 1966): 28–40. A new biography of Yancey would be welcome.

50. George Tucker, "On Duelling," in *Essays on Various Subjects of Taste, Morals and National Policy* (Georgetown, D.C.: Joseph Milligan, 1822), p. 250; see also pp. 258–59.

51. Louis T. Wigfall to John Manning, January 2, 1838; April 25, 1841; November [?], 1848, Manning-Chesnut-Williams MSS, SC, USC; see also Maxey Gregg to Manning, August 4, 1840, and John W. Cantry to Manning, May 19, 24, 1841, and other correspondence of 1841, ibid. See also Benjamin Franklin Yancey to Benjamin C. Yancey, November 5, 1852, and J. Pinckney to Benjamin C. Yancey, April 24, 1853, Yancey MSS, AlaDAH; King, *Wigfall*, chs. 1, 2, and passim. Wigfall, it will be recalled, had lost parents early and spent his life in quest of respectability, public acclaim, and patrons, but without much success. Like so many volatile duelists of that era, he suffered from depression.

52. Prentiss was a Yankee by birth and early training, but many Yankees were similarly attuned to traditional notions of honor and gentility; as is stressed throughout this work, the difference between Northerner and Southerner was often slight, although collectively the societies were changing at different rates. Prentiss and John A. Quitman, another emigrant from the North, found their temperaments and values most deeply appreciated in the South, and they naturally adapted themselves to the Southern style. See Joseph C. Baldwin, *The Flush Times of Alabama and Mississippi* (New York: Hill & Wang, 1957), pp. 144–62; Dallas C. Dickey, *Seargent S. Prentiss, Whig Orator of the Old South* (Baton Rouge: Louisiana State University Press, 1945), pp. 61–63, 383–84, 386–92; quotation in Joseph D. Shields, *The Life and Times of Seargent Smith Prentiss* (Philadelphia: Lippincott, 1884), p. 22; Foote, *Casket*, pp. 429–35.

53. Foote, *Casket*, pp. 435–42; Davis, *Recollections of Mississippi and Mississippians*, pp. 213–19; Eaton, *Mind of the Old South*, pp. 248–49: "He [McClung] was subject to fits of melancholy, when he would mount his spirited horse Rob Roy, ride to the cemetery, and throw himself upon a grave . . ." (p. 249). General John McGrath, Scrapbook, clipping from Baton Rouge *State-Times*, January 8, 1915, p. 9, LSU.

54. Lonnie J. White, ed., "The Pope-Noland Duel of 1831: An Original Letter of C. F. M. Noland to His Father," *ArkHQ* 22 (Summer 1963): 122–23. On other duels, see Lonnie J. White, "The Fall of Governor John Pope," *ArkHQ* 23 (Spring 1964): 74–84; idem, "The Election of 1827 and the Conway-Crittenden Duel," *ArkHQ* 19 (Winter 1960): 293–313; D. A. Stokes, Jr., "The First State Election in 1836," *ArkHQ* 20 (Summer 1961): 126–50; Diana Sherwood, "The Code Duello in Arkansas," *ArkHQ* 6 (Summer 1947): 186–97. W. Conard Gass, " 'The Misfortune of a High Minded and Honorable Gentleman': W. W. Avery and the Southern Code of Honor," *NCHR* 56 (July 1978): 278–97; discusses in detail the consequences of a fight between Samuel Flemming, a bully, and W. W. Avery, his indicted but acquitted killer, who thereafter suffered from depression and insomnia.

55. Tucker, "Density of Population," in *Essays*, p. 83. On duels see also Williams, *Dueling in the Old South*, with its useful bibliography.

Chapter Fourteen: Honor, Shame, and Justice

1. Michael S. Hindus, "Black Justice under White Law: Criminal Prosecutions of Black in Antebellum South Carolina," *JAH* 63 (December 1976): 575–76; see also Hindus's "Prison and Plantation: Criminal Justice in Nineteenth Century Massachusetts and South Carolina," (Ph.D. diss., University of California, Berkeley, 1975). Like most legally trained historians, Hindus takes "justice" for granted, as if there were some objective standards available in the past that conformed or should have conformed to present-day models. More theoretically interesting is Genovese's *Roll, Jordan, Roll*, pp. 49–70 (quotation from p. 27). Cf. A. E. Keir Nash, "A More Equitable Past? Southern Supreme Courts and the Protection of the Antebellum Negro," *North Carolina Law Review* 48 (February 1970): 197–242, and his other articles, as cited conveniently in Hindus, "Black Justice," 576 n; and Daniel J. Flanigan, "Criminal Procedure in Slave Trials in the Antebellum South," *JSH* 40 (August 1974): 537–64. As Hindus correctly observes, appeals decisions had little impact on local slave justice, especially in the older states, where freeholder and magistrate courts prevailed, in contrast to the newer ones, where juries took slave cases under juridical supervision.

2. The present thesis is a variation on a theme offered in Douglas Hay, "Property, Authority, and the Criminal Law," in Douglas Hay et al., eds., *Albion's Fatal Tree: Crime and Society in Eighteenth-Century England* (New York: Pantheon, 1975), pp. 17 ff. Hay's essay is one of the most truly outstanding examples of interpretive scholarship in many years.

3. See, for example, the very typical remarks of J. Brockenborough in *Commonwealth v. William Carver*, 5 Randolph (26 Va. Reports) at 633 (1828).

4. Rachel O'Connor to David Weeks, January 11, February 2, 17, 1830, Weeks MSS, LSU; for twentieth-century Southern crime figures, see Sheldon Hackney, "Southern Violence," *AHR* 74 (February 1969): 906–25. The 1830s were particularly violent, with slave insurrection scares in the South and street riots in the North. See Richard M. Brown, *Strain of Violence: Historical Studies of American Violence and Vigilantism* (New York: Oxford University Press, 1975), and Leonard J. Richards, *"Gentlemen of Property and Standing": Anti-Abolitionist Mobs in Jacksonian America* (New York: Oxford University Press, 1970). On nineteenth-century inner-city fatalities, see Roger Lane, *Death in the City: Suicide, Accident, and Murder in Nineteenth-Century Philadelphia* (Cambridge: Harvard University Press, 1979), pp. 116–18, 137–38, and table 22, p. 139.

5. Michael S. Hindus, "The Contours of Crime and Justice in Massachusetts and South Carolina, 1767–1878," *AJLH* 30 (July 1977): 218; see also Hindus, "Prison and Plantation," pp. 10, 92, 95, 108; Edward M. Steel, "Criminality in Jeffersonian America—A Sample," *Crime and Delinquency* 18 (April 1972): 150–59, esp. 157; Adams County Criminal Docket, 1829–1841, AdCC. Simple conviction ratios varied widely between Massachusetts and South Carolina: on murder, 72.6% (Mass.) and 50.5% (S.C.); assault, 82.5% (Mass.) and 79.6% (S.C.); riot, etc., 86.6% (Mass.) and 69% (S.C.); but for rape, 59.4% (Mass.) and 63.6% (S.C.). Figures from Michael S. Hindus, *Prison and Plantation: Crime, Justice, and Authority in Massachusetts*

and South Carolina, 1767–1878 (Chapel Hill: University of North Carolina Press, 1980), p. 91; cf. Hindus, "Prison and Plantation," pp. 134–35.

6. Stuart Lottier, "Distribution of Criminal Offenses in Sectional Regions," *Journal of Law and Criminology* 29 (September–October 1938): 329–44; Alvin L. Jacobson, "Crime Trends in Southern and Nonsouthern Cities: A Twenty-Year Perspective," *SF* 54 (September 1975): 226–42; William D. Miller, "Myth and New South Murder Rates," *MQ* 26 (Spring 1973): 143–53; H. C. Brearley, "The Pattern of Violence," in William T. Couch, ed., *Culture in the South* (Chapel Hill: University of North Carolina Press, 1934), pp. 678–92; Thomas S. Fitzgerald, "A Study of Crime in the City of Memphis, Tennessee," *Journal of the American Institute of Criminal Law and Criminology* 19 (August 1928): 1–124; Michael Russell, "Homicide and the Violent Ideal in Atlanta, 1865 to 1890," Paper kindly lent by author. Austin L. Porterfield, "Indices of Suicide and Homicide by States and Cities: Some Southern and Non-Southern Contrasts with Implications for Research," *ASR* 14 (August 1949): 481–90.

7. Bruce, *Violence and Culture;* B. B. Smith quoted in Weld, *Slavery as It Is,* p. 204.

8. [Scotch-Irishman], *The Mountain Whites of the South* (Pittsburgh: Presbyterian Banner, 1893); Tommy W. Rogers, "Origin and Cultural Assimilation of the Population of Louisiana," *MQ* 25 (Winter 1971–72): 45–67; Leyburn, *Scotch-Irish,* pp. 15, 45, 63–70; Moore, *Reminiscences of York,* p. 7; S. S. MacClintock, "Kentucky Mountaineers and their Feuds," parts 1 and 2, *AJS* 7 (July 1901): 1–28 and 7 (September 1901): 171–87; William L. Montell, *The Saga of Coe Ridge* (New York: Harper & Row, 1972); Thomas Henderson, "Moore County," (N.C.), Letterbooks, 1810–11, SHC, UNC; Paul H. Buck, "The Poor Whites of the Ante-Bellum South," *AHR* 31 (October 1925): 41–54.

9. Victor Turner, *Dramas, Fields, and Metaphors: Symbolic Action in Human Society* (Ithaca: Cornell University Press, 1974), pp. 201–2, 274.

10. Wesley Norris interview (1866?) in John Blassingame, ed., *Slave Testimony: Two Centuries of Letters, Speeches, Interviews and Autobiographies* (Baton Rouge: Louisiana State University Press, 1977), p. 467.

11. Lee to Custis Lee, July 2, 1859; in Jones, *Lee,* p. 102; Freeman, *Lee,* 1: 390–93; Myers, *Children of Pride,* pp. 935–39.

12. Beccaria quoted in Hans Speier, *Social Order and the Risks of War: Papers in Political Sociology* (Cambridge: M.I.T. Press, 1969), p. 47.

13. Olmsted, *Cotton Kingdom,* pp. 248–49.

14. Samuel Clark to his mother, August 2, 1845, Russwurm Family MSS, Tennessee Historical Society, at TSA.

15. Fuller, Diary, June 21, 1858, WLCL.

16. (Ivey), "Papers of No Use and Belonging to No Particular File," cab. 6, box 184, AdCC; Davis, *Barrow Diary,* p. 174; Inquest, June 21, 1848, Judge of Probate, Edgefield County, Coroner's Book of Inquisitions, WPA typescript, 43–44, SC, USC.

17. Harry Hammond to James H. Hammond, October [?], 1858, HBC MSS; Rev. C. C. Jones to Mary S. Jones, October 23, 1856, Myers, *Children of Pride,* pp. 255–56; Scarborough, *Ruffin Diary* 1: 110, 114–15, 355–56.

18. Mark Tushnet, "The American Law of Slavery, 1810–1860: A Study in the

Persistence of Legal Autonomy," *L&SR* 10 (Fall 1975): 119–84 is a persuasive discussion of slave law and social change, but others have been guided by prior political positions to some extent. Cf. A. E. Keir Nash, "The Texas Supreme Court and Trial Rights of Blacks, 1845–1860," *JAH* 58 (December 1971): 622–42; idem, "Negro Rights, Unionism, and Greatness on the South Carolina Court of Appeals: The Extraordinary Chief Justice John Belton O'Neall," *South Carolina Law Review* 21, no. 2 (1969): 141–90; idem, "Fairness and Formalism in the Trials of Blacks in the State Supreme Courts of the Old South," *Virginia Law Review* 56 (February 1969): 64–100; Nash, "A More Equitable Past?" pp. 197–242. Daniel J. Flanigan, "Criminal Procedure in Slave Trials in the Antebellum South" *JSH* 40 (November 1974): 537–64, is less sanguine about Southern justice than Nash, but still, like Genovese, *Roll, Jordan, Roll*, pp. 49–70, relics entirely upon appellate decisions.

19. Mississippi high court declaration in *State* v. *Jones*, 1 Walk. (Miss.) 83 (1820). Chaplin, Diary, February 19, 1849, SCHS; Olmsted, *Journey in the Seaboard Slave States* 2: 306.

20. On Sides and Bradshaw, see J. Patterson to Hutchins Burton, June 10, 1827, Gov. Pap., NCDAH; on Simpson case, see Inquest, March 19, 1846, Edgefield County, S.C., WPA typescript, pp. 57–58, SC, USC; on Emett case, see S. Miller to Montfort Stokes, January 5, 1831, Gov. Pap., NCDAH; see also Williams, *Vogues in Villainy*, p. 36.

21. Petition of citizens, March 16, 1858, and Galloway to J. J. Pettus, November 6, 1857, RG 27; J. E. Taliaferro to Pettus, August 21, 1860, ibid., MissDAH. General Charles C. Pinckney to Charles C. Pinckney, Jr., December 6, 1824, Pinckney Family MSS, LC.

22. Colcock, in *Hogg* v. *Keller et al.*, 2 Nott and McCord (S.C.) 113 (1821) at 114. *Land* v. *Johnson and Payne*, November 20, 1819, and *Vaughan* v. *Gardner*, April 16, 1823, Kershaw Dist., Court of Common Pleas (CCP), Journal, SCDAH.

23. Presentment of Grand Jury, Chowan County, North Carolina, April 14, 1836, N.C. Slave Papers, NCDAH; petition (on repeal of a law against teaching slaves to read the Bible), Sumter Dist., 1842, and pet. Abbeville Dist., 1838, with stern rebuttal by Frederick A. Porcher, Leg. Pap., SCDAH; pet. of Robert Bush, free black, to collect blacksmithing debts, denied, Leg. Pap., box 9, 1831, fldr. 1, TSA; John H. Tucker to T. D. Grimké, n.d., [1816], Misc. MSS, SCHS; Ira Berlin, *Slaves without Masters: The Free Negro in the Antebellum South* (New York: Random House, 1974), pp. 229–34.

24. R. F. W. Allston to General D. F. Jamison, December 24, 1858 (typescript), Allston Family MSS, SC, USC.

25. Maria Bryan to Julia A. D. Cumming, December 15, 1829, HBC MSS; see also J. G. Deveaux to Robert M. Deveaux, June 25, 1835, Singleton Family MSS, LC; *State* v. *Gorm*, Spartanburg Dist., CCP, Winter term, 1828, box 3, 1828–37, SCDAH; "Part of a letter of my mother to Uncle John, Sep 4, probably in 1849," Francis Nash MSS, SHC, UNC; *John Robinson* v. *Henry O'Neal*, Chowan County, 1736, N.C. Slavery Pap., NCDAH; Davis, *Barrow Diary*, p. 148.

For planters' reactions to yeoman violence against planters' slaves, see Grand Jury Presentment, Kershaw Dist., November 14, 1808, November 17, 1819; pet., Sumter Dist., December 14, 1807, Grand Jury Presentments, SCDAH; Laurensville (S.C.) *Herald,* May 31, 1850; Genovese, *Roll, Jordan, Roll,* p. 19; Stampp, *Peculiar Institution,* pp. 214–15; William Byrd to Lord Egremont, July 12, 1736, "Byrd Letters," p. 220; Sumter Dist., Pet., December 14, 1802, Grand Jury Presentments, Gen. Assembly, SCDAH.

26. R. F. W. Allston, Diary, January 14, 1860, SC, USC; *State* v. *Benjamin Wilson,* Spartanburg District, CCP, Fall sess., 1837, box 3; *State* v. *James Pamroy & David Eller; State* v. *John A. Harbers; State* v. *James M. Loper,* Barnwell Sess., Journal, 1841–56, 163, 343, SCDAH; *State* v. *James Jameson,* Barren County, Ky., CCP, March term, 1850, (1849–52), microfilm M–346, 293, KyHS. Cases 22 (quotation), 23, 25, Fairfield Dist., Magistrates & Freeholders Cases, 1–26 (1846–51), SC, USC.

27. Norfolk & Portsmouth *Herald,* April 24, 1802; see also Davis, *Barrow Diary,* July 2, 1840, p. 201; William Pratt, Diary, March 6, 1854, UKL; B. F. Thurell case, Lancaster (S.C.) *Ledger,* November 14, 1855; see also *Ledger* [from Pee Dee (S.C.) *Times*], September 5, 1855. Other wife murderers included ones reported in New Orleans *Bee,* May 12, 1828; Benjamin McReynolds, Diary, October 19, 1823, UKL; *Report . . . of the Trial of Thomas Gayner for the Alleged Murder of His Wife* (1810), pamphlet in SC, USC.

28. Pet., Charlotte County, November [?], 1818, (Preston), Gov. Pap., VSL; also, *State* v. *Green,* 4 Strob. (S.C.) 128 (1836). On infanticide, see Philip J. Resnick, "Murder of the Newborn: A Psychiatric Review of Neonaticide," *American Journal of Psychiatry* 126 (April 1970): 1414–20; idem, "Child Murder by Parents: A Psychiatric Review of Filicide," *American Journal of Psychiatry* 125 (September 1969): 77–78. The conditions described by Resnick, a forensic psychiatrist at University Hospitals, Case Western Reserve University, seem exactly opposite to the outward thrust of aggression in Southern mores; infanticide may be motivationally similar to suicide (children being seen as extensions of the self) rather than to stranger homicide. See also Peter C. Hoffer and N. E. H. Hull, *Murdering Mothers: Infanticide in England and New England, 1558–1803* (New York: New York University Press, 1981), pp. 145–64.

29. Quoted in Russell, "Homicide and the Violent Ideal," p. 8.

30. Henry P. Lundsgaarde, *Murder in Space City: A Cultural Analysis of Houston Homicide Patterns* (New York: Oxford University Press, 1977), table X, p. 230.

31. For a case of two brothers-in-law (both outsiders married to sisters) who fought for years, see General William Lenoir to his wife, July 20, 1828, Lenoir Family MSS, SHC, UNC. Husband-killing by wives could result in lynch action. See, for instance, Citizens of Warren County to H. G. Runnels, n. d., 1834, RG 27, MissDAH.

32. On brother versus brother-in-law strife, see for example the Lancaster (S.C.) *Ledger* (from Edgefield *Advertiser*), November 13, 1855; also, Inquest on Boone, November 14, 1855, Judge of Probate, Edgefield County, WPA typescript, pp. 103–4, SC, USC; E. B. Kennon to Rachel Mordecai, "Kennon-Mordecai Letters," VMHB 36 (July 1928): 238. On the relative Southern and Northern figures for affinal murder, cf. John C. Calhoun to Mrs. Floride Calhoun, September 7, 1810, "Calhoun Correspondence," 1: 119–20. Chesnut, *Diary from Dixie,* p. 126.

33. Maria Harford to Julia A. D. Cumming, January 14, 1827; November 14, 1843, HBC MSS. Drew Faust is currently preparing a major biography of James H.

Hammond and discusses these matters thoroughly. I have seen the relevant papers, but owing to archival restriction cannot make full use of the documents. However, see James Spann to Hammond, July 19, 1830; Hammond to Pierce Butler, July 21, September 5, 1831; to Daniel Johnson, December 19, 1831; letterbook, Hammond MSS, SC, USC, all of which are available; and S. A. Townes to G. F. Townes, August 8, 1836; June 22, 1837; G. F. Townes to S. A. Townes, October 7, 1834, Townes MSS, SC, USC. See also lawsuit dispute of William Flower and David Weeks, Flower to O'Connor, May 29, 1828, Weeks Family MSS, LSU. Quotation in Lancaster (S.C.) *Ledger*, November 14, 1855.

On the Jackson case, see the Raleigh *Register*, March 7, 1845; Pet. for Benjamin Bowens to Charles Wickliffe, n.d., box 55, jacket 285, Gov. Pap., KyHS; Pet. for George Broiles, July 18, 1828 (Houston), Gov. Pap., box 2, folder 2, TSA; Thomas P. Taul case, in Huntsville *Democrat* (Ala.), August 28, September 4, 1829.

34. *State* v. *Allen*, box 2, folder 1 (Carroll), Gov. Pap., esp. petition, n.d., (John Kennedy et al.), John A. McKinney to Houston, June 14, 1828; J. Powell to Houston, June 7, 1828; V[alentine] Sevier to Houston, June 7, 1828; J. A. Howard to Houston, June 27, 1828; Samuel Allen, aff., July 20, 1827, TSA. Howell Houston was never convicted of arson; the damaging testimony was restricted to the slave arsonist, so Houston was thereby protected from prosecution himself. On Allen's and Houston's marital connections and on earlier disputes between the pair, see *State* v. *Allen*, July 27, 1825 (Assault and Battery case), in Records of Greene County, Tennessee, Greene County Minutes, XII (1824–25), WPA typescript (1936), p. 86, TSA; Pollyanna Creekmore, ed., "Tennessee Marriage Record Books, III," *Greene County, 1783–1818* (Knoxville: Clinchdale Press, 1965), p. 2.

35. Brady entry in "Biographical Directory of Tennessee General Assembly, 1796–1967, preliminary no. 6, Rutherford County" (typescript), 1967, TSA; *State* v. *Keeble*, 1827, box 2, folder 1 (Carroll), Gov. Pap., TSA.

36. Charles C. Jones, Jr., to the Rev. Charles C. Jones, December 12, 1859, in Myers, *Children of Pride*, p. 546.

37. *Commonwealth* v. *Dick* (property of Charles Briggs), November 19, 1808, Southampton County (Cabell), Gov. Pap., box 157, VSL; *State* v. *Sam (property of Thomas Maxwell)* [c. 1834?], Davie County, Records, "Slaves, Criminal Actions, Wardens of the Poor, 1834–1927," North Carolina Slave Pap., NCDAH.

38. Fuller, Diary, October 16, November 15, 1857, WLCL; Davis, *Barrow Diary*, June 17, 1842, p. 262.

39. *State* v. *Elijah*, January term, 1840, Sup. Court Rec., Middle Tenn. Dist., TSA.

40. *State* v. *Henry*, December term, 1843, 7th Cir., box 71, Sup. Court Rec., Middle Tenn. Dist., TSA. On Gabriel rape case, see *Commonwealth* v. *Baker's Gabriel*, May 28, 1829; *Commonwealth* v. *Kinser's Gabriel*, June 28, 1829 (Giles), Gov. Pap., box 311, VSL. On Kelly-Swint feud, see W. L. Henderson to Montfort Stokes, October 15, 1831 (Stokes), Gov. Pap., NCDAH.

41. William Paley, *The Principles of Moral and Political Philosophy*, 2 vols. (New York: Collins, Keese, 1839) 2: 57; see also Douglas Hay, "Property, Authority, and the Criminal Law," in Hay et al., *Albion's Fatal Tree*, pp. 17, 26.

42. Blackstone, *Commentaries* 4: 17.

43. *Yazoo Banner* (Benton, Miss.), June 28, 1839.

44. Perry, Diary, April 9, 1836, SHC, UNC.

45. Quoted by Taylor, *Ante-Bellum South Carolina*, p. 42.

46. On the Tippett case, see Pet. to Hutchins Burton, April 7, 1827 (Burton), Gov. Pap., NCDAH. Hay, "Property, Authority and Criminal Law," pp. 56–63; Friedman, *History of American Law*, pp. 133–34.

47. Quotation from Davis, *Recollections of Mississippi*, p. 103. At a seminar at the Davis Center at Princeton the question of the legitimacy of challenges to the array or quashing of *venire* arose, leading me to investigate the matter more thoroughly. I am indebted to William L. Marbury, attorney at Piper & Marbury, Baltimore, for a thorough investigation of the issue as it developed in the Mississippi courts. He affirms the common-law tradition behind such pleas and is impressed, as I am, with the quality of the legal minds who drew up, pondered, and decided the complicated issues involved. See Marbury to Wyatt-Brown, memorandum, December 12, 1977, 1–12, in my possession; and Blackstone, *Commentaries*, 3: 349–85; 4: 352; *Byrd v. State*, 1 How. (2 Miss.) 163 (1834); *Shaffer v. State*, 1 How. (2 Miss.) 238 (1835); *Stevens & Pillet v. Richer*, 2 How. (3 Miss.) 522 (1837); *Woodsides v. State*, 2 How. (3 Miss.) 655 (1837). There is no modern study of the common law in Southern jurisprudence, but see William E. Nelson, *Americanization of the Common Law: The Impact of Legal Change on Massachusetts Society, 1760–1830* (Cambridge: Harvard University Press, 1975).

48. Quotation from *State v. Byrd*, 1 How. (2 Miss.) 163 (1834) at 181–82. Byrd was not convicted until a third trial, Seargent S. Prentiss assisting the prosecutor. On this case see also Foote, *Casket*, p. 204.

49. Rothman, *Discovery of the Asylum*; E. Bruce Thompson, "Reforms in the Penal System of Mississippi, 1820–1850," *JMH* 7 (January 1945): 51–74; Jack K. Williams, "Crime and Punishment in Alabama, 1819–1840," *AR* 6 (January 1953): 14–30; Waddy W. Moore, "Some Aspects of Crime and Punishment on the Arkansas Frontier," *ArkHQ* 23 (Spring 1964): 50–64. A thorough study of regional penal reforms is needed.

50. Clearly in Pet., October 6, 1825, Penal Pap., SCDAH. See also Salisbury (N.C.) *Western Carolinian*, July 25, 1820; Raleigh *Register*, April 7, 1946; Alice M. Earle, *Curious Punishments of Bygone Days* (Rutland, Vt.: Charles E. Tuttle, 1972); and Friedman, *History of American Law*, p. 517.

51. B. Branch to James P. Preston (Cobbs), February 3, 1818, box 243, Gov. Pap. (Preston), VSL; Howard Owens to McMinn, October 28, 1816 (Ellis Thomas); Thomas Ridley to McMinn (Aaron Gladden), March 10, 1816; Anderson Cheatham to McMinn, December 1, 1816 (Uriah Medlock); Hardy Weems to H. G. "Reynolds" [sic, Runnels] January 29, 1834; C. Farish to J. J. Pettus, February 6, 1860 (Solomon Morgan), Gov. Pap., MissDAH. See also Convict Record Book, RG 25, ser. 7, vol. 45, 1831–42, TSA for similar examples.

52. See various descriptions of inmates in Convict Record Book, RG 25, ser. 7, vol. 45, 1831–42, TSA; also A. V. Brown, chairman of Judiciary Committee, Report, 1831, Leg. Pap., Misc., TSA. Gerald W. Mullin, *Flight and Rebellion: Slave Resistance in Eighteenth Century Virginia* (New York: Oxford University Press, 1972), pp. 62, 80, 141, 147, 185 n36.

53. Phelps to Runnels, March 11, 1843, RG 27, MissDAH; Henry S. Foote, *The Bench and Bar of the South and Southwest* (St. Louis: Soule, Thomas & Wentworth, 1876), p. 34.

54. Eric J. Hobsbawm, *Primitive Rebels* (New York: W. W. Norton, 1959), presents the thesis that bad men as heroes represented "prepolitical" resentment by the poor of the rich. Phelps's claim to being a benefactor to the poor in Robin Hood fashion would seem to support the Marxian interpretation. Actually, however, it was the common admiration for primitive manliness that accounts for the awe and excitement surrounding figures such as Phelps and Jesse James. The free spirit of the criminal was hated, feared, and venerated.

55. Andrew A. Lipscomb and Albert E. Bergh, eds., *The Writings of Thomas Jefferson*, 20 vols. (Washington: Thomas Jefferson Memorial Association, 1904–5), 1: 221–22. Randolph to James P. Garnett, May 27, 1811, letterbook, Randolph MSS, LC.

56. See Bertram Wyatt-Brown, "Barn Burning and Other Snopesian Crimes," in Burton and McMath, *Southern Community* (forthcoming). Some themes and language in that essay have been incorporated into this chapter, with the permission of Greenwood Press and the editors.

Chapter Fifteen: Policing Slave Society

1. Rachel O'Connor to David Weeks, July 11, 1829, Weeks MSS, LSU. On an anti-insurrectionary frenzy in New York, see Daniel Horsmanden, *The New York Conspiracy; or, The History of the Negro Plot* . . . (Boston: Beacon, 1972); Ferenc M. Szasz, "The New York Slave Revolt of 1741: A Re-Examination," *New York History* 28 (July 1967): 215–30. On Louisiana, see Jack D. L. Holmes, "The Abortive Slave Revolt at Pointe Coupee, Louisiana, 1795," *LH* 11 (Fall 1970): 341–62; and Tommy R. Young, II, "The United States Army and the Institution of Slavery in Louisiana, 1803–1815," *Louisiana Studies* 3 (Fall 1974): 201–22. On the Stono Rebellion, see Peter H. Wood, *Black Majority: Negroes in Colonial South Carolina* . . . (New York: W. W. Norton, 1974). On North Carolina, see *State v. Duke, Cuff & Arthur*, May 3, 1798, Bertie County, North Carolina Slave Papers, NCDAH. Jeffrey J. Crow, "Slave Rebelliousness and Social Conflict in North Carolina, 1775 to 1802," *WMQ*, 3d ser. 37 (January 1980): 89–90, agrees that maroons did not constitute in themselves a major source of general revolt. But it should be added that they did represent a point of departure and example.

2. See Eugene D. Genovese, "The Treatment of Slaves in Different Countries: Problems in the Application of the Comparative Method," in Laura Foner and Eugene D. Genovese, eds., *Slavery in the New World*, (Englewood Cliffs, N.J.: Prentice-Hall, 1969), pp. 202–10, and other essays.

3. Genovese, *Roll, Jordan, Roll;* see also Raymond A. Bauer and Alice H. Bauer, "Day to Day Resistance to Slavery," *JNH* 27 (October 1942): 388–419; George M. Fredrickson and Christopher Lasch, "Resistance to Slavery," in Ann J. Lane, ed., *The Debate over 'Slavery'* (Urbana: University of Illinois Press, 1971), pp. 233–244, and other essays; George P. Rawick, *From Sundown to Sunup: The Making of the Black Community* (Westport, Conn.: Greenwood Press, 1972), pp. 95–121;

Kenneth M. Stampp, "Rebels and Sambos: The Search for the Negro's Personality in Slavery," *JSH* 27 (August 1971): 367–92. Compare, however, Genovese, *Roll, Jordan, Roll,* with his *From Rebellion to Freedom: Afro-American Slave Revolts in the Making of the Modern World* (Baton Rouge: Louisiana State University Press, 1979).

4. James Monroe to General Assembly, January 16, 1802, box 119, Gov. Pap., VSL; Richard Wade, *Slavery in the Cities: The South, 1820–1860* (New York: Oxford University Press, 1964), pp. 226–42, 250–52; Eugene D. Genovese, "The Slave States in North America," in David W. Cohen and Jack P. Greene, eds., *Neither Slave Nor Free* (Baltimore: Johns Hopkins University Press, 1972), pp. 258–77.

5. Byrd to Mr. Beckford, December 6, 1735, "Byrd Letters," p. 122; Withers to James Chesnut, August 19, 1848, Manning-Chesnut-Williams MSS, SC, USC.

6. Sarah Hicks Williams to Sarah and Samuel Hicks, October 10, 1858, in Bonner. "Plantation Experiences of a New York Woman," p. 389; Scarborough, *Ruffin Diary,* February 27, 1861, pp. 556–57. During the Civil War, though, fear of black passion against owners grew apace. See Woodward, *Chesnut's Civil War,* September 21, 24, October 7, 1861, pp. 198–99, 208–12.

7. Georges Lefebvre, *The Great Fear of 1789,* Joan White, trans. (New York: Vintage, 1973); John Brewer and John Styles, eds., *An Ungovernable People: The English and Their Law in the Seventeenth and Eighteenth Centuries* (New Brunswick: Rutgers University Press, 1979); and Lawrence Stone's review in *NYRB,* May 29, 1980, pp. 45–46; Norman Cohn, *The Pursuit of the Millennium* (New York: Oxford University Press, 1970).

8. Friedman, *History of American Law,* p. 63; Harold Garfinkel, "Conditions of Successful Degradation Ceremonies," *AJS* 61 (January 1956): 420–24; Kai T. Erikson, *Wayward Puritans: A Study on the Sociology of Deviance* (New York: John Wiley & Sons, 1966); Howard S. Becker, *The Outsiders: Studies in the Sociology of Deviance* (New York: Free Press, 1964), pp. 8–9; and John T. Kitsuse, "Notes on the Sociology of Deviance," in Howard S. Becker, ed., *The Other Side: Perspectives on Deviance* (New York: Free Press, 1964), pp. 9–21; Emile Durkheim, *The Rules of Sociological Method,* Sarah A. Solovay and John H. Mueller, trans.; George E. G. Catlin, ed. (New York: Free Press, 1964), p. 70.

9. Thomas C. Parramore, "The Great Slave Conspiracy," *The State* 39 (August 15, 1971): 7–10, 19; Freehling, *Prelude to Civil War,* pp. 25–48; Harvey Wish, "American Slave Insurrections before 1861," *JNH* 22 (July 1937): 299–310; Eric Foner, ed., *Nat Turner* (Englewood Cliffs, N.J.: Prentice-Hall, 1971), pp. 9–10; Mullins, *Flight and Rebellion,* pp. 124–39, 194–95; Herbert Aptheker, *American Negro Slave Revolts* (New York: International, 1974); *Virginia Gazette* (Richmond), January 12, February 16, May 29, 1802; Frank A. Cassell, "Slaves of the Chesapeake Bay Area and the War of 1812," *JNH* 34 (January 1949): 144–55; Bertram Wyatt-Brown, "The Abolitionists' Postal Campaign of 1835," *JNH* 50 (October 1965): 227–38; John Hartwell Cocke, Journal, January 1, 1857, Shields Deposit, UVa; Laurence Shore, "Making Mississippi Safe for Slavery: The Insurrection Panic of 1835," in Burton and McMath, *Southern Community.*

10. Dan T. Carter, "The Christmas Day Insurrectionary Scare of 1865," *JSH* 42 (August 1976): 345–64; William W. Rogers and Robert D. Ward, *August Reckon-*

ing: Jack Turner and Racism in Post-Civil War Alabama (Baton Rouge: Louisiana State University Press, 1973); James H. Inverarity, "Populism and Lynching in Louisiana, 1889–1896: A Test of Erikson's Theory of the Relationship between Boundary Crises and Repressive Justice," *ASR* 41 (April 1976): 262–80; and Ira M. Wasserman, Whitney Pope, and Charles Ragin, "Southern Violence and the Political Process," in *ASR* 42 (April 1977): 359–69; William I. Hair, *Carnival of Fury: Robert Charles and the New Orleans Riot of 1900* (Baton Rouge: Louisiana State University Press, 1976).

11. On brutalized slaves, see *DeBow's Review* 25 (July 1858): 51; John Blassingame, *The Slave Community: Plantation Life in the Antebellum South* (New York: Oxford University Press, 1979), p. 245.

12. Curtis, Diary, September 24, 1831, SHC, UNC.

13. Frank Carr to William Wirt, January 19, 1802, box 119, Gov. Pap. VSL.

14. [T. Hamilton], *The Late Contemplated Insurrection in Charleston, S.C. with the Execution of Thirty-Six of the Patriots* . . . (New York: n.p., 1850), p. 7; Richard C. Wade, "The Vesey Plot: A Reconsideration," *JSH* 30 (May 1964): 159–60; see also "A Colored American," in Robert S. Starobin, ed., *Denmark Vesey: The Slave Conspiracy of 1822* (Englewood Cliffs, N.J.: Prentice-Hall, 1970), pp. 168–69, also 209–42; *Southern Patriot* (Charleston), September 12, 1822, on sumptuary-custom violations by prosperous skilled blacks.

15. Davis, *Barrow Diary*, January 31, 1842, p. 250; Olmsted, *Cotton Kingdom*, p. 329; see also James R. Hamilton, Jr., Charleston mayor, in Starobin, *Vesey*, p. 97; Crow, "Slave·Rebelliousness," pp. 95–98; Scott Strickland, "Religion and African American Cultural Change: South Carolina, 1800–1865," paper presented Organization of American Historians, 1979, and idem, "Social Order and Slave Insurrection Panics: The Albemarle Sound Region of North Carolina, 1802," kindly lent by the author. Richard W. Byrd to John Tyler, May 30, 1810, box 166, Gov. Pap. (Tyler), VSL.

16. Donald G. Morgan, *Justice William Johnson, The First Dissenter: The Career and Constitutional Philosophy of a Jeffersonian Judge* (Columbia: University of South Carolina Press, 1954), pp. 137–39; [William Johnson], "Communication: Melancholy Effect of Popular Excitement," in Charleston *Courier,* June 21, 1822, and J. Hamilton, "To the Public" [a rejoinder to Johnson's article], in *Southern Patriot* (Charleston), June 22, 1822; see also, for Johnson's communication, Starobin, *Vesey*, pp. 67–70; and also Anna Hayes Johnson to Elizabeth E. W. Haywood, July 24, 1822, Ernest Haywood MSS, SHC, UNC. On dangers of insurrection in holiday seasons, see Calvin Jones to Montfort Stokes, December 28, 1830 (quotation), Gov. Pap. (Stokes), NCDAH; Robert Burton et al. to John Tyler, December 17, 1808; to answer this petition from Albemarle County, the Virginia lieutenant governor prepared a draft proclamation (December 19, 1808) for increased militia and slave patrol vigilance during the Christmas holidays. The governor's executive council, however, rejected dissemination of the proclamation, according to the Minutes of December 20, 1808, because of fear of exciting "unnecessary alarms" and stimulating an active "spirit of insurrection among the slaves." See box 158, Gov. Pap. (Tyler), VSL, for these documents.

17. *Southern Patriot* (Charleston), September 12, 1822. The author complained that he had lately met a return to the old pattern of black "impudence" whereas

"a few short weeks before" when the memory of executions was still fresh, blacks had been uncommonly deferential.

18. General John Reddick to Benjamin Williams, June 18, 1802, Gov. Pap. (Williams), NCDAH; Thomas Matthews, March 11; Richard Jones, January 2, 1802; E. Green, n.d., all to Monroe, box 120, Gov. Pap., VSL; Monroe to General Assembly, January 16, 1802, executive letterbook, VSL.

19. See Bertie County, North Carolina Slavery Pap. County Rec. NCDAH; see also Court of Oyer and Terminer, Nottoway County, January 7, 1802, in *CVSP* 9: 271–73 (not always accurate). Cf. Aptheker, *American Negro Slave Revolts*, and the error-filled Joseph C. Carroll, *Slave Insurrections in the United States, 1800–1865* (Boston: Chapman and Grimes, 1938), pp. 57–70.

20. John Burgywn to John Owen, November 30, 1830, executive letterbook (Owen), NCDAH; affidavit, Frances McDougle, July 16, 1821, box 268, Gov. Pap. (Pleasants), VSL.

21. Thomas Shackelford, Esq., *Proceedings of the Citizens of Madison County, Mississippi at Livingston in July 1835* . . . (Jackson: Mayson & Smoot, 1836), pp. 3–4, 5; see also Howard, *History of Virgil A. Stewart*, pp. 221–62; Colonel Christopher Tompkins to W. B. Giles, July 18, 1829, box 311, Gov. Pap. (Giles), VSL; Penick, *Great Western Land Pirate*, pp. 109–10.

22. *Commonwealth v. Tom and Glasgow*, Hanover County, April 29, 1802; quotation in John Mason, John Newell, William Fleet, et al., pet., May 2, 1802, box 122, Gov. Pap.; and deed of trust, Benjamin Pollard, August 26, 1802, Auditor's Records, VSL.

23. J. C. Cabell to John Hartwell Cocke, October 4, 1831; Cocke to Cabell, October 7, 1831, John Hartwell Cocke MSS, UVa; see also Cocke to Cabell, October 29, 1831, ibid.; Archibald Stuart to Cabell, January 16, 1832, J. C. Cabell MSS, UVa; Cocke to Sally Cocke, March 4, 1832, Shields Deposit, UVa; John C. Ehringham to R. R. Gurley, September 29, 1831, American Colonization Society MSS, LC.

24. Curtis, Diary, September 9, 10, 12, 1831, SHC, UNC; see also William Preston to Arthur Campbell, April 29, 1812, Campbell-Preston MSS, LC; Elizabeth Beverley Kennon to Lady Skipwith, June 9, 1810, Kennon MSS, VHS. Tennessee planter quoted by Eugene D. Genovese, "The Slave States of North America," in Cohen and Greene, *Neither Slave nor Free*, p. 275. See also Charles B. Dew, "Black Ironworkers and the Slave Insurrection Panic of 1856," *JSH* 41 (August 1975): 321–38, esp. 337–38.

25. Cocke, Journal, January 1, 1857, Shields Deposit, UVa. "To the Speakers of the House of Delegates, and of the Senate," December 7, 1801, in *The Writings of James Monroe* . . . , Stanislau H. Hamilton, ed., 7 vols. (New York: G. P. Putnam's Sons, 1900) 3: 311–12, also pp. 329, 345. Aptheker estimates that the Gabriel plot repression also cost the state over $14,000 in compensation to masters for convicted slaves: *American Negro Slave Revolts*, p. 233 n49.

26. John Price to John Floyd, September 21, 1831, box 321, Gov. Pap. (Floyd), VSL; Thomas H. Bayly to Monroe, January 30, 1802, *CVSP* 9: 277 and similar letters, 9: 278, 288, 297, 303. "An Old Citizen of Portsmouth" to Floyd, October 6, 1831, box 321, Gov. Pap. (Floyd), VSL.

27. Monroe to Jefferson, April 25, 1802, in *Writings of James Monroe* 3: 341.

28. Benjamin Williams to Charles Grandy et al., May 17, 1802, executive letter-book, Gov. Pap. (Williams), NCDAH; Governor's Message no. 2 to South Carolina Legislature, January 14, 1822, doc. A, 1822–24, pp. 1–28, SCDAH. Freehling, *Prelude to Civil War*, pp. 54 n6, 59–61, believes that no more than eighty slaves, Bennett's figures, were involved in South Carolina. Even that number may be too high.

29. Samuel Sawyer, encl. T. J. Haskins to Thomas Ruffin, September 2, 1831, Thomas Ruffin MSS, SHC, UNC; on Ruel Blake, see Shore, "Making Mississippi Safe"; Penick, *Great Western Land Pirate*, pp. 112, 124, 134–38.

30. Patrick Sharkey and James B. Kilbourn to Hiram G. Runnels, July 7, 1835, RG 27, Gov. Pap., MissDAH; *Yazoo Banner* (Benton, Miss.), July 26, 1839. Other communications to Runnels: William S. Jones, July 11, 1835; George Wyem, July 8, Patrick Sharkey, July 7; pet. from Vicksburg, July 10, 1835; and Runnels, Proclamation, July 13, 1835, all RG 27, Gov. Pap., MissDAH. Ruffin quoted in Mitchell, *Edmund Ruffin*, pp. 33–34.

31. B. Field to David Robertson, March 19, 1802, box 120, Gov. Pap., VSL.

32. James Wright, dep. to John G. Hill, magistrate, November 16, 1831, and other papers, Duplin County, North Carolina Slave Pap., NCDAH. Approximately forty slaves were either executed or deported during the 1802 Virginia panic, but the figure does not account for lynch-law action.

33. *Commonwealth* v. *Patrick and Cato*, Caroline County, March term, 1802, box 123; Thomas Oliver to Monroe, May 4, 1802, box 123; *Commonwealth* v. *Dick*, October 17, 1802, box 122, Gov. Pap., VSL.

34. *Commonwealth* v. *Randall and Cudge*, Isle of Wight County, September 6, 1802, box 122, Gov. Pap., VSL.

35. Henry Miller, Jr. to Joseph Desha, December 24, 1824, box 33, pardons, Gov. Pap. (Desha), KyHS; see also William J. Graves (quotation) to Desha, June 3, 1825, ibid.; *Commonwealth* v. *John*, Halifax County, April 19, 1802, box 123, Gov. Pap., VSL.

36. Bennett to Leg., August 10, 1822, printed doc., Gov. Pap., SCDAH. On slave-written documents, see Thomas Newton to Monroe, May 14, 1802; "White Pepil" (anon. letter), box 121, Gov. Pap. VSL; "Colerain" letter, reprinted Raleigh *Register*, July 6, 1802; "Negro Letter," Bertie County, N.C. Slave Pap.; William Williams to Gen. Stephen W. Carney, June 5, 1802; John Folk to Williams, June 6, 1802, Slave Pap., Misc. MSS, NCDAH. Some of these items were kindly supplied in copy form by Jeffrey J. Crow. E. P. Thompson, "The Crime of Anonymity," in Hay et al., *Albion's Fatal Tree*, explains the meaning of such documents: "The anonymous threatening letter is a characteristic form of social protest in any society which has crossed a certain threshold of literacy, in which forms of collective organized defence are weak, and in which individuals who can be identified as the organizers of protest are liable to immediate victimization." See pp. 255 and 255–344. Some of the letters in the 1802 rebellion scare in North Carolina and Virginia seem to have been written by blacks who fit Thompson's description. See particularly "White Pepil," cited above, which was written after Jerry Cornick's hanging (see account to follow). Other letters of prospective rebellion, however, may have been white men's work, as in the Jack Turner affair

of 1881. See Rogers and Ward, *August Reckoning;* and also Starobin, *Vesey,* p. 68.
37. See Starobin, *Vesey,* introduction, pp. 1–9 and passim, for the classic rejoinder to this argument, but it is not wholly convincing. A double standard is used. Postwar rape trials (Scottsboro, for instance) were palpably unfair and quite rightly mocked for being so. Yet supposedly by the same standards of justice and rigorous scholarly examination of evidence, insurrection trials presented in antebellum courts are presented as meeting the full criteria of historical verification when some historians review the proceedings. Crow, "Slave Rebelliousness," p. 86, cites the 1775 scare in which "considerable ammunition" was found. Individual slaves were also discovered to have guns in their possession (see John Folk to Benjamin Williams, June 6, 1802, North Carolina Slavery Pap., Misc. MSS, NCDAH). But in the first instance it is likely that maroons would obtain guns for their own protection and use but not necessarily to arouse the general slave populace, and in the second, that slaves in so violent a society would surreptitiously take possession of guns for personal defense and for hunting, but, again, not necessarily for widespread revolt. Rumors of large caches of arms abounded, of course, but seldom if ever, were they directly linked to those on trial and used as evidence of rebellion.
38. *Commonwealth* v. *Arthur,* Henrico County May 17, 1802, box 122; interview with Lewis, Nottoway jail, May 5, 1802, box 120: "I would not confess these things to no man under heaven or on earth if I did not expect to die. . . . I have given my life to you in that [confession] . . . and thousands of your Colour . . . I hope you white people may do well." Arthur, dep., May 17, 1802, box 121; E. Green to Monroe, n.d., box 120; P. Randolph to Monroe, May 8, 1802, box 120; Grief Green to Monroe, May 7, 1802, box 120; Monroe to Grief Green, May 1, June 5, 1802, executive letterbook (microfilm); William Rose to Monroe, encl. affidavits, May 17, 1802, box 121; Monroe to Colonel P. Goodwyn, June 19, 1802, box 121, Gov. Pap., VSL.
39. E.g., Aptheker, *American Negro Slave Revolts;* Genovese, *From Resistance to Revolt.*
40. *Commonwealth* v. *Ingraham's`Ned,* Norfolk County, Magistrates' Court, May 17, 1802, box 123, Gov. Pap., VSL.
41. Thomas Newton, Norfolk's Congressman, also thought Jerry Cornick was innocent: see Newton to Monroe, May 7, 1802; William Neusom to Monroe, May 19, 1802; George McIntosh to Monroe, May 19, 1802; Jerry's confession, May 2, 1802; Gov. Pap., VSL; McIntosh to John Y. Mason, November 25, 1848, John Y. Mason MSS, WMC. On McIntosh's biography, see "Slave Owners, Princess Anne County, 1810," *Lower Norfolk South Virginia Antiquary,* no. 1, pt. 3 (1895), p. 77; see also *WMQ,* 1st ser. 4 (July 1898): 110; "Genealogical Chart of Walke Family," *VMHB* 5 (July 1897): 88; "Slaveholders in Princess Anne County," *WMQ,* 1st ser. 2 (January 1894): 147; George McIntosh, Deed book 29, Princess Anne County, p. 49, book 31, August 3, 1811, Princess Anne County, p. 243 (microfilm), VSL; Norfolk and Portsmouth *Herald,* January 14, 1802 (advertisement); Sadie S. Kellam, "Cornick Family Genealogy," Kellam Family MSS, VHS.
42. Minute book, Norfolk County, May 17, 1802 (microfilm), VSL; copy in box 123, Gov. Pap. VSL; McIntosh to Monroe, May 19, 1802, ibid.

43. McIntosh to Monroe, May 19, 1802; *Commonwealth v. Ingraham's Ned,* May 17, 1802, box 123, Gov. Pap. VSL. On Boush's slaveholding, see "Slaveholders in Princess Anne," p. 147.

44. McIntosh to Monroe, May 19, 1802, box 123; James Bennett and McIntosh to Monroe, May 7, 1802, box 120, VSL. On Jarvis at courthouse, see Norfolk County, March 15, 1802, minute book #7, 1801-3 (microfilm), VSL.

45. "Concerning reprieve to Jeremiah & Ned, Advice," May 24, 1802; Monroe to Thomas Newton, May 12; to John Cowper, May 12, 1802; Cowper to Monroe, May 3, 18, 1802; Remonstrance, May 19, 1802, all in box 123; Monroe to Sheriff, Norfolk County, July 12, 1802, executive letterbook (microfilm), VSL.

46. Cowper to Monroe, June 1, 1802, box 121; Monroe to McIntosh, May 27, 1802, executive letterbook (microfilm), VSL.

47. Benjamin W. S. Cabell to John Floyd, October 6, 19, 1831, Gov. Pap., VSL; Jackson *Mississippian,* July 17, 1835; William Couper to William Couper, April 12, August 19, October 11, 1802, William Couper MSS, VHS.

48. Jeremiah to McIntosh, May 2, 1802 box 120, Gov. Pap., VSL.

Chapter Sixteen: Charivari and Lynch Law

1. Mark Twain, *Adventures of Huckleberry Finn,* Henry Nash Smith, ed. (Boston: Houghton Mifflin, 1958), pp. 119-24.

2. Thomas D. Clark, *The Southern Country Editor* (Indianapolis: Bobbs Merrill, 1948), p. 227; Brown, *Strain of Violence,* pp. 215-17; Howard, *History of Virgil A. Stewart,* p. 268; see also Michael P. Dougan, *Confederate Arkansas: The People and Politics of a Frontier State in Wartime* (University: University of Alabama Press, 1976), p. 5; Victor Turner, *The Forest of Symbols: Aspects of Ndembu Ritual* (Ithaca: Cornell University Press, 1981); see also Shaw, *American Patriots and Rituals of Revolution,* pp. 227-28, from which this discussion is largely derived.

3. *Langdon W. Moore: His Own Story of His Life* (Boston: private printing, 1893), p. 487; Brown, *Strain of Violence,* p. 173.

4. Foote, *Casket,* pp. 256-58.

5. C. Vann Woodward, *Tom Watson, Agrarian Rebel* (New York: Oxford University Press, 1963), pp. 437-50; Walter White, *Rope and Faggot* (New York: Arno, 1969), p. 172.

6. Violet Alford, "Rough Music or Charivari," *Folklore* 70 (December 1959): 505-18, esp. 505. Plutarch, *Moralia,* F. C. Babbitt, trans. (Cambridge: Harvard University Press, 1962), p. 177 [291 F]; see illustrations in Natalie Z. Davis, "The Reasons of Misrule: Youth Groups and Charivaris in Sixteenth-Century France," *Past and Present,* no. 50 (February 1971), illustration between pp. 56 and 57; Theo Brown, "The 'Stag Hunt' in Devon," *Folklore* 43 (June 1952): 104-9.

7. See K. J. Dover, *Greek Homosexuality* (Cambridge: Harvard University Press, 1978); Lidell, Scott, Jones, *Greek Lexicon:* "bepitched pathics" (*kinaidoi pepittokopemenoi*) were effeminized males of cowardly bearing—the pitch being used to remove surface hair. This reference has been very kindly supplied by Professor Donald Laing, Classics Department, Case Western Reserve University.

8. P. V. Glob, *The Bog People: Iron-Age Man Preserved*, Rupert Bruce-Mitford, trans. (New York: Ballantine, 1971), pp. 98, 103–32; Tacitus, *Germania*, pp. 116–18, passim.

9. Julian Pitt-Rivers, *The People of the Sierra* (Chicago: University of Chicago Press, 1954), pp. 169–77; Alford, "Rough Music," p. 508; Clement Eaton, "Mob Violence in the Old South," *MVHR* 29 (December 1942): 351–70.

10. See Thomas Rymer, *Foedara, Conventiones, Literae* . . . , 20 vols. (London: A. & J. Churchill, 1704–35) 1: 65: "Charta Richardi Regis Angliae de Statutis illorum qui mare ituri erant." William Andrews, *Old-Time Punishments* (Hull, Eng.: Wm. Andrew, 1890), pp. 193–96.

11. T. F. Grimké, *The South-Carolina Justice of the Peace* . . . (Philadelphia: R. Aithen & Son, 1796), p. 523.

12. E. K. Chambers, *The Medieval Stage*, 2 vols. (London: Oxford University Press, 1903) 1: 274–335; Robert Tallant, *The Romantic New Orleanians* (New York: Dutton, 1950), p. 123; Shaw, *American Patriots and Rituals of Revolution*, p. 204.

13. Davis, "Reasons of Misrule," *Past and Present*, no. 50 (February 1971), pp. 43, 55; Harnett T. Kane, *Queen New Orleans: City by the River* (New York: Morrow, 1949), p. 338; Herbert Asbury, *The French Quarter: An Informal History of the New Orleans Underworld* (New York: Knopf, 1936), p. 141.

14. Curtis, Diary, December 25, 1830, SHC, UNC. See also Newbell N. Puckett, *The Magic and Folk Beliefs of the Southern Negro* (New York: Dover, 1960), pp. 180–83; Lawrence W. Levine, *Black Culture and Black Consciousness: Afro-American Folk Thought from Slavery to Freedom* (New York: Oxford University Press, 1977), p. 56. Levine says almost nothing about black forms of charivari and skims over voodoo with barely a word. One must suspect, however, that conjure doctors used some kind of herbs with hallucinogenic effects that whites, observing the rituals associated with voodoo, considered to be both poisonous and subversive. On efforts to prevent these practices, including charivari, from stimulating slave revolts, see Kane, *Queen New Orleans*, p. 333. Much historical work is needed in this area of black life.

15. Randolph, *Ozarks*, pp. 57–58; see also William H. Haney, *The Mountain People of Kentucky* (Cincinnati: Robert Clarke, 1906), pp. 54–56; and Richard and Eva Blum, *The Dangerous Hour: The Lore of Crisis and Mystery in Rural Greece* (London: Chatto & Windus, 1970), pp. 17–19. Fallon's wedding described in John F. Darby, *Personal Recollections* (St. Louis: G. I. Jones, 1880), pp. 146–48.

16. Gouge quoted in Sharpe, "Defamation and Sexual Slander," p. 20.

17. Max Gluckman, "Gossip and Scandal," *Current Anthropology* 4 (June 1963): 307–16; Robert Paine, "What is Gossip About?: An Alternative Hypothesis," *Man* 2 (June 1967): 278–85; Peter J. Wilson, "Filcher of Good Names: An Enquiry into Anthropology and Gossip," *Man* 9 (March 1974): 93–102. Greer L. Fox, " 'Nice Girl': Social Control of Women through a Value Construct," *Signs* 2 (Summer 1977): 805–17. Americans never used the English brank or iron muzzle for compulsive gossippers—see Earle, *Curious Punishments of Bygone Days*, pp. 96–105—but the ducking stool was rather common in the seventeenth century, both in Northern and Southern colonies; see ibid., pp. 11–28, for an instrument designed for "slanderers, 'makebayts,' 'chyderers,' " and others, including wife-

beaters. See also Russell P. Dobash and R. Emerson Dobash, "Community Response to Violence against Wives: Charivari, Abstract Justice and Patriarchy," *Social Problems* 28 (June 1981): 563–81; Elizabeth Pleck, "Wife Beating in Nineteenth-Century America," *Victimology*, 4 (Fall 1979): 60–74.

18. On the Creole charivari, see Harnett T. Kane, *The Bayous of Louisiana* (New York: Morrow, 1943), 308–11; Asbury, *French Quarter*, 116–17 (quotation). On English charivari, see E. P. Thompson, " 'Rough Music': Le Charivari anglais," *Annales E.S.C.* 27 (March–April 1972): 285–312; on American "shivarees," see, C. L. Fernald, in *American Notes and Queries* 1 (October 13, 1888): 288; "S. S. R." and A. F. Chamberlain, in ibid., 1 (September 29, 1888): 263–64; Miles I. Hanley, " 'Serenade' in New England," *American Speech* 8 (No. 2 1933): 24–26, Mamie Meredith, " 'Billing the Bridal Couple' in Pioneer Days," ibid., pp. 22–24; Maurice Moore, "Reminiscences of York District, South Carolina," reprint, pp. 16–17, copy in LC.

19. Randolph, *Ozarks*, p. 55, on the girl driven out of the Arkansas settlement. Shorter, *Making of the Modern Family*, pp. 218–27. Enid Porter, *Cambridgeshire Customs and Folklore* (London: Routledge & Kegan Paul, 1969), pp. 8–10; Christina Hole, *English Folklore* (London: Botsford, 1940), pp. 23–25, both offering twentieth-century English examples. On the phenomenon of permitted premarital pregnancy, see Campbell, *Southern Highlander and His Homeland*, p. 132; and Randolph, *Ozarks*, pp. 57–60. Ely Green, *Ely: Too Black, Too White*, Elizabeth N. Chitty and Arthur Ben Chitty, eds. (Amherst: University of Massachusetts Press, 1970), p. 127. Herbert G. Gutman, *The Black Family in Slavery and Freedom, 1750–1925* (New York: Knopf, 1976), pp. 61–67, 78–79.

20. Charles C. Alexander, *The Ku Klux Klan in the Southwest* (Lexington: University of Kentucky Press, 1966), pp. 63–64; quotation, p. 34. *Attakapas Gazetteer* and St. Mary, St. Martin, and LaFayette *Advertiser*, April 26, 1834, from Westfield (Mass.), *Journal*.

21. Stone, *Family, Sex, and Marriage*, pp. 375, 503–4; Charlotte *Journal* in Hillsborough *Recorder*, March 28, 1845.

22. Quoted in Weld, *Slavery as It Is*, pp. 208–9.

23. O'Connor to Weeks, July 11, 1829, Weeks MSS, LSU.

24. William D. Valentine, Diary, April 3, 5, 8, 1838, SHC, UNC.

25. Gene A. Sessions, "Myth, Mormonism, and Murder in the South," *SAQ* 75 (September 1976): 212–25, esp. 218. On a Tory's charivari, see March 8, 1775 entry in *A British Fusilier in Revolutionary Boston, Being the Diary of Lieutenant Frederick MacKenzie, Adjutant of the Royal Welsh Fusiliers, January 5–April 30, 1775*, Allen French, ed. (Cambridge: Harvard University Press, 1926), p. 40. See also Roberts and Roberts, *Moreau de St. Mery's American Journey*, p. 57; and Shaw, *American Patriots and Rituals of Revolution*, passim.

26. Theodore Weld to Mrs. Marius Robinson, January 25, 1837; Reminiscence, Emily Robinson, n.d.; Marius Robinson to Emily Robinson, January 25, 1837; Marius Racine Robinson MSS, Western Reserve Historical Society, Cleveland; Russel B. Nye, "Marius Robinson: A Forgotten Abolitionist Leader," *OAHQ* 55 (1946): 138–54; idem, *Fettered Freedom: Civil Liberties and the Slavery Controversy, 1830–1860* (Urbana: University of Illinois, 1972), pp. 183, 187, 188. See also Amos Dresser, *Narrative of the Arrest, Lynch Law Trial, and Scourging of*

Amos Dresser at Nashville, Tennessee, August 1835 (Oberlin: n.p., 1835); *Anti-Slavery Record* (New York) 1: (January 1835–December 1837): 404–5; Robert H. Abzug, *Passionate Liberator: Theodore Dwight Weld and the Dilemma of Reform* (New York: Oxford University Press, 1980), p. 125; Julian A. Selby, *Memorabilia and Anecdotal Reminiscenes of Columbia, S.C. . . .* (Columbia: R. L. Bryan, 1905), p. 131.

27. Quotation on early Klan symbolism from William P. Randel, *The Ku Klux Klan: A Century of Infamy* (Philadelphia: Chilton Books, 1965), pp. 10, 20, 51; see illustrations throughout. Eyre Damer, *When the Ku Klux Rode* (Westport: Negro Universities Press, 1970 [1912]), p. 92. See also frontispiece to Albion W. Tourgee, *The Invisible Empire: A Concise Review of the Epoch* (Ridgewood, N.J.: Gregg Press, 1968 [1883]); and Allen W. Trelease, *White Terror: The Ku Klux Klan Conspiracy and Southern Reconstruction* (New York: Harper & Row, 1971), pp. 4–5, 53–54, passim. The red, black, and white of Klan costuming also, ironically, dominate ritual forms in the Ndembu and other African tribes, with similar (though not identical) meanings: white for "positive" qualities, black for "negative" ones, red for ambivalent elements. See Turner, *Forest of Symbols*, pp. 59–92, esp. p. 74. "It would seem probable that the notion of the colors is an inheritance from a remote (perhaps pre-Indo-European) past," Turner speculates. On the Indo-European meaning of red, see Onians, *Origins of European Thought*, pp. 535–36, 541–42.

28. See Matthews, *Kin and Neighbor*, pp. 94–124; Jethro Rumple, *A History of Rowan County, North Carolina . . .* (Salisbury, N.C.: J. J. Bruner, 1881), pp. 324–32; Michael O. Jones, "Folk Beliefs: Knowledge and Action," *Southern Folklore Quarterly* (December 1971), pp. 304–9; J. Slocumb in A. R. Newsome, ed., "Twelve North Carolina Counties in 1810–1811," *NCHR* 6 (July 1929); 308–9. See also Shaw, *American Patriots and Rituals of Revolution*, pp. 204–31, on the historic evolution of charivaris. Another approach is that of John P. Reid, "In a Defensive Rage: The Uses of the Mob, the Justification in Law, and the Coming of the Revolution," *NYULR* 49 (December 1974): 1043–91, who denies ambiguity in Whig enlistment of mobs.

29. *Joint Select Committee. The Condition of Affairs in the Late Insurrectionary States. Alabama. House Reports, no, 22, pt. 8* (Washington: Government Printing Office, 1872) 1: 118–19, 2: 757–58. On the wizard Klansmen in North Carolina, ibid., *North Carolina*, pp. 89–90. See also, *Georgia*, pp. 10 and 365. For similar views in the Klan of the 1920s see H. C. Nixon, *Possum Trot: Rural Community, South* (Norman: University of Oklahoma Press, 1941), p. 28.

30. Trelease, *White Terror,* passim; Nixon, *Possum Trot,* p. 28; Randel, *Ku Klux Klan,* pp. 8–17.

31. *New York Times,* December 7, 1899, quoted in Richard M. Brown, *American Violence* (Englewood Cliffs, N.J.: Prentice-Hall, 1970), pp. 107–8; Davis, *Barrow Diary,* June 17, 1842, p. 262. On the nature of such sacrifices see also Hutton Webster, *Taboo: A Sociological Study* (Sanford: Stanford University Press, 1948), pp. 218–19; Mircea Eliade, *The Sacred and Profane: The Nature of Religion* (New York: Harcourt, Brace, 1959), p. 92; Harold Garfinkel, "Conditions of Successful Degradation Ceremonies," *AJS* 6 (March 1956): 420–24. On a fairly recent lynching with celebratory overtones, see Edwin N. Smead, Jr., "The Lynch-

ing of Mack Charles Parker in Poplarsville, Mississippi, April 25, 1959," Ph.D. diss., University of Maryland, 1979, pp. 147, 155–60. Insufficient work has been done on the history of Pope's Day celebrations and their connection with effigy burnings and tar-and-tar-featherings in the Southern colonies.
32. Joseph Blotner, *Faulkner: A Biography*, 2 vols. (New York: Random House, 1974) 1: 15. George J. Holyoake, *Public Lessons of the Hangman* (London: Farrah, 1864), pp. 2–3; see also David D. Cooper, *The Lesson of the Scaffold* (London: Allen Lane, 1974), passim; Anon., Diary, Rockingham County, Virginia, 1861–1865, p. 85, DUL; Vicksburg *Register*, July 25, 1835.
33. Maxwell Geismar, *Mark Twain: An American Prophet* (Boston: Houghton Mifflin, 1970), pp. 233–37; Philip S. Foner, *Mark Twain: Social Critic* (New York: International, 1966), pp. 218–21.
34. Mary Douglas, *Purity and Danger: An Analysis of Concepts of Pollution and Taboo* (Baltimore: Penguin, 1970), p. 15; also pp. 116 and 168–69; Hugh D. Duncan, *Language and Literature in Society: A Sociological Essay on Theory and Method in the Interpretation of Linguistic Symbols* (New York: Bedminster Press, 1961), p. 92 (quotation); Sigmund Freud, *Totem and Taboo: Some Points of Agreement between the Mental Lives of Savages and Neurotics*, James Strachey, trans. (New York: W. W. Norton, 1950), 61–74; Anthony F. C. Wallace, *Religion: An Anthropological View* (New York: Random House, 1966), pp. 208–9; George H. Mead, "The Psychology of Punitive Justice," *AJS* 23 (March 1918): 577–602; Erikson, *Wayward Puritans*, pp. 3–19.
34. Freud quoted in H. Stuart Hughes, *Consciousness and Society: The Reorientation of Social Thought, 1890–1930* (New York: Vintage, 1958), pp. 143–44.

Chapter Seventeen: The Anatomy of a Wife-Killing

1. Merrill, *Jefferson's Nephews*; Robert Penn Warren, *Brother to Dragons: A Tale in Verse and Voices* (New York: Random House, 1953), which also concerns the Lewis's crime; Michel Foucault, ed., *I, Pierre Rivière, Having Slaughtered My Mother, My Sister, and My Brother . . . A Case of Parricide in the Nineteenth Century*, Frank Jellinek, trans. (New York: Pantheon, 1975); Weld, *Slavery as It Is*, included the Lewis case but not the Foster affair. On the Manning case, see Albert Borowitz, *The Woman Who Murdered Black Satin: The Bermondsey Horror* (Columbus: Ohio State University Press, 1981). Maria Manning, a Belgian woman, and her husband were hanged in Horsemonger Lane before at least 30,000 for the murder of her lover. Dickens portrays her in *Bleak House* as the murderous Frenchwoman Hortense.
2. Nancy A. Wood and Nancy Ligon, deps., n.d., and March 28, 1834, in *State v. James Foster, Jr.*, State Cases, June Term, 1834, cabinet 5, file 186, Judgments and Dismissions, Circuit Court Clerk's Office, AdCC (hereinafter *State v. Foster*.)
3. William Foster, dep., March 28, 1834, ibid. John C. Jones, *A Complete History of Methodism . . .*, 2 vols. (Nashville: Methodist Episcopal Church, South, 1887–1908) 1: 452–53.
4. David Sinclair McIntosh, dep., n.d., *State v. Foster*.

5. Ibid.; and McIntosh, dep., March 28, 1834.

6. Ibid.

7. Ferdinand L. Claiborne, dep., March 28, 1834, *State* v. *Foster;* Thomas P. Abernethy, "Aaron Burr in Mississippi," *JSH* 15 (February 1949): 9–21; John F. H. Claiborne, *Mississippi, as a Province, Territory and State* (Jackson: Power and Barksdale, 1880), 333–46.

8. Claiborne to Hiram G. Runnels, March 20, 1834, RG 27, MissDAH; Nancy Wood, Nancy Ligon, deps., n.d., and March 28, 1834, *State* v. *Foster.*

9. See Terry Alford, "Index and Chronology of South Carolina Fosters . . ." (typescript), 1972, kindly lent to the author. On the Mississippi migration of Fosters, see the entry for January 14, 1797, in Mary G. Bryan, comp., *Passports Issued by Governors of Georgia, 1810–1820* (Washington: National Geneological Society, no. 28, 1964); Alford, *Prince among Slaves*, pp. 39–40.

10. Consultation with Professor Terry Alford on December 3, 1981, reconfirmed my opinion that the John Foster branch of the family is by far the most difficult to trace. (Professor Alford has studied the family's history with great care.) But for some information on John Foster see Charles S. Sydnor, *A Gentleman of the Old Natchez Region: Benjamin L. C. Wailes* (Durham: Duke University Press, 1938), pp. 24, 28n; William D. Lum and Mrs. Lennie Schuchs, comps., *Reunion of Descendants of James Foster at Foster's Mound, Sunday, May 2, 1965* (n.p. 1965), p. 3, MissDAH; Alford, *Prince among Slaves*, pp. 40, 232; Walter Prescott Webb, ed., *The Handbook of Texas*, 2 vols. (Austin: Texas State Historical Association, 1952) 1: 636; Lester G. Bugbee, "The Old Three Hundred," *Quarterly of the Texas State Historical Association* 1 (July 1897–April 1898): 112; "A Record of Proceedings of the Washington Presbyterian Church Records, (1807–1861), Book 1, 1807–1818," microfilm, pp. 10, 11, 18, 23, MissDAH; Walter B. Posey, ed., "The First Session Book of the Oldest Presbyterian Church in Mississippi," *JMH* 10 (April 1948): 132–49.

11. Ingraham, *South-West* 2: 219.

12. Jones, *Complete History of Methodism* 1: 37–38, 454–55, 456, 460; 2: 315–16. *Wm. Foster ex. est. of Mary Gilbert, Nancy Gilbert, Wm. Gilbert* v. *Samuel King,* dr. 80, case #1021, 1831, AdCC; *Wm. Foster, admr., de ponis non est, &c* v. *Silas Dinsmore,* dr. 70, case 191–C, 1810 (typescript 1965), pp. 68–69, MissDAH; *Mississippi Statesman* and *Natchez Gazette,* February 22, 1827; *Mississippi Republican* (Natchez), June 12, 1821; John G. Jones, *A Concise History of the Introduction of Protestantism into Mississippi and the Southwest* (St. Louis: P. M. Pickard, 1866), pp. 163–72; also on Rachel's illiteracy, Jones, *Complete History of Methodism* 1: 657 and deed book L, 1820, p. 442, AdCC.

13. Ingraham, *South-West* 2: 208.

14. Col. Ferdinand L. Claiborne, "List of Gentlemen Little Nabobs of the Miss—— T——" [c. 1804], in Miss. Terr. file, Simon Gratz Collection, Pennsylvania Historical Society, Philadelphia, ref. courtesy of Professor Alford; see also Miss. Hist. Rec. Survey, "County Archives of Mississippi," no. 2, Adams County, vol. 2, entry #231, 234, typs. (1942), MissDAH; Alford, *Prince Among Slaves*, p. 76.

15. Anna G. Hayden, "Natchez under the Old Regime," in Maj. Steve Power,

comp. *The Memento: Old and New Natchez, 1700 to 1897* (Natchez: n.p., 1897), pp. 13–14; W. N. Foster, "The Family of Thomas Foster, of Natchez, Mississippi" (n.p., 1965), MissDAH. Alford, *Prince Among Slaves*, p. 40 (quotation).

16. Lum and Schuchs, *Reunion of Descendants*, pp. 10–12; see also genealogical table at the end of this chapter.

17. Sarah Foster, Will Book, no. 2, pp. 149–53, MissDAH.

18. Margaret Wilson, Diary, entry for January 3, 1837, M–L9 (microfilm), LSU. She called the plantation "Greenfield," a later name for Foster Fields.

19. Ephraim and Cassandra Foster, January 15, 1819, Deed Book B, pp. 142–44, Wilkinson County, Woodville, Miss., (supplied by Dr. Alford); Mortgage, Ephraim Foster to Elizabeth Greenfield, April 24, 1821, Deed Book L, 375, also ibid., pp. 571–74; and Book N, pp. 208, 419–420, AdCC; Jean Fly, ed., "Marriage and Death Notices in Natchez Newspapers," *JMH* 8 (October 1946): 182; Will of Sarah Foster, 1836, Will Record Book 2, 1832–54 (microfilm), ChanCo, AdCC, MissDAH; *Cassandra Foster v. Ephraim Foster*, 1824, Sup. Court of Chanc., case #452, drawer 73, MissDAH; *Heirs of Cassandra Foster Speed v. John Speed*, Sup. Court of Chanc., West Dist., #230, drawer 70, MissDAH; Ephraim Foster, Will, January 8, 1824, December 17, 1824, Will Book 1, p. 318, AdCC; *Mississippian and Natchez Advertiser*, March 27, 1824.

20. Obit., David S. McIntosh, *Southern Reformer* (Jackson, Miss.), August 23, 1845. See also Alford, *Prince among Slaves*, 93; Matilda Bacon and Maude T. Burson, "Family History (As I Remember· It)" (typescript), in possession of Lillian Quinn, Satucket, N.Y. (copy kindly lent by Professor Terry Alford); Fly, "Marriage and Death Notices," *JMH* 8 (October 1946): 182.

21. See indentures, Deed of Gift, to Samuel W. Wells, Nancy Wood, Barbara Barnard, Deed Book V, pp. 111, 112, 114, 365, 480, 524; to Caroline S. McIntosh (rather than to her husband; cf. the case of Frances Wells), Deed Book Y, pp. 38–39. Sarah's refusal is evident also in a review of James Foster's holdings; see *Foster v. Creditors*, Original Successions [O.S.], vol. 54, #1471 [p. 38, October 21, 1835] (hereinafter *Foster v. Creditors*), SMP.

22. See Martin Gold, "Suicide, Homicide, and the Socialization of Aggression," *AJS* 63 (May 1958): 651–66; H. C. Brearley, "The Pattern of Violence," in W. T. Couch, ed., *Culture in the South* (Chapel Hill, University of North Carolina Press, 1934), pp. 678–92; Raymond D. Gustil, "Homicide and a Regional Culture of Violence," *ASR* 36 (June 1971): 412–27; John S. Reed, *The Enduring South: Subcultural Persistence in Mass Society* (Lexington, Mass.: D. C. Heath, 1972), pp. 45–55.

23. See county receipt to Norwood, n.d., for $32.37½ for expenses incurred, *State v. Foster;* though undated, internal evidence of papers in the file suggests that Foster was in jail before the June term of the court.

24. Levi Foster to James Foster, Jr., September 29, 1829, Original Conveyances [O.C.], Book B, #429, p. 988 (from index, both lost); Lacy quoted in *Foster v. Creditors*, SMP; William Boyce, will, November 8, 1825, in Mary E. Sanders, comp., *Annotated Abstracts of the Successions of St. Mary Parish, Louisiana* (Lafayette: priv. print., 1972), pp. 72–73.

25. *Foster v. Creditors*, Book D, O.C., #2095, Plaintiff Schedule II, SMP.

26. See typed index, O.S., SMP; also four suits in Civil Suits, I, #278, pp. 698,

700, 720, Lafayette Parish Courthouse, Lafayette, La. No doubt there were also cases at Opelousas, St. Landry Parish, but the records are lost.

27. *Foster* v. *Creditors*, SMP; on use of liquor see *Levi Foster* v. *Joseph White*, C. S. #700, LaFayette Parish, La. For information about the identities of the Franklin gaming friends, see Sanders, *Annotated Abstracts*, (on Lockett) pp. 35, 40, 43, 47, 48, passim; (on Splane) pp. 81, 85, 87, 88, passim; (on Carlin) pp. 64, 72, 73, 88, passim; (on DeMaret) pp. 35, 36, 126, 145, 164; (on Moore) pp. 30, 35, 107, 148, 164, and in *A Biographical Congressional Directory . . . 1774–1911* (Washington: Government Printing Office, 1913), p. 872.

28. *Foster* v. *Creditors*, passim, SMP.

29. Ibid., pp. 2, 18, 21; *Burton Perry and Benjamin R. Gantt* [sic] v. *James Foster, Jr.*, O. S., vol. 44, #1273; *John Smith* v. *James Foster, Jr.*, vol. 44, #1284; *Alexander R. Splane* v. *James Foster, Jr.*, vol. 44, #1471, SMP.

30. Sanders, *Annotated Abstracts*, pp. 97, 157; *Foster* v. *Creditors*, pp. 20, 21, SMP.

31. *Foster* v. *Creditors*, pp. 18, 21, 22, SMP.

32. *Levi Foster* v. *James Foster, Jr.*, O. S. vol. 44, #1269; *Splane* v. *James Foster, Jr.*, vol. 44, #1471; *Splane* v. *James Foster, Jr.*, vol. 44, #1270, SM '.

33. Unfortunately the court records do not reveal Captain Bundick's first name, but see Robert Bruce L. Ardoin, comp., *Louisiana Census Records*. vol. 1, *Avoyelles and St. Landry Parishes, 1810 and 1820* (Baltimore: Genealogical Publications, 1970), p. 54, for Bundick families. A careful check of New Orleans ship registries as well as federal registries revealed no vessel called the *Calcasieu*. I was also unable to find its itinerary; the necessary issues of the *Attakapas Gazette* (St. Martinsville, La.) have been lost from the University of Texas (Austin) Library and no other copies are available (except the unhelpful November 13, 1833, issue in the Connecticut Historical Society, Hartford). Calcasieu, the county name for the Lake Charles region today, then was an Indian tribe in St. Landry Parish, the boundary of which then extended to the Texas line.

34. John Smith in *Foster* v. *Creditors*, p. 23; Moore in ibid., pp. 24, 25. See also *Foster* v. *Creditors*, p. 38, and *Dwight & Hartman* v. *Foster*, O. S. vol. 44, #1271, SMP.

35. Boyce, Lockett, Hungerford, bond, in *Dwight & Hartman* v. *Foster*, vol. 44, #1271; auction announcement for the schooner *St. Mary*, Benjamin Hudson, Sheriff, St. Mary Parish, April 8, 1835, O. C. book D, #2095, SMP; "Tableaux of Distribution," in *Foster* v. *Creditors* (for items cited and total evaluation), SMP; Mrs. Charles Rossmer, "Recollections," typed copy [c. 1945], kindly lent by Professor Terry Alford.

36. Consultations with genealogists Mrs. Clyde Alpha of Franklin, La., and Mrs. Lula Belle May Bowles of LaFayette cleared up the error of Mrs. Rossmer's recollection (see n35), which gave Susan Foster's maiden name as Susan Alpha. The Alphas were a long-established family in the area and Mrs. Rossmer assumed a connection with James Foster, Jr.'s, wife. But the Alphas did not arrive in St. Mary Parish until after 1840 (as the court records in Franklin confirm). It is true, though, that the Alphas, a Somerset County, Maryland, family (of Welsh and possibly Flemish extraction) moved to southern Indiana after Perryman Alpha returned from serving with General Jackson at the 1815 Battle of New Orleans. In 1832 Perryman left Jeffersonville, Indiana, and took his family to

Mobile, Alabama, where in that year he died in an accident at sea. According to the Indiana Censuses of 1820 and 1830, Alpha had a daughter of Susan Foster's birth year. (The census takers did not record dependents' names, only sex and age). The present-day Alpha family denies the existence of that female child, and Susan, they say, is not a family name. Perryman's son Independence (born July 4, 1821) settled about 1840 in Franklin, La. The clerk of court Woodson Wren, in taking a deposition from the Foster Fields residents, in mid-March, 1834, wrote Susan's maiden name as Al—— (the remaining letters being illegible). Alphin or possibly Alfhari may have been intended. (The Alphin family, located in southern Arkansas, descended from a tavern-keeper and gambler originally from western Virginia.) Without knowing the itinerary of the *Calcasieu*, however, I was unable to justify so extensive a search of county archives as one that might have led to accurate identification. The references for these investigations may be found in my unpublished version of the case.

37. *State* v. *Foster*, Docket book, 1829–1841, December term, 1834, p. 25, AdCC.

38. *Appletons' Cyclopaedia of American Biography* (New York: Appleton, 1892) 2: 732; Harriet De Cell and Joanne Prichard, *Yazoo: Its Legends and Legacies* (Yazoo, Miss.: Delta Press, 1976), pp. 69, 252, 414; Natchez *Newspaper and Public Advertiser*, April 25, June 6, July 13, 1826; Mississippi *Messenger*, August 18, 1807; Natchez *Ariel*, August 29, 1825, Joseph D. Shields, *Natchez: Its Early History* (Louisville: John P. Morton, 1930), pp. 237–54; James D. Lynch, *The Bench and Bar of Mississippi* (New York: Hale & Son, 1881), p. 132; Fly, "Marriage and Death Notices," p. 185; Rowland Dunbar, *Courts, Judges, and Lawyers of Mississippi, 1798–1935* (Jackson: Hederman Bros., 1935), p. 39; Yazoo *Banner* (Benton, Miss.), August 9, 1839; Vicksburg *Sentinel & Expositor for the Country*, August 13, 1839.

39. State Docket Book, 1829–41, December term, 1834, AdCC.

40. Huston to Editor, *Courier and New York National Enquirer*, August 25, 1833, and another statement of August 19, 1835, reprinted in *Mississippi Free Trader* (Natchez), August 28, 1844, kindly supplied by Laurence Shore of Johns Hopkins University. On the riots, see esp. Richards, "Gentlemen of Property and Standing."

41. Colonel James Creecy, *Scenes in the South, and Other Miscellaneous Pieces* (Washington: Thomas McGill, 1860), p. 54; see also Michael Ignatieff, *A Just Measure of Pain: The Penitentiary in the Industrial Revolution, 1750–1850* (New York: Columbia University Press, 1978), p. 66.

42. *Col. Crockett's Exploits and Adventures in Texas, Wherein is Contained a Full Account of His Journey from Tennessee and Thence Across Texas to San Antonio . . . Written by Himself* (London: R. Kennett, 1837), pp. 63–68.

43. Adams County Bd. of Police, Minutes, 1822-34, microfilm #40, MissDAH; Natchez *Courier*, January 9, 1835 (quotations).

44. Crockett, *Exploits*, p. 67; Claiborne, *Mississippi*, p. 259; Creecy, *Scenes in the South*, p. 55 (quotation).

45. Crockett, *Exploits*, p. 67.

46. *Ibid.*, pp. 67–68; Creecy, *Scenes in the South*, pp. 55–56; Natchez *Courier*, January 9, 1835.

47. Creecy, *Scenes in the South*, p. 56; Crockett, *Exploits*, p. 68; Natchez *Courier*, January 9, 1835.

48. Douglas, *Purity and Danger,* pp. 15, 116, 168–69; Emile Durkheim, "Deux lois de l'evolution penale," *L'Annes sociologique* 4 (1900–1901): 65–95, translated and annotated by Linda L. Robinson, Ph.D. diss., Case Western Reserve University, 1972. Max Weber, *Economy and Society,* Guenther Roth and Claus Wittich, eds., 2 vols. (New York: Bedminster Press, 1968) 1: 647–48; Garfinkel, "Conditions of Successful Degradation Ceremonies," pp. 420–24; George H. Mead, "Psychology of Punitive Justice," *AJS* 23 (March 1918): 577–602; Erikson, *Wayward Puritans,* pp. 3–19; Duncan, *Language and Literature in Society,* pp. 91–92; Roger Brown, *Social Psychology* (New York: Free Press, 1965), p. 501. For an ingenious interpretation of rites and punishment, see also Girard, *Violence and the Sacred.*

49. Crockett, *Exploits,* pp. 67–68.

50. James Foster, Jr., Deed of Gift, May 21, 1835, Deed Book W, 212–13, ChanCo, AdCC.

51. Rossmer, recollections.

52. Ernest Becker, *The Denial of Death* (New York: Free Press, 1975), pp. 133–37, from which this interpretation is largely derived.

BLANK PAGE

Index

CPSIA information can be obtained at www.ICGtesting.com
Printed in the USA
BVOW071610250912

301349BV00006B/150/A